COOK'S
ILLUSTRATED

~ 2000 ~

$29.95

Published by
Boston Common Press Limited Partnership
17 Station Street
Brookline, MA 02445

ISBN: 0-936184-48-5
ISSN: 1068-2821

To get home delivery of future issues of *Cook's Illustrated*, call 800-526-8442 inside the U.S., or 515-247-7571 if calling from outside the U.S.

In addition to the Annual Hardbound Editions, *Cook's Illustrated* offers the following publications:

The *How to Cook* series of single topic cookbooks
Titles include *How to Make a Pie, How to Make an American Layer Cake, How to Stir-Fry, How to Make Ice Cream, How to Make Pizza, How to Make Holiday Desserts, How to Make Pasta Sauces, How to Make Salad, How to Grill, How to Make Simple Fruit Desserts, How to Make Cookie Jar Favorites, How to Cook Holiday Roasts & Birds, How to Make Stew, How to Cook Shrimp & Other Shellfish, How to Barbecue & Roast on the Grill, How to Cook Garden Vegetables, How to Make Pot Pies & Casseroles, How to Make Soup, How to Cook Potatoes, How to Make Quick Appetizers, How to Make Sauces & Gravies, How to Sauté, How to Make Chinese Favorites, How to Make Muffins, Biscuits, & Scones, and How to Cook Chicken Breasts.* A boxed set of the first 11 titles in the series is available in an attractive, protective slip case. New releases are published every two months, so give us a call for our complete list of available titles.

The Best Recipe
This 576-page book is a collection of over 700 recipes and 200 illustrations from the first seven years of *Cook's*. We've included basics, such as how to make chicken stock, as well as recipes for quick weeknight meals and special entertaining. Let *The Best Recipe* become your indispensable kitchen companion.

Multi-Year Master Index
Quickly find every article and recipe *Cook's Illustrated* has published from the Charter Issue in 1992 through the most recent year-end issue. Recipe names, authors, article titles, subject matter, equipment testings, food tastings, cookbook reviews, wine tastings, and ingredients are all now instantly at your fingertips.

The Cook's Bible, The Yellow Farmhouse Cookbook, **and** *The Dessert Bible*
Written by Christopher Kimball and published by Little, Brown and Company.

To order any of the books listed above, call 800-611-0759 inside the U.S., or 515-246-6911 if calling from outside the U.S.

You can order subscriptions, gift subscriptions, and any of our books by visiting our online store at
www.cooksillustrated.com

COOK'S ILLUSTRATED INDEX 2000

COOK'S
ILLUSTRATED

Secrets of Broiling Chicken
How Do You Get Crispy Skin and Moist Meat?

Triple Coconut Macaroons
Moist, Not Sticky

Rating Soy Sauces
Supermarket Brands Don't Make the Grade

Perfect Fried Eggs
Yes, There Is a Right Way to Fry an Egg

Kitchen Thermometer Quick Tips
Test Breads, Puddings, and More

Mastering Beef Short Ribs
Take Out the Fat

Testing Paring Knives
Best Lemon Tart
Fresh Salmon Cakes
Streamlining Cassoulet
Winter Citrus Salads

$4.95 U.S./$6.95 CANADA

62805

0 232817 1

0 2>

CONTENTS

January & February 2000

COOK'S ILLUSTRATED

www.cooksillustrated.com

PUBLISHER AND EDITOR
Christopher Kimball

SENIOR EDITOR
John Willoughby

SENIOR WRITER
Jack Bishop

CORPORATE MANAGING EDITOR
Barbara Bourassa

ASSOCIATE EDITORS
Adam Ried
Maryellen Driscoll
Dawn Yanagihara

TEST KITCHEN DIRECTOR
Kay Rentschler

RECIPE DEVELOPMENT
Bridget Lancaster
Julia Collin

CONSULTING FOOD EDITOR
Jasper White

CONSULTING EDITOR
Jim Dodge

ART DIRECTOR
Amy Klee

PROJECT MANAGER
Sheila Datz

EDITORIAL PRODUCTION MANAGER
Nate Nickerson

COPY EDITOR
India Koopman

EDITORIAL INTERN
Brigitte Scott

MARKETING MANAGER
Pamela Caporino

SALES REPRESENTATIVE
Jason Geller

MARKETING ASSISTANT
Connie Forbes

CIRCULATION DIRECTOR
David Mack

FULFILLMENT MANAGER
Larisa Greiner

PRODUCTS MANAGER
Steven Browall

CIRCULATION ASSISTANT
Mary Connelly

VICE PRESIDENT
PRODUCTION AND TECHNOLOGY
James McCormack

SYSTEMS ADMINISTRATOR
Richard Cassidy

PRODUCTION ARTIST
Daniel Frey

JUNIOR WEB DEVELOPER
Nicole Morris

CONTROLLER
Mandy Shito

OFFICE MANAGER
Jennifer McCreary

SPECIAL PROJECTS
Deborah Broide

TROPICAL FRUIT

TROPICAL FRUITS There are literally hundreds of deliciously edible tropical fruits. Many, such as rambutans and jackfruits, originated in Southeast Asia, do not travel well, and have never been successfully grown in the American tropics. Those pictured here, however, are much more readily available in the United States. Many of them, including the glossy golden pepino, the oval guava, the large and familiar pineapple, the intensely floral passion fruit, and the delicately flavored cherimoya, originated in South America. The near-ubiquitous papaya, oddly enough, is actually of North American origin. Others, such as the flashy star-shaped carambola and a few of the many varieties of mango, can be grown in semitropical areas in the United States. Yet others, including the sweet-tart kiwano or horned melon of New Zealand, simply ship well.

COVER PAINTING: BRENT WATKINSON,   BACK COVER ILLUSTRATION: JOHN BURGOYNE.

For list rental information, contact The SpeciaLISTS, 1200 Harbor Blvd. 9th Floor, Weehawken, NJ 07087; (201) 865-5800; fax (201) 867-2450. Editorial office: 17 Station Street, Brookline, MA 02445; (617) 232-1000; fax (617) 232-1572. Editorial contributions should be sent to: Editor, *Cook's Illustrated.* We cannot assume responsibility for manuscripts submitted to us. Submissions will be returned only if accompanied by a large self-addressed envelope. Postmaster: Send all new orders, subscription inquiries, and change of address notices to: *Cook's Illustrated,* P.O. Box 7446, Red Oak, IA 51591-0446. PRINTED IN THE USA.

IN THE APPLE ORCHARD

The Red Delicious was discovered in Iowa in 1874 when a farmer repeatedly cut down a young apple tree only to have it reemerge the next season. Finally, figuring that anything that struggled against death so persistently might have a good reason to live, he tended the tree, grew the fruit, and entered it in competition at a state fair, where it won first prize. Later, a powerful nursery family from Missouri, the Stark Brothers, bought the Hawkeye (the apple's original name) and turned it into the ubiquitous, mediocre apple that it is today. After World War II, the Red Delicious became the staple of many growers, its classic shape and deep cherry color becoming synonymous with the American ideal of an apple. But we all know what it tastes like. It is, to borrow a phrase, a "gorgeous fraud"—the skin is thick and bitter and the fruit soft, sweet, and lacking in the tartness most apple growers and cooks find synonymous with a good eating apple.

The tale of the Red Delicious is one of serendipity—a tree grows from a chance seedling, barely escapes with its life, and then goes on to become the best-selling apple in history. But the tale of America's apple industry is less romantic. In the 19th century, apples were grown and consumed locally, with literally thousands of varieties on the market. Some apples were as small as cherries, some as large as grapefruit; some were pale white in appearance and others almost black; some even looked like potatoes and others like a sheep's nose (the Yellow Sheepnose). The Watermelon apple had bright red fruit, the Court Pendu Plat had rough, scabby skin (it would never sell today) but also a unique pecanlike sweetness, and others had lyrical names: Maiden Blush, Rainbow, Newtown Pippin, Wolf River, Fallawaters, Red Winter Pearmain, Summer Banana, and Esopus Spitzenberg. It was an industry that reflected the spirit of 19th-century America—a diversity of tastes and regions served by hard-working entrepreneurs who grafted and planted, fought scab and mildew, and battled the devastation wreaked by the apple moth and plum curculio, insects that had to be laboriously shaken from trees rather than killed easily through spraying.

In this half century, all that has changed. An industry spokesperson once told me, "There are only three kinds of apples in America today: red, yellow, and green." He meant that supermarket buyers know that consumers purchase on looks alone, the classic case of beauty only being skin deep. They prefer dark green Granny Smith apples (grannies came from Australia, and there once was a real Granny Smith) to light ones, yet the paler, somewhat yellow-skinned specimens are actually riper and sweeter. A collection of 19th-century apples would be a study in diversity; a crate of modern supermarket apples would be almost indistinguishable except for color: they all have the same shape, size, and smooth, glossy skin. Although not all "heirloom" apples were worth saving—many were bitter, had tough skin, or didn't store well—the apple business today is one of DNA engineering, no longer subject to the serendipity of a chance seed beating the odds to become a Golden Delicious or a McIntosh.

But we sometimes forget that there is more to apples than taste and texture. For Carlos Manning, who works 12-hour shifts at a mine in

Christopher Kimball

West Virginia, antique varieties have become a way of life. A few years back he had a craving for Red Winter Pearmain apples, he bought some seedlings, but the fruit didn't taste the same. He turned into an apple detective, seeking grafts from old trees that still bore good fruit. He has saved the Red Ben Davis apple, the Duchess of Oldenburg, the Rainbow, and, of course, the Red Winter Pearmain, which he found still growing in his great grandfather's abandoned orchard.

Like Manning, good cooks are hungry for taste but also for experience. In seeking that which is pleasing to the palate, the adventurous among us take walks in old orchards, grafting new experiences onto old, discovering bits and pieces of the past in the gnarled branches of old trees. In my Vermont orchard, I have come to realize that apples are mostly about trees, not fruit, about weather and early frosts, about drought and high winds, about plentiful years and those with poor harvests. I have planted a young tree for each of my four children: a Macoun for Whitney, a Northern Spy for Caroline, a Cortland for Charlie, and a Liberty for young Emily. We'll tend them together and watch them grow, making mistakes, to be sure, but planning the best we can for their future as well as ours. And when they are mature, we will have memories of the growing, of a time when we were young and the trees and the children were yet to take root, their immature scions still fragile but upstanding on a crisp April morning, yet to be tested by the weight of September's heavy fruit.

ABOUT COOK'S ILLUSTRATED

The Magazine Cook's Illustrated (ISSN 1068-2821) is published bimonthly (6 issues per year) by Boston Common Press Limited Partnership, 17 Station Street, Brookline, MA 02445. Copyright 2000 Boston Common Press Limited Partnership. Periodical postage paid at Boston, Mass. and additional mailing offices, USPS #012487. A one-year subscription is $29.70, two years is $55, and three years is $75. Add $6 postage per year for Canadian subscriptions and $12 per year for all other foreign countries. To order subscriptions in the U.S. call 800-526-8442; from outside the U.S. call 515-247-7571. Gift subscriptions are available for $24.95 each. Postmaster: Send all new orders, subscription inquiries, and change of address notices to: Cook's Illustrated, P.O. Box 7446, Red Oak, IA 51591-0446.

Magazine-Related Items Cook's Illustrated is available in annual hardbound editions for $24.95 each plus shipping and handling; each edition is fully indexed. Discounts are available if more than one year is ordered at a time. Individual back issues are available for $5 each. Cook's also offers a seven-year index (1993–1999) of the magazine for $12.95. To order any of these products, call 800-611-0759 inside the U.S. or 515-246-6911 from outside the U.S.

Books The Best Recipe, which features 700 of our favorite recipes from the pages of Cook's Illustrated, is available for $24.95. Cook's Illustrated also publishes a series of single-topic books, available for $14.95 each, which cover pie, American layer cake, stir-frying, ice cream, salad, simple fruit desserts, cookie jar favorites, holiday roasts and birds, stew, grilling, pizza, holiday desserts, pasta sauces, barbecuing and roasting on the grill, shrimp and other shellfish, cooking garden vegetables, pot pies and casseroles, soup, and sautéing. The Cook's Bible, written by Christopher Kimball and published by Little, Brown and Company, is available for $24.95. The Yellow Farmhouse Cookbook, also written by Christopher Kimball and published by Little, Brown and Company, is available for $24.95. To order any of these books, call 800-611-0759 inside the U.S. or 515-246-6911 from outside the U.S.

Reader Submissions Cook's accepts reader submissions for Quick Tips. We will provide a one-year complimentary subscription for each tip that we print. Send your tip, name, address, and daytime telephone number to Quick Tips, Cook's Illustrated, P.O. Box 470589, Brookline, MA 02447. Questions, suggestions, or submissions for Notes from Readers should be sent to the same address.

Subscription Inquiries All queries about subscriptions or change of address notices should be addressed to Cook's Illustrated, P.O. Box 7446, Red Oak, IA 51591-0446.

Web Site A searchable database of recipes, testings, and tastings from Cook's Illustrated, plus our ever-expanding online bookstore, information on great holiday gifts and gift subscriptions, and more can be found at http://www.cooksillustrated.com.

NOTES FROM READERS

Storing Parmesan

I was not surprised by the findings of your September/October 1999 Parmesan cheese tasting. My own curiosity led me to try a few different types of Parmesan, and, like you, I concluded that the real stuff, Parmigiano-Reggiano, was the best by far. The question I want to ask about this cheese is, what is the best way to store it so as to preserve its singular texture and flavor? Does the type of wrapping or the location in the refrigerator make any difference?

GREGORY TASIS
CAMBRIDGE, MASS.

➤ We consulted several of the sources who helped with research for the tasting article and got three different recommendations for wrapping Parmesan for storage. Before we even got to the question of wrapping, though, there were several points on which everyone agreed. First, it is best to buy small pieces of cheese that will get used up in the course of one or two meals, thus eliminating, or at least reducing, the need for storage. Assuming that there is some cheese left to store, everyone agreed that the relatively humid vegetable crisper was the best spot for it in the refrigerator.

In terms of storage, it was acknowledged that the cheese should be allowed to breathe, but just a little. Full and prolonged exposure to air oxidizes the cheese, which degrades both flavor and texture. So the cheese should be wrapped in a way that limits its breathing. The three specific wrapping recommendations we got from the experts were as follows: (1) wrap the cheese in a slightly moistened paper towel and then in a layer of aluminum foil (a method also recommended for large chunks of 2 to 3 pounds or more); (2) wrap the cheese in parchment paper and then in either plastic wrap or foil; and (3) simply wrap the cheese in parchment, wax paper, or butcher paper alone. To these ideas we added the two methods used most often by home cooks: (1) put the cheese in a zipper-lock bag and squeeze out the air before sealing, and (2) wrap the cheese directly in plastic wrap.

To determine which method works best, we wrapped five ¾-pound pieces of Parmigiano-Reggiano, all the same size and shape and all cut fresh at the same time from a single wheel, using each of the five methods. We then stored them in the vegetable crisper of our test kitchen refrigerator for six weeks. We monitored flavor and texture by tasting each piece every other day. Differences began to show up at the one-week mark, and all the subsequent tastings remained consistent. At one week, the sample wrapped in

paper towel and foil seemed slightly soft and chewy, the parchment-wrapped sample was starting to dry out a little, and some tasters felt they detected a faint "off," sour flavor in the plastic-wrapped sample (a new sheet of wrap was used every time the cheese was rewrapped after tasting). The best flavor and texture belonged to the cheese wrapped in parchment and then foil, though the cheese simply thrown in a zipper-lock bag was almost as good. And so it went. At the four-week mark, the paper towel and foil-wrapped cheese was downright mushy, the parchment-wrapped cheese was so dry we were calling it cheese jerky, and the plastic-wrapped cheese tasted distinctly sour and astringent. The parchment and foil-wrapped sample was still the best of show, followed closely by the zipper-lock bagged cheese. At the six-week mark, both of these samples were still fine.

Our conclusion, then, is to stick with the easiest method. If you must store a small piece of Parmesan, just toss the cheese into a small zipper-lock bag and squeeze out as much air as possible before fastening the seal.

Dry Jack Cheese

Your recent article about Parmesan cheese (see "Are Cheap Parmesans Any Good?" September/October 1999, page 26) was fascinating. It mentioned that Parmesan is a grana, or hard grating cheese. Another grating cheese I use is Dry Jack. I wondered where it falls on the spectrum of hard cheeses and how it compares with Parmesan?

MARIETTE HUGHES
MARYSVILLE, CALIF.

➤ *Associate editor Maryellen Driscoll, author of the piece on Parmesan, responds:* Steven Jenkins, cheese expert at the Fairway Market in New York City and author of *Cheese Primer* (Workman, 1996), told us that all granas are Italian cheeses. In fact, the word means "grain" in Italian. Dry Jack, a hand-crafted artisanal cheese from California, thus does not fall into the grana category. Nonetheless, Dry Jack is, as you point out, a hard cheese that grates beautifully and that shatters when cut with a knife.

After a side-by-side tasting of Dry Jack and Parmigiano-Reggiano in our test kitchen, we concluded that each has distinctive flavor and textural nuances. The Parmigiano-Reggiano was unanimously judged to be fruitier and nuttier than the Dry Jack, with a wider range of flavor notes from mild to sharp. This translated into a "stronger, more developed, complex flavor." By comparison, tasters considered the Dry Jack to

be more creamy, buttery, and rich, with a more "one-dimensional" flavor. Several people picked up "cheddarlike" characteristics in the texture and flavor. In sum, each cheese had its fans, and everyone agreed that "these are completely different cheeses."

Vella brand Bear Flag Dry Jack is available by mail for $10.95 per pound, plus shipping costs, from Formaggio Kitchen (244 Huron Avenue, Cambridge, MA 02138; 617-354-4750).

Freezing Red Wine for Cooking

Because I hate to waste red wine left over from cooking, I freeze it in small portions for use in stews and sauces and the like. This way, I don't have to waste wine by throwing it out if no one wants to drink it.

CAROLYN BAKER
HOLLAND, MICH.

➤ So many readers have suggested freezing red wine for cooking that we had to try it. Using a relatively inexpensive, mass-market French red table wine, we made side-by-side pan sauces with wine that had been frozen in ice cube trays for two weeks and wine from a freshly opened bottle. We made each sauce by reducing one-half cup wine to half of its volume over high heat and then swirling in three tablespoons of butter, one at a time, until the sauce was emulsified. Visually, the two sauces differed. The sauce made with frozen wine was lighter in color because many of the dark wine solids had been left behind in the ice cube tray when we turned out the wine cubes. As for flavor, though, not one of our tasters was able to detect any significant difference between the two. Both were delicious.

Sandy Block, a Master of Wine (certified by the Institute of Masters of Wine in London) based in Norwood, Massachusetts, said that chilling a red wine will indeed alter its flavor, probably more so in a complex, delicately balanced wine with many nuances of flavor. The fruit flavors in wine, Block explained, occur at the "middle" of the palate—that is, they are preceded and followed by other flavor sensations. He went on to say that when "red wines are brought to the freezing point, many of the organic compounds which are in solution, principally tannins, pigments, and other polyphenols, precipitate out as solids...causing the wine to lose flavor as well as balance. If a wine's flavors are multidimensional, with full body and strong tannins, they are sure to be flattened out a great deal by freezing, whereas those which are light and simple might not be harmed as much only because they have less to lose."

Thus, in making the decision whether or not

to freeze wine for cooking, consider the specific wine. With our simple red table wine, freezing to help reduce waste and introduce more spontaneity seems like a fine idea, but you won't catch us freezing cubes of Château Lafite-Rothschild.

Garnishing Vietnamese-Style Soups
While it is clear from the article "Shortcutting Vietnamese-Style Noodle Soups" in the March/April 1999 issue (page 18) that author Stephanie Lyness has a sharp palate, there are several points on which the article fell short. First, the class of soups she writes about has a name: *pho*. Second, though the recipes look great, one very important aspect of eating pho—and Vietnamese food in general—is lacking. Where are the condiments—the hoisin sauce, the bottle of Sriracha, the other chile sauces, the pickled chiles, the vinegar, the fish sauce—those additional flavors that the Vietnamese use to personalize their plates, so to speak?

R. W. LUCKY
SEATTLE, WASH.

➤ Of course you are correct that this is how pho is served in Vietnam. However, some of the Asian products you mention may be difficult to find in certain parts of the United States. To the greatest extent possible, we base *Cook's* recipes on widely available supermarket ingredients, which is one reason we chose not to explore the condiments typically served with these soups. In addition, we considered the soups to be highly flavorful and aromatic on their own; though no one here is a native Vietnamese, our American palates were fully satisfied. Nonetheless, there is an excellent mail-order source from which each of the items you mentioned—and many more—are available. That source is the Spice Merchant Oriental Cooking Secrets Catalog (4125 S. Highway 89, P.O. Box 524, Jackson Hole, WY 83001; 800-551-5999 or 307-733-7811; www.emall.com/spice).

Preservatives in Dried Apricots
I shop at a whole food store where many staples are available in bulk. On one recent shopping trip, when I was gathering ingredients to bake the *Cook's* coffee cake with apricot-orange filling (see "The Return of Yeast Coffee Cakes," November/December 1998, page 14), I bought dried apricots that were labeled unsulfured. They were brown, as opposed to the bright orange apricots I've seen in other stores. The filling tasted fine (though I didn't have a batch made with the other apricots for comparison), but it was ugly in color. Can you explain the difference? Does it matter for this recipe?

RICHARD OKIUYE
SAN FRANCISCO, CALIF.

➤ As you say, the brown apricots you purchased were unsulfured, whereas most of the prepackaged, bright orange dried apricots for sale in mainstream supermarkets have been treated with a preservative called sulfur dioxide. All of the food scientists we consulted agreed that sulfur both preserves the natural orange color of the fruit and fights against the development of mold. It does so by drastically slowing the activity of an enzyme in the apricots called polyphenoloxidase, which oxidizes other compounds in the plant tissue and creates brown and gray pigments. (Incidentally, the same browning compounds are also present in apples, pears, bananas, avocados, and potatoes, among other foods.) The use of sulfites is regulated by the Food and Drug Administration and is generally considered safe, though sulfites have been known to produce allergic reactions in some people, especially those who suffer from asthma.

We taste-tested prepackaged dried apricots preserved with sulfur dioxide side by side with some organic, unsulfured dried apricots we bought at a natural food store. Honestly, the unsulfured apricots were thoroughly unappealing—dry, shriveled, brown, and sour tasting. At a quick glance, one test cook mistook them for dried mushrooms. By comparison, the apricots treated with the preservative were bright orange, plump, moist, and sweet, by far the better choice for eating out of hand. Dr. Barry Swanson, professor of food science and human nutrition at Washington State University in Pullman, explained that the sulfur dioxide also limits the reaction of amino acids with glucose and other sugars in the fruit. This leaves a larger portion of the natural sugars in the fruit intact. So, in fact, apricots with sulfur dioxide may taste sweeter than their unsulfured counterparts.

Dr. Swanson did warn, however, that the two types of apricot may well have been different varieties, harvested at different stages of maturity, and dried for different lengths of time at different temperatures. In short, to make a definitive assessment, we would have to begin with the same product, and there is no guarantee that we did. We simply used what was available at stores in our neighborhood. Steve Kollars, director of product development for Sunsweet Growers in Yuba City, California, confirmed Dr. Swanson's hunch, saying that our samples were indeed different varieties. The sulfured apricots were grown in Turkey, and Mr. Kollars characterized them as more sweet and bland than the varieties grown in California, our unsulfured specimens, which he described as more acidic. With regard to texture, Mr. Kollars explained that that the use of preservatives allows the fruit to be processed with more moisture, making for a plumper end product.

All of the above information notwithstanding, we went ahead and made coffee cake fillings out of both types of apricot, and we were truly shocked by the results. The mixture made from the Californian unsulfured apricots was indeed brown—it looked more like prune filling than apricot—but the flavor was fantastic. It tasted bright and truly of apricot, with a great balance of tart and sweet. The mixture from the preserved Turkish apricots was an attractive orange, but its flavor was dull and overly sweet by comparison. If you can overlook the ugly brown color of the former and don't wish to snack on the apricots as you cook, we recommend Californian unsulfured fruit for this recipe. Look at the label on the bulk bin in the store where you make your purchase; the apricots' point of origin is usually listed.

WHAT IS IT?

My husband picked up this knife in a sale bin at a large variety store during a recent business trip to New York City. Nobody at the store knew its use...do you?

CAROLE DOVE
WAYCROSS, GA.

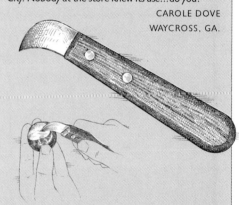

What you have is a chestnut knife. The inch-long, hook-shaped blade is designed to score the curved side of a chestnut with a single forward flick of the wrist. Before cooking fresh chestnuts in the shell in any manner (boiling and roasting are two popular methods), you must first pierce the shell, usually twice, to form an X so that steam can escape during cooking. Otherwise, pressure will build inside the shell as some of the chestnut's moisture vaporizes into steam, eventually causing the chestnut to explode.

The other benefit of puncturing the shell in this manner, especially when roasting chestnuts, is that the shell will begin to separate from the nut meat at the spot where it is slit, which facilitates peeling. In fact, the knife is handy as a peeling tool as well, but whenever you use it—whether to pierce or to peel—it is a good idea to protect the hand with which you hold the nut by wearing an oven mitt. One slip with the chestnut knife and its sharp, pointed blade could easily cut you.

The season for fresh chestnuts is September through February, which is also when chestnut knives are available in stores. Though they may not be pictured in the catalog, Williams-Sonoma (Mail Order Department, P.O. Box 7456, San Francisco, CA 94120; 800-541-2233) sells chestnut knives by mail for $5. Ask for item number 87-48454.

Quick Tips

Simplifying Stock Making

It's easy to make a mess when pouring stock from the pot into a strainer because the solids can make quite a splash when they slip out of the pot. To remove all the solids from the pot before further straining the liquid, Heidi Reichenberger of Brighton, Mass., and Florence Tan of Kensington, Md., both use a large pot with a pasta insert to make the stock. They simply place the meat, bones, and vegetables in the insert at the beginning of cooking and, when it's time to strain, lift the insert and its cargo out of the pot easily and neatly.

Working with Sticky Mixtures

The coconut macaroon mixture from the recipe on page 25 is rather sticky. The cooks in our test kitchen manage to handle this sticky problem by occasionally dipping their hands into a bowl of cold water kept right on the work surface. The water prevents the coconut mixture from sticking to their hands as they form the macaroons. This method works well for any sticky mixture, such as that for Rice Krispies Treats.

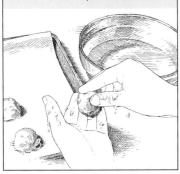

Two Ways with Deviled Eggs

A pasty, heavy texture in the yolk filling can be the downfall of otherwise good deviled eggs. Readers have suggested two options for avoiding this; one is particularly useful when making a large batch, one for a small batch.

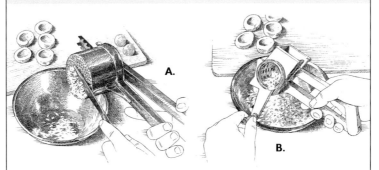

A. To keep her filling as smooth, light, and airy as possible (and to process many yolks at a time) Patricia Welch of Concord, N.H., presses the yolks gently through a potato ricer and uses a knife to shave the extruded yolk off the bottom of the ricer and into a bowl.

B. Maggie Carter of Downey, Calif., and Barb Holland of Markham, Ontario, both offered an alternative method that is especially well suited to smaller batches of yolks. They grate the yolks using the coarse drum of a Mouli grater. It's easy work, and the yolks stay light and fluffy—just be sure not to apply too much pressure on the hopper.

Easier Salad Spinning and Dough Mixing

Terri Walters of Wauwatosa, Wis., agreed with the results of our September/October 1999 testing of salad spinners, finding that models with a top-mounted turn crank rumble and vibrate in use. But Terri did offer this suggestion on how to make them a little smoother and easier to use.

A. Place the spinner in the corner of your sink. This increases your leverage by lowering the height of the turn crank. The extra leverage also acts to push the spinner down to the sink floor and into the sink walls, thereby stabilizing the spinner.

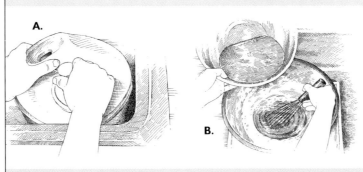

B. Nancy Hollerman of San Andreas, Calif., puts the same principle to work when she is hand mixing a dough or batter in a large mixing bowl. Placing the bowl on a wet dishcloth in the sink provides both a nonslip surface and extra leverage when stirring, which makes the whole operation easier.

Another Way to Steam Peppers

Kathy Somerville of Vancouver, British Columbia, found that cleaning the pan she used to roast peppers in the oven can be a real hassle because the juices of the peppers caramelize and harden into a sticky mess. To get around this problem, she started lining the baking sheet with tin foil. Then she realized that the foil could serve a double duty. Once the peppers are roasted, she tents the foil over the peppers and crimps to seal along the top and sides. Then the peppers can steam to loosen the skins in the same foil used for roasting.

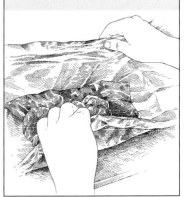

Homemade Cake Mixes

When preparing baked goods, most cooks inevitably haul several boxes and bags of dry ingredients out of their cupboards. While Joan Hensley of Porterville, Calif., has everything out, she'll prepare dry ingredient mixes for her next several cakes by setting up two or three zipper-lock bags in containers and folding their tops over the mouths of the containers to keep the bags open. While measuring the dry ingredients for the cake she's baking at the moment, she also measures ingredients into the bags. Once the bags are full and sealed, she labels them with the date, the name of the cake, and the location of the recipe and pops them into the freezer for future use.

Keeping the Remote Control Clean

Many cooks enjoy listening to music or watching TV as they cook. But sticky hands can make a real mess out of the remote control unit. Before Sig Albert of Berwick, Maine, starts cooking and messing up his hands, he wraps the remote control unit in a layer of clear plastic wrap. The buttons remain visible and operable but don't get smeared by sticky hands.

Stabilizing a Cutting Board

Placing a damp kitchen towel beneath a cutting board is an easy way to keep it from slipping all over the counter, but it leaves you with a damp, dirty kitchen towel to launder. Instead, Jennifer Zanis of Milan, Italy, uses a dampened sheet of paper towel. This works just as well and can be used to wipe down the counter, then simply be thrown away.

Tart Keeper

Wendy Provencher of Addison, Vt., recommends a one-gallon freezer bag to make a snug, tidy cover for an 8- or 9-inch unbaked tart shell. Just slip the tart pan into the bag and seal it. The tart shell can then be refrigerated or frozen until ready to use.

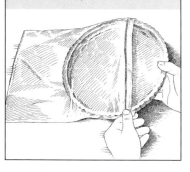

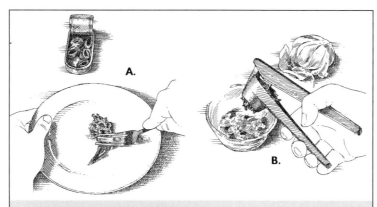

Two Easy Ways to Mince Anchovies

A. Kurt Gerhard of Waltham, Mass., makes quick work of mincing delicate anchovy fillets simply by using a dinner fork to mash them into a paste rather than trying to mince them with a chef's knife.
B. Adam Watson of New York, N.Y., accomplishes the same task by mashing the anchovy fillets in a garlic press. This is especially handy when you have already dirtied the press with garlic.

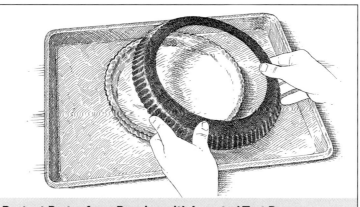

Protect Pastry from Burning with Inverted Tart Pan

Sometimes the edges of a tart shell will burn before the bottom can cook through and brown thoroughly. To protect the shell in these instances both Peter C. Christine of Alna, Maine, and S. Karen Britton of Bellevue, Wash., invert the ring of a second, larger tart pan over the endangered crust and continue baking.

Warming the Serving Bowl

Warm serving bowls are a nice touch for steamed vegetables and other foods. When Stephanie Kessler of Perham, Minn., is steaming her vegetables, she inverts the serving bowl over the covered steaming pot so it will heat up while the vegetables cook.

Sink Saver

With soapy, slippery hands, it's easy to drop a heavy pot or pan in the sink while you're washing it. If you have a porcelain or enameled sink, this can result in an ugly chip or crack. To protect her sink from this potential harm, Rebecca Orlikowski of South Milwaukee, Wis., lays several wooden spoons in it to cushion the blow in case she drops a pot or pan.

Cleaning Copper

Copper cookware is notorious for tarnishing quickly and, therefore, needing frequent polishing. Commercial copper polish requires a bit of scrubbing, but Charlene Gibbs of Bay Shore, New York, taught us that a thin layer of ketchup smeared on the copper and allowed to stand for about five minutes takes the tarnish with it when you rinse it off.

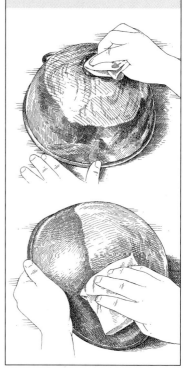

Adding Tiny Amounts of Liquid, Redux

After seeing Linda Burpee's version of this tip in the May/June 1999 Quick Tips, Theresa Gordon of Marblehead, Mass., offered the following refinement. Instead of using a drinking straw, she uses a baby's medicine dropper, which makes it easier to measure the liquid because the dropper is calibrated in units of 1/4 teaspoon. Squeeze the rubber bulb at the end of the dropper, then dip the tip just below the surface of the liquid in the bottle. Release the bulb slowly until you have trapped the desired amount of liquid inside the dropper.

The Best Pan-Fried Fresh Salmon Cakes

How do you get a delicate yet toothsome texture and a soft but clear salmon flavor? It's all in how you handle the fish and the binders.

≥ BY ADAM RIED WITH JULIA COLLIN ≤

We are, in many ways, lucky not to be frugal nineteenth-century New Englanders. One reason, which may have eluded you until now, is that we can use fresh, raw fish in our salmon cakes, if we choose. In America, fish cakes started out as thrifty New England fare, designed to use up salt-preserved or leftover cooked fish and potatoes. Back in the 1800s, the use of fresh fish would certainly have been regarded as a suspicious extravagance, if not downright odd.

Even today, the overwhelming majority of salmon cake recipes we researched started with cooked, or in some cases canned, salmon and used the traditional binder of cooked potato. The occasional recipe that did call for raw fish was usually titled Salmon Burgers. It was to these burgers that all of the tasters gravitated when we cooked up six different recipes for salmon cakes, patties, croquettes, and burgers to kick off our recipe development process. The chunky texture, the moistness, and the direct salmon flavor of the burgers appealed to all. From there, we thought, we could easily extrapolate our ideal salmon cake: toothsome, tender, and moist on the inside; crisp and golden brown on the outside; shapely; and firm and cohesive throughout. But there were many potholes on the road to that ideal. Salmon cakes often suffer from a texture that is either dry, overprocessed, and mushy or wet, loose, and underbound. Fresh salmon flavor may be close to absent, replaced by a distracting cacophony of ill-placed seasonings. The exterior coating may be lackluster. It was clear that to come up with the best possible recipe we would have to thoroughly test binders, seasonings, coatings, cooking mediums, and timing.

A Fresh Start

Based on our experience with three different brands of canned salmon, we wouldn't for a minute consider using that product as a base for our cakes. Full of bones and skin that made cleaning a real hassle, all three brands were utterly unappealing in terms of appearance, smell, taste, and texture. When it came to considering leftover cooked fish, we asked around among home cooks. Everyone we interviewed reported buying only as much fish as could be eaten in a single meal; leftover cooked fish is simply not something most people ever have on hand these days.

Don't bother refrigerating or freezing the cakes once they've been breaded. Just go ahead and cook them.

That was the first good reason we found to make these salmon cakes with fresh fish.

Despite the break with both tradition and the dictate of most current recipes, it was easy to find other good reasons for using fresh fish. The savings of time and effort were high on the list. We simply couldn't see the point of bringing home a beautiful, fresh salmon fillet and then going to the trouble of cooking it twice, once to make "leftovers" and then again to make the cakes. On top of that, we wanted to take advantage of the collagen, a structural protein found in raw fish (and meat) that melts when cooked and provides natural moisture and binding capacity. Both characteristics would be boons to the cakes' texture that precooking the salmon would eliminate. Last, the raw fish would provide a hedge against overcooking the cakes and, consequently, drying them out.

Having decided to use fresh fish, we next tried a couple of methods for breaking it down. Predictably, the food processor ground the fish too finely for our tastes, even when we proceeded with the greatest care. As it turned out, chopping the fish by hand was not difficult, and it provided a far greater margin of error in terms of overprocessing than did the food processor.

Bound, without Gagging

The collagen in the fish gave us a great head start in binding the cakes, but it couldn't do the job entirely on its own. Without additional binders the cakes had a chunky, heavy texture and such strong salmon flavor that some tasters were overwhelmed. Common choices for binders included eggs, either whole or yolks alone, and mayonnaise. Of the many egg combinations we tried, the yolks alone worked best. But when we tried mayonnaise, everyone preferred it over the egg yolks. Just two tablespoons of mayonnaise for the 1¼ pounds of chopped fish we were using added a noticeable creaminess to the cakes' texture and a welcome tang to the flavor. Any more, though, and the cakes began to get a little greasy.

Starchy products, including cooked potato, crushed crackers, dry and fresh bread crumbs, and bread soaked in milk, made up another category of binders worth testing. The cooked potato produced cakes that were rubbery and dry, and both the crushed crackers and dried bread crumbs became leaden and mushy by absorbing too much moisture from the fish, not to mention the fact that they gave the cakes a stale flavor. The milk-soaked bread showed well, but best overall were the fresh bread crumbs we made by simply mincing a piece of sturdy, white sandwich bread from which we had removed the crusts. The bread lightened and softened the texture of the cakes, making them smoother and more refined. Their flavor also benefited. On its own, the bread tastes slightly sweet, so it helped to balance out the strong flavor of the salmon and the creamy tang of the mayonnaise.

With the binding just right, we tried the various flavorings listed in our stack of test recipes. Maybe we're just purists, but the herbs, scallions, garlic, mustard, Worcestershire sauce, hot pepper sauce, and Old Bay seasoning all tasted out of place. In the end, the basic combination of onion, lemon juice, and parsley prevailed by providing simple, bright, fresh flavors. Some tasters objected to the crunch of the minced onion, but we quickly solved that problem by grating it to allow for better integration into the fish mixture.

Coating and Cooking

The next step was to find the crisp, light, golden coating of our dreams. Some recipes leave out the coating altogether, but the resulting cakes lacked interest and tasted too fishy. Flour alone soaked right into the fish mixture and became pasty when cooked. Dried bread crumbs alone were OK, but uninspiring. Our stellar coating involves a full breading treatment, called anglaise, which consists of flour, beaten egg, and bread crumbs, applied in sequence. Although making the coating does entail some extra work as well as more dirty dishes, the result is well worth it: a thin, toasty—even gorgeous—coating. A 15-minute stay in the freezer prior to breading, we found, firms the cakes slightly for easier handling and causes some of the surface moisture to evaporate, which helps the breading to adhere.

Perfecting the cooking procedure would be our last step. Temperature and timing were crucial to ensure that the breading browned but did not burn and that the cakes cooked through to the center without overcooking and drying out. Stovetop cooking over a medium-high flame in a large, heavy-bottomed skillet (at least 12 inches in diameter so as to accommodate eight cakes) proved to be our answer. Cooking the cakes in a generous quantity of vegetable oil—it should reach halfway up the cakes in the pan—for just two minutes per side produced a perfect golden crust and moist fish within, cooked just barely to medium. We tried the oven finish called for in many recipes and found it to be a useless extra step. We also experimented with other fats as a cooking medium, including olive oil, butter, clarified butter, and

a combination of butter and vegetable oil. But for its safety, ease of use, and convenience, vegetable oil alone remained our cooking medium of choice. Its neutral flavor allowed the balanced flavor of the fish mixture, the bright seasonings, and toasty breading of these salmon cakes to really shine.

PAN-FRIED FRESH SALMON CAKES
MAKES EIGHT 2¹⁄₂ BY ³⁄₄-INCH CAKES, SERVING 4

A big wedge of lemon is the simplest accompaniment to salmon cakes, but if you decide to go with dipping sauce, make it before preparing the cakes so the sauce flavors have time to meld. If possible, use panko (Japanese bread crumbs).

1¹⁄₄	pounds salmon fillet
1	slice high-quality white sandwich bread, such as Pepperidge Farm, crusts removed and white part chopped very fine (about 5 tablespoons)
2	tablespoons mayonnaise
¹⁄₄	cup finely grated onion
2	tablespoons chopped fresh parsley leaves
³⁄₄	teaspoon salt
1¹⁄₂	tablespoons juice from 1 lemon
¹⁄₂	cup all-purpose flour
2	large eggs, lightly beaten
1¹⁄₂	teaspoons plus ¹⁄₂ cup vegetable oil
³⁄₄	cup plain dried bread crumbs, preferably panko

1. Following illustration at left, locate and remove any pin bones from salmon flesh. Using sharp knife, cut flesh off skin, then discard skin. Chop salmon flesh into ¹⁄₄ to ¹⁄₃-inch pieces and mix with chopped bread, mayonnaise, onion, parsley, salt, and lemon juice in medium bowl. Scoop a generous ¹⁄₄-cup portion salmon mixture from bowl and use hands to form into a patty measuring roughly 2¹⁄₂ inches in diameter and ³⁄₄ inch thick; place on parchment-lined baking sheet and repeat with remaining salmon mixture until you have 8 patties. Place patties in freezer until surface moisture has evaporated, about 15 minutes.

2. Meanwhile, spread flour in pie plate or shallow baking dish. Beat eggs with 1¹⁄₂ teaspoons vegetable oil and 1¹⁄₂ teaspoons water in second pie plate or shallow baking dish, and spread bread crumbs in a third. Dip chilled salmon patties in flour to cover; shake off excess. Transfer to beaten egg and, using slotted spatula, turn to coat; let excess drip off. Transfer to bread crumbs; shake pan to coat patties completely. Return now-breaded patties to baking sheet.

3. Heat remaining ¹⁄₂ cup vegetable oil in large, heavy-bottomed skillet over medium-high heat until shimmering but not smoking, about 3 minutes; add salmon patties and cook until medium golden brown, about 2 minutes. Flip cakes over and continue cooking until medium

TECHNIQUE | SALMON SIZE

Chop the fish by hand into ¹⁄₄- to ¹⁄₃-inch pieces. It is easy to do and provides a wider margin of error than the food processor, which can turn the fish into mush in an instant.

golden brown on second side, about 2 minutes longer. Transfer cakes to plate lined with paper towels to absorb excess oil on surface, if desired, about 30 seconds, and then serve immediately, with one of the sauces that follow, if you like.

PAN-FRIED SMOKED SALMON CAKES

Follow recipe for Pan-Fried Fresh Salmon Cakes, substituting 8 ounces smoked salmon or lox, chopped into ¹⁄₄ to ¹⁄₃-inch pieces, for 8 ounces of fresh salmon and reducing salt to ¹⁄₂ teaspoon.

PAN-FRIED FRESH SALMON CAKES WITH CHEESE

Jasper White, *Cook's* consulting food editor and an acknowledged seafood authority, suggested adding a small amount of hard grating cheese to the salmon mixture to act as a binder. We admit to some initial skepticism about the idea, but to the delight of the test kitchen staff, every single taster enjoyed the cheese flavor with the fish.

Follow recipe for Pan-Fried Fresh Salmon Cakes, adding 2 tablespoons grated Parmesan or Asiago cheese to salmon mixture and reducing salt to ¹⁄₂ teaspoon.

CREAMY LEMON HERB DIPPING SAUCE
MAKES GENEROUS ¹⁄₂ CUP

¹⁄₂	cup mayonnaise, preferably homemade
2¹⁄₂	tablespoons juice from 1 lemon
1	tablespoon minced fresh parsley leaves
1	tablespoon minced fresh thyme leaves
1	large scallion, white and green part, minced
¹⁄₂	teaspoon salt
	Ground black pepper

Mix all ingredients in small bowl; season to taste with ground black pepper. Cover with plastic wrap and chill until flavors blend, at least 30 minutes.

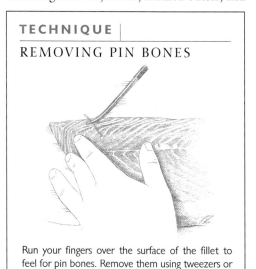

TECHNIQUE

REMOVING PIN BONES

Run your fingers over the surface of the fillet to feel for pin bones. Remove them using tweezers or needle-nose pliers.

How to Cook Beef Short Ribs

Here's how to get the fat out of these notoriously fatty but flavorful ribs, then braise them perfectly.

⇒ BY DAWN YANAGIHARA ⇐

In the supermarket meat case, short ribs are often overlooked, seldom understood, rather intimidating hunks of meat and bone that are frequently turned a cold shoulder. But braise them, and they become yielding, tender, and succulent. Then douse them with a velvety sauce containing all the rich, bold flavors from the braise, and they are as satisfying as beef stew, but with much more panache.

All of this, however, comes at a price: short ribs are outrageously fatty. The challenge is to get them to give up their fat. To find the best method of fat removal and to uncover the makings of a pot of soulful, flavorful short ribs, I armed myself with a good number of recipes and ribs galore, then embarked on a braise-athon.

Before You Braise

Whichever way you cut it, short ribs are just what their name says they are: "short ribs" cut from any part along the length of the cow's ribs. They can come from the lower belly section or higher up toward the back, from the shoulder (or chuck) area, or the forward midsection. They can be cut English or flanken style (see "Get Shorty," page 9), but no matter what, they're always fatty. Of course, the fat and connective tissue are also what make them so deeply flavorful, so to me, at least, they are worth dealing with.

The first step in most braises is browning the meat. Browning adds color and flavor, but in the case of short ribs it also presents an opportunity to render some of the excessive fat. I tried browning both on the stovetop and in the oven and quickly became a proponent of oven browning. As long as you own a roasting pan large enough to hold all of the ribs in a single layer, you can use the oven to brown them in just one batch. This eliminates the need to brown in multiple batches on the stove, which can create a greasy, splattery mess and result in burnt drippings in the bottom of the pot. In the oven, the ribs can brown for a good long time to maximize rendering. (Because they can also brown

The bacon-onion-parsnip garnish adds color, flavor, and texture.

unattended, you can use that time to prepare the other ingredients for the braise). The single inconvenience of oven browning is deglazing the roasting pan on the stovetop, which makes a burner-worthy roasting pan a prerequisite.

Like a beef stew, short ribs need aromatic vegetables. After having made a couple of batches with onions only, I chose to use a combination of onions, carrots, celery, and garlic for full, round flavor.

Braising liquids required only a cursory investigation. Homemade beef stock or broth was out of the question because just about no one makes it. And, based on previous tastings at this magazine, I discounted canned beef broth altogether. Canned chicken broth, however, offers sufficient backbone and, when enriched by the flavor and body contributed by the short ribs themselves, makes for a rich, robust sauce. I began the braise-athon using a combination of red wine,

chicken broth, and water. I eventually eliminated water, but the sauce, despite the abundance of aromatics and herbs, remained strangely hollow and lacking. All along I had been using a cheap, hardly potable wine. After stepping up to a good, solid one worthy of drinking, the sauce improved dramatically; it had the complexity and resonance that I was looking for. In trying other liquids, I found that a dark, mildly assertive beer—not a light lager—used in place of the wine also makes an excellent sauce.

If the braising liquid was to transform itself into the sauce I was after, it would need some thickening. After various experiments, I found that adding flour to the sautéed vegetables before pouring in the liquid resulted in a sauce that was lustrous and had the perfect consistency.

Get Fatty

Over the course of many hours of braising, I found that even an hour-long stint of browning in the oven was not enough to get the short ribs to relinquish all their fat. As they braise, they continue to release fat, which means that the braising liquid must be defatted before it is palatable. I found the easiest technique to be a two-day process, necessitating some forethought. Braise the ribs, let them cool in the liquid so that the meat does not dry out, remove them, strain the liquid, then chill the ribs and the liquid separately. The next day, spoon the solidified fat off the liquid's surface, and heat the liquid and the ribs together. This takes time, but braising usually does. Of course, the ribs can be made and served on the same day, provided that you allow the

TECHNIQUE | MANAGING THE FAT

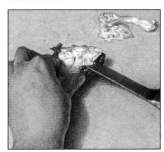

1. With a paring or boning knife, trim off the surface fat and silver skin from each rib.

2. After browning the ribs 45 minutes, remove liquid and fat with a bulb baster or pour off as shown here.

braising liquid to settle after straining so that the fat separates to the top, then carefully spoon off as much fat as possible. This isn't as easy or efficient as scooping off solidified fat, but it gets most of the job done.

SHORT RIBS BRAISED IN RED WINE WITH BACON, PARSNIPS, AND PEARL ONIONS
SERVES 6

If braising and serving the ribs on the same day, bypass cooling the ribs in the braising liquid; instead, remove them from the pot straight out of the oven, strain the liquid, then let it settle so that the fat separates to the top. With a wide shallow spoon, skim off as much fat as possible and continue with the recipe. Though this recipe and the one that follows call for widely available English-style short ribs, both recipes will also work with flanken-style short ribs. Serve the short ribs over noodles or mashed potatoes.

- 6 pounds bone-in English-style short ribs, trimmed of excess fat and silver skin, or bone-in flanken-style short ribs (see illustrations in "Get Shorty," right)
  Salt and ground black pepper
- 3 cups dry full-bodied red wine
- 3 large onions, chopped medium
- 2 medium carrots, chopped medium
- I large celery stalk, chopped medium
- 9 medium garlic cloves, chopped (about 3 tablespoons)
- 1/4 cup all-purpose flour
- 4 cups chicken stock or canned low-sodium chicken broth
- I can (14.5 ounces) drained canned chopped tomatoes
- 1 1/2 tablespoons minced fresh rosemary leaves
- I tablespoon minced fresh thyme leaves
- 3 medium bay leaves
- I teaspoon tomato paste

Bacon, Pearl Onion, and Parsnip Garnish
- 6 slices bacon (about 6 ounces), cut into 1/4-inch pieces
- 8 ounces frozen pearl onions (do not thaw)
- 4 medium parsnips (about 10 ounces), peeled and cut diagonally into 3/4-inch pieces
- 1/4 teaspoon sugar
- 1/4 teaspoon salt
- 6 tablespoons chopped fresh parsley leaves

1. Adjust oven rack to lower-middle position and heat oven to 450 degrees. Arrange short ribs bone-side down in single layer in large flame-proof roasting pan; season with salt and pepper. Roast until meat begins to brown, about 45 minutes; drain off all liquid and fat with bulb baster. Return pan to oven and continue to cook until meat is well browned, 15 to 20 minutes longer. (For flanken-style short ribs, arrange ribs in sin-

gle layer in large roasting pan; season with salt and pepper. Roast until meat begins to brown, about 45 minutes; drain off all liquid and fat with baster. Return pan to oven and continue to cook until browned, about 8 minutes; using tongs, flip each piece and cook until second side is browned, about 8 minutes longer). Transfer ribs to large plate; set aside. Drain off fat to small bowl and reserve. Reduce oven temperature to 300 degrees. Place roasting pan on two stovetop burners set at medium heat; add wine and bring to simmer, scraping up browned bits with wooden spoon. Set roasting pan with wine aside.

2. Heat 2 tablespoons reserved fat in large Dutch oven over medium-high heat; add onions, carrots, and celery. Sauté, stirring occasionally, until vegetables soften, about 12 minutes. Add garlic and cook until fragrant, about 30 seconds. Stir in flour until combined, about 45 seconds. Stir in wine from roasting pan, chicken stock, tomatoes, rosemary, thyme, bay leaves, tomato paste, and salt and pepper to taste. Bring to boil and add short ribs, completely submerging meat in liquid; return to boil, cover, place in oven, and simmer until ribs are tender, about 2 to 2 1/2 hours. Transfer pot to wire rack and cool, par-

Get Shorty

When I started testing short ribs, I went to the local grocery store and bought out their supply. What I brought back to the test kitchen were 2- to 4-inch lengths of wide flat rib bone, to which a rectangular plate of fatty meat was attached (see photo, below left). I also ordered short ribs from the butcher. Imagine my confusion when these turned out to be long, continuous pieces of meat, about 3/4 inch thick, that had been cut across the ribs and grain and that included two or three segments of rib bone (below right). The former, I learned, are sometimes called English-style short ribs and the latter are called flanken-style ribs.

— BONE —

English style   **Flanken style**

I began by braising both types of ribs. The ones from the butcher were favored by most tasters because the relatively thin, across-the-grain cut made the meat more pleasant to eat; the supermarket ribs were a bit stringier because they contained longer segments of "grain." Both types were equally tender and good, but considering the cost ($5.99 versus $2.99 per pound) and effort (special order) required to procure the butcher-cut specimens, I decided to go with the supermarket variety. —D.Y.

tially covered, until warm, about 2 hours.

3. Transfer ribs from pot to large plate, removing excess vegetables that may cling to meat; discard loose bones that have fallen away from meat. Strain braising liquid into medium bowl, pressing out liquid from solids; discard solids. Cover ribs and liquid separately with plastic wrap and refrigerate overnight. (Can be refrigerated up to 3 days.)

4. *To prepare garnish and finish dish*: In Dutch oven, cook bacon over medium heat until just crisp, 8 to 10 minutes; remove with slotted spoon to plate lined with paper towel. Add to Dutch oven pearl onions, parsnips, sugar, and salt; increase heat to high and sauté, stirring occasionally, until browned, about 5 minutes. Spoon off and discard solidified fat from reserved braising liquid. Add defatted liquid and bring to simmer, stirring occasionally; adjust seasoning with salt and pepper. Submerge ribs in liquid, return to simmer. Reduce heat to medium and cook, partially covered, until ribs are heated through and vegetables are tender, about 5 minutes longer; gently stir in bacon. Divide ribs and sauce among individual bowls, sprinkle each with 1 tablespoon parsley, and serve.

PORTER–BRAISED SHORT RIBS WITH PRUNES, BRANDY, AND LEMON ESSENCE
SERVES 6

Brandy-soaked prunes take the place of vegetables here, so this version is particularly suited to a mashed root vegetable or potato accompaniment.

Brandy, Prune, and Lemon Essence Garnish
- 1/2 cup brandy
- 8 ounces pitted prunes, each prune halved
- 2 teaspoons brown sugar
- 2 teaspoons grated zest from 1 lemon
- 6 tablespoons chopped fresh parsley leaves

1. Follow recipe for Short Ribs Braised in Red Wine with Bacon, Parsnips, and Pearl Onions, substituting 3 cups porter beer for the red wine, eliminating rosemary, and substituting 2 tablespoons Dijon mustard and 2 teaspoons Worcestershire sauce for the tomato paste. Continue with recipe through step 3.

2. *To prepare garnish and finish dish:* Bring brandy to boil in small saucepan; off heat, add prunes and let stand until plump and softened, about 15 minutes. Meanwhile, spoon off and discard solidified fat from braising liquid. Bring braising liquid to boil in Dutch oven over medium-high heat, stirring occasionally. Add prunes, brandy, and brown sugar; adjust seasoning with salt and pepper. Submerge ribs in liquid and return to simmer. Reduce heat to medium-low and cook until ribs are heated through, about 5 minutes longer; gently stir in lemon zest. Divide ribs and sauce among individual bowls, sprinkle each with 1 tablespoon parsley, and serve.

Rustic Potato-Leek Soup

For a country-style soup with the best flavor, we had to find the right variety of potato—
and use more of the leek than is traditional.

> BY KAY RENTSCHLER WITH BRIDGET LANCASTER

We love potatoes in any form, and leeks, with their gentle taste of onion, are among our favorite soup aromatics. And we have always liked the classic creamy soup that French cooks make from potatoes and leeks. But sometimes that recipe seems a little too refined. At times we want these two ingredients at their most basic; we want to eat them while resting our elbows on a scarred, wooden table, a cantankerous piece of bread in one hand. So for this story we decided to part company with the creamy French classic and take on the challenge of a more peasant-style French soup.

TECHNIQUE

CLEANING LEEKS

Leeks are often quite dirty and gritty, so they require thorough cleaning. There are two ways to do this. Both methods require that you first cut the dark green portion into quarters lengthwise, leaving the root end intact.

Hold the leek under running water and shuffle the cut layers like a deck of cards.

Slosh the cut end of the leek up and down in still water.

Ironically, the two ingredients that should make this soup great (potatoes and leeks) can also be its downfall. The potatoes should actually play only a supporting role; the leeks, gritty and time-consuming to clean though they are, are the real star of this soup. Cooking time is also crucial. Undercook the soup and the flavors will not meld; cook it too long and you will have a mixture of broken-down bits with little flavor or bite. These were the challenges we bore in mind when we set out.

We tested the potatoes first. Quickly eliminating high-starch, low-moisture baking potatoes, which broke down immediately, we duly rejected the flavorful, medium-starch Yukon Gold as well. These potatoes broke down, too—just not as quickly. We settled on waxy, low-starch Red Bliss potatoes, which held their texture and did not become waterlogged while cooking. Then we reduced the proportion of potatoes altogether, giving the leeks the leading role.

Next we wanted to pump up the flavor of the soup. We decided to use not only the white part of the leek but a substantial part of the green as well, and we left the chopped pieces large enough to create textural interest. A whopping four pounds of leeks used this way provided nonstop flavor. Water wasn't dynamic enough to stand up to it, so we used chicken broth instead.

But our real breakthrough came in the province of technique. We knew that potatoes and leeks would need different simmering times. Stewing the leeks over a low flame to coax out as much flavor as possible, we added the potatoes later, with the canned broth, then simmered them until almost tender. At that point we removed the pot from the heat, allowing the potatoes to finish cooking in the hot broth so they would not overcook and become mushy. The result: a soup with perfectly cooked potatoes, sweet and tender leeks, and an outspoken leek flavor. Because the potatoes were not cooked long enough to release their starch and thicken the broth, we added a little flour to cook with the leeks, giving the broth just the right amount of body to pull everything together.

COUNTRY-STYLE POTATO-LEEK SOUP

MAKES ABOUT 11 CUPS, SERVING 6 TO 8

Leeks differ. If yours have large desirable white and light green sections, use 4 pounds of leeks; if they're short on these parts, go with 5 pounds.

    6   tablespoons unsalted butter
  4–5   pounds leeks (see note above)
    1   tablespoon all-purpose flour
  5¼   cups chicken stock or canned low-sodium
        chicken broth
    1   bay leaf
  1¾   pounds red potatoes (about 5 medium), peeled
        and cut into ¾-inch dice
        Salt and ground black pepper

1. Cut off roots and tough dark green portion of leeks, leaving white portion and about 3 inches of light green. Clean leeks following illustrations at left. Slice in half lengthwise and chop into 1-inch sections. (You should have about 11 cups).

2. Heat butter in Dutch oven over medium-low heat until foaming; stir in leeks, increase heat to medium, cover and cook, stirring occasionally, until leeks are tender but not mushy, 15 to 20 minutes; do not brown. Sprinkle flour over leeks and stir to coat evenly ; cook until flour dissolves, about 2 minutes. Increase heat to high; whisking constantly, gradually add stock. Add bay leaf and potatoes; cover and bring to boil. Reduce heat to medium-low and simmer, covered, until potatoes are almost tender, 5 to 7 minutes. Remove pot from heat and let stand until potatoes are tender and flavors meld, 10 to 15 minutes. Discard bay leaf, season with salt and pepper; serve immediately.

COUNTRY-STYLE POTATO-LEEK SOUP
WITH KIELBASA

Eight ounces of cooked ham, cut into ½-inch dice, can be substituted for the sausage, if desired. Whichever you choose, season the soup with care, since both ham and kielbasa are fully seasoned.

Follow recipe for Country-Style Potato-Leek Soup. Before removing pot from heat, stir in 8 ounces kielbasa sausage, cut into ½-inch slices.

COUNTRY-STYLE POTATO-LEEK SOUP
WITH WHITE BEANS

Follow recipe for Country-Style Potato-Leek Soup, reducing potatoes to 2 medium (about ¾ pound). Before removing pot from heat, stir in 1 cup hot water and 1 cup canned cannellini beans.

Sweet Tart Pastry 101

Sweet tart pastry is both finicky and hard to roll out. Here is a recipe that is relatively foolproof, quick, and easier to handle.

⇒ BY KAY RENTSCHLER ⇐

Both of my Indiana grandmothers were expert pie bakers. Lucky for them: where they grew up, pies were the sole index of a woman's culinary expertise (except for the prized fudge recipe or two). But when I left the midsection of the country, I found eloquence in another turn of phrase: the strawberry tart. Sitting in a small French restaurant, virtually inhaling the glazed strawberries before me with my eyes and nose, and lining up the first bite so as to capture everything at once—chilled vanilla pastry cream, sweet strawberries, and crisp, buttery pastry—I was light years removed from a slice of raisin pie. This was heaven on a plate.

Over the years I have come to value the virtues of a traditional pie dough as much as those of its European cousin, known as *pâte sucrée* (literally, "sugar dough"). But many American pie bakers have yet to discover the virtues of sweet pastry dough. What is it, and how does it differ from regular pie dough? Does it deserve a place at our table? The answer is, emphatically, yes.

No fluting is required on this tart shell—you can finish the shell with one sweep of the rolling pin.

Sweetie Pie

While a regular pie dough is tender and flaky, a sweet tart dough is tender and crisp. Fine-textured, buttery rich, and crumbly, it is often described as cookielike. In fact, cookies are actually descendants of sweet pastry dough—a dough deemed so delicious by the French that it was considered worth eating on its own. There are also differences in the dough's relationship to the filling. Rather than encasing a deep hearty filling, a tart shell shares the stage with its filling. Traditional tart fillings—caramel, marzipan, pastry cream, or even jam, often adorned with glazed fresh fruits or nuts—would seem excessive if housed in a deeper pie. But these intense flavors and textures are perfect in thin layers balanced by a crisp, thin pastry. And a tart is elegant and understated, a dressy finish to a formal dinner. Whereas a slice of pie might request the company

of some cold milk, a tart would prefer espresso.

According to Bruce Healey, author of *The French Cookie Book* (Morrow, 1994), the proportions of ingredients for basic sweet pastry have not changed for a generation. These he offers as equal parts butter and sugar (one-half cup), twice as much flour, and one large egg. I made his basic dough and found little to quibble about. But if these proportions are standard, as he claims, then what accounts for all of the substandard pâte sucrées out there? I have eaten my share of thick, tough, and flavorless tart doughs. Many American recipes for these doughs call for too little butter or sugar, thus compromising texture, but more often poor technique is to blame.

I wanted to produce a crisp, flavorful pastry dough using the fastest and most foolproof method available. Though you can make sweet pastry as you would cookie dough, by creaming the butter and sugar together, then adding flour and finally egg, I found this technique too time-consuming. Like pie pastries, most sweet pastry

recipes direct the cook to cut butter into flour by hand or processor and then add liquid. Knowing cold butter and minimal handling to be critical to the success of this method, I headed straight for the food processor. Pulsing very cold butter with dry ingredients to obtain a fine, pebbly consistency took all of 15 seconds.

The addition of liquid was a trickier matter. I was reluctant to use a food processor, feeling it gave me less control. But the alternative, tossing the pebbly dough onto a countertop and fluffing the liquid in by hand, followed by a *fraisage*—the flattening of the dough in short strokes with the heel of the hand to incorporate ingredients—seemed tiresome and unnecessary to some of my colleagues. Though the manual method for adding liquid produced a marginally more delicate, tender dough, I found that in fact the difference was barely discernible—and only in side-by-side comparisons. Addition of liquid ingredients with the food processor took about 25 seconds. Armed with this quick, no-fuss technique, I wanted to tweak the major players in the dough to tease out the most tender, tastiest pastry imaginable.

The first to come under scrutiny were the butter and the sugar. The higher the proportion of butter in a pâte sucrée, the more delicate its crumb. I experimented with additional butter and found 10 tablespoons (five ounces) to be the maximum allowable for ease of handling. More butter simply made the dough too soft and did not improve its flavor or texture. As for the sugar, the traditional half cup did not seem overly sweet, and any less than that produced a dough lacking in flavor and tenderness. Most recipes recommend the use of superfine sugar (thought to be important for melting in a dough with so little liquid), but because no one ever has it in their pantry, I tried using confectioners' sugar, an ingredient most people do have on hand. I found that three-quarters cup gave me a crisper dough

A pie dough (left) derives its flakiness from relatively large pieces of butter in the dough. As the butter melts during baking, evaporation produces steam. The steam creates pockets in the dough, which makes it flaky. In a pastry dough (right), the butter is dispersed evenly throughout the dough, coating the flour and preventing it from absorbing liquid. The resulting dough is crumbly, rather than flaky.

than the one made with granulated sugar. Because I was using a food processor, the sugar did not need to be sifted but could be pulsed in with the other dry ingredients.

Next up for examination were the liquid ingredients. Though most recipes call for a whole egg, some call for a combination of egg yolk and cream. (As in any cookie dough, the egg lends structure to a dough that would otherwise be completely crumbly.) Testing these side by side, I discovered that the yolk and cream combination (one yolk and two tablespoons of cream) created a lovely crust with a degree of flakiness, a quality I value over the slightly firmer dough produced when using a whole egg alone. Finally, one-half teaspoon of vanilla in the liquid ingredients gave the baked crust a subtly complex flavor.

The last major player to be manipulated was the flour. Perfectly happy with my tests using all-purpose, I nevertheless performed a couple of tests using half all-purpose and half pastry flour, as well as half all-purpose and half cake flour. My reasoning was this: low-protein flours, such as pastry and cake flours (equal in protein percentage at about 8%, compared with all-purpose at about 11%) tend to retard gluten development, thus yielding a more tender dough. I was surprised to learn that in composition pastry and cake flours are identical; cake flour is simply bleached. To be honest, I liked the dough made with half pastry flour: it was a bit more tender and delicate than that made entirely with all-purpose and no more difficult to work with. But the improvement was not impressive enough to cause me to recommend the pastry flour, particularly since its acquisition requires a mail order or a vacation in South Carolina. The dough made with half cake flour had a pleasing texture as well, but less flavor: some of the taste was lost in the wash when the flour was bleached.

In the end, the proportions I was using left too much dough for my 9-inch tart pan. While many recipes calling for 1½ cups flour declared a yield of enough dough for one 9- or 11-inch tart, I scaled my proportions back to fit the pan.

Setting and Baking the Dough

Sweet pastry dough typically requires at least an hour of refrigerated resting time for the liquid ingredients to hydrate the dough fully and make it more manageable. In fact, an hour was the minimal wait required before rolling out this dough. A two-hour rest was even better. The butter gives the dough a nice plasticity if the dough is cold enough and makes rolling relatively easy. I knew it would be a challenge to roll out the dough directly on the counter with enough flour to keep it from sticking. I was able to convey it in one piece from counter to pan, but my success halted abruptly at the pan's edge. The baked shell was reminiscent of dried molding clay. Best results were obtained with minimal flouring and by rolling the dough out between double layers of wide parchment paper or plastic wrap without letting it become warm. Though many recipes suggest that a sweet pastry dough can simply be pressed into a pan, my tests did not support this recommendation. The patchwork technique made the crucial "even thickness" all but unattainable, and the imperfectly fused pieces did not have the same structural integrity as a correctly fitted, single sheath of dough. The patched crust

tended to crumble along the fault lines as it was unmolded or cut.

A half hour in the freezer "set" the dough nicely to prepare it for "blind baking" (baking the shell without any filling). A low oven rack and a baking sheet placed directly beneath the tart shell (to conduct heat evenly to the crust bottom) browned the tart beautifully. Because of the crust's delicate nature, the metal weights used to blind bake the tart are best left in place until the crust's edges are distinctly brown, about 30 minutes, at which point the weights can be removed and the tart moved to a higher rack for 5 more minutes to brown the top side of the crust.

This baked tart shell is a delight to eat. Firm and shapely before shattering under the impact of a fork, its crumb is buttery and light, its flavor superb. We consumed many pastry crusts during the course of testing—both filled and unfilled. Very few crumbs lived to see the inside of a trash barrel.

SWEET TART PASTRY (PÂTE SUCRÉE)
MAKES ONE 9- TO 9½-INCH TART SHELL

If the dough feels too firm when you're ready to roll it out, let it stand at room temperature for a few minutes. If, on the other hand, the dough becomes soft and sticky while rolling, don't hesitate to rechill it until it becomes easier to work with. Better to rechill than to add too much flour, which will damage the delicate, crisp texture of the dough. We find a French rolling pin (as pictured in

A Thing for Blonds

During the course of working on this recipe I was struck by two things: the first was how much better my pastry tasted deeply browned than lightly browned. This was not really surprising, as food scientists have long been aware that the volatile compounds arising from browning food produce a complex and pleasing range of flavors. How then to account for the second thing I was struck by—the American predilection for blond baked goods? So many pale fruit tarts, soft pale bread, and pale pliable cookies. In Europe, tart doughs are brown and crisp; bread crusts shatter rather than bend; cookies are crunchy. Why, I wondered, do we consistently underbake?

I took my inquiry to Stephen Schmidt, a food writer and historian. He agreed that Americans seem to favor soft white bread and soft moist textures, and he ventured some cautious speculation about the origin of this unfortunate tradition. In the mid-19th century, Schmidt said, Southern cooks wanted to demon-

strate that their biscuits and cookies were made with the finest white flour. Pale baked goods confirmed the quality of the ingredient in much the same way that a woman's pale complexion once confirmed her breeding. It is instructive to note that the best known flour in the South is called White Lily. Around the same time, Americans, unlike their European counterparts, became extremely interested in chemical leavenings: baking soda and powder. Chemical leavenings speed up baking times by lightening batters and doughs. Things are therefore done before they brown. Denser doughs, such as those used to make scones without baking powder or bread with just a little yeast, take longer to bake. When they're done, they're brown. —K.R.

illustrations) to be the most precise instrument for rolling tart pastry. Bake the tart shell in a 9- to 9½-inch tart pan with a removable bottom and fluted sides about 1 to 1⅛ inches high.

- 1 large egg yolk
- 1 tablespoon heavy cream
- ½ teaspoon vanilla extract
- 1¼ cups all-purpose unbleached flour, plus 1 tablespoon for dusting
- ⅔ cup confectioners' sugar
- ¼ teaspoon salt
- 8 tablespoons (1 stick) very cold unsalted butter, cut into twenty-four ¾-inch cubes

1. Whisk together yolk, cream, and vanilla in small bowl; set aside. Pulse to combine flour, sugar, and salt in bowl of food processor fitted with steel blade. Scatter butter pieces over flour mixture; pulse to cut butter into flour until mixture resembles coarse meal, about fifteen 1-second pulses. With machine running, add egg mixture and process until dough just comes together, about 25 seconds. Turn dough onto sheet of plastic wrap and press into 6-inch disk. Wrap in plastic and refrigerate at least 2 hours.

2. Unwrap dough; lightly flour large sheet of parchment paper or plastic wrap and place dough in center. Following illustrations 1–9,

roll out dough and line tart pan (see note preceeding recipe). Freeze dough 30 minutes.

3. Meanwhile, adjust one oven rack to upper-middle position and other rack to lower-middle position; heat oven to 375 degrees. Place chilled tart shell on cookie sheet; press 12-inch square of foil inside tart shell and fill with metal or ceramic pie weights. Bake on lower rack 30 minutes, rotating halfway through baking time. Carefully remove foil and weights by gathering edges of foil and pulling up and out. Transfer cookie sheet with tart shell to upper rack and continue to bake until shell is golden brown, about 5 minutes longer.

STEP-BY-STEP | ROLLING AND FITTING THE DOUGH

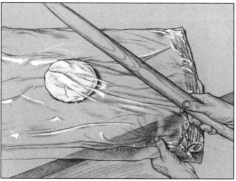

1. To facilitate rolling, flatten the dough with a rolling pin by rapping it smartly with one hand and spinning the dough with the other.

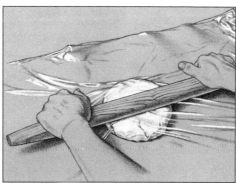

2. Roll the dough upward from the center and downward from the center with even pressure.

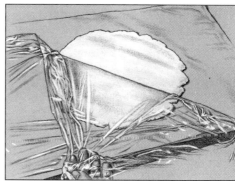

3. Spin the dough one quarter turn, repeating step 2 until dough is 13 inches in diameter and ⅛ inch thick. Loosen the dough from the plastic and flour again.

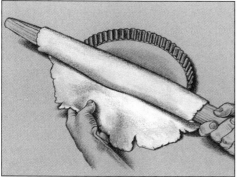

4. Ease the dough over the rolling pin and roll it up loosely. Unroll the dough on top of the tart pan.

5. Lift the edge of the dough with one hand and ease it into the corners of the pan with the other.

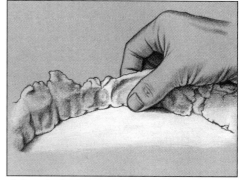

6. Press the dough into the fluted sides of the pan, forming a distinct seam along the pan circumference.

7. If some edges are too thin, reinforce the sides by folding the dough back on itself.

8. Run the rolling pin over the top of the tart pan to remove any excess dough.

9. The finished edge should be ¼ inch thick. If it is not, press the dough up over the edge and pinch.

Streamlining Cassoulet

Can you make a great cassoulet in a few hours without sacrificing
the deep, melded flavors that are characteristic of this dish?

≥ BY BRIDGET LANCASTER ≤

Every once in a while, a dish comes around that is so robust, so satisfying to every sense that we deem it comfort food. It warms us from the inside out and assures us that this winter, too, shall pass. Cassoulet is such a dish.

But for most cooks, the reasons to eat cassoulet outnumber the reasons to make it. Cassoulet can take three days to make, and the ingredients can be both hard to find and difficult to prepare.

The cassoulet originated in Langue-doc, France, and each area of the region touts its recipe as "the real thing." All versions of the dish contain white beans, but that is where the agreement ends. Some prefer pork loin in their cassoulet, others use a shoulder of lamb, while still others use a combination of both. Mutton, duck, pheasant, garlic sausage, and even fish can be found in the different variations.

But the best known and most often replicated type of cassoulet hails from Toulouse. This cassoulet must start with the preparation of confit. Meat or poultry, most often goose legs (the region of Toulouse also houses the foie gras industry, so goose is plentiful), is placed in a large container, sprinkled heavily with salt, and cured for 24 to 48 hours. This both preserves and tenderizes the meat. After this sojourn in salt, the meat is slowly simmered in its own fat, so that the flavor of the fat penetrates the spaces previously occupied by the juices. The finished confit may be used immediately or stored in an airtight container, covered in its own fat to prevent contamination.

But the intricacy of cassoulet doesn't end with the confit. Pork loin and mutton must be slow-roasted for hours to become fully tender, and garlic sausages freshly made. The beans must be presoaked and then simmered with pork rinds to develop flavor. Finally, the entire mixture has to be combined in an earthenware pot, topped with bread crumbs, and placed in a low-temperature oven to simmer slowly for several hours.

The result is nothing short of divine. But while this classic French peasant dish can be replicated at restaurants, it is definitely not a dish for the casual home cook. The time investment alone is impractical, and it can be difficult to achieve a

We devised a method that uses one pot rather than three.

perfect balance of flavor. On more than one occasion I have eaten cassoulets that were overwhelmed by salt or swimming in fat, most often because of the confit and sausages.

But I love this dish so much that I decided it would be worth the effort to try to streamline it without compromising its essential nature.

Ex-con(fit)

I decided to accept the hardest of the challenges first and conquer the confit. I eliminated the confit made from scratch as far too time-consuming. Assessing my other options, I created three cassoulets. One was prepared with braised duck leg confit (goose leg confit is less widely available) purchased through my butcher. The others I made with no confit at all, starting one version with sautéed and braised duck legs and the other with sautéed and braised chicken legs, which I wanted to use because they're so easy to find in the supermarket. The results were disheartening, although not surprising. The cassoulet made with the purchased confit was the clear favorite. Those made without it produced dishes more reminiscent of duck and chicken stews.

Unfortunately, ready-made con-

fit is not widely available, so I wanted to develop a recipe that wouldn't rely on it. Somewhat ironically, I arrived at the solution to the problem with some help from the confit itself.

Because confit is salt-cured and then cooked in its own fat, it retains an intense duck flavor when added to the cassoulet, contributing a rich, slightly smoky flavor that was noticeably absent from the dishes prepared with the sautéed duck and chicken. The texture of the dish made with confit was superior as well, the flesh plump with flavor yet tender to the bite; the sautéed and braised duck and chicken became tough and gave up all of their flavor to the broth. Taking an educated guess, I decided to adopt an approach often used at *Cook's* and brine the chicken. Because we had found when making other dishes that brining resulted in poultry that was both more moist and more flavorful, I reasoned that brining the chicken might bring it closer to the tender texture of confit. To approximate the confit's light smokiness, I decided to cook the legs briefly in bacon fat.

I quick-soaked the chicken legs for one hour in a concentrated salt and sugar solution, sautéed them quickly in rendered bacon fat, then braised them with the rest of the cassoulet ingredients. What resulted was just what I was hoping for: a suitable substitute for duck confit. The bacon added a smoky flavor, and it enhanced the flavors of the pork and sausage added later. The texture was spot-on for the confit; the chicken legs were plump and juicy; and the broth became well seasoned because of the brine. With this "mock" confit in hand, I proceeded.

CUTS | BLADE vs. CENTER LOIN

BLADE **CENTER LOIN**

Because the pork is stewed, the blade end of the loin (left) is preferable to the leaner center loin.

Red Meat and Beans

My next test involved figuring out which meats to use and how to avoid the issue of slow-roasting. I knew that I wanted to be true to the original recipe and use either fresh pork or lamb. I decided to try stewing the meat in liquid entirely on top of the stove. This method yielded great results in terms of tenderness, but the meat had none of the depth of flavor that occurs with roasting. Searing the meat in some of the rendered bacon fat that I had used with the chicken legs took care of that problem.

Because I was now stewing the meat, I needed to use cuts that were appropriate for this method. I tried pork loin, the choice in so many cassoulet recipes, but the loin became waterlogged and tasteless during stewing. A suggestion from my butcher led me to try a blade-end roast, which is the part of the loin closest to the shoulder. This cut, which has more internal fat than the center loin, retained the moisture and flavor that was lost with the other cut. To facilitate quicker cooking, I cut the roast into one-inch pieces. I used similar testing with the lamb. Lamb shoulder is the best cut for stewing, but it can be difficult to find in markets. I bought instead thick lamb shoulder chops, which I cut into one-inch pieces. Finally, perfectly tender meat without the effort of roasting.

Cassoulets traditionally use white beans. I wanted to make sure that the beans would retain their shape while adding a soft texture to the dish. Canned beans fell apart quickly, so I opted for dried beans. I tested four varieties, and the winner was the pale green flageolet bean. These small, French kidney-shaped beans have a creamy, tender texture and delicate flavor that perfectly enhanced the cassoulet. I also parcooked the beans on top of the stove along with the rendered bacon fat and the aromatics to let them absorb as much flavor as possible in little time, an effort to duplicate the depth of flavor in the original.

After ruling out the use of hard-to-find French sausages (and not willing to take the time to make my own), I found that both kielbasa and andouille sausages intensified the smokiness that I desired.

Keep It Simple

With the major problems out of the way, I was able to concentrate on streamlining the technique used to cook the dish. This proved to be quite simple. With the chicken, meat, and beans now modified for cooking on the stovetop, oven-braising became unnecessary. Cooking the dish entirely on the stove at a low simmer, with a quick finish in the oven to brown the bread crumbs, produced perfect results in a short amount of time. Stovetop cooking also necessitated the use of only one pot, down from the two to three used for the original. A little time management was all that was needed to keep the process moving swiftly. While the beans are parcooking, the chicken is soaking in the brine. The remaining ingredients are prepped and then ready to be used as needed. At last I had it: a quick cassoulet that was worthy of the name.

SIMPLIFIED CASSOULET WITH PORK AND KIELBASA
SERVES 8

To ensure the most time-efficient preparation of the cassoulet, while the chicken is brining and the beans are simmering, prepare the remaining ingredients. Look for dried flageolet beans in specialty food stores (or see Resources, page 32). If you can't find a boneless blade-end pork loin roast, a boneless Boston butt makes a fine substitution. Additional salt is not necessary because the brined chicken adds a good deal of it.

Chicken
- 1 cup kosher salt or 1/2 cup table salt
- 1 cup sugar
- 10 bone-in chicken thighs (about 3 1/2 pounds), skin removed

Topping
- 6 slices good-quality white sandwich bread, cut into 1/2-inch dice (about 3 cups)
- 3 tablespoons unsalted butter, melted

- 4 slices bacon (about 4 ounces)
- 1 pound dried flageolet or great Northern beans, picked over and rinsed
- 1 medium onion, peeled and left whole, plus 1 small onion, chopped
- 4 medium garlic cloves, 2 peeled and left whole, 2 peeled and minced
  Vegetable oil
- 1 pound boneless blade-end pork loin roast, trimmed of excess fat and silver skin and cut into 1-inch pieces
- 1 can (14.5 ounces) diced tomatoes, drained
- 1 tablespoon tomato paste
- 1 tablespoon chopped fresh thyme leaves
- 1 bay leaf
- 1/4 teaspoon ground cloves
  Ground black pepper
- 1 3/4 cups chicken stock or canned low-sodium chicken broth
- 1 cup dry white wine
- 1/2 pound kielbasa, halved lengthwise and cut into 1/4-inch slices

1. *Brining the chicken*: In gallon-sized zipper-lock plastic bag, dissolve salt and sugar in 1 quart cold water. Add chicken, pressing out as much air as possible; seal and refrigerate until fully seasoned, about 1 hour. Remove chicken from brine, rinse thoroughly under cold water, and pat dry with paper towels. Refrigerate until ready to use.

2. *Preparing the topping:* While chicken is brining, adjust oven rack to upper-middle position; heat oven to 400 degrees. Mix bread crumbs and butter in small baking dish. Bake, tossing occasionally, until light golden brown and crisp, 8 to 12 minutes. Cool to room temperature; set aside.

3. In heavy-bottomed, 8-quart Dutch oven, cook bacon slices over medium heat until just beginning to crisp and most fat has rendered, 5 to 6 minutes. Leaving bacon slices in pan, pour off bacon grease into heatproof measuring cup and reserve. Return pan to heat; add beans, 10 cups water, whole onion, and whole garlic cloves to pan with bacon. Bring to boil over medium-high heat; reduce heat to low, cover partially, and simmer, stirring occasionally, until beans are partially cooked and almost tender, 40 to 50 minutes. Reserving 1 1/2 cups cooking liquid, drain beans. Discard onion, garlic, and bacon.

3. Add vegetable oil to reserved bacon grease to equal 1/4 cup. In now-empty Dutch oven, heat bacon grease and vegetable oil over medium-high heat until shimmering. Add half of chicken thighs, fleshy-side down; cook until lightly browned, 3 to 4 minutes. Using tongs, turn chicken pieces and cook until lightly browned on second side, 2 to 3 minutes longer. Transfer chicken to large plate; repeat with remaining thighs and set aside. Drain off all but 2 tablespoons fat from pot. Return pot to medium heat; add pork pieces and cook, stirring occasionally, until lightly browned, about 5 minutes. Add chopped onion and cook, stirring occasionally, until softened, 3 to 4 minutes. Add minced garlic, tomatoes, tomato paste, thyme, bay leaf, cloves, and pepper to taste; cook until fragrant, about 1 minute. Stir in chicken stock, wine, and 1 cup of reserved bean cooking liquid; increase heat to medium-high and bring to boil, scraping up browned bits off bottom of pot with wooden spoon. Add chicken and beans; if liquid does not fully cover chicken and beans, add remaining 1/2 cup reserved bean cooking liquid. Reduce heat to low, cover, and simmer until chicken is cooked through and beans are tender, about 40 minutes.

4. Meanwhile, adjust oven rack to lower-middle position and heat oven to 425 degrees. Off heat, gently stir in kielbasa and sprinkle surface with bread crumbs. Bake uncovered until topping is golden brown, about 10 minutes. Let rest 10 minutes and serve.

SIMPLIFIED CASSOULET WITH LAMB AND ANDOUILLE SAUSAGE

Lamb, with its robust, earthy flavor, makes an excellent substitute for the pork. Andouille sausage adds a peppery sweetness that tasters loved.

Follow recipe for Simplified Cassoulet with Pork and Kielbasa, substituting 2 pounds lamb shoulder chops, trimmed, boned, and cut into 1-inch pieces, for pork, and substituting 8 ounces andouille sausage for kielbasa.

How to Use Your Kitchen Thermometer

To take much of the guesswork out of cooking, use your instant-read thermometer often—and use it right! BY DAWN YANAGIHARA

For the most part, cooking is pretty low-tech stuff. But sometimes modern gadgetry is actually useful. Nothing takes the guesswork out of cooking, for example, like an instant-read thermometer. That's why—both in the *Cook's* test kitchen and in my home kitchen—the thermometer is the second most reached-for item after a pair of tongs. In our story on testing instant-read thermometers a few years back (see "Digitals Top Instant-Read Thermometer Testing," July/August 1997), we explained that there are two basic types: digital and dial-face. Our favorite remains the digital because of its quick response time, easy-to-read display, and wide temperature range.

Within the digital category, there are basic instant-read thermometers and there are cooking thermometer/ timers. The latter have digital-display base units to which long, wire-connected metal probes are attached. Though not really meant to be used as instant-read thermometers because of their slow response times, they can be useful in their own right. You insert the probe in a roast just going into the oven, run the wire out the oven door, plug it into the base unit, and set the alarm to sound when the desired temperature is reached. As long as you keep the wire out of flame's way, this thermometer is also handy at the stovetop, where you can use it to check the progress of custards and other such delicate mixtures. The probe can be left to lean against the pot, the display easily readable, leaving your hands free to steady the pan and stir its contents simultaneously.

The less expensive dial-face ther-mometers, also known as dial-reads, should meet most cooks' needs, though they tend to register temperatures more slowly and their fine type can be hard to read. What's most important when using a dial-face thermometer is to remember that its probe must be inserted at least 1 to 1½ inches into the food to activate the temperature sensor. The sensors in digital thermometers, on the other hand, are located at the tip, making it easy to measure the temperature of shallow liquids.

If you've got a brand new instant-read thermometer—dial-face or digital—you may want to check its accuracy before putting it to use. To do so, insert the probe into boiling water; it should register 212 degrees Fahrenheit (but keep in mind that the boiling point of water drops about 1 degree with every 500-foot increase in altitude). An alternative method is to make a water and ice slush, in which the thermometer should register 32 degrees Fahrenheit. Because digital thermometers cannot be recalibrated, you'll need to take any degree discrepancy you find into account whenever you use the thermometer. Most dial-face versions can be recalibrated by adjusting the nut beneath the base of the head with a wrench or a pair of pliers. Make sure to recheck the accuracy of a dial-face thermometer if it is ever dropped or falls victim to any sudden, jarring motion.

Instant-read thermometers have many uses that are not so obvious. To ensure that you get good use and the most accurate readings out of yours, we've assembled a few tips based on our own experience in the test kitchen.

THERMOMETER BASICS

➤ To recalibrate a dial-face thermometer, insert the probe into boiling water—it should register 212 degrees Fahrenheit at sea level (see explanation, above). If it doesn't, adjust the nut just beneath the head with a wrench or a pair of pliers.

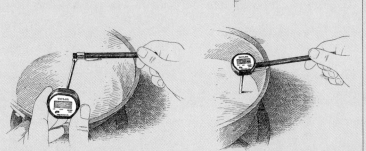

➤ Most instant-read thermometers are sold with a protective plastic sleeve with a metal clip (for clipping onto aprons) that forms a loop at the very top. To distance your hands from the heat of the food, slide the probe of the thermometer into the loop at the tip of the clip, and hold it upright using the sleeve.

MEAT

Whether cooking a burger or roasting a beef tenderloin, you should always take the temperature of the area of the meat that will be the last to finish cooking. This, naturally, is the thickest part of the meat or, if it is of uniform thickness, the center. Bones conduct heat, so if the meat you are cooking contains bone, make sure that the thermometer is not hitting it.

 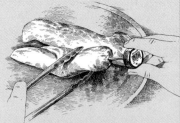

➤ Because it's easy to insert the thermometer too far or not far enough, the relative thinness of steaks, chops, and burgers can lead to erroneous readings when the thermometer is inserted straight down into the meat. Instead, insert the thermometer sideways into the center, taking care not to hit any bones.

➤ For narrow, cylindrical cuts of meat, such as a pork tenderloin or rack of lamb, lift the meat with a pair of tongs and insert the thermometer into the end, parallel to the meat itself.

Illustration: John Burgoyne

POULTRY

Poultry, when roasted whole, poses a unique problem because the breast is done at a lower temperature than the thigh.

➤ To take the temperature in the thickest part of the thigh, insert the thermometer at an angle into the area between the drumstick and the breast, taking care not to hit the bone.

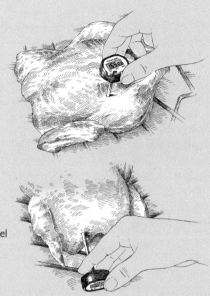

➤ To take the temperature in the thickest part of the breast, insert the thermometer from the neck end, holding the thermometer parallel to the bird.

➤ When cooking chicken pieces, use the same technique described for the breast, below left, lifting the piece with tongs and inserting the thermometer sideways into the thickest part of the meat, again taking care to avoid bone.

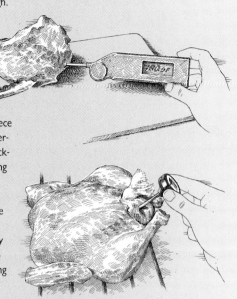

➤ If roasting a stuffed bird, the stuffing may lag behind the meat. Check its temperature by inserting the thermometer into the center of the cavity. (Stuffing is fully cooked at 165 degrees.)

BREAD

A thermometer is a useful tool to have at the beginning and final stages of baking bread.

➤ Use the thermometer to gauge the temperature of the liquid to which the yeast will be added. It should be between 105 and 115 degrees, warm enough to help dissolve and activate the yeast, but not so hot as to kill it.

➤ Recipes sometimes suggest taking the internal temperature of a loaf of bread to gauge when it's done. For bread that is baked free-form, tip the loaf up with a hand shielded by an oven mitt or potholder and insert the probe through the bottom crust into the center of the loaf.

➤ The simplest way to take the temperature of bread baked in a loaf pan is to pierce the thermometer through the top crust into the center. But it's not the best way, since it leaves behind a conspicuous hole. Instead, insert the thermometer from the side, just above the edge of the loaf pan, directing it at a downward angle toward the center of the loaf.

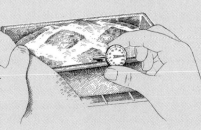

... AND MORE

An instant-read thermometer has other useful applications.

➤ Recipes for custards, curds, pastry creams, and other delicate or heat-sensitive mixtures on the stovetop often indicate at what temperature to take them off the heat. If you are cooking a small quantity and are having difficulty obtaining an accurate reading (this can be especially true with dial-face thermometers), tilt the pan or bowl so that the mixture collects to one side, creating enough depth to get an accurate reading.

➤ Butter is at the optimal temperature for creaming at 67 degrees, or cool room temperature. While it may seem persnickety, using an instant-read thermometer to determine the temperature of the butter can sometimes be helpful, especially, say, if it was just removed from the freezer. To do so, insert the probe into the length of the stick of butter.

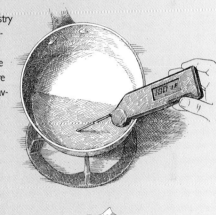

➤ An instant-read thermometer can also be used with cold foods. For example, before being churned, ice cream bases should be chilled to about 40 degrees. Cover the bowl containing the base tightly with plastic wrap, puncture the plastic with the thermometer probe, and then let the thermometer sit in the mixture, supported by the plastic.

Winter Salads with Oranges

Most salads made with oranges simply don't have enough orange flavor. We found two tricks to solve this problem.

≥ BY EVA KATZ WITH ADAM RIED ≤

In the midst of the earthy root vegetables and dark, rich braises and stews of winter cooking, our taste buds crave bright, rollicking flavors. The oranges that fill winter produce bins sate that appetite nicely, whether alone or as part of a lively salad. But too often these salads disappoint because the oranges fall by the wayside. Their flavor is fleeting, the pieces of orange getting lost among the salad greens. Our goal, then, was to develop salads in which the oranges had a distinctive presence alongside other vivid but complementary flavors.

Our first instinct was to beef up the orange flavor by including some fresh-squeezed juice in our vinaigrette dressings. Unfortunately, instinct failed us. A good vinaigrette depends on a balance of oil and acid, the latter usually supplied by either lemon or lime juice or vinegar, all of which have acidity levels of roughly 5 percent. According to Harold McGee in *The Curious Cook* (North Point Press, 1990), the acidity of oranges is only about 1.2 percent, so the flavor of the juice was not potent enough for a vinaigrette. In fact, we found that orange juice actually diluted our dressings and compromised their intense flavors. Next we tried fortifying the orange flavor by including some grated zest, the outer orange portion of the fruit's peel, where the flavorful citrus oils are concentrated. This approach brought a healthy orange flavor to the fore.

Many recipes for salads with oranges direct the cook to peel and slice the fruit, but we disliked the stringy membranes left in the slices. Instead, we used a paring knife to cut the orange sections free from the membrane, an easy process (see illustrations below) that produced consistently sized, jewel-like pieces of juicy orange for our salads. But then another problem cropped up: our beautiful orange sections disappeared to the bottom of the bowl when we tossed the salad, obliterating their visual and textural impact. The answer was to treat the fruit as a separate element altogether, spooning it over a bed of dressed greens rather than mixing everything together.

ESCAROLE AND ORANGE SALAD WITH GREEN OLIVE VINAIGRETTE
SERVES 4 TO 6

In this salad and those following, when arranging the orange segments on the greens, leave behind any juice that is released; it will dilute the dressing.

- 2 tablespoons sherry vinegar
- ½ cup chopped green olives
- 3 medium shallots, minced (about ¼ cup)
- 1 medium garlic clove, minced
- 1 teaspoon finely grated orange zest
- ⅓ cup olive oil
  Salt and ground black pepper
- 1 large head escarole, washed, dried, and stemmed (about 9 cups lightly packed)
- 2 large oranges, segmented (see illustrations)
- ½ cup slivered almonds, toasted in small dry skillet over medium heat until golden, about 7 minutes

1. Whisk vinegar, olives, shallots, garlic, and orange zest in large bowl; whisk in oil. Season to taste with salt and pepper. Add greens; toss to coat.

2. Divide dressed greens among individual plates, arrange a portion of orange segments on greens, and sprinkle with almonds. Serve immediately.

ORANGE-JÍCAMA SALAD WITH BUTTERHEAD LETTUCE AND HONEY-MUSTARD VINAIGRETTE
SERVES 4 TO 6

Boston and Bibb lettuces are the most widely available varieties of butterhead lettuce. Either would work well in this salad.

- 2 tablespoons red wine vinegar
- 3 medium shallots, minced (about ¼ cup)
- 1 tablespoon Dijon mustard
- 2 teaspoons honey
- 2 teaspoons finely grated orange zest
- ¼ cup olive oil
  Salt and ground black pepper
- 2 large heads butterhead lettuce, leaves separated, washed, dried, and torn into small pieces (about 9 cups firmly packed)
- 8 ounces jícama, peeled and sliced into ¼-inch matchstick pieces
- 2 large oranges, segmented (see illustrations)

1. Whisk vinegar, shallots, mustard, honey, and orange zest in medium bowl; whisk in oil. Season to taste with salt and pepper.

2. Pour all but 2 tablespoons dressing over greens; toss to coat. Toss jícama in remaining dressing. Divide dressed greens among individual plates; arrange a portion of jícama and orange segments on greens. Serve immediately.

AVOCADO-ORANGE SALAD WITH ROMAINE AND LIME-CUMIN DRESSING
SERVES 4 TO 6

- ¼ cup juice from 2 limes
- 2 small garlic cloves, minced
- 1 medium jalapeño chile, minced (about 1 tablespoon)
- 1 teaspoon cumin seed, toasted in small dry skillet over medium heat until fragrant and golden, about 4 minutes
- 1 teaspoon finely grated orange zest
- ¼ cup olive oil
  Salt and ground black pepper
- 2 medium heads romaine lettuce, leaves separated, washed, dried, and torn into small pieces (about 9 cups firmly packed)
- 1 cup cilantro leaves, washed, dried, and stemmed
- ½ medium red onion, sliced thin
- 1 avocado (preferably Haas), halved, pitted, and sliced ¼-inch thick
- 2 large oranges, segmented (see illustrations)

1. Whisk lime juice, garlic, jalapeño, cumin, and orange zest in medium bowl; whisk in oil. Season to taste with salt and pepper.

2. Pour all but 2 tablespoons dressing over lettuce and cilantro; toss to coat. Toss onion and avocado in remaining dressing. Divide dressed greens among individual plates; arrange a portion of onion, avocado, and orange segments on greens. Serve immediately.

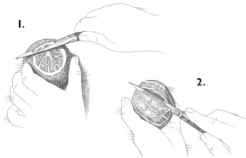

1. Slice off a small section at the top and bottom, stand the orange on end, and slice off the rind, including the white pith, following the contour of the fruit.
2. Free the sections by slicing along the membranes.

The Secrets of Broiling Chicken

Broiled chicken is quick and easy, but it doesn't have to be ordinary.

⊃ BY ANNE YAMANAKA ⊂

Although they certainly don't sound glamorous, broiled chicken parts can be fabulous when properly prepared: moist, well-seasoned, with a lovely caramelized flavor and crispy skin. Broiled chicken can also be made quickly and inexpensively, requiring little attention and the most basic of ingredients, making it the ultimate weeknight dinner.

The difficulties with broiling chicken are associated with cooking at such a high heat. If food is placed too close to the heating element, it can easily char on the outside long before it is cooked through at the center. Getting thin, crispy skin can also be a problem if the skin is not given time to slowly render its fat. To avoid these common problems, I knew I would have to figure out the optimal distance between the oven rack and the heat source, the best way to season the meat, and the parts of the chicken best suited to broiling. What I didn't anticipate was the fact that selecting the chicken itself would be just as important.

The Whole and the Parts

I began my investigation at the poultry section of the supermarket. There were way too many packages to choose from: boneless, skinless chicken breasts and thighs; skin-on, boneless chicken breasts; whole fryers; whole young chickens; chicken quarters…my head was spinning. Knowing that I had to narrow my field of focus, I chose to broil only bone-in, skin-on chicken. First, I like the contrast of crisp skin with broiled chicken meat, and I know that skin helps to keep the meat from drying out. Second, chicken cooked with the bone in seems to me to have a better, more meaty flavor. Finally, chicken sold this way is always less expensive than parts sold trimmed of skin and bone.

I began with whole young chickens, using the typical broilers weighing between three and five pounds and cutting them up myself. It didn't take long to realize that this was the best option in terms of both expense and the likelihood of getting pieces of chicken about the same size and weight for even cooking. But after breaking down six or seven chickens, I realized that for cooks with busy schedules, this was not the way to go. Time was a definite issue here.

The obvious next step was to try broiling with packaged whole, cut-up chickens. Unfortunately, there were many problems with this approach. To begin with, I often opened a package to find

We found three keys to getting perfectly crisp skin.

wings, breasts, and thighs of disproportionate sizes—so different, in fact, that it seems impossible that they all could have come from one bird. (See "Mismatched Parts," page 20.) I still had to do some butchering myself, too; most of the time the chicken came in quarters and so required that I separate the drumstick from the thigh. What's more, for some reason, the whole, cut-up chickens I found were not well butchered at all. The skin was often ragged. Haphazardly trimmed, it was sometimes there in excess, sometimes barely there at all. All this made for more work on my part while in the end still leaving me with an ugly finished product.

To simplify matters, I decided to try chicken packaged by parts, specifically breasts, thighs, or drumsticks. Packaged chicken breasts, like whole, cut-up chickens, are generally taken from roasters. As long as I broiled only breasts, the timing was not that much of a problem. Drumsticks, though, were hard to broil, because of their uneven shape. I decided that for dark meat I far preferred thighs for their combination of moist, succulent, flavorful meat and their relatively even thickness, which made them much easier to cook.

Ultimately, cutting up a whole young chicken yourself is best, but for cooks with little time to spare, packaged chicken thighs are the most appropriate chicken part for broiling—perfectly sized and least likely to dry out of all the different parts. If you really like white meat, breasts are doable as well.

Brining and Broiling

Because of my previous experience with poultry in the test kitchen at *Cook's,* I knew that brining could bring about a pronounced improvement in the flavor and texture of certain dishes. I tested brined chicken pieces (a brine of ¾ cup kosher salt and ¾ cup sugar) side by side with those simply sprinkled with salt and pepper. By unanimous vote, my tasters declared the brined chicken the winner: it was more moist, better seasoned, and better caramelized owing to the sugar in the brine.

Now I was ready to figure out the best way to broil. I decided that I would limit myself to the modern-style oven broilers in which the distance from the heat can be controlled. Many recipes I found said to broil the bird four to eight inches away from the heating element. This resulted in chicken with thick, charred, rubbery skin and meat that was not always cooked through. I tried broiling chicken at all levels in my wall oven (this one has rungs 4, 7, 10, and 13 inches away from the heating element). I found that chicken cooked on the bottom shelf (about 13 inches from the top of the oven) was best, staying moist and tender. To caramelize the chicken even more after it was almost completely cooked, I moved it up to the second shelf from the top for the final minute or two of broiling. This approach gave me chicken that closely resembled grilled chicken in both appearance and depth of meaty flavor.

Although the skin was now well browned, I still found it a touch too thick for my taste. I wanted the skin to be as crispy as cracklings, not in the least soggy or flabby. Remembering a technique I had learned when cooking ducks in a restaurant, I tried slashing the skin a few times before placing it in the oven to broil. This worked quite well. The skin rendered just a little more fat because of the extra surface area exposed to the heat of the broiler. I also discovered that starting the chicken skin-side down was key to getting the thin, crisp skin that I desired.

This way, I could finish the chicken with the skin side facing up, so it could crisp up under the direct heat of the broiler.

Broiled chicken is delicious plain, but it's also easy to jazz it up when you have more time to buy and prepare other ingredients. Because the chicken is brined, marinating is unnecessary. Instead, you can add variety by using glazes and sauces (such as barbecue sauce) in the last few minutes of the cooking process (the high sugar content in most sauces will burn under the heat of the broiler if put on at the beginning). In addition, aromatic pastes can be placed under the skin (to prevent singeing) to infuse flavor.

SIMPLE BROILED CHICKEN
SERVES 4

Though we recommend brining, you may bypass this step if pressed for time; simply skip step 1 and season the chicken generously with salt and pepper before broiling. This recipe will work only in broilers with adjustable racks, not fixed-height broilers. If you're making either the garlic rub or the dipping sauce (recipes follow) to flavor the chicken, prepare it while the chicken is brining.

- ¾ cup kosher salt or 6 tablespoons table salt
- ¾ cup sugar
- 1 chicken, 3 to 4 pounds, wings removed and reserved for another use, chicken cut into 2 thighs, 2 drumsticks, and 2 breast pieces
  Ground black pepper

1. In gallon-sized zipper-lock plastic bag, dissolve kosher salt and sugar in 1 quart of water. Add chicken and seal bag, pressing out as much air as possible; refrigerate until fully seasoned, about 1 hour. Remove from brine, rinse well, and dry thoroughly with paper towels.

2. Meanwhile, adjust one oven rack to lowest position and other rack to upper-middle position (top rack should be about 5 inches from heating element; bottom rack should be 13 inches away); heat broiler. Line bottom of broiler pan with foil and fit with slotted broiler-pan top. Following

CUTS | MISMATCHED PARTS

"Frankenchicken"   Home-butchered bird

Parts from a packaged whole cut-up chicken (left) vary considerably in size. Those from a bird we butchered (right) fit together properly.

illustration at left, make three diagonal slashes in skin of each chicken piece with sharp knife (do not cut into meat). Season both sides of chicken pieces with pepper and place skin-side down on broiler pan.

3. Broil chicken on bottom rack until just beginning to brown, 12 to 16 minutes. Using tongs, turn chicken skin-side up and continue to broil on bottom rack until skin is slightly crisp and thickest part of breast meat registers 160 degrees on an instant-read thermometer, about 10 minutes (if some chicken parts are browning too quickly, cover only those pieces with small pieces of foil). Transfer breast pieces to plate and cover with foil to keep warm. Continue to broil thighs and drumsticks on bottom rack until thickest part of meat registers 165 degrees on an instant-read thermometer, about 5 minutes longer. Return breast pieces skin-side up to pan and move pan to upper rack; broil until chicken is dark spotty brown and skin is thin and crisp, about 1 minute. Serve immediately.

SIMPLE BROILED CHICKEN BREASTS

Follow recipe for Simple Broiled Chicken through step 2, substituting 4 bone-in, skin-on chicken breast halves (about 3 pounds) for whole chicken. Broil chicken on bottom rack until just beginning to brown, 12 to 16 minutes. Using tongs, turn chicken skin-side up and continue to broil on bottom rack until skin is slightly crisp and thickest part of meat registers 160 degrees on an instant-read thermometer, about 10 minutes. Move pan to upper rack; broil until chicken is dark spotty brown and skin is thin and crisp, about 1 minute. Serve immediately.

SIMPLE BROILED CHICKEN THIGHS

Follow recipe for Simple Broiled Chicken through step 2, substituting 8 bone-in, skin-on chicken thighs (about 3 pounds) for whole chicken. Broil chicken on bottom rack until just beginning to brown, 12 to 16 minutes. Using tongs, turn chicken skin-side up and continue to broil on bottom rack until skin is slightly crisp and thickest part of meat registers 165 degrees on an instant-read thermometer, about 15 minutes. Move pan to upper rack; broil until chicken is dark spotty brown and skin is thin and crisp, about 1 minute. Serve immediately.

GARLIC, LEMON, AND ROSEMARY RUB

- 5 medium garlic cloves, minced
- 2 teaspoons grated zest plus ¼ cup juice from 1 lemon
- 1 tablespoon minced fresh rosemary leaves
  Ground black pepper
- 3 tablespoons extra-virgin olive oil

TECHNIQUE
FOR CRISPIER SKIN

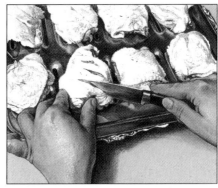

Make three diagonal slashes in the skin of each chicken piece to help render the fat.

Combine garlic, lemon zest, rosemary, and pepper to taste in small bowl. Combine lemon juice and oil in second small bowl. Follow recipe for Simple Broiled Chicken, Simple Broiled Chicken Breasts, or Simple Broiled Chicken Thighs, spreading a portion of garlic rub under skin before slashing skin and brushing chicken with lemon juice and oil before moving chicken to upper rack to crisp skin.

SPICY JAMAICAN JERK DIPPING SAUCE

- ¼ cup juice from 2 limes
- ¼ cup lightly packed brown sugar
- 1 medium garlic clove, skin left on
- 1 medium habanero chile
- 2 medium scallions, white and green parts, minced
- ½ medium onion, minced
- 1 1½-inch piece fresh ginger, minced (about 1½ tablespoons)
- ½ teaspoon dried thyme
  Pinch ground allspice

Stir together lime juice and brown sugar until dissolved in small bowl; set aside. Toast garlic and habanero in small dry skillet over medium heat, shaking pan frequently, until blistered, about 8 minutes. Peel and mince garlic; seed and mince habanero. Combine garlic, habanero, scallions, onion, ginger, thyme, and allspice in second small bowl, stir in 2 tablespoons lime-brown sugar mixture; set aside as dipping sauce for cooked chicken. Follow recipe for Simple Broiled Chicken, Simple Broiled Chicken Breasts, or Simple Broiled Chicken Thighs, brushing chicken pieces with remaining lime/brown sugar mixture before moving to upper oven rack to crisp skin. Serve chicken, passing dipping sauce separately.

Anne Yamanaka lives and cooks in Torrance, California.

How to Fry Perfect Eggs

The trick is to have the pan at the perfect temperature, add the eggs all at once—and use a cover.

⇒ BY JEANNE MAGUIRE ⇐

Anyone can make fried eggs—but few and far between are the cooks who can make them perfectly every time. For most of us, they are sometimes great and sometimes second rate at best. While my efforts are usually at least passable, I decided to eliminate the guesswork and figure out how to best and most easily fry the perfect egg every time. For me, this means an egg with a white that is firm, not runny, and a yolk that sets up high and is thick but still runny.

For starters, I thought it made sense to investigate the hardware. After testing skillets made from aluminum, hard-anodized aluminum, stainless steel, and well-seasoned cast iron in addition to one with a nonstick coating, my initial feeling was confirmed: there is no point in frying eggs in anything but a nonstick pan.

Next I examined the degree to which the pan should be heated before the eggs are added. I learned that there is a point at which the temperature of the pan causes the egg to behave just as I want it to. When an egg lands in a pan that's at the correct temperature, it neither runs all over the place nor sputters or bubbles; instead, it just sizzles and sets up into a thick, restrained oval. Getting the taste and texture of the white just right depends on achieving this correct set point. A white that's too spread out becomes overcooked, rubbery, and tough, while a white that browns at the edges as soon as it hits the pan ends up tasting metallic—at least to me.

I needed to devise a plan that would incorporate this crucial setting temperature, no matter what type of pan or what cooktop a cook was using. To begin, I placed the pan on a low setting and let it heat for a full five minutes. I had discovered that while eggs might set up well initially if a pan is not completely heated, they then tend to overcook at the finish; five minutes ensures a thorough preheating of the pan. Next I added the butter, which I allowed to melt, foam, and subside before adding the egg. I knew immediately that the pan was too hot—the white sputtered into huge bubbles, and the butter had even started to brown. Fast-forward to the next egg. This time I put the heat below the low setting. And this time I hit the mark: I added the egg just as the butter foam subsided, and it set up perfectly. On this perfect setting the butter took exactly one minute to melt, foam, and subside.

Now that the egg was sitting pretty, I moved on to the next part of the cooking process. Thumbing through cookbooks, I found directions for basting with butter, adjusting the temperature, and covering the eggs as techniques to get the desired thick and runny yolk. Eggs basted with butter were too rich and the process was fussy. Adjusting the heat to get the white and yolk cooked properly was actually pretty difficult. In all cases I ended up with the bottom too browned and the yolk too runny.

I moved on to using a cover during the cooking process. After putting two eggs in the skillet, I put on the lid and allowed the eggs to cook for 2 minutes. One of my eggs was cooked perfectly, but the other was slightly undercooked. I realized that with such a short cooking time, I had to get the eggs into the pan together at the same time. I tried the covered skillet method one more time. This time I broke each of the eggs into a cup before starting the process. This allowed me to empty the eggs into the skillet at virtually the same time. This method worked beautifully. The steam created when the pan was covered produced whites that were firm but not at all rubbery and yolks that were thick yet still runny. Since not all folks want a runny egg, I also experimented with other stages of doneness. It took 2½ minutes for a set but soft yolk, and 3 minutes for a light-colored, cooked-through yolk.

It's worth mentioning at this point that the fat used is meant to be a flavoring agent as well as lubricant. I tried several kinds. Canola oil had too little flavor, olive oil had too much, but both bacon fat and butter were delicious. For two eggs in a nine-inch skillet, I found that 1½ teaspoons of either of these fats works well. A quick sprinkle of salt and freshly ground pepper before throwing on the cover is also recommended—seasoning after the eggs are cooked does not impart as much flavor.

It seems to me after a bit of trial and error that the perfectly fried egg is attainable by all. I, for one, will sleep soundly and take the stairs with confidence, knowing I can greet the day sunny side up.

FRIED EGGS FOR TWO

A nonstick skillet is essential because it ensures an easy release of the eggs. Since burners vary, it may take an egg or two before you determine the ideal heat setting for frying eggs on your stovetop.

Follow the visual clue in the recipe and increase the heat if necessary. If you've just fried up some bacon or happen to have some bacon grease around, use it in place of the butter for really tasty fried eggs. Unlike butter, however, bacon grease will not go through visual changes that you can use to gauge the pan's heat.

2   large eggs
1½   teaspoons cold unsalted butter
   Salt and ground black pepper

1. Heat 8- or 9-inch heavy-bottomed nonstick skillet over lowest heat for 5 minutes. Meanwhile, crack open 1 egg into cup or small bowl; crack remaining egg into second cup or small bowl. Add butter to skillet, let it melt and foam. When foam subsides (this process should take about 1 minute; if butter browns in 1 minute, pan is too hot), swirl to coat pan.

2. Working quickly, pour one egg on one side of pan and second egg on other side. Season eggs with salt and pepper; cover and cook about 2 minutes for runny yolks, 2½ minutes for soft but set yolks, and 3 minutes for firmly set yolks. Slide eggs onto plate; serve.

FRIED EGGS FOR FOUR

Follow recipe for Fried Eggs for Two, using a 10-inch heavy-bottomed nonstick skillet, cracking open 2 eggs into each cup, and increasing butter to 1 tablespoon. Increase cooking times to about 2½ minutes for runny yolks, 3 minutes for soft but set yolks, and 3½ minutes for firmly set yolks.

Jeanne Maguire lives and cooks in Massachusetts.

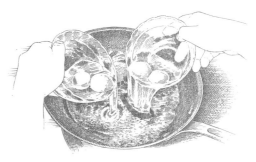

Crack the eggs into two cups and slide the eggs into the hot skillet simultaneously.

The Best Lemon Tart

We adjusted the ingredients to produce a lemon tart with a silken texture, the perfect balance of tart and sweet, and a taste that isn't too "eggy."

⇒ BY KAY RENTSCHLER ⇐

With its minimal interplay of ingredients and straight forward style, the lemon tart achieves a near-transcendent simplicity of form and content. Light, refreshing, and beautiful, when it's good, it is very, very good—but when it's bad, you wish you'd ordered the check instead. Despite its apparent simplicity, there is much that can go wrong with a lemon tart. It can slip over the edge of sweet into cloying; its tartness can grab at your throat; it can be gluey or eggy or, even worse, metallic-tasting. Its crust can be too hard, too soft, too thick, or too sweet. If by chance you bring more than one of these flaws to bear on a single tart, the results are horrific.

There is more than one way to fill a tart, of course. I considered briefly but dismissed the notion of an unbaked lemon filling—a lemon pastry cream or a lemon charlotte. In each case, the filling (the former containing milk and thickened with eggs and flour, the latter containing cream and thickened with eggs and gelatin) is spooned into a baked tart shell and chilled. Not only did I find the flavor of these fillings too muted and their texture too billowy, but I realized that I wanted a proper tart, one in which the filling is baked with the shell. (See "Sweet Tart Pastry 101," page 11.) To me, that meant only one thing: lemon curd, and a thin, bracing layer of it at that.

Lemon Curds New and Old

Originally an old English recipe that was to be eaten like a jam and called lemon cheese, lemon curd is a stirred fruit custard made of eggs, lemon juice, sugar, and, usually, butter. Cooked over low heat and stirred continuously, the mixture thickens by means of protein coagulation. The dessert owes its bright flavor not to lemon juice but to oils released by finely grated peel, the equivalent of a lemon twist in a vodka martini. Butter further refines a lemon curd's flavor and texture. The result is a spoonable custard that can

Sometimes simpler is better. A heavy nonreactive saucepan was less fussy than a double boiler and produced a curd that was just as lovely.

be spread on scones or used as a base for desserts. When baked, its color deepens and it "sets up," remaining supple and creamy yet firm enough to be sliceable. It is intense, heady stuff, nicely modulated—if you must—by a cloud of whipped cream.

In my mind, several variables warranted exploration. Most straightforward was the ratio of sugar to lemon juice. I wanted just enough sugar to offset the acid. More complex was the proportion of eggs. Egg yolks contain both cholesterol and lecithin, which act as emulsifiers and create a satiny texture. Whole eggs contain albumin as well, the protein in the egg white that is responsible for "setting" a custard. What, I wondered, would produce the best texture—whole eggs, the egg yolks alone, a combination of egg yolks and whole eggs, or maybe even whole eggs plus egg whites? Temperature is the critical factor in coaxing a custard to thicken without curdling, and the slower the journey, the more forgiving the process. Cook the eggs

too quickly and you won't know when to pull back: the heat within will have gathered force and taken the curd to the breaking point even if you've pulled the pan off the stove. Chemical reactions, too, accelerate at higher temperatures. Then what, exactly, is the correct temperature for cooking this stirred custard? Would a double boiler be necessary to produce a fine curd, or could I simply proceed with care (and proper equipment) over direct heat? As for the butter, should it be added at the outset of cooking or stirred in at the end?

Ways with Curds

I began by following the usual *Cook's* protocol of preparing a number of classic recipes. For an 8- or 9-inch tart I estimated that I would need about 3 cups of filling. The traditional lemon curds all contained between 1 and 1½ cups sugar, but the amount of lemon juice varied widely, between ½ and 1½ cups. There was also quite a bit of play between whole eggs and yolks, with the average falling between 8 and 10 eggs total. Though the recipes were divided on the matter of using direct heat versus a double boiler, most were quite cavalier about cooking time, with visual descriptions of the desired final texture ranging from "thick" to "very thick" to "like whipped cream." Only two mentioned cooking temperatures: 160 and 180 degrees, a rather wide range when dealing with eggs. Some recipes added butter at the beginning of the cooking time; others preferred to whisk it in later.

During my early experiments, certain proportions emerged easily. The balance of sweetness and tartness I sought came in at roughly two parts sugar to one part lemon juice. Four full tablespoons finely grated lemon zest (strained out after cooking, along with any hardened bits of egg whites from the eggs) packed enough lemon punch without having to linger in the final custard, where it would become bitter or usurp the silky texture. A pinch of salt brightened the flavor. Four tablespoons of butter were perfect, smoothing taste and refining texture. Adding cold butter chunks to the still-liquid curd proved superior to whisking the butter in after stovetop cooking. Though the latter curd looked glossy and beautiful before it was baked, the butter aerated the filling, causing it to rise in the oven and overrun the shell's borders.

Holding the proportions of the above ingredients constant, I made a number of lemon curds testing various combinations of whole eggs and yolks. Somewhat surprisingly, the curds that tasted great in a spoon were not always the ones that tasted best baked. The curd made with whole eggs alone had a light texture in the spoon and a gorgeous sheen, but it had a muted color and a texture most tasters described as "mayonnaise-like" when baked. The curd made with whole eggs and whites had a smooth, translucent surface but firmed up too much, while the curd made with an equal ratio of whole eggs to yolks was faulted for being cloyingly rich. In the end, most tasters preferred a curd made principally with yolks and only a couple of whole eggs for structure: creamy and dense with a vibrant color, it did not become gelatinous when baked, as did those curds made with all whole eggs, but it did set up enough to slice. Its flavor also lingered and teased. This made sense to me because fats carry flavors and hold them on the palate. Egg yolks are high in fat.

But the most interesting discovery was still to come. Remembering a lemon mousse I had made, I wanted to see what a softening splash of cream might do to the curd. Adding cream before cooking the curd on the stovetop gave it a cheesy flavor. But three tablespoons of cold, raw cream stirred in just before baking proved a winning touch. It cooled the just-cooked curd, blunted its acidity, and lightened its final baked

TECHNIQUE

STIRRING THE CURD

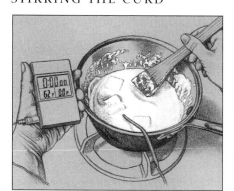

Stir the curd constantly until it has the consistency of a thin dessert sauce and registers 170 degrees on an instant-read thermometer.

texture to a celestial creaminess. If you don't get around to baking a crust, buy some fresh berries and grab a spoon.

Finally, I made identical tarts in the two available depths of 9-inch tart pans; the thinner ¾-inch version was the unanimous winner.

CLASSIC LEMON TART
SERVES 8

Once the lemon curd ingredients have been combined, cook the curd immediately; otherwise it will have a grainy finished texture. To prevent the curd from acquiring a metallic taste, make absolutely sure that all utensils coming into contact with it—bowls, whisk, saucepan, and strainer—are made of nonreactive stainless steel or glass. Since the tart pan has a removable bottom, it is more easily maneuvered when set on a cookie sheet. If your prebaked tart shell has already cooled, place it in the oven just before you start the curd and heat it until warm, about 5 minutes. Serve the tart with lightly whipped cream, the perfect accompaniment to the rich, intensely lemon filling.

1	9- to 9½-inch fully baked warm tart shell (see recipe, pages 12–13)
7	large egg yolks, plus 2 large eggs
1	cup plus 2 tablespoons sugar
⅔	cup juice from 4 to 5 medium lemons, plus ¼ cup finely grated zest
	Pinch salt
4	tablespoons unsalted butter, cut into 4 pieces
3	tablespoons heavy cream

1. Adjust oven rack to upper-middle position and heat oven to 375 degrees. Place tart pan with shell on cookie sheet.

2. In medium nonreactive bowl, whisk together yolks and whole eggs until combined, about 5 seconds. Add sugar and whisk until just combined, about 5 seconds. Add lemon juice, zest, and salt; whisk until combined, about 5 seconds. Transfer mixture to medium nonreactive saucepan, add butter pieces, and cook over medium-low heat, stirring constantly with wooden spoon, until curd thickens to thin sauce-like consistency and registers 170 degrees on an instant-read thermometer, about 5 minutes. Immediately pour curd through single-mesh stainless steel strainer set over clean nonreactive bowl. Stir in heavy cream; pour curd into warm tart shell immediately.

3. Bake until filling is shiny and opaque and until the center 3 inches jiggle slightly when shaken, 10 to 15 minutes. Cool on wire rack to room temperature, about 45 minutes. Remove outer metal ring, slide thin metal spatula between bottom crust and tart pan bottom to release, then slip tart onto cardboard round or serving plate. Cut into wedges and serve.

Science in a Shell

When we began this story, we wondered how such a high proportion of eggs in the presence of a relatively small amount of liquid could produce the creamy, silken texture of lemon curd, while the same proportion of eggs and cream, for example, would simply scramble.

We suspected from previous experience that it had something to do with acid content. So we did a little experiment. We placed one egg in each of three separate pans over medium heat and added two tablespoons of rice wine vinegar to one pan, two tablespoons of lemon juice to the second pan, and the same amount of water to the third pan. The egg stirred with vinegar (top, right) cooked quickly and remained pale yellow and very creamy. The egg stirred with lemon juice (center) turned a more lemony yellow, took longer to cook, and, though it also remained creamy, formed a more solid gel than the egg cooked with vinegar. The egg stirred with water (bottom) took

Rice Wine Vinegar

Lemon Juice

Water

almost twice as long to cook as the first egg and contained distinctly coagulated bits of bright yellow egg—just like scrambled eggs.

Dr. Eric A. Decker, associate professor of food chemistry at the University of Massachusetts, explained what happened. Egg proteins, he said, are tangled bundles of amino acids. Each bundle carries a similar electrical charge, which causes them to repel each other. Applying heat causes the bundles to unravel, at which point they are inclined to pull together and form a clump. In the process of clumping, the amino acid molecules squeeze out any liquid that comes between them. This is known as curdling.

Introducing an acid to the egg proteins can increase their electrical charges. Consequently, when the proteins are heated and unwind they are even more strongly repelled from one another and are inclined to interact more with the liquid. The effect is to create a layer of liquid between the ribbons of protein, like a sandwich. This creates what we know as a gel, the effect that we pleasantly experienced with our lemon curd ("curd" is a misnomer in this case). The vinegar created a similar but different effect because different acids have different degrees of ability to change the charge on the proteins. Thus the lemon juice, while encouraging an egg to cook and form a solid, keeps the solid moist and creamy. — K.R. and Maryellen Driscoll

Unlocking the Secrets of Coconut Macaroons

Most coconut macaroons are achingly sweet, sticky mounds of semicooked dough that don't taste much like coconut. We set out to make something better.

≥ BY CHRISTOPHER KIMBALL ≤

Coconut macaroons are a bit like broughams. In the age of horse-pulled transport, a brougham was a light closed carriage with seating for either two or four. When Detroit got hold of this term, realizing that nobody had a clue as to what a real brougham was, they appropriated it, transforming the brougham from an elegant 19th-century conveyance into a rather pedestrian, motor-powered two-door sedan. Macaroons have undergone a similar transformation. A thousand years ago they were baked almond paste, and by the 19th century they had become quite elegant (and very popular) cone-shaped cookies flavored with real coconut. But today they have deteriorated into lackluster mounds of beaten egg whites and coconut shreds or, at their worst, nothing more than a baked mixture of condensed milk and sweetened coconut.

When I began looking at recipes for modern coconut macaroons, I found that they varied widely. In addition to different kinds of coconut and sweeteners, they often called for one or more of a wide range of ingredients, including extracts such as vanilla or almond, salt, flour, sugar, sweetened condensed milk, and even an egg or two in extreme variations.

I was sure that somewhere among these second-rate cookies was a great coconut macaroon waiting to be found, with a pleasing texture and real, honest coconut flavor. I decided to find it.

Getting the Basics

The initial recipe testing included five recipes. What came out of the oven that day ranged from dense, wet cookies to light, if not dry, mounds of coconut. In the former category were recipes that used unbeaten egg whites mixed with sweetened coconut and sugar. (One of them, a Brazilian macaroon, even included whole eggs and produced a gooey, cavity-inducing cookie with a strong caramel flavor but nary a hint of coconut.) A recipe calling for beaten egg whites resulted in a light, airy, meringue-style cookie, pleasantly delicate but totally lacking in coconut flavor or chew. The test winners were simple enough: unbeaten egg whites mixed with sugar, unsweetened coconut, salt, and vanilla. But even

It's easiest to form the cookies into rough haystacks after dropping small mounds of dough onto the parchment paper–lined trays.

these lacked coconut flavor and were a bit on the dry side, not sufficiently chewy or moist. We set out to find a happy medium among our test recipes.

Sweetened versus Unsweetened

Our testing had shown us that the choice of sweetened versus unsweetened coconut had a major effect on texture. The unsweetened variety resulted in a less sticky, more appealing texture, but it made the cookies just a bit too dry. Flour—we tried both cake and all-purpose—was helpful in eliminating the stickiness of cookies made entirely with sweetened coconut, but it also made the cookies a bit too dense. Looking for a way past this roadblock, we decided to test a combination of sweetened and unsweetened coconut. This worked very well, giving the cookies a somewhat more luxurious texture without making them wet or heavy.

We also found, to our surprise, that the sweetened coconut had more flavor than unsweetened, so the coconut flavor was turned up a notch. A scientist who works with the Baker's

brand of coconut, which is sweetened and flaked, explained this phenomenon. He said that fresh coconut is 53 percent moisture; unsweetened, which is dried, is 3 to 5 percent moisture; and sweetened and flaked coconut (which is dried before being flaked and then rehydrated) is 9 to 25 percent moisture. Unlike most fruits that are quite sweet, coconut is mostly fat and, when dried, is rather tasteless, unlike dried apples or apricots. Hydrating dried coconut therefore adds flavor, as does the addition of sugar. Although one could add both more moisture and more sweetness to a macaroon batter and then use dried, unsweetened coconut, the coconut itself would still be less flavorful than sweetened coconut flakes.

Another key issue was the ratio of coconut to unbeaten egg whites. Testing showed that cookies made with 3½ cups of coconut and only one egg white were dense and heavy; three cups of coconut to four egg whites seemed a better ratio.

To add still a bit more moisture to the cookies, we tried using corn syrup instead of sugar as a sweetener and found that the cookies were slightly more moist, held together a bit better, and were pleasantly chewy. Melted butter was tried but discarded since it masked the flavor of the coconut, as did sweetened condensed milk.

We still felt that the cookies were a bit light in coconut flavor. To remedy this, we tried adding cream of coconut, and we hit the jackpot. The coconut flavor was superior to any of the cookies we had made to date. Finally, a coconut macaroon with real coconut flavor. (Since cream of coconut is sweetened, we did have to decrease the amount of corn syrup. For more information on this and similar products, see "What Is Coconut Milk?" on page 25).

Putting these cookies together is easy. No need even to whip the egg whites. The liquid ingredients are whisked together, the dry ingredients are mixed, and then the two are combined. We found

What Is Coconut Milk?

Coconut milk is not the thin liquid found inside the coconut itself—that is called coconut water. Coconut milk is a product made by steeping equal parts shredded coconut meat and either warm milk or water. The meat is pressed or mashed to release as much liquid as possible, the mixture is strained, and the result is coconut milk. The same method is used to make coconut cream, but the ratio of coconut meat to liquid is higher, about 4 to 1. (The cream that rises to the top of coconut milk after it sits awhile is also referred to as coconut cream.) Finally, cream of coconut—not to be confused with coconut cream—is a sweetened product based on coconut milk but which also contains thickeners and emulsifiers. Cream of coconut and coconut cream are not interchangeable in recipes, since the former is heavily sweetened and the latter is not.

To find out firsthand how coconut milk, coconut cream, and cream of coconut stack up, we made coconut milk and cream in the test kitchen and compared them with commercial products. For the first test batch, we made coconut milk with water. (One cup fresh coconut meat was ground in a food processor with one cup of warm water. The mixture steeped for one hour and then was strained.) Next, we made a batch with milk, using the same method. The coconut cream was made using the same method, but with a higher ratio of meat to water: 2 cups of fresh coconut meat to 1/2 cup of water. We then did a blind taste test, pitting our homemade products against canned cream of coconut and canned coconut milk.

Both the canned and the homemade coconut milks were very thin, with only a modest amount of coconut flavor (although the coconut milk made with cow's milk rather than water was superior). The homemade coconut cream, though made with water, was quite good: thicker, creamier, and somewhat more flavorful than the coconut milk. The canned cream of coconut was very sweet and syrupy, really inedible right out of the can, with sugar being the predominant flavor. However, we found that it can be used in baking with good results.   – C.P.K.

it best to refrigerate this dough for 15 minutes to make it easier to work with, but in a pinch you can skip this step. In an effort to produce a nicely browned, crisp exterior, we experimented with oven temperatures and finally settled on 375 degrees; the bottoms tended to overcook at 400 degrees, and lower temperatures never produced the sort of browning we were after.

Because I am partial to huge, two-fisted cookies, I like using one-quarter cup of batter for each cookie. This also produces the best contrast between crispy exterior and moist interior. However, since most of our test cooks preferred a slightly daintier confection, our final recipe calls for a smaller cookie. We also found that these cookies are great when the bottom third is dipped in chocolate. Since the cookie is not overly sweet, the chocolate is a nice complement, not a case of sending coals to Newcastle.

TRIPLE COCONUT MACAROONS
MAKES ABOUT 4 DOZEN 1-INCH COOKIES

Cream of coconut, available canned, is a very sweet product commonly used in piña colada cocktails. Be sure to mix the can's contents thoroughly before using, as the mixture separates upon standing. Unsweetened desiccated coconut is commonly sold in natural food stores or Asian markets. If you are unable to find any, use all sweetened flaked or shredded coconut, but reduce the amount of cream of coconut to 1/2 cup, omit the corn syrup, and toss 2 tablespoons cake flour with the coconut before adding the liquid ingredients. For larger macaroons, shape haystacks from a generous 1/4 cup of batter and increase the baking time to 20 minutes.

1	cup cream of coconut
2	tablespoons light corn syrup
4	large egg whites
2	teaspoons vanilla extract
1/2	teaspoon salt
3	cups unsweetened, shredded, desiccated (dried) coconut (about 8 ounces)
3	cups sweetened flaked or shredded coconut (about 8 ounces)

1. Adjust oven racks to upper-middle and lower-middle positions and heat oven to 375 degrees. Line two cookie sheets with parchment paper and lightly spray parchment with nonstick vegetable cooking spray.

1. Using your fingers, form the cookies into loose haystacks. Moisten your fingers with water if needed to prevent sticking.

2. If desired, dip the bottom half-inch of the baked cookies into melted chocolate, tapping off excess chocolate with your finger.

2. Whisk together cream of coconut, corn syrup, egg whites, vanilla, and salt in small bowl; set aside. Combine unsweetened and sweetened coconuts in large bowl; toss together, breaking up clumps with fingertips. Pour liquid ingredients into coconut and mix with rubber spatula until evenly moistened. Chill dough for 15 minutes.

3. Drop heaping tablespoons of batter onto parchment-lined cookie sheets, spacing them about 1 inch apart. Form cookies into loose haystacks with fingertips (see illustration 1, above), moistening hands with water as necessary to prevent sticking. Bake until light golden brown, about 15 minutes, turning cookie sheets from front to back and switching from top to bottom racks halfway through baking.

4. Cool cookies on cookie sheets until slightly set, about 2 minutes; remove to wire rack with metal spatula.

THE BEST CHOCOLATE–DIPPED TRIPLE COCONUT MACAROONS

Using the two-stage melting process for the chocolate helps ensure that it will be at the proper consistency for dipping the cookies.

Follow recipe for Triple Coconut Macaroons. Cool baked macaroons to room temperature, about 30 minutes. Line two cookie sheets with parchment paper. Chop 10 ounces semisweet chocolate; melt 8 ounces in small heatproof bowl set over pan of almost-simmering water, stirring once or twice, until smooth. (To melt chocolate in microwave, heat at 50 percent power for 3 minutes and stir. If chocolate is not yet entirely melted, heat an additional 30 seconds at 50 percent power.) Remove from heat; stir in remaining 2 ounces chocolate until smooth. Holding macaroon by pointed top, dip bottom and 1/2 inch up sides of each cookie in chocolate, scrape off excess with finger (see illustration 2), and place on cookie sheet. Refrigerate until chocolate sets, about 15 minutes.

Patience Pays Off for Soy Sauce

We found that the best soy sauce was the one that sat outdoors for three years.

⇒ BY MARYELLEN DRISCOLL ⇐

A well-made soy sauce has not one but a colorful range of culinary faces. In a dipping sauce it can provide a quick, bright flavor hit that dances off the food it coats. In a braise its presence might be more surreptitious, an underbelly of flavor nuances. In whatever application, when it is good, its flavors should resonate the way sound does from a gong struck by a padded hammer. There should be a beginning, a middle, and an end, none of them clashing.

Soy sauce is a complex seasoning with an ancient history. Originating more than 2,500 years ago in China, it was first used as a preservative and quickly moved on to become a flavoring. In the seventh century Buddhist priests introduced it to Japan as a replacement for meat- and fish-based seasonings. Over the centuries, it has become one of the defining flavors of both cuisines.

In the United States, though, it is only within the past 20 years that soy sauce has emerged as a kitchen staple. Introduced to the market when stir-frying became popular, American cooks have learned to use it in many styles of cooking. This has resulted in a proliferation of soy sauce products on store shelves. Because *Cook's* had not conducted a rating of soy sauces since publishing its second issue—May/June 1994—it seemed time to revisit this important liquid seasoning.

The Nature of the Sauce

As with any tasting, the starting point was to attain a basic understanding of the product.

Like wine, soy sauce consists of simple ingredients transformed by the process of fermentation. The process typically begins when a blend of soybeans and roasted wheat is inoculated with a mold called *Aspergillus*. The mixture matures in vats for three days, long enough for a culture known as *koji* to develop. The culture is then transferred to fermentation tanks where it is mixed with salt and water to produce a liquidy mash. The mash ferments, or "brews," for as little as several months or as long as several years. The liquid element of the fermented mash is then filtered out and bottled up as soy sauce. The fermentation process produces literally hundreds of new compounds with complex flavors.

At least that is true of soy sauces made in the traditional way, as just described. As you might suspect, however, there are many soy sauce producers that shortcut this age-old process. The label on some soy sauces states that they are "naturally brewed" or "traditionally brewed." Unfortunately, the Food and Drug Administration sets no standards for such labels, so they can mean anything. But you can detect synthetically brewed soy sauces—the kind that can be produced in less than a week's time—by reading the label. In the making of these sauces, hydrolyzed vegetable protein (versus whole soybeans) and hydrochloric acid are boiled together for 15 to 20 hours. Caramel, salt, and corn syrup are typically added for coloring and flavor. So you can easily identify this type of soy sauce by looking for hydrolyzed vegetable protein on the label's ingredient list.

Although soy sauce originated in China, most of the soy sauces found on U.S. store shelves are from Japan or are made Japanese-style in the United States. Sometimes called *shoyu*, they are typically brown-amber in color. They have a relatively thin consistency and are considered to be sweeter and brighter in flavor than the Chinese versions because they are made with a higher proportion of wheat. Chinese soy sauces, which tend to be very dark, lend a deeper, richer color to a dish. They also tend to have more full-bodied flavor, though some can be as light as Japanese-style soy sauces. The synthetic soy sauces on the market typically have Chinese-sounding names, such as La Choy, and are dark in color but otherwise unrepresentative of Chinese soy sauces.

Tamari is a Japanese soy sauce that tends to confuse many consumers—and rightfully so. By definition, it contains no wheat, but many products that call themselves "tamari" do contain wheat. In general, tamari tends to be richer and stronger in flavor than other Japanese soy sauces. So it is generally better used in braises or other cooking applications than served as is.

To keep the blind tasting within reason, we limited it to widely distributed brands and further limited it to consist of a representation of the basic available types. The tasting was two-tiered: First each product was tasted plain with unseasoned sweet rice and silken tofu for dipping. Then each product was used to marinate chicken pieces, which were stir-fried for tasters to assess.

A Winning Nature

In general, the soy sauces that did well in our tasting were pleasingly distinct and balanced in flavor. They were neither overpowering nor blasé.

Saltiness was acceptable so long as this was not the only personality trait. All of the soy sauces that were disliked in the plain tasting failed to gain approval in the stir-fry test. Not all of the soy sauces recommended performed consistently in both tastings. The clear favorite, however, an organic soy sauce by Eden Foods, was remarkably consistent.

It was interesting to find out that the winner, Eden Selected Shoyu Soy Sauce, which is made in Japan, is brewed outdoors in cedar vats for about three years so that the fermenting soy sauce is subjected to seasonal changes in temperature. Sally Gralla, a spokesperson for Eden Foods, explained that most soy sauces are brewed indoors in steel tanks for a shorter period of time, about one year.

According to Dr. Daniel Y. C. Fung, professor of food science at Kansas State University, the amount of time a soy sauce is given to ferment can be a contributing factor to its palatability. But that's not everything. Wheat and soybeans are very complex food systems, he says. When bacteria, yeast, and mold start growing, they produce a large variety of compounds that will create a great diversity of flavors. The grade of wheat or soybean, the type or quality of mold starter, the temperature at which the wheat is roasted, the amount of salt used in the brine, the amount of air let into the vats during aging…all can affect the fine balance of flavors in soy sauce. "It is a science as well as an art to make soy sauce," says Fung. "Much like winemaking."

All of the above can also contribute to the ability of the sauce to retain flavor during cooking (or, as we found with many soy sauces, the inability to retain flavor). At the heart of soy sauce flavor are amino acid compounds, some of which are volatile. These are the compounds that give the sauce its aroma, says Dr. Ronald Schmidt, professor of food science at the University of Florida in Gainesville. Add heat to the mix, and these aromatic compounds quickly dissipate. Depending on the soy sauce, this can significantly reduce the taste experience—which tasters actually found to be advantageous with the particularly awful-tasting products.

Finally, it was no surprise that the one synthetic soy sauce in the tasting ranked miserably low. Sadly, this is the sort of soy sauce most Americans were first able to access. Fortunately, we found, plenty of other choices are now available.

TASTING SOY SAUCE

The following products are listed in order of ranking, with the top-scoring product listed first. The blind tasting of the following soy sauces took place in two sittings. First, each was served plain with unseasoned sweet rice and silken tofu for dipping. In the second blind tasting, cubes of chicken were tossed in a measured amount of each soy sauce as well as a small amount of sugar. The chicken was then stir-fried along with a modest amount of minced garlic and ginger. In both tastings, the soy sauces were rated on flavor "favorability," intensity of overall flavor and salt flavor, and overall likability. Tasters were also asked to make general comments on aroma, consistency, complexity, and any specific flavor characteristics. The scores for overall likability from both tests were averaged to calculate ranking, based on the decision that we were seeking the best multipurpose soy sauce. The first tasting panel consisted of 15 tasters, including magazine staff, Jean Chan of Nancy's Café, and Barry Chui and Rebecca Li of Yokohama, both located in Brookline Village, Mass. Twelve magazine staff attended the stir-fry tasting.

HIGHLY RECOMMENDED

Eden Selected Shoyu Soy Sauce MADE IN JAPAN

➤ **$2.59 for 10 fluid ounces**

Tasters decisively ranked this "distinct" soy sauce number one in both taste tests. The flavor was "toasty, caramel-y, and complex," not wimpy. Rich, yet clean and balanced, with "vivid" flavor. The salt flavor was tangible but not overpowering. Primarily available in whole food stores.

RECOMMENDED

San-J Reduced Sodium Tamari Natural Soy Sauce
MADE IN THE UNITED STATES

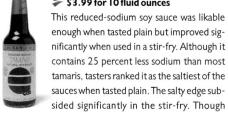

➤ **$3.99 for 10 fluid ounces**

This reduced-sodium soy sauce was likable enough when tasted plain but improved significantly when used in a stir-fry. Although it contains 25 percent less sodium than most tamaris, tasters ranked it as the saltiest of the sauces when tasted plain. The salty edge subsided significantly in the stir-fry. Though labeled as a tamari, its makers do add a trace amount of wheat to this sauce. Available in whole food stores and some supermarkets.

Naturally Brewed Higeta Honzen Soy Sauce
MADE IN JAPAN EXPRESSLY FOR WILLIAMS-SONOMA

➤ **$7.50 for 12.6 fluid ounces**

The tag on the fancily packaged bottle touts this soy sauce as "the preferred seasoning" in "the finest and most exclusive restaurants in Japan." It did catch the attention of many of our tasters. One described it as "enhancing the flavor without standing out or underrepresenting itself" in the stir-fry. As a dipping sauce, it was more "intense," with a somewhat bitter finish. Available in Williams-Sonoma stores.

Eden Organic Tamari Soy Sauce Traditionally Brewed MADE IN JAPAN

➤ **$4.49 for 10 fluid ounces**

This tamari was full-bodied, complex, and "almost fruity," but it still "doesn't set off all my taste buds," wrote one taster. "A respectable level of salt." "Very savory, almost meaty," rounded and smooth. A solid finish in both taste tests. Available in whole food stores.

Kikkoman MADE IN THE UNITED STATES

➤ **$1.59 for 10 fluid ounces**

Recommended—with reservations. This was the best among the supermarket standards and tied for first in the dipping sauce taste test, where it was described as "more rounded than others" and "kind of perky." It was definitively salty, but most tasters found it to their liking. When tasted in a stir-fry, it lost its pizazz; tasters described it as "a true nonpresence." Available in supermarkets.

San-J Organic Whole Soybean Shoyu
MADE IN THE UNITED STATES

➤ **$2.49 for 10 fluid ounces**

This Japanese-style soy sauce (brewed in Virginia) stood out as saltier than many of the others, even though its sodium level was no different. Sweet and slightly bitter. What some people called "mellow" others called "flat." There was nothing objectionable about this soy sauce, but nothing great to say about it either. Available in whole food stores and some supermarkets.

NOT RECOMMENDED

Pearl River Bridge Superior Soy Sauce MADE IN CHINA

➤ **$2.55 for 18.6 fluid ounces**

When tasted plain this Chinese soy sauce was described as unpalatably fishy—"like the parking lot of a wholesale fish pier." Tasters also complained of metallic notes and too much salt flavor. (One tablespoon of this soy sauce contains 1,590 milligrams of sodium. Most others contain just under 1000 milligrams per tablespoon.) No one, however, complained of off flavors or a fishy taste in the stir-fry test. Available in specialty food stores and some supermarkets.

Yamasa Naturally Brewed MADE IN JAPAN

➤ **$2.99 for 34 fluid ounces**

Popular in Japanese restaurants, this rich, amber-colored soy sauce contradicted itself. When tasted plain as a dipping sauce, tasters objected to it, saying it was "too strong," "harsh," or "spikey" and "a bit chemical." In the stir-fry it was mild and shallow. "I can't really taste it," complained one taster. Available in supermarkets and Japanese markets.

Eden Organic Tamari Soy Sauce Naturally Brewed
MADE IN THE UNITED STATES

➤ **$2.99 for 10 fluid ounces**

This tamari was aged for just six months in an accelerated brewing process. The drawbacks were glaring. One taster thought it tasted like burnt bacon, others found it "harsh" and "overpowering." These offenses dissipated when the sauce was heated up in a stir-fry; there, however, it had "hardly any flavor." Available in whole food stores.

Ka-Me Dark Chinese Soy Sauce
MADE IN THE UNITED STATES

➤ **$1.59 for 12 fluid ounces**

Tasters said it all. "No gusto." "Incomplete." "Weak, almost watery." "Nondescript and rather wimpy." In sum, "it could use more flavor." This soy sauce did contain only 500 milligrams of sodium per tablespoon, less than even the one low-sodium soy sauce in the tasting. One taster of Chinese descent said that this would be used in Chinese cooking as a coloring agent more than a flavor enhancer. Available in supermarkets.

Westbrae Shoyu Traditionally Brewed
MADE IN CANADA

➤ **$3.79 for 12.7 fluid ounces**

The only shoyu that did not make the cut. Made from organic ingredients, as a dipping sauce it was brashly offensive. "Wave after wave of nasty aftertastes." It "gave me the shivers it was so bad." In the stir-fry it became a nonentity, described as "one-dimensional," "flat," and "empty." Contains only 700 milligrams of sodium per tablespoon (versus almost 1,000 milligrams for the average soy sauce). Available in whole food stores.

La Choy Soy Sauce MADE IN THE UNITED STATES

➤ **$1.99 for 10 fluid ounces**

Where to begin? This was the only synthetically made soy sauce in the tasting, and it showed. Tasters did not mince words in their descriptions: "awful," "crude," "chemical," and "heinous"; like "very bad jarred beef" or "burnt wood." Maybe we should have tried using it for dipping french fries, as is recommended on the bottle's inside label. Available in supermarkets.

Testing All-Purpose Paring Knives

An inexpensive stamped model performs on a par with the forged knives that are the industry's standard bearers.

⇒ BY ADAM RIED ⇐

When I went to cooking school, students were told that we'd need only two knives for our courses, a chef's knife and a paring knife. But that doesn't really limit the field all that much. Take paring knives. There are dozens of versions with blades and handles in different sizes and shapes and made from different materials. Some are marketed for specific tasks such as trimming, fluting, mincing, and peeling round items, but most are designed to be "all-purpose." Prices vary from a modest $5 plus change to a grand $50, which invites the obvious question for a home cook: Is the most expensive knife really 10 times better than the cheapest model? To find, out, we gathered a group of seven "all-purpose" knives and put them through their paces.

The First Cut

After pretesting knives with blades of various lengths, we decided to stick with those having blades measuring as close as possible to 3½ inches, which we determined to be the most versatile size. We also decided to steer clear of knives with serrated edges because they cannot be honed with a steel or run through most home electric knife sharpeners.

Our next decision was whether to test knives with forged or stamped blades or to test both types. Forged blades, which are generally more expensive and considered to be of higher quality, are made by heating a crude piece of steel to more than 2,000 degrees Fahrenheit and beating it into the shape of a blade using a mold and a forging hammer. It is then ground down, tempered by repeated heating and cooling, sharpened, and finished in many, many time-consuming, labor-intensive, expensive steps. One sign that a knife has probably been forged is the presence of a bolster, a thick collar of metal between the blade and the handle. Stamping, on the other hand, is less expensive, starting with a large sheet of metal from which crude blades are cut out, much like cookie shapes are cut from rolled dough. The finishing steps are similar to those of forging.

In the final analysis, we decided to test knives across the range of price and quality. As a result, our final lineup included seven knives: forged, high-carbon stainless steel knives with ergonomically molded handles from two famous German cutlery makers; a Japanese forged model with a unique metal handle; and four inexpensive knives with stamped blades and handles made variously of plastic, wood, and rubber.

With the knives selected, five testers used each of them for a number of cutting and paring jobs for which a chef's knife, even a small one of 6 inches, would likely be too large and clumsy. The tasks included peeling and slicing turnips; peeling and mincing shallots; coring tomatoes; peeling, quartering, and coring apples; and peeling and sectioning oranges. In addition, over the course of several weeks the test kitchen staff used the knives for a wide range of tasks, such as cutting small pieces of coconut, peeling and mincing fresh ginger, and slicing lemons, limes, and hard-cooked eggs.

The Final Cut

To our surprise, forging and stamping were not determining factors in the performance of a knife. Though an expensive forged knife did manage to edge out an inexpensive stamped knife for first place, we did not find a strict correlation between manufacturing technique and performance. Unlike a chef's knife, a paring knife is by its very nature used for lighter tasks, where weight and balance are not crucial (it doesn't take a huge effort to peel an apple or slice a tomato). So our testers found that the extra weight and balance afforded by the forging process and the bolster did not add up to a distinct advantage. We vetted this theory with several knife experts, who agreed. "Provided you have a good-quality blade, you don't necessarily need a weighty paring knife," said Norman Weinstein, a knife-skills instructor at Peter Kump's New York Cooking School in New York City. "The handle should fit well in your hand and feel comfortable, but you don't need heft for coring and peeling."

As Weinstein said, what matters most is the feel of the knife in your hand. Is the handle smooth or rough? Comfortably shaped or awkward? Do your fingers rest safely on the handle, or are they threatened by the blade in any way? Does the knife as a whole feel solid or flimsy? This important factor, however, is also the most open to subjective interpretation. For most of the knives we tested, assessments of handle comfort varied from user to user, so this is where you should acknowledge your own personal preference when shopping. Both the Wüsthof and the Henckels had ergonomically designed, molded handles that testers with medium-sized hands found perfectly comfortable; exceptionally large- and small-handed testers found them less so. Likewise, opinions were divided on the very light, slim handle of the Forschner (one large-handed tester objected) and on the square wooden handle of the Chicago Cutlery (some testers simply disliked wooden knife handles,

The Paring Knives We Tested

RECOMMENDED

Wüsthof-Trident Grand Prix
This joyously agile knife is the clear winner.

Forschner (Victorinox) Fibrox
Very flexible blade pleased most users.

Zwilling J. A. Henckels Four Star
A comfortable, consistent performer; handle more popular than blade.

NOT RECOMMENDED

Progressive Int'l
Completely serviceable when new, but doesn't take an edge well.

Chicago Cutlery
Performs all tasks serviceably but excels at none.

Global
"Awkward" design with an "awesomely sharp" blade.

Oxo Good Grips
Huge, bulky handle and overly stiff blade.

RATING 3½-INCH PARING KNIVES

The prices listed are retail—paid in Boston stores and through national mail-order catalogs—but generally reflect a standard discount of 20 to 25 percent off full retail prices. Expect prices in your area to vary depending on the discounts offered by local stores. See Resources, page 32, for price and availability of top-choice models. Testers' comments augment the categorical ratings with general observations, including grip comfort, blade rigidity and flexibility, and perceived construction quality.

Brand	Price	Blade type/ length	Handle	Blade	Edge Resto-ration	Peeling Turnips	Mincing Shallots	Coring Tomatoes	Paring Apples	Paring Oranges	Testers' Comments
RECOMMENDED											
Wüsthof-Trident Grand Prix Utility Knife	$27.99	Forged/ 3½ inches	★★★	★★★★ ★	★★★	★★★ ★	★★★	★★★ ★	★★★ ★	★★★ ★	"This knife just wants to go," exclaimed one tester. Its thin, "surgically sharp" blade won praise for easy movement, precision, and a welcome degree of flexibility. Some testers had to saw through shallots; all other tasks were performed almost flawlessly.
Forschner (Victorinox) Fibrox	$5.95	Stamped/ 3¼ inches	★★	★★★	★★★	★★★ ★	★★★	★★★ ★	★★★ ★	★★★ ★	The lightest knife in the group, the Forschner was loved by most for its svelte figure and diminutive presence. The blade was too flexible for some, while others noted the flex was great for moving around the curves of a turnip and coring apples and tomatoes. Overall, a great value.
Zwilling J. A. Henckels Four Star	$19.99	Forged/ 3 inches	★★★ ★	★★★	★★★	★★★	★★★	★★	★★★	★★★ ★	Less blade flex than Wüsthof or Forschner, but this knife felt "solid," "stable," and "high-quality." Sharpness was adequate, but some testers noted a bit of "drag" cutting through hard foods like turnips.
NOT RECOMMENDED											
Progressive International Stainless Steel Paring Knife	$5.49	Stamped/ 3½ inches	★★★	★★★	★	★★★	★★★	★★★	★★★ ★	★★★	Most testers "liked it more than they thought they would." Flexible blade was "perfect for paring apples" and performed perfectly well in other tasks. Rating downgraded owing to poor edge restoration and construction; blade and handle were not firmly attached.
Chicago Cutlery Walnut Tradition Utility/Parer, Item # 107SP	$9.99	Stamped/ 3⅜ inches	★★	★★	★★	★★	★★★	★★★	★★★	★★★	Some testers liked the square shape and wood surface of the handle, while others found both uncomfortable; blade was somewhat too dull for all but one tester.
Global 10-cm Paring Knife, ZModel GS-7	$32.40	Forged/ 3⅞ inches	★★	★★★	★★	★★	★★★	★★	★	★★★	Sleek, gorgeous, and razor sharp, but impractical for paring. Handle considered awkward by most testers, and stiff blade difficult to maneuver around curves for peeling or coring. The blade cannot be honed on a regular sharpening steel. One tester, who favors large knives, quickly become a Global fan—but a lonely one.
Oxo Good Grips—11	$6.99	Stamped/ 3½ inches	★	★	★	★	★★	★	★★	★★	"Big" and "clunky" handle won no fans, nor did the very stiff blade. "This knife is seriously difficult to manipulate… feels like I'm using an axe," commented one tester.

while others didn't seem to mind).

There was accord about the two knives in the group with unusual handles: because of them, testers downgraded the knives drastically. While the Oxo Good Grips was praised for the feel of its soft rubber handle, both large- and small-handed testers rated the knife poorly overall because of its huge grip, which felt "way too big and unnatural." Our test kitchen staff observed another annoying trait of the Oxo: it is difficult to distinguish the cutting edge of the blade at first glance. The shape of the blade tricks the eye, and our staffers found themselves regularly starting to cut with the wrong side of the blade. The other big loser when it came to handles was the Global knife. All of the testers noted how the unusual shape of the handle required them to choke up on it, which put their thumbs within dangerous proximity of a sharp and prominent point at the heel of the blade. This awkward hand position also made the knife so difficult to control that one tester called the Global "perilous for paring."

Another important performance factor was maneuverability, which was determined largely by the relative flexibility of the blade. The most flexible blade in the group belonged to the Forschner, followed by Wüsthof, Progressive International, and Henckels. These knives were the easiest to work into tight spots, such as tomato cores and orange sections, and around the round surfaces of turnips and apples. The superflexibility of the Forschner blade did make one tester uncomfortable, however, because he considered it flimsy. Stiffer blades, such as those of the Global, Chicago Cutlery, and Oxo knives, offered a very minor advantage for slicing and mincing, but these are secondary tasks for parers.

As with any kind of knife, of course, sharpness was also an important factor. The factory edge on each of the knives tested, forged and stamped alike, was sharp enough to use without incident. Just out of the box, though, the Global and the Wüsthof were the sharpest, with the Oxo bringing up the dull rear. Regardless of the factory edge, however, any knife will dull with use, and our two sharpness leaders seemed to dull faster than the rest of the pack. The good news was that the edges on most of the knives were easy to restore by honing on a sharpening steel, a characteristic referred to in kitchen parlance as "taking an edge." The Global, however, required a ceramic or diamond steel for honing, another big disadvantage.

In sum, the forged knives from Wüsthof and Henckels regained their edges well and felt the most solid and stable in use, but that feeling of quality comes at a price. Their cost is, respectively, three and five times as much as that of the inexpensive stamped Forschner. Although this knife did feel superlight and unsubstantial in the hands of some testers, the Forschner is agile, easy to use, and takes an edge as well as its expensive competition.

Cream of Tomato Soup
NOV./DEC. '99

When we called for just a "pinch" of allspice to heighten flavor in our cream of tomato soup, we meant the intuitive—an amount that's small enough to be picked up between your thumb and forefinger. So we were intrigued (and amused) when Amco Corporation recently came out with measuring spoons for a "pinch," a "dash," and a "smidgen." We called the Office of Weights and Measures at the Department of Commerce's National Institute of Standards and Technology and found out that in fact there is no standardized measurement for a pinch or a dash or a smidgen. Many cookbooks define a pinch as 1/16 of a teaspoon. Amco's pinch measured 1/8 of a teaspoon. That would have to be a pinch from someone with extraordinarily large digits. Our conclusion: the spoon idea is cute, but a cook's own fingers are best.

A New Thermometer
New to the realm of instant-read thermometers is the Raytek MiniTemp Noncontact Thermometer with laser sighting and infrared technology. Having seen it featured in the food section of the *New York Times*, we quickly sent for one. We had 10 fun-filled minutes with it, taking the temperature of everything in sight—from a carton of milk to some dogs walking by in the alley behind the office. It didn't take long to realize that this gadget would be of limited use in the home kitchen, however, because it measures only surface temperatures, not internal temperatures. And at $139, it's anything but a cheap thrill.

Salmon Cakes PAGE 6
In our recipe for salmon cakes, a small amount of vegetable oil is beaten in with the egg dip used to coat the chilled salmon patties before covering them in bread crumbs. We were looking for as thin a coating as possible and found the added bit of oil—as opposed to the traditional all-egg dip—did the trick.

Cassoulet PAGE 14
We are big fans of brining and found this technique particularly effective in making the chicken legs in our cassoulet plump and juicy, reminiscent of confit. The trouble is that the chicken wants to float at the top of the brine because salt water increases buoyancy. To make sure your chicken is not bobbing halfway out of the brine, press as much air as possible out of the zipper-lock bag holding the brine and the bird. Or, if you're brining in a plastic tub or a bowl, simply fit a plate, another sealed bag of water, or some other simple weight over the chicken to keep it immersed.

Hard-Cooked Eggs MAR./APR. '99
We have found that if you hard-boil eggs and leave them to sit in the refrigerator for a few days, they can sometimes be tougher to peel. When this happens, it helps if you let them sit in a bowl of warm water for 10 minutes. Then just crack the shell extensively and peel.

Electric Knife Sharpeners
MAR./APR. '97

While some electric knife sharpeners do a great job of restoring a knife's edge, we have found that they cannot sharpen all the way to the bolster of a chef's knife. Over time, this results in two problems: the blade end near the handle grows duller and duller, and it also begins to stick out as the rest of the blade gets shaved away. That's not much help considering the bolster end is often what gets the most use. We periodically take our chef's knives to a professional sharpening service. To find a knife-sharpening service, look in your Yellow Pages under "cutlery," "knives," or "sharpening services." Be wary of places that sharpen lawn mower blades as well as kitchen knives. We take our knives to Stoddard's, a cutlery store that actually accepts knives for sharpening through the mail (see Resources, page 32). The other bonus you get when having a professional sharpen your knife is that he or she can improve a damaged blade without shaving it down to nothingness, which is always a possibility with an electric model.

Automatic Drip Coffee Makers
NOV./DEC. '98

Many people store their ground coffee in the freezer or refrigerator. Because having the water at the proper temperature is a key factor in brewing coffee in drip coffee makers, we wondered what effect cold coffee would have on the process—could the beans' aromatic oils adequately release? To find out we made three pots of coffee by the same method, using freezer-cold coffee, coffee from the fridge, and room-temperature coffee (all coffee had been stored in airtight jars for 2 weeks). In a side-by-side tasting, the pot brewed with room temperature coffee did have a fuller, rounder flavor than the other two, but the difference was subtle and went almost undetected when cups of the coffee were doctored with milk. So it's a gamble. If you go through coffee quickly, room temperature storage might be best. Whichever storage method you choose, coffee should always be stored in an airtight container.

Pancakes JAN./FEB. '96
A couple staff members and a few readers, too, have noticed that melted butter clumps up when added to the buttermilk mixture in this pancake recipe. We decided to see if the clumps make any difference in the end product. The pancakes made with perfectly smooth batter were just as they should be—light and fluffy. Those made with butter-clumped batter were still nice and airy, maybe a bit greasier, though not remarkably so. The trick is to have the buttermilk and milk at room temperature before adding the butter mixture.

TESTING UPDATE: Instant-Read Thermometers

Owen Instruments Thermapen 5   **Taylor** Digital Pocket Thermometer Model 9840   **Polder** Cooking Thermometer/Timer

In our July/August 1997 issue, we rated instant-read thermometers. The top three models were the Owen Instruments Thermapen 5, the Taylor Digital Pocket Thermometer Model 9840, and the Polder Cooking Thermometer/Timer. Hundreds of additional test kitchen hours later, we stand by our ratings but have a few comments to add. Since our original testing, the top-rated Owen Thermapen has been redesigned so that it shuts off automatically. (It has always turned on when the probe is swung out. Now it shuts off—randomly, we might add—after anywhere between three and eight minutes if the probe is not folded back in place.) We find, to our frustration, that it always shuts down when you need it most. Innovation failed to deliver improvement here. We also noticed that our second choice, the Taylor 9840, now has a slower read-response time, so we reach for the Thermapen first if we're measuring something so hot that we don't want to hold our hands too close to it for long. The third-place Polder, originally downgraded owing to its short battery life (the thermometer never turns off), turned out to need batteries less frequently than we had expected. But because it's not strictly an instant-read thermometer (it is also a timer) and because the 45-inch wire connecting the probe to the reading panel can be awkward to use, we still prefer either the Owen or the Taylor. See Resources, page 32, for mail-order information.

Baking In the New Year

Three new entries into the baking cookbook sweepstakes have
varying degrees of success. BY CHRISTOPHER KIMBALL

Alice Medrich's Cookies and Brownies
Alice Medrich
Warner Books, 123 pages

This is a straightforward, no-nonsense collection of recipes that are both familiar and appealing—chocolate chip cookies, snickerdoodles, macaroons, ginger snaps, and so on. Medrich's goal, as described in her introduction, is to develop recipes that turn out high-quality, consistent results from baker to baker, a difficult task indeed given the fact that cookies are notoriously tricky, with small variations in ingredients leading to huge differences in outcomes. (I think I would rather promise a cure for world hunger—the odds would be better.) The layout is clear, the writing concise, and the collection of recipes large enough to be satisfying for the American home baker without being the last or most comprehensive word on the subject.

PROS: The recipes are generally reliable, and some of the cookies and brownies were truly outstanding. Silhouettes of different cookies all printed on the same page are useful—sort of a cookie glossary at a glance.

CONS: Why purchase this particular book? Medrich fans would say because the recipes are excellent and the instructional information so thorough that missteps by the home baker will be rare. We agree. Even so, we occasionally found the directions a bit lacking. For example, in the introduction, Medrich makes a point of telling us to spoon flour into a measuring cup, indicating that the weight will be quite different from what it would be if using the more common dip-and-sweep method. The problem is that people often don't bother to read the front matter of a book and so will no doubt proceed to dip and sweep. If the author is setting out to produce foolproof recipes, she needs to deal with even these sorts of editorial issues.

RECIPE TESTING: We tested seven recipes from this book; two were slam-dunk winners, and the others ranged from very good to disappointing. The New Classic Brownies were the best basic brownies we have ever tasted, made with an innovative method in which the baking pan is taken hot from the oven and put directly into an ice bath. This one recipe might be worth the price of the book. The Mexican Wedding Cakes were also terrific, and the Coconut Macaroons delivered

sweet, gooey-on-the-inside cookies as promised. Chocolate-Hazelnut Meringue Kisses were good but not exceptional, and Lemon Bars were a bust: the baking time was off, they were hard to cut and serve, and our tasters found them too acidic. Turtle Bars promised "gooey chewy caramel," but instead we got incredibly sweet bars with a crystallized brown sugar layer.

Butter, Sugar, Flour, Eggs
Gale Gand, Rick Tramonto, Julia Moskin
Clarkson N. Potter, 288 pages

This book was spawned by a Chicago restaurant, Brasserie T, and the name of the book derives from the authors' love of ingredients—"bricks of smooth, creamy butter, snowy mountains of sugar…and the golden glow of fresh egg yolks." Chapters are organized by ingredient, and the recipe titles have enormous appeal: Brooklyn Blackout Cake, Marzipan Torte with Ginger, Raspberry Cream Tart. It makes one want to quit work early and rush home to the kitchen. Although the chatty tone reminds one of an overly friendly but knowledgeable waiter named Bob, the recipe notes are down-to-earth and useful, explaining foods such as ganache and crème anglaise in simple terms. The book also contains 32 pages of color food photography.

PROS: If you are tired of the same old dessert offerings, this book has plenty of good ideas. The authors have a warm, personal tone that some will like and others will find a bit over the top.

CONS: This book is a great source for ideas, but not for the inexperienced baker; these recipes need more testing. The ingredient amounts often seem questionable, and the recipe writing is occasionally sketchy.

RECIPE TESTING: We tested five recipes and would consider making only one of them a second time. The Vanilla Panna Cotta was a snap to make but proved rubbery, using a whopping one tablespoon of gelatin. Pecan Toffee had a bevy of problems, while the Marzipan Torte with Ginger was too oily. There was an error in the ingredient list for a butter cake, and the inside of the cake was leaden and tough—not worth eating. On the bright side, a butterscotch pudding was good, although we found that the caramelization took a lot less time than the recipe predicted

The Family Baker
Susan Purdy
Broadway Books, 248 pages

This is a warm, friendly collection of personal recipes with no pretense of being either perfect or visually stunning. It reminds me of a time when bakers played with their food, putting recipes together with a sense of whimsy, as Purdy does in this book, with recipe titles such as Rice Krispies Candy Cones and the Ice Cream "Sand" Castle. That said, though, I will add that the bulk of the recipes, from Mom's Apple Pie to Classic Peanut Butter Cookies, are straightforward. There are eight pages of color photographs.

PROS: This is a professionally written and tested cookbook that the author compiled without the burden of having to prove anything. Put another way, it is a charming collection of personal recipes without all the bloody hype. Purdy knows her way around the kitchen, and her love of the connection between family and food is heartfelt and perfectly expressed. In the introduction she manages to convey in spare prose the power of recipes to invoke the spirit of family members. The recipes are generally thorough, providing plenty of detail.

CONS: The layout of the recipes could be improved. The ingredients are listed in small type that some may find hard to read. In addition, there is a great deal of information about equipment, advance preparation, and the like that, while useful, makes the recipes seem a bit more complicated than they really are.

RECIPE TESTING: This book fared a great deal better than the second book we tested. Butter Mints were fun to make and turned out perfectly. Rosemary-Honey Cookies were simple and wonderful, although some of our tasters were less than enthusiastic about the use of rosemary in a sweet context. Cornmeal Crisps were outstanding, lighter and crispier than similar recipes we have tried. To-Live-for Chocolate Mousse Cake was a disappointment, though, with a bitter crust and a spongy texture. Old-Fashioned Coconut Layer Cake was a mixed bag—the artificial coconut extract smelled like suntan lotion, and there were a couple of minor missteps in the recipe, but the cake still tasted good in the end.

Most of the ingredients and materials necessary for the recipes in this issue are available at your local supermarket, gourmet store, or kitchen supply shop. The following are mail-order sources for particular items. Prices listed below were current at press time and do not include shipping or handling unless otherwise indicated. We suggest that you contact companies directly to confirm up-to-date prices and availability.

Paring Knives

All three of the top-rated paring knives in the article on page 28 are available by mail order through **Professional Cutlery Direct (242 Branford Road, North Branford, CT 06471; 800-859-6994; www.cutlery.com).** The top recommended Wüsthof-Trident Grand Prix Utility Knife, order number CI01W, sells for $27.95. The runner-up Forschner (Victorinox) Fibrox, order number CI01F, sells for $5.50. The third-place finisher, a Zwilling J. A. Henckels Four Star, order number CI01H, sells for $19.99.

Thermometers

In the magazine's new section, Kitchen Notes, found on page 30, we updated *Cook's* July/ August 1997 rating of instant-read thermometers. The top model, Owen Instruments Thermapen 5, is not readily available in stores but can be ordered for $59.95 from **The Baker's Catalogue (King Arthur Flour, P.O. Box 876, Norwich, VT 05055-0876; 800-827-6836; www.kingarthurflour.com).** The Taylor 9840 and the Polder can be found in many major cookware stores. You can also order them, for $18.90 and $29.99, respectively, from **A Cook's Wares (211 37th Street, Beaver Falls, PA 15010-2103; 800-915-9788; www.cookswares.com).**

Mail-Order Knife Sharpening

If you cannot locate a professional knife sharpener in your area, Stoddard's, a Boston cutlery store founded in 1800, will accept knives by mail for sharpening service. If you choose this option, use common sense when packaging to protect the knife's edge—and the mail carrier. Do not tape up your blade. Use the original plastic or cardboard sheath in which the knife was purchased if you still have it. Wrap in newspaper and pack in a sturdy corrugated box in such a way that the knife won't shift position. If your blade edge is not badly dulled, you can expect to be charged the following for sharpening: $1.50 for a paring knife, $2.25 for a knife that is up to 8 inches, $2.75 for a 10-inch knife, and $3 for a knife that is longer than 10 inches. Mail to **Stoddard's (50 Temple Place, Boston, MA 02111; 617-426-4187)** and enclose your name, address,

and phone number. The store will contact you regarding billing information. Allow up to 10 days for your knife to be serviced. Stoddard's also sharpens scissors and poultry shears and offers a wide selection of cutlery by mail order.

Matfer Exoglass Spoon

One of our favorite basic kitchen tools has become the Matfer "Do Anything" Spoon. At a glance, it looks like your ordinary wooden mixing spoon. This multipurpose kitchen tool, however, is made of exoglass, a nonporous, waterproof material that is heat resistant up to 430 degrees Fahrenheit. This means that unlike a wooden spoon, it does not stain or darken, warp, or absorb flavors. And, unlike a metal spoon, it does not scratch nonstick surfaces. It is also dishwasher safe. Made in France, it can be ordered by mail (stock #648352) for $4.99 from **Kitchen Etc. catalogue services (Department TM, 32 Industrial Drive, Exeter, NH 03833; 800-232-4070; www.kitchenetc.com).**

Confit

In preliminary tests for the recipe for simplified cassoulet (page 14), we were able to track down some duck confit through a Boston butcher who primarily supplies restaurants. Understandably, the average store and the average butcher do not carry this specialty item. If you are in the market for confit, we recommend ordering by mail from D'Artagnan, a leading purveyor of poultry and game. D'Artagnan sells duck leg confit for $6.95 a leg—or $30 for a package of six. A bucket of 60 legs preserved in fat sells for $200. D'Artagnan does not use any preservatives or nitrites, and the duck meat is never pumped with water. The confit has a shelf life of one month. Order directly from **D'Artagnan (280 Wilson Avenue, Newark, NJ 07105; 800-327-8246; www.dartagnan.com).**

Flageolets

Of the four varieties of beans we tested for the cassoulet recipe on page 15, we liked flageolets best for their tender, creamy texture and subtle flavor. Dried flageolets are typically sold in specialty food stores. You can also order them by mail from **Indian Harvest Specialtifoods (909 Paul Bunyan Drive SE, P.O. Box 845, Bemidji, MN 56619-0845; 800-294-2433; www.indianharvest.com or www.beanbag.net).** A 1½ pound bag sells for $6.95.

Tapered Rolling Pin

When developing a recipe for sweet pastry dough (see page 11), test kitchen director Kay Rentschler found that it was much easier to con-

trol the dough and work with precision when using a tapered rolling pin. The simple design of this French-style rolling pin, a solid wooden dowel with tapered ends instead of handles, can give the cook a more immediate feel for the condition, shape, and evenness of the dough when rolling it out. The tapered shape means it rotates easily, a particular plus when trying to work dough in a circle. The **Sur La Table catalog (1765 Sixth Avenue South, Seattle, WA 98143-1608; 800-243-0852; www.surlatable.com)** carries a 20-inch tapered pin made of lightweight beechwood that sells for $9.95.

United States Postal Service
Statement of Ownership, Management, and Circulation

1. Publication Title		2. Publication Number		3. Filing Date
Cook's Illustrated		1 0 6 8 - 7 8 2 1		10/1/99
4. Issue Frequency		5. Number of Issues Published Annually		6. Annual Subscription Price
Bi-Monthly		6		$29.70

7. Complete Mailing Address of Known Office of Publication (Not printer) (Street, city, county, state, and ZIP+4)   Contact Person
b Boston Common Press, 17 Station St., Brookline, MA 02445   Telephone 617-232-1000

8. Complete Mailing Address of Headquarters or General Business Office of Publisher (Not printer)
Same as Above

9. Full Names and Complete Mailing Addresses of Publisher, Editor, and Managing Editor (Do not leave blank)
Publisher (Name and complete mailing address)
Christopher Kimball, Boston Common Press, 17 Station St., Brookline, MA 02445

Editor (Name and complete mailing address)
Same as Publisher

Managing Editor (Name and complete mailing address)
Barbara Bourassa, Boston Common Press, 17 Station St., Brookline, MA 02445

10. Owner (Do not leave blank. If the publication is owned by a corporation, give the name and address of the corporation immediately followed by the names and addresses of all stockholders owning or holding 1 percent or more of the total amount of stock. If not owned by a corporation, give the names and addresses of the individual owners. If owned by a partnership or other unincorporated firm, give its name and address as well as those of each individual owner. If the publication is published by a nonprofit organization, give its name and address.)

Full Name	Complete Mailing Address
Boston Common Press Limited Partnership	500 Boylston St., Boston, MA 02116
(Christopher Kimball)	

11. Known Bondholders, Mortgagees, and Other Security Holders Owning or Holding 1 Percent or More of Total Amount of Bonds, Mortgages, or Other Securities. If none, check box.   ☐ None

Full Name	Complete Mailing Address
N/A	

12. Tax Status (For completion by nonprofit organizations authorized to mail at nonprofit rates) (Check one)
The purpose, function, and nonprofit status of this organization and the exempt status for federal income tax purposes:
☐ Has Not Changed During Preceding 12 Months
☐ Has Changed During Preceding 12 Months (Publisher must submit explanation of change with this statement)

13. Publication Title	14. Issue Date for Circulation Data Below
Cook's Illustrated	Sept./Oct. 1999

15.	Extent and Nature of Circulation	Average No. Copies Each Issue During Preceding 12 Months	No. Copies of Single Issue Published Nearest to Filing Date
a.	Total Number of Copies (Net press run)	399,223	408,046
b. Paid and/or Requested Circulation	(1) Paid/Requested Outside-County Mail Subscriptions Stated on Form 3541. (Include advertiser's proof and exchange copies)	284,610	289,974
	(2) Paid In-County Subscriptions (Include advertiser's proof and exchange copies)	0	0
	(3) Sales Through Dealers and Carriers, Street Vendors, Counter Sales, and Other Non-USPS Paid Distribution	52,613	55,643
	(4) Other Classes Mailed Through the USPS	0	0
c.	Total Paid and/or Requested Circulation (Sum of 15b. (1), (2),(3),and (4))	337,223	345,617
d. Free Distribution by Mail (Samples, complimentary, and other free)	(1) Outside-County as Stated on Form 3541		
	(2) In-County as Stated on Form 3541	4,485	4,251
	(3) Other Classes Mailed Through the USPS		
e.	Free Distribution Outside the Mail (Carriers or other means)	401	375
f.	Total Free Distribution (Sum of 15d. and 15e.)	4,886	4,626
g.	Total Distribution (Sum of 15c. and 15f)	342,109	350,243
h.	Copies not Distributed	57,114	57,803
i.	Total (Sum of 15g. and h.)	399,223	408,046
j.	Percent Paid and/or Requested Circulation (15c. divided by 15g. times 100)	98.6%	98.7%

16. Publication of Statement of Ownership
☑ Publication required. Will be printed in the Jan./Feb. 2000 issue of this publication.   ☐ Publication not required.

17. Signature and Title of Editor, Publisher, Business Manager, or Owner   Date 10/1/99

I certify that all information furnished on this form is true and complete. I understand that anyone who furnishes false or misleading information on this form or who omits material or information requested on the form may be subject to criminal sanctions (including fines and imprisonment) and/or civil sanctions (including civil penalties).

Instructions to Publishers
1. Complete and file one copy of this form with your postmaster annually on or before October 1. Keep a copy of the completed form for your records.
2. In cases where the stockholder or security holder is a trustee, include in items 10 and 11 the name of the person or corporation for whom the trustee is acting. Also include the names and addresses of individuals who are stockholders who own or hold 1 percent or more of the total amount of bonds, mortgages, or other securities of the publishing corporation. In item 11, if none, check the box. Use blank sheets if more space is required.
3. Be sure to furnish all circulation information called for in item 15. Free circulation must be shown in items 15d, e, and f.
4. Item 15h., Copies not Distributed, must include (1) newsstand copies originally stated on Form 3541, and returned to the publisher, (2) estimated returns from news agents, and (3), copies for office use, leftovers, spoiled, and all other copies not distributed.
5. If the publication had Periodicals authorization as a general or requester publication, this Statement of Ownership, Management, and Circulation must be published; it must be printed in any issue in October or, if the publication is not published during October, the first issue printed after October.
6. In item 16, indicate the date of the issue in which this Statement of Ownership will be published.
7. Item 17 must be signed.

Failure to file or publish a statement of ownership may lead to suspension of Periodicals authorization.

PS Form 3526, September 1998 (Reverse)

RECIPE INDEX

Classic Lemon Tart **PAGE 23**

The Best Chocolate-Dipped Coconut Macaroons **PAGE 25**

Simplified Cassoulet **PAGE 15**

Short Ribs Braised in Red Wine **PAGE 9**

Pan-Fried Fresh Salmon Cakes **PAGE 7**

Country-Style Potato Leek Soup **PAGE 10**

PHOTOGRAPHY: CARL TREMBLAY   PROP STYLING : MYROSHA DZIUK

Guava

Carambola "Star Fruit"

Mango

Cherimoya "Custard Apple"

Pepino

Kiwano "Horned Melon"

Passion Fruit

Papaya

Pineapple

TROPICAL FRUIT

NUMBER FORTY-THREE

MARCH & APRIL 2000

COOK'S
ILLUSTRATED

High-Roast Chicken Perfected
Crisp Skin, Moist Meat, No Smoke

Meaty Tomato Sauce
Which Cut of Meat Works Best?

Digital Scale Testing
Absolute Accuracy Takes Back Seat

Supermarket Chicken Broth Wins Tasting
Expensive Natural Products Lose

Devil's Food Cake
For Rich, Velvety Texture, Use Boiling Water

The Ultimate Homemade Baguette

Oatmeal Worth Eating

Exploring Rice Pilaf

Cooking Supermarket Spinach

Cake Frosting 101

Roasting Boneless Leg of Lamb

$4.95 U.S./$6.95 CANADA

CONTENTS

March & April 2000

COOK'S ILLUSTRATED

www.cooksillustrated.com

PUBLISHER AND EDITOR
Christopher Kimball

SENIOR EDITOR
John Willoughby

SENIOR WRITER
Jack Bishop

CORPORATE MANAGING EDITOR
Barbara Bourassa

ASSOCIATE EDITORS
Adam Ried
Dawn Yanagihara

TEST KITCHEN DIRECTOR
Kay Rentschler

RECIPE TESTING AND DEVELOPMENT
Bridget Lancaster
Julia Collin

CONSULTING FOOD EDITOR
Jasper White

CONSULTING EDITORS
Maryellen Driscoll
Jim Dodge

ART DIRECTOR
Amy Klee

PROJECT MANAGER
Sheila Datz

EDITORIAL PRODUCTION MANAGER
Nate Nickerson

COPY EDITOR
India Koopman

EDITORIAL INTERN
Brigitte Scott

MARKETING MANAGER
Pamela Caporino

SALES REPRESENATIVE
Jason Geller

MARKETING ASSISTANT
Connie Forbes

CIRCULATION DIRECTOR
David Mack

FULFILLMENT MANAGER
Larisa Greiner

PRODUCTS MANAGER
Steven Browall

CIRCULATION ASSISTANT
Mary Connelly

VICE PRESIDENT
PRODUCTION AND TECHNOLOGY
James McCormack

SYSTEMS ADMINISTRATOR
Richard Cassidy

PRODUCTION ARTIST
Daniel Frey

JUNIOR WEB DEVELOPER
Nicole Morris

CONTROLLER
Mandy Shito

OFFICE MANAGER
Jennifer McCreary

SPECIAL PROJECTS
Deborah Broide

For list rental information, contact The SpeciaLISTS, 1200
Harbor Blvd. 9th Floor, Weehawken, NJ 07087; (201) 865-
5800; fax (201) 867-2450. Editorial office: 17 Station Street,
Brookline, MA 02445; (617) 232-1000; fax (617) 232-
1572. Editorial contributions should be sent to: Editor, *Cook's
Illustrated*. We cannot assume responsibility for manuscripts
submitted to us. Submissions will be returned only if accompanied by a large self-addressed envelope. Postmaster: Send all
new orders, subscription inquiries, and change of address
notices to: *Cook's Illustrated*, P.O. Box 7446, Red Oak, IA
51591-0446. PRINTED IN THE USA.

ALLIUMS The amazing allium family includes a variety of the most commonly used seasonings in
the world. Spanish onions, purple onions, and marble-sized pearl onions are well-known to every
cook in America, but recently sweeter versions have become more common. These include the
Vidalias of the American South and the flat, ovoid cipollini of Italy, which are called wild onions but
are actually bulbs of the grape hyacinth. In the same way, standard-sized garlic is often sold these
days side by side with elephant garlic, which is actually a closer relative of the leek and is much less
pungent than true garlic. Shallots have a mild onion flavor with subtle overtones of garlic. Leeks,
chives, scallions, and ramps (which are also known as wild leeks and are native to North America),
differ from other alliums in that their green shoots as well as their bulbs are often used in cooking.

COVER PAINTING: BRENT WATKINSON,   BACK COVER ILLUSTRATION: JOHN BURGOYNE.

THE NEW NEW THING

In *The New New Thing,* Jim Clark, founder of Netscape and celebrated Silicon Valley entrepreneur, crosses the Atlantic on his $30 million sailboat, a vessel controlled by millions of lines of computer software code rather than sailors. Outside, the wind changes direction, the sea rises, and the enormous mainsail develops a rip that aborts the journey. Inside, Clark is totally absorbed by the glowing screen of a Silicon Graphics workstation, completely unaware of the forces of nature. After the maiden voyage, he soon loses interest in his 150-foot toy, moving on to the new new thing, an even bigger boat with more computers.

I have found that children, unlike Jim Clark, take great pleasure in the unchanged. Once they find an activity they like, they repeat it endlessly. As G. K. Chesterton wrote in *Orthodoxy,* "grown-up people are not strong enough to exult in monotony." The word *monotony,* of course, is the problem. My children simply shout "Do It Again!" with no thought that repetition and pleasure are somehow separate. For my 2 year old, joy is the 100th reading of *Goodnight Moon;* for my 4 year old it is playing pirate; for my 10 year old it is the perfect bowl of homemade oatmeal prepared just so each morning; and for my 9 year old it is yet one more game of Clue before bedtime.

Many of us might label this obsession with the familiar as no more than immaturity; a young, insecure child always seeks comfort in routine. However, the corollary is that the rest of us take no comfort at all in the familiar, since we are always seeking what is next. I am reminded of a story told by a Zen teacher, Steve Hagen. A crowd is seated around a sumptuous banquet, the table filled with meats, fruits, fish, vegetables, wine, and sweets, everything one could desire, yet the guests are slowly starving to death. They don't realize that food is what they need. They have forgotten how to see.

I wonder if this lack of vision is perhaps the greatest attribute of modern times. In the 19th century, a "tourist" experienced foreign lands at a snail's pace, a trip to Europe taking months and encounters with locals frequent, since one traveled by the blessed tedium of coach and train rather than at jet speed. The travel itself was the adventure, not the destination. In cooking, of course, we have pared down our expectations to the food itself, the experience of cooking being of little import. Like modern tourists, we are focused on the destination and miss the journey entirely.

Perhaps we have lost, as Chesterton put it, "the eternal appetite of infancy." In modern times, to be called infantile is be singled out as a fool unsophisticated in the ways of the world. Perhaps we ought to regard the label of childishness as a compliment, a term worthy of someone who can wallow in the indulgence of the moment and see things for what they are. I support this new definition with the example of nature itself, the ultimate study in repetition.

Christopher Kimball

The sun rises every morning, yet poets have not found that simple act monotonous. Homer, in *The Odyssey,* starts each chapter with the words, "The rosy red fingers of dawn…" Is one more perfect Black-Eyed Susan not worth a glance? Should we tire of the thrill of winter's first snow? Is the sight of a wild apple tree in full bloom not breathtaking? Nature refreshes itself through repetition; renewal is part of an endless cycle.

My 2-year-old daughter bends down to peep through the oven window, hands on knees, saucer eyes wide with expectation, glimpsing, I am thinking, a bit of the eternal. I stop to watch, realizing that I have forgotten how to see the mystery of life in the rise of angel food or in the upward push of a baking biscuit. Standing by the stove, we could all travel like this newly minted being, slipping into the stream of life through the familiar, finding everything we seek within our four walls. For cooks, the yeast of life is to be had on the cheap, with the slap of dough or the foam of batter. It is a journey best taken with baby steps, one at a time, until we find ourselves face to face with our heart's desire, that which is timeless but also familiar. If we could but see like a child, we would set out on journeys never thinking only of the destination. We would all be happy cooks, I expect, busy in the kitchen, discovering the unexpected in the midst of the familiar.

ABOUT COOK'S ILLUSTRATED

Expanded Web Site Coming in March 2000, the new *Cook's* Web site will feature original editorial content not found in the magazine and searchable databases for recipes, equipment tests, food tastings, buying advice, cookbook reviews, and quick tips. The site will also feature our online bookstore, e-mail newsletter, online cooking courses, and a message board. Visit the site at **cooksillustrated.com**.

The Magazine *Cook's Illustrated* (ISSN 1068-2821) is published bimonthly (6 issues per year) by Boston Common Press Limited Partnership, 17 Station Street, Brookline, MA 02445. Copyright 2000 Boston Common Press Limited Partnership. Periodical postage paid at Boston, Mass. and additional mailing offices, USPS #012487. A one-year subscription is $29.70, two years is $55, and three years is $75. Add $6 postage per year for Canadian subscriptions and $12 per year for all other foreign countries. To order subscriptions in the U.S. call 800-526-8442; from outside the U.S. call 515-247-7571. Gift subscriptions are available for $24.95 each. Postmaster: Send all new orders, subscription inquiries, and change of address notices to: *Cook's Illustrated,* P.O. Box 7446, Red Oak, IA 51591-0446.

Magazine-Related Items *Cook's Illustrated* is available in annual hardbound editions for $24.95 each plus shipping and handling; each edition is fully indexed. Discounts are available if more than one year is ordered at a time. Individual back issues are available for $5 each. *Cook's* also offers a seven-year index (1993-1999) of the magazine for $12.95. To order any of these products, call 800-611-0759 inside the U.S. or 515-246-6911 from outside the U.S.

Books *The Best Recipe,* which features 700 of our favorite recipes from the pages of *Cook's Illustrated,* is available for $24.95. *Cook's Illustrated* also publishes a series of single-topic books, available for $14.95 each, which cover pie, American layer cake, stir-frying, ice cream, salad, simple fruit desserts, cookie jar favorites, holiday roasts and birds, stew, grilling, pizza, holiday desserts, pasta sauces, barbecuing and roasting on the grill, shrimp and other shellfish, cooking garden vegetables, pot pies and casseroles, soup, sautéing, and potatoes. *The Cook's Bible,* written by Christopher Kimball and published by Little, Brown and Company, is available for $24.95. *The Yellow Farmhouse Cookbook,* also written by Christopher Kimball and published by Little, Brown and Company, is available for $24.95. To order any of these books, call 800-611-0759 inside the U.S. or 515-246-6911 from outside the U.S.

Reader Submissions *Cook's* accepts reader submissions for Quick Tips. We will provide a one-year complimentary subscription for each tip that we print. Send your tip, name, address, and daytime telephone number to Quick Tips, *Cook's Illustrated,* P.O. Box 470589, Brookline, MA 02447. Questions, suggestions, or submissions for Notes from Readers should be sent to the same address.

Subscription Inquiries All queries about subscriptions or change of address notices should be addressed to *Cook's Illustrated,* P.O. Box 7446, Red Oak, IA 51591-0446.

Cornstarch in the Crust

I enjoyed Susan Logozzo's article "The Best Lemon Bars" in the May/June 1998 issue, and the lemon bars I made using the recipe were excellent. But I do have a question. Why did the crust ingredients include one-quarter cup of cornstarch? What quality does the cornstarch impart to the crust that flour alone does not provide?

JULIA EDWARDS LONG
HONOLULU, HAWAII

➤ Cornstarch helps make the crust tender and delicate. Flour contains two proteins, glutenin and gliadin, which link together and develop into sheets of gluten when liquid is added and mixed into the flour. The gluten, in turn, gives baked goods strength and structure. The formation of gluten is essential to the success of yeast breads, puff pastry, and pastry for cream puffs or popovers, all of which require enough strength and structure to withstand the rising process.

On the other hand, too much strength is a potential problem in doughs and batters for cookies, cakes, quick breads, muffins, and pie crusts. Tenderness is prized in these products, so the development of gluten is undesirable. Adding cornstarch to the lemon bar crust mixture was one way to keep the gluten in check. Because cornstarch contains no protein, it does not promote gluten development. In addition, cornstarch is ground finer than flour, so it contributes a delicate, tender, melt-in-your-mouth quality to the crust. Note also that this crust mixture contains no liquid beyond the water present in the butter, that it has very fine confectioners' sugar rather than plain granulated sugar, and that it is not kneaded or mixed beyond simply incorporating the ingredients. All of these tactics are designed to keep gluten development to a bare minimum.

Tweaking Tomato Sauce

Jack Bishop's "Quick, Fresh Tomato Sauce" in the September/October 1999 issue was very good. One small but important change we suggest is to refrain from adding pasta cooking water when mixing the sauce with the pasta. Rather, liquefy one medium, cored, peeled, and seeded tomato in a blender or food processor and add it in place of the water. This brightens both the flavor and the color of the sauce.

ED AND ELLEN GAGNON
BURLINGTON, N.C.

I enjoyed reading about tomato sauce in a recent issue of *Cook's*. I noticed that the garlic in this sauce was sautéed, as it is in most sauces of this type. I took a cooking class in which the chef told us not to sauté garlic but to add it after adding the liquid—in this case, tomatoes. This way, the garlic remains more flavorful and aromatic.

SHEILA ANN LEFORS
WILSONVILLE, ORE.

➤ We took both of these ideas back to the test kitchen and made tomato sauces with the last of the late-season local tomatoes this past fall. In both cases, our tasters agreed with the readers' assertions. A pureed tomato used in place of the cooking water to help marry the sauce with the pasta does brighten the tomato flavor, and adding the garlic along with the tomatoes produces a stronger garlic flavor in the final dish.

Certainly the latter involves no more effort when preparing the recipe, and if you like a strong garlic flavor, we recommend it. We are not as convinced, though, about the return on the investment of coring, seeding, skinning, and pureeing a tomato. While it doesn't take a lot of effort, we did find the process to be a minor nuisance. For one thing, so small an amount of tomato was tricky to puree smoothly because it easily stuck to the sides of the food processor bowl, requiring repeated stops to scrape it down. We had an easier time and equally good results by replacing the pasta water with the juice we collected while seeding the tomatoes.

Fresh Salmon Cakes

My family loves salmon cakes, so I was pleased to read your recent article on the subject (see "The Best Pan-Fried Fresh Salmon Cakes," January/February 2000)—especially because I, like your authors, start with fresh fish. In my opinion, these cakes are more moist and succulent than those made with cooked fish. The article briefly mentioned collagen as the reason for this, and I wondered if you had any more information.

ERIKA AUSTIN
ELGIN, ILL.

➤ Collagen, we learned from Dr. Denise Skonberg, assistant professor of food science at the University of Maine in Orono, is a structural protein present in the flesh, cartilage, and bones of fish (and other animals). Collagen acts as connective tissue; it holds together the muscle segments in the flesh, and it holds the flesh to the bones. When the collagen melts (which it does at a much lower temperature in fish than in meat), it tenderizes the flesh by providing lubrication between the fibers. Because collagen is also somewhat sticky when it melts, it contributes to the binding of ingredients as well.

Parchment versus Wax Paper

Many *Cook's* baking recipes, and even some for other dishes such as the spiced nuts in the November/December 1999 issue, call for parchment paper. Generally, I don't keep parchment in supply. Is it really worth buying, or can I simply substitute wax paper?

IRMA DEJON
NEWTON, MASS.

➤ In most cases, wax paper should not be substituted for parchment. This is because parchment can withstand oven temperatures up to about 425 degrees without burning, while wax paper (which, according to the Reynolds Consumer Products Division Web site, is tissue paper treated with a triple coating of paraffin wax) will smoke when subjected directly to oven heat.

We tested wax paper in three situations in which we'd normally use parchment: to line a cookie sheet for baking cookies, to line the bottom of a cake pan to help release the cake, and to cover pie dough for rolling out. As we suspected, the wax paper lining the cookie sheet smoked in a 350-degree oven. We had better luck with the wax paper in the cake pan. The batter completely covered the paper, which didn't burn because it was not exposed to any direct heat. The cake easily released from the pan, the spent wax paper peeled off the bottom of the cake with no trouble, the texture of the crust was fine, and it had no traces of residual wax from the paper. Last, we rolled out pie dough between sheets of wax paper. While the wax paper did prevent the dough from sticking to both the work surface and the rolling pin, several testers agreed that they preferred either parchment or plastic wrap because they both stuck to the dough a little less than did the wax paper.

In short, parchment is a better "all-purpose" cooking paper than wax paper, so if we were going to keep only one of the two around, parchment would be our choice. We could think of only two instances (neither one a regular occurrence in our kitchen) when we might choose wax paper over parchment. First was packing cookies in a tin. Wax paper works better here because it is more pliable than parchment and provides better cushioning. Second was wrapping sandwiches, although our first preference in this case would usually be a plastic sandwich bag.

Parchment, often packaged for consumers in rolls just like other common kitchen wraps and papers, is becoming more widely available in well-stocked supermarkets. You can also mail-order it from *The Baker's Catalogue* (King Arthur Flour, P.O. Box 876, Norwich, VT

05055-0876; 800-827-6836; www.kingarthur flour.com). The cost is $8.95 for a 33-foot roll that is 15 inches wide and $14.96 for a 100-count box of 16½ by 12¼ -inch sheets, sized to fit perfectly in a standard half-sheet baking pan.

Preserving Champagne's Effervescence

I have been told that you can keep an opened bottle of champagne fresh and bubbly for hours —one person even claimed for days—by sticking the handle of a spoon down the neck of the bottle. Honestly, I am quite skeptical about this. Do you know if it's true?

JEFFREY LEMLEY
BEAVER, PA.

➤ Several readers suggested the same idea to us recently, so we had to try it. Based on our experience, your skepticism is well-founded. In case the quality of the wine might affect its keeping characteristics, we conducted our test with two types of champagne, a relatively inexpensive Korbel and a moderately priced Tattinger. After drinking (at the end of the work day, of course) half of two bottles of each, we placed spoon handles down the necks of one bottle of each type and recorked the other bottle of each with champagne stoppers. (A champagne stopper is a plated steel bottle top with a gasket and two hinged wings that fold down to lock beneath the lip of the bottle, thereby expanding the gasket in the neck of the bottle to seal it tightly.) The next morning, about 15 hours after opening the bottles, we checked them. The champagne in the bottles with the spoons still had some bubbles, but they were quite small and slow moving. By comparison, the champagne in the bottles with the stoppers had many more bubbles, and they were both larger and far more active.

We confirmed our findings with a representative of the Champagne Wines Information Bureau in New York City, who said that she had heard of the spoon method and had also found it to be unsuccessful. She went on to say that while champagne is best drunk when the bottle has been freshly opened, the key to preserving any leftovers is to limit the contact between the wine and air. To accomplish this, she suggested using a champagne stopper in the original bottle or, if you have a smaller bottle on hand, transferring the leftovers to it for storage. When we later compared leftover champagne kept in a standard 750 milliliter bottle with some that we had poured into a smaller bottle (we chose another common size of champagne bottle, a 375 milliliter half bottle, over the 187 milliliter "split," which holds one quarter the amount in a standard bottle), both sealed with a champagne stopper, we actually found the former to be more effervescent. The reason was that the

champagne lost some of its carbon dioxide gas, the source of its effervescence, as it was being poured from the standard bottle into the half bottle for storage.

Ceramic Knife Blades

I noticed that you rated paring knives in the last issue (see "Testing All-Purpose Paring Knives," January/February 2000). I hear more and more about knives with ceramic blades as opposed to traditional steel. Your group of paring knives did not include any of these, and I wondered if you have any experience with them one way or another.

HOWARD TEYMORE
SCOTTSDALE, ARIZ.

➤ As you point out, most knife blades are made of steel, but one Japanese company, Kyocera, does specialize in blades made of zirconium oxide, an especially strong type of ceramic. The primary advertised benefit of ceramic blades is their ability to stay sharp without honing for a much longer period of time than steel blades. We were intrigued when we read about them, so we actually included a Kyocera three-inch paring knife in our original lineup of paring knives for the testing. The knife won many fans; in fact, it scored high enough to rank fourth overall. Despite its high marks, though, this knife failed to make our final cut. Here's why.

The Kyocera's instructions provide a laundry list of activities to avoid with this knife. Not only can you not sharpen it in a conventional sharpener, but you must also not use it to chop, pry, flex, scrape, or cut frozen foods or hard crusts of bread; dropping the knife or knocking it against china or flatware are also forbidden. Our experience proved the warnings true. The tip of the blade chipped off when it hit a bowl in the dish drainer, and then an even larger piece chipped

off as we cut through hard coconut meat. At $36, the Kyocera was the most expensive parer in the group, and though testers praised it for its precision, it was far from an "all-purpose" paring knife. Knives in our test kitchen (and, we'd wager, in most busy home kitchens) are rarely treated with the utmost care, and, in the words of one tester, the Kyocera was "definitely not a knife with which you can be careless." In addition, the handle was judged "too slippery" and "rounded" by most testers for a truly comfortable grip.

Cake-Pan Depth

Some *Cook's* staff members have become concerned that the 1½-inch depth of the Ekco Baker's Secret Non-Stick Round Cake Pan, the winner of our November/December 1999 cake-pan testing (see "$4 Cake Pan Wins Testing," page 28), may be too shallow to accommodate the full amount of batter produced by some cake recipes. In most instances, the batter should reach just over halfway up the sides of the pan. There was further worry that 1½-inch-deep pans might be too short to provide optimal baking conditions for genoise and other sponge cake batters, which are leavened exclusively by eggs and which must cling to and climb the sides of the pan to rise fully. We were relieved when we tested our September/October 1998 sponge cake recipe in pans with both 1½- and 2-inch sides and found little or no difference in the height or texture of the cakes from both pans.

If you have run into trouble because the Ekco pans will not hold all of your batter, please accept our apologies, and keep in mind that several of the other recommended choices from that article, including the All-Clad, Calphalon, Kaiser, and both Chicago Metallics, have a depth of 2 inches.

WHAT IS IT?

While poring over Scottish and other British Isles cookbooks to research the oatmeal story on page 22, consulting editor Maryellen Driscoll discovered this strange Scottish wooden utensil used expressly for stirring oatmeal and other hot porridges while they cook. Called a spurtle, it is about 13 inches long and shaped vaguely like a small baseball bat. Once known as a porridge stick, the spurtle was used in the time before oatmeal was processed as it is today. For that oatmeal to soften and become edible, it had to be cooked for a long time, often overnight, in a cauldron suspended over a fire. The spurtle was used to do the frequent stirring necessary to prevent the formation of large, unpalatable lumps. In this age of processed oatmeal, however, the spurtle, Driscoll read, is used for just the opposite reason: to create "knotty tams," or toothsome little lumps, in the porridge. She found this to be quite true. She also discovered that stirring occasionally with the handle end of a wooden spoon as the oatmeal cooks creates the same effect—a satisfying, pleasantly lumpy texture.

If you want to try out the real thing, we did locate one mail-order source, Sunrise Woodcrafts (RR#4, River John, Nova Scotia B0K 1N0 Canada; 902-351-3886; www.sunrisewoodcrafts.ns.ca). The company sells handmade wooden spurtles for $9.95 (U.S.), plus $3.50 (U.S.) for shipping. Incidentally, according to the Sunrise Woodcrafts Web site, in some districts of Scotland a spurtle is called a thieval.

Quick Tips

Preventing Scorched Pans

Sometimes a cook can become distracted and forget about a pan on the stove. For D. J. Paul of Los Angeles, Calif., this was especially true when he was using a steamer basket set over a small amount of water in a pan. Then he figured out an easy way to save his pans. He adds a few old glass marbles to the pan along with the water. If the water level drops too low, the marbles rattle around, and the racket reminds him to add more water.

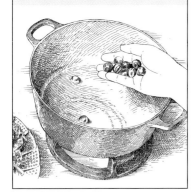

Quick-Chilling Soups or Stews

One joy of soups and stews is that you can make them ahead to serve the next day. But they should be fully cooled before being refrigerated for the night, and Loretta Fisher of Anacortes, Wash., has found a quick, easy way to speed up that process. Fill a large plastic beverage bottle almost to the top with water and freeze it. Then use the frozen bottle to stir the soup or stew in the pot; the ice will cool it down rapidly.

A. **B.**

Keeping Artichokes Upright and Stable

When cooking artichokes, it is important to keep them upright in the pan as they cook. In the Quick Tips section of the July/August 1998 issue, Nancy Peterson of Clarkdale, Ariz., shared her method of propping up the artichokes with help from the band of a canning jar lid. Loretta and Ben Ciutto of Hampton Bays, N.Y., found another solution that does not require canning jar lids. Instead, the Ciuttos use onions in one of two possible ways (A or B):
A. Place small whole or halved onions between the chokes to prop them up.
B. Cut very thick slices (about 1½ inches) from medium onions and use your fingers to pop the outer three or four rings free from the rest of the slice. Then use those rings just as you would the canning jar lid, setting them on the bottom of the pan and placing one artichoke on each.

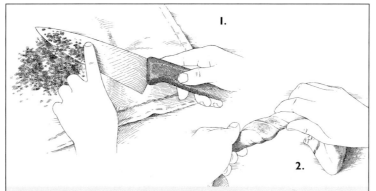

1. **2.**

Extralong-Lasting Chopped Parsley

Chopped parsley is an easy, attractive garnish for many dishes, but it's a nuisance to chop at the very last minute, when you've got steaming-hot plates of food to serve to hungry guests waiting at the table. Ausma Balinkin, of Cincinnati, Ohio, has a secret for chopping parsley well ahead of time that keeps it looking bright and fresh for sprinkling and garnishing.
1. Chop the parsley finely, then place it in the center of a clean kitchen towel.
2. Wrap the towel around the parsley, and then twist both ends very, very tightly, until you see green parsley juice bleeding through the cloth. Twist as tightly as you can to extract as much juice as possible. The dried parsley will stay fresh-looking for hours.

More Bacon Grease Disposal Tips

After reviewing the March/April 1999 Quick Tip on using paper towels to soak up the fat in the pan after browning ground beef and the September/October 1999 Quick Tip on saving small cream containers for discarding bacon grease, Susan Trantham of Lufkin, Tex., shared her method of using tongs and tissue paper for dealing with bacon grease. Crumple up a wad of tissue paper (which you may have saved after opening a package in which the paper was used as cushioning), grab it with tongs, and use it to swab the extra grease from the pan. It may take a couple of wads, but the grease is always soaked up, making the pan easier to clean.

Drip-Free Ladling

Christopher Jones-Thibodeaux of New Orleans, La., keeps drips and spills to a minimum when ladling liquid by doing the following: Before lifting the filled ladle up and out of the pot, dip the bottom back into the pot, so the liquid comes about halfway up the ladle. The tension on the surface of the soup grabs any drips and pulls them back into the pot.

Cleaning a Garlic Press

Dirty garlic presses are notoriously challenging to clean. Rebecca Savage of Dallas, Tex., discovered that an old toothbrush, kept handy at the sink, makes it much easier to clean the garlic press (as well as tight or hard-to-reach spots on other dirty kitchen utensils).

Defatting Soups and Stews

Using a gravy separator to defat liquids is effective, but, admittedly, it's sometimes a pain. And forget about using one to defat a chunky stew. Elaine Klempay of Canfield, Ohio, offers this alternative method. Place a large lettuce leaf on the surface of the liquid in the pot; it will absorb excess fat, and then you can remove and discard it.

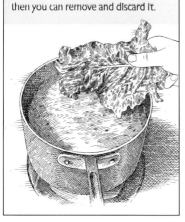

Easy, Even Lattice Strips

To give a handsome look to a lattice-top pie, test kitchen director Kay Rentschler uses a thin, inch-wide metal ruler to line up both the length and width of the lattice.

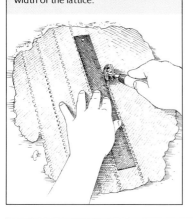

Securing the Silverware Tray

Most silverware organizers are shorter than the drawers they are placed in. The result is that the organizer and its contents slide to the back of the drawer every time you open it. Tired of pulling the organizer forward whenever she needed a fork, Bonnie Frederick of Pullman, Wash., devised the following simple plan to anchor the organizer.

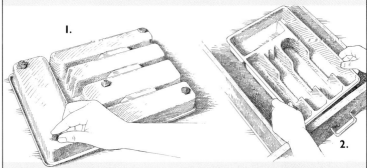

1. Buy a small amount of poster tack, putty, or even florist's clay at a flower shop or craft store and affix several small pieces of it to the bottom of the silverware organizer.
2. Press the tray into place in the drawer. It will stay put, with no more sliding when you open and shut the drawer.

Extralarge Trivet

Many cooks, especially those whose kitchens have countertops that cannot accommodate hot pots and pans, have problems finding a spot to put down a hot roasting pan right out of the oven. F. Narvaez, of Minneapolis, Minn., had the same problem until she discovered that she could place an overturned jelly roll pan on the counter and use that as a trivet on which to rest a hot roasting pan or Dutch oven.

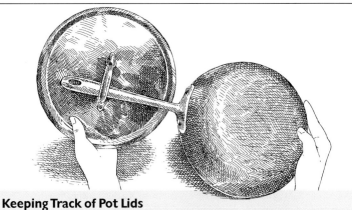

Keeping Track of Pot Lids

Most home cooks we know have one drawer for the lids to all of their pots and pans. Disorganization is thus the order of the day, and fishing out the right lid becomes a real nuisance. Helen Yanagihara of Honolulu, Hawaii, who hangs her pots from a rack, has discovered an alternate system for keeping lids with their pots. Slide the loop handle of the lid right onto the handle of its matching pan, then hang the pan from the rack.

Removing Squash Seeds in One Swoop

Digging through the seed cavity of a winter squash to remove the seeds and strings can be a tedious task, even with a large serving spoon. Eric Pallant of Meadville, Pa., discovered that the type of ice cream scoop shaped like a cupped hand has just the right shape and sharpness to cut out all of the seeds and strings without damaging the flesh. And because it's larger than a spoon, it can remove more in a single swipe.

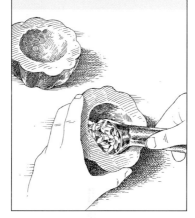

Containing Raw Chicken

The possibility of raw chicken contaminating any surface it touches is a real concern for many cooks. This can be especially tricky when washing and drying the chicken before preparing it to be cooked; the slippery chicken can slide right off a cutting board onto the counter or soak through any number of protective layers of paper towel on which it's been placed. Denise Garcia of New York City used to wrestle with this mess until she discovered that a metal colander was ideal for containing the chicken while washing it.

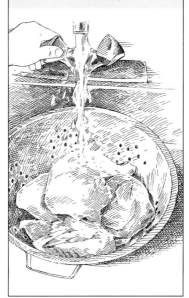

Roasting Boneless Leg of Lamb

How do you get a crisp crust and a perfectly cooked interior?

⇒ BY BRIDGET LANCASTER ⇐

While at the super-market meat case one rainy Sunday, I came across a neatly packaged bundle. It was a whole lamb leg, boned, rolled, and tied. The label said it was "great for grilling"—something I already knew since that is my preferred method for cooking a leg of lamb. But as the April weather in Boston was not conducive to grilling, I had to find another way.

The thought of an easy supper was exciting. Since the butcher had done all of the hard work, I figured that all I had to do was season the lamb, throw it in the oven, and check on it occasionally. But the roast, to my disappointment, cooked to a brown, rubbery mass. Even worse, the outer layer of fat began to smoke, filling the kitchen with an odious aroma that penetrated the meat, giving it that familiar and offensive "gamey" flavor. This was not acceptable. I knew how fabulous grilled lamb leg tasted. Now I wanted great flavor, but I also wanted a roast elegant enough for a small dinner party, something more reminiscent of lamb chops—tender and juicy, with a crust to complement the delicately flavored meat. Could I really get all that from a boneless leg of lamb?

Whole boneless legs can weigh 8 to 9 pounds; great for a crowd, but impractical for a small, elegant dinner. More practical were boneless half legs, which weigh 3 to 5 pounds. We found the sirloin (top) to be more tender than the shank (lower) end, but both roast beautifully.

After settling on the half leg, I decided to experiment with oven temperatures. I usually roast lamb at 375 degrees. But since other *Cook's* contributors had been successful in slow-roasting beef, I wanted to give it a try with my lamb, too. But lamb cooked at 250 degrees turned to mush. After some investigation, I learned that this transformation was due to an enzyme found in meat that targets myosin, a substance that gives meat its firmness. The enzyme breaks down the myosin when the internal temperature of the meat is between 95 and 135 degrees. Slow-roasting at 250 degrees allows for the complete collapse of the myosin. Because lamb is so tender to begin with,

We found that we preferred putting a simple spice or herb mixture, rather than a complex stuffing, inside the rolled lamb.

this turns the meat to mush.

A 450-degree oven, on the other hand, overcooked the lamb exterior. The best lamb was the half leg roasted at 400 degrees. But because I wanted a crisp crust, I cooked the lamb at 450 to 500 degrees to start and then reduced the temperature to 375 degrees to finish.

This oven-searing method brought me closest to my goal, but the exterior fat still smoked and gave the meat that unwanted gamey flavor. Taking a cue from *Cook's* previous experience with lamb (see "Roasted Rack of Lamb," May/June 1999), I tried pan-searing the lamb on the stovetop before putting it in to the oven to finish. The results were perfect. The direct heat jump-started the cooking of the lamb's exterior, producing a crisp crust in a matter of minutes. The flesh, meanwhile, remained very tender, and although there was still a little smoke, the meat picked up none of the gamey flavor produced with oven searing. Using a roasting rack allowed the lamb to cook evenly on all sides once transferred to the oven.

With my cooking method of choice established, I was ready to test flavorings. I started out intending to stuff the roast but soon dispensed with that idea. This was not only too much work, the stuffing also overshadowed the lamb. Instead, I found that a simple rub of aromatics worked best; just enough herbs and garlic to enhance but not overpower the flavor of the lamb. A savory crumb crust also proved to be a perfect addition to the roast, making it reminiscent of the delicate lamb chops that I love. Unlike chops, however, lamb leg is tied, which means that a crust will disintegrate when you cut the string after the roast comes out of the oven. I solved this problem by cutting the twine and placing the crust on the lamb midway through cooking, after it had roasted long enough to hold its shape.

On the Lamb

Lamb is a hard sell in the United States. According to the American Meat Institute, we eat less than 1 1/2 pounds of lamb per person each year. Lamb gets a much more favorable reception abroad. And we wondered why. Is imported grass-fed lamb that much more tender and less "lamby" than domestic grain-fed lamb?

To find out, we held a blind taste test of imported lamb legs from New Zealand, Australia, and Iceland, along with domestic lamb. Our tasters included both lamb enthusiasts and the lamb-averse.

Icelandic   Domestic

Tasters didn't find any of the roasts "gamey" or overly tough, and they found all of them to be juicy. The Australian lamb had the strongest lamb flavor. The meat was chewy and dark, indicating older lamb, a trait not offensive to the lamb lovers in our group. The New Zealand lamb had a bold lamb flavor, but some tasters disliked the texture, finding it "stringy" and "more like ham." The domestic lamb (above, right) was milder in taste; many thought it more reminiscent of roast beef than lamb. Tasters thought that the domestic lamb's texture was a bit chewy, but not unpleasantly so. The lamb from Iceland (above, left), which is new to the U.S. market, was the smallest lamb by far. It also had the most delicate flavor—too delicate for those tasters who enjoyed a stronger lamb flavor (one referred to the Icelandic lamb as "lamb lite"). All found the texture of the Icelandic lamb to be the most tender by far. As one taster noted, it "cut like butter." –B.L.

ROAST BONELESS LEG OF LAMB WITH GARLIC, HERB, AND BREAD CRUMB CRUST
SERVES 4 TO 6

- 3 tablespoons olive oil
- 3 medium garlic cloves, peeled
- 3 tablespoons fresh rosemary leaves
- 2 tablespoons fresh thyme leaves
- ¼ cup fresh parsley leaves
- ⅓ cup grated Parmesan cheese (about 1 ounce)
- 1 cup coarse fresh bread crumbs
- 1 3½- to 4-pound boneless half leg of lamb, untied (if tied when purchased), trimmed of surface fat, and pounded to even ¾-inch thickness (see illustration 1), at room temperature
  Salt and ground black pepper
- 1 tablespoon Dijon mustard

1. Adjust oven rack to lower-middle position and heat oven to 375 degrees. Meanwhile, in workbowl of food processor fitted with steel blade, process 1 teaspoon of olive oil with garlic, rosemary, thyme, and parsley until minced, scraping down bowl with rubber spatula as necessary, about 1 minute. Remove 1½ tablespoons herb mixture to small bowl and reserve. Scrape remaining mixture into medium bowl; stir in cheese, bread crumbs, and 1 tablespoon olive oil, and set aside.

2. Lay lamb with rough interior side (which was against bone) facing up on work surface; rub with two teaspoons olive oil, and season generously with salt and pepper. Spread reserved 1½ tablespoons herb mixture evenly over meat, leaving 1-inch border around edge. Following illustrations 2 and 3, roll roast and tie (see How to Tie a Roast, below). Season tied roast generously with salt and pepper, then rub with remaining 1 tablespoon oil.

3. Place roasting rack on rimmed baking sheet. Heat 12-inch heavy-bottomed skillet over medium-high heat until very hot, about 3 minutes. Sear lamb until well browned on all sides, about 2 minutes per side; then, using tongs, stand roast on each end to sear (see illustration 4), about 30 seconds per end. Transfer to rack and roast until instant-read thermometer inserted into thickest part registers 120 degrees, 30 to 35 minutes.

STEP-BY-STEP | KEY STEPS IN PREPARING THE LAMB

1. Cover the lamb with plastic wrap and pound to a uniform ¾-inch thickness.

2. Cover with the herb mixture, then roll into a tight cylinder.

3. Tie the roast into a neat package, following steps shown below left.

4. Holding the leg with tongs, sear the two ends until well browned.

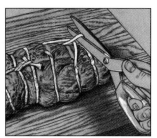

5. When the lamb is midway through cooking, remove it from the oven and carefully remove the twine.

6. Coat the lamb with the herb/crumb mixture, pressing well to ensure that it sticks.

Transfer lamb to cutting board; following illustration 5, remove and discard string. Brush lamb exterior with mustard, then, following illustration 6, carefully press herb and bread crumb mixture onto top and sides of roast with hands, pressing firmly to form a solid, even coating that adheres to the meat. Return coated roast to rack; roast until instant-read thermometer inserted into thickest part of roast registers 130 to 135 degrees (medium-rare), 15 to 25 minutes longer. Transfer meat to cutting board, tent with foil, and let rest 10 to 15 minutes. Cut into ½-inch slices and serve.

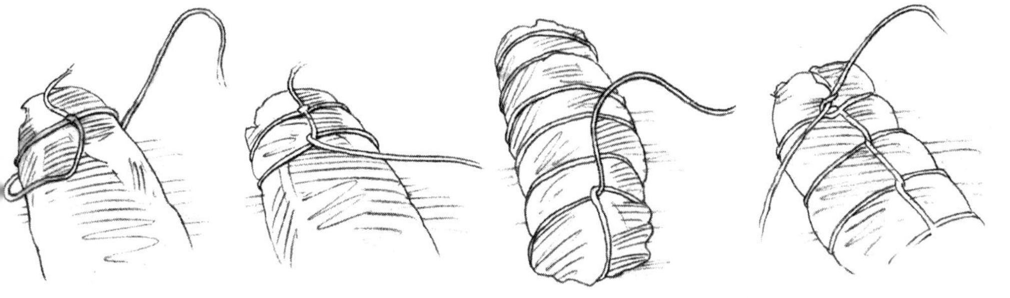

INDIAN-SPICED ROAST BONELESS LEG OF LAMB WITH HERBED ALMOND-RAISIN CRUST

Garam masala, an Indian spice blend, can be found in specialty food stores and well-stocked grocery stores, or can be mail-ordered.

- 3 medium garlic cloves, peeled
- ¼ cup fresh mint leaves
- ¼ cup fresh cilantro leaves
- 1 piece fresh ginger (about 1 inch), peeled and quartered
- 1 teaspoon garam masala
- ¼ teaspoon ground coriander
- ¼ teaspoon ground cumin
- 2 tablespoons olive oil
- ¼ cup slivered almonds
- ¼ cup raisins
- 1 3½- to 4-pound boneless half leg of lamb, untied (if tied when purchased), trimmed of surface fat, and pounded to even ¾-inch thickness (see illustration 1), at room temperature
  Salt and ground black pepper
- 1 tablespoon plain yogurt

1. Adjust oven rack to lower-middle position and heat oven to 375 degrees. Meanwhile, in workbowl of food processor fitted with steel blade, process garlic, mint, cilantro, ginger, ½ teaspoon garam masala, ⅛ teaspoon ground coriander, ⅛ teaspoon ground cumin, and 1 teaspoon olive oil until herbs are minced, scraping down bowl with rubber spatula as necessary, about 1 minute. Remove 1½ tablespoons herb mixture to small bowl and reserve. Add almonds and raisins to food processor workbowl; continue processing until finely ground, about 45 seconds, and transfer to small bowl. Combine yogurt with remaining ½ teaspoon garam masala, ⅛ teaspoon ground coriander, and ⅛ teaspoon ground cumin; set aside.

2. Continue with recipe above from step 2, substituting yogurt mixture for mustard in step 3 and almond/raisin crust for bread crumbs

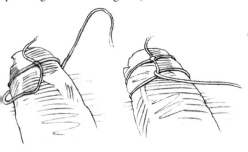

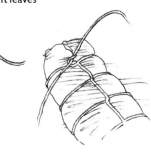

How to Tie a Roast Slip a 5-foot piece of twine under the lamb roast and tie a double knot, then loop the long end of twine under and around the roast. Run the long end through the loop and repeat this procedure down the length of the roast. Roll the roast over and run the twine under and around each loop. At the end, tie to the original knot.

Perfecting Egg-Lemon Soup

Just the right combination of four common ingredients makes an exceptional soup.

≥ BY ADAM RIED WITH JULIA COLLIN ≤

American mothers, Jewish or otherwise, have not cornered the world market on chicken soup. Greek mothers, for instance, regularly transform four simple ingredients—chicken stock, rice, eggs, and lemon—into a surprisingly elegant, deeply satisfying soup called *avgolemono*. For those who have never encountered it, this egg-lemon soup is the essence of simple home cooking, based on ingredients as common in American pantries as they are in Greek ones. Flavorful chicken stock is simmered with rice, accented with lemon, and thickened to a suave, creamy consistency and golden hue with beaten eggs. Season simply with a little salt, and you have a soup as fit to start a fancy holiday meal as it is to comfort a flu or soothe frayed winter nerves. For these reasons alone, egg-lemon soup is worth incorporating into your culinary repertoire.

Straightforward though it is, there are issues to investigate with egg-lemon soup. First, the texture must be rich and soft, not thin or frothy or pasty, all of which it sometimes is. Also, the soup should be free of tough bits of cooked egg, which would mar its luxurious texture. Finally, you want a full, lemony flavor—more than just acidity—to balance the savory flavor of the stock.

Fine-Tuning Texture

That eggs are responsible for the smooth texture of this soup was one of only two points of accord found in all of the recipes we researched, which originated not only in Greece but also in Middle Eastern and North African countries, where versions of this soup are also part of the national cuisine. There was considerable debate, however, over the number of eggs, whether to use them whole or separated, whether to whip separated whites to a foam, how long to beat the yolks, and whether to beat them by hand or with a blender or food processor.

Initial tests based on two quarts of stock and two eggs demonstrated that whole eggs produced better body than yolks alone but that the yolks produced a superior flavor. At the same time, we ruled out separating the eggs and whipping the whites, as well as using a machine to beat yolks or whole eggs, because both led to soups that were unappealingly foamy and aerated, with weak body and a pale color. The two-egg soup was a little too thin for us, though, so from there we tinkered with different numbers of eggs and extra yolks until we finally settled on two whole

For a Turkish-style garnish, mix 2 teaspoons sweet paprika and 3 tablespoons melted butter, then swirl a bit on the surface of each serving.

eggs plus two yolks as the foundation of our ideal texture and color.

Next we had to ponder even finer points concerning the eggs. First was their temperature. Some recipes warned that the eggs must be at room temperature if they are to marry successfully with the stock. While we had absolutely no problem thickening the soup with eggs right out of the refrigerator, we did find that eggs that sat unchilled for 15 or 20 minutes yielded a marginally smoother soup. The upshot? If you remember, remove the eggs from the refrigerator a few minutes ahead of time, but don't give it a second thought if you forget. Likewise, several recipes insisted on beating the eggs for up to five minutes before introducing the stock, but we found this extra effort unwarranted. Not only was it harder to do than beating them lightly and quickly, but it created undesirable foam and faded the color of the soup. Like whipping the eggs in a machine, longer beating added too much air.

Think Thick

In classic French cooking, any agent used to thicken or bind a soup, sauce, or stew is called a *liaison*. Common liaisons include flour, starch, roux, cream, the butter-flour mixture called *beurre manié*, and, as in the case of egg-lemon

soup, eggs and yolks. The method used to introduce the liaison into the stock was the second point of agreement in the recipes we researched. Known as *tempering*, this process consists of first beating the eggs lightly and then slowly beating in some of the hot stock. This mixture is then added to the remaining hot stock to finish the soup. The effect of tempering is to elevate the temperature of the eggs gradually so that they don't seize up and form curds in the soup.

According to Elisa Maloberti, a test kitchen representative from the American Egg Board in Park Ridge, Ill., the added stock dilutes the eggs, with the extra water molecules in effect separating the protein molecules. The protein molecules then have to move faster to find each other and link up, or coagulate, thus raising the temperature at which coagulation occurs. Just to cover all the bases, we tried skipping the tempering process. Sure enough, we produced chunks of scrambled eggs floating in watery soup. Eggs normally coagulate at roughly 150 degrees Fahrenheit, and simmering stock can approach 200 degrees.

One recipe, however, offered a variation on the tempering technique. Rather than adding the stock to the eggs in a thin stream, this recipe called for dumping the stock into the eggs, just as long as it was added in small portions. So we tried it, adding one-half cup of stock at a time. The eggs didn't curdle, but the texture of the soup did suffer a little bit. The smoothest soups resulted from the tried-and-true method of trickling the stock in gradually.

The rice cooked in the stock also plays a minor role in the thickening process. Shirley Corriher, author of *Cookwise* (William Morrow, 1997) and a *Cooks'* food science advisor, explained that the rice leaches some of its starch into the stock as the grains swell and cook. Those loose starch molecules act to slightly increase the coagulation temperature of the eggs by becoming part of the network of denatured proteins that join together to do the work of thickening. The presence of the starch in the protein network also provides some buffer against curdling the eggs should the soup overheat during the final cooking process. So, in a sense, the rice helps to stabilize the entire mixture.

With the texture just where we wanted it, we turned our attention to the flavor. In most of the soups we'd made so far, the lemon flavor was fleeting. It came and went on the palate in almost the same instant. We tried various amounts of lemon juice, but adding more than one-quarter cup made the soup taste harsh. Extra acidity was not the answer here. Though none of the recipes we consulted had mentioned it, we tried adding lemon zest—the yellow outermost part of the peel—to the equation. The addition of zest from 1½ lemons, simmered in the stock with the rice, was a stunning success, giving the soup a refreshing tang and full lemon resonance. This flavor stayed with us. Adding bay leaves and a trace amount of spice to the stock brought even greater depth of flavor. Cardamom, in particular, added a real finesse.

With so few ingredients, the stock plays the leading role when it comes to the flavor of egg-lemon soup. That's why we were sadly disappointed with soup made from canned low-sodium chicken broth. "Weak and tinny" was the consensus of our tasters. There's no question that the very best egg-lemon soup is made with a robust, homemade stock. While making stock is not difficult, it is time-consuming, so we were lucky to have the details of a quick chicken stock worked out by Pam Anderson in her March/April 1996 story "Quick Homemade Chicken Soup." A traditional long-cooked stock can simmer for up to five hours, but the version in the recipe below can be completed in less than one hour, and the flavor is excellent.

GREEK EGG-LEMON SOUP (AVGOLEMONO)
MAKES ABOUT 8 CUPS, SERVING 6 TO 8

Homemade chicken stock gives this soup the best flavor and body; in a pinch, use low-sodium canned chicken broth. The longer the final soup cooks after the eggs have been added, the thicker

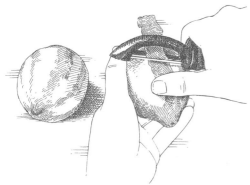

Large Strips of Zest Run a vegetable peeler from pole to pole to remove long, wide strips of zest.

it becomes. About 5 minutes of heating produces a soft, velvety texture; any longer and the soup begins to turn pasty. Scallions and fresh mint, individually or together, make simple and flavorful garnishes. Serve the soup immediately; it thickens to a gravylike consistency when reheated.

- 2 quarts chicken stock, preferably homemade (see recipe at right)
- ½ cup long-grain white rice
- 1 bay leaf
- 4 green cardamom pods, crushed, or 2 whole cloves
  Zest strips from 1½ medium lemons (about 12 1 inch x 4-inch pieces); see illustration, below left
- 1½ teaspoons salt
- 2 large eggs, plus 2 yolks, preferably at room temperature
- ¼ cup juice from zested lemons
- 1 large scallion, sliced thin, and/or 3 tablespoons chopped fresh mint leaves

1. Bring chicken stock to boil in medium non-reactive saucepan over high heat. Add rice, bay leaf, cloves or cardamom, lemon zest, and salt; reduce heat to medium and simmer until rice is tender and stock is aromatic from lemon zest, 16 to 20 minutes. With slotted spoon, remove and discard bay leaf, cloves or cardamom, and zest strips; increase heat to high and return stock to boil, then reduce heat to low.

2. Whisk eggs, yolks, and lemon juice lightly in medium nonreactive bowl until combined. Whisking constantly, slowly ladle about 2 cups hot stock into egg mixture; whisk until combined. Pour egg-stock mixture back into saucepan; cook over low heat, stirring constantly, until soup is slightly thickened and wisps of steam appear, 4 to 5 minutes. Do not simmer or boil. Divide soup among serving bowls, sprinkle with scallion and/or mint; serve immediately.

EGG-LEMON SOUP WITH CINNAMON AND CAYENNE

This variation, the test kitchen favorite, is based on a Tunisian-style egg-lemon soup detailed in Mimi Sheraton's *The Whole World Loves Chicken Soup* (Warner Books, 1995).

Follow recipe for Greek Egg-Lemon Soup, substituting one 2-inch stick cinnamon and a pinch of cayenne for cloves or cardamom.

EGG-LEMON SOUP WITH SAFFRON

Follow recipe for Greek Egg-Lemon Soup, adding a pinch (about ¼ teaspoon) saffron threads, crushed between fingertips, to stock along with rice, bay leaf, cloves or cardamom, salt, and zest.

TECHNIQUE
TEMPERING THE EGGS

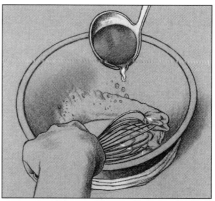

Whisking constantly, trickle the hot stock mixture into the beaten eggs with a ladle.

EGG-LEMON SOUP WITH CHICKEN

Follow recipe for Greek Egg-Lemon Soup, Egg-Lemon Soup with Cinnamon and Cayenne, or Egg-Lemon Soup with Saffron, adding two boneless, skinless chicken breasts (about 12 ounces total) cut into ½-inch cubes to stock along with rice, seasonings, and zest.

QUICK HOMEMADE CHICKEN STOCK
MAKES ABOUT 2 QUARTS

If chicken necks and backs are not available at your market, substitute chicken wings. A cleaver is best for hacking the chicken parts, though a heavy chef's knife will also do.

- 1 tablespoon vegetable oil
- 1 medium onion, chopped medium
- 4 pounds chicken backs and necks, hacked with cleaver into 2-inch pieces
- 2 quarts boiling water
- 2 teaspoons salt
- 2 bay leaves

1. Heat oil in large stockpot over medium-high heat until shimmering; add onion and sauté until softened slightly, 2 to 3 minutes. Transfer onion to large bowl. Add half of chicken pieces to pot; sauté until no longer pink, 4 to 5 minutes. Transfer cooked chicken to bowl with onion. Repeat with remaining chicken pieces. Return onion and chicken pieces to pot. Reduce heat to low, cover, and cook until chicken releases its juices, about 20 minutes. Increase heat to high; add boiling water, salt, and bay leaves. Return to simmer, reduce heat to medium-low, then cover and barely simmer until broth is rich and flavorful, about 20 minutes.

2. Strain broth and discard solids. Spoon off fat and discard. (Stock can be covered and refrigerated up to 2 days or frozen for several months.)

High-Roast Chicken Perfected

High oven temperatures produce crisp, brown skin—as well as dry-as-cardboard breast meat and five-alarm smoke. We solve the problems.

> BY DAWN YANAGIHARA <

At the pinnacle of simple food is roast chicken. With an oven and a chicken as the only requisites, it's an easy answer to the weeknight cooking conundrum. Whenever I roast chicken, I stick by the technique I learned in cooking school: 375 degrees right-side up, left-side up, then breast up. It's a safe and sound method that yields pretty good results. But I was wanting something better. I'd heard mentioned the "high-roasting" technique for chicken in which the bird is roasted at temperatures in excess of 450 degrees. It's reputed to produce a better bird, with skin that is crisp and tanned to a deep golden hue. And, presumably, it would get dinner on the table quickly.

The only drawback I could foresee was that the breast meat might be prone to overcooking at such high temperatures. At any rate, an improved roast chicken would be more than welcome in my house. I decided to see what this high-roasting thing was all about.

Where There's Smoke, There's Chicken

In her book *Roasting: A Simple Art* (Morrow, 1995), Barbara Kafka suggests roasting a 5- to 6-pound bird at 500 degrees for about an hour. While it seemed to me rather pyromaniacal, I have heard several people swear by her method. So along with roasting birds at 425 and 450 degrees, I gave it a go. However, I decided to use 3½- to 4-pound birds because they are the size most commonly found in grocery stores.

When the birds came out of the oven, the differences between them were marked. The 500-degree bird was a looker, with beautiful, deep brown, crisp skin. The other two were splotchy and only mildly attractive. And, of course, the inevitable had occurred: the breast meat on all the birds had been torched; as the thighs sauntered up to the finish line, the more delicate breast meat overcooked. And, worst of all, with 450- and 500-degree oven temperatures, I chased everyone, coughing and hacking, out of the kitchen with billows of smoke.

To remedy the uneven cooking, I tried several adjustments, from preheated roasting pans to dif-

Thinly sliced potatoes—our solution to the smoky perils of high roasting—produce a superb side dish to the brown, crisp-skin chicken.

ferent configurations of oven temperatures, all to no avail. The obvious solution was to rotate the bird, as I had learned to do in school, so that the breast would spend some time shielded from the intense oven heat while the thighs would receive the exposure they needed to catch up. After trying this technique, however, I vetoed it. I was after deep browning and crisp skin, neither of which were produced by this method. For that, the bird needs to spend all or at least most of the roasting time breast up.

I suspected that the fix lay in butterflying the chicken—that is, removing the backbone, then opening and flattening the bird. That would give the thighs greater exposure to the heat, increasing the odds that they would cook at the same rate as the breast. In addition, all areas of skin would be face-up to facilitate even browning and crisping. I tried it, and it worked like a charm. The thighs actually raced ahead of the breast meat and finished first.

While butterflying a chicken is actually an easy task—it takes all of a couple of minutes—I worried that it was too much to ask of the home cook on a weeknight. And yet the results had been so good. My tasters and I concurred that roast butterflied chicken was roast chicken elevated to a whole new level in terms of both appearance and doneness. Consequently, I put my hesitations aside and con-

centrated on determining the best roasting temperature for the butterflied bird. Again, for the best browned, most crispy, and nicest looking bird, 500 degrees was the optimal temperature.

But there was still that smoking problem. I tried putting water in the pan beneath the bird (which was set on a rack), but this steamed the chicken and prevented the skin from crisping. I tried bread slices, soaked wood chips, and even uncooked rice to catch the drippings, but they all turned to charcoal before the chicken was done. Then I tried potatoes. They burned in spots, dried out in others, and stuck to the pan but showed mouth-watering potential; tasters lined up for any morsel of crispy potato that could be salvaged. Even better, by creating a buffer and absorbing some of the drippings, the potatoes kept the fat from hitting the hot pan bottom, where it would normally sizzle and burn on contact. I knew that with some finessing, the answer to the smoking problem could also provide a great side dish.

I assumed that the potatoes would need some protection as they cooked to keep them from burning and drying out. A broiler pan came to the rescue. With its slotted top and its ample bottom pan, which nicely accommodated the potatoes, it was just what the chicken and potatoes ordered. The potatoes in the broiler pan had turned a deep brown and were as crisp as potato chips but far tastier. A foil lining on the pan bottom helped with potato removal and cleanup, and that was that. Not surprisingly, the potatoes won their own fans, who, waiting for the daily potato call, began to regard the chicken as the side dish.

The Finer Points

Now that I had solved the major problems of high-roast chicken, I began to wonder if I could take this method to further new heights.

Though the butterflied chickens had been emerging from the oven with crisp skin, I noticed that as they sat waiting to be carved, the breast skin would become soggy. I began searching for a way to keep it crisp. I tried basting with oil, basting with butter, putting butter under the skin, putting chicken fat under the skin, and finishing the cooking under the broiler, but I found only one thing that worked. When my colleagues heard what it was, they rolled their eyes: drying the chicken uncovered overnight in the refrigerator. I borrowed the technique from recipes for crispy-skin Chinese roasted duck. Letting the bird dry uncovered in the fridge allows surface moisture to evaporate; the skin becomes dry and taut and so crisps more readily in the heat of the oven. It took a couple of side-by-side tastings to convince my tasters and, frankly, myself that air drying worked and was worth the effort. And even though we agreed that it is worth the trouble, it remains an option—that is, you can skip it and still have a great roast chicken.

The other step in preparation for roasting that makes a significant improvement in the flavor and texture of the bird is—no surprise here—brining. The salt in the brine permeates the chicken, so the meat is evenly seasoned and full-flavored. Brining also keeps the breast meat moist and tender, providing a cushion if it overcooks a bit (though there's little chance of that happening with a butterflied bird). Brining solutions are formulated in concentrations to fit the duration of the brine; I chose to go with a very concentrated one-hour brine that can be done the evening you intend to roast the bird or, if you plan ahead, the night before, so that the bird can dry overnight in the refrigerator. But there is also a quick solution. In the course of testing different types of birds I was glad to discover that kosher chickens, which are salted during processing to draw out fluids, provide an excellent alternative to brining for those cooks with time constraints.

With technique resolved, I wanted to work flavorings into the roast chicken. Clearly, anything on the surface of the chicken would burn at 500

degrees. Instead, garlic, herbs, and other bold flavors mixed with some softened butter and placed under the chicken skin before roasting added subtle, welcomed flavor not only to the chicken but to the potatoes below as well.

When all was said and done, I had roasted four dozen chickens and more than 60 pounds of potatoes. But I had accomplished what I set out to do: I had four-star, perfectly browned roast chicken with spectacular skin—and potatoes, too.

CRISP-SKIN HIGH-ROAST BUTTERFLIED CHICKEN WITH POTATOES
SERVES 4

If you prefer not to brine, use a kosher chicken—it is salted and has a taste and texture similar to a brined bird. For extracrisp skin, after applying the flavored butter (if using), let the chicken dry uncovered in the refrigerator 8 to 24 hours. Russet potatoes have the best potato flavor, but Yukon Golds have beautiful color and better retain their shape after cooking. Either works well in this recipe. A food processor makes quick and easy work of slicing the potatoes.

- 1 cup kosher salt (or ½ cup table salt) (for brine)
- ½ cup sugar
- 1 whole chicken, 3½ to 4 pounds, preferably free-range or other high-quality chicken such as Bell and Evans, giblets removed and reserved for another use, fat around cavity removed and discarded

- 1 recipe flavored butter for placing under skin, optional (recipes follow)
- 2½ pounds (4 to 5 medium) russet or Yukon Gold potatoes, peeled and sliced ⅛ to ¼ inch thick
   Nonstick vegetable cooking spray
- 1½ tablespoons olive oil
- ¾ teaspoon salt (for potatoes)
   Ground black pepper

1. Dissolve salt and sugar in 2 quarts cold water in large container. Immerse chicken and refrigerate until fully seasoned, about 1 hour. Meanwhile, adjust oven rack to lower-middle position and heat oven to 500 degrees. Line bottom of broiler pan with foil and spray with nonstick vegetable cooking spray. Remove chicken from brine and rinse thoroughly under cold running water. Following illustrations 1 through 6, butterfly chicken, flatten breastbone, apply flavored butter (if using), and position chicken on broiler pan rack; thoroughly pat dry with paper towels.

2. Toss potatoes with 1 tablespoon oil, salt, and pepper to taste in medium bowl. Spread potatoes in even layer in foil-lined broiler pan bottom. Place broiler pan rack with chicken on top. Rub chicken with remaining 1½ teaspoons oil and sprinkle with pepper.

3. Roast chicken until spotty brown, about 20 minutes. Rotate pan and continue to roast until skin has crisped and turned a deep brown and an instant-read thermometer registers 160 degrees in thickest part of breast, 20 to 25 minutes longer. Transfer chicken to cutting board. With potholders, remove broiler pan rack; soak up excess grease from potatoes with several sheets paper towels. Remove foil liner with potatoes from broiler pan bottom and invert foil and potatoes onto cookie sheet or second cutting board. Carefully peel back foil, using a metal spatula to help scrape potatoes off foil as needed. With additional paper towels, pat off remaining grease. Cut chicken into serving pieces and serve with potatoes.

CHIPOTLE BUTTER WITH LIME AND HONEY
MAKES ABOUT 3 TABLESPOONS

In a small bowl, mash together 2 tablespoons softened unsalted butter, 1 medium garlic clove pressed with garlic press, 1 teaspoon honey, 1 teaspoon very finely grated lime zest, 1 medium chipotle chile en adobo—seeded and minced to a paste—and 1 teaspoon adobo sauce.

MUSTARD-GARLIC BUTTER WITH THYME
MAKES ABOUT 3 TABLESPOONS

In a small bowl, mash together 2 tablespoons softened unsalted butter, 1 medium garlic clove pressed with garlic press, 1 tablespoon Dijon mustard, 1 teaspoon minced fresh thyme leaves, and ground black pepper to taste.

STEP-BY-STEP | PREPARING TO ROAST

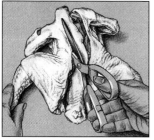

1. Cut through bones on either side of backbone, then remove and discard backbone.

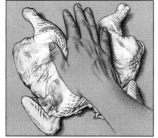

2. Flip chicken over as shown and use the heel of your hand to flatten breastbone.

3. If using a compound butter, slip your fingers between skin and breast, loosening the membrane.

4. Scoop some of the butter onto a spoon, slide it under breast skin, and push off with your fingers.

5. Work butter under skin to cover breast evenly. Repeat steps 4 and 5 with each drumstick and thigh.

6. Transfer to broiling rack and push leg up to rest between thigh and the breast.

The Ultimate Homemade Baguette

Why bother making baguettes at home? Months of testing and research resulted in a homemade baguette recipe that was actually worth the trouble.

⊰ BY KAY RENTSCHLER ⊱

In 1988, when I left the United States for Germany, a decent cup of coffee or a good loaf of bread were about as rare in Boston as a friendly bureaucrat in Berlin. I felt deeply grateful—tucked in the glow of a café, unmindful of the perpetual twilight known as winter in northern Europe—to sip a dark, fragrant cup of coffee (no refill), while sawing my *Brötchen* in half German-style before buttering it.

Five years later, when I returned, everything had changed: good coffee was a chain reaction and artisan bakeries were on the rise. Americans had realized that one satisfying cup of coffee is worth four refills at a fraction of the cost and that bread that puts up a fight when grappled with is a lot more fun to eat than the sliced stuff that collapses like an accordion. There were startling changes afoot in American bread baking. Banished, for example, were the ubiquitous milk and butter that every white bread recipe had boasted, to say nothing of sugar. Bakers like Joe Ortiz recognized and wrote about the benefits to flavor and texture in using less yeast. People were talking about bread with an open texture and the best way to use steam to get a great crust. No longer white bread with a French twist, the baguette was its own raison d'être.

But the question remains: Why make baguettes at home? There are many reasons. First, despite the minor revolution described above, it's still damned hard to find a really good one at your local bakery. And, if you like to bake, it is a uniquely challenging and therefore uniquely satisfying experience. At *Cook's*, the topic of French baguette had long been contemplated as promising but risky. Everyone agreed that a great baguette was made from just four ingredients—flour, water, yeast, and salt—and that it must express excellence in its chief characteristics—crust, crumb, flavor, and color. We agreed that it would have a thin, shattering crust of the deepest golden brown; an open, airy texture; a light, moist crumb; and fully developed flavor. Where we parted ways was on the question of whether you could actually create an outstanding baguette

Overnight fermentation produces a cracklingly crisp crust with a blistered surface and a flavor that's outstanding.

at home in a regular oven. Some were skeptical; I dismissed their skepticism. I had baked many baguettes and felt comfortable mixing and shaping doughs. I was an experienced baker, wasn't I? Halfway through testing I was well on my way—to proving the naysayers right.

In fact, at the beginning of this investigation I knew just enough to give myself a false sense of confidence. I discovered that in bread making, little errors along the way can gang up on you in the end. I learned that the most well-meaning recipes offer neither adequate explanations of their instructions nor methods for trouble shooting, and that the quality of bread produced often reflects these omissions. But, best of all, I learned that you can make a great baguette at home. This, then, is a story of small mistakes and big discoveries.

The Rise, the Bloopers, and the Blunders

The first problem I had to figure out was, as bakers say, "rising" the dough. Real bread doughs (as opposed to quick breads, which are chemically leavened with baking soda or powder) depend on commercial yeast or a natural leavener to help them rise. Modern French bread uses a direct-rise

method—one in which flour and water are mixed with commercial yeast, given a rise, punched down, shaped, allowed to rise again, and baked. But I found that an older method, one that prevailed before commercial yeast became affordable, appealed to me more.

This method, known as a *pre-ferment*, uses a small amount of yeast to rise a portion of the dough for several hours or overnight. The pre-ferment becomes a dough when it is refreshed with additional flour, yeast, and water, given some salt as well, mixed, and set to rise again.

I tried a number of apparently authentic French baguette recipes, using both the direct-rise and the pre-ferment methods. Although none of these baguettes swept me off my feet, the flavor and texture of the breads made from pre-fermented dough were definitely superior. Among the two or three types of pre-ferments, I chose the sponge method, which basically calls for a thinnish mixture of flour and water and a small amount of yeast. These ingredients are easily stirred together, and the resulting relatively liquid structure encounters little physical resistance to fermentation, so it rises fully (or ripens) in hours, not days.

Having determined my basic approach, I put together a rough recipe and began making bread. Because I wanted enough dough for two baguettes, I started with a total of three cups of

Bread Flour? Don't Bother

There is much discussion among bakers about the type of flour to use in bread making. Some sources recommend a high-gluten flour, which is alleged to produce bread of a lighter consistency. But with its 12 or 13 percent protein content, this flour is labeled "made for bread machines" with some justification: this was tough stuff to knead by hand, and it put a heavy-duty mixer through its paces to the point of overheating. The results were nothing special. Other sources insist that a French-style flour with its softer wheat (King Arthur makes one) is necessary for achieving the flavor of a true French baguette. Some tasters liked the bread made from this flour, but it didn't really distinguish itself as the front-runner. Nor did combinations of flours produce bread of startling superiority. I decided to stick with unbleached all-purpose King Arthur flour. —K.R.

flour, using about a cup of it in the pre-ferment. Initially cavalier about the volume of water I stirred into the sponge (generally about one cup, with between one-third and one-half cup additional water in the final dough), my mishaps convinced me that correct early ratios of flour to water are critical to the behavior of the bread in later stages and that a scale was essential to ensure consistent results. As it turns out, what looks like a cup of flour may be more or less on a given day, depending on factors such as the humidity and the way the measuring cup is filled. Six ounces of flour, on the other hand, is always six ounces.

Any given bread type, moreover, has a correct proportion of ingredients. In a system known as the "baker's percentage," these proportions are predicated on the weight of the flour, which is judged to be 100 percent, with the other ingredients lining up behind. A correct baguette dough, for instance, is said to have a hydration of 62–65 percent. This means that for every 1 pound of flour, there will be between .62 and .65 pounds of water. I found it necessary to weigh both flour and water to make sure the sponge had the correct consistency when I was ready to mix the dough. I settled on six ounces of both flour and water for the pre-ferment stage; this gave me a sponge that was soft but still firm enough to require additional water when I mixed the dough.

As for the yeast, I knew that I wanted to use as little as possible for greatest flavor development—using a lot of yeast results in bread that tastes more of yeast than of the flavorful byproducts of fermentation—but I wasn't sure just how little. While I also knew the sponge should have doubled in volume and be pitted with small bubbles when ripe, I didn't know exactly how long this might take—it could reach this stage in as little as three hours or take as many as eight. Finally, I determined that a pinch of dry instant yeast was equal to the task of rising the sponge and one-half teaspoon enough to refresh the body of the dough. But I remained in a quandary about fermentation time until I came across Daniel Wing's exemplary book *The Bread Builders* (see Kitchen Notes, page 30) and his explanation of "the drop." This term refers to a sponge rising and then falling under its own weight. Far from representing deflation or exhaustion of the yeast, which seems logical and which I had previously supposed, the drop revitalizes the sponge and is a sign that the sponge is ready for action. The drop is a critical visual clue. By using warm water and a pinch of yeast, my sponge rose and dropped in about six hours in a 75-degree room.

Hands Only, Crash, and Windowpane

The second phase of bread making is kneading, or mixing. Mixing unites wet and dry ingredients and transforms them from shaggy ball of dough to satiny orb. My preferred partner was the standing mixer outfitted with a dough hook. The thought of a food processor blade whizzing through my dough seemed antithetic to the slow, measured pace of kneading. But I wasn't keen on performing the entire operation by hand, either. Seasoned bakers will be familiar with the notion of gluten development, wherein flour and water join to form an interlocking protein structure that traps the gas that makes the dough rise. Kneading is the means to this end, and most recipes instruct the baker to knead the dough until it is smooth and elastic; others suggest a period of time by which mixing should be complete.

Because I was not yet employing the baker's percentage and never knew precisely what consistency my dough would have, my mixing times were arbitrary. If a dough was too wet and required additional flour, that dough was subjected to a protracted mixing time, while drier doughs got pulled from the mixer much sooner. What should have been a precise system with predictable results became essentially a crapshoot for me, and every time I pulled baguettes out of the oven, I was baffled and frustrated. Often my crumb was dense and rubbery, sometimes the loaves looked flat and sad. Clearly, many variables bore investigation, but my wanton approach to measuring and mixing left me directionless—and increasingly concerned.

New information got me back on track. One thing I had not realized was how easily bread dough can overheat in a mixer. For the dough hook to engage my small amount of dough, I had to mix at high speed. The sticky blob I ended up with once or twice was, I learned, a direct result of overheating—the dough was irreparably damaged and the character of the bread destroyed. By kneading with a dough hook instead of my hands, I had unwittingly distanced myself from some important tactile permutations that were taking place: the dough's temperature, its increasing elasticity and stretchiness, and its surface tackiness. At this point, I switched to hand kneading and began to experience the dough's transformation in a measured and controlled way. The process was pleasurable as well.

I never supposed I would be sprinkling a dough with water instead of flour. I had often

made wet doughs—thinking the resulting crumb would be more open and moist—only to throw flour on them near the end. But this is a poor approach, as Daniel Wing cautions. Rather than working its way into the dough, the flour slides around on the surface. Real friction must be generated for proper gluten development. A relatively dry dough, vigorously hand-kneaded, on the other hand, welcomes incremental additions of water to bring it to the correct hydration. I discovered that a method of kneading I had used in Germany for strudel dough, known as *crashing* (in which the dough is picked up and flung repeatedly against the counter), worked beautifully to incorporate water (see illustrations, page 14). The doughs I produced using this technique had a texture far more satiny than did the wet doughs to which I added flour, and the bread had a far nicer crumb as well.

But perhaps the single most important contribution to my understanding of mixing came from Peter Reinhart's book *Crust and Crumb* (see Kitchen Notes, page 30), in which he describes a technique known as *windowpaning*. In windowpaning, when you think the dough is fully kneaded, you stretch a small amount between your fingers. If it can be stretched until

STAGES | THE RISE AND FALL OF A PRE-FERMENT

In the beginning stages, a pre-ferment shows no evidence of rising or bubbling (left). Its middle phase is characterized by substantial swelling and surface bubbling (center). The final stage, or "drop," is characterized by a slight sinking of the sponge, leaving a higher edge around the circumference of the bowl. At this point the sponge is ready to use.

it is very thin, almost translucent, the dough has been adequately kneaded and can be set to rise (see illustration below). Should it tear while being stretched, more kneading is required.

With the baker's percentage and the windowpane technique now firmly part of the plan, my testing began to show significant improvement.

The next steps in bread making, which precede the final rise, are punching down and shaping. A fully risen dough should feel puffy and will not long bear the imprint of a finger. But punching down, experts agree, is a misleading term, inviting more force than is desirable. A gentle fist to the center of the dough does the trick. It is now ready to be scaled or divided and given a rough shape. I knew from experience that a covered rest of about 20 minutes is necessary to relax the dough again, giving it some workability. Attempts to shape long thin baguettes from freshly punched-down dough are frustrating because the dough feels tough and uncooperative and snaps back at you.

It's Cool

Having gotten this far, I had no idea that my most exciting discovery was right around the corner—in the refrigerator. Traditional wisdom holds that the second rise takes place in a warm, draft-free spot to encourage rapid rising and is accomplished in about half the time required for primary fermentation. So I was intrigued when I read about cool fermentation in Peter Reinhart's book. Cool fermentation retards, or slows down, the second rise—the formed loaves go into the refrigerator overnight and are baked the following day. With this method, the dough is thought to become better hydrated, to develop more flavor, and to achieve greater volume. Refrigeration also maintains humidity around the loaves, which keeps a skin from forming on the surface and inhibiting the rise. But surely the most dramatic contribution cold fermentation makes is to the crust.

TECHNIQUE

ACHIEVING WINDOWPANE

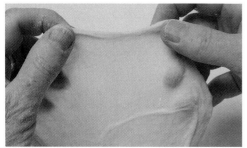

A well-kneaded dough can be stretched into a nearly translucent membrane.

Crashing the Dough Really a form of kneading, crashing is a good way to incorporate additional water into the dough. The dough is flung vigorously and repeatedly against the countertop.

The first baguettes I baked using overnight fermentation leapt beyond anything I had yet experienced. The surface of the crust was pitted with tiny bubbles and gave a sharp thrilling crackle when torn. Shards of crust sprayed the counter to reveal a creamy interior. But it was the flavor of the crust that rocketed this bread to stardom: it was incomparable. Though the French, Reinhart told me, believe a baguette's surface should be smooth and unblistered, I was untroubled by this breach of tradition. To me, this bread was the ultimate.

It's Hot

The final step in bread making is, of course, baking. Home baking is plagued by the problems that attend home ovens, which can neither deliver nor maintain heat in the same way that stone or brick does. I tried a number of baguette pans, both perforated and black (thought to improve browning), but by far the best means of conducting heat to the bread proved to be a large pizza stone, preheated for a full 45 minutes in a hot oven. A stone is the closest home ovens can get to hearth ovens. Transferring the baguettes to the stone was another matter. Precise placement is crucial: once dough meets stone, there is no turning back—or over, as it were. I tried different approaches with calamitous results. Ultimately, the best approach proved to be using parchment paper and an inverted sheet pan to let the baguettes rise, then sliding the baguettes—paper and all—onto the stone.

Realizing that the goal of baking baguettes is to get a deep, golden brown crust in the short period of time it takes to finish the bread, I began experimenting with oven temperatures. Temperatures below 500 degrees produced inadequate browning of the crust or overbaked the interior. Even an initial temperature of 500 degrees accompanied by temperature reduction after a few minutes did not produce the color I wanted. Some recipes suggest leaving the bread in the oven for a few minutes after baking with the oven turned off to help set the crust, but my 12-ounce baguettes needed full, steady heat all along. In the end, 15 minutes at 500 degrees produced the crust and color I desired as well as a moist interior. The final temperature of the bread was around 208 degrees.

Ironically, this research and testing (well over 100 baguettes), distilled down to the four ingredients I began with—and my hands. It speaks to the deceptive simplicity of yeasted doughs: basic ingredients, the magic of yeast, a firm and gentle touch, and time can produce one of the greatest aromas and most satisfying foods in the world.

BAKERY-STYLE FRENCH BAGUETTES
MAKES TWO 15 BY 3-INCH BAGUETTES

For this recipe you will need an instant-read thermometer, a scale, a lame (see Resources, page 32) or a single edge razor blade, a rectangular pizza stone, and a spray bottle filled with water. We prefer SAF instant or Perfect Rise yeast, but other instant dry yeasts work as well. For the sponge, the ideal ambient temperature is 75 degrees; if it is cooler, fermentation will take longer. This recipe will yield baguettes for breakfast; the following version uses altered rising times so that the baguettes are baked in time for dinner. In either case, begin the recipe the day before you intend to serve the bread; the baguettes will emerge from the oven 20 to 24 hours after you start the sponge. Do not add flour while kneading or shaping the dough. The baguettes are best served within 2 hours after baking.

Sponge
- ⅛ teaspoon instant dry yeast or ¼ teaspoon regular dry yeast
- 6 ounces (by weight) bottled or spring water, 110 to 115 degrees
- 6 ounces unbleached all-purpose flour, preferably King Arthur

Dough
- ½ teaspoon instant dry yeast or ¾ teaspoon regular dry yeast
- 4 ounces (by weight) bottled or spring water, 75 degrees, plus additional 2 teaspoons water if necessary
- 10 ounces unbleached all-purpose flour, preferably King Arthur
- 1 teaspoon salt

Glaze
- 1 large egg white, beaten with 1 tablespoon water

1. *For the sponge:* Combine yeast, water, and flour in medium bowl and stir together with wooden spoon to form thick batter. Scrape down bowl with rubber spatula. Cover with plastic wrap and punch a couple of holes in plastic wrap with paring knife; let stand at room temperature. After 4 or 5 hours, sponge should be almost doubled in size and pitted with tiny bubbles. Let stand at room temperature until surface shows slight depression in center, indicating the drop (see "Rise and Fall of a Pre-ferment," page 13), 2 to

3 hours longer. The sponge now is ready to use.

2. *For the dough:* To sponge, add yeast and all but 2 tablespoons water. Stir briskly with wooden spoon until water is incorporated, about 30 seconds. Stir in flour and continue mixing with wooden spoon until a scrappy ball forms. Turn dough onto countertop and knead by hand, adding drops of water if necessary, until dry bits are absorbed into dough, about 2 minutes. Dough will feel dry and tough. Stretch dough into rough 8 by 6-inch rectangle, make indentations in dough with fingertips, sprinkle with 1 tablespoon remaining water (see illustration 1), fold edges of dough up toward center to encase water, and pinch edges to seal. Knead dough lightly, about 30 seconds (dough will feel slippery as some water escapes but

bowl, and replace plastic wrap. Let rise until doubled in bulk, about 1½ hours.

4. Decompress dough by gently pushing a fist in center of dough toward bottom of bowl (see illustration 2); turn dough onto work surface. With dough scraper, divide dough into two 12-ounce pieces. Working one at a time, with second piece covered with plastic wrap on work surface, cup hands stiffly around dough and drag in short half-circular motions toward edge of counter (see illustration 3) until dough forms rough torpedo shape with taut rounded surface, about 6½ inches long. (As you drag the dough, its tackiness will pull on the work surface, causing the top to scroll down and to the back to create a smooth, taut surface.) Repeat with second piece of dough.

Dough will have formed cylinder about 12 inches long. Roll dough cylinder seam-side down; gently and evenly roll and stretch dough until it measures 15 inches long by 2½ inches wide (see illustration 7). Place seam-side down on prepared baking sheet. Repeat with second dough piece. Space shaped dough pieces about 6 inches apart on baking sheet. Drape clean dry kitchen towel over dough and slide baking sheet into large clean garbage bag; seal to close. Refrigerate until dough has risen moderately, at least 12 but no longer than 16 hours.

6. *To bake:* Remove one oven rack from oven; adjust second oven rack to lowest position. Place pizza stone on rack in oven and heavy rimmed baking sheet on oven floor. Heat oven to 500 degrees. Remove baking sheet with baguettes from refrigerator and let baguettes stand covered at room temperature 45 minutes; remove plastic bag and towel to let surface of dough dry, then let stand 15 minutes longer. The dough should have risen to almost double in bulk and feel springy to the touch. Meanwhile, bring 1 cup water to simmer in small saucepan on stovetop.

7. With a lame or single-edge razor blade, make five ¼-inch deep diagonal slashes on each baguette (see illustration 8). Brush baguette with egg white and mist with water. Working quickly, slide parchment sheet with baguettes off baking sheet and onto hot pizza stone. Pour simmering water onto baking sheet on oven floor and quickly close oven door. Bake, rotating loaves front to back and side to side after 10 minutes, until deep golden brown and instant-read thermometer inserted into center of bread through bottom crust registers 205 to 210 degrees, about 5 minutes longer. Transfer to wire rack; cool 30 minutes.

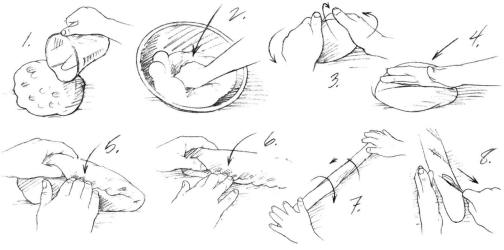

How a Baguette Comes Together Add the remaining water (1), then gently punch the dough down to degas it (2). Round the dough with half-circular motions (3), then use the side of your hand to form an indentation (4). Roll the sealed upper edge over your thumb (5), then repeat this process several times to form a seam (6). Stretch and roll the dough into a baguette shape (7), then slash it diagonally (8).

will become increasingly pliant as the water is absorbed). Begin crashing (see illustrations, page 14) and kneading dough alternately until soft and supple and surface is almost powdery smooth, about 7 minutes. Stretch dough again into rough 8 by 6-inch rectangle and make indentations with fingertips; sprinkle dough with salt and remaining tablespoon water. Repeat folding and sealing edges and crashing and kneading until dough is once again soft and supple and surface is almost powdery smooth, about 7 minutes. If dough still feels tough and nonpliant, knead in 2 additional teaspoons water.

3. Test dough to determine if adequately kneaded by performing window-pane test (see illustration, page 14). If dough tears before stretching thin, knead 5 minutes longer and test again. Gather dough into ball, place in large bowl, and cover with plastic wrap. Let stand 30 minutes, then remove dough from bowl and knead gently to deflate, about 10 seconds; gather into ball, return to

Drape plastic wrap over dough on work surface; let rest to relax dough, 15 to 20 minutes.

5. Meanwhile, line an inverted rimmed baking sheet with parchment paper. Working one at a time, with second piece covered with plastic wrap, roll torpedo seam-side up and press indentation along length of dough with side of outstretched hand (see illustration 4). Working along length of dough, press thumb of one hand against dough while folding and rolling upper edge of dough down with other hand to enclose thumb (see illustration 5). Repeat folding and rolling 4 or 5 times until upper edge meets lower edge and creates seam (see illustration 6); press seam to seal.

DINNER BAGUETTES

The altered rising times in this version help get the baguettes on the table at the same time as dinner.

Follow recipe for Bakery-Style French Baguettes, starting the sponge at about noon and using 75-degree water; let sponge rise 5 to 6 hours, then refrigerate overnight, 12 to 14 hours. In step 2, make dough using 110-degree water. Continue with recipe to knead, rise, and shape. Place shaped and covered dough in refrigertor until slightly risen, 7 to 10 hours. Continue with recipe from step 6.

Bakery-Style French Baguettes	SPONGE	DOUGH	SHAPED DOUGH
Begin: 8 A.M. to 12 NOON **Bake:** The following morning.	Rise at room temperature 6 to 7 hours.	Rise at room temperature 30 minutes; deflate, then rise 1½ hours longer.	Rise in refrigerator 12 to 16 hours; let stand 1 hour at room temperature before baking.
Dinner Baguette			
Begin: 12 NOON to 4 P.M. **Bake:** The following afternoon.	Rise at room temperature 5 to 6 hours, then refrigerate 12 to 14 hours.	Rise at room temperature 30 minutes; deflate, then rise 1½ hours longer.	Rise in refrigerator 7 to 10 hours; let stand 1 hour at room temperature before baking.

Cake Frosting 101 BY DAWN YANAGIHARA

Tired of complicated cake decorating instructions that ignore the basics? Here is what you need to know to trim, frost, and decorate a cake without a pastry bag.

An iced cake with straight, smooth sides, perfectly level top, and clean, sharp corners is a blank canvas for piped embellishments or for simpler adornments, such as toasted nuts. For most occasional cake bakers, though, creating a perfect coat of icing on a layer cake is no easy task. Here we walk you through the process of trimming and splitting a cake into layers, icing it, and then finishing it with a few simple decorating techniques. Don't worry—you won't need a pastry bag or tips, just a little patience.

We recommend that you equip yourself with a few tools that can make all the difference in the finished appearance of the cake and minimize your frustration: a long serrated knife for trimming and cutting, a 10-inch flexible icing spatula, cardboard rounds, and, ideally, a rotating cake stand (see Resources, page 32). For an alternative to the rotating cake stand, improvise by setting a dinner plate upside down on top of an upside-down cake pan. The cake won't spin freely, as it does on a rotating cake stand, but this arrangement does elevate the cake and gives you an edge to grip and spin.

LEVELING AND SPLITTING THE CAKE

A cake can be cut into layers, or cakes baked separately can be layered together. Either way, level cakes are much easier to ice than mounded ones that must be supplemented with an overabundance of icing. Use a long serrated knife to level an uneven cake and/or to cut it into layers. When the cake has cooled completely, set it on a cardboard round that is cut about 1/8 inch larger than the cake. Place the cake close to the edge of the counter for more clearance when cutting.

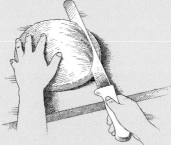

1. First, determine the cake's lowest point. Steady the cake by gently pressing an outstretched hand on its surface. Holding the knife parallel to the work surface and using a steady sawing motion, begin cutting at the same level as the cake's lowest point, slicing off the mound. Remove the trimmed area.

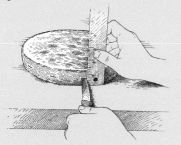

2. If you are cutting the cake into layers, measure the height of the cake (that has been leveled, if necessary) and cut a small incision into the side with a paring knife to mark the desired thickness of your layers. Repeat every 3 or 4 inches around the circumference of the cake.

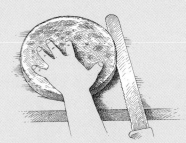

3. With a serrated knife held parallel to the work surface, cut superficially into the cake. Then, with an outstretched palm gently pressed on the surface, slowly spin the cake away from you while pulling the knife toward you. The goal is to connect the incisions and score the cake, not slice it, to create a clearly defined midpoint.

4. Following the midpoint marking, cut deeper and deeper in the same manner. Gradually move the knife closer to the cake's center with each rotation. When the knife progresses past the cake's center, the cut is complete. Carefully slide the knife out, then remove the cake from the cardboard round.

ICING THE CAKE

When filling and icing a cake with a buttercream frosting, the challenge is to prevent crumbs from catching in the icing. Cold icing is difficult to spread and pulls on the surface of the cake, so if you've made the icing ahead and chilled it, give it ample time to warm and soften. Also, placing the cake's sturdy bottom crust face-up on the top layer minimizes crumbs and provides distinct, clean edges that are easy to ice. Finally, applying a base coat, or "crumb coat," of icing seals in loose crumbs so that they do not mar the cake's appearance.

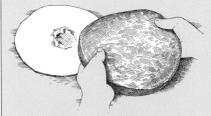

1. To anchor the cake, spread a dab of frosting in the center of a cardboard round cut slightly larger than the cake. Center the upper layer of a split cake crust-side up or one cake of separately-baked layers bottom-side up on the cardboard round. Spread a dab of frosting on the center of the cake stand, then set the cardboard round with the cake on the stand.

2. Place a large blob in the center of the cake and spread it to the edges with an icing spatula. Imagine that you are pushing the filling into place rather than scraping it on as if it were peanut butter on a slice of toast. Don't worry if crumbs are visible in the icing; since the filling will be sandwiched between layers, these crumbs will not be noticeable.

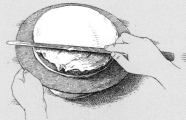

3. To level the icing and remove any excess, hold the spatula at a 45 degree angle to the cake and, if using a rotating cake stand, turn the cake. If you're not using a rotating stand, hold the spatula at the same angle, and, starting at the edge farthest away from you, gently drag the spatula toward you. It will take a few sweeps to level the icing.

4. Using a second cardboard round, slide the top cake layer crust-side up on top of the frosted bottom layer, making sure that the layers are aligned. Press the cake firmly into place.

Illustration: John Burgoyne

ICING THE CAKE (continued)

5. A thin base coat of icing helps seal in crumbs. To coat the top, place a blob of icing in the center of the cake and spread it out to the edges, letting any excess hang over the edge. Don't worry if it is imperfect. Smooth the icing as in step 3 above.

6. Scoop up a large dab of icing on the spatula's tip: Holding the spatula perpendicular to the cake spread the icing on the side of the cake with short side-to-side strokes. Repeat until the entire side is covered with a thin coating. Refrigerate the cake until the icing sets, about 10 minutes.

7. Apply a final thick coat of icing to the top and the sides, following the steps above, making sure that the coat is even and smooth. When icing the sides, apply a coat thick enough to cover and conceal the cardboard round. Dipping the spatula into hot water will help create a smooth coat.

8. As you ice the top and sides, a ridge will form along the edge where they meet. After you've finished icing, hold the spatula at an angle, and, with a very light hand, starting at the farthest edge of the cake, smooth the ridge toward the center. Rotate the cake and repeat until the ridge no longer exists.

SOME FINISHING TOUCHES

With a perfectly coated cake, you've got a base on which to apply some finishing touches to give the cake a polished look. The following techniques work best with buttercream icings.

Powdered Sugar and Cocoa

Powdered sugar will gradually dissolve, so unless you're using nondissolving sugar, decorate the cake just before serving. When using stencils of any sort—store-bought or improvised, like those below—freeze the cake for 15 minutes before decorating; chilling sets up the icing so that the stencil will not stick.

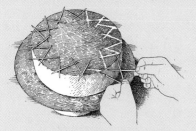

➤ Consulting editor and baker Jim Dodge suggests arranging toothpicks on the perimeter of the cake in a crisscross pattern, with a slight overhang. Dust the cake's surface with cocoa or powdered sugar, then remove the toothpicks.

➤ For a different effect you can also arrange the toothpicks in a pattern similar to the spokes of a wheel.

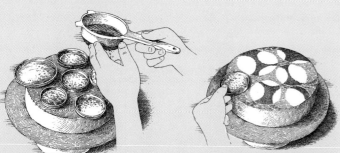

➤ For a two-tone geometric circle pattern, gather about six jar lids, varying in size from small to medium. Place the lids face down on the surface of the cake in a random arrangement, letting some hang over the edge. Dust the cake with cocoa or confectioners' sugar.

➤ Remove the lids, grasping them by the lip and lifting straight up. Rearrange them randomly again, then dust with a contrasting color, using confectioners' sugar, cocoa, or very finely ground nuts, such as pistachios, hazelnuts, or almonds. Remove the lids.

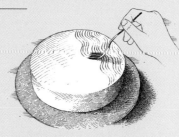

Fork Designs

➤ Use the tines of a dinner fork to make wave designs in the icing. Wipe the fork clean intermittently.

➤ You can also use a fork to make wavy patterns on the sides of the cake.

Nuts

Nuts add flavor to a cake as well as textural and visual appeal. Pressed onto the cake's sides, they also cover any imperfections. Sliced almonds, chopped pistachios, walnuts, and pecans all make attractive and flavorful finishing touches.

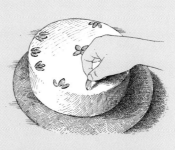

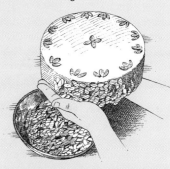

➤ The shape and color of sliced almonds lend themselves to simple, elegant designs. First, lightly dust the surface of the cake with powdered sugar. Halve several intact almond slices with a paring knife. Arrange the halved and additional whole almond slices in a fleur-de-lis design around the perimeter of the cake.

➤ To press nuts onto the side of a cake, lift the cake off the stand and hold it by the cardboard round beneath. Using one hand to hold the cake above the bowl containing the nuts, use the other to press nuts into the icing, letting the excess fall back into the bowl. You will need about one cup of nuts to cover the sides of a 9-inch cake.

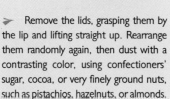

Meaty Tomato Sauce

What's the best method for adding meat to a basic tomato sauce? We tested eight cuts of meat and found that ribs make the most flavorful sauce.

≥ BY JACK BISHOP ≤

I can still remember the basement kitchen in the home of my first and only cooking teacher. It was 16 years ago this month that Giancarlo taught me how to make ravioli, gnocchi, and other handmade pastas while I was living in Florence. One of my most vivid memories from those fun days of marketing and cooking was the simple sauce Giancarlo would make from canned tomatoes and a stray piece of meat.

The meat (pork chop) was browned, the fat drained, and the sauce built in the empty pan. Then the browned meat was added back to the sauce, the pan covered, and the sauce simmered slowly until the meat was fall-off-the-bone tender. Finally, the meat was shredded and stirred into the sauce, which was then served over rigatoni, with a good sprinkling of grated cheese.

Last winter I began playing around with this recipe again. It soon became clear that the choice of meat was the most important issue.

I tried pork chops from the blade, loin, and sirloin. Even the fattiest chops were dry and tough after braising. I wanted the meat to almost melt when added to the tomato sauce. I needed a piece of meat with more marbling so that it would not dry out during braising.

I thought about something from the shoulder—either picnic or Boston butt—since this part of the pig has more fat than the loin, where most chops come from. The problem with these shoulder roasts was their size; the smallest at my market was four pounds. Nevertheless, I cut a pound of this meat into stewlike chunks and proceeded. This meat was more yielding when cooked and had a better flavor. However, the sauce tasted a bit wan; the meat had not done a really good job of flavoring the tomato sauce.

At this point I turned to spareribs, which are fattier than roasts from the shoulder. The braised meat from spareribs was better than the Boston butt—it was unctuous, almost gelatinous. Best of all, the tomato sauce really tasted meaty. The bones had flavored the sauce in a way that meat alone couldn't. But spareribs are sold in an entire rack that weighs three or more pounds. I needed only four or five ribs for a batch of sauce. That meant spending $9 on a rack of ribs and using half for my sauce and freezing the rest. Was there a more economical way to make this peasant sauce?

I paid $1.99 per pound for country-style ribs and was able to find a small packet with just 1½ pounds of ribs—enough for one batch of sauce with no leftovers. The sauce made with country-style ribs was similar to the spareribs sauce.

Now I wondered if this sauce could be made with beef. Short ribs are roughly equivalent to spareribs or country-style ribs. (On the cow, ribs cut from the belly, called the plate, as well as those cut from the back are called short ribs.) The sauce made with short ribs was delicious, too. It's just important to remember that short ribs must be simmered longer than pork ribs, since they are thicker.

RUSTIC SLOW-SIMMERED TOMATO SAUCE WITH MEAT

MAKES ABOUT 3½ CUPS, ENOUGH TO SAUCE 1 POUND PASTA

This sauce can be made with either beef or pork ribs. Depending on their size, you will need 4 or 5 ribs. To prevent the sauce from becoming greasy, trim all external fat from the ribs and drain off most of the fat from the skillet after browning. This thick, rich, robust sauce is best with tubular pasta, such as rigatoni, ziti, or penne. Pass grated Pecorino (especially nice with pork) or Parmesan cheese at the table. The sauce can be covered and refrigerated for up to 4 days or frozen for up to 2 months.

- 1 tablespoon olive oil
- 1½ pounds beef short ribs, or pork spareribs or country-style ribs, trimmed of fat
  Salt and ground black pepper
- 1 medium onion, minced
- ½ cup red wine
- 1 can (28 ounces) whole tomatoes, drained, juice reserved, tomatoes chopped fine

1. Heat oil in 12-inch, heavy-bottomed skillet over medium-high heat until shimmering. Season ribs with salt and pepper and brown on all sides, turning occasionally with tongs, 8 to 10 minutes. Transfer ribs to plate; pour off all but 1 teaspoon fat from skillet. Add onion and sauté until softened, 2 to 3 minutes. Add wine and simmer, scraping pan bottom with wooden spoon to loosen browned bits, until wine reduces to a glaze, about 2 minutes.

2. Return ribs and accumulated juices to skillet; add tomatoes and reserved juice. Bring to a boil, then reduce heat to low, cover, and simmer gently, turning ribs several times, until meat is very tender and falling off the bones, 1½ hours (for pork spareribs or country-style ribs) to 2 hours (for beef short ribs).

3. Transfer ribs to clean plate. When cool enough to handle, remove meat from bones and shred with fingers, discarding fat and bones. Return shredded meat to sauce in skillet. Bring sauce to a simmer over medium heat and cook, uncovered, until heated through and slightly thickened, about 5 minutes. Adjust seasoning with salt and pepper. To serve, toss sauce with drained pasta.

TOMATO-PORK SAUCE WITH ROSEMARY AND GARLIC

Follow recipe for Rustic Slow-Simmered Tomato Sauce with Meat, using pork spareribs or country-style ribs. Substitute 3 medium garlic cloves, minced, for onion, and add 2 teaspoons minced fresh rosemary to skillet along with garlic; sauté until softened and fragrant, about 30 seconds. Continue with recipe.

TOMATO-BEEF SAUCE WITH CINNAMON, CLOVES, AND PARSLEY

Follow recipe for Rustic Slow-Simmered Tomato Sauce with Meat, using beef short ribs and adding ½ teaspoon ground cinnamon, pinch ground cloves, and 2 tablespoons minced fresh parsley leaves to softened onion; sauté until spices are fragrant, about 30 seconds longer. Continue with recipe.

CUTS | PORK RIBS

Spareribs   **Country-style ribs**

Spareribs (left) come from the belly of the hog. Country-style ribs come from the backbone of the animal, where the shoulder and loin meet.

Cooking Tough Supermarket Spinach

We discover that thick, tough supermarket spinach is often superior to delicate flat-leaf spinach when used in side dishes.

⇒ BY EVA KATZ WITH ADAM RIED ⇐

Compared with some of the intriguing cooking greens available these days, spinach can be easy to pass by as old hat, even mundane. But this traditional European-derived green has an appealing earthy, mineral taste that provides an ideal foil for bold, sharp flavors like sherry vinegar, hot pepper, garlic, and goat cheese.

Though we prefer the tender, relatively flat leaf spinach sold in bundles for making salads, we decided to use the ubiquitous cellophane-wrapped, dark green, crinkly leaf variety in these dishes. First, this is by far the most common type of spinach, available almost everywhere, almost all the time. Since this is what most people have access to, we wanted to figure out how to make great dishes with it. Second, the small leaves of flat-leaf spinach, which are so fantastic in salads, give up a lot of liquid as they cook, which makes them less well suited for recipes of this type.

We had a great head start in terms of choosing a cooking method. In a *Cook's* September/October 1994 article, "Cooking Tender Greens," Pam Anderson and Karen Tack thoroughly investigated blanching, steaming, microwaving, and wilting. We repeated their tests and agreed that wilting was the most straightforward method and produced the best texture. To wilt, just place the leaves, still a little damp from their washing, into a pot with a small amount of hot fat over medium-high heat, and cover the pot. The water clinging to the leaves is all that's required to cook them, breaking down the huge volume of raw leaves to a manageable quantity of cooked spinach in just three to five minutes. It is important, though, to use the largest Dutch oven you have—or even a stockpot—to accommodate the bulky spinach when raw, and to stir it several times as it wilts so the leaves cook evenly.

SPINACH WITH GARLIC CHIPS AND PEPPER FLAKES
SERVES 6 TO 8

Do not heat the oil before adding the garlic; heating them together over gentle heat helps reduce the risk of burnt, bitter garlic.

- 3 tablespoons olive oil
- 6 medium garlic cloves, sliced very thin (about 1/4 cup)
- 1/4 teaspoon red pepper flakes
- 3 bags spinach (10 ounces each), stemmed, washed thoroughly, and partially dried, with some water left clinging to leaves
- Salt and ground black pepper

Heat oil and garlic in large Dutch oven or stockpot over medium heat; cook, stirring occasionally, until garlic is golden and very crisp, 10 to 12 minutes. Remove garlic chips with slotted spoon to paper towel–lined plate. Add pepper flakes to oil; sauté until oil is flavored and fragrant, about 1 minute. Add spinach; toss to combine with oil. Cover pot, increase heat to medium-high, and cook, stirring occasionally, until spinach is tender and wilted but still bright green, 3 to 5 minutes. Off heat, season with salt and pepper, and toss with reserved garlic chips.

SPINACH WITH PANCETTA, WHITE BEANS, AND BALSAMIC VINEGAR
SERVES 6 TO 8

- 1 tablespoon olive oil
- 4 ounces pancetta or bacon, cut into 1/4-inch pieces
- 3 large garlic cloves, minced (about 2 tablespoons)
- 1 can (15 1/2 ounces) Great Northern or white kidney beans, drained and rinsed
- 3 bags spinach (10 ounces each), stemmed, washed thoroughly, and partially dried, with some water left clinging to leaves
- Salt and ground black pepper
- 1 tablespoon balsamic vinegar

Heat oil in large Dutch oven or stockpot over medium heat until shimmering; add pancetta or bacon and sauté until crisp, 5 to 6 minutes. Remove pancetta or bacon with slotted spoon to paper towel–lined plate. Add garlic to oil; sauté until light golden and fragrant, about 30 seconds. Add beans and spinach; toss to combine with oil and garlic. Cover pot, increase heat to medium-high, and cook, stirring occasionally, until spinach is tender and wilted but still bright green, 3 to 5 minutes. Off heat, season with salt and pepper, and add vinegar and pancetta or bacon.

SPINACH WITH CARAMELIZED ONIONS, PINE NUTS, AND DRIED APRICOTS
SERVES 6 TO 8

- 1 tablespoon olive oil
- 1 tablespoon butter
- 1 large red onion, chopped medium
- 1 teaspoon sugar
- 2 large garlic cloves, minced
- 2 anchovy fillets, rinsed
- 1/4 cup chopped dried apricots
- 1 tablespoon sherry vinegar
- 3 bags spinach (10 ounces each), stemmed, washed thoroughly, and partially dried, with some water left clinging to leaves
- Salt and ground black pepper
- 1/3 cup pine nuts, toasted in small dry skillet over medium heat until golden and fragrant, about 5 minutes

Heat oil and butter in large Dutch oven or stockpot over medium heat until foaming, about 2 minutes. Add onion and sugar; sauté until soft and golden, 10 to 12 minutes. Add garlic and anchovies; sauté, mashing anchovies to paste with wooden spoon, until fragrant, about 1 minute. Add apricots, vinegar, and spinach; toss to combine with onion mixture. Cover pot, increase heat to medium-high, and cook, stirring occasionally, until spinach is tender and wilted but still bright green, 3 to 5 minutes. Off heat, season with salt and pepper; toss in pine nuts.

SPINACH WITH SAUTÉED SHALLOTS AND GOAT CHEESE
SERVES 6 TO 8

- 3 tablespoons olive oil
- 2 large shallots, sliced (about 1/2 cup)
- 2 teaspoons grated zest from 1 large lemon
- 3 bags spinach (10 ounces each), stemmed, washed thoroughly, and partially dried, with some water left clinging to leaves
- Salt and ground black pepper
- 2 ounces goat cheese, crumbled (about 1/3 cup), at room temperature

Heat oil in large Dutch oven or stockpot over medium heat until shimmering; add shallots and sauté until golden, 3 to 4 minutes. Add lemon zest and spinach; toss to combine with oil and shallots. Cover pot, increase heat to medium-high, and cook, stirring occasionally, until spinach is tender and wilted but still bright green, 3 to 5 minutes. Off heat, season with salt and pepper, toss in crumbled goat cheese; let stand until cheese warms and softens, 1 to 2 minutes.

Exploring Rice Pilaf

Traditional recipes insist that for a truly great pilaf you must soak or at least repeatedly rinse the rice before cooking. Is this really necessary or just an old wives' tale?

∋ BY ANNE YAMANAKA ∈

A few years ago when eating in a Persian restaurant, I became instantly enamored of its rice pilaf. Fragrant and fluffy, perfectly steamed, tender but still retaining an al dente quality, this was the type of rice I loved. Still better, this rice had gained flavor and texture from the other, more intensely flavored ingredients that had been added to it. Excited, I decided to find the best way to make rice pilaf that was this good in my own kitchen.

My first step was to define rice pilaf. According to most culinary sources, it is simply long-grain rice that has been cooked in hot oil or butter before being simmered in hot liquid, typically either water or stock. In Middle Eastern cuisines, however, the term *pilaf* also refers to a more substantial dish in which the rice is cooked in this manner and then flavored with other ingredients—spices, nuts, dried fruits, and/or chicken or other meat. To avoid confusion, I decided to call the simple master recipe for my dish "pilaf-style" rice, designating the flavored versions as rice pilaf.

I also discovered in my research that there are many different ways to cook rice pilaf. Most of these methods were traditions from the Middle East, from which this dish hails. Most recipes stipulated that the rice had to be soaked or at least rinsed prior to cooking in order to produce a finished rice with very separate, very fluffy grains, the characteristic that virtually defines the dish. With my recipes in hand, I started testing.

Right Rice, Right Ratio

The logical first step in this process was to isolate the best type of rice for pilaf. I immediately limited my testing to long-grain rice, since medium and short-grain rice inherently produce a rather sticky, starchy product and I was looking for fluffy, separate grains. Searching the shelves of my local grocery store, I came upon a number of different choices: plain long-grain white rice, converted rice, instant rice, jasmine, basmati, and Texmati (basmati rice grown domestically in Texas). I took a box or bag of each and cooked them according to a standard, stripped-down recipe for rice pilaf, altering the ratio of liquid to rice according to each variety when necessary.

Each type of rice was slightly different in flavor, texture, and appearance. Worst of the lot was the

A short, wide, heavyweight pan, such as a large saucepan or sauté pan with straight sides, encourages even cooking and equal distribution of liquid throughout the rice grains.

instant rice, which was textureless and mushy and had very little rice flavor. The converted rice had a very strong, off-putting flavor, while the jasmine rice, though delicious, was a little too sticky for pilaf. Plain long-grain white rice worked well, but basmati rice was even better: each grain was separate and long and fluffy, and the rice had a fresh, delicate fragrance. Though the Texmati produced similar results, it cost three times as much as the basmati per pound, making the basmati rice the logical choice. That said, I would add that you can use plain long-grain rice if basmati is not available.

In culinary school I was taught that the proper rice to liquid ratio for long-grain white rice is 1 to 2, but many cooks I know use less water, so I decided to figure it out for myself. After testing every possibility, from 1:1 to 1:2, I found that I got the best rice using 1⅔ cups of water for every cup of rice. To make this easier to remember, as well as easier to measure, I increased the rice by half to 1½ cups and the liquid to 2½ cups.

Give It a Rinse

With my rice/water ratio set, I was ready to test the traditional methods for making pilaf, which

called for rinsing, soaking, or parboiling the rice before cooking it in fat and simmering it to tenderness. Each recipe declared one of these preparatory steps to be essential in producing rice with distinct, separate grains that were light and fluffy.

I began by parboiling the rice for three minutes in a large quantity of water, as you would pasta, then draining it and proceeding to sauté and cook it. This resulted in bloated, waterlogged grains of rice. To be sure that I wasn't adding more liquid than necessary, I weighed the rice before and after parboiling to measure the amount of water the rice had absorbed, then subtracted that amount from the water in which the final cooking was done. After trying this with both basmati and domestic long-grain white rice and still coming up with waterlogged rice, I eliminated parboiling as part of my cooking method.

Rinsing the rice, on the other hand, made a substantial difference, particularly with basmati rice. I simply covered 1½ cups of rice with water, gently moved the grains around using my fingers, and drained the water from the rice. I repeated this process about four or five times until the rinsing water was clear enough for me to see the grains distinctly. I then drained the rice and cooked it in oil and liquid (decreased to 2¼ cups to compensate for the water that had been absorbed by or adhered to the grains during rinsing). The resulting rice was less hard and more tender, and it had a slightly shinier, smoother appearance.

I also tested soaking the rice before cooking it. I rinsed three batches of basmati rice and soaked them for five minutes, one hour, and overnight, respectively. The batch that soaked for five minutes was no better than the one that had only been rinsed. Soaking the rice for an hour proved to be a still greater waste of time, since it wasn't perceptibly different from the rinsed-only version. Soaked overnight, however, the rice was noticeably better. It was very tender, less starchy, and seemed to have longer, more elegant grains than the other batches I'd prepared. Though the difference was subtle, this batch of rice was definitely more refined than the others. (Keep in mind that rice soaked overnight needs to be cooked in only two cups of liquid, compensating for the amount of water absorbed while it soaks overnight). Soaking overnight takes some forethought, of course, so if you don't think of it a day ahead of time, simply rinse the rice well; this also delivers a good pilaf.

Thus far, I had allowed the rice to steam an additional 10 minutes after being removed from the heat to ensure that the moisture was distributed throughout. I wondered if a longer or shorter steaming time would make a big difference in the resulting pilaf. I made a few batches of pilaf, allowing the rice to steam for 5 minutes, 10 minutes, and 15 minutes. The rice that steamed for 5 minutes was heavy and wet. The batch that steamed for 15 minutes was the lightest and least watery. I also decided to try placing a clean dish towel between the pan and the lid right after I took the rice off the stove. What I found was that this produced the best results of all, while reducing the steaming time to only 10 minutes. It seems that the towel (or two layers of paper towels) prevents condensation and absorbs the excess water in the pan during steaming, producing dryer, fluffier rice than those steamed without the towel.

Fat and Flavorings

In culinary school, we were taught to use just enough fat to cover the grains of rice with oil, about one tablespoon per cup of rice. I was therefore surprised to see that many of my Middle Eastern recipes called for as much as one-quarter cup of butter per cup of rice. I decided to do a test of my own to determine the optimal amount of fat. Using butter (since I like the extra flavor and richness that it lends to the rice), I tried from 1 to 4 tablespoons per 1½ cups of rice. Three tablespoons turned out to be optimal. The rice was buttery and rich without being overwhelmingly so, and each grain was shinier and more distinct than when cooked with less fat.

I also wondered if sautéing the rice for different amounts of time would make a difference, so I sautéed the rice over medium heat for one minute, three minutes, and five minutes. The pan of rice that was sautéed for five minutes was much less tender than the other two. It also had picked up a strong nutty flavor. When sautéed for one minute, the rice simply tasted steamed. The batch sautéed for three minutes was the best, with a light nutty flavor and tender texture.

At the end comes the fun part—adding the flavorings, seasonings, and other ingredients that give the pilaf its distinctive character. You need to pay attention when you add these ingredients, though, since different types work best when added at different stages. I found that dried spices, minced ginger, and garlic, for example, are best sautéed briefly in the fat before the raw rice is added to the pan. Saffron and dried herbs are best added to the liquid as it heats up, while fresh herbs and toasted nuts should be added to the pilaf just before serving to maximize freshness, texture (in the case of nuts), and flavor. Dried fruits such as raisins, currants, or figs can be added just before steaming the rice, which gives them enough time to heat and become plump without becoming soggy.

SIMPLE PILAF–STYLE RICE
SERVES 4 AS A SIDE DISH

If you like, olive oil can be substituted for the butter depending on what you are serving with the pilaf. Soaking the rice overnight in water results in more tender, separate grains. If you'd like to try it, add enough water to cover the rice by 1 inch after the rinsing process in step 1, then cover the bowl with plastic wrap and let it stand at room temperature 8 to 24 hours; reduce the amount of water to cook the rice to 2 cups. For the most evenly cooked rice, use a wide-bottomed saucepan with a tight-fitting lid.

1½	cups basmati (or long-grain) rice
2¼	cups water
1½	teaspoons salt
	Ground black pepper
3	tablespoons unsalted butter
1	small onion, minced (about ½ cup)

1. Place rice in medium bowl and add enough water to cover by 2 inches; using hands, gently swish grains to release excess starch. Carefully pour off water, leaving rice in bowl. Repeat four to five times, until water runs almost clear. Using a colander or fine mesh strainer, drain water from rice; place colander over bowl and set aside.
2. Bring 2¼ cups water to boil, covered, in small saucepan over medium-high heat. Add salt and season with pepper; cover to keep hot. Meanwhile, heat butter in large saucepan over

After the rice is cooked, cover the pan with a clean dish towel and allow it to sit for 10 minutes.

medium heat until foam begins to subside; add onion and sauté until softened but not browned, about 4 minutes. Add rice and stir to coat grains with butter; cook until edges of rice grains begin to turn translucent, about 3 minutes. Stir hot seasoned water into rice; return to boil, then reduce heat to low, cover, and simmer until all liquid is absorbed, about 16-18 minutes. Off heat, remove lid, and place kitchen towel folded in half over saucepan (see illustration below); replace lid. Let stand 10 minutes; fluff rice with fork and serve.

RICE PILAF WITH CURRANTS
AND PINE NUTS

Toast ¼ cup pine nuts in small dry skillet over medium heat until golden and fragrant, about 5 minutes; set aside. Follow recipe for Simple Pilaf-Style Rice, adding ½ teaspoon turmeric, ¼ teaspoon ground cinnamon, and 2 medium garlic cloves, minced, to sautéed onion; cook until fragrant, about 30 seconds longer. When rice is off heat, before covering saucepan with towel, sprinkle ¼ cup currants over rice in pan (do not mix in). When fluffing rice with fork, toss in toasted pine nuts.

INDIAN–SPICED RICE PILAF WITH
DATES AND PARSLEY

Follow recipe for Simple Pilaf-Style Rice, adding 2 medium garlic cloves, minced, 2 teaspoons grated fresh ginger, ⅛ teaspoon ground cinnamon, and ⅛ teaspoon ground cardamom to sautéed onion; cook until fragrant, about 30 seconds longer. When rice is off heat, before covering saucepan with towel, add ¼ cup chopped dates and 2 tablespoons chopped fresh parsley (do not mix in); continue with recipe.

RICE PILAF WITH VERMICELLI

If you're using soaked rice for this variation, use 3 cups of water.

Break 4 ounces vermicelli into 1-inch pieces (you should have about 1 cup); set aside. Follow recipe for Simple Pilaf-Style Rice, increasing water to 3¼ cups and melting only 1½ tablespoons butter in saucepan over medium heat; add vermicelli and cook, stirring occasionally, until browned, about 3 minutes. Remove to small bowl and set aside. Sauté onion in remaining 1½ tablespoons butter in now-empty saucepan; add 2 medium garlic cloves, minced, ½ teaspoon ground cumin, ½ teaspoon ground coriander, and pinch allspice to sautéed onion; cook until fragrant, about 30 seconds longer. Add vermicelli along with rice; continue with recipe.

Anne Yamanaka lives and cooks in Torrance, California.

The Best Bowl of Oatmeal

After making 50 batches of oatmeal, we make porridge worth eating again by using steel-cut oats and a simple toasting method that greatly enhances flavor.

≥ BY MARYELLEN DRISCOLL ≤

The midwinter muse of belly-warming oatmeal has been a source of bewitchment for me over the years. It started back at 4-H camp, where they'd dish out pasty mounds of the stuff. It was no remedy for homesickness. Leftovers were suspected to have been recycled as glue substitute in arts and crafts.

Two decades later I finally did have great oatmeal—the details of which are regrettably vague. I am certain I was in Scotland. But at the time my attention was fixed, I confess, on a young man whom I was visiting. Ultimately, the romance died, but pinings for that great steaming bowl of oatmeal lingered.

After a bit of research I found I had much to explore if I was to re-create that great oatmeal experience in my home kitchen, from the kind of oats used to the cooking technique to the method of stirring. I began by first considering the oats.

Pour some milk or cream over the oatmeal or, like the Scottish, dunk each spoonful into a separate bowl of cold milk or cream.

The Goldilocks Syndrome

Oats are a cool-climate grain crop that make for excellent animal feed but must be cleaned, toasted, hulled, and cleaned again if they are to be used for human consumption. This process makes what are called oat groats. Similar in appearance to brown rice, oat groats are not readily available in stores and make more of a nutty rice-type dish than a creamy cereal food.

The oat cereal product most familiar to American households—next to Cheerios—is rolled oats, an American innovation of the late 19th century. Rolled oats are made by steaming oat groats and flattening them with large rollers. In supermarkets you will find two types of rolled oats—quick-cooking and regular, also known as old-fashioned. Quick-cooking are cut into smaller pieces before rolling and are rolled thinner than the regular variety so that the cereal takes just one minute to cook versus five. In the *Cook's* test kitchen, we tried making hot cereal with both.

The quick-cooking were a bit powdery and had no real flavor but did create a pleasant mushy consistency. In a matter of minutes, however, the bowl of oatmeal cooled and gelled into a flabby paste. Hot oatmeal from Quaker old-fashioned oats turned out a slightly more bulky bowl of cereal but

was still insubstantial, drab, and flecky in texture. We did try regular rolled oats purchased in the bulk section of a natural food store. They were noticeably more golden in color than the Quaker variety and had better flavor. As I later learned, the rolled oats sold in natural food store bulk bins are often flash-toasted during processing.

Instant oats, often sold in individual flavor packets, are a slightly different species. These are made with cut groats that have been precooked and dried before being rolled. So, amazingly, all you must do is stir a packet into boiling water for an immediate fix. We found the trade-off to be a bowl of gelled oat chaff that's quick to lose its moisture and heat.

As it turns out, many Scottish and Irish cooks scorn American rolled oats, saying they make a sloppy bowl of "porridge." I figured I should carefully consider the opinion of these renowned oat eaters. In these countries, oatmeal is made from steel-cut oats—groats that have been cut into a few pieces but have not been otherwise processed or rolled. Also known as Scotch oats, Irish oatmeal, or pinhead oats, they can typically be found in the bulk foods section of natural food stores. Supermarkets carry pricey canned varieties, but all of the tins we tried were stale.

Making hot oatmeal from steel-cut oats took considerably longer than with regular rolled oats (about 25 to 30 minutes total), but the outcome was very much worth the wait. The hot cereal had

a faint nutty flavor, and while its consistency was surprisingly creamy, it was also toothsome; there was a firm core to the soft oat granules that whimsically popped between your teeth when chewed.

If Goldilocks had been among my tasters, I figured she'd tell me this oatmeal was most like Papa Bear's, only it wasn't quite "juuuust right." There was still some fine-tuning needed to determine how to bring out the best texture and flavor of these oats.

Toast, Butter, and Milk

Taking a clue from the flash-toasting technique of the natural food store's rolled oats, I tried toasting the steel-cut oats. This definitely helped to accent the nutty flavor. Because oats are high in oil content and thus quick to burn, I found toasting them in a skillet as opposed to the oven provided better control. And, to no great surprise, toasting the oats with a little butter in the skillet lent them a sweet, rounded nutty flavor, with an aroma like butterscotch.

As for the cooking method, I tried a variety of approaches: adding to boiling water then dropping to a simmer, boiling constantly, simmering only, starting in cold water, covered versus uncovered, and so on. The ultimate goal was to determine which method would create the creamiest bowl of oatmeal without being too mushy.

Starting in cold water is supposed to make the creamiest oatmeal. It did, but it was mushy, too. There was no kernel pop. Tasters agreed that the cereal needed to be more toothsome. Starting in boiling water and dropping to a simmer did just that—but so did simmering only, and that made

TECHNIQUE

TOASTING OATMEAL

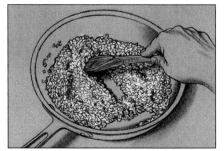

Toasting in a skillet accents the oats' nutty flavor.

Hold the Salt, Please

Almost all of the recipes that called for steel-cut oats also called for the addition of salt to the oatmeal only after it had cooked for at least 10 minutes. After trying a batch in which I added the salt to the water before adding the oats, I found out there was good reason for this practice—salt added beforehand hardened the meal and prevented the grains from swelling.

To find out why, I contacted Professor Chuck Walker, who teaches a course on breakfast cereal technology at Kansas State University. He explained that under slow-cooking conditions and without the addition of salt, a lot of starch and pentosans, a group of naturally occurring gums, leach out through the oats' cell walls. While all cereal grains contain pentosans, oats have an unusually large amount. These gums love water, so they prefer to leach out into the cooking water, which is why oats make for such a creamy hot cereal. Like the pentosans, salt is also strongly attracted to water. So if it is added at the beginning of the cooking process, it essentially will compete with the starch and gums for the water. This is why you get a less creamy cereal.　　—M. D.

for a creamier oatmeal, too, with just five or so more minutes in cooking time.

I did try simmering with the pot covered to see if that might speed up the process some. The outcome was disappointingly gummy. And cooking over a double boiler, as recommended in many cookbooks produced early in the (20th) century, made for a soupy, loose consistency and an even longer cooking time. In sum, the best method seemed to be a steady uncovered simmer on medium-low heat.

Many cookbooks suggest soaking the oats before cooking, anywhere from five minutes to overnight. Because I was planning on toasting the oats, I had to factor this in. Soaking the oats for five minutes before toasting caused them to clump up in the skillet, and the final outcome was a less creamy oatmeal. Soaking for five minutes after toasting made for a thick, creamy bowl of oatmeal, but no more thick and creamy than that made from the toasted oats that had not been soaked—and the cooking time was no different, either. Just to test, I did try presoaking without toasting. Made this way, the oatmeal was quite pasty.

With the cooking technique down, all I needed to test was the cooking medium. I had been using water only. A few recipes used milk, but my oatmeal was so creamy with just water I thought milk would push it over the top. When completely replacing the water, milk was indeed over the top, as well as quick to burn the pan bottom. A ratio of 3 parts water to 1 part milk, however, added a pleasant roundness in texture and flavor to the oatmeal.

Stir Moderately, Then Rest

Many oatmeal recipes require frequent stirring. Surprisingly, I found that when oats are cooked slowly at a moderate simmer they do not need constant attention for the first 20 minutes of cooking time. It is in the final five to eight minutes, when the hot cereal has swelled and just a bit of liquid remains on top, that the pot must be stirred to blend the liquid and oats and to prevent sticking. I found that the last eight minutes is also the best time to stir in the salt (see "Hold the Salt, Please," left) and, if they are to be added, raisins, so that they plump. Following an old tradition, I confirmed that the rounded handle end of a wooden spoon is the best stirring tool (see "What Is It?" page 3). Stirring with the usual end of a spoon, like stirring early in the cooking process or stirring frequently, results in a mushier, less toothsome oatmeal.

Finally, I found that a rest period is essential after cooking because the consistency changes significantly with just slight cooling. The creamy grains pull together like a pudding. For this reason it's important that the oatmeal still be a bit liquidy when it is pulled off the heat. It holds its heat well during the resting period, but much liquid evaporates. If you cover the pot during the five-minute rest period, moisture condenses on the lid and drips back down on the hot cereal, so it's better without the lid.

PERFECT OATMEAL
SERVES 3 TO 4

Many supermarkets sell prepackaged steel-cut oats, but we found they were often stale and always expensive. A better option is to purchase them in the bulk section of a natural food store. To double the recipe, use a large skillet to toast the oats; increase the cooking time to 10 to 15 minutes once the salt has been added. If desired, pass maple syrup or brown sugar separately when serving, or try the topping below.

3　cups water
1　cup whole milk
1　tablespoon unsalted butter
1　cup steel-cut oats
1/4　teaspoon salt

1. Bring water and milk to simmer in large saucepan over medium heat. Meanwhile, heat butter in medium skillet over medium heat until just beginning to foam; add oats and toast, stirring constantly with wooden spoon, until golden and fragrant with butterscotch-like aroma, 1 1/2 to 2 minutes.

2. Stir toasted oats into the simmering liquid, reduce heat to medium-low; simmer gently, until mixture thickens and resembles gravy, about 20 minutes. Add salt and stir lightly with spoon handle. Continue simmering, stirring occasionally with wooden spoon handle, until oats absorb almost all liquid and oatmeal is thick and creamy, with a pudding-like consistency, about 7 to 10 minutes. Off heat, let oatmeal stand uncovered 5 minutes. Serve immediately, with the following topping, if desired.

HONEYED FIG TOPPING WITH VANILLA AND CINNAMON
MAKES ABOUT 1 CUP, ENOUGH FOR 4 SERVINGS OATMEAL

5　ounces dried figs (about 1 cup), each fig quartered and stemmed
1 1/2　tablespoons honey
1/8　teaspoon vanilla extract
1/8　teaspoon ground cinnamon

Bring figs, honey, 1 1/2 tablespoons water, vanilla, and cinnamon to simmer in small saucepan over medium-high heat; cook until liquid reduces to glaze, about 4 minutes. Spoon a portion over individual bowls of hot oatmeal; serve immediately.

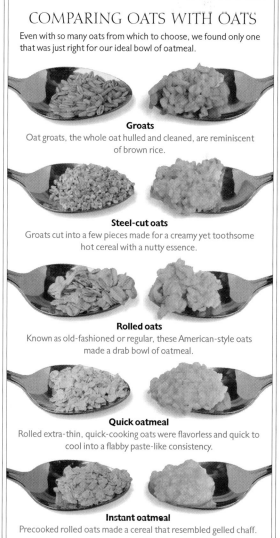

COMPARING OATS WITH OATS

Even with so many oats from which to choose, we found only one that was just right for our ideal bowl of oatmeal.

Groats
Oat groats, the whole oat hulled and cleaned, are reminiscent of brown rice.

Steel-cut oats
Groats cut into a few pieces made for a creamy yet toothsome hot cereal with a nutty essence.

Rolled oats
Known as old-fashioned or regular, these American-style oats made a drab bowl of oatmeal.

Quick oatmeal
Rolled extra-thin, quick-cooking oats were flavorless and quick to cool into a flabby paste-like consistency.

Instant oatmeal
Precooked rolled oats made a cereal that resembled gelled chaff.

The Best Devil's Food Cake

The secrets to this moist, velvety chocolate cake are Dutch-processed cocoa, boiling water, baking soda, and sour cream.

⇒ BY CHRISTOPHER KIMBALL ⇐

When was the last time that you played with your food? I don't mean starting a food fight. I am thinking about baking up a Minnehana, Butterfly, Sunshine, or Watermelon Cake, confections that derived their names from their color, their shape, or both. If you like flowers, you could make a Daisy, Black-Eyed Susan, Daffodil, or Chrysanthemum Cake. If you were in a religious frame of mind you might make a Scripture Cake, but if you were in a lighter mood you might bake up a Wacky or Crazy-Mixed-Up Cake. This craze for fancy cake names dates back to the latter part of the nineteenth century. But only one cake has survived from that period to ours, the Devil's Food Cake. Its success is a testament to its utter simplicity and, being a moist chocolate cake, it has had lasting appeal.

The obvious question is, "Just what is this cake?" The short answer is that the name refers to the color of the cake, not the texture, taste, shape, or fancy decorations. One group of food historians would argue that Devil's Food is a black cake; others would point to a reddish hue—cocoa naturally contains red pigments—as the distinguishing characteristic. For those who argue for black cakes, there is the Satan Cake, a cake made in the late nineteenth century that was probably synonymous with devil's food and was an obvious counterpoint to angel food. Those who favor a reddish cake would offer the "flames of hell" as the working analogy and the fact that the devil is often portrayed as a red, not a black, figure. Related to this type of devil's food cake is the Red Velvet Cake, which is usually chocolate and contains red food coloring; the Mahogany Cake, which includes molasses; and the Oxblood Cake, which is also reddish.

The problem with defining the Devil's Food Cake, beyond the obvious issue of color, is that over time the recipe has been changed and embellished to the point where different recipes have little in common. To get a better handle on the situation, we pulled together two dozen or so recipes from cookbooks and the Internet, and our test kitchen baked the most promising five. The blind tasting that followed helped us put together a good working definition of our ideal Devil's Food Cake. Although some of the recipes were similar to a regular chocolate cake (crumbly, a bit dry, and milder in flavor), we found the

A bit of sour cream gives the cake a richer taste and moister texture.

essence of devil's food to be a very moist, velvety texture combined with an intense chocolate experience. In addition, the better cakes were very dark, almost black. Here was a chocolate cake that was rich in both color and texture.

The next question was how to construct the ideal recipe. Despite their several differences, we first noted that all the recipes were constructed using the basic layer cake method. Butter and sugar were creamed, and then eggs were beaten in, followed by flour, cocoa, milk or water, and other ingredients. The next thing we noticed was that the majority of recipes for this cake called for both cocoa and baking soda (not baking powder), and that many also suggested the addition of melted chocolate. Almost all of them used boiling water as the liquid of choice, although recipes from the early 1900s preferred milk, sour milk, or buttermilk. So the four key ingredients—those which really stood out in our research—were chocolate, cocoa, baking soda, and water.

The first issue was whether both chocolate and cocoa were necessary for the best flavor. The one cake out of five that used only cocoa was the

driest and most tasteless. Clearly, a bit of chocolate was a must, and we finally settled on four ounces after testing smaller and larger amounts. As expected, the cake that used milk instead of water had less flavor, since milk tends to dull the flavor of chocolate. (Think of milk versus dark chocolate.) Baking soda was the leavener of choice in virtually every recipe we found, but we tested this anyway. To our great surprise, the baking powder cake produced a totally different product. It was much lighter in color, and, more to the point, it was fudgy, almost like a brownie. It shared none of the delicate, velvety texture that we had come to expect of a classic Devil's Food.

We also tested the proper amount of baking soda and settled on one teaspoon: higher quantities caused the cake to fall in the center, and amounts smaller than one teaspoon didn't provide enough lift.

We continued our testing to refine the recipe and found that a mixture of cake flour and all-purpose was best. The all-purpose provided structure, while the addition of the cake flour made the cake a bit more delicate. On a lark, we made one cake by whipping the egg whites separately from the yolks, but the result was a much too flimsy cake that could not support the large amount of water called for in most recipes—so it sunk. We played with the number of eggs, trying two, three, and then four. The middle road proved best—three eggs was just right. White sugar was tested against brown sugar and the latter won, improving the flavor. (I noted later that many devil's food recipes call for brown sugar, whereas those for regular chocolate cakes tend to list regular white sugar.)

Although we had tested milk and buttermilk against water—the water produced a more intense chocolate experience—we tried adding sour cream to the recipe and were impressed. It deepened the flavor, added substance to the texture, and provided a richer taste experience, the chocolate flavor lingering in the mouth and coating the tongue.

Finally, we wondered if boiling water was really necessary. To find out, we made a cake with room-temperature water and found that it made virtually no difference. But when we tested dissolving the cocoa in the boiling water (as opposed to simply mixing it in with the flour), we found that this significantly enhanced the cocoa's flavor.

We had finally discovered the essence of a great Devil's Food Cake. Unlike chocolate cake, which is usually made from milk and has a higher proportion of fat (butter), Devil's Food provides a velvety, more intense chocolate experience. And it is a particularly dark cake when made with Dutch-processed cocoa; supermarket cocoa will give it a redder hue. (See "Is Dutch-Processed Cocoa Really Better?" below.) It is, ultimately, a singular cake in its devotion to a pure chocolate experience, subordinating everything to this simple but tasty proposition.

MOIST AND TENDER DEVIL'S FOOD CAKE
MAKES THREE 8-INCH CAKES

Regular, or natural, cocoa like Hershey's can be used with good results, though the cakes will bake up a bit drier, redder, and with slightly less chocolate flavor.

- 4 ounces unsweetened chocolate, chopped
- ¼ cup Dutch-processed cocoa
- 1¼ cups boiling water
- ¾ cup all-purpose flour
- ¾ cup cake flour
- 1 teaspoon baking soda
- ¼ teaspoon salt
- 8 ounces (2 sticks) unsalted butter, softened, plus extra for greasing pans
- 1½ cups packed dark brown sugar
- 3 large eggs, room temperature
- ½ cup sour cream
- 1 teaspoon vanilla extract

1. Adjust oven rack to upper- and lower-middle positions; heat oven to 350 degrees. Meanwhile, grease three 8-inch cake pans with butter and line bottom of each pan with parchment paper round. Combine chocolate and cocoa in medium bowl; pour boiling water over and whisk until smooth. Sift together flours, baking soda, and salt onto large sheet parchment or waxed paper; set aside.

2. Place butter in bowl of standing mixer and beat at medium-high speed until creamy, about 1 minute. Add brown sugar and beat on high until light and fluffy, about 3 minutes. Stop mixer and scrape down bowl with rubber spatula. Increase speed to medium-high and add eggs one at a time, beating 30 seconds after each addition. Reduce speed to medium; add sour cream and

vanilla and beat until combined, about 10 seconds. Stop mixer and scrape down bowl. With mixer on low, add about one third of flour mixture, followed by about one half of chocolate mixture. Repeat, ending with flour mixture; beat until just combined, about 15 seconds. Do not overbeat. Remove bowl from mixer; scrape bottom and sides of bowl with rubber spatula and mix gently to thoroughly combine.

3. Divide batter evenly among cake pans, smooth batter to edges of pan with rubber spatula. If baking three 8-inch cakes, place two pans on lower-middle rack and one on upper-middle rack. Bake until skewer inserted in center comes out clean, 20 to 23 minutes for 8-inch cakes. Cool on wire rack 15 to 20 minutes. Run knife around pan perimeter to loosen. Invert cakes onto large plate; peel off parchment, and reinvert onto lightly greased rack. Cool completely before icing.

VANILLA BUTTERCREAM FROSTING
MAKES ABOUT 4 CUPS, ENOUGH TO ICE ONE 8-INCH, 3-LAYER CAKE

The whole eggs, whipped until airy, give this buttercream a light, satiny-smooth texture that melts on the tongue.

- 4 large eggs
- 1 cup sugar
- 2 teaspoons vanilla extract
  Pinch salt
- 1 pound (4 sticks) unsalted butter, softened, each stick cut into quarters

1. Combine eggs, sugar, vanilla, and salt in bowl of standing mixer; place bowl over pan of simmering water. Whisking gently but constantly, heat mixture until thin and foamy and registers 160 degrees on instant-read thermometer.

2. Beat egg mixture on medium-high speed with whisk attachment until light, airy, and cooled to room temperature, about 5 minutes. Reduce speed to medium and add butter, one piece at a time. (After adding half the butter, buttercream may look curdled; it will smooth with additional butter.) Once all butter is added, increase speed to high and beat 1 minute until light, fluffy, and thoroughly combined. (Can be covered and refrigerated up to 5 days.)

COFFEE BUTTERCREAM FROSTING
MAKES ABOUT 4 CUPS, ENOUGH TO ICE ONE 8-INCH, 3-LAYER CAKE

Dissolve 3 tablespoons instant espresso in 3 tablespoons warm water. Follow recipe for Vanilla Buttercream Frosting, omitting vanilla and beating dissolved coffee into buttercream after butter has been added.

Is Dutch-Processed Cocoa Really Better?

Dutch-processed cocoa is less acidic (or more alkaline) than a regular cocoa such as Hershey's. The theory is that reducing the acidity of natural cocoa enhances browning reactions, which in turn result in a darker color. Because the red pigments in cocoa become more visible in a more acidic environment, the more acidic natural cocoa is supposed to produce a redder cake. Manufacturers also claim that the process of Dutching cocoa results in a smoother, less bitter chocolate flavor.

To determine the veracity of these claims, we conducted a head-to-head test of three Dutch-processed cocoas—Droste, King Arthur Flour's "black" cocoa (made from beans that are roasted until they are almost burnt), and Pernigotti, a very expensive brand sold at Williams-Sonoma stores—against Hershey's natural cocoa.

All three Dutch-processed cocoas produced darker cakes with more chocolate flavor than the Hershey's, bearing out our research. The Hershey's cocoa also produced a much redder cake, just as promised. But we also noticed textural differences in the cakes. The cake made with Hershey's was dry and airy without much complexity of flavor. Among the cakes made with Dutch-processed cocoa, the cake made with the expensive Pernigotti produced a very moist, soft crumb; that made with Droste was a bit dry with a more open crumb; and the "black" cocoa cake was very dense, almost spongy, although incredibly chocolatey as well.

So if you want a richer-tasting, darker, more velvety cake, use Dutch-processed cocoa, keeping in mind that quality matters. Those who must have a reddish color can go with regular cocoa, but the taste and texture will suffer somewhat.

– C.P.K.

The three Dutch-processed cocoas   The "natural" cocoa

Swanson Wins Chicken Broth Tasting

Mass-produced chicken broths with flavor enhancers beat out simpler, more natural products in blind tastings.

⋗ BY MARYELLEN DRISCOLL ⋖

Despite the importance of good chicken stock to a wide array of dishes, few home cooks actually take the time to make it these days. The convenience of commercial chicken broth is inarguable. But the likelihood that it will taste any good at all is questionable.

Since the magazine's blind tasting of commercial chicken broths six years ago, scores of new products have appeared in stores. We wanted to know if improvements had followed suit. Did the increasing choice of ready-to-serve broths carry an improved, more definitive chicken flavor and aroma? Were they clear golden yellow in color and full bodied in consistency, like a good homemade broth? To find out, we pulled together a wide variety of new products to taste along with the top four broths from the 1994 blind tasting.

Hen Picked

Like homemade broths, commercial broths are made from the meat and bones of chickens, only chicken of a kind that's different from what we are accustomed to cooking at home. We mainly cook with meat birds, meaty breeds of chickens raised for about eight weeks and subsequently sold as roasters and broilers in the butcher section of the supermarket. The chickens used in commercial broths are hens, or egg layers. Hens are effectively productive for only one to two years. After that, says Katherine Kotula, food scientist at the University of Connecticut, they are not suited to be sold as meat because they are typically skinny birds, having spent all their energy producing eggs. But because they are older and have been more active than young meat birds, they can be more flavorful, and, most important, they contain a higher density of the connective tissue known as *collagen*. When heated with moisture, collagen converts to gelatin and provides broth with body. So, basically, the food industry makes use of retired hens to flavor their broths—much like our grandmothers did.

But they sure must not be using the same ratio of bird to water as our grandmothers. Few of the commercial broths in our tasting came close to the full-bodied consistency of a successful homemade broth. Many lacked even a hint of chicken flavor. And, disappointingly, none of the new products on the market outdid the top four broths in the 1994 tasting. Interestingly, these top four broths are all products of the Campbell Soup Company, of which Swanson is a subsidiary. We tried to find out more about why Campbell's broths are superior to so many others, but the giant soup company declined to respond to questions, explaining that its recipes and cooking techniques are considered proprietary information.

Chicken Little

Many of the answers, however, could be found on the products' ingredient labels. As it turned out, the top two broths happened to contain the highest levels of sodium. As Kenneth Hall, a professor of food science at the University of Connecticut duly notes, salt has been used for years in the food industry to add taste to foods having less than optimum flavor. The top two products also contained the controversial monosodium glutamate (MSG), a very effective flavor enhancer.

Sadly, most of the products that had lower levels of salt and did not have the benefit of other food industry flavor enhancers simply tasted like dishwater. Their labels did indicate that their ingredients included "chicken broth" or "chicken stock" or sometimes both. But calls to both the Food and Drug Administration and the U.S. Department of Agriculture revealed that there are no standards of definition for chicken broth or stock, so that an ingredient label indicating that the contents include chicken broth or chicken stock could mean anything as long as some chicken is used. As we found out in our beef broth tasting, that means little—little chicken, little flavor.

Ingredients aside, we found one more important explanation for why most commercial broths simply cannot replicate the full flavor and body of a homemade broth. Most broths are sold canned, which entails an extended heating process carried out to ensure a sterilized product. The immediate disadvantage of this processing, says Hall, is that heat breaks down naturally present flavor enhancers found in chicken protein. And prolonged heating, which is necessary for canning, causes a loss of additional volatile flavors and at the same time concentrates flavor components that are not volatile, such as salt.

The only new development we found to have any positive effect on the flavor of chicken broth was the aseptic packaging favored by some manufacturers (see "Package Deal," below). So until there are some unforeseen new advances in food science, we recommend either making your own chicken broth or sticking with one of the Campbell's products, preferably in an aseptic package.

Package Deal

A few national brands of chicken broth have begun to offer the option of aseptic packaging. Compared with traditional canning, in which products are heated in the can for up to nearly an hour to ensure sterilization, the process of aseptic packaging entails a flash heating and cooling process that is said to help products better retain both their nutritional value and their flavor. On learning this, I decided to have a small blind tasting among *Cook's* editorial and test kitchen staff to see if they could detect more flavor in the products sold in aseptic packaging. Of the recommended broths in the tasting, only Swanson broths are available in aseptic packaging, and even these are not yet available nationwide. We tasted Swanson's traditional and Natural Goodness chicken broths sold in cans and in aseptic packages. The results fell clearly in favor of the aseptically packaged broths; both tasted cleaner and more chickeny than their canned counterparts. So if you are truly seeking the best of the best in commercial broths, choose one of the two Swanson broths sold in aseptic packaging. An opened aseptic package is said to keep in the refrigerator for up to two weeks (broth from a can is said to keep refrigerated for only a few days). One drawback of the aseptic packages is that they contain more than two cans' worth of broth. So they are not practical for those who keep commercial broth on hand for the occasional recipe that calls for just a quarter cup of broth. 　　　　　　　　　—M. D.

Broths in a box

TASTING CHICKEN BROTH

The broths below are ranked in order of tasters' preference. They were rated on aspects of flavor and consistency as well as for overall likeability. Each broth was served warm to a panel of 20 tasters, including magazine staff and three chef instructors and one student from the culinary arts program at Newbury College in Massachusetts. The leading four brands below were also the leading brands in the magazine's blind tasting of chicken broths six years ago. The remainder are broths that have come onto the market since the earlier tasting or for other reasons were not included in that tasting. The following commercial chicken broths were excluded from the tasting because they were rated poorly in the January/February 1994 blind tasting: College Inn (traditional and lower salt), Health Valley, Knorr bouillon, Minor's base, Shelton's, and Walnut Acres.

RECOMMENDED

Swanson Chicken Broth

➤ **89 cents for 14.5-ounce can**
AVAILABLE IN SUPERMARKETS

Although this major brand had a slightly less assertive chicken flavor than runner-up Campbell's, it was preferred for having a more harmonious balance of flavor components. "Best by far!" commented one taster. "Actually tastes like chicken," another said. Other comments: "Pleasant and perfectly fine," "No offensive tangential flavors." "Very even balance between chicken, vegetables, and salt." The broth's consistency was somewhat thin, and it was pale in color. Contains MSG.

Campbell's Chicken Broth

➤ **99 cents for 10.5-ounce can**
AVAILABLE IN SUPERMARKETS

This Campbell's broth was voted as having the most chicken flavor. Medium gold in color, it was also voted the second most salty, and it does in fact contain about three times as much sodium as its Healthy Request counterpart. Tasters' reactions ranged from "It could pass in a pinch" to "This is so much better." There was "a touch of fat on the surface," said one taster, "but that's probably why it tastes good." Contains MSG.

Swanson Natural Goodness Chicken Broth

➤ **89 cents for 14.5-ounce can**
AVAILABLE IN SUPERMARKETS

The appeal of this broth may be due to the fact that it was not too strong tasting. Delicate, balanced, and smooth, it "would remain very neutral as an ingredient in a recipe," one taster observed. Some tasters found the flavor watery and "not chickeny enough." This broth contains one third less sodium than the winning standard Swanson broth. In sum: "Not bad."

Campbell's Healthy Request Chicken Broth

➤ **89 cents for 16-ounce can**
AVAILABLE IN SUPERMARKETS

The chicken flavor in this broth is light, but so is the salt level—30 percent less sodium than regular Campbell's chicken broth. "I would want to reduce it before using it because it is so bland," commented one chef. Other frequently used flavor descriptors: mild, vegetal, sweet. A couple of tasters noted that the aroma was a turn-off—"like wet dog." This broth's body was thin.

Hain All Natural Chicken Broth

➤ **$1.29 for 14.5-ounce can**
AVAILABLE IN NATURAL FOOD STORES AND SOME SUPERMARKETS

This was the only recommended broth that listed no manufactured flavor enhancers on its label. Tasters were not enthralled, but they also did not want to dismiss this product. "OK chicken flavor—at least it has some light body." Other comments included, "Definitely not among the worst" and "At least it's not disgusting."

Progresso Chicken Broth

➤ **85 cents for 16-ounce can**
AVAILABLE IN SUPERMARKETS

Best described as merely acceptable. "This could be used in cooking (i.e., stuffings), but not in a soup," wrote one taster, who was in the majority. Oddly, a number of tasters picked up a chlorine flavor. Contains MSG.

NOT RECOMMENDED

Pritikin Chicken Broth

➤ **$1.79 for 14.5-ounce can**
AVAILABLE IN SUPERMARKETS

The response to this relatively new product was not good. It was watery, lacked depth, and yet had a fatty mouthfeel. "Dishwater city. How can they sell this as chicken broth?" said one taster. "Like weak perfume in a veggie stock," commented another. This broth contained one of the lowest sodium levels—50 percent less than Swanson Natural Goodness.

Dominique's Chicken Broth

➤ **$1.99 for 13.75-ounce can**
AVAILABLE IN GOURMET STORES

Tasters were opposed to what tasted primarily like colored salt water with a weak vegetal undertone. "If I had a sore throat, I might use this for gargling," summed up one taster.

Pacific Organic Chicken Broth

➤ **$1.99 for 32-ounce aseptic box**
AVAILABLE IN NATURAL FOOD STORES AND SUPERMARKETS

This product was downgraded for tasting too bland and having a dishwater appearance and consistency. "I can taste some chicken somewhere off in the far distance, but in between is this distracting murky quality." Others described it as uninteresting, vegetal, and tasteless.

Williams-Sonoma Chicken Cooking Stock

➤ **$6 for 10.5-ounce jar**
AVAILABLE IN WILLIAMS-SONOMA STORES

This broth had a rich, brown tealike color and nice clarity, but the flavor was bewildering—harsh, off, and peculiarly sour, "like pickled chicken stock." It was "as if it had vinegar or lemon juice added." "Gives me heartburn," bemoaned one taster. As for its potential in a recipe, one taster said, "This would ruin anything it goes into."

Pacific All Natural Chicken Broth

➤ **$1.99 for 32-ounce aseptic box**
AVAILABLE IN NATURAL FOOD STORES AND SUPERMARKETS

"Complete dishwater," commented one taster. This broth was also described as tasting bland, like "stale corn chips," and very metallic. It had a pale, cloudy appearance.

Perfect Addition Unsalted Rich Chicken Stock

➤ **$2.99 for 16 ounces**
AVAILABLE IN GOURMET AND NATURAL FOOD STORES

This was the only frozen broth product in the tasting. It was also the only unsalted product. Its originality miserably failed to deliver much of anything different. It tasted "like nothing—maybe tainted water," "like heated water that has been run through dirty metal." As one taster concluded, "Needs salt—needs chicken!"

Glace de Poulet Roasted Chicken Stock

➤ **$4.59 for 1.5-ounce packet**
AVAILABLE IN GOURMET STORES

"Hey, how did beef broth get slipped into this tasting?" said one taster among many. This product was the most expensive and least liked. Its flavor was extremely strong but shallow, tomatoey, slightly smoky—"like burnt caramel"—and bitter. Because of the rich mahogany color and the absence of chicken flavor, we double-checked: it was chicken. This product is sold concentrated. It makes about four cups of broth.

How to Buy a Digital Scale

To our surprise, accuracy is less important than readability and capacity.

⇒ BY ADAM RIED ⇐

In our test kitchen, we weigh most baking ingredients, meats such as whole chickens or parts (most recipes call for, say, a three- to four-pound chicken rather than simply "one medium chicken"), as well as fruits and vegetables for cooking. An apple pie, for example, would look uninspiring if it were filled with only 2½ pounds of apples instead of four pounds, which is why a recipe that simply calls for "X" number of medium apples without a specific weight can be risky. If you were to choose apples that were smaller than those intended by the recipe writer, you'd end up with a flat, disappointing pie.

This is why *Cook's* reviewed 13 kitchen scales some 4½ years ago (see "For Kitchen Scales, Go Electronic," September/October 1995). Testers preferred electronic models with digital readouts because they were easier to read and seemed more accurate than the mechanical models with dial displays. The natural question then was, which electronic scale is best? To find out how things look now, we recently scrutinized eight popular models, ranging in price from just over $25 to $125, and discovered a few surprising differences that made some units easier to use than others.

As always, our tests were based on real-world cooking tasks, things we do regularly with the test kitchen scales. Specific tests included weighing bread dough and ground beef directly on the weighing platform (covered with plastic wrap), weighing burgers on a dinner plate, weighing chocolate, weighing cake batter into pans to make sure they contained equal amounts, and doubling cake batter ingredients. In addition, we tested each scale using calibrated laboratory weights.

Design and Features

Perhaps the biggest advantage of digital scales over dial-face models is readability. Some digitals, however, are easier to read than others. We found that readability depends equally on the design of the scale and the size of the display. Scales with large displays that angled steeply and were set far away from the weighing platform were the easiest to read, because the display was not hidden beneath the rim or in the shadow of the vessel on the platform, be it a dinner plate, cake pan, or mixing bowl. For these reasons, and because its weighing platform was elevated far above the scale base, the Soehnle Cyber was the exemplar in terms of design and readability. The Cuisinart and the Salter were also particularly easy to read.

A few other features made some scales easier to use than others. For instance, the two Soehnles tested had the largest weighing platforms, at roughly 7 inches, which could accommodate a large portion of ground meat or a raw chicken without letting anything spill onto the base. That feat would be much less likely on either the Measurement Specialties or the Terraillon, with their comparatively small 5-inch platforms. For the sake of comparison, the platform on the pro-

fessional electronic scale in our test kitchen measures a full 11 inches wide.

Large capacity was another feature we valued highly. The Soehnle Cyber, Salter, Cuisinart, and EKS were the best of the lot, all with 11-pound capacities, which meant they could easily weigh a large roast. The Sunbeam and the Terraillon, on the other hand, could handle weights up to only 4½ pounds, and the Measurement Specialties was rated for only two pounds, so you couldn't even weigh a large chicken on it. These facts alone made these scales pretty useless for cooking, as far as we were concerned.

All of the scales but one, the Measurement Specialties, offered a metric conversion feature, and every single scale offered something called a tare feature, which allows you to set the scale back to zero with a container such as a mixing bowl on the platform, thus giving you a reading on the weight of the food alone. All of the scales also had an automatic shut-off feature. While this is certainly a good way to preserve battery life, we found it annoying when the scale shut itself off after a short cycle of less than two minutes, often before we were finished adding ingredients to the bowl. Guilty on this count were the Measurement Specialties, the Terraillon, and the EKS. The Soehnle Cyber provided a reliable margin of about five minutes, and after measuring the shut-off times for five rounds, we found that the Cuisinart and the Sunbeam, which both claim 1

The Digital Scales We Tested

BEST SCALE: Soehnle Cyber Electronic
The runaway winner, despite high price tag and minor quirks.

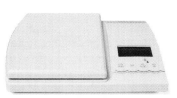

Salter Electronic Aquatronic
Well laid out, good readability even when using big bowls.

Cuisinart Precision Electronic Scale
Ridge can trap food particles and be challenging to clean.

Soehnle Magnum Electronic Scale
Middle-of-the-road performer.

EKS Electronic Scale
Very accurate, but textured weighing platform is hard to clean.

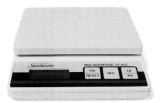

Sunbeam Deluxe Digital Scale
Low capacity, failure to return to zero gave low ratings.

Measurement Specialties Thinner
Super accuracy, but flimsy feel, small platform, and no metric conversion.

Terraillon Electronic Food Scale
Display difficult to read with mixing bowl, cake pan, or plate on scale.

RATING DIGITAL KITCHEN SCALES

We tested eight digital kitchen scales and rated them according to the criteria listed below. Display visibility was the most important criterion in the ratings. Capacity and the size of the measuring platform were the next most important criteria.

DISPLAY VISIBILITY: Determined by the size of the display and its position and angle relative to the weighing platform.
CAPACITY: The greater, the better.
PLATFORM SIZE: Larger platforms were considered more useful and rated higher.

EASE OF USE: Consisted of the size and sensitivity of the operating buttons, the relative difficulty of converting the readout from U.S. to metric and back, and ease of cleaning.
ACCURACY: Tests were conducted using 4-ounce, 8-ounce, 1-pound, 4-pound, and 8-pound laboratory weights. Readouts that were accurate within 0.2 ounce were rated good, between 0.2 and 0.4 ounce rated fair, and more than 0.4 ounce rated poor.
MEASURING INCREMENTS: Scales that measured in decimal points were preferred over those that measured in fractions, which are less precise.

Brand	Price	Display Visibility	Capacity	Platform Size	Ease of Use	Accuracy	Measuring Increments	Testers' Comments
BEST SCALE **Soehnle** Cyber Electronic Kitchen Scale, Model 8048	$124.95	★★★	★★★ 11 lb./5 kg.	★★★ 7³/₄" diam.	★★	★★★	★★★	Detachable glass measuring platform especially easy to clean, but metric conversion feature was excruciatingly difficult to use. Did not always return to zero when weight was removed from scale.
Salter Electronic Aquatronic The Baker's Dream, Model 3007	$59.95	★★★	★★★ 11 lb./5 kg.	★★ 5¹/₄" x 6¹/₂"	★★	★	★★	Despite compromised accuracy, Salter was well liked for its long 5-minute automatic shut-off time, fluid weight feature, and rubber feet, which prevent sliding. On the downside, as with Cuisinart, ridge between weighing platform and base can trap food particles.
Cuisinart Precision Electronic Scale, Model SA-110A	$69.95	★★★	★★★ 11 lb./5 kg.	★★ 6¹/₂" x 5¹/₄"	★★	★	★★	Good display and long 6-minute automatic shut-off time; rubber feet help prevent sliding.
Soehnle Magnum Electronic Baking & Domestic Scale, Model 8038 63	$64.95	★★	★★ 9 lb. 15 oz./5 kg.	★★★ 7" diameter	★★★	★★	★★★	Good accuracy, generous weighing platform size, and decimal weighing increments were pluses, but scale slides around on surface and flat display can be hard to read.
EKS Electronic Scale	$69.00	★★	★★★ 11 lb./5 kg.	★★ 6¹/₂" x 4⁷/₈"	★	★★★	★★	Display starts in metric and must be changed to U.S. standard every time, which is irritating, as is short automatic shut-off time.
Sunbeam Deluxe Digital Scale, Model 6025	$49.99	★★	★ 4 lb. 6 oz./2 kg.	★★ 5³/₄" x 4³/₄"	★★	★★★	★★★	Good accuracy, but low capacity could pose problem for some users. Scale often did not return to zero when weight was removed.
Measurement Specialties Thinner Electronic Food/Diet Scale, Model MS-11	$26.92	★★	★ 2 lb. 1 oz.	★ 5" diameter	★★	★★★	★★★	Intended for dieting, so display reads out in ounces only, not pounds. Despite 2-pound capacity claim, we found actual capacity to be 10 pounds. Lowest price tag.
Terraillon Electronic Food Scale, Model BE225-T	$44.95	★★	★ 4 lb. 6 oz./2 kg.	★ 5" diameter	★★★	★★★	★★	Good accuracy, but low capacity and small weighing platform held it back. Also, unimpressive automatic shut-off time, and did not always return to zero when weight was removed.

minute shut-off times, turned in respective times between 6 minutes 15 seconds and 9 minutes 20 seconds and between 2 minutes 20 seconds and a whopping 16 minutes 56 seconds.

Last, we preferred scales that displayed weight increments in decimals, including both Soehnles, the Sunbeam, and the Measurement Specialties. Decimals were easier to work with when scaling recipes up or down, and they had a minor advantage in terms of accuracy because they measured in increments of one tenth of an ounce, or 0.1, in the lower weight ranges. The scales that displayed fractions—the Salter, Cuisinart, EKS, and Terraillon—measured in increments of one-quarter ounce, or 0.25, in those ranges.

Accuracy

Philosophically, we feel that every scale should be perfectly accurate all the time. Realistically, we found otherwise. In fact, after extensive testing with calibrated laboratory weights, only one of the scales tested, the EKS, proved to be absolutely accurate every time. Up through four

pounds, the scale with the largest average inaccuracy, just a hair over 0.25 ounce, was the Cuisinart. The others were off by about 0.2 ounce, or even less. In the higher weight ranges of eight pounds or more, the margins of inaccuracy increased to just above 0.5 ounce for both Soehnles and to a full ounce for both the Salter and the Cuisinart. We noted with all of the scales that placing them on a very flat, solid surface helped produce a sure reading. If the surface was at all unstable or wobbly, the readings would fluctuate from one increment to the next.

Philosophy aside, all of our scales were accurate enough in the lower weight ranges for most home cooks, particularly when making savory dishes. No one would be able to tell, for instance, if your meatloaf contained 7.75 ounces of ground pork rather than 8 ounces. Even in baking, inaccuracy of 0.25 ounce would be all right, as long as you were measuring flour or sugar or butter as opposed to ingredients used in tiny amounts, such as salt or leaveners. Not a single home cook we asked ever weighs salt or leaveners.

We were not surprised that the professional baker/authors we contacted, including Flo Braker, Susan Purdy, and Rose Levy Beranbaum, felt differently. To them, complete accuracy was paramount, especially for cakes, and they agreed that an inaccuracy of 0.125 (one-eighth) ounce is all they could possibly tolerate—and even that grudgingly. They also noted that bakers who strive for total precision weigh ingredients in grams because it's more accurate than ounces and that they use a completely different kind of scale.

But back to our digital scales. For its sleek and thoughtful design, good accuracy, and superior readability, the handsome but expensive Soehnle Cyber was the star of this show. Understandably, though, many cooks may be reluctant to drop $125 on a scale. In that case, both the Salter and the Cuisinart offer optimal readability and 11-pound capacities for about $70 or less. Although their accuracy was impressive, we'd pass on both the Measurement Specialties and the Terraillon because their capacities were low and it was simply too difficult to use their small weighing platforms.

⇒ BY KAY RENTSCHLER ⇐

Do You Like Your Coffee Maker? Food Processor?

NOV./DEC. '98; SEP./OCT. '97

We are interested in information about items tested in past issues of the magazine. If you have purchased and regularly use the food processor or coffee maker models listed below, please let us know what you think. Have they stood up over time? Which features have you found useful or unnecessary? Please mail responses to Equipment Follow-Up, *Cook's Illustrated,* 17 Station St., Brookline, MA 02445

Food Processors:
Kitchen Aid Ultra Power KFP 600
Cuisinart Pro Custom 11, DLC 8-S
Automatic Coffee Maker:
Krups ProAroma 12 Time
w/NaturActiv Filter, Model 453

Fried Egg Controversy

NOV./DEC. '99

When we started testing fried eggs for the story in our November/December 1999 issue, some strident discussions arose about what constitutes perfect texture—and we're not talking about the yolk here, we're talking about the white. Yes, there was a large faction of test cooks and editors who confessed to preferring their egg whites fried to a frizzy, grizzled halo. The rest of us found that notion perfectly vile. We

wanted our egg whites snowy white and set to firmness, not really "fried" at all.

As it turns out, there are safety issues at play here that support the opinion of the second group. According to a spokesperson for the American Egg Board, frying an egg over low heat does more than deliver a handsome, practically coddled egg—it also ensures that the egg will be properly cooked through. Those frizzy edges preferred by some are a sign of high skillet heat, which causes the outside egg proteins to coagulate quickly but may leave the inside of the egg untouched by heat and, subsequently, less safe to eat. In addition, the lacy brown edges represent destroyed protein, a nutritional wasteland. Sorry, guys. Time to turn down the heat.

Road Test: Standing Mixer Update

MAY/JUNE '96

Our earlier assessment of free-standing mixers (see "Rating Free-Standing Mixers," May/June 1996) gave superior marks to three products: the Rival Select KM210B; the KitchenAid K5SS; and the K5SS's little brother, the KitchenAid K45SS. Since asking readers to evaluate the performance of these mixers in June of last year, lots of mail has

arrived at our office. Letters from KitchenAid users outnumbered those from Rival users by a ratio of about 20 to 1—an indication of KitchenAid's high name recognition and solid following.

KitchenAid K45SS

KitchenAid users praised the sturdiness, reliability, and robust health of their machines and gave customer service unanimously high marks. The only substantive complaints were from users of the roomier and pricier K5SS, who faulted its nontilting head and the required use of a plastic pouring shield when adding ingredients to a running mixer. Many people also remarked that mixing on even the lowest setting sent dry ingredients flying out of the bowl.

In terms of mixing bread doughs, a number of KitchenAid users reported problems with heavier doughs, occasioning machine burnouts. When we used bread flour to mix our baguettes in the test kitchen, we noticed that even the K5SS became winded and overly warm. The KitchenAid company advises against exceeding speed 2 when kneading doughs. But in our case, the small amount of dough we'd mixed received only glancing blows with the dough hook on speed 2—engagement insufficient to get much kneading done. We had to up the speed to 6.

Among Rival mixer users, most praised the machine's powerful engine. But we received a number

of letters from readers who had purchased this mixer on the strength of our recommendation and were disappointed to discover the unbearable noise it generates. In fact, virtually every letter from Rival owners, even those who liked their machines, mentioned its obstreperous motor.

Natural Cleansers for Cast Iron

MAY/JUNE '97

We use cast-iron pans a lot. We found them to be the best option, for example, when cooking pan-fried steak (see "The Secrets of Panfrying Steaks," May/June 1997). Unfortunately, these pans need to be dried and stored away from water or they will rust. Let's say someone leaves a wet skillet on top of your crêpe pan—you'll soon find dimes of rust spotting its surface. Time for an early burial in the trash can? Thankfully, no: there are ways and means to restore your pan to good health.

Having spent several years working in restaurants, I know that cast iron routinely suffers abuse brought about by early rushes and exhausted dishwashers. The solution? A warm bath of vegetable oil and a brisk rub with kosher salt. Simply pour the oil into the offending pan to a depth of one-half inch, then place the pan over a medium-low flame for about five minutes. Remove the pan from the heat, and toss in a half cup of kosher salt. Using a potholder to grip the hot handle, scrub the pan's face with a thick cushion of paper towels. The warm oil will have opened the pores on the pan's interior surface, and the kosher salt will have an abrading, loofah-like effect on rust and leftover bits of food. Rinse the pan under hot running water, dry well, and repeat, if necessary. Your pan is now ready for the fussiest of crêpe batters. And a better hiding place.

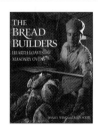
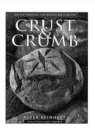

San Francisco Dreamin'

Three new cookbooks present the best of "California cuisine" in ways that are accessible to home cooks. BY CHRISTOPHER KIMBALL

The San Francisco Bay Area, along with the wine country just north of it, has been discovered repeatedly by various immigrant groups. In the last 20 years this culinary Eden has been discovered once again, this time by a host of young chefs on the forefront of a culinary revolution that might be described as café style: utterly fresh ingredients, simply prepared, and casually served. Back in the early 1980s, many New York foodies were taken aback at the simplicity of the fare (combined with the size of the check) found at notable eateries such as Chez Panisse. Yet over time this bold, clean approach to food has won over the hearts and stomachs of both gourmets and gourmands around the world. It owes a great debt to the flourishing immigrant communities of San Francisco, but the food is also very American—generally unpretentious, more suited to a lingering lunch than a gourmet's four-star dinner. Here are three new cookbooks that admirably represent this trend and, thankfully, present a style of cooking within the reach of most practiced home cooks.

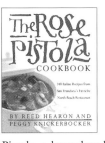

THE ROSE PISTOLA COOKBOOK
Reed Hearon and Peggy Knickerbocker
Broadway Books, 276 pages

Reed Hearon, a San Francisco restaurateur, named his North Beach restaurant after Rose Pistola, a legendary bar owner from the neighborhood. Like the restaurant, this book has a lot of charm. The recipes in the book, on which well-known food writer Peggy Knickerbocker collaborated with Hearon, are usually simple, most taking a page or less, and the book is sprinkled with black-and-white photos of the North Beach neighborhood, then and now.

PROS: The charm of this well-written book is the appeal of its North Beach neighborhood—great food, interesting people, and a rich history. The recipes are, for the most part, simple in name and execution, as is the color photography. The overall design is fine but not inspired.

CONS: Some of the recipes are so simple that one gets the feeling that making them with substandard supermarket ingredients would be a waste of time, while others called for hard-to-find ingredients such as squid ink and harissa.

RECIPE TESTING: The results were mixed. Roast Sage-Stuffed Quail with Walnut Sauce, hardly one of the simpler offerings, lacked clear instructions, the onions burned to a black dust, and the rosemary sprig added nothing to the dish. Calamari Meatballs were interesting, but the 14 anchovies made them a bit too fishy for some tasters, and the meatballs fell apart readily during cooking. Chicken under a Brick was very good but nothing new, and the directions could have been clearer. Broiled Radicchio with Gorgonzola was great, and Braised Broccoli with Anchovy and Garlic was good but lacking in sauce. (We had to add water during cooking.) Warm, Soft Chestnut Pudding curdled and tasted more of honey than chestnut.

THE TRA VIGNE COOKBOOK
Michael Chiarello
Chronicle Books, 214 pages

One of my most memorable meals was an alfresco lunch at Tra Vigne with founder Cindy Pawlcyn. It was an afternoon of luxurious simplicity, the dishes simple in concept but surprising in flavor. The design of this oversized cookbook admirably captures the feeling of Tra Vigne with a pleasing blend of color and black and white photography. One gets the sense that the food here is more complex and demanding than the fare at Rose Pistola.

PROS: This is a nice coffee table book, and the food sounds great. A mix of simple recipes (Roasted Butternut Squash Soup) with the more complex (Roasted Eggplant and Onion Raviolini with Roasted Tomato Sauce) makes for a compelling range of recipes.

CONS: The design of the book makes it difficult to use for actual cooking; the ingredients are printed in a light gray type, and the size of the page is such that it is hard to grasp the recipe at a glance. Many of the recipes require additional preparations, such as roasted garlic paste or roasted, peeled, and seeded peppers, which is typical of restaurant cooking.

RECIPE TESTING: Autumn Fruit and Frisée Salad was outstanding but did call for panettone croutons, an ingredient that we were not about to make from scratch, and none were available locally. The Sicilian Harvest Salad was a home run. The sug-

gestion to use only the outside radicchio leaves, however, makes no sense for home cooks. Polpette of Potato with Avocado, Red Onion, and Cucumber was excellent and easy to make, but the Stuffed Chicken Thighs were too much trouble for the result. Fennel-Spiced Prawns required six hours of marinating and ended up being overcooked.

CHEZ PANISSE CAFÉ COOKBOOK
Alice Waters
HarperCollins, 267 pages

When so many other chefs were toque-deep in convoluted "New American" cuisine, Alice Waters was busy organizing a community of local growers, bakers, chefs, and hungry customers at her landmark Berkeley restaurant, Chez Panisse. The main restaurant was often populated by out-of-towners on expense accounts, while the upstairs café was more of a local hangout with a simpler, less expensive menu. This book mirrors the café's devotion to simplicity and good taste, with classic typography, charming decorative illustrations, and relatively short, straightforward recipes. This is a quiet, sure-footed book, the sort of work that can be produced only by an author who is sure of herself and her art.

PROS: This is the food we all love to eat, and the simple design of the book makes it easy to use. The food is a far cry from "meals in minutes," but everything looks worth the effort.

CONS: Those of us far from Berkeley tend to feel a bit cheated when recipes call for fresh chervil, assorted heirloom tomatoes, wild nettles, and shelled fava beans. Although most of the recipes are simply presented, some are time-consuming and depend on access to the freshest ingredients.

RECIPE TESTING: In short, we loved the recipes. An Oyster Stew with Thyme and Fennel was creamy, mild, and exceedingly easy to make, although some felt that the oysters themselves deserved more prominence in the final dish. An Avocado and Beet Salad delivered just as promised with clear instructions; it has now become part of our salad repertoire. Chocolate-Almond Cookies were also outstanding, with excellent instructions, and the Bolognese Sauce was superb. The only dud was the Panna Cotta, which had an unappealingly loose, Jell-O-like texture.

RESOURCES

Most of the ingredients and materials necessary for the recipes in this issue are available at your local supermarket, gourmet store, or kitchen supply shop. The following are mail-order sources for particular items. Prices listed below were current at press time and do not include shipping or handling unless otherwise indicated. We suggest that you contact companies directly to confirm up-to-date prices and availability.

Digital Scale

Superior display visibility, greater weighing capacity, large platform size, and a high accuracy rating were just some of the features that made the Soehnle Cyber Electronic Kitchen Scale, Model 8048, our winner and favorite among the eight scales that we tested (see page 28). Its round glass measuring platform is detachable, making it a cinch to clean, and it offers measurements in both U.S. standard and metric increments. With its sleek, triangular, chrome-fronted display panel, the Soehnle Cyber is attractive enough to be left on any countertop, making it more likely to be used than one stored away in a cabinet. It measures approximately 10 inches long, 7½ inches wide, and 3 inches high, and it runs on a lithium battery included with the scale. You can order the Soehnle Cyber Electronic Kitchen Scale, item #9553-04, by mail for $124.95 from **Professional Cutlery Direct (242 Branford Road, North Branford, CT 06471; 800-859-6994; www.cutlery.com)**. The purchase code is CI03. The runner-up in the ratings, the Salter Electronic Aquatronic: The Baker's Dream, Model 3007, which has a more modest price, also features superior display visibility and a large capacity. Its long automatic shut-off time of five minutes gives it an advantage over many of the other scales tested, and its white plastic exterior is easy to wipe clean. The scale measures about 8 inches long, 7 inches wide, and 1½ inches high, and it requires one 9-volt battery (not included). The Baker's Dream, item #4030, can be ordered for $59.95 from **The Baker's Catalogue (P.O. Box 876, Norwich, VT 05005-0876; 800-827-6836; www.kingarthurflour.com)**

Bread Lame

Slashing shaped baguette dough before baking is not only aesthetically important for the finished product, it also allows the dough to expand evenly as it bakes to prevent bursting of the crust. While many people use a knife or razor blade to score the dough, these tools can easily tear the dough instead of producing slashes of even depth. To obtain the most even slashes, we have found the best tool by far to be a bread lame. A lame resembles a small, square spoon but has a double-edged stainless steel blade attached to a plastic handle. You can order one, item #2804, for $5 ($3 shipping within the continental U.S., includes free catalog) by contacting **A Cook's Wares (211 37th Street, Beaver Falls, PA 15010-2103; 800-915-9788; www.cookswares.com)**.

Flexible Icing Spatula

While care and precision are key for icing a cake to smooth perfection, the correct tools can make the job a lot easier. For the cake frosting tips on pages 16 and 17, the *Cook's* test kitchen likes a flexible, 10-inch icing spatula to expedite the icing process. Manufactured by the F. Dick Company of Esslingen, Germany, the icing spatula consists of a stamped, stainless steel blade housed in a sturdy black plastic handle. It can be mail-ordered for $26.80 from **A Cook's Wares (211 37th Street, Beaver Falls, PA 15010-2103; 800-915-9788; www.cookswares.com)**. Ask for item #4056.

Rotating Cake Stand

Using a rotating cake stand certainly eases the process of icing and decorating a cake, and it can help get the job done quickly. After icing many cakes for the cake frosting tips on pages 16 and 17, the *Cook's* test kitchen found its favorite to be a cake-decorating turntable with a large, 12-inch-diameter disk that glides smoothly on its heavy, cast-iron base, allowing even the largest of cakes to be iced with ease. The cake-decorating turntable, item #ABCT, costs $53 and can be ordered from **Bridge Kitchenware (214 East 52nd Street, New York, NY 10022; 800-274-3435 [in New York call 212-838-1901]; www.bridgekitchenware.com)**.

Steel-Cut Oats

Busy workdays and rushed meals can leave one longing for a warm, leisurely breakfast come Sunday morning. While testing which oats to use in our oatmeal recipe on page 23, we found that all oats are not created equal. Steel-cut oats produced the best oatmeal, with a creamy consistency and toothsome texture. Also sold as Scotch oats, pinhead oats, and Irish oatmeal, steel-cut oats are sold in many gourmet shops and natural food stores. If you cannot locate a source near you, try **Walnut Acres Organic Farms (Penns Creek, PA 17862-0800; 800-433-3998; www.walnutacres.com)**, which sells Irish oatmeal, item #20104, in 1-pound bags for $1.99 and in 3-pound bags for $5.69.

Pernigotti Cocoa

As we found when testing the recipe on page 25, using the right cocoa in a devil's food cake can have a big impact on the finished product. We prefer Dutch-processed cocoa for the velvety texture and rich taste it gives the cake. Dutch-processed cocoa is made by a adding a small amount of an alkaline solution to cocoa beans or chocolate liquor, both of which are acidic by nature. This raises the pH to a more neutral state. The result is cocoa with a smooth and rounded flavor. While all of the Dutch-processed cocoas produced a dark, rich cake, we found Pernigotti cocoa to be superior, yielding a cake with a moist, soft crumb and decadent flavor. Although not available through the company's catalog, you may purchase a 13.5-ounce can of Pernigotti cocoa for $10.50 at Williams-Sonoma stores nationwide. Call **800-541-1262** or log onto their Web site **(www.williams-sonoma.com)** to find a store location near you.

Basmati Rice

In our rice pilaf story on page 20, we found that not all rice works well when making pilaf. Among the varieties of long grain rice that we tested, basmati produced the pilaf with the most desirable texture and taste. Fluffy, separate grains of rice and a fresh delicate fragrance and flavor are characteristic of fine basmati. Recently, many supermarkets and natural food stores have begun to carry basmati. If you cannot find it in your area, however, you can order authentic Indian basmati from the **Spice Merchant (4125 S. Highway 89, P.O. Box 524, Jackson Hole, WY 83001; 800-551-5999)**. A 1-pound bag, item #ND401, sells for $3.25, while a 5-pound bag, item #ND411, sells for $14.95.

Cardboard Cake Rounds

Icing a cake directly on a plate has many disadvantages. A rimmed plate can impede the process of icing the sides of the cake to smooth perfection, and the plate edges can be streaked with icing or wisps of cocoa powder, making it unsuitable for presentation. Whether used with a dab of frosting to anchor a cake layer or simply as a lightweight surface to turn out a just-baked cake (a task that can be awkward with a heavy plate), cardboard cake rounds can make the job a lot easier and are essential for properly and efficiently icing a cake. You can order packages of six round cake boards from **Bridge Kitchenware (214 East 52nd Street, New York, NY 10022; 800-274-3435 [in New York call 212-838-1901]; www.bridgekitchenware.com)**. The 8-inch diameter package of six, item #ABKP-CB-8, sells for $1.20, and a 9-inch diameter package of six, item #ABKP-CB-9, sells for $1.65.

RECIPE INDEX

High-Roast Butterflied Chicken with Potatoes **PAGE 11**

Greek Egg-Lemon Soup **PAGE 9**

Roast Boneless Leg of Lamb with Garlic, Herb Crust **PAGE 7**

Mini Penne with Rustic Slow Simmered Tomato-Beef Sauce **PAGE 18**

Devil's Food Cake **PAGE 25**

Bakery-Style French Baguette **PAGE 14**

PHOTOGRAPHY: CARL TREMBLAY

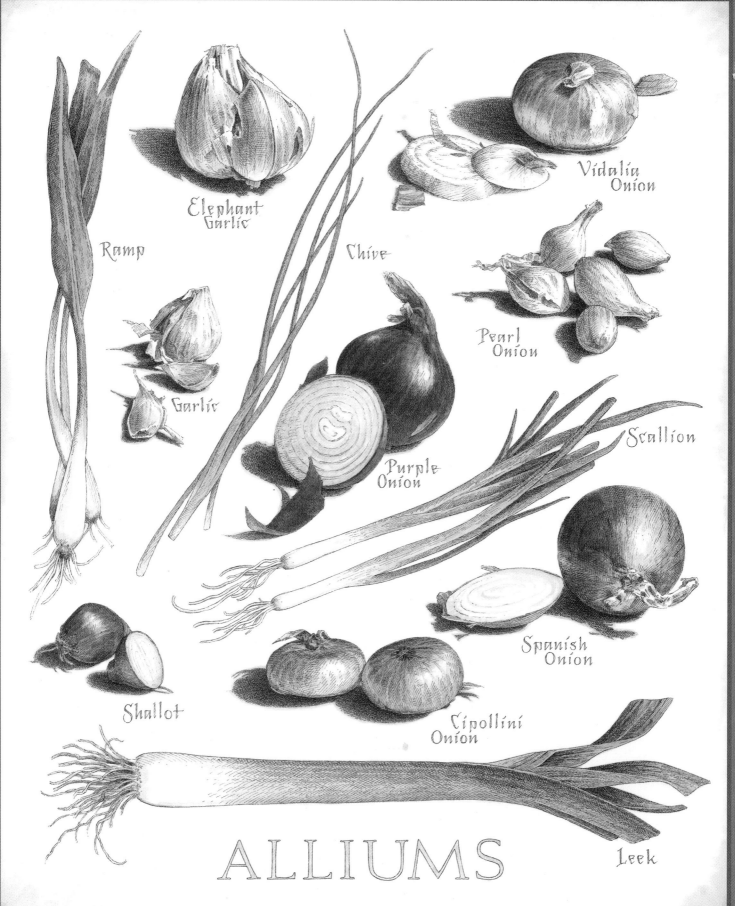

Ramp

Elephant
Garlic

Chive

Vidalia
Onion

Pearl
Onion

Garlic

Purple
Onion

Scallion

Spanish
Onion

Shallot

Cipollini
Onion

ALLIUMS

Leek

NUMBER FORTY-FOUR

MAY & JUNE 2000

COOK'S
ILLUSTRATED

Perfect Pasta Every Time
We Test Every Trick in the Book

Chewy, Fudgy Brownies
Velvety Texture, Deep Chocolate Flavor

The Best Beef Kebabs
Cooking Both the Meat and the Vegetables Right

Quick (but Great) Biscuits
Simplest Method Works Best

Basic Blenders Beat Upscale Rivals
Modern Gadgets Don't Impress

How to Grill Pork Tenderloin

Summer Berry Gratin
Sweet Pea Soup
Great Home Fries
Deviled Eggs
Chicken Marsala

$4.95 U.S./$6.95 CANADA

CONTENTS

May & June 2000

COOK'S ILLUSTRATED

www.cooksillustrated.com

PUBLISHER AND EDITOR
Christopher Kimball

SENIOR EDITOR
John Willoughby

SENIOR WRITER
Jack Bishop

CORPORATE MANAGING EDITOR
Barbara Bourassa

ASSOCIATE EDITORS
Adam Ried
Dawn Yanagihara
Raquel Pelzel

TEST KITCHEN DIRECTOR
Kay Rentschler

RECIPE TESTING AND DEVELOPMENT
Bridget Lancaster
Julia Collin

CONSULTING FOOD EDITOR
Jasper White

CONSULTING EDITOR
Jim Dodge

CONTRIBUTING EDITORS
Maryellen Driscoll
Elizabeth Germain

ART DIRECTOR
Amy Klee

PROJECT MANAGER
Sheila Datz

EDITORIAL PRODUCTION MANAGER
Nate Nickerson

COPY EDITOR
India Koopman

EDITORIAL INTERN
Melissa Brown

MARKETING MANAGER
Pamela Caporino

SALES REPRESENTATIVE
Jason Geller

MARKETING ASSISTANT
Connie Forbes

CIRCULATION DIRECTOR
David Mack

FULFILLMENT MANAGER
Larisa Greiner

PRODUCTS MANAGER
Steven Browall

CIRCULATION ASSISTANT
Mary Connelly

VICE PRESIDENT OPERATIONS AND TECHNOLOGY
James McCormack

SYSTEMS ADMINISTRATOR
Richard Cassidy

PRODUCTION ARTIST
Daniel Frey

WEB MASTER
Nicole Morris

WEB TEST COOK
Shona Simkin

CONTROLLER
Mandy Shito

OFFICE MANAGER
Jennifer McCreary

SPECIAL PROJECTS
Deborah Broide

For list rental information, contact The SpecialLISTS, 1200 Harbor Blvd. 9th Floor, Weehawken, NJ 07087; (201) 865-5800; fax (201) 867-2450. Editorial office: 17 Station Street, Brookline, MA 02445; (617) 232-1000; fax (617) 232-1572. Editorial contributions should be sent to: Editor, *Cook's Illustrated*. We cannot assume responsibility for manuscripts submitted to us. Submissions will be returned only if accompanied by a large self-addressed envelope. Postmaster: Send all new orders, subscription inquiries, and change of address notices to: *Cook's Illustrated*, P.O. Box 7446, Red Oak, IA 51591-0446. PRINTED IN THE USA.

BASIL There are many varieties of basil with quite different characteristics. Most familiar to American cooks is the highly fragrant and minty sweet basil. Genovese and Napoletano basils share the general flavor profile of sweet basil and also have similar leaves. Lettuce leaf basil has large, ruffled leaves and a light, spicy, faintly astringent flavor. At the other end of the flavor spectrum are Spicy Globe basil, in which we noted sweet hints of berry along with assertive spice; cinnamon basil, which we found to taste strongly of clove; and Thai basil, which has a distinctly licorice flavor. Sweet Dani is a type of lemon basil, while both African Blue and Holy basil are bitter, astringent, and better for ornamentation than seasoning. Dark Opal and Red Rubin varieties, though beautiful, taste weedy and vegetal.

COVER (*Rhubarb*): BRENT WATKINSON, BACK COVER (*Basil*): JOHN BURGOYNE

COFFEE HOUR

Christopher Kimball

The Methodist church in our Vermont town was built in the 1870s. It is a modest church that holds no more than 150, although any sort of crowd is unusual these days. It was built on the edge of a cornfield, just off the main road into Beartown and not far from the river that contains the old Baptist hole, a small but deep spot used for baptisms. The congregation usually runs to no more than 25 on a given Sunday, our family sometimes making up a good percentage of those present. The walls are made of pressed tin painted white, the windows are high and narrow with the original, imperfect glass, the Green Mountains filtered in small bubbles of distortion, a child's attention held by the play of light and wavy glass. The artwork, Christ Blessing Little Children and Suffer Little Children to Come unto Me, are modest, inexpensive prints of the same biblical event. A few plaques also adorn the walls; the most practical reads, "Oil Burner Installed in May of 1972, John W. Lunquist." Out in the small foyer, there is a smattering of mementos from the church's history: a Perkins Hollow Report Card from 1916 and photographs of Old Home Day, 1964, depicting hearty, broad-faced women with easy smiles and large flower-print dresses serving up a picnic on long tables draped in oilcloth.

Each of our children has been introduced to the congregation in turn, at first as sleeping infants and then, as they have grown older, as impatient preschoolers, fiddling with the broken hymnal rack or giving a younger sister a sharp pinch during Amazing Grace. When they reach the age of 3, our children are excused with the other children, after the first hymn, for Sunday school. They join the kids' choir, taking turns with a solo or, when they are younger, simply standing in front, trying to mouth the half-remembered words. Eventually, each is presented with his or her own Bible, resplendent in its bright cardinal-red jacket and inscribed with the child's name, a gift from the minister and the congregation.

But the Bible is soon forgotten in the rush to coffee hour, an important social event in our small town. The coffee pot is plugged in just before the collection, the percolating drumbeat reaching out into the congregation with its own offering. After the closing benediction, the Victorian pump organ starts up, the connecting doors open, and the congregation flows into the back room, in which there stands a long picnic table covered in clear plastic and set with yellow coffee mugs, with perhaps a leftover cake from yesterday's birthday party, a basket of homemade nutmeg doughnuts, or, on disappointing Sundays, simply a store-bought strudel. Small hands grab at the sweetest offerings, coffee is poured, the crowd disperses into groups of two or three, and the business of visiting gets under way. In the country, the telephone is no substitute for socializing, the typical call lasting just seconds and consisting of a few clipped "ayuhs" and "nopes." A good chat is reserved for chance roadside meetings or for Sunday mornings over a cup of coffee.

For the adults, coffee hour is a time to catch up with neighbors and to share the latest gossip.

But for the children, it is an invitation to run out the back door to start a game of hide-and-go-seek behind the white-washed two-holer. These moments make good memories, but I hope that our children will also recall the view from the tall church window, an ash-gray wood cabin sitting just above a brown field in spring, a sea of lime-green stalks poking through last year's stubble. In the distance, the outline of the Green Mountains is just visible, the clouds skimming lightly over them on a Sunday morning, the sun suddenly spotlighting our country sanctuary. In a warm corner of our family's oak pew, I daydream that each of the kids will take with them the sound of the furnace turning on and off in December and the back-and-forth cadence of In the Garden. When they are grown, I imagine the songs floating out through the windows like swallows, beckoning them to a homecoming. The simple melodies from the Estey organ will reach out and they will pause, recalling a father taking their hand when they were still children to walk with them and talk with them, and tell them that they are his own.

If you like the editorials in Cook's Illustrated, *you might also enjoy* Dear Charlie, *an award-winning collection of letters written by Christopher Kimball to his children describing family life on a small mountain farm. Order at www.cooksillustrated.com or by calling 800-611-0759.*

ABOUT COOK'S ILLUSTRATED

Visit our expanded Web site The new *Cook's* Web site features original editorial content not found in the magazine as well as searchable databases for recipes, equipment tests, food tastings, buying advice, step-by-step technique illustrations, and quick tips. The site also features our online bookstore, cooking courses, a question and answer message board, and a sign-up form for our free e-Notes cooking newsletter. Join us online today at cooksillustrated.com.

The Magazine *Cook's Illustrated* (ISSN 1068-2821) is published bimonthly (6 issues per year) by Boston Common Press Limited Partnership, 17 Station Street, Brookline, MA 02445. Copyright 2000 Boston Common Press Limited Partnership. Periodical postage paid at Boston, Mass. and additional mailing offices, USPS #012487. A one-year subscription is $29.70, two years is $55, and three years is $75. Add $6 postage per year for Canadian subscriptions and $12 per year for all other foreign countries. To order subscriptions in the U.S. call 800-526-8442; from outside the U.S. call 515-247-7571. Gift subscriptions are available for $24.95 each. Postmaster: Send all new orders, subscription inquiries, and change of address notices to: *Cook's Illustrated*, P.O. Box 7446, Red Oak, IA 51591-0446.

Cookbooks and other products *Cook's Illustrated* also offers cookbooks and magazine-related items for sale through our bookstore. Products offered include annual hardbound editions of the magazine, a seven-year (1993–1999) reference index for the magazine, the How To Cook Master Series of single subject cookbooks, as well as copies of *The Best Recipe, The Complete Book of Poultry, The Cook's Bible,* and *The Yellow Farmhouse Cookbook.* Prices and ordering information are available by calling 800-611-0759 inside the U.S. or 515-246-6911 from outside the U.S. or visiting our bookstore at www.cooksillustrated.com.

Back issues of *Cook's Illustrated* are available for sale by calling 800-611-0759 inside the U.S. or 515-246-6911 from outside the U.S.

Questions about your book order? Visit our customer care page at www.cooksillustrated.com, or call 800-611-0759 inside the U.S. or 515-246-6911 from outside the U.S.

Reader submissions *Cook's* accepts reader submissions for Quick Tips. We will provide a one-year complimentary subscription for each tip that we print. Send your tip, name, address, and daytime telephone number to Quick Tips, *Cook's Illustrated*, P.O. Box 470589, Brookline, MA 02447. Questions, suggestions, or submissions for Notes from Readers should be sent to the same address.

Questions about your subscription? Visit our customer care page at cooksillustrated.com where you can manage your subscription, including changing your address, renewing your subscription, paying your bill, or viewing answers to frequently asked questions. You can also direct questions about your subscription to *Cook's Illustrated*, P.O. Box 7446, Red Oak, IA 51591-0446, or call 1-800-526-8442.

What Is Silver Skin?

Most recipes for preparing either pork or beef tenderloin advise you to remove a membrane called the silver skin. The last time I followed these directions, I began to wonder just what is a silver skin, and why am I bothering to cut it off?

BERTIN TREMBLAY
SILLERY, QUEBEC

➤ The silver skin is a swath of connective tissue made primarily of collagen that is located between the tenderloin muscle and the fat that covers its surface. Functioning like support hose, the silver skin provides the muscle with supplemental structural integrity. Kathryn Kotula, assistant professor of animal science at the University of Connecticut, explained that the silver skin protects the animal's muscles while allowing them to slide back and forth, giving the animal free range of movement.

Since the tenderloin is composed of one muscle, the silver skin is especially prominent, being that muscle's primary link to the bone. Other cuts of meat also have silver skin (among other types of connective tissue), but if the cut is composed of sections of many different muscles, as are, for example, many chuck roasts—with pieces from the neck, shoulder, and first few ribs—the silver skin is often buried in the interior of the roast, making it and the other bits of connective tissue virtually impossible to remove.

The reason it is good to remove the silver skin from a tenderloin before cooking it, as we recommend in the recipe for grilled pork tenderloin on page 7 in this issue, relates mostly to the cooking method. Because tenderloin is so tender and lean, it is best cooked using a "dry heat" method, such as grilling or roasting, for a relatively short time. Exposed to hot dry oven heat with no added liquid, the collagen fibrils of the silver skin shrink to roughly one-third their original length. As they do so, they not only take on an unappetizing texture but also cause the long, straight, narrow tenderloin to buckle into a slight curve. A chuck roast, on the other hand, is generally cooked with liquid, at a more moderate heat, and for a longer time, which enables the liquid to help the collagen melt into gelatin that tenderizes the meat. The moisture given off by a tenderloin during roasting or grilling is not sufficient to gelatinize the collagen, so you'd end up with a distorted and gristle-lined tenderloin rather than an elegant roast.

Short of fully removing the silver skin, which is quite simple to do, you can compromise by nicking it crosswise at regular intervals with a sharp knife, as indicated in our November/

December 1998 roast beef tenderloin recipe. This leaves some of the exterior fat in place. We tested this technique as well as complete removal of the silver skin on both pork and beef tenderloins. Especially with the pork, we preferred the meat with no silver skin at all. Though nicking does prevent the meat from buckling, the silver skin toughens and becomes chewy. The nicked silver skin also became somewhat tough and chewy on the beef tenderloins, but we were willing to accept that in return for the extra flavor afforded by the exterior fat, which would have been lost along with the silver skin. Even without that flavor boost, the roast is still a treat, so it is fine to remove the silver skin if you'd rather not encounter its chewy texture.

Garlic Bread Style

I am usually very pleased with your magazine, but I would like to comment on your recent article about garlic bread (see "Perfecting Garlic Bread," September/October 1999, page 19). For too many years I've read garlic bread recipes and never been satisfied. When I was a child, my father made what I consider to be perfect garlic bread. He baked thick slices of Italian bread in the oven until very well toasted, and then rubbed peeled fresh garlic over the hard surface of the toast. The bread was finished with a drizzle of olive oil. No butter, no cheese, and no toasting the garlic. That strong, pungent, and to some, "bitter aftertaste" was just what we wanted.

HANK RICCIO
STRATFORD, CONN.

➤ As its name suggests, the Classic American Garlic Bread recipe we developed for that article represented our idea of American garlic bread, a distinct style that is, at its best, rich, buttery, mellow, and full-flavored, the kind of side dish we associate with a good steak house.

You describe a different style of garlic bread altogether, which, incidentally, also appeals strongly to some of our editors here. Your dish is true to the Italian notion of garlic bread, which, for lack of a more technical term, you could call bruschetta style. *Cook's* covered this topic in a September/October 1996 article called "Bruschetta: Italian Garlic Bread," which begins, "Authentic Italian garlic bread, called bruschetta, is never squishy or soft. Crisp toasted slices of country bread are rubbed with raw garlic, brushed with extra-virgin olive oil (never butter), then slathered with various ingredients."

If you remove the toppings from that equation, it becomes exactly the type of garlic bread you describe. Though this is no secret to Italians who

have made bruschetta for generations, it tastes best when the bread is grilled over a fire until golden brown on both sides, as opposed to broiled.

Ready, Set…Slaw!!

The article about salting cabbage to draw out excess moisture (see "Crisp Cabbage Salads," September/October 1999, page 18) was enlightening, and this has become an important new procedure in my kitchen. As I cook only for two, however, I've discovered that cabbage, shredded and salted as the article directs, will last almost a full week in the refrigerator, maintaining both crispness and flavor. With very little effort, I now have cabbage ready at a moment's notice with absolutely no waste because I make only as much salad as we can eat.

EDGAR DUNHAM
ADVANCE, N.C.

➤ We confirmed your discovery in the test kitchen by shredding half a head of cabbage, tossing it with 1 teaspoon of salt, refrigerating it, and checking it daily over a five-day period for flavor, texture, and liquid loss. Taking a cue from our earlier finding that greens keep best when stored right in the salad spinner used to dry them, we chose to store the salted cabbage in a spinner, too, because it allows the liquid to drain out through the perforations in the inner basket. (For more information on storing greens, see "Storing Greens," sidebar to the article "The Spin Cycle: Rating Salad Spinners," September/October 1999 issue, page 28.)

The initial water loss, about one tablespoon in the first four hours, was the greatest. After that, our cabbage lost less than one teaspoon per day. Though the cabbage got marginally drier as each day passed, both texture and flavor stood up well and were acceptable through the third day. By the fourth day, while the texture was still crisp and dry, the flavor of cabbage had begun to develop a faint but unpleasantly sulfurous note, so it could no longer be used for salad.

Habanero and Scotch Bonnet Chiles

I enjoyed the broiled chicken with spicy Jamaican jerk dipping sauce from the January/February 2000 issue of *Cook's*, but I have a question about the peppers used in the sauce. The recipe calls for habanero, yet the Jamaicans tend to use Scotch Bonnet peppers in their dishes. Was there a mistake in the recipe, or, as some people have told me, are habanero and Scotch Bonnet one and the same?

HALLY STIEF
SWARTHMORE, PA.

➢ Technically speaking, no; the habanero and Scotch Bonnet are not the same pepper. Practically speaking, though, for the purposes of most home cooks, there is very little difference between them and they can be used interchangeably in recipes. Both peppers receive the very highest heat rating, between 100,000 and 500,000 units on the Scoville scale, which is the most common way of measuring chile heat. In comparison, the jalapeño rates in the range of 3,000 to 8,000 Scoville heat units. Though we could not detect significant flavor differences through all that scorching heat when we tasted the habanero and Scotch Bonnet side by side, Mark Miller, in *The Great Chile Book* (Ten Speed Press, 1991), describes the habanero as having distinct "tropical fruit tones" and the Scotch Bonnet as "fruity and smoky." We tried both in the Spicy Jamaican Jerk Dipping Sauce recipe (see "The Secrets of Broiling Chicken," January/February 2000, page 19) and found them to be, in fact, very close in both flavor and heat. Two tasters did note, however, that they found the sauce made with habaneros to be somewhat fruitier than the Scotch Bonnet sauce, which one taster described as slightly earthy.

Though habaneros and Scotch Bonnets often look alike in both shape and color, a classic habanero is roughly 2 inches long, 1 to 1½ inches wide, and shaped like a lantern with a pointed end (see upper left illustration). When ripe, the color ranges from orange to orange-red to red. Scotch Bonnets, which can be green, yellow, or orange, hail from Jamaica and are wider than they are long, measuring approximately 1 to 1½ inches long and 2 to 2½ inches wide (see lower right illustration). The name Scotch Bonnet refers to the pepper's relatively flat, wide shape, which resembles the beretlike Scottish cap called a tam-o'-shanter.

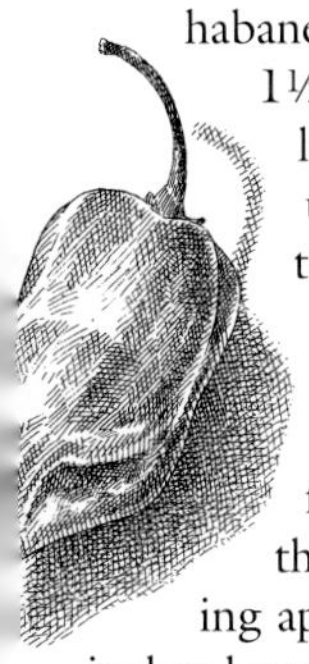

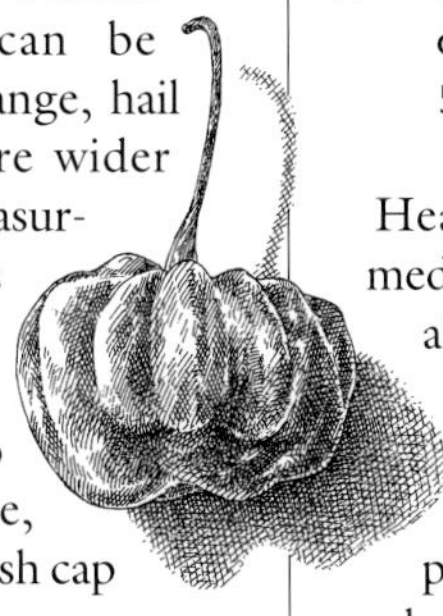

Fried Egg Technique

I thoroughly enjoyed Jeanne Maguire's "Perfect Fried Eggs" article in the January/February 2000 issue. One suggestion I might make, however, is to add one teaspoon of water (for two eggs) to the pan just before you slide in the eggs. The resulting steam not only facilitates the cooking of the tops of the whites but also creates a thin, whitish coating over the tops of the yolks. The coating does not harden the yolks but ensures that the entire top of the eggs cook evenly, with no jelly-like white or yolk surface. The steam may take a few seconds off the cooking time.

ROLLAND QUICK
TROPHY CLUB, TEXAS

➢ Author Jeanne Maguire ran across this technique in her research and tried it during the process of developing her recipe. When we got your letter, we re-created Maguire's tests. There is no question that a little bit of steam in the pan helps set the tops of the eggs. What is at issue is how that steam is created. You generate it by adding the teaspoon of water; we do so by covering the pan as the eggs cook. In our side-by-side tests, we found the difference between those fried with the water and without, and both with covers, negligible. In both instances, the tops of the whites were perfectly set, and the yolk tops were just barely filmed with white.

Oatmeal Topping Erratum

Owing to space considerations, two recipes originally developed for the "Best Bowl of Oatmeal" story in our March/April issue were omitted. We failed, however, to remove the recipe titles from the recipe index. We apologize for any confusion and, in response to requests from many of you, have printed the recipes below.

BANANA–RUM TOPPING WITH TOASTED PECANS

MAKES ABOUT 1 CUP, ENOUGH FOR 4 SERVINGS OATMEAL

- 1 tablespoon butter
- 1 tablespoon packed brown sugar
- 1/4 cup dark rum
- 1 medium ripe banana, sliced into 1/4-inch coins
- Pinch ground allspice
- 1/4 cup pecan pieces, toasted in small dry skillet over medium-low heat until fragrant, about 5 minutes

Heat butter and sugar in small skillet over medium-high heat until melted and bubbling, about 1 minute. Off heat, stir in rum; return skillet to heat and simmer mixture until reduced and syrupy, about 1 minute. Stir in banana, allspice, and pecans. Spoon a portion over individual bowls of hot oatmeal; serve immediately.

CRANBERRY–ORANGE TOPPING WITH CIDER AND BROWN SUGAR

MAKES ABOUT 3/4 CUP, ENOUGH FOR 4 SERVINGS OATMEAL

Use more or less brown sugar to sweeten the oatmeal to your liking.

- 3 ounces dried cranberries (about 3/4 cup)
- 3/4 cup apple cider
- 1/8 teaspoon grated zest from 1 orange
- 2–4 tablespoons brown sugar

Bring cranberries, cider and orange zest to simmer in a small saucepan over medium-high heat; cook until cranberries are softened and plumped, about 4 minutes. Sprinkle brown sugar over individual bowls of hot oatmeal and top with cranberry mixture; serve immediately.

WHAT IS IT?

Last fall, a group of neighbors and I cleaned out the storage area at our community center. There were several boxes of discarded kitchen utensils, including this item. Neither my friends nor I know what this is, and we thought you might be able to help.

TERRY KENNEY
FINDLAY, OHIO

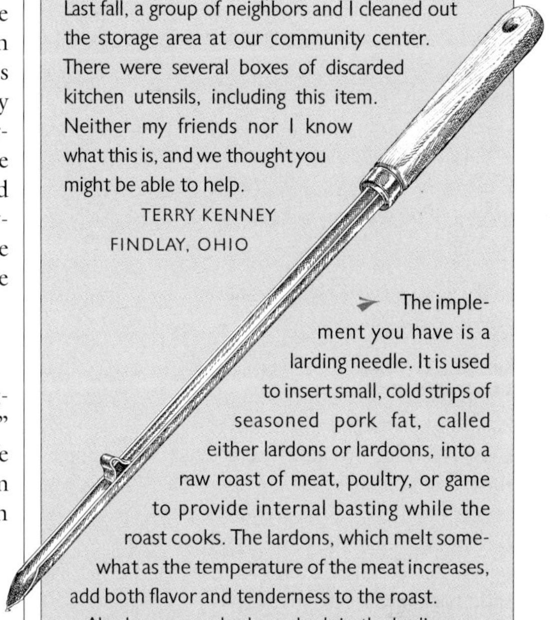

➢ The implement you have is a larding needle. It is used to insert small, cold strips of seasoned pork fat, called either lardons or lardoons, into a raw roast of meat, poultry, or game to provide internal basting while the roast cooks. The lardons, which melt somewhat as the temperature of the meat increases, add both flavor and tenderness to the roast.

Also known as a larder or lardoir, the larding needle is a long (anywhere from 6 to 12 inches), rather thick, stainless steel skewer with a point at one end for piercing meat. At the other end is a wooden or metal handle. The body of the needle is hollow and open along one side, so it acts as a trough. The method is to lay a lardon in the trough and push the larding needle all the way through the meat, going with the grain. If all works according to plan, the lardon will stay in the meat as you draw the needle back out. You then repeat this process every couple of inches along the length of the roast—which is just what we did in the test kitchen.

We cooked three eye of round beef roasts side-by-side, one larded using the needle, the second larded by the common method of inserting the fat into slits made on the surface of the meat with a sharp paring knife, and the third unadorned. The needle allowed us to dispense with this task much more easily and quickly than the paring knife did, and the resulting meat was more tender and flavorful because the lardons were inserted deep into the roast rather into the surface only. Not surprisingly, both larded roasts were superior to their plain counterpart.

Other versions of the larding needle are curved, while some include a clip to hold the lardon. Kitchen Arts (161 Newbury Street, Boston, MA 02116; 617-266-8701) sells the type pictured above for $6.95 each, plus $6.00 for shipping and handling. Incidentally, that shipping cost covers up to 12 needles, in case you want to order a few spares.

Quick Tips

Basting Brush Care

It can be very difficult to get a basting brush that has been dipped in oil or sauce thoroughly clean, and, as a result, the bristles often remain sticky and sometimes even get smelly as the brush sits in a drawer between uses. Harry Lipman of New York City has discovered a better way to care for them.

1. Wash the dirty bristles thoroughly with dish soap and very hot water, then rinse well and shake dry.

2. Place the brush, bristles pointing down, into a cup and fill the cup with coarse salt until the bristles are covered. The salt draws the moisture out of the bristles and keeps them dry and fresh between uses. Next time you need the brush, simply shake off the salt and you're ready to go.

Counter Saver

On some types of countertop surfaces, such as old-fashioned Formica, you run the risk of damaging the counter by setting a hot pot down on it. Linda Stone of Chatsworth, Calif., has found a great way to protect her counter while gaining valuable work space next to her stovetop. Purchase an attractive 12 by 12-inch tile and position it next to your stovetop to use as a trivet. This way, pots coming off of a burner can go onto the trivet, leaving the burner free for another pot.

Keeping Deviled Eggs Stable for Transport

Preparing beautiful deviled eggs requires care, so it goes without saying that the cook hopes the eggs arrive at their destination looking as perfect as they did the moment they left the kitchen. The eggs that Lynn Cheesebrough of Laramie, Wyo., makes always survive the trip because she has discovered a foolproof method for keeping them upright.

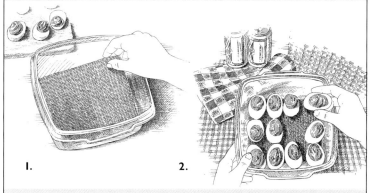

1.   2.

1. Cut a clean piece of rubberized shelf or drawer liner (available at hardware stores) to the size of the dish you'll use to hold the eggs. Make sure you choose a dish with relatively high sides—a square plastic storage container with a lid is perfect.

2. Lay the fitted liner on the bottom of the dish and stock it with enough eggs to fill it in a single layer. The liner keeps the eggs from sliding when the dish is moved.

Smallwares Holder for Dishwasher

After her son, Alex, gave up drinking from a bottle, managing editor Barbara Bourassa converted the cagelike bottle paraphernalia washer in her dishwasher into a catchall for small items such as pastry tips and brushes, measuring spoons, and pot lids.

Easier Rice Rinsing

While rinsing rice to make the pilaf recipe in the March/April 2000 issue, Steven Thoma of Tuscaloosa, Ala., discovered that by covering the bowl of rice with his mesh splatter screen he could rinse, then pour off water, and still keep all the rice in the bowl for the next rinse.

Evenly Toasting Pine Nuts

Many cooks know that pine nuts are difficult to toast evenly on the stovetop; the slightest interruption during the process can result in burning. Beverly Shortridge of Walla Walla, Wash., found that she could produce perfect, uniformly toasted pine nuts in her hand-cranked stovetop popcorn popper. Turning the crank keeps the nuts in constant motion, so they toast evenly.

Pot Lid Storage Redux

After reviewing Helen Yanagihara's method for keeping track of pot lids in the March/April 2000 issue, Linda Stone of Chatsworth, Calif., wrote in to share her own trick. Set an adjustable V-rack for roasting to the widest setting, and stand the pot lids up in the slots between the wires of the rack.

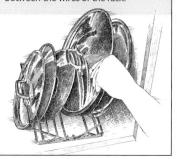

Send Us Your Tip We will provide a complimentary one-year subscription for each tip we print. See page 1 for information.

Preventing Lumps in Polenta

Polenta fanciers know that adding the cornmeal to the water too quickly can result in lumpy polenta. Most recipes advise pouring the meal into the water in a slow, steady stream, but Andrew Benkard of Princeton Junction, N.J., goes one step further—and never has lumps in his polenta. By holding a metal colander filled with cornmeal over the pot of boiling water and tapping it gently, the meal falls slowly and steadily into the water.

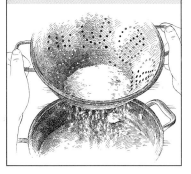

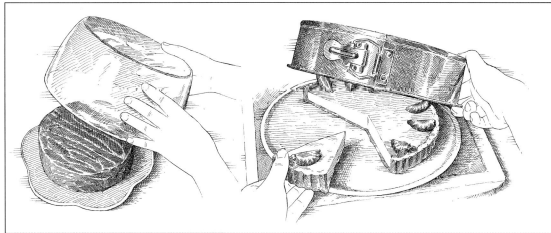

Two Improvised Cake and Tart Covers

Few things are as disappointing to a baker as the occasion when something somehow falls onto an iced cake or finished pie and ruins its appearance.

Susan Kwong of Moraga, Calif., protects her cakes from this potential misfortune by turning the outside bowl of her salad spinner upside down and placing it over the cake.

Kris Shacklette of Woodbridge, Va., gave us a similar tip. Instead of using a salad spinner bowl, she inverts a springform pan to cover the leftovers of a tart in the refrigerator. This not only protects the tart from being crushed but maximizes fridge space by providing a solid platform on which to stack other items.

Bulk Tortilla Storage

The tortillas sold in bulk packages at warehouse-type supermarkets are much less expensive than the smaller packages sold at the grocery store. But if you freeze the whole package, you'll end up ripping many tortillas as you try to free just a couple of them from the frozen block. Ellen Sandberg of North Vancouver, British Columbia, discovered a better way to handle the tortillas. Before freezing the tortillas in a single pile, separate them with sheets of waxed or parchment paper, then place them in freezer bags and freeze as usual. The paper between the tortillas makes it much easier to pull individual ones from the frozen pile.

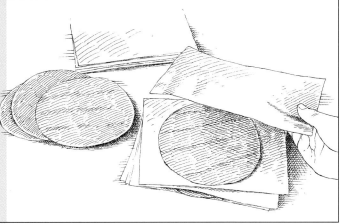

Milk Carton as Counter Saver

Louise Hasegawa of Torrance, Calif., uses empty milk cartons to keep chicken or fish parts off her counter while she is skinning or slicing them.

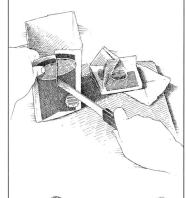

Another Way to Dry Homemade Pasta

Richard Piro's November/December 1999 tip about hanging homemade pasta to dry over clean broom handles prompted Sandra Sawyer of Hanover, Pa., to send us her idea about drying pasta. Sandra hangs her pasta over the bars of a wooden indoor adjustable clothes rack.

Better Dipping

Recipes for biscuits or cookies often call for dipping the cutter in flour between cuttings. Recipe developer Bridget Lancaster recommends refilling the one-cup measure you've already used with more flour for dipping. It saves dirtying another bowl, and the shape and size are perfect.

Cutting Scallions

Slicing or chopping scallions with a knife often crushes their natural tube configuration, which not only adds to preparation time but also spoils their appearance. While developing an appetizer recipe in which the appearance of the scallion pieces was important, test kitchen director Kay Rentschler got around this problem by using scissors to cut neat, intact pieces of scallion.

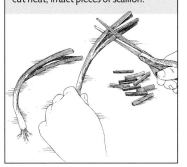

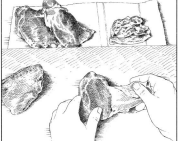

She cuts the top and bottom of the carton and slits it up the side so that it opens flat. She then lays the flattened carton next to her cutting board to keep the chicken or fish she is preparing from contaminating the counter.

How to Grill Pork Tenderloin

Pork tenderloin is often dry and bland. For a tender, juicy roast, brine it for one hour and then grill over a two-level fire.

⇒ BY ADAM RIED ⇐

Grilling is a terrific way to cook pork tenderloin, a sublimely tender cut that benefits especially from the flavor boost provided by fire. But grilling a tenderloin does have its challenges. The chief problem is how to achieve a rich, golden, caramelized crust without destroying the delicate texture of the meat by overcooking it. What level of heat is best, and exactly how long should a tenderloin cook? There's also the important question of flavor. Will grilling alone flavor the meat adequately, or should you pull another flavor-building trick from your culinary magic hat?

The tenderloin's natural leanness is one reason for its popularity. Though this is good news for diners concerned about fat intake, it can cause problems during cooking. Marbling (threads of intramuscular fat) contributes a lot of flavor to meat, and the tenderloin has next to none. Marbling also helps to ensure juiciness, since the fat between the muscle fibers melts during cooking. Without that extra measure of protection, the long, slender, quick-cooking tenderloin can overcook and dry out much faster than fattier cuts. To guard against this problem, we cook the tenderloin short of the USDA's recommended 160-degree internal temperature, to just medium so it will retain a slight rosy hue in the center.

The tenderloin's internal temperature will climb about 5 degrees once it comes off the grill. Remove it at 145 degrees and give it about 5 minutes to reach 150 degrees before serving.

Grilling Details

Before setting match to charcoal, I reviewed numerous grilled tenderloin recipes and found most to be more confusing than enlightening. Many recipes were vague, offering ambiguous directions such as "grill the tenderloins for 10 to 12 minutes, turning." Those which did provide detail disagreed on almost every point, from method (direct or indirect heat, open or covered grill) to heat level (hot, medium-hot, medium, or low), timing (anywhere from 12 to 60 minutes), and internal temperature (from 145 to 160 degrees).

Direct grilling over hot, medium-hot, medium, and low fires constituted my first series of tests. While the meat certainly cooked over all of these fires, it didn't cook perfectly over any of them. The low fire failed to produce the essential crust. Each of the other fires produced more of a crust than we wanted by the time the internal temperature of the tenderloins had reached 145 degrees. Even the medium fire, which took 16 minutes to cook the tenderloin to 145 degrees, charred the crust a little too much by the time the meat had cooked through.

It was clear at this point that some indirect cooking on a cooler area of the grill would be necessary to allow the tenderloin to cook through without burning. Building the right type of fire was easy; you simply bunch the hot coals in one half of the grill and leave the other half empty. A medium-hot fire seared the meat steadily and evenly in 2½ minutes on each of four sides, but the internal temperature at this point usually hovered around 125 degrees. To finish cooking, I moved the tenderloin to the cooler part of the grill and waited for the internal temperature to climb. And I waited, and waited some more. About 10 seemingly endless minutes and countless temperature checks later, the meat arrived at 145 degrees. I tried speeding the process up by covering the grill for that portion of the cooking, which did save a few minutes, but it also produced a faintly tinny, burnt, resinous flavor in the meat, no doubt from the residue on the inside of the grill cover.

To address this problem, I borrowed an idea from the article "How to Grill Bone-In Chicken Breasts," written by *Cook's* senior editor John Willoughby and chef/restaurateur Chris Schlesinger (July/August 1997). After finding that the grill cover gave their chicken breasts a similarly undesirable taste, they tried covering the meat with an overturned disposable aluminum roasting pan. What worked for the chicken breasts also did the trick for pork tenderloin, which I seared directly over medium-hot coals for 2½ minutes per side, then moved to a cooler part of the grill and covered with a pan. In just 2½ minutes under the pan, the tenderloin reached 145 degrees internal without picking up either off flavors or additional char on the crust.

A Little Extra Flavor

The well-developed crust did the tenderloin a world of good, but I knew there were other flavor development methods to try, including marinating, dry and wet rubs, and brining.

Marinating, which required at least two to three hours and often up to 24, simply took too long, especially for an impromptu weeknight meal. Next I tried both dry and wet rubs. My tasters' favorite dry spice rub for pork was quick to throw together and gave the tenderloin a fantastic, flavorful crust; the recipe is included below. We also had success with wet rubs. They are easy to make, have strong flavors, and give the pork a lovely, crusty, glazed effect.

As good as these methods were, though, the meat still lacked seasoning at its center. So I tried brining. Since it takes close to an hour to make a

Preflavored Pork

rub and any side dishes, prepare the fire, and heat the grill rack, I reasoned that the tenderloins could spend that time—but no more—sitting in a brine. I started out with a simple salt water brine, which seasoned the meat nicely throughout. Then, picking up on the subtle sweetness I liked in the dry and wet rubs, I added some sugar to the brine. The results were spectacular. The brine had ensured robust flavor in every bite of each slice of meat.

CHARCOAL-GRILLED PORK TENDERLOIN
SERVES 6 TO 8

Pork tenderloins are often sold two to a package, each piece usually weighing 12 to 16 ounces. The cooking times below are for two average 12-ounce tenderloins; if necessary, adjust the times to suit the size of the cuts you are cooking. For maximum time efficiency, while the pork is brining, make the rub and then light the fire. If you opt not to brine, bypass step 1 in the recipe below and sprinkle the tenderloins generously with salt before grilling. Use a rub whether or not the pork has been brined—it adds flavor and forms a nice crust on the meat.

- 3 tablespoons kosher salt (or 1 1/2 tablespoons table salt)
- 3/4 cup sugar
- 2 cups hot water, plus 2 cups cold water
- 2 pork tenderloins, 1 1/2 to 2 pounds total, trimmed of silver skin
- 1 recipe wet flavor rub or 1 recipe spice rub (recipes follow)

1. In medium bowl, dissolve salt and sugar in hot water; stir in cold water to cool mixture to room temperature. Add tenderloins, cover bowl with plastic wrap, and refrigerate until fully seasoned, about 1 hour. Remove from brine, rinse well, and dry thoroughly with paper towels; set aside.

2. Meanwhile, ignite 1 large chimney using about 6 quarts of charcoal and burn until coals are completely covered with a thin coating of light gray ash, 20 to 30 minutes. Spread coals evenly over one half of grill bottom, position grill rack, and heat until medium-hot (you can hold your hand 5 inches above grill surface for three to four seconds). Scrub rack with wire grill brush.

3. If using wet rub, rub tenderloins with rub mixture. If using dry spice rub, coat tenderloins with oil and rub with spice mixture. Place tenderloins directly over coals and cook until well browned on all four sides, about 2 1/2 minutes per side. Move tenderloins to cool part of grill and cover with overturned disposable aluminum roasting pan; continue to cook until instant-read thermometer inserted in thickest part of tenderloin registers 145 degrees or until it is still slightly pink at center when cut with a paring knife, 2 to 3 minutes longer. Transfer tenderloins to cutting board, cover with disposable aluminum pan, and let rest 5 minutes. Slice crosswise into 1-inch-thick pieces and serve.

GAS-GRILLED PORK TENDERLOIN

Follow recipe for Charcoal-Grilled Pork Tenderloin through step 1. When pork is almost done brining, turn all burners on gas grill to high, close lid, and heat grill until hot, 10 to 15 minutes. Continue with recipe from step 3 to season tenderloins with rub. Cook with grill lid closed until well browned on three sides, about 3 1/2 minutes per side, then cook on fourth and final side until well browned and instant-read thermometer inserted into thickest part of tenderloin registers 145 degrees or until meat is slightly pink at the center when cut with paring knife, about 2 1/2

minutes. Transfer tenderloins to cutting board, tent loosely with foil, and let rest 5 minutes. Slice crosswise into 1-inch-thick pieces and serve.

ORANGE–GARLIC WET RUB
MAKES 1/2 CUP, ENOUGH FOR 2 TENDERLOINS

If you have no orange marmalade, substitute an equal amount of honey.

- 1 tablespoon zest grated from 1 large orange
- 2 large garlic cloves, minced (about 1 tablespoon)
- 1 tablespoon chopped fresh sage leaves
- 1 tablespoon extra-virgin olive oil
- 1 tablepoon orange marmalade
- 1/2 teaspoon ground black pepper
- 1/4 teaspoon salt

Mix all ingredients together in small bowl.

ASIAN BARBECUE WET RUB
MAKES 1/3 CUP, ENOUGH FOR 2 TENDERLOINS

If you don't have Asian chile paste, substitute 1/2 teaspoon dried red chile flakes.

- 2 large garlic cloves, minced (about 1 tablespoon)
- 1 piece fresh ginger (2 inches), minced (about 2 tablespoons)
- 2 medium scallions, white and green parts, minced (about 3 tablespoons)
- 2 tablespoons light brown sugar
- 1 tablespoon hoisin sauce
- 1 tablespoon Asian sesame oil
- 1 teaspoon Asian chile paste
- 1/4 teaspoon five spice powder
- 1/4 teaspoon salt

Mix all ingredients together in small bowl.

FRAGRANT DRY SPICE RUB FOR PORK
MAKES ENOUGH FOR 2 TENDERLOINS

In this case, coat the pork with the oil to help the spice rub adhere to the meat.

- 1 tablespoon fennel seeds
- 1 tablespoon cumin seeds
- 1 tablespoon coriander seeds
- 3/4 teaspoon ground cinnamon
- 1 1/2 teaspoons dry mustard
- 1 1/2 teaspoons light brown sugar
- 1/4 teaspoon ground black pepper
- 2 tablespoons olive oil (for rubbing on pork before applying spice rub)

Toast fennel, cumin, and coriander over medium heat in small skillet, shaking pan occasionally to prevent burning, until fragrant, 3 to 5 minutes. Cool to room temperature, mix with remaining ingredients (except oil), and grind to powder in spice grinder.

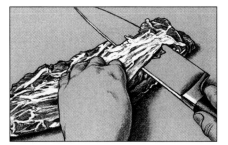

Home Fries at Home

Diced, precooked Yukon Gold potatoes make terrific home fries when sautéed in a heavy skillet until deep golden brown and crisp.

⇒ BY ELIZABETH GERMAIN ⇐

When I began trying to uncover the secret of the ultimate home fries, I went right to the source—to diners. But soon I learned that the problems with this dish are often the same, no matter where they are consumed. Frequently, the potatoes are not crisp, there is too much grease, and the flavorings are either too bland or too spicy. I decided to figure out just how to make great home fries in the home kitchen.

My first step—which was not as easy as I had expected—was to define home fries. I found plenty of definitions in cookbooks, reference books, and conversations with friends and colleagues, but no two were exactly the same. After plenty of research and plenty of cooking, I felt I could define home fries as individual pieces of potato that are cooked in fat in a frying pan on top of the stove and mixed with caramelized onions. I also knew what they should look and taste like: they should have a crisp, deep golden brown crust and a tender interior with a full potato flavor. The potatoes should not be greasy but instead feel crisp and moist in your mouth. Now I could figure out the other factors, such as how to cut the potatoes and whether or not they should be precooked, knowing that I would always choose the option that would yield the texture and flavor I wanted.

Although there are dozens of varieties, potatoes can be divided into three major categories based on their relative starch content. Experience has taught me that high-starch potatoes (like russets) make

A large, heavy pan lets you brown the potatoes without burning them, and a wooden or heatproof plastic spatula turns them without breaking the crust.

the best baked potatoes and French fries, while low-starch potatoes (all red-skinned and new potatoes) are the top choice for boiling, making salads, and roasting. Medium-starch potatoes (like all-purpose and Yukon Gold) have a combination of these traits. Because the cooking method and the type of potato used are so intimately interconnected, I decided it made sense to try each cooking method with all three types of potatoes.

I knew the potatoes would end up in a skillet with fat, but would it be necessary to precook them, as my research suggested? I began testing with the simplest approach: dice them raw and cook them in a hot skillet with fat. But in test after test, no matter how small I cut them, it proved challenging to cook raw potatoes all the way through and obtain a crisp brown crust at the same time. Low temperatures helped cook the inside, but the outside didn't get crisp. High temperatures crisped the outside, but the potatoes had to be taken off the heat so soon to prevent scorching that the insides were left raw. I decided to precook the potatoes before trying them in a skillet.

Because a common approach to home fries is to use leftover baked potatoes, I baked some of each type, stored them in the refrigerator overnight, then diced them and put them in a skillet with fat. These tests were disappointing. None of the resulting home fries had a great potato flavor. They all tasted like leftovers, and their texture was somewhat gummy. The exterior of the red potatoes was not crisp, although they looked very good, and the starchier russet potatoes fell apart.

Next I tried starting with freshly boiled potatoes. Potatoes that were boiled until tender broke down in the skillet, and the inside was overcooked by the time the exterior was crisp. So I tried dicing and then braising the potatoes, figuring I could cook them through in a covered pan with some water and fat, remove the cover, let the water evaporate, and then crisp up the potatoes in the remaining fat. Although this sounded like a good idea, the potatoes stuck horribly to the skillet.

Finally, I considered a technique I found in Lydie Marshall's book *Passion for Potatoes* (HarperPerennial, 1992). In her recipe Sauté of Potatoes Bonne Femme, Marshall instructs the cook to cover diced raw potatoes with water, bring the water to a boil, then immediately drain the potatoes well and sauté them. With this approach, the potatoes begin cooking briefly without absorbing too much water, which is what makes them sus-

VARIETIES | YUKON GETS THE GOLD

Yukon Gold   **All-Purpose**   **Red Bliss**   **Russet**

Our favorite choice for home fries is the medium-starch Yukon Gold, with all-purpose, another medium-starch variety, coming in second. Neither the low-starch Red Bliss nor the high-starch russet makes the grade for this dish.

ceptible to overcooking and breaking down.

I tested this technique with russets, Red Bliss potatoes, and Yukon Golds. Eureka! It worked better with all three varieties of potato than any of the other methods I had tried. The Yukon Golds, though, were the clear favorite. Each individual piece of potato had a crisp exterior, and the inner flesh was tender, moist, and rich in potato flavor. Its appearance was superior as well, the golden yellow color of the flesh complementing the crispy brown exterior. The russets were drier and not as full flavored but were preferred over the Red Bliss by all of the tasters I had gathered. These potatoes were somewhat mushy and tasted disappointingly bland.

I decided to test another medium-starch potato. All-purpose potatoes also browned well and were tender and moist on the inside, but they lacked the rich buttery potato flavor and yellow color of the Yukon Golds, which remained the favorite.

Having discovered the ideal cooking method and the preferred potato variety, I moved on to the best way to cut the potato. I found sliced potatoes much harder to cook than diced ones. A pound of sliced potatoes stacks up three or four layers deep in a large skillet. The result is uneven cooking, with some slices burning and others remaining undercooked. Countless tests had convinced me that one of the keys to success in cooking home fries is to cook the potatoes in a single layer. When a pound of potatoes is diced, one cut side of each potato piece can have contact with the skillet at all times. I tested dices of various size and found the half-inch cube to be ideal: easy to turn and to eat, characterized by that pleasing combination of crispy outside and soft fleshy inside.

Deciding whether or not to peel the potato was easy. All tasters preferred the texture and flavor added by the skin, and leaving it on also saves time and effort.

Thus far I had determined that letting the potatoes sit undisturbed in hot fat to brown was critical to a crisp exterior. Three tablespoons turned out to be the ideal amount of fat for one pound of potatoes. I also found it best to let the potatoes brown undisturbed for four to five minutes before the first turn, then to turn them a total of three or four times. When sampling potatoes cooked in different frying mediums, I found that a 50-50 combination of butter and oil offered the best of both worlds, providing a buttery flavor with a decreased risk of burning. Refined corn and peanut oils, with their nutty overtones, were the first choice.

Soft, sweet, and moist, onions are the perfect counterpoint to crispy potatoes, but I had to determine the best way to include them. Tests showed the easiest and most efficient way also produced the best results—dice the onions and cook them first. More flavor can be added with help from paprika, parsley, red or green bell peppers,

For the "Home Fries with Bell Peppers and Cumin" recipe, go to Cook's Extra at cooksillustrated.com.

or cayenne pepper, as you wish. Whatever your choice, these are going to be home fries worth staying home for.

DINER-STYLE HOME FRIES
SERVES 2 TO 3

If you need to double this recipe, instead of crowding the skillet, cook two batches of home fries separately. While you make the second batch, the first can be kept hot and crisp by spreading them on a cookie sheet and placing them in a 300-degree oven. The paprika adds a warm, deep color, but can be omitted. An alternative is to toss in 1 tablespoon minced parsley just before serving the potatoes.

2½   tablespoons corn or peanut oil
1   medium onion, chopped small
1   pound (2 medium) Yukon Gold or all-purpose
    potatoes, cut into ½-inch cubes
1¼   teaspoons salt
1   tablespoon unsalted butter
1   teaspoon paprika
    Ground black pepper

1. Heat 1 tablespoon oil in 12-inch heavy-bottomed skillet over medium-high heat until hot but not smoking. Add onion and sauté, stirring frequently, until browned, 8 to 10 minutes. Transfer onion to small bowl and set aside.

2. Meanwhile, place diced potatoes in large saucepan, cover with ½ inch water, add 1 teaspoon salt, and place over high heat. As soon as water begins to boil, about 6 minutes, drain potatoes thoroughly in colander.

3. Heat butter and remaining 1½ tablespoons

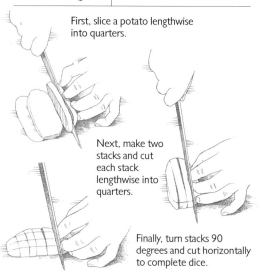

First, slice a potato lengthwise into quarters.

Next, make two stacks and cut each stack lengthwise into quarters.

Finally, turn stacks 90 degrees and cut horizontally to complete dice.

oil in now-empty skillet over medium-high heat until butter foams. Add potatoes and shake skillet to evenly distribute potatoes in single layer; make sure that one side of each piece is touching surface of skillet. Cook without stirring until potatoes are golden brown on bottom, about 4 to 5 minutes, then carefully turn potatoes with wooden spatula. Spread potatoes in single layer in skillet again and repeat process until potatoes are tender and browned on most sides, turning three to four times, 10 to 15 minutes longer. Add onions, paprika, remaining ¼ teaspoon salt, and pepper to taste; stir to blend and serve immediately.

Elizabeth Germain is a personal chef and writer focusing on food for well-being. She lives in Cambridge, Mass.

Out of Hot Water and into the Frying Pan

To gain a clearer understanding of what happens to the starch and moisture content of diced potatoes when they are cooked first in water and then in fat, I spoke with Shirley Corriher, author of *Cookwise* (Morrow, 1997).

Corriher explained that potato starch granules are composed of layer upon layer of tightly packed starch molecules. When the potatoes are first put in cold water, nothing happens to the starch molecules. As the water heats, it warms the molecules and starts seeping in between the layers. The hotter the water gets, the more rapidly it works its way into the softer areas of the granules, causing them to expand. Finally, near the boiling point, the starch molecules swell so much that they burst. By removing the diced potatoes just as the water begins to boil, the water absorption is stopped before the granules have a chance to explode.

When the just-boiled potatoes come into contact with hot fat, the starch granules on the surface expand immediately and absorb water from the inside of the potato. The moisture rushing to the surface creates the sizzling sound, and the expanding granules begin to seal the surface. If the surface is sealed and too much moisture remains stuck inside, the texture of the potato will be mushy; if there is not enough moisture on the inside, the texture will be dry and mealy; if there is no moisture left on the inside and the surface has not sealed, the starch granules will begin to absorb fat and the potatoes will be greasy. Medium-starch potatoes such as Yukon Golds have an ideal moisture content in that when a crisp crust has formed, just enough water is left to create a moist, tender inside.   — E.G.

Starch in cold water

Starch in heated water

Starch in boiling water

Beef Kebabs Done Right

Most beef kebabs are disappointing, with overcooked meat and vegetables that are either raw or mushy. Using inexpensive beef, we set out to find a simple one-skewer recipe that cooked everything perfectly.

≥ BY ANNE YAMANAKA ≤

When I entertain during the summer months, I like to set up the grill and cook simple, casual meals for friends and family, especially grilled steak. Serving premium steaks to a half dozen guests, though, really begins to add up if you entertain often. Beef and vegetable kebabs always seem like a great, more affordable alternative. Indeed, the mere concept of grilled beef and vegetable kebabs is brilliant. Cut beef into small pieces, skewer along with flavorful, aromatic vegetables, and grill over a live fire—the juices emitted during cooking flavor the vegetables, and the vegetables in turn add flavor to the pieces of beef, while both are seared by the intense heat and infused with the smoke of the grill.

Unfortunately, the idea of the kebab is often more appealing than the kebab itself. The reason is that while the concept of kebabs is simple, the pitfalls of grilling on skewers are many. To begin with, it's very easy to pick the wrong cut of beef. There are dozens of choices. It's also not very hard to overcook the meat when it's cut into smaller pieces. Or you can grill the skewers over a heat that's too intense and end up with meat that's charred on the outside and raw on the inside and vegetables that are just plain raw. When not seasoned carefully, the kebabs can taste dull and bland.

My goal was simple. I was looking for a straightforward, easy recipe that highlights the juiciness and flavor of beef, that lets the vegetables cook through without getting mushy, and that allows the meat to become richly caramelized on the outside but to cook from medium-rare to medium at the center. To reach my goal, I needed to answer a number of questions: How can you prepare and grill the beef to get a decently caramelized surface without overcooking the meat? How can you ensure that the vegetables cook through so that they aren't still raw when the beef is cooked to the right temperature? And what are the cuts of beef that will give tender, flavorful kebab meat without breaking the bank? I set out to answer these questions.

Making the Cut

I knew that choosing the right cut of beef was the most important of all of these factors. I also knew that I didn't want to spend a fortune on the meat;

By selecting only certain vegetables and cutting them just right, we avoided the mushiness caused by precooking.

to pay the price for premium cuts of meat such as tenderloin, rib eye, or strip steak and then turn them into kebabs seemed wasteful. I wondered, though, if cheaper cuts of meat would be tender enough to use as kebab meat. I also wanted a cut of meat that wasn't too hard to cut into little pieces. In some cuts of meat, fat and sinew are abundant, making it extremely hard to make evenly sized pieces of meat to skewer. No matter how great the meat was, I wasn't going to spend hours trimming and cutting intermuscular fat and connective tissue to make kebabs. It had to be a simple, quick process.

So I began skewering and grilling different cuts of meat from the less expensive parts of the steer. From the chuck I tried the mock tender steak, clod steak, and top blade steak; from the

round I tested steaks cut from the top, bottom, and eye of round muscles; from the plate came the skirt and flank steak; and from the sirloin portion I tried a top sirloin steak.

The cuts from the round portion of the cow were quite dry and chewy, with a weak, livery beef flavor. The skirt and flank steak were both flavorful and juicy, but their flat configuration and loose grain made them almost impossible to grill along with vegetables and even harder to cook to a medium or medium-rare. They are much more fit for satay, in which long, thin strips of meat are skewered.

Not surprisingly, all but one of the non-premium cuts from the chuck were too tough. I say it is not surprising because this part of the steer—the neck, arm, and shoulder—is well known to be flavorful but quite tough, best suited for stewing and braising. This was definitely true of the clod steak and mock tender steak. But the top blade steak was a different matter entirely—well marbled, intensely beefy, and surprisingly tender and suitable for grilling. It was my first choice for skewers.

My second choice was the top sirloin. This steak comes from the sirloin portion of the cow, just behind the short loin, which is the source of premium steaks such as porterhouse, filet mignon, and New York strip. The sirloin is made up of several muscles, the most tender of which is the top sirloin, from which this particular steak is cut.

So at the end of this first round of testing, I had two steaks that offered a reasonable texture and great beefy flavor at a reasonable price: top blade steak, also known as flatiron steak ($3.28/pound), and top sirloin steak ($4.99/pound). Both were also were quite easy to cut into even-sized, skewerable pieces of meat.

Flavoring and Cutting

Though the top sirloin and top blade steaks were relatively flavorful and tender on their own, I hoped that marinating the steaks would not only flavor the kebabs but also add some moisture. Thus far, I had approached the kebabs as I would a steak: I began simply, by seasoning with salt and pepper only. While the results were decent, the steak was a touch dry and bland. Most kebab recipes call for marinating the meat in an acidic marinade that supposedly tenderizes the meat before grilling. I tried both an acidic and a nonacidic (oil-based) marinade and marinated meat pieces in both, for one hour, two hours, and four hours.

In all three cases the acidic marinade produced meat that was mushier on the surface but not noticeably more tender than the meat in the oil-based marinade. The oil-based marinade didn't really change the texture of the meat, but the olive oil in it kept the meat from drying out on the grill and served as a great flavor vehicle for garlic, salt, and pepper. The lime juice in the acidic marinade, however, did contribute a nice flavor. I decided that instead of marinating the meat in the acid, I would marinate the meat in an oil-based marinade and squirt a little lime juice onto the kebabs after they came off the grill. I liked the results. The meat was tender yet still firm, and the lime juice tasted fresher when added to the meat just before serving.

The next step was to figure out how best to cut the steaks for skewering. As many meat connoisseurs know, beef cooked past medium becomes dry and tough. I wanted my kebabs to be cooked to medium-rare or, at most, to medium. This meant that the cubes of beef would have to be relatively large. After a few rounds of grilling, I noticed that any beef cut into pieces smaller than one inch was very hard to keep from overcooking. One the other hand, pieces of beef cut this large took quite a bit of time to marinate fully. The meat

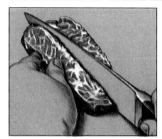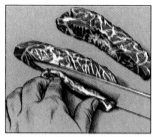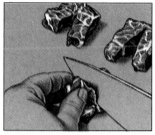

I. Halve each steak lengthwise, leaving gristle on one half.

2. Cut away the gristle from the half to which it is still attached.

3. Cube meat, and cut each cube almost through at center.

that wasn't marinated overnight tasted a little bland because the seasoning didn't penetrate the surface very much.

After researching a number of kebab recipes, I came upon one from Paula Wolfert's *The Cooking of the Eastern Mediterranean* (Harper Collins, 1994) in which cubes of lamb are butterflied (cut open and flattened) before being skewered for kebabs. This, I thought, might produce a more flavorful kebab. Because the pieces of meat would have more surface area, more marinade might penetrate the surface in a shorter period time. I tested this theory out and was pleased to find the meat more flavorful; it was also easier to eat and less chewy. Unfortunately, since the meat was also thinner after being butterflied, it was getting cooked to the well-done stage. To combat this problem, I simply butterflied the meat, marinated it, and then put it on the skewers as if it were still a cube. This technique worked perfectly. Now the meat was easier to eat and packed with flavor all the way through to the center, and it was also nicely caramelized without being overcooked at the interior.

Cooking the Vegetables

The final problem that most of us encounter when making meat and vegetable kebabs is getting both components to cook at the same rate. I noticed that if I cut my vegetables too thick, they ended up raw at the center. My first thought was to skewer the meat and vegetables separately, but after trying a few batches of kebabs this way, I realized that both the meat and the vegetables tasted much better when cooked together on the skewer.

The logical solution to the problem was to precook the vegetables. I ruled out both parboiling and presteaming because each meant dirtying another pan and making something complicated out of a dish that should, in my mind, be simple. The only precooking idea that made any sense to me was to microwave the vegetables before grilling.

After figuring out the appropriate timing in the microwave for each vegetable, I began cooking and skewering. I found this process to be extremely labor intensive; not only did I have to cut and microwave the vegetables, but the onions and peppers were slightly soft and wet, which made it hard to skewer them neatly. The kebabs already required a good deal of preparation—cutting and butterflying the meat, cutting the vegetables, and skewering both. Adding another step made it just too complicated.

Surprisingly, even though the precooked vegetables were softer at the center after grilling, I didn't necessarily find them more appealing than those grilled from the raw stage. In fact, some of the vegetables, including the onions and bell peppers, maintained a pleasant tender-crisp texture (sort of like that of a stir-fry) when skewered raw, and I found this to be a nice contrast with the texture of the meat. Vegetables like mushrooms, eggplant, and zucchini, which need to be cooked completely through to be palatable, were not satisfactory when skewered raw. Instead of trying to precook these vegetables, I decided to omit them. To add variety to the skewer, I added chunks of pineapple; they grill well, add a nice sweetness and fruitiness to the kebabs, and, most important, don't need to be cooked through to the very center, as do eggplant and mushrooms. In the case of the onions and peppers, the trick is to cut them to the right dimensions (see illustrations, page 12) so that they don't come off of the grill undercooked.

Top Blade Steak

Top Sirloin

Our first choice for kebabs is the inexpensive but very tender chuck top blade steak (left); top sirloin is an acceptable substitute.

Lighting My Fire

There were two options for grilling the kebabs: cooking over a single-level fire and cooking over a two-level fire (in which one side of the grill is hotter than the other). Thinking that simpler is better, I started with a single-level fire. Because I wanted the kebabs to cook quickly—to brown the surface and retain as much juice as possible—I started with a medium-hot fire. While the meat cooked this way came out relatively well browned, I thought it might be even better if cooked over a hotter fire. Instead of covering the entire grill with the hot charcoal, I used the same amount and covered only three-quarters of the grill bottom. This produced a more intense fire when cooking directly over the charcoal, searing the outside of the kebabs more successfully. The result was richly caramelized meat, with a perfectly cooked, juicy interior. A two-level fire was not necessary for these kebabs.

Finally, I had a great beef and vegetable kebab recipe that fulfilled my expectations for both the meat and its accompaniments. The beef was well flavored and seasoned, juicy but not overcooked, and well caramelized. The vegetables were cooked through, not raw or soggy. These were kebabs I could count on.

CHARCOAL-GRILLED BEEF KEBABS
SERVES 4 TO 6 AS A MAIN COURSE

My favorite cut of beef for kebabs is top blade steak (known sometimes as blade or flatiron steak), but you can also use top sirloin. If you do, ask the butcher to cut the top sirloin steak between 1 and 1¼ inches thick (most packaged sirloin steaks are thinner). If desired, add 2 teaspoons minced fresh rosemary, thyme, basil, or oregano to the garlic and oil mixture for this marinade. For maximum efficiency, prepare the fruit and vegetables while the meat is marinating.

Marinade
- ¼ cup extra-virgin olive oil
- 3 medium garlic cloves, minced
- ¾ teaspoon salt
- ½ teaspoon ground black pepper

- 2 pounds top blade steaks (about 4 to 5 steaks), trimmed of fat and prepared according to illustrations 1 through 3, page 11

Fruit and Vegetables
- 1 pineapple (about 3½ pounds), trimmed and cut according to illustrations
- 1 medium red bell pepper (about 5½ ounces), prepared according to illustrations
- 1 medium yellow bell pepper (about 5½ ounces), prepared according to illustrations
- 2 tablespoons extra-virgin olive oil
  Salt and ground black pepper
- 1 large red onion (about 10 ounces), prepared according to illustrations
  Lemon or lime wedges for serving (optional)

Kebab Preparation

Pineapple

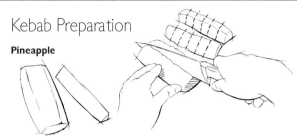

Trim both ends of pineapple and peel. Halve lengthwise, reserve one half for another use, and halve remaining half lengthwise. Remove woody triangular core, then cut each piece crosswise into six chunks.

Onion

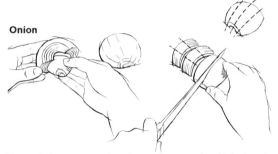

Trim ends from onion and peel away dry outer skin. Halve lengthwise. Peel out and discard inner core. Slice each onion half lengthwise into four pieces, then cut each piece crosswise into thirds.

Peppers

Cut away two wide planks of pepper on opposite sides of core, then cut away two remaining smaller sections. Cut smaller sections crosswise into thirds. Cut each of the larger sections into nine pieces.

Skewering

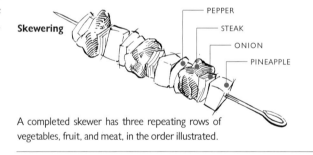

PEPPER
STEAK
ONION
PINEAPPLE

A completed skewer has three repeating rows of vegetables, fruit, and meat, in the order illustrated.

1. *For the marinade:* Combine oil, garlic, salt, and pepper in large bowl. Add steak cubes and toss to coat evenly. Cover and refrigerate until fully seasoned, at least one hour or up to 24 hours.

2. Ignite 1 large chimney (about 6 quarts, or 5 pounds) of charcoal and burn until covered with thin coating of light gray ash, about 20 minutes. Empty coals into grill and spread over three-quarters of grill surface. Position grill rack over coals; heat until hot, about 5 minutes. Scrape rack clean with wire brush.

3. *For the fruit and vegetables:* Toss pineapple and peppers with 1½ tablespoons olive oil in medium bowl and season with salt and pepper. Brush onions with remaining oil and season with salt and pepper. Using eight 12-inch metal skewers, thread each skewer with a pineapple piece, a stack of onion, a cube of meat (skewering as if it were an uncut cube), and one piece of each kind of pepper, and then repeat this sequence two more times. Brush any oil remaining in bowl over skewers.

4. Grill kebabs directly over coals, uncovered, until meat is well browned, grill marked, and cooked to medium-rare, about 7 minutes (or about 8 minutes for medium), turning each kabob every 1¾ minutes to brown all sides. Transfer kebabs to serving platter, squeeze lemon or lime wedges over kebabs, if desired; serve immediately.

GAS-GRILLED BEEF KEBABS

Follow step 1 in recipe for Charcoal-Grilled Beef Kebabs. Turn all burners on grill to high, close lid, and heat grill until hot, 10 to 15 minutes. With wire brush, scrape cooking grate clean. Continue with recipe by completing step 3, and then grill kebabs, covered, until well browned, grill marked, and cooked to medium-rare, about 8 minutes (or about 9 minutes for medium), turning each kabob every 2 minutes to brown all sides.

BEEF KEBABS WITH ASIAN FLAVORS

Follow recipe for Charcoal-Grilled Beef Kebabs or Gas-Grilled Beef Kebabs, substituting 3 tablespoons vegetable oil and 1 tablespoon Asian sesame oil for olive oil in marinade and adding 1½ teaspoons minced fresh ginger, 2 tablespoons soy sauce, 1 teaspoon sugar, ½ teaspoon red chile flakes, and 2 minced scallions to oil and garlic mixture. Continue with recipe, substituting an equal amount of vegetable oil for olive oil for fruit and vegetables.

SOUTHWESTERN BEEF KEBABS

Follow recipe for Charcoal-Grilled Beef Kebabs or Gas-Grilled Beef Kebabs, adding ½ teaspoon ground cumin, ½ teaspoon chili powder, 1 minced chipotle chile en adobo, and 2 tablespoons minced cilantro leaves to oil and garlic mixture.

Anne Yamanaka lives and cooks in Torrance, California.

Chicken Marsala Perfected

The secrets? The right pan, lots of heat, sweet Marsala—and no stock.

⋟ BY JULIA COLLIN ⋞

Marsala has never been a glamorous wine. It bears the name of its hometown, a seaport on the western coast of Sicily, once mockingly dubbed "the dump" by Italians from neighboring wine-making regions. In the early 1800s, a marketing campaign touted Marsala as a less expensive alternative to Madeira and sherry. As sales soared, it quickly made its way into Italian kitchens, where classic dishes such as chicken Marsala were created. Nowadays, chicken Marsala is an Italian restaurant staple. After having several disappointing encounters with this dish involving watery sauces, flaccid mushrooms, and pale, stale chicken, I realized that chicken Marsala was being taken for granted. It was in need of a rescue.

While all of the recipes I found listed the same three ingredients—breast of chicken, mushrooms, and Marsala—their cooking methods differed. Some called for simmering the chicken and mushrooms in Marsala, which resulted in flavors that were waterlogged and bland. Others recommended cooking everything in separate pans, creating not only a messy kitchen but a dish with disjointed flavors. Yet others had the cook sauté everything in the same pan, but sequentially. The clear winner turned out to be the classic, in which the meat is sautéed first and then moved to a warm oven while the browned bits left in the pan are splashed with wine and mounted with butter to create a sauce. With this decided, I focused on perfecting the sautéed chicken and developing the sauce.

In his article "How to Sauté Chicken" (*Cook's*, September/October 1993), Stephen Schmidt explained that the most important steps include getting the skillet incredibly hot and patting the chicken dry with paper towels before dusting with a light coating of flour. Using these pointers as a guide, I sautéed with a variety of oils and with butter to find that vegetable oil was the least likely to burn and splatter.

My next task was to figure out how to get the mushrooms crisp and brown without burning the drippings left from the sautéed chicken. One way to do this, I thought, would be to add more fat to the pan and scrape the browned bits off the bottom before cooking the mushrooms. So I tried cooking small pieces of pancetta (Italian bacon that has been cured but not smoked) directly after the chicken. Just as I had thought, the fat rendered from the pancetta prevented the chicken drippings from burning while providing

the oil necessary for sautéing the mushrooms—not to mention adding a meaty, pepper-flavored punch to the sauce, which I now felt prepared to tackle.

Since there are several types and grades of Marsala wine, I conducted a taste test before doing any cooking, trying imported and California brands of both the sweet and dry varieties. I favored an imported wine, Sweet Marsala Fine, for its depth of flavor, smooth finish, and reasonable price tag. By reducing the wine, I found the silky, plush texture I was looking for in the final sauce. Knowing that stock is traditionally added to pan sauces for depth of flavor and body, I tested a variety of stock-to-Marsala ratios. Again and again my tasters preferred a sauce made only from wine, slightly reduced. The stock simply got in the way of the Marsala's distinctive zip.

All I needed to do now was round out the final flavors. Some lemon juice tempered the Marsala's sweetness, while one clove of garlic and a teaspoon of tomato paste rounded out the middle tones. Last, I found that four tablespoons of unsalted butter whisked in at the end added a dreamlike finish and beautiful sheen. Here was a chicken Marsala that no one would take for granted.

We preferred the sweet Marsala (left) over the dry (right) for the body, soft edges, and smooth finish it added to the sauce.

CHICKEN MARSALA
SERVES 4

- 1 cup all-purpose flour
- 4 boneless, skinless chicken breasts (about 5 ounces each)
- Salt and ground black pepper
- 2 tablespoons vegetable oil
- 2½ ounces pancetta (about 3 slices), cut into pieces 1 inch long and ⅛ inch wide
- 8 ounces white mushrooms, sliced (about 2 cups)
- 1 medium garlic clove, minced (about 1 teaspoon)
- 1 teaspoon tomato paste
- 1½ cups sweet Marsala
- 1½ tablespoons juice from 1 small lemon
- 4 tablespoons unsalted butter, cut into 4 pieces, softened
- 2 tablespoons chopped fresh parsley leaves

1. Adjust oven rack to lower-middle position,

place large heatproof dinner plate on oven rack, and heat oven to 200 degrees. Heat 12-inch heavy-bottomed skillet over medium-high heat until very hot (you can hold your hand 2 inches above pan surface for 3 to 4 seconds), about 3 minutes. Pat chicken breasts dry. Meanwhile, place flour in shallow baking dish or pie plate. Season both sides of chicken cutlets with salt and pepper; working one piece at a time, coat both sides with flour. Lift breast from tapered end and shake to remove excess flour; set aside. Add oil to hot skillet and heat until shimmering. Place floured cutlets in single layer in skillet and cook until golden brown, about 3 minutes. Using tongs, flip cutlets and cook on second side until golden brown and meat feels firm when pressed with finger, about 3 minutes longer. Transfer chicken to heated plate and return plate to oven.

2. Return skillet to low heat and add pancetta; sauté, stirring occasionally and scraping pan bottom to loosen browned bits until pancetta is brown and crisp, about 4 minutes. With slotted spoon, transfer pancetta to paper towel–lined plate. Add mushrooms and increase heat to medium-high; sauté, stirring occasionally and scraping pan bottom, until liquid released by mushrooms evaporates and mushrooms begin to brown, about 8 minutes. Add garlic, tomato paste, and cooked pancetta; sauté while stirring until tomato paste begins to brown, about 1 minute. Off heat, add Marsala; return pan to high heat and simmer vigorously, scraping browned bits from pan bottom, until sauce is slightly syrupy and reduced to about 1¼ cups, about 5 minutes. Off heat, add lemon juice and any accumulated juices from chicken; whisk in butter 1 tablespoon at a time. Season to taste with salt and pepper, and stir in parsley. Pour sauce over chicken and serve immediately.

Cooking Perfect Pasta Every Time

Perhaps no simple cooking task is accompanied by more tips and tricks than boiling pasta. We decided to put them all to the test.

⇒ BY MARYELLEN DRISCOLL ⇐

A well-known chef once confessed to me that he did not know what difference it made to add olive oil to the water when cooking pasta—but he always did it anyway, because that's what his Italian grandmother did. Like this chef, many of us follow pasta cooking methods blindly. So at *Cook's* we decided to take a keen look at the method and rituals around cooking dried pasta. After collecting all the recipes we could find, from chefy to folkloric, the primary questions we ended up with were these: Do you have to start with cold water? Is salt necessary in the cooking water? How about oil? How thoroughly do you drain the pasta? What happens if you rinse after draining? Does the type of pan matter?

Of Water, Oil, and Salt

I had always been told that it is important to start with cold water when cooking pasta but confess that I haven't always followed that rule. Certainly the temptation to fill a pasta pot with hot tap water is strong. Depending on how hot your tap water is, it can cut in half the time it takes the pot of water to reach a boil. But tradition holds that this is a bad idea, that it can make the pasta taste less fresh or give it an "off" taste.

But when we cooked side-by-side batches of pasta starting with cold tap water and hot tap water, no one on our tasting panel could tell the difference. So I talked to Darren Fitzgerald, general manager of Aqua Science, a water treatment consulting firm in Clifton Park, New York. Fitzgerald said that the common misconception is that hot tap water can pick up "off" tastes from a hot water heater. Hot tap water does have the potential to taste "off," he said, but this depends more on the water itself than on your hot water heater. When being heated, organic compounds in water, such as iron or manganese, can oxidize; this oxidation has the potential to cause discoloring or an "off" taste. So I tried the side-by-side test again at my home, where the water is problematically hard. I still did not taste a difference.

Of course the other nagging question around water, pasta, and corner cutting is, how much water is enough? Many cooks tend to skimp, for the obvious reason that the less water you use the faster it comes to a boil. To start testing this variable, we cooked a pound of pasta in two quarts of water and discovered two major problems straight

An inexpensive pasta fork is the only pasta gadget we liked.

off. First, the water tends to foam up and boil over the pan edges. Second, the pieces of pasta are more inclined to stick together.

Dr. Patricia Berglund, director of the Northern Crops Institute in Fargo, North Dakota, explained the reasons behind these problems. Pasta, Berglund explained, consists primarily of starch but also contains about 10 percent protein. For dried pasta to make the change from its brittle state to a tender, toothsome noodle, the starch granules must absorb enough hot water to make them burst, thereby giving pasta its tenderness, while the small amount of protein "sets up" to provide the noodle with its characteristic "bite." I noticed that between absorption and evaporation a quart or more of water can be lost in the process of cooking one pound of pasta. During the cooking process, a lot of starch also leaches out into the cooking water. Without enough water to dilute the leached starch,

Berglund said, the pieces of pasta will be more inclined to stick together and the water will foam up, which is precisely what we observed. So we recommend that you not skimp on the water—use at least four quarts per pound of pasta.

While ample water proved key to preventing pasta from sticking, we also found (no great surprise) that frequent stirring makes a difference. It is particularly important to stir the moment the pasta goes into the water. Otherwise, pasta can get remarkably comfortable stuck to the pan bottom or nestled up against its kind. In most cases any kind of spoon or even a pair of tongs will do for stirring. For long noodles, like spaghetti, I found the tines of a pasta fork to be most effective in separating the strands that tend to stick together (see "Pasta Paraphernalia," page 15).

Of course, what many people do to prevent sticking is add oil to the boiling water. We tried this repeatedly and determined that oil definitely did not minimize pasta's sticking potential while cooking. What best keeps noodles from sticking is not oil, but cooking in a large quantity of water—and the method of saucing. Americans tend to fill a bowl with pasta and then glop the sauce on top. Italians toss the just-cooked pasta and the sauce together. This evenly distributes the sauce and, in effect, helps to prevent sticking.

As with oil, opinions vary widely about whether salt should be added to the cooking water. Other than contributing to flavor, salt had no discernible effect on the pasta or the cooking process itself; in fact, the small amounts of salt we added to the water never increased the boiling point. As for flavor, every participating taster found the addition of one tablespoon of salt to be over the top once you tossed an already-seasoned sauce with the pasta. While a couple of tasters preferred no salt at all in the water, the overall opinion was that 1½ teaspoons salt to 4 quarts of water worked best to round out the pasta flavor.

When Is It Done?

Most important to the cooking process is determining when the pasta is done, or al dente. We cooked up a number of pasta types made by a variety of manufacturers and found that overall, the timing on the box instructions tends to be too long. We also found that the old, curious trick of tossing a noodle against the wall (which really only applies to spaghetti or fettucine noodles) isn't very accurate. The most surefire test is simply biting into the pasta starting about three minutes before the package directions indicate doneness. Under-cooked pasta will have a clearly visible white core, making it crunchy in the center. When it's al dente, which translates as "to the tooth," it should have some bite to it but still be tender throughout. The white core may be just faintly visible.

While there is no exact science to determining doneness and each person has different preferences as to when pasta is "done," taste-testing the pasta once or twice every minute within the last few minutes of cooking helps a cook to gain a better sense for when the pasta is "just right." The pasta will continue to soften a bit as you drain and sauce it, so pull it off the flame about 30 seconds before you think it will be perfectly cooked.

The only time you might want to rinse drained pasta is if you plan on making pasta salad. Rinsing flushes starch from the surface of the noodles, which causes two problems. First, starch helps the sauce adhere to the pasta; without it, the sauce can drain off and pool at the bottom of the bowl. Second, rinsing cools down the noodles, which are best served hot.

Finally, some pasta aficionados warn against shaking the strainer after draining the pasta. As with the recommendation against rinsing, there is some cause for this. Shaking drains off some of the starchy moisture that helps the sauce cling to the pasta. But don't worry if by impulse you shake the strainer; it is no grave offense. I found that you lose only about two tablespoons of liquid.

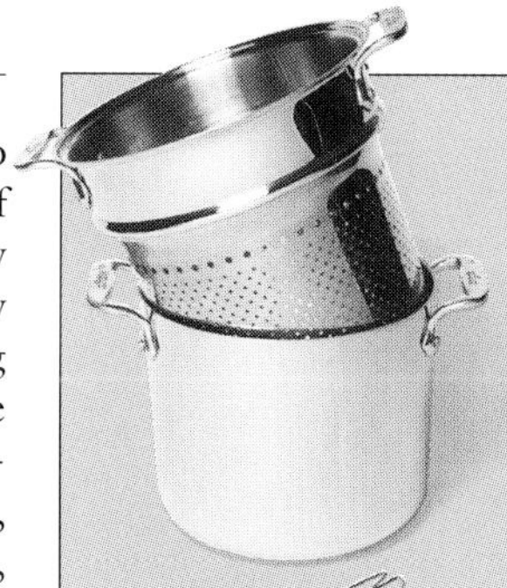

HOW TO COOK PASTA

It's best to combine pasta and sauce when both are hot and fresh, so if your sauce requires long cooking, have it nearly complete when you start cooking the pasta. For many simple sauces, such as the one below, pasta and sauce can be cooked simultaneously.

Bring 4 quarts water to rolling boil in 6-quart (or larger) stockpot or Dutch oven. Add 1½ teaspoons salt and 1 pound dried pasta; stir to separate noodles. Cover pot and return to boil. Remove cover and boil pasta, stirring frequently to keep noodles separate and tasting for doneness 3 minutes short of cooking time indicated on box. If not done, taste every 30 seconds until pasta is just shy of al dente—that is, the noodles are tender but resist slightly more than desired (an opaque white core should be faintly visible in the noodle you bit into). If necessary for sauce, reserve ½ cup pasta cooking water (as suggested in following sauce recipe); drain pasta in large colander for 30 seconds without shaking. Transfer

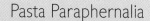

Pasta Paraphernalia

Nowadays cookware stores and catalogs contain a mind-boggling array of pots, utensils, and gadgets for cooking pasta. I tried a wide variety and was surprised by what I found out.

Pot with Perforated Insert I have to confess that I don't understand the growing popularity of these "pasta pots." I tried both the eight-quart "Multi Pot," which goes for about $45, and the All-Clad seven-quart "Pasta Pentola," selling at a steep $269.

To get four quarts of water in the Multi-Pot insert, you must fill the pan with six quarts of water. If you do that, we found, the pot is prone to boiling over. The All-Clad insert is an inch smaller in diameter than the 8½-inch diameter pot and sits 6 inches below the pan edge. It has a deceptive 2½-inch lip that sits above the pot edge, making it look as if it has a much greater capacity. In fact, as it turns out, the insert to this seven-quart, $200-plus pot has a capacity for holding only three quarts of water; add any more and the water begins to boil over.

Mesh Inserts The inexpensive mesh inserts sold in cookware stores proved much too small to be useful. They also tend to bob out of the water, which creates a suction at the bottom of the pan. When the suction releases, gurgles of boiling water are hurled from the pan.

Pasta Pronto This pan takes a different approach to the issue of straining pasta. It has a perforated "strainer lid" with handles that swivel to hold the lid in place. It seems clever, but the handles do not actually lock the lid in place, your grip does. Once you tilt the pan to strain, the grip can become awkward. I lost my grip once, and my sink was not so clean that I dared try to salvage the fallen noodles.

Strainer Plate Similarly risky was a crescent-shaped perforated stainless plate meant to fit around the pot edge for straining. We found that it fit comfortably only with pans of certain sizes, and, again, sureness of grip was essential.

Pasta Rakes The tines on the wooden versions of these rakes, designed to retrieve pasta, tend to fall out over time. The tines on the stainless variety are welded in. But why spend $24 on a single-purpose utensil when a $5 pair of tongs works just fine?

Pasta Tongs Again, why pay $14 on a pasta-particular utensil when an inexpensive pair of all-purpose tongs will toss and serve just as well? In addition, the handle on this utensil is too short for fetching noodles out of hot cooking water.

Pasta Forks This is the only pasta-specific tool that we found to be useful. It effectively combs through long, sticky strands of noodles to separate them. The wood variety tends to be clunky and is prone to splitting with use, but both the plastic and stainless steel versions work fine. —M.E.D.

pasta to now-empty cooking pot or to warm serving bowl; toss with sauce and serve immediately.

PASTA WITH GARLIC, OIL, AND TOASTED BREAD CRUMBS
SERVES 4 TO 6 AS A MAIN COURSE

Choose a long, slender pasta shape such as linguine or spaghetti for this sauce.

1	pound dried linguine or spaghetti
1½	teaspoons salt (for pasta), plus 1 teaspoon for sauce
1	tablespoon unsalted butter
¼	cup dry bread crumbs
½	ounce Parmesan cheese, grated (about 2 tablespoons)
3	medium garlic cloves, minced (about 1 tablespoon)
¼	cup extra-virgin olive oil
½	teaspoon red pepper flakes
¼	cup dry vermouth
	Ground black pepper

1. Adjust oven rack to middle position, place large ovensafe serving bowl on rack, and heat oven to 200 degrees. Prepare pasta according to "How to Cook Pasta," reserving ½ cup pasta cooking water before draining.

2. Heat butter in heavy-bottomed 10-inch skillet over medium-high heat until foaming. Add bread crumbs and cook, stirring frequently, until golden brown, toasted, and fragrant, 2 to 3 minutes. Transfer crumbs to small bowl and mix in cheese and ½ teaspoon minced garlic; set aside. Wipe out now-empty skillet with large wad of paper towels.

3. Mix remaining minced garlic with 1 teaspoon water. Heat olive oil, garlic, and pepper flakes in cleaned skillet over medium heat until fragrant, about 2 minutes. Add vermouth, reserved pasta cooking water, remaining 1 teaspoon salt, and pepper to taste; cook to blend flavors, about 1 minute longer. Toss pasta and sauce in warm serving bowl; sprinkle bread crumbs over and serve immediately.

An Illustrated Guide to Tender Steaks

There are a lot of steaks to choose from, which can make things very confusing. Here's exactly what you get for your money when you buy each particular steak.

BY DAWN YANAGIHARA WITH JOHN WILLOUGHBY

It's not easy to select a steak from the supermarket meat case. Steaks come in all different shapes and sizes, are sold at varying prices, and are often slapped with bold, bright "Great for Grilling" stickers that vie for your attention. To further confuse matters, steak cuts often go by different regional names. Consequently, turning to cookbooks is sometimes of no help, and asking a supermarket butcher for a steak by name can result in frustration. Marketers have also invented fanciful names for different steaks, further muddying the water.

Here we try to make sense of it all. We identify the most common tender steaks found in the supermarket,

explain what section of the steer each comes from, and advise you about its qualities and most common aliases. We also rate the steak cuts for tenderness and flavor (★★★★ being best) and cost ($$$$ being most expensive).

The term *steak* refers to any thin cut of meat, but not all steaks are suitable for quick high-heat grilling, searing, or pan-frying. Here we limit ourselves to those steaks that are best suited for a quick sear in a hot pan or a sizzling stint on a grill. We have not included hanger and skirt steaks, both of which we like, because they are almost impossible to find in grocery stores. London broil is often gone missing, too, but for a different reason: London broil is not a

particular type of steak but a method of cooking and cutting the meat. If you see steak in the supermarket that is labeled "London Broil," it may be anything from a shoulder steak to a top round steak.

Making the Grade

There are eight USDA (U.S. Department of Agriculture) beef grades, but most everything available to consumers falls into the top three: Prime, Choice, and Select. The grades classify the meat according to fat marbling and age, which are relatively accurate predictors of palatability; they have nothing to do with freshness or purity. Grading is strictly voluntary on

the part of the meat packer. If it is graded, the meat should bear a USDA stamp indicating the grade, but it may not be visible. Ask the butcher when in doubt.

In our blind tasting of rib-eye steaks from all three grades, Prime ranked first for its tender, buttery texture and rich beefy flavor; it was discernibly fattier. Choice came in second, with solid flavor and a little more chew. The Select steak was tough and stringy, with flavor that was only "acceptable." The lesson here is this: when you're willing to splurge, a Prime steak is worth the money, but a Choice steak that exhibits a moderate amount of marbling is a fine and more affordable option.

CONSUMER BEEF GRADES

Prime
Prime meat is heavily marbled with intramuscular fat, which makes for a tender, flavorful steak. A very small percentage (about 2 percent) of graded beef is graded Prime. Prime meats are most often served in restaurants or sold in high-end grocery stores and butcher shops.

Choice
The majority of graded beef is graded Choice. Choice beef is moderately marbled with intramuscular fat, but within the category there are varying levels of marbling.

Select
Select beef has little marbling. The small amount of intramuscular fat can make Select meats drier, tougher, and less flavorful than the two higher grades.

CHARACTERISTICS OF PRIMAL CUT STEAKS

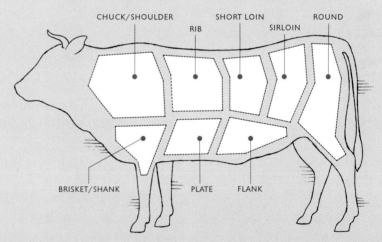

CHUCK/SHOULDER • RIB • SHORT LOIN • SIRLOIN • ROUND • BRISKET/SHANK • PLATE • FLANK

Chuck Steaks The chuck section, or shoulder area, includes ribs 1 through 5 as well as the shoulder blade bone. Most steaks cut from the chuck area are not suitable for grilling or quick high-heat cooking—some chuck steaks are downright tough and others may contain unpleasant amounts of gristle and fat.

Rib Steaks The rib section is located just behind the chuck, or shoulder area, and contains ribs 6 through 12. Its claim to fame is the prime rib roast. The steaks from the rib section are of high quality, with a rich, smooth texture and pockets of fat in the meat.

Short Loin Steaks The short loin section is located behind the rib section, in the middle area of the back. Steaks cut from the short loin are of very high quality. The

tenderloin, renowned for its buttery texture, extends through the short loin and is found in the T-bone and porterhouse steaks that are cut from this section.

Sirloin Steaks The sirloin section is just behind the short loin section and is sometimes referred to as the hip area. Sirloin steaks are fairly large but thin, and the meat is only moderately tender with decent flavor. The meat tends to be lean and rather dry, but it is a good value.

Flank Steak The flank is located on the underside belly area, directly below the short loin and sirloin. Steaks from this section have a rich, beefy flavor but must be sliced thinly and on the bias to counteract their chewy texture and long grain.

Top Blade

TENDERNESS ★ ★ ★
FLAVOR ★ ★ ★
COST $

➤ These small steaks are cut from the shoulder area of the cow. Top blade steaks are tender, but each has a line of gristle running down the center. They are inexpensive and perfectly suited to grilling or sautéing. Top blade steak is often called flatiron steak or blade steak.

RIB STEAKS

Rib

TENDERNESS ★ ★ ★
FLAVOR ★ ★ ★
COST $ $ $

➤ Imagine a prime rib roast at a hotel buffet or banquet. A rib steak is a steak cut from that rib roast, with the curved rib bone attached. Rib steaks are less prevalent than the boneless version, the rib eye.

Rib Eye

TENDERNESS ★ ★ ★
FLAVOR ★ ★ ★
COST $ $ $

➤ A rib-eye steak is a rib steak with the bone removed. Sans bone, the steak has an oval shape with a narrow strip of meat that curves around one end. Rib-eye steaks, like other steaks from the rib section, contain large pockets of fat and have a rich, smooth texture. Rib eye is often known as Spencer steak in the West and Delmonico steak in New York.

SHORT LOIN STEAKS

Top Loin

TENDERNESS ★ ★ ★
FLAVOR ★ ★ ★
COST $ $ $

➤ This long, narrow, triangular steak may be sold bone-in or boneless. Its most common bone-in alias is shell steak. Boneless top loin is also known as strip steak, hotel steak, sirloin strip steak (don't be confused—it's not cut from the sirloin, see below), Kansas City strip, and New York strip. The top loin steak is a bit chewy, with a noticeable grain, and is slightly less fatty than the rib or rib-eye steak.

Tenderloin

TENDERNESS ★ ★ ★ ★
FLAVOR ★
COST $ $ $ $

➤ The tenderloin, a long, cylindrical muscle that is the most tender meat on the cow, may be cut into a number of different steaks, each of which has its own name but all of which are very expensive, since Americans prize tenderness above all else in their steaks. Chateaubriand is a 3-inch-thick steak cut from the thickest part of the tenderloin, usually large enough to serve two. Filet, filet mignon, or tenderloin steak is typically 1 to 2 inches thick, cut from the narrow end of the tenderloin. Tournedos are the smallest tenderloin steaks, about an inch thick, cut toward the tip end. Tenderloin steaks are extremely tender but are not known for having much beefy flavor.

T-Bone

TENDERNESS ★ ★ ★
FLAVOR ★ ★ ★
COST $ $ $

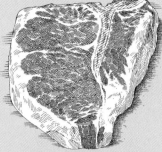

➤ The T-shaped bone in this steak separates the long, narrow strip of top loin and a small piece of tenderloin. Since it contains top loin and tenderloin meat, the T-bone is well balanced for texture and flavor.

Porterhouse

TENDERNESS ★ ★ ★
FLAVOR ★ ★ ★
COST $ $ $

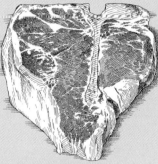

➤ The porterhouse is really just a huge T-bone steak with a larger tenderloin section. It is cut farther back in the animal than the T-bone steak. Like the T-bone, the porterhouse, with both top loin and tenderloin sections, has well-balanced flavor and texture.

SIRLOIN STEAKS

Round-Bone or Shell Sirloin

TENDERNESS ★ ★
FLAVOR ★ ★
COST $

➤ Several steaks are cut from the sirloin, or hip, section; moving from the front to the rear of the steer, they are pin- or hip-bone steak, flat-bone steak, round-bone steak, and wedge-bone steak. Of these, the round bone is best; the others are rarely found in supermarkets. Shell sirloin steak is simply a round-bone sirloin steak that has had the small piece of tenderloin removed. It is most commonly found in the Northeast and is sometimes called New York sirloin. Do not confuse sirloin steaks with the superior top loin steak, which is sometimes called sirloin strip steak.

Top Sirloin

TENDERNESS ★ ★
FLAVOR ★ ★
COST $

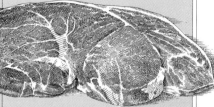

➤ This steak is merely a boneless shell sirloin steak. It is sometimes sold as boneless sirloin butt steak or top sirloin butt center cut steak. Again, do not confuse this steak with top loin steak, which is sometimes called sirloin strip steak.

FLANK STEAK

Flank

TENDERNESS ★ ★
FLAVOR ★ ★ ★ ★
COST $ $

➤ Flank steak is a large, thin, flat cut with a distinct longitudinal grain. To minimize the stringy, chewy nature of flank steak, it should not be cooked past medium and should always be sliced thinly across the grain. It is usually sold whole, although some grocery stores package flank steaks cut into smaller portions. Flank steak is sometimes called jiffy steak.

Illustration: John Burgoyne

Sweet Pea Soup

Partially ground frozen peas cooked with lettuce leaves make a quick, all-season sweet pea soup.

≥ BY KAY RENTSCHLER ≤

This simple soup is a pleasing pale, creamy green and full of subtle flavor nuances.

With the changing season, one warmth I welcome is a soup of pureed peas and lettuce. Coming out of winter, my palate numbed by garlic and red wine, I find the mild but satisfying flavors of this soup a lovely change from heavier fare.

A classic soup, sweet pea soup was originally prepared by stewing fresh blanched peas, leeks, and tendrils of lettuce briefly in butter, moistening them with white veal stock, and passing them through a fine sieve. The soup was then finished with cream and seasoned with fresh chervil.

I wanted to come up with a quick and delicious version of this soup, minus the laborious techniques, so I looked at several modern versions. Many introduced new ingredients, largely dismissing the veal stock in favor of chicken and adding split peas or sugar snap peas to the mix. Most also moved into the arena of frozen peas. Lacking in gelatinous veal stock, these new recipes were obliged to include a bit of thickener in the form of egg yolk, potatoes, or flour. Fresh mint typically replaced chervil. Of the handful of such recipes that I tried, though, most either completely lacked pea flavor or attained this flavor only by sacrificing color or body.

What I was looking for was something different—an easy version of this popular soup that had the same fundamental virtues as the original. Flavor, color, and texture all bear equally on the success or failure of this soup. My challenge was to cook the pea quickly enough to preserve its vivid color and to achieve a puree of spectacular smoothness without incurring the loss of flavor sometimes associated with sieving away vegetable bits in short-cooked soups.

The obvious starting point was the pea itself. For those of us without gardens, the long-awaited season of fresh peas is often disappointing. Grocery store pods can conceal tough, starchy pellets worthy of neither the price they command nor the effort they occasion. So when I began this recipe, I headed not down the garden path but up the frozen foods aisle.

From the pea I ventured to aromatics. Because the flavor of the peas is delicate and easily overwhelmed, I wanted to minimize any additions. Experimenting with onions, leeks, and shallots sautéed in butter (unquestionably the most pea-compatible fat in terms of flavor), I found onions a bit too strong, but shallots and leeks equally agreeable—delicate and sweet, like the peas themselves.

The means of introducing peas to the soup now became critical. The fun of eating whole peas—breaking through the crisp, springy hull to the sweet pea paste—goes missing in a smooth pea soup, where the listless hulls become an impediment to enjoyment and so must be removed altogether. I discovered that only the starchy centers of the peas can be pureed and that in sautéing or simmering them first to soften their skins, I invariably overcooked them. Additions such as sugar snap peas or snow peas sounded interesting but actually added little flavor.

It occurred to me that if I pureed the peas before putting them into the soup and infused them briefly in the simmering liquid, I might get to the heart of the pea right off. Toward that end I processed partially frozen peas in the food processor and simmered them briefly in the soup base to release their starch and flavor quickly. At this juncture, finding the puree a trifle thin, I doubled back and added two tablespoons of flour to the sautéed aromatics to give the base a little body. A few ounces of Boston lettuce added along with the peas gave the soup a marvelous frothy texture when pureed. (To achieve optimal texture, the soup still needed to be passed through a sieve.) A bit of heavy cream, salt, and pepper was the only finish required.

CREAMY GREEN PEA SOUP
MAKES ABOUT 6 1/2 CUPS, SERVING 4 TO 6

Remove the peas from the freezer just before starting the soup so that when you are ready to process them, as the stock simmers, they will be only partially thawed. To preserve its delicate flavor and color, this soup is best served immediately.

    4   tablespoons unsalted butter
    8   medium shallots (about 5 ounces), minced
        (about I cup), or I medium leek, white and light
        green parts chopped fine (about 1 1/3 cups)
    2   tablespoons all-purpose flour
 3 1/2 cups canned low-sodium chicken broth
 1 1/2 pounds frozen peas (about 4 1/2 cups), partially
        thawed at room temperature for 10 minutes
        (see note above)
   12   small leaves Boston lettuce (about 3 ounces)
        from I small head, leaves washed and dried
  1/2   cup heavy cream
        Salt and ground black pepper

1. Heat butter in large saucepan over low heat until foaming; add shallots or leeks and cook, covered, until softened, 8 to 10 minutes, stirring occasionally. Add flour and cook, stirring constantly, until thoroughly combined, about 30 seconds. Stirring constantly, gradually add chicken broth. Increase heat to high and bring to boil; reduce heat to medium-low and simmer 3 to 5 minutes.

2. Meanwhile, in workbowl of food processor fitted with steel blade, process partially thawed peas until coarsely chopped, about 20 seconds. Add peas and lettuce to simmering broth. Increase heat to medium-high, cover and return to simmer; simmer 3 minutes. Uncover, reduce heat to medium-low, and continue to simmer 2 minutes longer.

3. Working in 2 batches, puree soup in blender until smooth; strain into large bowl. Rinse out and wipe saucepan; return pureed mixture to saucepan and stir in cream. Heat mixture over low heat until hot, about 3 minutes. Season to taste with salt and pepper; serve immediately.

Croutons make a nice topping for this soup. For our "Buttered Croutons" recipe, go to Cook's Extra at cooksillustrated.com.

Best Deviled Eggs

We set out to perfect this traditional picnic standby.

≥ BY BARBARA BOURASSA AND BRIDGET LANCASTER ≤

When we set out to develop this recipe, we had in mind the deviled eggs of our childhood: perfectly cooked nests of egg whites cradling a creamy filling, made with simple ingredients and quickly whipped together. We remembered a filling balanced with the flavor of mayonnaise and a hint of spiciness, but no dominant egg overtones. We knew we didn't want a smooth, pasty, monotonous filling any more than we wanted a version reminiscent of chunky egg salad.

Since we were starting with the *Cook's* recipe for hard-cooked eggs (see "The Best Way to Hard-Cook an Egg," March/April 1999), we knew that half the work was already done. In that article, Maryellen Driscoll discovered the perfect way to hard-cook an egg: Place the eggs in cold water, bring the water just to a boil, remove the pan from the heat and let the eggs sit in the water for 10 minutes, then give them a brief rest in a bath of ice water. Our challenge was to find a recipe that would make the most of our perfectly cooked eggs.

We started by testing the main ingredient in most deviled egg recipes—mayonnaise. We tested eggs made with our favorite commercial mayonnaise (Hellmann's), Miracle Whip salad dressing, salad cream (a sweet British condiment similar in consistency to sour cream), butter (several recipes called for butter in addition to or instead of mayonnaise), and homemade mayonnaise. The eggs made with salad cream were acidic and offensive, while the eggs made partially or wholly with butter were dry and bland, and the homemade mayonnaise just wasn't worth the trouble. When it came to salad dressing versus mayonnaise, the results were mixed. In the interviews conducted after the tasting, we learned that the testers had chosen the eggs made with the ingredient they had grown up with and still associated with deviled eggs. But the majority went with mayonnaise, and that is what we preferred.

To be "deviled," the eggs needed some spiciness. Since mustard was the prevalent source of spicy flavor in most recipes, we made that our next test. We tested French's mustard (found on hot dogs everywhere); dry, or powdered, mustard; Dijon mustard; grainy mustard; and brown mustard. The winner was cracked country-style mustard, preferred just ahead of whole-grain mustard for its finer texture.

Next we turned to vinegar, another ingredient common to many recipes for deviled eggs. After testing six, we chose cider vinegar. In this case, 1½ teaspoons was just right; add more and that's all you'll taste.

Having made the "big" decisions, we moved on to the accent flavors. We tested sour cream, curry, Worcestershire sauce, and cayenne pepper. The version with sour cream dulled the impact of the accompanying ingredients, and even the smallest amount of curry dominated all the other flavors, so we left both out of our final recipe. Worcestershire sauce added a touch of savory pungency. Cayenne pepper is a good substitute, if you like a bit of heat.

While testing the easiest manner in which to fill the egg whites, we found that stuffing them as close to serving time as possible was key to a fresh, bright flavor. If last-minute preparation is not possible, prepare the eggs up to one day ahead and store the whites in an airtight container and the filling in a sealed zipper-lock plastic bag. Snip the corner of the bag, as shown below when ready to use.

CLASSIC DEVILED EGGS
MAKES 1 DOZEN FILLED EGG HALVES

If all of your egg white halves are in perfect shape, discard two. During testing we found it usual for a couple to rip at least slightly, which worked out well because it meant the remaining whites were very well stuffed. If you have a pastry bag, you can use it to fill the eggs with a large open-star tip or a large plain tip. If not, follow the directions below to improvise with a zipper-lock plastic bag.

- 7 large eggs, cold
- ¾ teaspoon grainy mustard
- 3 tablespoons mayonnaise
- 1½ teaspoons cider vinegar (or vinegar of your choice)
- ¼ teaspoon Worcestershire sauce
  Salt and ground black pepper

1. Place eggs in medium saucepan, cover with 1 inch of water, and bring to boil over high heat. Remove pan from heat, cover, and let stand 10 minutes. Meanwhile, fill medium bowl with 1 quart cold water and about 14 ice cubes (one tray). Transfer eggs to ice water with slotted spoon; let sit 5 minutes.

2. Peel eggs and slice each in half lengthwise with paring knife. Remove yolks to small bowl.

Arrange whites on serving platter, discarding two worst-looking halves. Mash yolks with fork until no large lumps remain. Add mustard, mayonnaise, vinegar, Worcestershire, and salt and pepper to taste; mix with rubber spatula, mashing mixture against side of bowl until smooth.

3. Fit pastry bag with large open-star tip. Fill bag with yolk mixture, twisting top of pastry bag to help push mixture toward tip of bag. Pipe yolk mixture into egg white halves, mounding filling about ½ inch above flat surface of whites. Serve immediately.

DEVILED EGGS WITH ANCHOVY AND BASIL

Rinse, dry, and finely chop 8 anchovy fillets. Mince 2 tablespoons basil leaves. Follow recipe for Basic Deviled Eggs, mixing anchovy fillets and 2 teaspoons minced basil into mashed yolks along with mustard, mayonnaise, vinegar, Worcestershire, and salt and pepper. Continue with recipe, sprinkling filled eggs with shredded basil.

DEVILED EGGS WITH TUNA, CAPERS, AND CHIVES

Drain and finely chop 2 ounces canned tuna (you should have about ½ cup). Rinse and drain 1 tablespoon capers; chop 1 tablespoon chives. Follow recipe for Basic Deviled Eggs, mixing tuna, capers, and 2 teaspoons chives into mashed yolks along with mustard, mayonnaise, vinegar, and salt and pepper. Omit Worcestershire. Continue with recipe, sprinkling filled eggs with remaining teaspoon chives.

Filling the eggs
If you don't own a pastry bag, spoon the yolk mixture into a sealable plastic bag. Snip a small piece from one corner of the bag and then gently squeeze the filling through the hole into the egg halves.

Quick Cream Biscuits

With high rise and light texture, biscuits made with a simple combination of heavy cream, flour, baking powder, and salt beat out more complicated recipes.

⇒ BY CHRISTOPHER KIMBALL ⇐

Biscuits made with cream rather than butter or shortening not only turn out lighter and fluffier, but are simpler to make as well. In fact, even confirmed non-bakers can easily make them.

Biscuits are the ultimate American bread. They are at home when baked in a Dutch oven over a campfire as well as in the most expensive restaurant oven. They were and are integral to Southern cooking, in which they have often been referred to as hot scratch biscuits, and they were standard fare in chuck wagons headed west and on New England farms. They even became part of music folklore in 1941 when the King Biscuit Flour Hour, a radio show devoted to the blues, made its debut.

Biscuits are also among the simplest of all breads. They are made from a mixture of flour, leavener (baking powder, soda, or sourdough starter), salt, fat (lard, butter, bacon fat, or vegetable shortening), and liquid (milk, buttermilk, sour milk, melted butter, or cream). To make them, one cuts fat into the dry ingredients, as when making a pie dough; the liquid is then stirred in until a dough forms. Biscuits are usually rolled out and cut, although they can also be shaped by hand or dropped onto a baking sheet by the spoonful.

So what's the problem? Well, for many cooks, cutting the butter or vegetable shortening into the flour is a nonstarter because they are not comfortable with the process. In addition, rolling out the dough is one of those recipe directives that immediately puts off many prospective bakers. As one food writer friend of mine said recently, "If I have to roll out dough, I won't make it." Others seem bewitched by refrigerated doughs such as Poppin' Fresh, which were introduced in the early 1950s and quickly supplanted the homemade version. The question is then, is there a great recipe for homemade biscuits that can be made quickly and easily and that does not require cutting fat into flour or rolling out dough?

I began with a basic recipe calling for two cups flour, two teaspoons baking powder, one tablespoon sugar, and one-half teaspoon salt. Now I had to figure out what to add to this mixture instead of butter or vegetable shortening to make a dough. I decided to try plain yogurt, sour cream, milk, milk combined with melted butter, and whipped heavy cream, an idea I borrowed from a scone recipe.

The biscuits made with yogurt and sour cream were a bit sodden in texture, those with the milk and milk/butter combination were tough and lifeless, and the whipped cream biscuit was too light, more confection than biscuit. This last approach also required another step—whipping the cream—which seemed like too much trouble for a simple recipe. So I tried using plain heavy cream, without whipping, and this biscuit was the best of the lot. (Cream biscuits are not my invention. I was introduced to them by James Beard, who includes such a recipe in his seminal work *American Cookery* (Little, Brown, 1972).

Next, I decided to do a blind tasting in the

STEP-BY-STEP | TWO WAYS TO SHAPE BISCUITS

For Rounds: Shape the dough into a round and cut with a biscuit cutter.

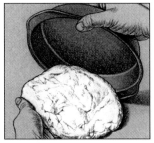

For Wedges: Press the dough into an 8-inch cake pan, then turn the dough out and cut it into 8 wedges.

Unlike traditional biscuits, cream biscuits benefit from relatively rough treatment. The biscuit at left, which was kneaded for 30 seconds before baking, rose higher than the one on the right, which was handled gently.

Cook's test kitchen, pitting the cream biscuits against my usual recipe, which requires cutting butter and vegetable shortening into the flour. The result? Being both lighter and more tender, the cream biscuits won.

Still, I was running into a problem with the shape of the biscuits—they spread far too much during baking. I have always followed Nika Hazelton's advice in *American Home Cooking* (Viking Press, 1980), where she warns the home cook against overworking the dough. In my experience (and hers) the best biscuits are made from dough that is handled lightly. But cream biscuits, being less sturdy than those made with butter or vegetable shortening, become soft and "melt" during baking. In this case, I thought, a little handling might not be such a bad thing.

So I baked up two batches: the first dough I patted out gingerly; the second dough I kneaded for 30 seconds until it was smooth and uniform in appearance. The results were remarkable. The more heavily worked dough produced much higher, fluffier biscuits than the lightly handled dough, which looked short and bedraggled.

I still ran into a problem, however, when one batch of biscuits had to sit for a few minutes while I waited for the oven to heat up. During baking, the dough spread, resulting in biscuits with bottoms too wide and tops too narrow. The solution was to pop the biscuits into the oven immediately after cutting. (I also tried preheating the baking sheet, but this only produced overcooked, almost burnt bottoms.) As for dough thickness, ¾ inch provides a remarkably high rise, more appealing than biscuits that start out ½ inch thick. I also discovered that it was best to add just enough cream to hold the dough together. A wet dough does not hold its shape as well during baking.

Although I find it easy enough to quickly roll out this dough and then cut it into rounds with a biscuit cutter, you can simply shape the dough with your hands or push it into the bottom of a standard loaf pan or an 8-inch cake pan. The dough can then be flipped onto the work surface and cut into squares or wedges with a knife or dough scraper.

I also tested making drop biscuits, a method in which the dough is simply scooped up and dropped onto a baking sheet. When I tried them with this batter, though, the biscuits did not rise very well and their shape was inferior. It was also more time-consuming to drop the batter in individual spoonfuls than to simply shape the dough in one piece.

My final ingredient tests included the sugar—the tasters felt that one tablespoon was a bit much, so we dropped it to two teaspoons—and the baking powder, which we found we could reduce to one teaspoon with no decrease in rise. For oven temperature, I tried 375, 400, and 425 degrees, and the latter was best for browning.

Now I had the simplest of biscuit recipes: whisk together the flour, baking powder, sugar, and salt in a medium bowl, add 1½ cups of heavy cream, form the dough, knead it for 30 seconds, cut it, and bake for 15 minutes at 425 degrees. The results will surprise you.

QUICK AND EASY CREAM BISCUITS
MAKES EIGHT 2½-INCH BISCUITS

Bake the biscuits immediately after cutting them; letting them stand for any length of time can decrease the leavening power and thereby prevent the biscuits from rising properly in the oven.

> 2 cups all-purpose flour
> 2 teaspoons sugar
> 1 teaspoon baking powder
> ½ teaspoon salt
> 1½ cups heavy cream

1. Adjust oven rack to upper-middle position and heat oven to 425 degrees. Line baking sheet with parchment paper.

2. Whisk together flour, sugar, baking powder, and salt in medium bowl. Add 1¼ cups cream and stir with wooden spoon until dough forms, about 30 seconds. Transfer dough from bowl to countertop, leaving all dry, floury bits behind in bowl. In 1 tablespoon increments, add up to ¼ cup cream to dry bits in bowl, mixing with wooden spoon after each addition, until moistened. Add these moistened bits to rest of dough and knead by hand just until smooth, about 30 seconds.

3. Following illustrations in box, page 20, cut biscuits into rounds or wedges. Place rounds or wedges on parchment-lined baking sheet and bake until golden brown, about 15 minutes, rotating baking sheet halfway through baking.

CREAM BISCUITS WITH FRESH HERBS

Use the herb of your choice in this variation.

Follow recipe for Quick and Easy Cream Biscuits, whisking 2 tablespoons minced fresh herbs into flour along with sugar, baking powder, and salt.

CREAM BISCUITS WITH CHEDDAR CHEESE

Follow recipe for Quick and Easy Cream Biscuits, stirring ½ cup (2 ounces) sharp cheddar cheese cut into ¼-inch pieces into flour along with sugar, baking powder, and salt. Increase baking time to 18 minutes.

CREAM BISCUITS WITH CRYSTALLIZED GINGER

Follow recipe for Quick and Easy Cream Biscuits, adding 3 tablespoons minced crystallized ginger to flour along with sugar, baking powder, and salt. Before baking, brush tops of biscuits with 1 tablespoon heavy cream and sprinkle with 1 tablespoon sugar.

Cinnamon Swirl Cream Biscuits
MAKES 8 MEDIUM BISCUITS

> 1 recipe Quick and Easy Cream Biscuits, prepared through step 2 and rolled into a 9 by 12-inch rectangle, about ⅜ inch thick
> 2 tablespoons dark brown sugar
> 2 teaspoons ground cinnamon
> 1 tablespoon butter, melted
> 1 tablespoon egg white
> ½ cup confectioners' sugar
> Dash vanilla extract

1. Stir together brown sugar and cinnamon in small bowl; set aside.

2. Brush surface of dough rectangle with melted butter and sprinkle evenly with brown sugar mixture. Following illustrations at right, roll, cut into 8 rounds, flatten, and arrange biscuits in ungreased 10-inch pie plate; bake until golden brown, about 25 minutes.

3. While biscuits are baking, whisk together egg white, confectioners' sugar, and vanilla in small bowl until smooth and glossy, about 1 minute. Following illustration at right, spread icing over hot biscuits.

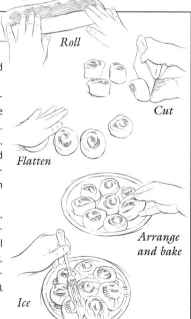

Roll

Cut

Flatten

Arrange and bake

Ice

Chewy, Fudgy Brownies

Baking brownies with a moist, velvety texture, a hint of chew, and deep chocolate flavor is no piece of cake. The secret lies in the perfect balance of ingredients and three different types of chocolate.

⇒ BY DAWN YANAGIHARA ⇐

Americans are passionate about brownies. Some are passionate about eating them, about a brownie's rich, chocolatey decadence. Others are passionate about a recipe, scrawled on a stained index card bequeathed to them by their mother, guaranteeing people like me that this family heirloom produces the best brownie of all.

I've sampled good brownies, I think, but I know I've never encountered my brownie paragon. And yet somehow I know exactly how the perfect brownie ought to taste and look. Those light cakey versions are not for me. I imagine a moist, dark, luscious interior with a firm, smooth, velvety texture that your teeth easily glide through but meet just a little resistance in chewing. My perfect brownie must pack an intense chocolate punch and have deep, resonant chocolate flavor, but it must fall just short of overwhelming the palate. It must not be so sweet as to make your teeth ache, and it must certainly have a thin, shiny, papery crust and edges that crisp during baking, offering a contrast with the brownie's moist center. With all of this in mind, I began my quest, determined to meet my brownie ideal.

My baking sense told me that the taste and texture of the brownies I sought lay in a delicate balance of the five ingredients basic to all brownie recipes: chocolate, flour, sugar, butter, and eggs. After gathering a number of recipes that promised to deliver a fudgy brownie, I made a select six that confirmed my expectations. The varying proportions of these five ingredients produced batches of brownies that were soft and pasty; dry and cakey; or chewy, like a Tootsie Roll. Chocolate flavor was divergent, too, ranging from intense but one-dimensional jolts to weak, muted passings on the palate. My next step was to cobble together a composite recipe that would incorporate the best traits of these six recipes. It would serve as the foundation for all of my testing.

These chewy, fudgy brownies are incredibly rich, so we recommend that you cut them into small squares for serving.

The two essential qualities I was looking for in these brownies were a chewy, fudgy texture and a rich chocolate flavor. I went to work on flavor first. After making the six initial test recipes and reading earlier *Cook's* articles on cream cheese brownies (January/February 1999) and chocolate cookies (September/October 1999), I knew that unsweetened chocolate was a good source of assertive chocolate flavor. Semisweet and bittersweet chocolates don't have much chocolate punch because of the large amount of sugar they contain. But this is also why they are smoother and milder. One of my favorite recipes from the initial test yielded a brownie with exceptional chocolate flavor; this recipe combined unsweetened and bittersweet chocolates, so to the composite recipe I tried adding varying amounts of the two chocolates. (Semisweet and bittersweet chocolates are not identical but can be exchanged for one another in many recipes depending on what's available at the supermarket; I'll refer to semisweet from here on because it's what I used when testing the recipes.)

Too much unsweetened chocolate and the brownies were sour and acrid, too much semisweet chocolate and they were one-dimensional and boring. I found that 5 ounces of semisweet and 2 ounces of unsweetened created just the right flavor balance. Next I thought to add some cocoa powder, which typically adds flavor but no harshness. I was pleased with this combination. The unsweetened chocolate laid a solid, intense chocolate foundation, the semisweet provided a mellow, even, sweet flavor, and the cocoa smoothed any rough edges and added depth and complexity. I tried both Dutch-processed cocoa and natural cocoa and found them to work equally well.

I then fiddled with the type and quantity of sugar needed to sweeten the brownies, given the amount and types of chocolate and cocoa they contained. In addition to white sugar, I tried brown sugar to see if it might add flavor, but it didn't. I also tried a bit of corn syrup, thinking it might add moistness and chew, but it only made the brownies wet and gummy and the crust dull (see "Crustily Ever After," page 23). Satisfied that white sugar was the best sweetener for the job, I tested varying amounts. I knew I didn't want overly sweet brownies. Too little sugar, though, left the brownies with a chocolate flavor that was dull, muted, and flat, much like mashed potatoes without salt. Just the right degree of sweetness was provided by 1¼ cups sugar; the flavor of the brownies was now spot-on.

Chew, Chew

Satisfied with the flavor of the brownies, I moved on to refining the texture, starting with flour. My composite recipe contained ¾ cup flour, but wanting to exhaust all reasonable quantities, I baked brownies with as little as ¼ cup and up to 1¼ cups, increasing the quantity in ¼ cup increments. The batch with the least amount of flour was like goopy, sticky, chocolate-flavored Spackle, so pasty it cemented your mouth shut. The one with 1¼ cups flour had good chew, but it verged on dry, and the chocolate flavor was light and muted. One cup was perfect. The chocolate flavor remained deep and rich, and the texture was fudgy, smooth, and dense, the moist crumb putting up a gentle resistance when chewed.

Butter was up next. Melting butter, rather than creaming it with sugar and eggs, makes for a dense, fudgy texture. Creaming produces an aerated batter, which bakes into lighter, cakier brownies. Had I questioned this baker's axiom after the initial test, in which all of the six recipes employ the melted butter technique, any doubts would be dispelled. But now the question of how much butter remained.

Semisweet chocolate contains more fat than unsweetened chocolate, yet many recipes that call exclusively for one type of chocolate frequently call for the same amount of butter (some 16 tablespoons) per cup of flour. As it stood, my working recipe used semisweet and unsweetened chocolate, cocoa, 1 cup flour, and 10 tablespoons butter. The texture of the brownies this recipe produced was moist and dense, albeit a bit sodden and pasty. Improvement came with eight tablespoons of butter. Minus these two tablespoons, the brownies shed their soggy, sodden quality but still remained moist and velvety.

With butter and flour set, I went to work on eggs. I tried as few as two and as many as six. Two eggs left the brownies dry and gritty and compromised the chocolate flavor. With four or more eggs, the brownies baked into cakey rubber erasers with an unattractive, high-domed, dull matte crust. Three was the magic number—the brownies were moist and smooth, with great flavor and delicate chew.

Toward a Still Better Brownie

I finalized the recipe by making adjustments to vanilla and salt and then began to examine other factors that might have an impact on the brownies. First I tried baking in a water bath, a technique used for delicate custards, reasoning that gentle heat might somehow improve texture. Not so. I got a grainy, sticky, puddinglike brownie.

I experimented with midrange oven temperatures. Three-hundred-fifty degrees did the job and did it relatively quickly, in about 35 minutes (many brownies bake for nearly an hour). As is the case with most other brownies, if baked too long, these brownies run the risk of drying out; they must be pulled from the oven when a toothpick inserted into the center comes out with some sticky crumbs clinging to it.

STEP-BY-STEP | LINING AND LIFTING

1. Line the baking pan with two sheets of foil placed perpendicular.

2. Use the foil handles to lift the cooked brownies from the pan.

After making more than 50 batches, I really began to appreciate an aspect of brownies quite beside their rich flavor and texture—with only a couple of bowls, a whisk, and a spatula, the batter can be mixed and in the oven in 10 minutes.

CHEWY, FUDGY TRIPLE CHOCOLATE BROWNIES
MAKES SIXTY-FOUR 1-INCH BROWNIES

Either Dutch-processed or natural cocoa works well in this recipe. These brownies are very rich, so we prefer to cut them into small squares for serving.

- 5 ounces semisweet or bittersweet chocolate, chopped
- 2 ounces unsweetened chocolate, chopped
- 8 tablespoons (1 stick) unsalted butter, cut into quarters
- 3 tablespoons cocoa powder
- 3 large eggs
- 1 1/4 cups sugar
- 2 teaspoons vanilla extract
- 1/2 teaspoon salt
- 1 cup all-purpose flour

1. Adjust oven rack to lower-middle position and heat oven to 350 degrees. Spray 8-inch square baking pan with nonstick vegetable cooking spray. Fold two 12-inch pieces of foil lengthwise so that they measure 7 inches wide. Fit one sheet in bottom of greased pan, pushing it into corners and up sides of pan; overhang will help in removal of baked brownies. Following illustration 1, above, fit second sheet in pan in same manner, perpendicular to first sheet. Spray foil with nonstick cooking spray.

2. In medium heatproof bowl set over a pan of almost-simmering water, melt chocolates and butter, stirring occasionally until mixture is smooth. Whisk in cocoa until smooth. Set aside to cool slightly.

3. Whisk together eggs, sugar, vanilla, and salt in medium bowl until combined, about 15 seconds. Whisk warm chocolate mixture into egg mixture; then stir in flour with wooden spoon until just combined. Pour mixture into prepared pan, spread into corners, and level surface with rubber spatula; bake until slightly puffed and toothpick inserted in center comes out with a small amount of sticky crumbs clinging to it, 35 to 40 minutes. Cool on wire rack to room temperature, about 2 hours, then remove brownies from pan using foil handles (see illustration 2, above). Cut

into 1-inch squares and serve. (Do not cut brownies until ready to serve; brownies can be wrapped in plastic and refrigerated up to 5 days.)

For our "Chocolate Espresso Brownies" variation, go to Cook's Extra at cooksillustrated.com.

Summer Berry Gratin

What could be simpler than buttered and sugared bread crumbs tossed over fresh berries and then baked for just 15 minutes?

≥ BY KAY RENTSCHLER ≤

Whether teardrop, globed, or beveled, ruby, indigo, or magenta, fresh berries are the jewels in summer's crown. I'm not talking about those specimens available year-round—boxcar strawberries with blanched centers, mouth-withering blueberries, blackberries with no juice. Instead, I refer to the procession of late spring and summer berries—those ripe, fleshy, sweet, perfumed, finger-staining, succulent specimens that return every year and visit us but briefly. You know the ones.

Nothing makes a person feel more virtuous than driving off with a crate of just-picked berries, and nothing feels more extravagant than eating enough of them out of hand to induce torpor. In the aftermath of our indulgence, most of us set about earnestly sealing freezer bags or making pies and cobblers, muffins and pancakes, jams and preserves—the traditional but often time-consuming projects associated with these dainty bites.

Sometimes, though, it's nice to strike a balance between the hastily improvised "berries and cream" ending to a meal and a fully orchestrated lattice-top pie. A fitting alternative is the fruit gratin. Quicker than a crisp, dressier than a shortcake, a gratin is a layer of fresh fruit piled into a shallow baking dish, gussied up with crumbs or sweetened fresh cheese, and run under a broiler. The topping browns and the fruit is warmed just enough to juice a bit.

I wanted to travel the simplest route to this summer dessert. So even though gratins can be made with all types of summer fruits, I confined my subject matter to berries (easy, no slicing), my topping to crumbs (easy, no mixing) and my ingredients to a minimum (five, to be precise).

I discovered straight off that a dish of this simplicity requires much attention. The berries, in whatever combination, had to be perfect: ripe, dry, unbruised, and clean. Woody and unyielding berries delivered indifferent results. No flavors coalesced, no juices were exchanged, nothing happened. Overripe or moldy berries, on the other hand, which found their way in among the others, disgraced the flavor of the gratin instantly. What's more, to cook correctly and to look and taste good, the berries needed to be of relatively similar size. Smallish strawberries halved once lengthwise complemented the other berry shapes.

Strawberries, raspberries, and blueberries were superb when used alone; they were also compatible in combination. Blackberries tasted best when paired with raspberries or blueberries. (For anyone lucky enough to have access to fresh currants, they would doubtless be wonderful with any of the other berries.) Four cups of berries—whatever the selection—fit nicely into a 9-inch glass or porcelain pie plate.

Then there were the crumbs. Cake and muffin crumbs—even stale ones—collapsed into the filling and disappeared. French chef Jacques Pépin uses dry croissant crumbs in his raspberry gratin. Translate croissant into American English and you come up with, well, white bread. So I tried both dried and fresh bread crumbs and dried and fresh croutons.

The dried breadcrumbs were granular and texturally at odds with the soft flesh of the berries. Croutons, too, were somewhat standoffish. Weary of this unproductive fussing, I took three pieces of soft white bread and tossed them into the food processor with a couple tablespoons of sugar and a little chunk of soft butter. The resulting fluffy crumbs embraced the berries like a fresh snowfall. Once broiled, the surface of the crumbs became lightly crunchy and the undercoat soft enough to absorb the berries' juices. I modified this combination only slightly by switching from white sugar to light brown and by adding a pinch of ground cinnamon—both for a small flavor bonus.

The berries themselves needed just a bit of sweetness to brighten them and coax forth their juices. A modest tablespoon of white sugar brought them to the fore. Many of my tasters also liked a tablespoon of kirsch (a clear cherry brandy) or another eau de vie tossed with the berries and sugar. Taken together on a spoon, the flavors of the gratin were soft but deeply pleasing. The clear berry tastes shone forth against the light, buttery crumbs, and the berries and crust formed a nice textural counterpoint.

Broiling the gratin, as I had been, required more vigilance than I deemed suitable, and often the browning of the crust was uneven. I thought perhaps a moderately high oven heat lasting a bit longer might melt the berries slightly and brown the crust more evenly while also needing less monitoring. This proved to be true: a 400-degree oven and 15 or 20 minutes gave me a chance to put the coffee on and whip a bit of cream or soften vanilla ice cream before the dome of the crust grew deep golden and the berries warm and fragrant.

FRESH BERRY GRATIN
SERVES 4 TO 6

Though a mixture of berries offers a wonderful combination of color, flavor, and texture, it's also fine to use just one or two types of berries. One-half pint of fresh berries equals about one cup of fruit. Later in the season, ripe, peeled peach or nectarine slices can be used in combination with blueberries or raspberries. We recommend using only fresh fruit, but if you must use frozen, raspberries are the best option. Do not thaw them before baking. Avoid using a metal pie pan that may react with the acidity of the fruit and impart an "off" metallic flavor. Serve the fruit gratin with lightly sweetened whipped cream or vanilla ice cream.

Fruit Mixture
- 4 cups mixed raspberries, blueberries, blackberries, and strawberries (hulled and left whole if small, halved lengthwise if medium, quartered lengthwise if large)
- 1 tablespoon sugar
- 1 tablespoon kirsch (optional) or other eau de vie
  Pinch salt

Topping
- 3 slices sandwich bread, each slice torn into quarters
- 2 tablespoons unsalted butter, softened
- 1/4 cup lightly packed light or dark brown sugar
  Pinch ground cinnamon

1. Adjust oven rack to lower-middle position and heat oven to 400 degrees. Toss fruit gently with sugar, kirsch (if using), and salt in medium nonreactive bowl and transfer to 9-inch glass or ceramic pie pan.

2. Pulse bread, butter, sugar, and cinnamon in bowl of food processor fitted with steel blade until mixture resembles coarse crumbs, about ten 1-second pulses. Sprinkle crumbs evenly over fruit and bake until crumbs are deep golden brown and fruit is hot, 15 to 20 minutes. Cool on wire rack 5 minutes and serve.

Basic Blenders Beat Upscale Rivals

Fancy features and a high price tag do not guarantee great performance.

⇒ BY ADAM RIED ⇐

Blenders today are far sleeker and more advanced than the harvest gold clunker I've used for nearly 20 years. To its credit, though, despite being neither a beauty nor a technological tour de force, old faithful has faultlessly churned out daiquiris every summer since it was new.

Nonetheless, modern blenders occasionally beckon me with their electronic touch-pad controls, great range of speeds, redesigned jars, and pulse and ice-crushing functions. The bells and whistles don't come cheap, though: many units cost $100 or more. Do all of these features really add up to a better blender that is worth the extra expense? To find the answer, we tested the ability of eight popular models—Oster, Hamilton Beach, Farberware, Krups, Waring, Cuisinart, Sunbeam, and KitchenAid—to perform such everyday kitchen tasks as making smoothies and frozen drinks, pureeing chunky ingredients into a smooth soup, crushing ice, processing berries into sauce, and making pesto.

Why a Blender?

Food processors do everything blenders do and more, such as mincing, chopping, grating, slicing, and shredding. So it would be perfectly reasonable for a cook to ask, "Well, why bother with a blender, then?" As multitalented as food processors are, blenders are better at processing liquids and solids together to form a fine, smooth, well-aerated puree and at liquefying solids. A blender, for instance, will process cooked vegetables and broth into a finer puree than a food processor, making the texture of the finished soup silky. Blenders are also better than food processors at combining ice, fruit, juice, and yogurt to make smoothies. A food processor will leave small chunks of ice, whereas a

blender will break up the ice and fruit into particles tiny enough for the drink to live up to its name.

Several design elements account for this. One important factor is the shape of the blender jar. Because food processor workbowls are relatively wide and low, the food that gets thrown off the moving blade tends to stick to the sides of the bowl. By comparison, tall, narrow blender jars force the food up because there is less space for it to move laterally. This upward motion, combined with the rapid spinning of the blades, creates a vortex within the jar that allows for the incorporation of more air, which gives the end product a fluffier, smoother consistency. In our experience in the test kitchen, blender jars also form tighter seals than food processor bowls—another benefit when processing liquids. A rubber gasket forms a seal between the base of the blender jar and the blade assembly, and a tight-fitting lid seals the mouth of the jar. (Despite its secure seals, you should not fill a blender jar more than halfway; this ensures that the contents will have ample room to move as they are blended.)

John Rousso, engineering manager for Windmere Durable Holdings (parent company to Windmere and Household Products, the makers of Black & Decker Household Products), stressed the importance of one component of blender jar design—the flutes. Flutes are vertical protrusions on the inside of the blender jar (see photo above), which, in Rousso's words, "collapse the vortex" inside the jar, thus redirecting the material being thrown against the jar walls back down onto the blade. This fosters increased contact between the food and spinning blades.

Kristin Verratti, product manager of food products for Household Products, reported that the configuration of the blade assembly also matters. Most food processors have a blade with two cutting edges at different levels, one tight against the

bottom of the workbowl and one that is elevated slightly. The blades on most blenders, on the other hand, have four cutting edges oriented on two, and sometimes three or four, planes (usually, two of the cutting edges reach down toward the base of the jar and two reach up toward the top). This way, the material in the jar hits four cutting edges instead of two.

Frivolous Features

We were a little surprised to find that even in this digital age, electronic touch-pad controls made for little improvement over old-fashioned raised buttons. The flat touch pad is certainly easier to clean than the buttons, (around which it is undeniably difficult to maneuver a sponge or cloth), but it is not easier to operate. Of the four blenders tested that did have electronic controls—the Farberware, Cuisinart, Krups, and KitchenAid—three operated only if two buttons—"on" and a speed button—were pushed. Only the Krups required the use of just one button, though to be fair to the Farberware, it would operate in the low-speed range with the touch of a single button; a push of the second button served to bump it up to the high-speed range.

We also found that you had to really pound on the buttons of the Farberware to get them to work. The fact that the touch pads were easier to clean did not compensate for these annoyances.

A wide variety of speeds was another feature that failed to dazzle us. Most of our tests, including those for smoothies, frozen drinks, soups, and berry puree, were performed at high speed, while crushing ice and making pesto were done at low speeds and/or with the pulse feature, which was included on all of the units tested except the Waring. Even the industry experts we interviewed agreed that only low, high, and pulse were essential; the inclusion of a broad range of speeds beyond those may be more useful for marketing than for cooking.

Jar designs vary in two principal ways—shape and material. The jars on the Krups, Cuisinart, Waring, Sunbeam, and KitchenAid units had straight sides rather than the angled sides famil-

TESTING | PERFECT PUREE

A good blender produces a perfectly smooth puree (left). Some of the less efficient blenders we tested failed to break down large chunks of food, as shown in puree at right.

BEST BLENDER
Oster Designer 12-Speed Osterizer
Noisy, but solid and effective.

Hamilton Beach BlendMaster 14 Speed
A good performer, but had the shortest
power cord of all.

Farberware Millennium 14 Speed
Good performer with sub-par touch-pad controls.

Krups Power Xtreme
Middle-of-the-road performance in
an attractive package.

Waring Kitchen Classics
Classic and beautiful, but expensive and
an uneven performer.

Cuisinart SmartPower 7 Speed
Excelled at crushing ice, but not much else.

Sunbeam 6 Speed Easy Clean
Cheap to buy, but you get what you pay for...
mediocre construction and performance.

KitchenAid 5 Speed Ultra Power
Sleek and handsome, but also expensive and
disappointing in every test.

jar on older designs (the Waring jar was much narrower overall than the other four). We did not find these jars any easier to use, scrape down, or pour from than the old standards, nor were their mouths appreciably wider than most of the others. In fact, because these jars have wider bases, the distance between the jar walls and the blades was roughly ½ inch more than in our top three blenders, which had jars with angled sides (or, in the case of the Oster, jar walls that angle in steeply at the base). A narrower base translates into less space between the blade and the jar walls and therefore greater contact between the blade and the food.

Blender jars also come in several materials: stainless steel is common for bar blenders and not great for culinary uses because you cannot see through it. Most blender jars are glass, and although glass is heavier than the other choice,

plastic, we prefer it because it is less likely to get scratched. After observing how badly scratched the plastic bowls on the test kitchen food processors have become, we were also concerned that plastic blender jars might scratch and therefore retain food flavors and odors over time. Among the eight blenders tested, only the Sunbeam had a plastic jar. One jar we particularly disliked, though, was the KitchenAid, because it lacked a pouring spout. We also found it difficult to align the base and body of the jar properly when screwing them together. The unfortunate result was that the jar tended to leak from the bottom. This was the case with two of the three KitchenAid 5-speed units we tested.

Conclusions
Overall, we found electronic touch-pad controls to be a nuisance, a broad range of speeds

to be unnecessary, and newfangled, wide-bodied, straight-sided jars to offer no advantage over traditional jars with angled sides. Unfortunately though, even all the right design features don't guarantee first-rate performance. None of our blenders excelled in every single test. Chopping ice evenly and easily, which any blender should be able to do, stymied our two top choices, the Oster and the Hamilton Beach. Otherwise, both models were reasonably priced at around $40 and sailed through all the other tests with aplomb. Only the Krups and the Cuisinart did a great job crushing ice, but otherwise they turned in spotty performances. The losers of the bunch were the Sunbeam and, to our surprise, the costly, handsome KitchenAid. Looks like the harvest gold wonder in my kitchen at home stays on daiquiri duty again this summer.

RATING BLENDERS

We tested eight blenders and rated them according to the criteria listed below. They are listed in order of preference. The majority of people we asked reported using their blenders primarily to make smoothies and frozen drinks, so these became our most (and equally) important tests.

PRICE: Retail prices paid in Boston-area stores and national mail-order catalogs.

CAPACITY: The bigger, the better. Note, however, that blender jars should never be filled to the top, so the figures here are intended for comparison only.

SMOOTHIES: We combined 1½ cups semifrozen mango chunks (thawed at room temperature for 1 hour), 1 cup orange juice, ½ cup strained berry puree, and ½ cup plain yogurt and set the blender on high speed—usually called "liquefy"—for 30 seconds. Blenders that produced a fine, smooth puree that left little or no pulp in a strainer when passed through it were rated good; somewhat coarser purees that left noticeable pulp in a strainer were rated fair; and those which produced a very coarse, bulky puree that left noticeable chunks of fruit in the strainer were rated poor.

FROZEN DRINKS: We combined one semifrozen 10-ounce can of frozen drink mix (thawed at room temperature for 90 minutes) and 10 ounces of water, added three cups of ice cubes, and then set the blender on high speed for 40 seconds. Blenders that produced a smooth, even slush that passed through a strainer completely were rated good; if the drink was acceptably smooth but left small granules of ice in a strainer, the blender was rated fair; and if the drink left any large chunks of ice or whole cubes in the strainer, the blender was rated poor.

SOUP PUREE: We cooked 1 cup sautéed minced shallots and 1½ pounds broccoli florets and stems—peeled, trimmed, and cut into pieces no larger than ¾ inch, in four cups of liquid until completely tender, about 10 minutes. The total quantity of this mixture was 7 cups. We allowed it to cool for 5 minutes and then pureed it in two batches of 3½ cups each, for 30 seconds, on high speed. Blenders that produced a smooth, lump-free puree that passed through a sieve completely were rated good; if the puree left any noticeable pieces of broccoli in the strainer, the blender was rated fair, and if lots of nearly whole pieces of broccoli were left in the strainer, the blender was rated poor.

CRUSHED ICE: We tried crushing 14 cubes of ice, with no liquid added, using the ice-crushing mode if the blender had one and otherwise using the pulse mode. If the blender pulverized all the cubes into reasonably small, even shards, it was rated good; if the size of the ice pieces was very uneven and some of the cubes remained in pieces about one-third to one-half their original size, the blender was rated fair; and if whole cubes were left, the blender was rated poor.

BERRY PUREE: We cooked 12 ounces of hulled fresh strawberries in a modest amount of sugar syrup until they softened, about 5 minutes, and processed them, still warm, at medium speed—usually labeled "mix" or "shred"—for 20 seconds. If the puree was utterly smooth and passed through a strainer leaving no residue other than seeds, the blender was rated good; if medium-sized pieces of berry were left in the strainer, the blender was rated fair; and if large pieces or whole berries were left, the blender was rated poor.

PESTO: Most people make pesto in a food processor because it breaks down the basil easily, but for cooks who don't own one, we wanted to find out if a blender was a viable alternative. We processed three cloves of minced garlic, ¼ cup chopped walnuts, 2 packed cups fresh basil and parsley leaves, and 7 tablespoons olive oil any way we could, usually using a combination of pulse, low, medium, and high speeds and stopping frequently to push the mixture down onto the blades. If the blender was eventually able to break the ingredients down into a paste, it was rated good; if only a portion of the ingredients broke down, the blender was rated fair; and if essentially whole leaves and nuts were left in the jar by the time our patience ran out, the blender was rated poor.

COMMENTS: Testers' observations related to button responsiveness, jar handle comfort, and perceived construction quality augment the testing results.

Brand	Price	Speeds	Capacity	Smoothie	Frozen Drink	Soup Puree	Crushed Ice	Berry Puree	Pesto	Testers' Comments
BEST BLENDER **Oster** Designer 12-Speed Osterizer Blender, Model 6663	$39.99	12	5 cups	★★★	★★★	★★★	★	★★★	★★★	Good fit between base and jar, comfortable jar handle, and especially good pouring spout. But what a racket it makes.
Hamilton Beach BlendMaster 14 Speed Blender, Model 54200R	$39.99	14	5 cups	★★★	★★★	★★★	★	★★★	★★★	Not a sleek or stellar design—jar sometimes wobbles on base and buttons are especially close together and difficult to clean— but it does get the job done.
Farberware Millennium 14 Speed Electronic Professional Blender, Model FPB600	$79.99	14	6 cups	★★★	★★★	★★★	★	★★★	★★★	Small, hidden side power switch is easy to overlook and leave on. Electronic touch-pad controls required hard mashing to operate.
Krups Power Xtreme, Model 572	$79.99	6	6 cups	★★	★★★	★★	★★★	★★	★	Best-designed electronic touch-pad control of all because it operates with one touch instead of two.
Waring Kitchen Classics Blender, Model PBB201	$129.99	2	5 cups	★★	★★★	★★★	★	★★	★	Simplest design and longest cord—6 feet!—of the bunch. Great for purees with plenty of liquid, but not so good for drier dishes. No pulse feature.
Cuisinart SmartPower 7 Speed Electronic Blender, Model SPB-7	$79.99	7	5 cups	★★	★★	★	★★★	★	★	Electronic touch-pad buttons were responsive but irritating because you must press two buttons—"on" and the speed of your choice—to operate blender.
Sunbeam 6 Speed Easy Clean Blender, Model 4142-8	$29.99	6	6 cups	★	★	★★★	★	★	★	Noisy unit looks and feels flimsy, but it out-pureed KitchenAid at less than one-third the price. Only unit with a plastic jar.
KitchenAid 5 Speed Ultra Power Blender, Model KSB5	$99.99	5	5 cups	★	★★	★	★★	★	★	Difficult to unscrew jar base and even more difficult to screw it back on so that the gasket seals. Have to press two buttons on the touch pad to operate blender.

Whole Peppercorns Grind Competition to Dust

Once a peppercorn is cracked, its volatile components begin to disperse, resulting in loss of flavor. The good news is that whole peppercorns are often less expensive than ground.

⇒ BY MARYELLEN DRISCOLL ⇐

As the long-reigning King of Spice, once equal in value to gold, pepper has become a kitchen table constant. So it can be surprising to learn that these hard, dry, blackish kernels we know as pepper are derived from long, thin spikes of ripe green berries that grow on a vine reaching up to 100 feet long. Once picked, the berries are typically spread out on concrete slabs or straw mats, where they dry for a number of days in the sun, changing from taut green balls to dark, wrinkled, dense kernels. Not to be confused with chile pepper (*Capsicum annuum*), black pepper (*Piper nigrum*) grows in warm, moist climates all over the world, typically within about 15 degrees of the equator. My kitchen supply of pepper has been abundant for years thanks to a two-gallon stash a relative brought back from Vietnam in a grocery bag. Sadly, that windfall recently ran dry and I was faced with choosing my next pepper. Although most of us tend to think that black pepper is black pepper, there are actually several varieties. The most readily available include Vietnamese pepper, Lampong (from the island of Sumatra), Sarawak (from Malaysia), and Malabar and Tellicherry (both are from India). Among spice experts, each has gained a reputation for its particular attributes.

Neither a supermarket brand nor sometimes even a gourmet store brand is likely to specify from what part of the world its pepper was sourced. They simply advertise their product as "black pepper" and leave you with the choice of whole or preground.

So for a spice that we use virtually every day, and with a wide variety of foods, it's hard not to wonder if we have taken pepper too much for granted and are missing out on a greater taste experience. Perhaps we should be seeking out black pepper from a particular region of a particular country. Or, at the other end of the spectrum, perhaps all this fuss over grinding fresh whole peppercorns is not really providing us with improved flavor. We decided to hold a blind tasting to sort it all out.

We included in our tasting the two preeminent national supermarket brands as well as the above-mentioned varieties, which were ordered from specialty spice and gourmet stores. We skipped some varieties of black pepper, such as Brazilian and Ponape, because they proved too difficult to find on a retail level. Even some of those we did include in the tasting can be hard to track down (see Resources, page 32).

We also left out white pepper, which comes from the same plant as black pepper but is harvested when the berries are further ripened; they are then soaked, rubbed to remove their shells, and dried. Also excluded from our tasting were green peppers, which are unripe pepper berries, and pink peppercorns, which are not true peppercorns at all. They come from a tree.

Wholesome Goodness

Overall, our tasting confirmed that fresh ground pepper is far superior to pepper purchased already ground. The latter carried minimal aroma and tended to taste sharp and dull, lacking in complexity. Those whole peppers that were fresh ground just before the tasting contained bold as well as subtle flavors and aromas that were both lively and complex.

As for differences between the varieties of whole peppers that were tasted fresh ground, we found them to be distinct yet subtle. All were appreciated for their particular characteristics (see chart, page 29), receiving high scores within a close range of one another. Based on these results, we concluded that what is important is not so much which variety of pepper you buy but how you buy it.

This is good news, since the most readily available sources, the supermarket brands, can vary as to which type of black pepper they package. This is because black pepper is sold on the world market through exporters and traders who purchase the best of what is available. Depending on the time of year, black pepper from some regions has yet to be harvested, so it is not available, while others are. McCormick/Schilling informed us, however, that for its "gourmet" line (identified by the glass jar with the green lid) the company always uses either Malabar or Lampong pepper varieties. Unfortunately, the label on the jar never indicates the variety, so we could not be certain which of the two we tasted.

Michele Anna Jordan, author of *Salt and Pepper* (Broadway, 1999), found our tasting results consistent with her findings on black pepper. In general, she said, all black pepper is good, no matter the variety. That is not to say that it can't be even better. Because pepper is sold as a commodity, U.S. buyers demand more consistency in delivery, price, and cleanliness than in quality or flavor, says Jordan.

Jordan was also able to explain why we found the most noticeable differences in pepper to be between fresh ground whole pepper and commercially ground pepper. When a peppercorn is cracked, the volatile chemical components that give pepper its bold aroma as well as its subtle characteristics immediately begin to disperse. These more subtle flavors often include pine and citrus. So with time (and cracking), what remains is the predominant nonvolatile compound in black pepper, piperine. Piperine is the source of black pepper's renowned pungency and is what gives it its characteristic hot, sharp, and stinging qualities. It is also said to stimulate saliva and gastric juices, creating the sensation of hunger.

Knowing this, one of the easiest ways for a home cook to improve his or her cooking is simply by buying whole pepper and grinding it fresh with each meal. That way, instead of merely experiencing the sharp sensation that ground pepper has to offer, you will unleash a spectrum of flavors from earthy to exotic.

There are a couple of tips for buying pepper. As with any spice, purchase it from a reputable source that has high product turnover, so that you know you are buying a fresh product. The appearance of the peppercorns can also be an indicator of quality. Peppercorns that were not dried quickly enough take on a white tint to their dark color (not to be confused with white peppercorns) and will not be as flavorful. According to William Penzey of Penzeys Spices in Muskego, Wisconsin, a retail and mail order spice source, quality black pepper should have a dark, shiny appearance and not be sitting in a lot of dust.

TASTING BLACK PEPPER

The following peppers are listed in order of ranking. All those in the recommended category received relatively close score results. The peppers were evaluated for their aroma, heat, flavor complexity, and overall likeability. Those peppers purchased whole were cracked within a half hour before the tasting. All of the peppers were offered plain but with the option of being tasted on plain white rice. The panel consisted of 15 tasters, including magazine staff as well as Jim Burke, chef/owner of the Tuscan Grill in Waltham, Massachusetts; Abe Faber, owner of Clear Flour Bakery in Brookline, Massachusetts; and Chris Schlessinger, chef/owner of the East Coast Grill in Cambridge, Massachusetts, who is coauthor with John Willoughby of several cookbooks, including the forthcoming *How to Cook Meat* (Morrow, 2000). For availability of specific pepper varieties listed below, see Resources, page 32.

RECOMMENDED

McCormick/Schilling Whole Black Pepper (sold in glass jar)
➤ $4.19 for 1.87 ounces

The premium black pepper offered by this national name brand proved a strong favorite among tasters. It carried a full and robust piney aroma with citrus notes many tasters pinpointed as orange. Its flavor was described as "lively" and "penetrating" with "nice complexity." It had a respectable heat level and a musty element in its character. "Very subtle, complex and very warm and nice," one taster noted. Though we could not be certain which pepper variety was in the jar we tasted, a company spokesperson said this line always consists of either Malabar or Lampong pepper. Available in supermarkets on the East Coast under the McCormick label and on the West Coast under the Schilling label.

Kalustyan Vietnam Black Pepper
➤ $2.49 for 4 ounces

Black pepper is a relatively new trade item for Vietnam. This sample carried a moderately intense aroma that was

sweet and musty with earthy notes. It tasted mild, was noticeably smoky, and was said to nave a "very distinct woody flavor" as well as a "nice gritty, complex flavor." Its heat was neither fiery nor immediate, "but then later it catches up to you." Although this pepper scored well overall, it was controversial, having as many fans as tasters who were indifferent to it.

Kalustyan Lampong Black Pepper
➤ $3.49 for 4 ounces

Lampong, the primary black pepper from Indonesia, is grown on the island of Sumatra. It carried a strong, bright, and pungent aroma described as "penetrating" and "fruity" as well as "woody." Its flavor was not as characteristically pungent as expected based on its aroma and carried "some interesting fruity undertones." It was also described as "clean" and "peppy," with high flavor notes and a "bright heat" that was "fairly hot but not to the point of hurting."

Penzeys Malabar Black Pepper
➤ $2.99 for 2.5 ounces

This well-respected variety from India had a bold, rich fragrance with elements of fresh pine and a "strong citrus essence" that a few tasters described as lemony. Its flavor was "sharp," "woodsy," and "biting," with "lots of back-of-the-palate heat" that "builds and carries pleasantly."

Penzeys Tellicherry Black Pepper
➤ $3.09 for 2.2 ounces

From India, this pepper is purposely left to

mature on the vine until the berries begin to pick up a red hue. Because of the maturity of the berries, they tend to be larger than other varieties and are reputed to carry more developed flavor. The sample we tasted packed a lot of heat. The aroma was characterized as straightforward and mild. Overall, it had a "nice big bite" that some tasters really liked. "Quite pungent and robust" with an "intense heat at the end."

Penzeys Sarawak Black Pepper
➤ $3.29 for 2.4 ounces

Grown in the Malaysian state of Sarawak on the island of Borneo, this pepper was marked by a particularly fresh, "friendly" aroma that carried notes of hickory, fruit, pine, and fresh flowers as well as a musty essence. The flavor was surprisingly light. Its heat development was slow and lingering; "not hot compared to others."

McCormick/Schilling Whole Pepper (sold in plastic jar)
➤ $2.29 for 2.37 ounces

Considered the least premium pepper in the McCormick/Schilling line, this pepper nonetheless held up reasonably well. The aroma was particularly musty, which reminded more than one taster of fresh garden dirt. Its flavor was equally musty as well as biting and pungent — a "characteristic black pepper flavor." Available in supermarkets.

NOT RECOMMENDED

McCormick/Schilling Pure Ground Black Pepper (sold in tin)
➤ $1.89 for 2 ounces

Of all the ground pepper samples, this familiar tin can carried the most flavor but was still deemed bland. Its aroma was "flat" and "not very penetrating," as was the overall flavor. It carried a unique minty quality and a low, slow heat that tasters considered lacking. Its finish was "drab." Available in supermarkets.

Spice Island Whole Black Pepper
➤ $3.89 for 2.4 ounces

This well-known brand name pepper was penetratingly hot but otherwise deemed "average—nothing special." It carried a piney/woody and somewhat sweet aroma. The flavor was described as "mossy," "blah," "dry" and "dusty." More than one taster said they could not "get past the bitterness." Available in supermarkets.

Spice Island Fine Ground Black Pepper
➤ $4.68 for 2.3 ounces

The aroma of this ground pepper was pungent and dull, reminding many tasters of the pepper packets found in fast-food restaurants. The flavor was equally uninteresting to tasters, who described it as "weak," having "no complexity" and only a light, latent heat. "I can't imagine this would add any interest to foods," wrote one taster. Available in supermarkets.

McCormick/Schilling Ground Black Pepper (sold in glass jar)
➤ $4.39 for 1.62 ounces

This pricey ground pepper carried a sharp aroma that lacked distinction. It had "no interesting flavor characteristics to speak of," one taster asserted. Most tasters had little more to say other than to describe it as "dull." It carried a medium level of heat. Available in supermarkets.

⇒ BY KAY RENTSCHLER ⇐

An Electric Mixer for Folding?

Desserts such as génoise, which call for folding flour into whipped eggs and sugar, are among the most difficult recipes for home cooks. Why? Because hand-folding flour into a light batter takes up to 20 strokes that can easily damage the egg foam. This results in a dense, compact cake, lacking the high, light structure desired in a génoise and other egg foam cakes. But during work on an in-progress dessert book, *Cook's* publisher Christopher Kimball broke ranks with tradition by folding flour into a génoise batter with the mixer itself. The resulting cake emerged higher than those folded by hand. The test kitchen confirmed these results by making a half-dozen génoise, some folded by hand, others by machine. In side-by-side comparisons, the mixer-folded génoise beat out the hand-folded génoise every time. How is this done? By sprinkling the flour on top of the egg foam, then engaging the mixer on low speed for 10 seconds. The whisk attachment is then disengaged and used to make a couple of final strokes by hand.

Getting Even with Phyllo

Among the pluses of phyllo-wrapped concoctions—sweet or savory—is their tidy, make-ahead freezeability. But phyllo dough can also be maddening. Often, despite efforts to keep the brittle sheets moist and supple, commercial phyllo refuses to cooperate. Having recently worked on phyllo appetizers at the magazine, we can offer a few temper-sparing tips.

Phyllo dough comes frozen. The instructions on the brand we were using called for defrosting the dough for 12 hours in the refrigerator; eager to begin, we headed for the microwave. Big mistake. The sheets hung together like strips of wallpaper. Defrosting at room temperature proved problematic as well—the sheets gummed in the center and cracked on the outside. The recommended 12-hour fridge defrost yielded mostly whole and pliant sheets. Another tip: a clean plastic spray bottle filled with a 3-to-1 ratio of melted butter to vegetable oil is a timesaver. The oil keeps the butter thin enough to spray, freeing the cook from the constant dipping and dripping of the pastry brush. Should the butter begin to congeal, toss the plastic bottle in the microwave for a few seconds. Cutting stacked sheets? Use scissors instead of a knife. Perhaps most important: phyllo brands vary enormously in quality. Try to find one you like

and, er, stick with it. Athenos is a nationally available brand that we have found to be quite reliable.

Berry Good Indeed

Our berry gatherings for summer berry gratin (page 24) put us up against a couple of annually recurring problems: how to clean fresh berries and how to store them. Though raspberries, blackberries, and blueberries grow on bushes out of dirt's way, rambling strawberries are often sandy. Rather than rinsing them and bruising their delicate flesh, we found the best method of cleaning strawberries is to wipe each berry lightly with a dampened paper towel or to brush it softly with a mushroom brush. Raspberries and blackberries are so delicate that they are difficult to wash at all (in my opinion, local berries don't need washing), but blueberries can be turned into a colander and sprayed lightly with water. If you find yourself with a surfeit of fresh berries, the best thing to do is to place the unwashed, unhulled berries in a single layer on a rimmed baking sheet lined with a clean kitchen towel. Cover them with a second towel and refrigerate. You will have extended their lives by days.

Revenge of the Electric Knife

Working recently on an appetizer book as well as a few delicate desserts for an office party, the test kitchen discovered that the once-reviled electric knife actually makes a formidable kitchen companion. Possessed of both delicacy and clout, it can cut through a crust of country bread without damaging the crumb, race through a frozen mousse cake,

glide through a sticky pecan tart, and sail through a fruit-filled sponge roll. We found our new friend to be equally indispensable for slicing slender canapés and quesadillas. There are currently five models available in the United States. We plan to test them in the near future.

Hold the Fat, Please

What's the next best thing to grilling? When it comes to steaks, at least, our choice is pan-searing. While broiler cooking means hauling the screeching broiler rack in and out of the oven to check the meat, cooking on the stovetop gives you access and control, and it gives your steak an outstanding crust. The trick is to heat a heavy skillet—preferably cast iron—on its own for a full four minutes. No fat. A nicely marbled steak, such as a 1½-inch-thick rib-eye, needs no additional fat. Just blot it with paper towels to dry the surface and give it a rub with salt and pepper. Then toss it into the pan and let it sear for 2½ minutes undisturbed; turn the steak and sear the second side for 2½ minutes. That's rare. The caramelization of the crust may astound you. When cooking a steak that has less marbling, such as a rump steak, brush the dry steak with olive oil before putting it in the pan. You may never broil again.

Flat for the Fridge

In her story on high-roast chicken (March/April 2000), Dawn Yanagihara first brines, then butterflies a 3½-pound chicken, and roasts it to lacquered mahoghany finish in a 500-degree oven. A reader wrote to remark that the brining vessel took up the free space in her refrigerator. She recommended butterflying the chicken first, then brining it. With the chicken flattened, it fit comfortably in a large zipper-lock bag along with the brining solution. Dawn emphasizes that the chicken must lie flat on the refrigerator shelf to maintain its shape.

Ties that Bind

In developing our recipe for deviled eggs, we cooked, peeled, and halved close to 200 eggs. For every dozen or so there were one or two eggs in which the cooked yolk nudged up so close to the outer wall that the white tore when we removed the yolk. As it turns out, the yolk of a freshly laid egg is nearly round and almost perfectly centered by cord-like strands of egg white known as chalazae, which anchor the yolk in place. The shell of an aging egg—particularly one stored for any period of time at room temperature—absorbs air, thinning the egg white and weakening the chalazae. The yolk is then free to move off center. Our advice: buy the freshest eggs possible. (Minor caveat: fresh eggs may be slightly more difficult to peel.)

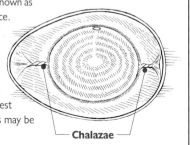

Chalazae

Vegetarian Cooking for Carnivores

Two new cookbooks sell vegetarian cooking for the taste,
not the politics. BY CHRISTOPHER KIMBALL

Vegetarianism as a lifestyle ain't what it used to be. Deborah Madison, the reigning queen of this culinary niche and author of *Vegetarian Cooking for Everyone* (Broadway Books, 1997), admits to a taste for red meat and has, on occasion, been seen consuming a sizzling steak in public. Mollie Katzen, author of *The Moosewood Cookbook* (Ten Speed Press, 1977), espouses wholesome cooking, "whether that contains meat or not." And Madhur Jaffrey has now turned her considerable talents to the subject of vegetarian cooking, but from an international perspective, bringing numerous ethnic specialties together in one giant tome. Vegetarian cooking is growing up, shedding tie-dye for L.L. Bean and taking on a more sophisticated, less politically sensitive palate. At last, it seems, vegetarian cooking can be welcomed into the fold of legitimate culinary pursuits now that it is first and foremost about taste and technique rather than health and politics.

WORLD VEGETARIAN
Madhur Jaffrey

Clarkson Potter, 758 pages

This book is huge, a tome that is weighty in scope as well as in sheer mass. Madhur Jaffrey, author of a dozen cookbooks, including *A Taste of India* (Atheneum, 1985) and *Madhur Jaffrey's Indian Cooking* (Barrons, 1982) has lived all over the world and brings considerable experience to the task at hand. The design is straightforward—no fanciful illustrations or decorative colors—although the book does include 16 pages of color photos.
PROS: Few cookbooks exude the experience and professionalism of the author, but this work by Madhur Jaffrey is clearly one of them. Her command of the subject is inspiring, leaving one to

wonder how one person could have gained such a wealth of seemingly firsthand knowledge in a single lifetime. She has eaten chickpea curry in Port of Spain, and scrambled Indian cheese at truck stops in Punjab, and slurped Javanese noodles in Malaysia. Most of her recipes are clear, detailed, and informative.
CONS: To live up to the title of "world" vegetarian cooking, Jaffrey has to cover a lot of bases. When she is working with a cuisine with which she has considerable personal experience, the book shines. When she is on less solid footing—Italian or American cooking, for example—the book is more pedestrian.
RECIPE TESTING: Of the 10 recipes we tested, seven were winners, a notably high percentage by our test kitchen's standards. Corn Tortillas Stuffed with Cheese were fun to make and delicious, and the recipe was extremely well written. Scrambled Eggs with Onion and Tomato were simple but excellent, and a Persian pilaf was very good, even though the recipe was complicated and the results not quite as fantastic as the author promised. Egg Whites with Peas was a weird but satisfactory dish (lightly beaten whites are sautéed with cooked peas and scallions, then thickened with cornstarch), a tabbouleh made with arugula was a revelation, a cabbage dish made with rice and currants was a bit confusing but tasty, and butternut squash cooked with sage was simple and good enough for this year's Thanksgiving table. Less impressive were a homemade Indian cheese, a yogurt dish spiced with, among other things, pimento-stuffed green olives (a frightful pairing), and a Tuscan zucchini pie that was easy to make and delicate in flavor but nothing extraordinary.

THE NEW ENCHANTED BROCCOLI FOREST
Mollie Katzen

Ten Speed Press, Paperback, 303 pages

Mollie Katzen has been something of a cultural icon ever since she authored *The Moosewood Cookbook* in 1977 (followed by *The Enchanted Broccoli Forest* in 1982, both published by Ten Speed Press). Unlike Jaffrey, who brings you the world, Katzen brings you herself—her work is intensely personal. This is reflected in the design of her books, which are rooted in the artistic vernacu-

lar of *The Whole Earth Catalog*. (*Still Life with Menu Cookbook*, published in 1988, is an exception to this rule, being considerably more sophisticated in both design and content.) With a hand-scripted style of typography and cute illustrations, her books speak to the 1960s in all (or at least some) of us.
PROS: If you live in Burlington, Vermont, or Bend, Oregon, you probably love Mollie Katzen. She is true to her style, she is charming, and your original copies of *Moosewood* and *Enchanted Broccoli* are well thumbed and highly regarded. When you open the cover of a Mollie Katzen book, you enter a different world, one that is animated, communal, and highly original.
CONS: Jaffrey is the consummate grown-up, while Katzen still plays with her food. (*Enchanted Forest,* for example, is named after a recipe for broccoli "trees" planted in an herbed rice pilaf.) When preparing some of the recipes in *The New Enchanted Broccoli Forest*, we thought more about cooking with our kids than cooking for a dinner party. That doesn't mean that Katzen doesn't occasionally hit a culinary home run. It's just that the food is relatively unsophisticated; my five-year-old would love her bubble gum–colored strawberry mousse. If the style of her cookbooks has remained much the same, so, too, has the substance of many of the recipes. The original books relied heavily on dairy (eggs, cheese, sour cream, and yogurt are ubiquitous), and this book, too, depends a good deal on these ingredients for texture and flavor.
RECIPE TESTING: Overall, we had very mixed results—from the sublime to the inedible—and the recipe directions were often either unclear or inaccurate. We made two breads, a chocolate honey cake quick bread and a cottage cheese dill bread. Both were disappointing, and the baking times were either too short or too long. The fresh strawberry mousse was rubbery in texture and mediocre in flavor—great for kids, but not one adult went back for seconds. The chilled marinated cauliflower was a huge hit, however. It was easy to make, and the recipe was right on the mark. The cold mushroom soup was refreshing and tasty, but the recipe directions were problematic on many fronts. Finally, although the filling in Katzen's recipe for rugelach was on the dry side, the dough is wonderful. Made with cottage cheese, the baked dough was almost as good as puff pastry and a whole lot easier to make. This one recipe may be worth the price of the book.

Most of the ingredients and materials necessary for the recipes in this issue are available at your local supermarket, gourmet store, or kitchen supply shop. The following are mail-order sources for particular items. Prices listed below were current at press time and do not include shipping or handling unless otherwise indicated. We suggest that you contact companies directly to confirm up-to-date prices and availability.

Blenders

Although blenders are being replaced by food processors in many home kitchens, there are numerous applications in which a blender outperforms its replacement. We put eight blenders to the test for our story on page 25. Along with rating the blenders on jar capacity and design, we created a battery of tests that included blending smoothies and frozen drinks, pureeing broccoli soup, crushing ice, pureeing fresh, just-cooked strawberries, and making homemade basil and parsley pesto.

Our winner, the Oster Designer 12-Speed Osterizer Model 6663, earned a "good" rating in all categories but one. The Osterizer produced perfect pesto, pulverizing all ingredients, including walnuts, and it pureed fruit and soup to smooth perfection. Smoothies and frozen drinks made with the Oster left none of the pulp or ice granules that other blenders refused to break down. Only crushing ice gave the Oster pause, but because ice crushing was reported to be low on people's list of priorities for blender use, the Oster still placed first.

The Oster blender offers 12 speed options, and its glass container, which has a five-cup capacity, fits well in its white plastic base. Jar and base together, the blender measures about 13½ inches high; the base is 5½ inches wide, and 8 inches deep. Many department stores and kitchen stores carry Oster brand blenders, but if you can't find one in a store near you, you can order it from **Kitchen Etc. (32 Industrial Drive, Exeter, NH 03833; 800-232-4070; www.kitchenetc.com).** The blender sells for $39.99.

Peppercorns

Although pepper is often forgotten in favor of its kitchen companion, salt, no other seasoning can enhance and finish a dish the way that pepper does. We set out to develop a series of tastings that would help us uncover the subtle (and sometimes not so subtle) nuances of different varieties of peppercorn. We loved Vietnamese black pepper for its smoky and complex flavor and the Lampong black pepper for its fruity and clean flavor. Tellicherry black pepper was favored by those looking for heat in their pepper, and Sarawak black pepper had a light floral flavor enjoyed by many.

Luckily, two of our preferred choices—Malabar and Lampong—are sold in most supermarkets nationwide. McCormick/Schilling Whole Black Pepper, which consists of either Malabar or Lampong pepper, is packaged in glass or plastic jars. We also found two excellent sources for those who prefer a specific variety of peppercorn. **Penzeys Spices (P.O. Box 933, Muskego, WI 53150; 800-741-7787; www.penzeys.com)** offers whole Sarawak, Tellicherry, and Malabar Black Peppercorns. Sarawak peppercorns come in a 2.4-ounce glass jar (item #56652) for $3.29 or in a 4-ounce bag (item #56640) for $3.79. Tellicherry peppercorns are sold in a 2.2-ounce jar (item #56052) for $3.09 or in a 4-ounce bag (item #56049) for $2.99. The Malabar peppercorns are sold in a 2.5-ounce glass jar (item #56157) for $2.99 or a 4-ounce bag (item #56144) for $2.79. **Kalustyan's (123 Lexington Avenue, New York, NY 10016; 212-685-3451; www.forspice.com)** sells Vietnamese and Lampong whole black peppercorns. The Vietnamese pepper comes in a 4-ounce bag and sells for $2.49. Sarawak pepper is sold in a 4-ounce bag for $3.49.

Metal Skewers

Nothing is worse than waiting patiently for a juicy, perfectly cooked kebab to come off the grill only to bite into a skewer of charred, smoky bamboo. Of course, soaking the wooden skewers can help to alleviate the problem, but who ever thinks that far ahead? After testing the kebab recipe on page 12, we found that metal skewers were the way to go. They are reusable, dishwasher-safe, and, best of all, need no soaking. We found the size of the skewers to be important as well. Skewers shorter than 12 inches don't allow for the full complement of meat and vegetables that we like to see on our kebabs, while anything longer than 14 inches tends to get caught in the grill grates, making it awkward and sometimes dangerous to turn the kebabs. Our preference is to use 12- to 14-inch metal skewers. **Kitchen Etc. (32 Industrial Drive, Exeter, NH 03833; 800-232-4070; www.kitchenetc.com)** carries a set of six metal kebab skewers that are 13½ inches long and have a metal loop at one end for easier turning. The skewers are chrome-plated metal and sell for $3.99.

Square Cake Pan

For the chewy, fudgy brownie recipe on page 23, we tried a multitude of 8-inch square baking pans made of various materials and with varying sides. Although the brownies baked up consistently in every pan, we liked the perfectly flat surface and clean, sharp corners and edges of the brownies baked in a straight-sided pan. **Bridge Kitchenware Corp. (214 East 52nd Street, New York, NY 10022; 800-274-3435 [in the New York area call 212-838-1901]; www.bridgekitchenware.com)** sells an 8-inch square baking pan, item BBAA-SC-82, for $8.99. It is made of professional-weight anodized aluminum and is 2 inches deep.

Pasta Equipment

When consulting editor Maryellen Driscoll set out to learn how to make the perfect pot of pasta (see page 14), she was amazed at the vast array of pasta-specific products on the market. She found that high-end pasta pots with perforated inserts have capacities too small for the amount of water needed to perfectly cook pasta.

The only pasta-specific utensil she found helpful was a pasta fork made of either metal or plastic. While a pair of all-purpose tongs did their part by securely grabbing strands of pasta out of the hot water, the pasta fork was able to do this and more. Its toothlike, spoon-shaped end was able to comb through even the stickiest batch of pasta, separating any strands that stuck together. Although you can find inexpensive plastic pasta forks at many supermarkets, they can sometimes bend or torque out of shape while in use. **A Cook's Wares (211 37th Street, Beaver Falls, PA 15010-2103; 800-915-9788; www.cookswares.com)** offers a full line of pasta forks. Included in their selection is a 13-inch, black, heat-resistant nylon pasta fork from Calphalon, item #3297, which sells for $6.00 and is ideal for use with nonstick pots. For those who see cost as no object, All-Clad offers an 11½ inch stainless steel pasta fork for $20.00 (item #305U).

Biscuit Cutters

While testing the biscuit recipe on page 21, we were reminded of how aggravating it can be to pick through an overcrowded kitchen drawer only to fail to find the perfect-sized biscuit cutter. One way around this problem is to purchase a set of cutters in graduated sizes; the smallest is usually used for canapés and the largest for buns and large cookies. **Kitchen Arts (161 Newbury Street, Boston, MA 02116; 617-266-8701)** carries a large selection of biscuit and cookie cutters. We especially like the 12-piece set from Ateco, containing tinned steel cutters ranging from 7/8 to 4 7/16 inches in diameter. Because they neatly nest in their own metal case, you can rest assured that they won't get banged around and misshapen in a crowded kitchen drawer. The set costs $24.95, including shipping and handling.

RECIPES

May & June 2000

Grilled Pork Tenderloin

Diner-Style Home Fries

Grilled Beef Kebabs

Chicken Marsala

Perfect Pasta

Creamy Green Pea Soup

www.cooksillustrated.com

Cook's Illustrated has just launched its new Web site and we invite you to join us. Simply log on at www.cooksillustrated.com. Although much of the information is free, database searches are for site subscribers only. *Cook's Illustrated* readers are offered a 20% discount.

Here is what you can do on our site:

Search Our Recipes: We have a searchable database of all the recipes from *Cook's Illustrated*.

Search Tastings and Cookware Ratings: You will find all of our reviews (cookware, food, wine, cookbooks) plus new material created exclusively for the Web site.

Find Your Favorite Quick Tips.

Get Your Cooking Questions Answered: Post questions for *Cook's* editors and fellow site subscribers.

Take a Cooking Course Online: Take online cooking courses from *Cook's* editors and receive personalized instruction.

Check Your Subscription: Check the status

of your subscription, pay a bill, or give gift subscriptions online.

Visit Our Bookstore: You can purchase any of our cookbooks, hardbound annual editions of the magazine, or posters via the Internet.

Subscribe to e-notes: Our free e-mail companion to Kitchen Notes offers cooking advice, test results, buying tips, and recipes about a single topic each month.

Find Out About Our New Public Television Cooking Show: Coming to public television soon, America's Test Kitchen will take you into the *Cook's Illustrated* test kitchen.

Get All the Extras: The outtakes from each issue of *Cook's* are available at Cook's Extra, including step-by-step photographs.

Deviled Eggs

Quick and Easy Cream Biscuits

Chewy, Fudgy Brownies

Fresh Fruit Gratin

Spicy Globe

Thai

Napoletano

Sweet

African Blue

Holy

Dark Opal

Lettuce Leaf

Red Rubin

Genovese

Cinnamon

Sweet Dani

BASIL

NUMBER FORTY-FIVE

JULY & AUGUST 2000

COOK'S
ILLUSTRATED

Great Grilled Burgers
Shaping the Patty Is Key

Quick, All-Purpose Barbecue Sauce
Use Simple Pantry Ingredients

Lattice-Top Fresh Peach Pie
Juicy, Not Soupy

Fresh Pasta Rating
Are Supermarket Brands Any Good?

The Best Grill-Roasted Chicken
"Beer Can" Chicken Takes Top Honors

Testing Bread Knives
Blade Shape Makes the Difference

Fluffy Rice Salad

Rich, Creamy Corn Pudding

Stuffed Zucchini

Grilled Vegetable Salads

Ultimate Panna Cotta

Fresh Herb Primer

$4.95 U.S./$6.95 CANADA

CONTENTS

July & August 2000

COOK'S
ILLUSTRATED

www.cooksillustrated.com

PUBLISHER AND EDITOR
Christopher Kimball

SENIOR EDITOR
John Willoughby

SENIOR WRITER
Jack Bishop

CORPORATE MANAGING EDITOR
Barbara Bourassa

TEST KITCHEN DIRECTOR
Kay Rentschler

ASSOCIATE EDITORS
Adam Ried
Dawn Yanagihara
Raquel Pelzel

ASSOCIATE EDITOR,
ONLINE EDUCATION
Becky Hays

RECIPE TESTING AND DEVELOPMENT
Bridget Lancaster
Julia Collin

WEB TEST COOK
Shona Simkin

ASSISTANT EDITOR
Shannon Blaisdell

CONSULTING FOOD EDITOR
Jasper White

CONSULTING EDITOR
Jim Dodge

CONTRIBUTING EDITORS
Maryellen Driscoll
Elizabeth Germain

ART DIRECTOR
Amy Klee

PROJECT MANAGER
Sheila Datz

PRODUCTION MANAGER
Nate Nickerson

COPY EDITOR
India Koopman

EDITORIAL INTERN
Melissa Brown

MARKETING MANAGER
Pamela Caporino

SALES REPRESENTATIVE
Jason Geller

MARKETING ASSISTANT
Connie Forbes

CIRCULATION DIRECTOR
David Mack

CIRCULATION MANAGER
Larisa Greiner

PRODUCTS MANAGER
Steven Browall

CIRCULATION ASSISTANT
Mary Connelly

CUSTOMER SERVICE
REPRESENTATIVES
Adam Dardek
Jacqui Valerio

VICE PRESIDENT OPERATIONS
AND TECHNOLOGY
James McCormack

SYSTEMS ADMINISTRATOR
Richard Cassidy

PRODUCTION ARTIST
Daniel Frey

WEB MASTER
Nicole Morris

CONTROLLER
Mandy Shito

OFFICE MANAGER
Jennifer McCreary

SPECIAL PROJECTS
Deborah Broide

For list rental information, contact The SpecialLISTS, 1200 Harbor Blvd. 9th Floor, Weehawken, NJ 07087; (201) 865-5800; fax (201) 867-2450. Editorial office: 17 Station Street, Brookline, MA 02445; (617) 232-1000; fax (617) 232-1572. Editorial contributions should be sent to: Editor, *Cook's Illustrated*. We cannot assume responsibility for manuscripts submitted to us. Submissions will be returned only if accompanied by a large self-addressed envelope. Postmaster: Send all new orders, subscription inquiries, and change of address notices to: *Cook's Illustrated*, P.O. Box 7446, Red Oak, IA 51591-0446. PRINTED IN THE USA.

BERRIES The familiar raspberry, blackberry, and strawberry are members of the rose family, with all of the fragrance that the name implies. Mulberries, which look much like blackberries but have a sweeter taste, are not cultivated in the United States but do grow wild in much of the country. Huckleberries and blueberries are often confused, but the former are slightly more tart than their blue cousins, with thicker, glossier skin and small, hard seeds at their center. Currants and gooseberries, which come from the same family, are more often cooked than eaten raw, although white currants are sweet enough to eat out of hand. Elderberries, which are quite sour, are best served in jam or wine.

COVER (Cantaloupe): BRENT WATKINSON,   BACK COVER (Berries): JOHN BURGOYNE

WHERE THE WILD THINGS ARE

I first saw the moose last August—or, to be more precise, heard its thunderous hoofbeats as it ran over the rise of our upper hayfield. I was up early checking the orchard and, startled by the unusual noise, looked up, expecting to see one of my neighbor's large Belgians, escaped once again from its summer pasture. Instead, I saw the moose standing stock still at the highest point in the field, looking straight down at me; curious, huge, and immobile. It turned and galloped away, up from the swampy hollow and back into the forest.

A week later I was camped out in a small yellow tent with my five-year-old son, Charlie, and awoke after midnight to the same heavy pounding and then a great snort, the noise a deer makes when it is startled. I stepped out of the tent barefoot, onto cold wet grass, and heard the great animal inhaling buckets of air through its cavernous nostrils, like a prehistoric leaf-eater. We listened to each other for a bit, and then my son turned in his sleep, and I went back to bed.

This year during sugaring season I was setting out sap buckets and came across the moose, this time lying down like a Holstein in our upper field, indifferent to my passing, and only slightly curious. Then things turned downright silly. Two weeks later, a neighbor, Nancy, found herself trapped in our house when the moose stuck its huge head under the porch roof and peered in through the back door to the mudroom, seeming to wait for her to come out. She was a prisoner for an hour until her son happened by and chased the moose away. She ran part of the way home, afraid the animal might run after her, but the moose just stood in the field, curious, and, as I like to tell the story, lovesick.

In the weeks that followed, the moose became a local celebrity, stopping cars on the dirt road that runs by our farm. One neighbor mentioned something about his taste for moose steaks, "bigger than a hubcap and better tasting than beef." Another wondered if the moose had a brain disease that made it too friendly. Still others said that moose are just plain dumb. One morning I walked down to our lower hayfield and stood awhile. The moose, curious, edged closer, and I, not looking at it directly, got within about 10 feet after a half hour of disinterested shuffling. We had a nice visit before breakfast, and then we went our separate ways.

Months later, after the moose had returned to the wild, Charlie got up from the dinner table and went for his boots. "Where are you headed?" I asked. "Come on, Dad, we're going up to the cabin." It was a cold, moonless spring night with a light rain. The nice warm bed upstairs seemed inviting. "Come on, you promised." A bit reluctantly, I found our sleeping bags and ponchos, the rolled-up foam bedding, and the lanterns. I even loaded up my 22, not much of a rifle when it comes to stopping a coyote or a moose, but it made the trip more of an adventure. Leaving my wife and three young daughters on the back porch, Charlie and I set out, up the logging road through the woods to our small hunting cabin.

The road was muddy and the rain pelted down on my rubber hood, making a soft, hollow sound. The lights from the farmhouse faded and the woods turned a deep ocean black, the pale

Christopher Kimball

lantern light illuminating wet silvery bark and wriggling in the gusty wind. I could see moose tracks on the road, huge round prints when seen next to the sharp, cloven hoof prints of deer. The woods smelled of warm rot and spearmint. Charlie pulled me along as we went deeper into the night, far from the hum of the furnace and the ticking of bedside clocks. We were headed into cold and unfamiliar territory, yet my son was strangely heroic, comfortable with his night visions. He was guiding me into his world, a place where sons come face to face with their dreams and fathers rediscover the unknown.

Late that summer, it was another dark night, and I made a stew from the last of the rabbits frozen from last year's hunting season. The cast-iron Dutch oven, filled as it was with game, freshly cut rosemary, white wine, and homegrown potatoes plucked from the root cellar, reminded me once again of the wild things. Over dessert, I asked Charlie if he was ready to take a return trip to the cabin, but on this night he was content to head for a bit of bedtime reading with his mom. I was disappointed that the summer of wild things had run its course, the moose having disappeared and life having now returned to normal. But one of these days, I am going to take my son back to that cabin, past dark shapes in the woods and four-legged shadows at the edge of vision. For now, I'll dream of the two of us, hand in hand, as we walked backward through time, a son leading his father home through the black, wet night.

ABOUT COOK'S ILLUSTRATED

Visit our expanded Web site The *Cook's* Web site features original editorial content not found in the magazine as well as searchable databases for recipes, equipment tests, food tastings, buying advice, illustrations of step-by-step techniques, and quick tips. The site also features our online bookstore, cooking courses, a question-and-answer message board, and a sign-up form for our free newsletter, *e-Notes*. Join us online today at www.cooksillustrated.com.

The Magazine *Cook's Illustrated* (ISSN 1068-2821) is published bimonthly (6 issues per year) by Boston Common Press Limited Partnership, 17 Station Street, Brookline, MA 02445. Copyright 2000 Boston Common Press Limited Partnership. Periodical postage paid at Boston, Mass., and additional mailing offices, USPS #012487. A one-year subscription is $29.70, two years is $55, and three years is $75. Add $6 postage per year for Canadian subscriptions and $12 per year for all other foreign countries. To order subscriptions in the U.S. call 800-526-8442; from outside the U.S. call 515-247-7571. Gift subscriptions are available for $24.95 each. Postmaster: Send all new orders, subscription inquiries, and change of address notices to *Cook's Illustrated*, P.O. Box 7446, Red Oak, IA 51591-0446.

Cookbooks and other products *Cook's Illustrated* also offers cookbooks and magazine related items for sale. Products offered include annual hardbound editions of the magazine, a seven-year (1993–1999) reference index for the magazine, the How to Cook Master Series of single-subject cookbooks, as well as copies of *The Best Recipe*, *The Complete Book of Poultry*, *The Cook's Bible*, and *The Yellow Farmhouse Cookbook*. Prices and ordering information are available by calling 800-611-0759 inside the U.S. or 515-246-6911 from outside the U.S. or by visiting our online bookstore at www.cooksillustrated.com. Back issues of *Cook's Illustrated* are available for sale by calling 800-611-0759 inside the U.S. or 515-246-6911 from outside the U.S.

Questions about your book order? Visit our customer care page at www.cooksillustrated.com, or call 800-611-0759 inside the U.S. or 515-246-6911 from outside the U.S.

Reader submissions *Cook's* accepts reader submissions for quick tips. We will provide a one-year complimentary subscription for each tip that we print. Send your tip, name, address, and daytime telephone number to Quick Tips, *Cook's Illustrated*, P.O. Box 470589, Brookline, MA 02447. Questions, suggestions, or submissions for Notes from Readers should be sent to the same address.

Questions about your subscription? Visit our customer care page at www.cooksillustrated.com, where you can manage your subscription, including changing your address, renewing your subscription, paying your bill, or viewing answers to frequently asked questions. You can also direct questions about your subscription to *Cook's Illustrated*, P.O. Box 7446, Red Oak, IA 51591-0446, or call 1-800-526-8442 inside the U.S. or 515-247-7571 from outside the U.S.

Treat Basil Gingerly

The other day I was listening to National Public Radio and heard a chef talking about cutting herbs. He claimed that if you cut basil crosswise it will darken, but if you cut it lengthwise it will not. I can't figure out any reason why this might be true, but I figured if he was saying it on the radio, there must be something to it. Can you enlighten me?

DANA VERBOTEN
OAKLAND, CALIF.

➤ To determine whether the degree to which basil darkens is related to the method by which it is cut, we started with a few tests of our own. We stacked fresh basil leaves into two piles and rolled each into tight, cigar-style rolls from which thin, even strips (called chiffonade) are most efficiently cut. We rolled one stack from tip to stem and the other from side to side, and then sliced both rolls into thin ribbons with a freshly honed chef's knife. The basil that was rolled from side to side and cut crosswise darkened in seconds at both the cut edge and in its interior creases. The basil that was rolled from tip to stem and therefore sliced lengthwise darkened at a much less dramatic rate and showed less overall damage. We then cut two additional stacks, keeping one flat and cutting it with the knife and tearing the other by hand; in each case, the leaves hardly blackened at all.

A plant researcher at Cornell University explained that when basil is cut, oxygen mixes with chemical compounds called polyphenols on the surface cells of the leaf, which causes the darkening and bruised appearance. Even the simple act of rolling the basil breaks vascular tissue and fibers on the surface of the leaves and causes discoloration. That explains why the leaves left flat hardly darkened when cut. In addition, we learned that the reason the crosswise-cut basil rolls darkened more than the lengthwise-cut rolls is that in side-to-side rolling the leaves are cut "across the grain," which causes more breakage of vascular tissue and greater surface damage.

So for basil that will retain its fresh green appearance for the long haul, your best bet is to keep the leaves flat and delicately rip or cut them rustic style. If you're after thin, ribbonlike strips for garnish, roll the leaves from tip to stem and cut. (See "Harvesting, Using, and Storing Fresh Herbs," pages 16–17.)

Devil's Food Cake Run Amok?

I was excited to try *Cook's* recent devil's food cake recipe (see "The Best Devil's Food Cake,"

March/April 2000), but as I read the recipe carefully, I thought that the total amount of flour, 1½ cups, seemed like too little. This recipe was not consistent with other cakes I regularly make. Is it correct?

DIANE KOSS
BURLINGTON, VT.

➤ The recipe is correct at 1½ cups of flour. Producing a luxuriously moist and intense chocolate devil's food cake was a primary concern. To achieve the deep, resonant flavor we wanted, we used high proportions of unsweetened chocolate and cocoa. Because both of these are dry ingredients, the amount of flour in the recipe is less than that in many other types of chocolate cake. This is not entirely unusual for devil's food cakes, and the texture of those we tested with this quantity of chocolate and more flour was compromised.

Other readers, including Dave Waugh of Columbia, Mo., noted that the cake layers were thin. This is a delicate batter that will not support a large volume per pan. Hence the batter is divided among three 8-inch cake pans designed to stack into a single three-layer cake. The cakes that we baked for this report rose to just over 1 inch high, yet when they were layered and frosted, they resulted in a tall and impressive confection. In fact, many "homemade" cake layers of any quality may seem thin when compared with the layers produced from packaged cake mixes, which tend to tower owing to their ample and powerful chemical leavening. To our palates, however, such cakes lack in flavor what they offer in majesty.

One Fold, Two Fold, Three Fold, Four

The labels on the large bottles of vanilla extract available in warehouse stores and food service industry supply houses sometimes include the terms "one fold" or "two fold" and so on. What does "fold" mean in this case?

BETH McDERMOTT
NEWTON, MASS.

➤ "Fold" refers to the flavor strength of vanilla extract as dictated by the Food and Drug Administration. According to current FDA standards, one-fold (single-strength) vanilla extract must be made from 13.35 ounces of vanilla beans at 25 percent moisture per gallon of liquid solvent.

Understanding how vanilla extract is produced clarifies the picture. Industry literature published by the flavor division of McCormick and Company in Hunt Valley, Md., outlines in

detail the four-stage manufacturing process used to transform cured vanilla beans into extract. First, the beans are chopped or shredded, and then they are soaked in an alcohol and water solution that "extracts" their flavor. The precise formula of the solution and the method, duration, and temperature of the extraction vary with the manufacturer. The term "fold" derives from the third stage of the process, which may be called concentration, adjustment, or folding. Here some or all of the alcohol and water solvent is removed, and the remaining extract is adjusted for flavor strength. Most often, vanilla extracts available at the retail level are one fold, or single strength, though some mail-order spice houses offer double-strength (or two-fold) extracts.

Double-strength extracts are adjusted so they contain the "extractive matter" of 26.70 ounces (or two times 13.35 ounces) of vanilla per gallon of solvent. Three-fold extract would contain three times the 13.35-ounce-unit of vanilla beans per gallon of liquid. When using two- or three-fold vanilla, adjust the amount used in the recipe accordingly.

Incidentally, the final stage of the manufacturing process is called solvent recovery, in which the residual solvent is recovered from the spent vanilla bean solids used to make the extract.

Vanilla Extract, and Not

What is the difference between alcohol-based vanilla extract and the nonalcoholic, glycerin-based versions?

STERLING HAIDT
LOS ALTOS, CALIF.

➤ The answer to this question hinges on a different facet of the FDA's measurement standard for vanilla extract, discussed above in "One Fold, Two Fold, Three Fold, Four." We contacted Matthew Nielsen, vice president of Nielsen-Massey Vanillas in Waukegan, Ill., and Rick Brownell, vice president of vanilla products for Virginia Dare Extract Company in Brooklyn, N.Y., and both noted immediately that according to the FDA standard, vanilla extract must contain no less than 35 percent ethyl alcohol by volume. If the solution contains less than 35 percent alcohol, which is of course the case with alcohol-free, glycerin-based products, the FDA defines that substance as vanilla flavoring. Vanilla flavoring allows those consumers who want to avoid alcohol a source of natural vanilla flavor without having to use vanilla beans.

Though both Nielsen and Brownell said that glycerin-based vanilla flavorings are used more commonly for commercial applications than for retail sale, we found two such products, called vanilla flavoring and cookbook vanilla, in local markets. Phillip Sprovieri, vice president of sales for Flavorchem/The Spicery Shoppe in Downer's Grove, Ill., explained that glycerin is a vegetable oil derivative, and, sure enough, the texture of our glycerin-based vanillas was viscous and a little slick, while the flavor was quite sweet. Brownell said that some manufacturers may add trace amounts of glycerin to their alcohol-based extracts because its sweetness helps to mask the few harsh overtones in the vanilla.

Dr. Susan Brewer, associate professor of food chemistry at the University of Illinois in Urbana, explained that glycerin evaporates at a much higher temperature than alcohol. Brownell also mentioned the evaporation point, explaining that some commercial vanilla users detect a stronger vanilla aroma during baking with the extract and associate that aroma with a loss of vanilla flavor. Glycerin-based products give off a milder vanilla aroma during baking. We confirmed this empirically by baking sequential batches of simple sugar cookies, one with vanilla flavoring, followed by another with vanilla extract. Sure enough, everyone in the kitchen did note a stronger vanilla aroma from the extract-based cookies.

We experimented further in the test kitchen by making side-by-side batches of panna cotta (see "The Secrets of Panna Cotta," page 22 of this issue), one with true alcohol-based vanilla extract and the other with glycerin-based vanilla flavoring. Our tasters agreed that the panna cotta made with extract had a deeper, more multidimensional vanilla flavor that lasted on the palate. The panna cotta made with the glycerin-based vanilla packed a strong initial hit of vanilla flavor that dissipated quickly. The latter was also unanimously judged sweeter. Tasters' comments about the two batches of cookies ran along the same lines.

Our advice, then, is to stick with true, alcohol-based vanilla extracts if you have no objection to the alcohol. They are not only widely available, but they offer a more refined vanilla flavor as well.

Toasting Rolled Oats, Too

I agree with *Cook's* that steel-cut oats cooked slowly and with little stirring produce the best bowl of oatmeal (see "The Best Bowl of Oatmeal," March/April 2000). Still, while a 30-minute cooking process may be fine for weekends, I just don't have time for that on weekday mornings. So I was interested in improving my weekday breakfast bowl of quicker cooking rolled oats. I experimented with *Cook's* method of toasting the oats in butter before adding the liquid (which I warmed in the microwave while I was toasting the oats) and then stirring only minimally near the end of cooking and, boy, was I amazed at the change in my bowl of oats! They were nuttier in flavor, and I liked the texture better. With my quick-cooking rolled oats tasting better than ever, I can indulge in weekday oatmeal without even thinking of opening a package of the instant stuff.

CAROL FOY
SPICEWOOD, TEXAS

➤ When you switch from steel-cut to rolled oats, the sacrifice in both flavor and texture is significant, but we certainly understand the time constraints of a busy school- or working-day morning. Your idea about toasting rolled oats led us into the test kitchen for some investigation, and, sure enough, we noticed the difference, too. In a side-by-side tasting, everyone on our tasting panel picked up a slightly richer, deeper, nuttier flavor in the oatmeal that had been made with oats toasted in butter. The improvement was most pronounced in the oatmeal made with just water and somewhat subtler in oatmeal cooked in a combination of water and milk.

Garam Masala

We recently tried the Indian-spiced version of the roasted boneless leg of lamb (see "Indian-Spiced Roast Boneless Leg of Lamb with Herbed Almond-Raisin Crust," March/April 2000) and found it delicious, but I have a question. One of the ingredients is garam masala, which is listed only as an Indian spice blend. Can you give me more information about its specific ingredients? I'd like to try blending my own at home.

SHELLY THOMAS
FREDERICK, MD.

➤ Garam masala, which means "hot mixture," is a northern Indian combination of dry-roasted, ground spices used in a wide range of dishes. Often used as a base to which other spices are added, the exact composition of the mixture varies with the tastes of the cook. The most common ingredients include black peppercorns, cinnamon, cloves, cardamom, coriander, cumin, dried chiles, fennel, mace, nutmeg, and bay leaves. Ginger and caraway seeds also make frequent appearances, and we have encountered recipes that call for saffron, sesame seed, and ajowan. As evidence that the proportions of the spices vary from cook to cook, Monisha Bharadwaj says in her book *The Indian Pantry* (Kyle Cathie Limited, 1996) that "there are as many recipes for [garam masala] as there are households in India." All of the other spice merchants, Indian cooks, and cookbook authors we contacted agreed. Our sources agreed further that bottled, commercial mixtures tend to be less aromatic and more mellow than a batch you toast and grind fresh at home.

Blender Blunder

An unfortunate editorial mix-up caused us to print a picture of the wrong Hamilton Beach blender in our May/June 2000 story "Basic Blenders Beat Upscale Rivals." The model that we tested and wrote about was the 14-speed BlendMaster, model 54200R. The blender we inadvertently pictured was its less expensive cousin, the seven-speed BlendMaster, model 57101R. We apologize for the confusion.

WHAT IS IT?

A friend recently brought this item to me as a gift. An elderly Japanese woman in her neighborhood had passed away, and she bought it at the yard sale held at her neighbor's house. It was among the other kitchen equipment, but no one there could identify it for sure, and I thought you might be able to.

ANNETTE BAUERMANN
DAVENPORT, IOWA

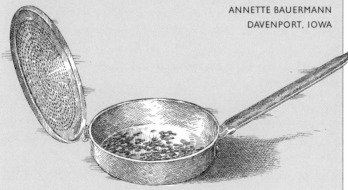

Your pan is a sesame seed toaster, designed specifically for that task. If you have explored Japanese cooking, then you've probably toasted sesame seeds in a skillet on the stovetop for a number of dishes. Toasting deepens the seeds' flavor considerably, so it is almost always done before they are added to a dish. Heated sesame seeds often pop right out of an uncovered skillet, hence the hinged, vented lid on this pan to keep them in place. Generally, sesame toasters are made of tinned steel and measure about 4½ inches in diameter and 1 inch in depth. Although the lid on your sesame toaster is made of perforated steel, lids on other versions are fashioned out of wire mesh screen, as it is on the model we found for sale at Buck's 5th Avenue (209 Fifth Avenue S.E., Olympia, WA 98501; 360-352-9301; b5th@earthlink.net (e-mail); www.culinaryexotica.com). The toaster comes with 2 ounces of either sesame or coriander seeds and costs $11.95, plus shipping and handling.

Quick Tips

Homemade Charcoal Fire Starter

Using a chimney starter is our favorite way to start a charcoal fire in the grill. Herbert Lewis of Woodbridge, Conn., suggests the following method for making your own inexpensive chimney starter at home. (This method can also be found in *Thrill of the Grill* [Morrow, 1990] by John Willoughby and Chris Schlesinger.)

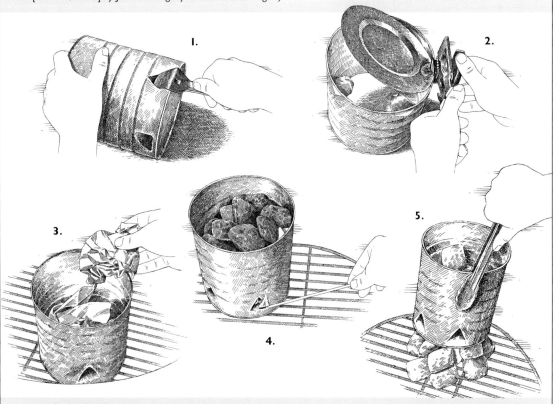

1. Using a church-key can opener, punch six holes in an empty 39-ounce coffee can along the lower circumference of the unopened end.
2. Remove the unopened end of the can with a can opener.
3. Set the can on the grill's charcoal rack with the triangular holes at the bottom. Load the can about one-half full with crumpled paper, then top it off with charcoal.
4. Insert a long match through one of the triangular holes at the bottom to set the paper on fire.
5. Several minutes later, when the coals are well lit, use tongs to grasp the top of the can and lift it upward to empty the contents onto the charcoal rack. Place more coals loosely around and on top of the burning coals to build up a cooking fire.

Stabilizing a V-Rack on a Gas Grill

When grill-roasting a turkey (see "Foolproof Turkey on the Grill," November/ December 1999), a V-rack is needed to hold the bird. LeeAnne McCabe of Ipswich, Mass., ran into trouble when the base of her V-rack slipped through the bars of her gas grill rack. She devised the following solution. Place a wire cooling rack (or, even better, a wire cooling rack with a grid design) on the grill so that its bars run perpendicular to the bars on the grill rack. This provides a stable surface for the V-rack.

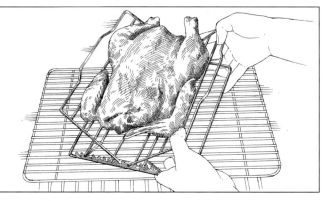

Soaking Bamboo Skewers

Although we thread most meats on metal skewers, many cooks like bamboo skewers. Soaking them before grilling helps to delay the burning (of the bamboo, not the food). Leslie Saltsman of Potomac, Md., found it difficult to keep the skewers submerged in water until she developed this easy method: Fill an empty two-liter soda bottle with water, slip the skewers inside, and screw the cap in place. The skewers will remain fully submerged and pop out when the bottle cap is removed.

Ready-Made Wood Chip Trays

While fashioning a wood chip tray from aluminum foil to use in grill-roasting a turkey on a gas grill (see "Foolproof Turkey on the Grill," November/ December 1999), Steve Ackley of San Antonio, Texas, thought he might save himself the trouble of making the tray by using a small, disposable aluminum pie plate (or a disposable aluminum pan in another shape). He fills the pie plate with the wood chips and, before preheating the grill, sets the pie plate on the burner that is to remain lit. The plate becomes scorched during the course of grilling, but, unlike our homemade foil tray, it can be reused. In addition, it's easier to manipulate a plate, which is stiffer than a homemade foil tray.

Keeping Pizza Crisp

Fresh tomato is a popular pizza topping, but its high moisture content can turn a crisp crust soggy in no time. Louis Maverick of Reno, Nev., has come up with the following solution. He spins the tomato slices or chunks in the salad spinner to draw out much of the water before topping the pizza.

Frozen Lemon Slices

When Carissa Robertson of Tyler, Texas, finds lemons on sale, she buys an ample supply and freezes them for garnishing glasses of water and other drinks. To follow her example, slice the lemons, lay the slices flat on a parchment-covered baking sheet and freeze, then store frozen in a zipper-lock bag.

Shakable Salt

Cooks who live in hot, humid climates will tell you that salt clumps up in the shaker, making it difficult to sprinkle. Lisa Louise Yuen of New York, N.Y., wrote to offer one popular method for keeping the salt dry and ready to sprinkle. Just add a few grains of uncooked rice to the shaker; the rice, which is more hygroscopic than salt, will absorb excess moisture.

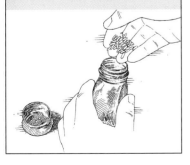

Easiest Fish Transfer

The recipe for hot-smoked salmon in the July/August 1999 issue produced delicious results, but, as Shawn Grimes of Rochester Hills, Mich., pointed out, transferring the cooked side of salmon intact from grill rack to serving platter can be a challenge. Grimes proposed the following adjustment to our technique to make the transfer of the fish a little easier.

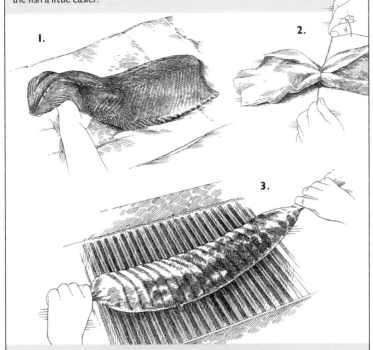

1. Place the salmon on a length of cheesecloth that is about 4 to 6 inches longer than the fillet on each side.
2. Wrap the fish carefully, tie the cheesecloth shut at both ends with string, and grill as directed.
3. Though the cheesecloth will turn brown, the overhang creates handles that extend over the edges of the grill, making it much easier to lift the fish than when using two spatulas, as we originally suggested. Grimes's technique also reduces the risk of damaging the fish.

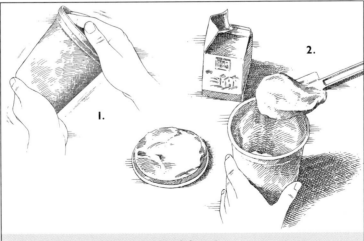

Whipped Cream Shaken, Not Stirred

Topping desserts with freshly whipped cream while on a picnic or wherever a whisk or electric mixer is unavailable is not an impossibility. Paige and Josh Hochschild of Mecosta, Mich., have developed a way to whip cream using nothing more than a plastic food container with a tight seal.

1. Pour 1 cup of whipping cream into a 2-cup capacity plastic food storage container.
2. Shake vigorously until the cream is whipped, about 3 minutes.

Leak-Free Ice Cream Cones

Small children and adults who savor ice cream cones know that the melting ice cream often leaks out from the tip of the cone. Three readers, Christine Sapp of Columbus, Ohio, Lisa Jionzo of Mendon, Mass., and Thomas Saaristo of Chicago, Ill., all use the same trick to prevent the leak. They place a mini-marshmallow or upside-down Hershey's Kiss in the cone before loading it up with ice cream, creating a barrier between the melting ice cream and the cone tip.

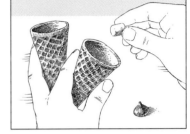

Easiest Tea Bag Removal

A big fan of iced tea, Catherine Carm of Brunswick, Maine, enjoys using *Cook's* recipe for it (July/August 1999) and found the recommended tea bag removal technique to be helpful. She took that same idea one step further and came up with the easiest way of all to remove the tea bags.

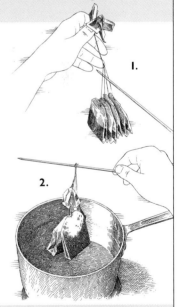

1. Tie the tea bag strings together, then slide a skewer through the knot before tightening it.
2. Position the skewer across the top of the pan, with the tea bags dangling in the water. When the tea has finished brewing, remove the skewer and the tea bags simultaneously.

Grilling Great Hamburgers

Burgers often come off the grill tough, dry, and bulging in the middle.
To our surprise, making a shallow depression in the center of the patty
was the first step toward a great burger.

≥ BY ADAM RIED WITH JULIA COLLIN ≤

Perfectly flat burgers make an ideal bed for toppings and are just plain easier to eat.

I'll admit it: I have, at times, considered becoming a vegetarian. I could give up steaks and pork chops and leg of lamb, but when I bite into a juicy grilled hamburger with all the trimmings, I'm back with the carnivores.

I'm not talking about one of those pasty, gray "billions served" or "have it your way" specimens. And I'm not talking about the typical backyard barbecue burger, either. You know the one I mean, because we've all made them. This burger is tough, chewy, and dry, and, after one flip with a spatula, more of its crust—if it formed one at all—sticks to the grill than to the patty. And of course there's the shape—domed, puffy, and round enough to let all the condiments slide right off. The ideal grilled burger, however, is alto-gether different: moist and juicy, with a texture that's tender and cohesive, not dense and heavy. Just as important, it's got a flavorful, deeply caramelized, reddish brown crust that sticks to the meat, and a flat shape to hold the goodies.

Given the vagaries of a live fire, this combination of traits is not always easy to achieve. Beyond choosing the right type of ground beef, seasoning it correctly, and sizing and forming the patties carefully, I knew that we had to determine the right type of fire, optimal cooking times, and the best way to flip the burger.

The Meat Matters

Virtually every burger recipe I researched recommended chuck as the cut of choice for robust beefy flavor and juiciness (this portion of the cow includes the neck, the shoulder down to the top of the foreshank [the front leg], and the ribs, up to and including the fifth). Most recipes also suggested starting with a solid piece of chuck, such as a roast or large steak, and asking the butcher to grind it for you as opposed to buying packaged, preground beef. Testing for this article and previous testing at *Cook's* (see "A Better Burger," July/August 1995) bore this out. Our current and past tests also confirmed the ideal ratio of fat to lean as 20 percent fat/80 percent lean. With this level of agreement, the issue of what meat to use was settled.

Knowing that the type of fire and cooking times would depend on the thickness and diameter of the patties, we experimented with size and shape first. In our experience, the crust that formed on patties that were made too thick—anything much over 1 inch—became tough and chewy by the time the interior had cooked enough. So we shaped 5-ounce portions of meat into patties that were 1 inch, ¾ inch, and ½ inch thick. Once cooked, these burgers looked especially round and puffed, rather like a tennis ball in shape, clumsy both to top with condiments and to eat. The reason all burgers puff a little when they cook, according to Dr. Susan Brewer, associate professor of food chemistry at the University of Illinois in Urbana, has to do with the connective tissue, or collagen, that is ground up along with the meat. When the connective tissue in the patty heats up to roughly 130 degrees, it shrinks. This happens on the top and bottom flat surfaces first, and then on the sides, where the tightening acts like a belt. When the sides tighten, the interior meat volume is forced up and down, so the burger puffs.

The thinner ½-inch-thick patty produced fairly good results, but the unexpected slam-dunk winner was a patty we formed with a slight depression in the middle, so that the edges were thicker than the center (the edges were ¾ inch thick, the center ½ inch thick). Test cook Bridget Lancaster had encountered this trick in a restaurant kitchen, and it was quite a success. The burger cooked evenly from the edges to the center and was neither puffy nor cumbersome to eat. In fact, the puffing effect during cooking pushed the center up to almost the same height as the edges, so the burger was level—all the better for accommodating ketchup and other trimmings. Using this technique, we went on to try patties weighing in at 4, 6, and a whopping 8 ounces. The 6-ounce burgers, which were about 4½ inches in diameter, were our tasters' choice—generous without being huge or overwhelming.

Another tip on making the patties that we'd found in many recipes was to avoid overhandling the meat. This, too, was good advice. When we really mashed a patty into shape so that the white flecks of fat melded with the red lean into a blurry pink, the resulting burger was dense and less tender. Visually, the red lean and flecks of white fat should remain separate and distinct. Resist the temptation to press the meat hard into a perfectly uniform patty.

Fire and Flip

The prized flavor of the fire is just one reason that burgers and grills are so well matched. Heat is the other reason. Burgers require a good blast of heat if they are to form a crunchy, flavorful crust before their interior overcooks. Nevertheless,

while many of the recipes we looked at advised cooking the burgers over a hot fire, we suspected we'd have to adjust the heat because our patties were quite thin in the middle. Sure enough, a hot fire made it too easy to overcook the burgers. We found that a medium-hot fire (you can hold your outstretched hand 5 inches above the grill rack for just three to four seconds) formed a crust quickly and easily while also providing a wider margin of error in terms of cooking the center. Nonetheless, burgers cook quickly—needing only 2 to 2½ minutes per side—so don't walk away from the grill while they're on it. We also tried a medium fire, which produced a sub-par crust. Because burgers cook through so fast, there was no reason to try an indirect fire. Likewise, we found no need to use the grill cover to help retain heat.

Make depressions in the patties by gently pressing down in the center with your index, ring, and middle fingers. The resulting burger (right), while thick, is also flat and evenly cooked.

Patties made with the same amount of meat but formed without a depression, such as the one at left above, resulted in burgers with a distinct bulge in the center.

While researching recipes we came across a couple of grilling tricks that panned out well. The best was to lightly grease the grill rack with

Our "National Condiment"

An occasional brush with vegetarianism is not my only confession. While good burgers certainly stand on their own merits, I go for them largely because they deliver my longest standing, truest culinary love: ketchup. Most of what I ate as a child was doused with it, and while I have over the years matured into tastes for bitter greens, stinky cheeses, and other prickly adult flavors, my devotion to ketchup has never faltered.

Andrew Smith's book *Pure Ketchup: A History of America's National Condiment* (University of South Carolina Press, 1996) fueled my obsession. Smith writes that there is considerable confusion about the origin of ketchup. Food historians have associated it most often with Asia, specifically with the Chinese *kê-tsiap* or *fan-kei chop*, Malay or Javanese *kitjap*, and Indonesian *kecap*. What is certain is that what we now know as ketchup was originally a salty, fermented medium for preserving or pickling ingredients, primarily fish.

British explorers first encountered this spicy sauce in Asia at the end of the 17th century, and early 18th-century British ketchup recipes were often anchovy-based. By the mid-18th century, though, the three predominant types of ketchup were fish, walnut, and mushroom, though shellfish, berries, fruit, and beans were also used as ketchup bases. By the turn of the 19th century, cooks in the fledgling United States had added tomatoes to that list, and the popularity of tomato ketchup skyrocketed soon thereafter. By 1896 the *New York Tribune* reported that tomato ketchup was "the national condiment," available "on every table in the land." Devotion to our national condiment has remained strong over the last 100 years. According to the Chicago market research firm Information Resources, Americans consumed more than 604 million pints of it in 1999.

Yet it's no secret that not all ketchups are created equal; any kid can tell you that. A sweep though four local markets turned up 10 kinds of tomato ketchup, not including specially flavored (roasted red pepper, roasted garlic, Tabasco, and maple syrup, to name a few), no-salt types, and the local and store-name brands that we left behind.

Hein | Del Monte | Hunt's

Add to that two fancy varieties of mail-ordered ketchup and one batch we made fresh in the test kitchen, and we had 13 kinds to try in a side-by-side tasting. They included the big three national brands, Heinz, Hunt's, and Del Monte; organic, fruit-sweetened, or otherwise all-natural brews from Muir Glen, Walnut Acres, Westbrae Natural, and World's; specialty and mail-order ketchups from Grand Lyon, Uncle Dave's Vermont Kitchen, Fox's Fine Foods, American Spoon Foods, and the El Paso Chile Company; and a homemade version from Cindy Pawlcyn's *Fog City Diner Cookbook* (Ten Speed, 1993). With mounds of hot french fries at the ready, we set to work.

It wasn't much of a surprise that the winner was Heinz. For all tasters but one Heinz ranked either first or second, and they chose words such as "classic," "balanced," "smooth," "glossy," and "perfect" to describe it. Some tasters commented that it was a trifle salty and "superprocessed," but they didn't consider these qualities to be faults in ketchup. A tiny bit sweeter than Heinz, Del Monte took second place, ranking among the top three choices of most tasters. Hunt's earned an honorable mention as the top choice of two tasters.

As a group, the "natural" ketchups struck tasters generally as overly thick and grainy in texture, with a muted, unbalanced flavor. In the Walnut Acres ketchup, tasters noticed overwhelming spice, and in the Westbrae they tasted too much vinegar; the Muir Glen was thought to taste overly "cooked and dull." World's ketchup garnered consistently unfavorable comments and brought up the rear in this group. The specialty ketchups did not fare much better, with tasters similarly noting excess spice, off colors and textures, and distinctly vegetal flavors. Even our homemade ketchup fell short, with tasters judging it far too sweet and chunky, more like "tomato jam" than ketchup.

In color, consistency, and flavor, none of the interlopers could match the ketchup archetype, Heinz. In fact, in answer to the question "Please characterize your ideal ketchup" on the tasting sheet, one respondent wrote simply "Heinz." —A.R.

a wad of paper towels dipped in oil; this allows the crust to stick to the burger instead of the grate when the patty is flipped over. The oiled grill also allowed us to flip the burgers with a long-handled barbecue spatula rather than tongs, which can gouge the delicate meat. Another good piece of advice is to refrain from pressing on the patties with the spatula as they cook. Rather than speeding their cooking, pressing on the patties served only to squeeze out their juices. Last, if you are intent on producing really rare burgers, freeze the patties for 30 minutes before putting them on the grill. When we tried this, the inside remained red while a beautiful crust formed on the outside.

CHARCOAL-GRILLED HAMBURGERS
SERVES 4

Weighing the meat on a kitchen scale is the most accurate way to portion it. If you don't own a scale, do your best to divide the meat evenly into quarters. Eighty percent lean ground chuck is our favorite for flavor, but 85 percent lean works, too. If you start with a chuck roast or steak, ask the butcher to grind it twice and expect some weight loss—2 to 3 percent in our experience—to the grinder. Toasting the buns is an easy extra flourish; just split them open and lay the halves cut-side down on the grill rack for the last 45 to 60 seconds of the hamburgers' cooking time.

  1½   pounds 80 percent lean ground chuck
  1   teaspoon salt
  ½   teaspoon ground black pepper
      Vegetable oil for oiling grill rack
      Buns and desired toppings

1. Ignite about 6 quarts (1 large chimney or about 6 pounds) charcoal and burn until coals are completely covered with thin coating of light gray ash, 20 to 30 minutes. Spread coals evenly over grill bottom, position grill rack above the coals, and heat until medium-hot (you can hold your hand 5 inches above grill surface for no longer than 3 or 4 seconds).

2. Meanwhile, break up ground chuck with your hands in medium bowl. Sprinkle salt and pepper over meat; toss lightly with hands to distribute seasonings. Divide meat into four 6-ounce portions. Gently toss one portion of meat back and forth between hands to form loose ball. Lightly flatten into patty ¾ inch thick and about 4½ inches in diameter. Gently press center of patty down until about ½ inch thick, creating a slight depression in each patty; repeat with remaining portions of meat.

3. Scrape hot grill rack clean with wire brush. Lightly dip wadded paper towels in vegetable oil; holding wad with tongs, wipe grill rack. Grill patties, uncovered, without pressing down on them,

until well seared on first side, about 2½ minutes. Flip burgers with metal barbecue spatula; continue grilling about 2 minutes for rare, 2½ minutes for medium-rare, or 3 minutes for medium. Serve immediately.

GAS-GRILLED HAMBURGERS

Turn all burners on gas grill to high, close lid, and heat until very hot, 10 to 15 minutes. Follow recipe for Charcoal-Grilled Hamburgers from step 2, grilling patties 3 minutes per side for rare, 3 minutes on the first side and 3½ minutes on the second side for medium-rare, or 3 minutes on first side and 4 minutes on second side for medium.

GRILLED HAMBURGERS WITH GARLIC, CHIPOTLES, AND SCALLIONS

Toast three medium unpeeled garlic cloves in small dry skillet over medium heat, shaking pan occasionally, until fragrant and color deepens slightly, about 8 minutes. When cool enough to handle, peel and mince cloves. Follow recipe for Charcoal- or Gas-Grilled Hamburgers, mixing garlic, 1 tablespoon minced chipotle chile en

adobo, and 2 tablespoons minced scallion into meat along with salt and pepper.

GRILLED HAMBURGERS WITH PORCINI MUSHROOMS AND THYME

Cover ½ ounce dried porcini mushroom pieces with ½ cup hot tap water in small microwave-safe bowl; cover with plastic wrap, cut several steam vents with paring knife, and microwave on high power for 30 seconds. Let stand until mushrooms soften, about 5 minutes. Lift mushrooms from liquid with fork and mince using chef's knife (you should have about 2 tablespoons). Follow recipe for Charcoal- or Gas-Grilled Hamburgers, mixing porcini mushrooms and 1 teaspoon minced fresh thyme leaves into meat along with salt and pepper.

GRILLED HAMBURGERS WITH COGNAC, MUSTARD, AND CHIVES

Mix 1½ tablespoons cognac, 2 teaspoons Dijon mustard, and 1 tablespoon minced fresh chives in small bowl. Follow recipe for Charcoal- or Gas-Grilled Hamburgers, mixing cognac mixture into meat along with salt and pepper.

Hamburger Helpers?

We formed plenty of burger patties while working on this story, and, while it's really not much of a problem to pat them out by hand, we did begin to wonder about all the gadgets out there specifically designed for this task. Could they really make a simple process even simpler? Were they good enough to earn a space in the already-crammed drawers of our test kitchen? We scooped up four different patty-forming models at our local kitchen gadget emporia and went to work.

All of the presses easily accommodated our six-ounce portions of meat. After pressing a number of patties in each, the only general advantage we could recognize was that they saved your hands from becoming too greasy by limiting contact with the meat. As advantages go, this was pretty thin. Most cooks we know relish the feel of food in their hands and would not be offended by getting their hands a little greasy.

The patties made with both the Acme Burger Maker and the East Hampton Industries (EHI) Square Hamburger Press were somewhat tattered around the edges, though this was certainly not detrimental to the final product. In fact, when we sampled the cooked burgers, we noticed very little textural difference between those formed by hand and those formed with a press. The top and bottom interior surfaces on both the EHI press and another Acme product, the Acme Hamburger Patty Maker, were ribbed so as to give the patty surfaces more texture, but we failed to see any real benefit therein. Furthermore, their release of the burger was extremely poor. The press we liked best was the Fox Run Craftsmen Hamburger Press, model 5434. This press turned out patties of the ideal size and shape and released them easily. The handle on top of the press was an added bonus, because it could be used to press the dent into the tops of the patties.

If you're squeamish about touching ground meat, this press was definitely the best of the four we tried. Still, we have to admit that none of these presses has found its way into our permanent collection of kitchen gadgets. —A.R.

Acme Burger Maker EHI Square Hamburger Press Acme Hamburger Patty Maker Fox Run Craftsmen Hamburger Press

Grilled Vegetable Salads

A medium-hot fire and some light dressings turn varied mixes of onions, peppers, zucchini, and eggplant into simple summer salads.

⇒ BY JACK BISHOP ⇐

Grilled vegetable salads make an excellent warm-weather side dish for chicken, fish, or meat. Most grilled vegetable salads taste best at room temperature, after the cooked vegetables and seasonings have had a chance to blend.

The problem for most cooks is figuring out how to use the same fire to grill-roast peppers or char onions for salad and then cook chicken parts or tuna steaks. On a gas grill, your strategy is simple: Grill the vegetables, let them cool, assemble the salad, and then just fire up the grill again when you want to cook dinner.

Grilling on charcoal requires more planning. Vegetables should be cooked over a medium-hot fire (you should be able to hold your hand 5 inches above the grill rack for no more than three to four seconds). If you don't mind serving the main course at room temperature, you can cook it first (when the fire is hot) and then cook the vegetables as the fire begins to cool down. If you work really quickly, this strategy can work.

An easier plan is to build the fire, let it die down a bit, then grill your vegetables. Once the vegetables come off the grill, add a handful of unlit coals. While waiting for the fire to become hot again, assemble the salad, which can then sit around while you grill the main course. This second strategy is a bit more work (adding coals is a bother), but it keeps you from having to work frantically on the vegetable salad while you worry about the main course cooling down too much.

Another concern when preparing grilled vegetable salads is the dressing. Because the vegetables must be oiled generously before grilling to prevent sticking (use extra-virgin olive oil for the best flavor) the dressing must be light or the salad will taste greasy.

GRILLED PEPPERS WITH SHERRY VINEGAR, GREEN OLIVES, AND CAPERS
SERVES 4 TO 6

Use a mix of red and yellow peppers, if possible. The Spanish flavors in this dish work especially well with grilled fish, pork, or chicken.

    4   medium red and/or yellow bell peppers (about
        1 1/2 pounds)
    1   tablespoon sherry vinegar
    2   tablespoons extra-virgin olive oil
        Salt and ground black pepper
    6   large green olives, pitted and chopped (about 1/4 cup)
    1   tablespoon drained capers
    1   tablespoon minced fresh parsley leaves

Grill peppers over medium-hot heat (you can hold your hand 5 inches above grill surface for 3 to 4 seconds), turning several times with tongs, until skins are blistered and charred on all sides, about 15 minutes. Transfer peppers to medium bowl and cover with plastic wrap; let steam to loosen skins. Remove skins; core and seed peppers, then cut into strips 1 inch wide. Return pepper strips with accumulated juices to bowl. Add vinegar, oil, and salt and pepper to taste; toss gently. Arrange peppers on large platter and scatter with olives, capers, and parsley. (Can be covered and set aside for 3 hours.)

GRILLED ONION AND TOMATO SALAD
SERVES 4

The sweetness of grilled onions is an excellent foil for the acidity of the tomatoes. Use a high-quality, aged balsamic vinegar. This salad is especially good with steaks or burgers.

    3   medium-large red onions (about 1 1/4 pounds),
        cut into rounds 1/2 inch thick, rounds left intact
    3   tablespoons extra-virgin olive oil
        Salt and ground black pepper
    3   small, ripe tomatoes (about 1 pound), cored
        and cut into wedges 3/4 inch thick
    10 large fresh basil leaves, chopped coarse
    2   teaspoons balsamic vinegar

1. Insert 2 toothpicks into sides of each onion round to keep layers intact on grill. Lay onion rounds on large baking sheet and brush both sides with 2 tablespoons oil. Season generously with salt and pepper.

2. Grill onions over medium-hot heat (you can hold your hand 5 inches above grill surface for 3 to 4 seconds), turning once until lightly charred, about 6 minutes per side. Transfer onions to cutting board and cool slightly. Remove and discard toothpicks. Cut onion rounds in half and place in serving bowl; toss gently to separate layers. Add tomatoes, basil, and salt and pepper to taste; drizzle with remaining 1 tablespoon oil and the vine-gar. Toss gently and serve. (Can be covered and set aside for 1 hour.)

GRILLED EGGPLANT SALAD WITH THAI FLAVORS
SERVES 4 TO 6

Salting the eggplant before cooking removes excess moisture; we prefer to use kosher salt for its large grains, which can be easily wiped off afterwards. Use small red Thai chiles if you can find them, but any hot chile will work. Leave the seeds in for extra heat, but remove them if you prefer milder food. Serve this salad with grilled fish, chicken, or beef.

    4   tablespoons juice from 1 or 2 limes
    2   small hot red or green chiles, minced
    4   teaspoons sugar
    2   teaspoons soy sauce
    1   teaspoon Asian fish sauce
    1   medium garlic clove, minced (about 1 teaspoon)
    4   medium eggplants (about 2 pounds), cut
        lengthwise into planks 1/2 inch thick
    1   tablespoon kosher salt
    3   tablespoons peanut oil
        Salt and ground black pepper
    2   medium scallions, white and light green parts,
        sliced thin
    2   tablespoons minced fresh cilantro leaves
    1/4 cup roasted unsalted peanuts, chopped

1. Combine lime juice, chiles, sugar, soy sauce, fish sauce, and garlic in small bowl; set aside to blend flavors and allow sugar to dissolve.

2. Meanwhile, lay eggplant on large baking sheet. Sprinkle both sides with kosher salt; let stand 30 minutes. Using paper towels, wipe off salt and pat eggplant dry. Brush both sides with oil; season with ground black pepper. Grill over medium-hot heat (you can hold your hand 5 inches above grill surface for 3 to 4 seconds), turning once, until dark and crisp, about 5 minutes per side. Transfer eggplant to large cutting board and cool to room temperature. Cut eggplant into 1/2-inch squares.

3. Combine chopped eggplant, scallions, and cilantro in large serving bowl. Drizzle dressing over vegetables and toss to combine. Adjust seasonings. Sprinkle with peanuts and serve. (Can be covered and set aside for 1 hour.)

The Best Grill-Roasted Chicken

Rub the bird with spices and flip it just once for crisp, bronzed skin and flavorful, moist meat. (And then try cooking it on a beer can.)

≥ BY JACK BISHOP ≤

Millions of cooks will grill all manner of chicken parts this summer, from breasts and wings to thighs and drumsticks. If you're one of them, you can follow the guidelines published in previous issues of *Cook's* (July/August 1996 and July/August 1997) and pull pieces of chicken off the grill that boast mahogany skin and moist, flavorful meat.

There's only one problem with this scenario: Chicken parts don't spend enough time on the grill to pick up much smoke flavor. Since the smoky taste is one of the main reasons I like to grill, I often grill a whole chicken. When grilled over indirect heat (coals banked to one side, with the chicken over the cool part of a covered grill), the bird cooks in about an hour, giving it plenty of time to pick up a good hit of smoke.

Unlike grill-roasting a turkey, where the size of the bird really complicates things (see November/December 1999), grill-roasting a chicken turns out to be a fairly straightforward matter. On reading through various recipes while researching this story, however, I did notice some variations in technique. Wanting to determine the very best technique, I decided to test the important variables, including how to arrange the coals, whether or not to use a V-rack, when and how to turn the bird, and how to flavor it.

One or Two Piles of Charcoal?

When grill-roasting large birds (such as turkeys) or big cuts of meat (such as ribs or brisket), the standard setup is to fill half of a kettle grill with charcoal and to leave the other half empty. The food is placed on the cool side of the grill, and the kettle is covered. Because one side of the food faces the lit coals, the bird or meat will cook unevenly unless it is rotated at least once. (I found that a turkey must be rotated twice for even cooking.) Rotating is simple enough, but the heat dissipates when the lid is removed, and you often have to add more coals, which is a pain.

Since a chicken is so much smaller than a

Moist white meat, fully cooked dark meat, and crispy skin make the ideal chicken.

turkey or brisket, I wondered if the lit coals could be banked on either side of the kettle grill and the chicken cooked in the middle. After several tests, I concluded that this arrangement works fine, with some caveats.

First, the coals must be piled fairly high on either side to form relatively tall but narrow piles. I split the coals between either side of the grill and ended up piling the lit briquettes three or four levels high. If the coals are arranged in wider, shorter piles, the cool spot in the middle of the grill won't be large enough to protect the bird from direct heat.

Second, don't use too much charcoal. When I split a whole chimney (about 70 briquettes) into two piles I burned the chicken. Reducing the number of coals to just 50 kept the temperature inside the grill between 325 and 375 degrees, the ideal range for grill-roasting. (In addition to charcoal, you will also need three or four wood chunks. The wood chunks, which should be soaked in water so that they burn more slowly, flavor the chicken and add heat to a charcoal fire.

If you omit them, your grill will be too cool.)

Third, you must use a relatively small chicken. I found that the skin on a large roaster scorches long before the meat cooks through. A broiler/fryer (see "Broilers, Fryers, Roasters, Capons, and Hens" on page 11) is a must.

Last, keep the vents in the lid halfway open so the fire burns at a fairly even pace. If the vents are open all the way, the fire burns too hot at the outset—thereby scorching the bird's skin—and then peters out before the chicken has cooked through.

With the heat attacking the chicken from two sides, the bird cooks evenly, so there's no need to rotate it. (On gas grills, where just one lit burner is used to cook by indirect heat, you will need to rotate the bird.) After my initial tests, however, I did conclude that it was necessary to flip the bird over once during the hour-long cooking process. The skin on top of the bird cooks faster than the skin touching the rack. (Although this seems counterintuitive, repeated tests confirmed this observation.) Because the side of the bird that finishes right-side up tends to look better (grill marks fade and the skin bronzes more evenly), I decided to start the chicken breast-side down.

When I cook a turkey on the grill, I always cradle it in a V-rack, which keeps the skin from scorching and promotes even cooking. I prepared several chickens with and without V-racks and found that those placed right on the grill rack browned better and cooked just fine. Again, because a chicken is small, the bird spends much less time on the grill than a turkey and the skin is less likely to burn.

Flavoring the Chicken

With my technique perfected, I focused on the chicken and flavoring options. As expected, I found that brining the chicken in a salted water solution helps it retain moisture while cooking and is recommended. The one exception is a kosher bird, which is salted during processing and cooks up moist—and perfectly seasoned—without brining.

During the course of my testing, I tried brushing the chicken with melted butter and olive oil before and during grilling. Although a buttered bird browned marginally better than an oiled one, I don't recommend using either. Birds coated with a spice rub cooked up both more crisply and better looking than greased birds.

My last set of tests concerned the addition of smoke. Developing this recipe convinced me that wood chips aren't worth the hassle. On charcoal, wood chunks burn two to three times longer than the chips and give foods a much better smoked flavor. Since wood chunks won't burn in a gas grill, in the past I've resorted to placing soaked chips in a foil tray over the lit burner. Sometimes the chips burn just fine and you get some smoke flavor. Other times the chips are exhausted by the time the grill is preheated and the food placed on the rack. If you are serious about smoke flavor, use charcoal. Fortunately, a spice-rubbed chicken is so flavorful that tasters were more than happy with the gas-grilled variation.

CHARCOAL GRILL–ROASTED WHOLE CHICKEN
SERVES 4

If you choose not to brine, skip that part of step 1 and season the bird generously with salt inside and out before rubbing with spices. Or, better yet, use a kosher chicken (which is salted during processing). For added accuracy, place a grill thermometer in the lid vents as the chicken cooks. The temperature inside the grill should be about 375 degrees at the outset and will fall to about 300 by the time the chicken is done.

    1   cup kosher salt
    1   whole broiler/fryer (about 3 1/2 pounds)
    3   tablespoons spice rub (recipes follow)

1. Dissolve salt in 2 quarts cold water in large container. Immerse chicken in salted water and refrigerate until fully seasoned, about 1 hour. Remove chicken from brine and rinse inside and out with cool running water; pat dry with paper towels. Massage spice rub all over chicken, inside and out. Lift up skin over breast and rub spice rub directly onto meat (see illustration, above right).

2. While chicken is brining, soak 4 medium-sized wood chunks in water to cover for 1 hour; drain. When chicken is almost done brining, fill large chimney starter two-thirds full with charcoal (about 4 quarts, or 50 briquettes) and ignite; burn until briquettes are covered with light gray ash, 15 to 20 minutes.

3. Empty coals into grill. Divide coals in half to form two piles on either side of grill; use long-handled tongs to move any stray coals into piles (see illustration 1, right). Nestle 2 soaked wood chunks on top of each pile (see illustration 2, right). Position grill rack over coals and cover grill. Heat rack for 5 minutes, then scrape clean with wire brush. Position bird, breast-side down, in middle of rack, over portion of grill without any coals. Cover, opening grill lid vents halfway. Grill-roast for 30 minutes.

4. Working quickly to prevent excessive heat loss, remove lid and, using 2 large wads of paper towels, turn chicken breast-side up. Cover and grill-roast until instant-read thermometer inserted into thickest part of thigh registers 170 to 175 degrees, 25 to 35 minutes longer. Transfer chicken to platter or carving board, tent loosely with foil, and let rest 15 minutes. Carve and serve.

GAS GRILL–ROASTED WHOLE CHICKEN

Wood chunks are not suitable for gas grills, and wood chips, which don't add much smoky flavor, are more trouble than they're worth. Instead, rely on the spice rub alone; it will supply ample aroma and flavor. While grill-roasting, adjust the lit burner as necessary to maintain a temperature of 325 to 350 degrees inside the grill.

Follow step 1 of Charcoal Grill-Roasted Whole Chicken to brine chicken and apply spice rub. Light grill and turn all burners to high; cover and heat grill 15 minutes. Turn off all but one burner. Place chicken, breast-side down, over cool part of grill; close lid and grill-roast for 35 minutes. Turn chicken breast-side up, so that the leg and wing that were facing away from lit burner are now facing toward it. Close lid and

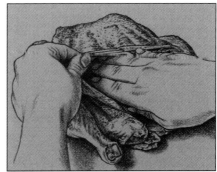
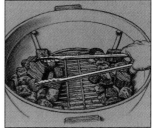

continue grill-roasting until thermometer inserted into thickest part of thigh registers 170 to 175 degrees, 30 to 40 minutes longer.

GRILL-ROASTED WHOLE CHICKEN WITH BARBECUE SAUCE

If you like, barbecue sauce can be used along with the Fragrant Dry Spice Rub. Wait until the bird is almost done to brush on the barbecue sauce, so that it does not scorch. For a quick and easy homemade barbecue sauce, see the recipe for Simple Sweet and Tangy Barbecue Sauce on page 13.

Follow recipe for Charcoal or Gas Grill-Roasted Whole Chicken; after rotating chicken breast-side up, roast only until instant-read thermometer inserted into thickest part of thigh registers 160 degrees, about 15 minutes. Working quickly to prevent excessive heat loss, brush outside and inside of chicken with ½ cup barbecue sauce. Cover and continue grill-roasting until instant-read thermometer inserted into thickest part of thigh registers 170 to 175 degrees, 10 to 15 minutes longer.

FRAGRANT DRY SPICE RUB
MAKES ABOUT ½ CUP

This rub and the one that follows were developed by grilling experts John Willoughby and Chris Schlesinger.

- 2 tablespoons ground cumin
- 2 tablespoons curry powder
- 2 tablespoons chili powder
- 1 tablespoon ground allspice
- 1 tablespoon ground black pepper
- 1 teaspoon ground cinnamon

Combine all ingredients in small bowl. (Extra rub can be stored [or frozen] in an airtight container for several weeks.)

CITRUS–CILANTRO WET SPICE RUB
MAKES ABOUT 3 TABLESPOONS

For extra spiciness, add up to ½ teaspoon cayenne pepper.

- ½ teaspoon ground cumin
- ½ teaspoon chili powder
- ½ teaspoon paprika
- ½ teaspoon ground coriander
- 1 tablespoon juice from 1 orange
- 1½ teaspoons juice from 1 lime
- 1½ teaspoons extra-virgin olive oil
- 1 small garlic clove, minced very fine
- 1 tablespoon minced fresh cilantro leaves

Combine all ingredients in small bowl. Use immediately.

Beer Can Chicken

As I was working on this story, a friend who spends many weekends at barbecue cook-offs told me about beer can chicken. On the barbecue circuit, she said, this is how beer can chicken is done: The bird is rubbed with spices and then an open, partially filled beer can is inserted into the main cavity of the chicken. The chicken is grill-roasted on the can, which functions as a vertical roaster.

I decided to try this wacky idea, convinced I would have something silly to write about. I culled a half-dozen recipes for beer can chicken (sometimes called drunken chicken) from the Internet, and they all followed the same basic formula, with some variation in the spice rub and the liquid inside the can. I decided to stick with my favorite rub and a can of cheap beer for my first test. My plan was to roast the bird in the morning and then have barbecued chicken for dinner. If beer can chicken was a bust, there still would be time to make something else.

I should have had more confidence in my friend's opinion. The bird came off the grill looking beautiful, with a deeply tanned, crisp skin. And the flavor was fantastic. Although I had a hard time tasting the beer, the spices had penetrated deep into the meat. The chicken was so good that my wife and I polished off the whole bird for lunch, which left us empty-handed for dinner.

Beer can chicken has a number of things going for it. The beer in the open can creates steam as the chicken roasts. This steam keeps the meat incredibly juicy. The moist heat also gives the meat an unctuous, rich quality. If you have ever steamed or braised a chicken, you know what I mean. Some people may not like this texture—the meat is a bit slippery. Personally, I find moist, unctuous meat preferable to the dry, shredding quality of chicken cooked by dry heat.

The beer can chicken was also better seasoned with spices—almost right down to the bone—than any chicken I had ever eaten. For the best flavor, I found it imperative to rub the spices inside the cavity (where the steam is generated) and under the breast skin.

Since my first test was such a success, I wondered about some of the variables I had uncovered in my research. I focused on the liquid in the can first, adding some barbecue sauce to the beer in one test, adding chopped aromatic vegetables to the beer in another, and using Guinness (a rich, dark beer) in a third test. In all cases, tasters couldn't detect much difference from the first bird steamed over a can of cheap beer without any additions.

I then replaced the beer with lemonade in one test and white wine in another. Tasters were able to detect a lightly sweet, lemon flavor in the bird cooked over lemonade. With the white wine, I rubbed a garlic, rosemary, and olive oil paste into the bird. This bird was a dud. The skin was not nearly as crisp and the flavor of the garlic and rosemary was confined to the surface. Furthermore, tasters thought the wine had not done much for the bird.

For one last test, I emptied a soda can and filled it with water, then rubbed the bird with spices as before. Although the differences were not dramatic, the flavor was a bit washed out and less appealing. Evidently, the beer was contributing something to the bird in addition to steam.

One last note: Chickens that weigh about 3½ pounds are ideal for this recipe. The cavity in smaller birds is too narrow to hold a beer can, and larger birds won't fit upright in most grills. —J.B.

GRILL-ROASTED BEER CAN CHICKEN
SERVES 4

If you prefer, use lemonade instead of beer. Fill an empty 12-ounce soda or beer can with 10 ounces (1¼ cups) of lemonade and proceed as directed.

- 1 cup kosher salt
- 1 whole broiler/fryer chicken (about 3½ pounds)
- 3 tablespoons spice rub (see recipes, left)
- 1 12-ounce can beer

1. Follow recipe for Charcoal Grill-Roasted Whole Chicken through step 1 to brine chicken and apply spice rub. Light charcoal or gas grill as recipe directs.

2. Open beer can and pour out (or drink) about ¼ cup. With church key can opener, punch two more large holes in top of can (for a total of three). Slide chicken over can so that drumsticks reach down to bottom of can and chicken stands upright (see illustration, right).

3. Place chicken and beer can on cool part of grill, using ends of drumsticks to help steady bird. Cover and grill-roast, rotating bird and can 180 degrees at halfway mark to ensure even cooking, until instant-read thermometer inserted into thickest part of thigh registers 170 to 175 degrees, 70 to 90 minutes.

4. With a large wad of paper towels in each hand, transfer chicken and can to platter or tray, making sure to keep can upright. Let rest 15 minutes; using paper towel wads, carefully lift chicken off can and onto platter or cutting board. Discard remaining beer and can. Carve chicken and serve.

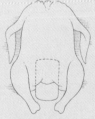

With the legs pointing down, slide the chicken over the open beer can. The two legs and the beer can form a tripod that steadies the chicken on the grill.

All-Purpose Barbecue Sauce

How can you make a quick, all-purpose barbecue sauce from pantry ingredients without sacrificing either complex flavor or that smooth, thick texture?

≥ BY ANNE YAMANAKA ≤

Just look on the shelves of your supermarket, and you'll find dozens of bottled versions of tomato-based barbecue sauce. But most of them are distractingly sweet and full of starchy additives that give them a gummy texture and harsh chemical flavors.

Homemade barbecue sauce is the natural answer to the bottled stuff, and some recipes that I've made are quite good. Unfortunately, though, you can't usually make these recipes in a pinch, since most of them either take hours to make or have ingredient lists that run the length of a novel, including many that most of us don't have on hand. I've tried other recipes that are quicker and easier to make, but they all fell short of my expectations. Some tasted more like a mixture of ketchup and a few spices than a true barbecue sauce, while others were too strong, either cloyingly sweet or overly sour. In addition, most of the homemade sauces had annoying chunks of onion floating around that gave the sauce a nice flavor but an unappealing texture.

I wanted a sauce that was easy to make in a pinch, using ingredients that I always have on hand ("pantry" ingredients), without compromising complexity of flavor or the smooth, thick texture that I expect from a barbecue sauce. I also wanted it to have the right balance of competing tastes—sweet and sour, spicy and smoky.

Most of the good recipes I'd found before used two or more tomato products, up to three sweeteners (brown sugar, molasses, pineapple juice), and a handful of spices and condiments. I was sure that by sticking with ingredients that gave me the most bang for my buck I could lose a few of these ingredients without sacrificing too much. So I began streamlining my list, paring it down to as few ingredients as I could without compromising complexity of flavor.

First I needed to know which tomato product would contribute the best texture and flavor. I made batches of sauce with the following: ketchup, tomato paste, tomato puree, canned tomatoes in juice, canned tomato sauce, chili sauce, and various combinations of tomato products. Not surprisingly, ketchup was the best for barbecue sauce because no other tomato product could contribute its combination of sweetness, tartness, and glossy smooth texture. Those sauces made solely with canned tomato products didn't cook down in the amount of time that I wanted

and so made slightly watery sauces, reminiscent of marinara in texture. To be sure that the sauce could not be improved by adding another tomato product, I tried ketchup and other options in various combinations. Happily, I found that ketchup used by itself provided the best base.

After tasting a number of sauces that included combinations of brown sugar, honey, and molasses (I had ruled out plain sugar and corn syrup in earlier tests), it was clear that molasses was the best sweetener for the job, contributing not just sweetness but also rich color and a spicy, slightly astringent, almost smoky flavor that was most welcome in the sauce.

Vinegar, condiments (other than ketchup), aromatics, and spices played a secondary role in the sauce. Apple cider vinegar was my first choice among a number of vinegars for its fruitiness and clear, bright flavor. I also liked prepared mustard, which lent a radishlike sharpness; Worcestershire sauce, which combined tartness and an unusual tamarind flavor; and hot pepper sauce (as in Tabasco), which added spiciness and acidity all at once. Using prepared mustard meant that I could omit dried mustard as an ingredient, paring down the list even further.

I found only a few spices really necessary to boost the flavor of the sauce: chili powder, black pepper, and a touch of cayenne to add a kick. Liquid smoke was another matter altogether. Some tasters liked the flavor, while others felt it had an artificial flavor. In the end I decided to include liquid smoke in my recipe because its smokiness gives the sauce a more authentic flavor; acknowledging that some people just don't like it, I made it an optional ingredient.

Based on my first tests I had ruled out vegetables such as green bell peppers and celery because I didn't like their vegetal flavor. I did like the flavors of onion and garlic in the sauce, but I didn't like the texture of the sauce when made with chunks of onion. I figured an easy solution would be to run the sauce through a blender after cooking. I was wrong. The texture after blending was grainy, not the smooth, glossy concoction I had envisioned. I briefly considered onion powder, but after trying a batch of sauce with it, I went back to the chunky sauce. A colleague in the Cook's test kitchen suggested pureeing the raw onion in the food processor, straining out the juice, adding the juice to the sauce, then cooking.

I was skeptical at first, thinking that the process would be too labor-intensive. But after trying it, I realized that it was actually just as quick as chopping an onion, taking only a few seconds to process and strain. This method produced the heady onion flavor I liked without adding any unpleasant chunkiness; the result was the viscous, glossy, smooth texture I had been hoping for.

Finally, I had a recipe for a great sauce, not only better than bottled but more complex and rich tasting than more complicated recipes.

SIMPLE SWEET AND TANGY BARBECUE SAUCE
MAKES ABOUT 1½ CUPS

1	medium onion, peeled and quartered
1	cup ketchup
2	tablespoons cider vinegar
2	tablespoons Worcestershire sauce
2	tablespoons Dijon mustard
5	tablespoons molasses
1	teaspoon hot pepper sauce, such as Tabasco
¼	teaspoon ground black pepper
1½	teaspoons liquid smoke (optional)
2	tablespoons vegetable oil
1	medium garlic clove, minced (about 1 teaspoon)
1	teaspoon chili powder
¼	teaspoon cayenne pepper

1. Process onion and ¼ cup water in workbowl of food processor fitted with steel blade until pureed and mixture resembles slush, about 30 seconds. Strain mixture through fine-mesh strainer into liquid measuring cup, pressing on solids with rubber spatula to obtain ½ cup juice. Discard solids in strainer.

2. Whisk onion juice, ketchup, vinegar, Worcestershire, mustard, molasses, hot pepper sauce, black pepper, and liquid smoke (if using) in medium bowl.

3. Heat oil in large nonreactive saucepan over medium heat until shimmering but not smoking. Add garlic, chili powder, and cayenne pepper; cook until fragrant, about 30 seconds. Whisk in ketchup mixture and bring to boil; reduce heat to medium-low and simmer gently, uncovered, until flavors meld and sauce is thickened, about 25 minutes. Cool sauce to room temperature before using. (Can be covered and refrigerated for up to 7 days.)

How to Make Rice Salad

For light, fluffy, separate rice that doesn't turn sticky as it cools, toast it, then cook it with the "pasta" method. To avoid a mushy salad, spread the rice out to cool.

⇒ BY MARYELLEN DRISCOLL ⇐

A few summers ago I took a road trip in a pickup truck with a farmer friend and his chicken-killing dog, Buck. Traveling from the Great Smoky Mountains to coastal New England, we ate dinner at Arby's, camped in a dirt parking lot, and always drove with the windows rolled down. By the time we arrived at our destination, nothing could have seemed more refreshing to me than a shower. But a large bowl of rice salad served alongside grilled shellfish topped that. Unlike the soggy, gummy, over-dressed rice salads I'd had in the past, this one was light, bright, and studded with the flavors of summer. It was a welcome change of pace from the standard seasonal fare of pasta salad, coleslaw, and green salad.

Rice salads, we found, are best when only lightly dressed.

Since then I've tried a number of rice salad recipes with hopes of replicating that experience. After a series of failures, I began to wonder if my judgment that one day had been skewed by a journey's worth of fast food and service station coffee.

The concept of making rice salad seems quite simple. Yet the problems it presents appear to be twofold. For starters, this understated grain does not hold up to assertive flavors the way a pasta salad can. And it is readily bogged down by a vinaigrette that would be well suited to a green salad.

Even more troubling than the delicate dance of flavors is the texture of the rice. Long-grain rice normally just isn't good cold; it tends to turn hard, clumpy, and slightly crunchy. Short-grain rice holds up better as it cools, but it has a sticky heaviness about it that I didn't want in a rice salad. If I were to rediscover that tender, fluffy, and light rice salad I once sampled, I needed to isolate a cooking method for long-grain rice that would preserve its fresh-from-the-pan characteristics once cooled.

I began with the technique prescribed for cooking rice pilaf in the March/April 2000 issue of *Cook's*. This made for a nice pilaf dish, but its buttery flavor was ill suited to a rice salad, and as the rice cooled it lost its appealing fluffiness. A similar master recipe for long-grain white rice in the May/June 1996 issue produced similar results—great when hot from the pot but pasty, dense, and slightly crunchy once cooled.

Stymied, I started testing every method of cooking rice imaginable. While many methods cooked up great rice, inevitably, the quality deteriorated upon cooling.

What I finally realized was the source of these failures is in fact the component of long-grain rice that makes it cook up fluffy: amylose, one of the two primary starches contained in rice. As it turns out, when long-grain rice cools, the long amylose molecules form rigid crystals that squeeze liquid out and turn the rice rock-hard. Technically speaking, this is called retrogradation. I realized that if I were going to come up with a palatable rice salad, I would need to apply some kind of sorcery to the starch.

In a last-ditch effort, I tried cooking the long-grain rice with the "abundant water" technique, in which rice is boiled in a large volume of water, just like pasta, until it is toothsome and cooked through but has not yet begun to fray. At this point, the water is simply strained out. The drawback of this technique is that it tends to turn out rice that tastes waterlogged. This is true. Yet the light and separate texture of the rice it delivered held up so well after cooling that I did not dare disregard this method. Instead, I added a couple of steps to the process to cope with the waterlogging problem.

Taking a cue from the pilaf recipe, I toasted the rice before boiling to tease out its nutty essence. Actually, its aroma might be better likened to that of popcorn. I did this, however, without the oil, since I found that oil made the rice heavy and greasy in salad form. (Another bonus is that all that's needed to clean the pan is a swipe with a dry towel.)

After the rice was boiled, I spread it across a baking sheet to cool it off. This creates a great deal of surface area, which allows the excess moisture to evaporate. Spreading out the rice to cool also prevents it from clumping, as it would if left to rest in a bowl. An added bonus is that because the rice cools to room temperature in about 10 minutes, salad assembly can be done quickly.

TECHNIQUE | THE BEGINNING AND THE END

Start by toasting the rice in a hot skillet for about five minutes. Then, when the rice has been cooked, cool it on a baking sheet.

Rice salads are not meant to be doused in oil and vinegar. Just a small amount does the trick. This also permits you to use a dark-colored vinegar, such as balsamic, without discoloring the rice.

Rice salad is particularly conducive to flavors that are politely understated, not especially bold or loud. It is a side dish that should taste light, not at all filling, yet every forkful should have character. Rice salads pair up particularly well with grilled fish or chicken and are best served at room temperature. Toss the rice with the dressing about 20 minutes before serving so that the subtle flavors have time to develop. If you dress it too far ahead, the rice absorbs the flavor and mutes it. The rice in this salad does stand up to refrigeration. Simply let it rest at room temperature for 30 minutes before serving.

BOILED RICE FOR RICE SALAD
MAKES ABOUT 6 CUPS COOKED RICE

Taste the rice as it nears the end of its cooking time; it should be cooked through and toothsome, but not crunchy. Be careful not to overcook the rice or the grains will "blow out" and fray. Aromatic basmati rice works well in any of the rice salads, but regular long-grain rice works fine, too.

- 1½ cups long-grain or basmati rice
- 1½ teaspoons salt

1. Bring 4 quarts water to boil in large stockpot. Meanwhile, heat medium skillet over medium heat until hot, about 3 minutes; add rice and toast, stirring frequently, until faintly fragrant and some grains turn opaque, about 5 minutes.

2. Add salt to boiling water and stir in toasted rice. Return to boil and cook, uncovered, until rice is tender but not soft, 8 to 10 minutes for long-grain rice or about 15 minutes for basmati. Meanwhile, line rimmed baking sheet with foil or parchment paper. Drain rice in large fine-mesh strainer or colander; spread on prepared baking sheet. Cool while preparing salad ingredients.

CURRIED RICE SALAD WITH CAULIFLOWER, MANGO, AND CASHEWS
SERVES 6 TO 8

- 2 tablespoons peanut oil
- ½ small head cauliflower, cut into small florets (about 2 cups)
- 1 tablespoon curry powder
- 1 teaspoon salt
- ¼ cup currants
- 1 recipe Boiled Rice for Rice Salad
- ½ cup raw cashews, chopped and toasted in small dry skillet over medium heat until golden and fragrant, about 2 minutes
- 1 medium mango, peeled and diced fine
- 3 tablespoons minced chives
- ¼ teaspoon ground black pepper

Heat oil in medium skillet over high heat until shimmering but not smoking. Add cauliflower, curry powder, and ½ teaspoon salt; cook, stirring constantly, until fragrant and curry powder adheres to cauliflower, about 1 minute. Add currants and ¼ cup water; reduce heat to medium-high and continue to cook until water evaporates and cauliflower is tender, about 3 minutes. Transfer cauliflower to large bowl; add rice, cashews, mango, chives, pepper, and remaining ½ teaspoon salt to bowl and toss thoroughly to combine. Let stand 20 minutes to blend flavors and serve.

RICE SALAD WITH ORANGES, OLIVES, AND ALMONDS
SERVES 6 TO 8

- 2 tablespoons olive oil
- 1 small garlic clove, minced (about ½ teaspoon)
- ¼ teaspoon grated zest plus 1 tablespoon juice from 1 small orange
- 2 teaspoons sherry vinegar
- 1 teaspoon salt
- ½ teaspoon ground black pepper
- 1 recipe Boiled Rice for Rice Salad
- ⅓ cup coarsely chopped pitted green olives
- 2 medium oranges, peeled and cut into segments
- ⅓ cup slivered almonds, toasted in small dry skillet over medium heat until fragrant and golden, about 2 minutes
- 2 tablespoons fresh oregano, minced

Stir together oil, garlic, orange zest and juice, vinegar, salt, and pepper in small bowl. Combine rice, olives, oranges, almonds, and oregano in large bowl; drizzle oil mixture over and toss thoroughly to combine. Let stand 20 minutes to blend flavors and serve.

RICE SALAD WITH PINEAPPLE, JÍCAMA, AND PUMPKIN SEEDS
SERVES 6 TO 8

If you're unable to find pumpkin seeds, substitute unsalted sunflower seeds.

- 2 tablespoons vegetable oil
- 1 medium jalapeño chile, seeded and minced (about 1 tablespoon)
- ½ teaspoon grated zest plus 1 tablespoon juice from 1 lime
- 1 small garlic clove, minced (about ½ teaspoon)
- 1 teaspoon honey
- 1 teaspoon salt
- ½ teaspoon ground black pepper
- 1 recipe Boiled Rice for Rice Salad
- ½ small pineapple, peeled, cored, and diced medium (about 1 cup)
- 5 ounces jicama, peeled and diced medium (about 1 cup)
- ⅓ cup pumpkin seeds, toasted in small dry skillet over medium heat until fragrant and lightly browned, about 1 minute
- 2 medium scallions, white and green parts, sliced thin
- 3 tablespoons minced fresh cilantro leaves

Stir together vegetable oil, jalapeño chile, lime zest and juice, garlic, honey, salt, and black pepper in small bowl. Combine rice, pineapple, jícama, pumpkin seeds, scallions, and cilantro; drizzle oil mixture over and toss thoroughly to combine. Let stand 20 minutes to blend flavors and serve.

RICE SALAD WITH CHERRY TOMATOES, PARMESAN, PEAS, AND HAM
SERVES 6 TO 8

- 2 tablespoons extra-virgin olive oil
- 1 tablespoon balsamic vinegar
- 1 small garlic clove, minced (about ½ teaspoon)
- 1 teaspoon salt
- ½ teaspoon ground black pepper
- 1 recipe Boiled Rice for Rice Salad
- ½ cup frozen peas, thawed
- 6 ounces cherry tomatoes, quartered and seeded (about 1 cup)
- 1 ounce thin-sliced cooked deli ham or prosciutto, chopped fine (about ¼ cup)
- 1 ounce Parmesan cheese, shredded (about ¼ cup)
- ¼ cup shredded fresh basil leaves

Stir together oil, vinegar, garlic, salt, and pepper in small bowl. Combine rice, peas, tomatoes, ham, Parmesan, and basil in large bowl; drizzle oil mixture over and toss thoroughly to combine. Let stand 20 minutes to blend flavors and serve.

Harvesting, Using, and Storing Fresh Herbs

Many gardeners raise herbs but don't know how to pick, use, and store them properly to maximize their fresh scent and flavor. Here are 20 tips that show you how.

BY KAY RENTSCHLER

To discover how best to harvest herbs both during and at the end of the season and how best to store them, we made an excursion to Plimoth Plantation in Plymouth, Mass., where we spoke with resident horticulturist John Forti. He offered invaluable advice on a wide variety of culinary herbs.

Knowing the Nomenclature

Tender annuals like basil, cilantro, and summer savory are so called because they will not survive a frost and are planted new from seed or small plants every year. Woody perennials like sage and winter savory, so called because of their branching habit and woody stems, can survive much colder temperatures and return year after year.

Whether for immediate use or end-of-season preservation, there are right and wrong ways to harvest specific herbs. Once they are out of the ground, it's important to handle them properly.

Illustration: John Burgoyne

HARVESTING AND STORING HERBS FOR SHORT-TERM USE

Frequent harvesting and use of fresh herbs throughout the season will help keep plant growth manageable and make your garden a pleasure to look at.

During the summer months, the herbs in kitchen gardens should be harvested to encourage growth. The young, flavorful leaves of tender annuals should be harvested above leaf buds, where the plant branches out. Tender annuals such as basil can be harvested simply by pinching them back.

Once a plant's energy goes into the flower, the flavor in the leaves can diminish and become bitter. Annuals such as basil (pictured here), summer savory, and cilantro will live longer if their flowers are pinched back.

Wait to harvest parsley (shown above) and other such herbs, including summer savory, until roots have developed and the plant is strong enough for regrowth. You can use a scissors or a knife to cut the herbs, or you may twist and pull off with your hands.

Perennials that have flowered, like the thyme pictured here, should not be harvested back to their branching growth. Instead, harvest fresh young leaves directly below the flowery tops.

Woody perennials such as rosemary (pictured here) should be harvested at the point at which new branches grow off a central stem (note position of fingers at left) rather than along a central stem; harvesting a central stem slows down new growth.

To clean fresh herbs, submerge them in a sink or large bowl (depending on the quantity of herbs) filled with cool salted water (about 2 tablespoons salt per sinkful). The salt water will drive away any insects without damaging the plant itself. Remove the herbs from the standing water, and dry in a salad spinner. To dry herbs completely, blot with paper towels.

Perennials such as sage and thyme are able to tolerate cold outdoor temperatures (12 degrees Fahrenheit), and thus can be stored in the refrigerator. We recommend plastic containers with tight lids. Stack the clean, dry herbs in loose layers separated by parchment paper or paper towels to allow for maximum air flow between them, and seal tightly. Smaller amounts of herbs can be placed in food storage bags.

HARVESTING AND STORING HERBS FOR LONG-TERM STORAGE

Harvest a plant when it is in its prime and looks vigorous. When considering long-term storage, remember that not all herbs freeze well; some are superior dried.

At the end of the year, an annual such as summer savory (pictured here) can be harvested right to the ground or can be pulled completely out of the ground, roots and all. It is, however, a good idea to leave one or two annuals in their beds; they will reseed and come back much earlier the following year.

Harvest perennials (such as marjoram shown here), completely to the ground with a knife or scissors. With woody perennials, like sage or winter savory, harvest no more than one-third of the plant so as not to compromise its health and vigor the following year.

Rosemary (pictured here), like other perennials, takes well to a pot and can be brought indoors over the winter. Such plants demand cool but well-lit indoor locations; they will not thrive on a warm windowsill.

We froze thyme, oregano, sage, tarragon, parsley, and dill for more than three months to gauge the effects on their freshness. Though tarragon and parsley experienced some discoloration, they still smelled and tasted fresh. The other herbs froze very well. Clean and dry the herbs as pictured above and layer them in tightly sealed plastic containers to insulate the delicate herbs from freezer odors. (They can be packed quite tightly; there's no need for the air flow required when these herbs are refrigerated.) Herbs can be frozen for up to four months.

Herbs such as sage, winter savory, mint, rosemary, marjoram, and oregano are well suited for drying as well as freezing. The classic method is to tie them in bunches by their stems (pictured) and hang them upside down in a cool, dry place for three weeks. We also tried drying clean herbs on oven racks in a closed gas oven for four days. The residual heat from the pilot light produced dried herbs still bright green in color and with vivid, fresh flavor. After drying, seperate the leaves from the stems and store in glass jars.

USING FRESH HERBS

Once they are harvested, herbs may need to be plucked or chopped before use.

Herb Bouquets
Refrigerator temperatures are too frigid for annuals such as basil and cilantro. They are best held for a day or two in a container of water set at room temperature.

Removing Tiny Leaves
To pluck leaves from stems—whether fresh or dried—hold the stem and run your fingers down the stem in a shredding motion, severing leaves from stem. Tiny leaves, such as thyme, may be used as they are; larger leaves, such as basil, should be plucked from the stem and chopped or torn.

Cutting Chives
Though many recipes call for snipped chives, we find snipping useful only for harvesting. To cut them finely, gather them tightly in one hand and mince finely with the other, turning your fingertips under to shield your fingers from the blade.

Cutting Large Leaves
For herbs with larger leaves, such as basil and mint, the most attractive and least damaging cut is the chiffonade.

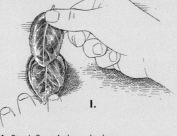

1. Stack 3 or 4 clean dry leaves.
2. Roll them tightly like a cigar, then slice the cigar thinly lengthwise.

Herb Flowers
If you let your herbs flower, that doesn't mean they are no longer useful. Herb flowers are actually delicious, tasting like the essence of the herb itself but with a little added sugar. To use them, pluck the blossom or trumpet of the flower from its green backing. Having sampled these herb flowers, we agree with Forti's assessment of some of their best culinary uses.

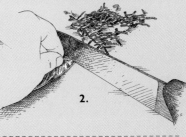

BASIL FLOWERS:
salads and tomato dishes
CHIVE FLOWERS:
omelets and grilled meats
MARJORAM FLOWERS:
herb butters and vegetable dishes
SUMMER SAVORY:
hummus
THYME FLOWERS:
most everything
WINTER SAVORY:
fowl or Middle Eastern food

Really Good Stuffed Zucchini

Preroasting readies the squash for hearty fillings and a fast finish.

⇒ BY JULIA COLLIN ⇐

In my experience, stuffed zucchini has either been a healthy but bland attempt at a vegetarian dinner or a thrifty, last-ditch effort to use up some leftovers. Either way, the dish has never garnered any points with me. I prefer the delicate flavor of zucchini in basic preparations: sautéed with a little garlic, thrown on the grill, or lightly roasted in the oven. I wondered, however, if I had been premature in giving this stuffed vegetable a bad rap. Realizing that a simple summer recipe would make a handy addition to my repertoire, I set out to create a stuffed zucchini worth making.

To start, I tried several recipes out of my favorite cookbooks. One after another, however, each turned out to be a disappointment. Simpler recipes stuffed raw zucchini with rice and vegetables and threw it in the oven. Not only did these zucchini take a while to cook through, but the filling on top dried out while the filling on the bottom absorbed the zucchini's moisture and became mushy. Other recipes blanched the squash in water or stock before they were stuffed, draining the zucchini of flavor and leaving behind a dull, limp shell. Still others filled the squash raw and baked it in a tomato juice or sauce that succeeded only in imparting a tinned, tomato flavor. As for the fillings, most recipes used precooked rice, which absorbed the moisture in the zucchini, thereby creating a toothless texture and monotonous flavor. The reasons for my longstanding bias against this stuffed vegetable were now more obvious than ever. To make a dish worth eating, I had to figure out how to par-cook the zucchini before stuffing it, then find something exciting to stuff it with.

The moisture in the zucchini was clearly the biggest problem. Roasting, with its hot, dry heat, seemed a promising way to lose this moisture while also precooking the squash. I experimented by roasting zucchini whole, roasting it halved, and roasting it halved and seeded. The whole zucchini took too long to cook and steamed itself soggy. Although the halved squash cooked in less time, the seeds still held onto some moisture, leaving behind a soggy shell. The seeded squash, on the other hand, retained the toothsome texture I was looking for and also developed a more concentrated flavor. With the heat of the oven able to hit the flesh of the zucchini directly, more moisture evaporated, intensifying the flavor.

Next I did side-by-side roasting tests. When the zucchini were roasted cut-side up, the mois-

The potatoes for the filling can be roasted alongside the zucchini, making the whole process quite easy.

ture that did not evaporate pooled in the hollow space once occupied by the seeds and later seeped into the stuffing, making it watery. When roasted cut-side down, however, the squash dripped moisture onto the hot roasting pan, where it turned to steam. Some of this steam got trapped underneath the overturned squash, speeding up the cooking process. Using a preheated pan further reduced the roasting time while creating a flavorful, golden brown crust along the rim. Salt and pepper brought out flavor, while olive oil prevented sticking. With its lightly browned edges and toothsome texture, the seeded squash, roasted cut-side down on a preheated pan, was by far the best of class. Now I could turn my attention to the filling.

Right off the bat I set up a few guidelines. I wanted to use ingredients that I would likely have on hand, and I wanted to prepare the filling while the squash roasted. I also wanted a filling that would transform the squash into a light meal or an elegant side dish. To start, I tried

using a simple combination of sautéed vegetables and cheese, but my tasters were left wanting something more substantial. I then tested fillings made with rice, couscous, bread cubes, bread crumbs, and roasted potatoes. The rice and couscous, two predictable choices, tasted fine, but the bread cubes and bread crumbs were mushy and wanting in texture. Somewhat unexpectedly, the roasted potatoes stole the show, giving the dish a satisfying oomph that none of the contenders could match. After trying several varieties of potatoes, including russets, Yukon Gold, and Red Bliss, I found that Red Bliss, a high-moisture/low-starch potato, had the best texture when roasted. Best of all, both the squash and the potatoes roasted at about the same speed when placed on preheated pans in a 400-degree oven.

To get the summery flavor mix I was after, I added some fresh tomatoes, a bit of sautéed garlic, and some slightly caramelized onions along with fresh basil. I also found that a little cheese

All the Gourdy Details

Although the Spanish are credited with introducing squash to Europe, believing them to be melons, it was the Italians who actually downsized the huge gourds into the delicate, green vegetable they termed *zucchini* in the 18th century. This dainty new vegetable, with its elegant flavor and tender flesh, was intended to be eaten before it matured and was immediately popular in France as well as Italy. The English acquired the vegetable through the French and therefore call them *courgettes*, whereas Italian immigrants brought them to America, so we have always called them by their Italian name.

According to Vincent Laurence of White Flower Farms in Litchfield, Conn., there is no noticeable difference in flavor among the different types of zucchini, although different parts of the world prefer different shapes and shades of green. While consumers in the United States prefer straight, dark green zucchini; consumers in Syria prefer a tapered, pale gray zucchini to which the edible blossoms are still attached. Although only one type of zucchini is usually available at the grocery store, you can grow more exotic and unusual types from seed. —J.C.

helped to bind the filling. After trying eight different types of cheese, my tasters voted unanimously for Monterey Jack cheese (it edged out even the Parmesan). The flavor of the Jack cheese was evident without being overpowering, and it melted and browned nicely along the top. I finally had a stuffed zucchini worth making; it was even worth serving to company.

STUFFED ZUCCHINI WITH TOMATOES AND JACK CHEESE

SERVES 4 AS A MAIN DISH OR 8 AS A SIDE DISH

Buy firm zucchini with tiny prickly hairs around the stem end; the hairs are a sign of freshness.

- 4 medium zucchini (about 8 ounces each), washed
- Salt and ground black pepper
- 4 tablespoons olive oil
- 3 medium Red Bliss potatoes (about 1 pound), cut into ½-inch cubes
- 1 medium onion, chopped fine
- 5 large garlic cloves, minced
- 3 medium tomatoes (about 1¼ pounds), seeded and chopped
- ⅓ cup chopped fresh basil leaves
- 6 ounces Monterey Jack cheese, shredded (about 1½ cups)

1. Adjust one oven rack to upper-middle position and second oven rack to lowest position, then place a rimmed baking sheet on each rack and heat oven to 400 degrees.

2. Meanwhile, halve each zucchini lengthwise. With small spoon, scoop out seeds and most of flesh so that walls of zucchini are ¼ inch thick (see illustration below). Season cut sides of zucchini with salt and pepper, and brush with 2 tablespoons oil; set zucchini halves cut-side down on hot baking sheet on lower rack. Toss potatoes with 1 tablespoon olive oil, salt, and pepper in small bowl and spread in single layer on hot baking sheet on upper rack. Roast zucchini until slightly softened and skins are wrinkled, about 10 minutes; roast potatoes until tender and lightly browned, 10 to 12 minutes. Using tongs, flip zucchini halves over on baking sheet and set aside.

3. Meanwhile, heat remaining tablespoon oil in 12-inch skillet over medium heat until shimmering but not smoking, about 2 minutes. Add onion and cook, stirring occasionally, until softened and beginning to brown, about 10 minutes. Increase heat to medium-high; stir in garlic and cook until fragrant, about 30 seconds. Add tomatoes and cooked potatoes; cook, stirring occasionally, until heated through, about 3 minutes. Off heat, stir in basil, ½ cup cheese, and salt and pepper to taste.

4. Divide filling evenly among squash halves on baking sheet, spooning about ½ cup into each, and pack lightly; sprinkle with remaining cheese. Return baking sheet to oven, this time to upper rack, and bake zucchini until heated through and cheese is spotty brown, about 6 minutes. Serve immediately.

STUFFED ZUCCHINI WITH CORN, BLACK BEANS, AND CHIPOTLE CHILES

- 4 medium zucchini (about 8 ounces each), washed
- Salt and ground black pepper
- 4 tablespoons olive oil
- 1 medium Red Bliss potato (about 5 ounces), cut into ½-inch cubes
- 1 medium onion, chopped fine
- 1 cup fresh corn kernels cut from 2 medium ears
- 5 large garlic cloves, minced
- 3 medium chipotle chiles en adobo, minced (about 3 tablespoons)
- 2 medium tomatoes (about 12 ounces), seeded and chopped
- 1 can (15 ounce) black beans, drained and rinsed (about 1½ cups)
- ⅓ cup chopped fresh cilantro leaves
- 6 ounces Monterey Jack cheese, shredded (about 1½ cups)

1. Follow recipe for Stuffed Zucchini with Tomatoes and Jack Cheese through step 2.

2. Heat remaining tablespoon oil in 12-inch skillet over medium heat until shimmering but not smoking, about 2 minutes. Add onion and cook, stirring occasionally, until softened and beginning to brown, about 10 minutes. Increase heat to medium-high; stir in corn and cook until almost tender, about 3 minutes. Add garlic and chipotle chiles; cook until fragrant, about 30 seconds. Stir in tomatoes, black beans, and cooked potatoes; cook, stirring occasionally, until heated through, about 3 minutes. Off heat, stir in cilantro and ½ cup cheese and salt and pepper to taste.

3. Continue with recipe for Stuffed Zucchini with Tomatoes and Jack Cheese from step 4.

STUFFED ZUCCHINI WITH CURRIED LAMB, MANGO, AND CURRANTS

- 4 medium zucchini (about 8 ounces each), washed
- Salt and ground black pepper
- 4 tablespoons olive oil
- 1 medium Red Bliss potato (about 5 ounces), cut into ½-inch cubes
- 1 medium onion, chopped fine
- 5 large garlic cloves, minced
- 2 tablespoons curry powder
- Pinch ground cayenne
- ½ cup dried currants
- ½ pound ground lamb
- 1½ cups plain yogurt
- 2 medium tomatoes (about 12 ounces), seeded and chopped
- ½ mango, peeled and cut into ⅜-inch pieces (about ½ cup)
- ⅓ cup chopped fresh parsley leaves

1. Follow recipe for Stuffed Zucchini with Tomatoes and Jack Cheese through step 2.

2. Heat remaining tablespoon oil in 12-inch skillet over medium heat until shimmering but not smoking, about 2 minutes. Add onion and cook, stirring occasionally, until softened and beginning to brown, about 10 minutes. Increase heat to medium-high; stir in garlic, curry powder, and cayenne and cook until fragrant, about 30 seconds. Add currants and lamb, breaking lamb into bite-sized pieces with wooden spoon; cook, stirring occasionally, until lamb begins to brown, about 3 minutes. Stir in yogurt 2 tablespoons at a time, allowing it to sizzle and most of the moisture to cook off with each addition (this process should take about 5 minutes). After last addition, simmer mixture until almost all liquid has evaporated, about 5 minutes. Stir in tomatoes, mango, and cooked potatoes; cook, stirring occasionally, until heated through, about 3 minutes. Off heat, stir in parsley and salt and pepper to taste.

3. Continue with recipe for Stuffed Zucchini with Tomatoes and Jack Cheese from step 4, omitting step of sprinkling with cheese.

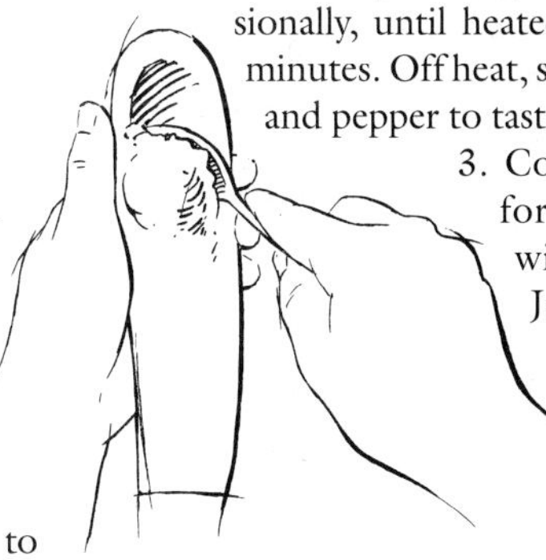

SEEDING With a small spoon, scoop out the seeds and most of flesh so the walls of the zucchini are ¼ inch thick.

Rich and Creamy Corn Pudding

Precooked corn and a brief reduction of heavy cream result in a pudding that is creamy, not watery.

⇒ BY JEANNE MAGUIRE ⇐

While it's hard to imagine tiring of fresh corn on the cob, it recently occurred to me that there may well be another way to preserve the fresh, sweet flavor of just-picked corn. The answer turned out to be a savory corn pudding. Actually more like custard, corn pudding is a combination of eggs, milk, and cream graced with a generous helping of freshly cut kernels. I set out to find a recipe for a tender, creamy custard with lots of corn flavor that would make a satisfying addition to my seasonal menu.

I originally thought that this dish would be a no-brainer. Many American cookbooks include recipes for corn pudding, and while some call for cheese and herbs and others add chiles, they invariably boil down to a combination of milk, cream, eggs, and corn. Given the consistency of the recipes, I was quite surprised to find that my first batch of puddings were all failures: each and every one curdled and wept, producing an unwanted pool of watery liquid.

It seemed obvious that the corn in the pudding was the source of the escaping liquid. The question was how to get rid of the moisture in the corn without losing that fresh corn flavor essential to the dish.

After experimenting with various options, I settled on a simple two-step approach. First I cooked the corn kernels in a little butter, just until the moisture in the pan had almost evaporated. Then I eliminated a bit more of the corn's liquid by simmering the kernels in heavy cream. Because heavy cream, unlike milk or even light cream, can be cooked at a boil without curdling, I reasoned that it would be safe to simmer the corn together with the cream that was already part of the recipe. When I tried this method, I was very happy with the results. When I made the pudding with corn that was briefly sautéed and then simmered with heavy cream to make a

Corn pudding this light and creamy can only be made with fresh corn; frozen corn made a dull tasting, soggy pudding.

thick mixture, I had a dish with great flavor but no seeping liquid.

Now I was ready to move on to balancing flavors. The first thing I noticed about my now smooth and creamy custard was the corn—there was too much of it. To reduce the corn-to-custard ratio, I cut back from four cups of corn to three. This helped, but there still seemed to be too many large kernels intruding on the tender custard. Perhaps pureeing some of the corn, I thought, would smooth out the texture without sacrificing any of the intense corn flavor. But pureeing did the job too well; I wanted the pudding to have some chew, and now it didn't have enough. Next I tried grating some of the corn directly off the cobs on the coarse side of a box grater. This method gave me just what I was looking for in terms of flavor as well as texture.

Now that I had solved the problem of weeping and developed a satisfying texture for the pudding, I thought it was just a bit too rich. I decided to try using whole eggs alone. First I tried three eggs and liked the pudding better than the version with two whole eggs and two yolks. Next I tried four whole eggs, and this version was even

better. The two extra whites seemed to lighten the dish, and the custard remained smooth and tender—just what I wanted.

CREAMY CORN PUDDING
SERVES 6 AS A SIDE DISH

- 6   medium ears fresh corn, husks and silk removed
- 3   tablespoons unsalted butter, plus extra for greasing baking dish
- 2/3 cup heavy cream
- 1 1/2 teaspoons salt
- 1   teaspoon sugar
- 1/4 teaspoon ground cayenne
- 1 1/3 cups whole milk
- 4   large eggs, beaten lightly
- 1   tablespoon cornstarch

1. Cut kernels from 5 ears of corn into medium bowl, then scrape cobs to collect milk in same bowl (you should have about 2½ cups kernels and milk). Grate remaining ear corn on coarse side of box grater (you should have about ½ cup grated kernels). Add grated kernels to bowl with cut kernels.

2. Adjust oven rack to lower-middle position, place roasting pan or large baking dish on rack, and heat oven to 350 degrees. Generously butter 8-inch square baking dish. Bring 2 quarts water to boil in kettle or saucepan.

3. Heat large heavy-bottomed skillet over medium heat until hot, about 2 minutes. Add butter; when foaming subsides, add corn kernels and grated corn. Cook, stirring occasionally, until corn is bright yellow and liquid has almost evaporated, about 5 minutes. Add cream, salt, sugar, and cayenne; cook, stirring occasionally, until thickened and spoon leaves a trail when pan bottom is scraped, about 5 minutes. Transfer corn mixture to medium bowl. Stir in milk, then whisk in eggs and cornstarch. Pour mixture into buttered baking dish.

4. Set dish in roasting pan or large baking dish on oven rack; fill outer pan with boiling water to reach halfway up inner pan. Bake until center jiggles slightly when shaken and pudding has browned lightly in spots, 20 to 25 minutes. Remove baking dish with pudding from water bath; cool 10 minutes and serve.

Jeanne Maguire lives and cooks in Massachusetts.

Fresh Margaritas

Put away that blender. For the ultimate margarita, mix premium tequila with fresh juice and zest, and shake it yourself.

≷ BY BRIDGET LANCASTER ≶

During the hot summer months, the margarita all but replaces the martini as America's favorite cocktail. Indeed, our obsession with margaritas has helped make the United States the world's leading consumer of tequila. Unfortunately, the typical margarita tends to be a slushy, headache-inducing concoction made with little more than ice, tequila, and artificially flavored corn syrup. At their best, though, margaritas are the perfect balance of tequila, orange liqueur, and fresh lime juice, shaken briskly with crushed ice and served on the rocks (with salt if preferred). I wanted to see if I could produce this ideal cocktail, balancing the distinctive flavor of tequila with a hint of orange and a bright burst of citrus.

As tequila is a margarita's most important ingredient, I started the testing there. I made margaritas with all types of tequila, using both super-premium 100 percent blue agave (agave is the plant from which tequila is distilled) as well as mixed tequilas, to which cane or corn syrup is often added.

Two types of tequila known as silver (or white) and gold, are not aged; their young alcoholic flavor gave the margarita a raw, harsh flavor. Margaritas made with the prized aged and very aged tequilas were extremely smooth, but their distinct tannic taste, produced as they age up to six years in oak casks, dominated the cocktail. *Reposado* or "rested" tequila, made from 100 percent blue agave and aged for 12 months or less, was the favorite. Its slightly mellow flavor blended perfectly with the other ingredients.

Next I tested orange-flavored liqueurs. Both Grand Marnier and Cointreau were delicious, but many tasters thought their robust flavor too pronounced and "boozy" for a margarita. Triple Sec, an orange liqueur with a lower alcohol content, made a more delicate contribution.

Finally, the citrus juice. Margaritas are traditionally made with fresh-squeezed lime juice, but some tasters thought the flavor too acidic. Those made with only lemon juice ended up tasting a little too much like lemonade. An equal mixture of both lime and lemon juice produced a margarita that was very refreshing, but too mild. So I turned to the method *Cook's* had used to make fresh lemonade (see "First-Rate Lemonade," July/August 1998). For that recipe, we found that mashing thinly sliced lemons extracted their

full flavor. While this technique greatly boosted the citrus flavor in the margaritas, the oil from the white pith was too bitter, giving the drink a medicinal flavor. Steeping just the zest of the lime and lemon in their juices for 24 hours deepened the citrus flavor without adding any bitterness. Adding sugar to the steeping mixture countered any remaining harshness from the citrus.

In testing the proportions of the three main ingredients, I found that my tasters favored an equal portion of each, quite different from the tequila-heavy concoctions I had consumed in the past. My last test was to try the margarita in a salt-rimmed glass. This was clearly a question of individual taste. So salt the glass or not, as you and your guests prefer.

THE BEST FRESH MARGARITAS
MAKES ABOUT I QUART, SERVING 4 TO 6

The longer the zest and juice mixture is allowed to steep, the more developed the citrus flavors in the finished margaritas. We recommend steeping for the full 24 hours, although the margaritas will still be great if the mixture is steeped only for the minimum 4 hours. If you're in a rush and need to serve margaritas immediately, omit the zest and skip the steeping process altogether.

4	teaspoons grated zest plus ½ cup juice from 2 to 3 medium limes
4	teaspoons grated zest plus ½ cup juice from 2 to 3 medium lemons
¼	cup superfine sugar
	Pinch salt
2	cups crushed ice
I	cup 100 percent agave tequila, preferably *reposado*
I	cup Triple Sec

1. Combine lime zest and juice, lemon zest and juice, sugar, and salt in large liquid measuring cup; cover with plastic wrap and refrigerate until flavors meld, 4 to 24 hours.

2. Divide 1 cup crushed ice between 4 or 6 margarita or double old-fashioned glasses. Strain juice mixture into 1-quart pitcher or cocktail shaker. Add tequila, Triple Sec, and remaining crushed ice; stir or shake until thoroughly combined and chilled, 20 to 60 seconds. Strain into ice-filled glasses, serve immediately.

We like our margaritas without salt, but with a nice balance of flavors, not dominated by the tequila.

FRESH PINEAPPLE MARGARITAS

The pineapple flavor in this variation makes the zest and steeping process in the recipe above unnecessary.

Peel and core 1 small ripe pineapple (about 3½ pounds); cut half the pineapple into rough 2-inch chunks (reserve remaining half for another use). Puree in workbowl of food processor fitted with steel blade until smooth and foamy, about 1 minute. Follow recipe for the Best Fresh Margaritas, omitting zest and steeping process, reducing lemon and lime juices to ¼ cup each, and adding ½ cup pureed pineapple to juice mixture.

FRESH RASPBERRY MARGARITAS

For strawberry margaritas, substitute an equal amount of hulled strawberries for the raspberries.

Follow recipe for the Best Fresh Margaritas, omitting zest and steeping process and pureeing 1 cup fresh raspberries, lime and lemon juices, sugar, and salt in workbowl of food processor fitted with steel blade until smooth. Strain mixture into pitcher or cocktail shaker; continue with recipe, reducing Triple Sec to ½ cup and adding ½ cup Chambord (or desired raspberry liqueur) to juice and tequila mixture in pitcher.

The Secrets of Panna Cotta

What makes this simple chilled Italian cream great? Balanced proportions, sound technique, and a light hand with the gelatin.

⇒ BY KAY RENTSCHLER WITH JULIA COLLIN ⇐

Panna cotta seems to have entered the world on tiptoe—or on wing. It is included in neither Waverly Root's book *The Food of Italy* (1971) nor in Marcella Hazan's *Classic Italian Cook Book* (1973). In fact, no one seems to know much about it. Yet from virtual anonymity 25 years ago, panna cotta has achieved star status in restaurants around the country, becoming the popular successor to tiramisu.

Though its name is lyrical, the literal translation of panna cotta, "cooked cream," does nothing to suggest its ethereal qualities. In fact, panna cotta is not cooked at all. Neither is it complicated with eggs, as is a custard. Instead, sugar and gelatin are melted in cream and milk, and the whole is then turned into individual ramekins and chilled. It is a virginal dessert, a jellied cream of pure alabaster. It forms a richly neutral backdrop for everything it touches: strawberry coulis, fresh raspberries, light caramel, chocolate sauce.

That, I should say, describes the ideal panna cotta. There are others.

Panna cotta is about nothing if not texture. The cream must be robust enough to unmold but delicate enough to shiver on the plate. My mission, therefore, was to find correct proportions for four simple ingredients and the most effective way to deal with the gelatin.

I began by preparing five recipes from well-known Italian cookbooks. Each of them used like ingredients in varying proportions and dealt with the ingredients similarly. Two called for powdered sugar (favored in Italian confections). A couple simmered the cream; others merely warmed it. One recipe whipped half the cream and folded it into the base. Procedurally, the recipes were extremely straightforward.

Upon tasting the different recipes, it was clear they fell into two groups. Those with higher proportions of milk were slippery and translucent, their flavor elusive and flat. Those with more cream had a rich mouthfeel and a creamier, more

The rich yet neutral flavor of this dessert lends itself to many different garnishes—pictured here, raspberry sauce and fresh raspberries.

rounded flavor. What united these recipes most noticeably, however, was a toothsomeness, a slight rubbery chew. It was the result of too much gelatin (see "Supportive Friend, Tough Opponent," below).

It would be practical, I decided, to design the recipe around a single packet of gelatin. Given this amount, I knew I would need to establish the volume of liquid required to set up the cream. But before that I had to determine the best proportion of cream to milk, critical in terms of mouthfeel. Preliminary tastings put us on the side of a 3-to-1 ratio of cream to milk.

Over the next week my colleague and I made dozens of panna cotti. We were surprised to find textural inconsistency between batches that should have been identical. Some were flabby, others stalwart. Serendipity saved the day when I realized that the amount of gelatin included in a packet is not consistent but in fact varies widely from one packet to another. (See "The En-

velope, Please," page 23.) As soon as we began measuring gelatin by the teaspoonful, things began looking up.

In addition to proportions, there was chilling time to consider. Preparation and chilling times should be brief and the dessert quick to the table. My first priority, therefore, was to create the best dessert to emerge within the shortest chilling time, a panna cotta that would be firm, say, in the space of a few hours. By inversing the amount of gelatin in increments of ⅛ teaspoon, from 2 to 3 teaspoons, I found that 2¾ teaspoons produced a firm enough, yet still fragile finished texture after four hours.

Yet I wanted the option of an overnight version as well. Knowing that gelatin grows more tenacious over time—transforming what was a lilting mousse one evening into a bouncing sponge the next—I figured there must also be a statute of limitations on its grip. At what point would the gelatin stop advancing? Research indicated maximum rigidity was reached after about 18 hours. At this point my colleague and I recorded the textural changes occasioned by incremental decreases in gelatin and discovered that an implausibly small decrease (⅛ teaspoon) put the overnight texture on a par with the four hour version.

With flexible time options in place, I moved on to technique. Because gelatin's response is hastened by cold temperatures, it seemed reasonable to keep most of the liquid cold. Why heat all the milk and cream when I only needed hot liquid to melt the gelatin and sugar? I gave the milk this assignment, pouring it into a

Supportive Friend, Tough Opponent

Gelatin is a flavorless, nearly colorless substance derived from the collagen in connective tissue and bones, extracted commercially and dehydrated. It works on the same principle in reverse as a meat stew that you put in the fridge hot and remove the next day as a solid one-piece mosaic; when you heat the stew up, the collagen melts and the stew reverts to its liquid state. Commercial gelatin begins dry in granular or leaf form and must first be rehydrated in cool liquid—where it absorbs about three times its weight—then melted, and finally cooled. Gelatin has clout when cold. Depending on the length of cooling time and the concentration of the solution, gelatin molecules form anything from a weblike gel—in the case of panna cotta, for example—to a solid block that can be cut with a knife—as illustrated by cafeteria Jell-O cubes. –K.R.

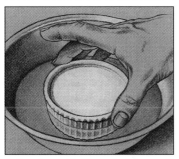

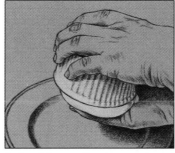

1. Pour 1 cup of boiling water into a small, wide-mouthed bowl, dip a ramekin into the water, count to three, and lift the ramekin out of the water.

2. With a moistened finger, press lightly around the periphery of the cream to loosen the edges. Dip the ramekin back into the water for another three-count.

3. Invert the ramekin over your palm and loosen the cream by cupping your fingers between the cream and the edges of the ramekin.

4. Gently lower the cream onto the plate.

saucepan, sprinkling the gelatin over it, then giving the gelatin five minutes to swell and absorb liquid. Knowing that gelatin sustains damage at high temperatures, I heated the milk only enough to melt the gelatin—a couple of minutes, stirring constantly—then added the sugar off heat to dissolve. The gelatin did not melt perfectly, and I thought I might have to increase the milk's temperature. Instead, I doubled the softening time to 10 minutes, and the problem was solved.

To do its job of firming the liquid to a gel, melted gelatin must be mixed with other recipe ingredients while its molecules have enough heat energy to move through the mixture. By combining ingredients hastily in the past, I had often precipitated gelatin seizures, causing the melted gelatin to harden into chewy strings, which ruined the texture of the dessert rather than enhancing it. So I stirred the cold cream slowly into the milk to temper it.

In cooking school I learned to stir gelatin-based desserts over an ice bath—allowing the gelatin to thicken somewhat under gentle agitation—before refrigerating them to set. Besides supporting nuts, fruit, or vanilla bean throughout, this process was said to produce a finer finished texture. Hoping to avoid this step in a recipe that was otherwise so easy, I presented tasters with side-by-side creams, one stirred first over ice, one simply refrigerated. They unanimously preferred the texture of the panna cotta chilled over ice, describing it as "lighter, creamier, and smoother." Given the results, the extra 10 minutes required did not seem unreasonable to me.

Now it was fine-tuning time. First place for flavor accents went to vanilla, particularly in the company of fruit sauces. We preferred whole bean to extract and Tahitian to Madagascar (for more on vanilla, see Kitchen Notes, page 30).

This is a gorgeous anytime, anywhere dessert, proving that you don't have to be flocked, layered, filigreed, or studded—you don't even have to be chocolate—to win.

CLASSIC PANNA COTTA
SERVES 8

Serve panna cotta very cold with strawberry or raspberry sauce or lightly sweetened berries. Though traditionally unmolded, panna cotta may be chilled and served in wine glasses and sauced on top. If you would like to make the panna cotta a day ahead, decrease the gelatin to 2 5/8 teaspoons (2 1/2 teaspoons plus 1/8 teaspoon), and chill the filled wine glasses or ramekins for 18 to 24 hours.

    1   cup whole milk
    2 3/4 teaspoons gelatin
    3   cups heavy cream
    1   piece vanilla bean, 2 inches long, slit
         lengthwise with paring knife (or substitute
         2 teaspoons extract)
    6   tablespoons granulated sugar
         Pinch salt

1. Pour milk into medium saucepan; sprinkle surface evenly with gelatin and let stand 10 minutes to hydrate gelatin. Meanwhile, turn contents of two ice cube trays (about 32 cubes) into large bowl; add 4 cups cold water. Measure cream into large measuring cup or pitcher. With paring knife, scrape vanilla seeds into cream; place pod in cream along with seeds and set mixture aside. Set eight wine glasses or 4-ounce ramekins on baking sheet.

2. Heat milk and gelatin mixture over high heat, stirring constantly, until gelatin is dissolved and mixture registers 135 degrees on instant-read thermometer, about 1 1/2 minutes. Off heat, add sugar and salt; stir until dissolved, about 1 minute.

3. Stirring constantly, slowly pour cream with vanilla into saucepan containing milk, then transfer mixture to medium bowl and set bowl over ice water bath. Stir frequently until thickened to the consistency of eggnog and mixture

registers 50 degrees on an instant-read thermometer, about 10 minutes. Strain mixture into large measuring cup or pitcher, then distribute evenly among wine glasses or ramekins. Cover baking sheet with plastic wrap, making sure that plastic does not mar surface of cream; refrigerate until just set (mixture should wobble when shaken gently), 4 hours.

5. Serve panna cotta in wine glasses, or, following illustrations 1 through 4, unmold panna cotta from ramekins and serve immediately.

The Envelope, Please

Between batches of panna cotta, we scratched our heads and asked what to make of the vagaries in texture produced when using identical recipes. Whereas one batch of cream might have the resilience of an eraser, another would be wobbly and frail. Squinting to find an 800 number on an unopened twin pack (in pursuit of an authority at Knox), what I noticed instead was far more instructive: the two packets appeared to contain noticeably different amounts. Measuring the contents of several envelopes yielded teaspoon measures as little as 1 3/4 and as great as 2 7/8. Anne Smith, a spokesperson for the parent company of Knox, Nabisco, told me the packets were machine-filled and acknowledged that their individual weight could vary by plus or minus 5 percent. Using a gram scale, we weighed more than 50 individual gelatin packets and found weight discrepancies as great as 20 percent. In fact, in two separate packages of four we found eight different weights. When a recipe calls for an envelope of gelatin, it is expecting a quarter of an ounce, which measures precisely 2 1/2 teaspoons. Making a texture-sensitive delicate dessert? Dump a couple of envelopes into a bowl and get out your measuring spoons. —K.R.

Lattice-Top Fresh Peach Pie

We went in search of a pie with a filling that was juicy but not soupy, a well-browned bottom crust, and an easy-to-make lattice top.

> BY JEANNE MAGUIRE AND KAY RENTSCHLER

L iving in the country has its drawbacks. Take winter, for example: I'm buried in a snowbank while my friends in the city step out to restaurants or catch the latest movie. But come summer, things change. Afternoons in my neck of the woods are long and relaxed, and I can stroll up the hill to a neighborhood orchard and buy peaches that taste the way they did when I was a kid. Unlike those urban prisoners, I might even manage to bake some into a pie.

My occasional disappointment with peach pies in the past has taught me to wait for peach season and then buy only intoxicatingly fragrant peaches, peaches ripe enough when squeezed to make you swoon. But even ripe peaches vary in juiciness from season to season and from peach to peach, making it difficult to know just how much thickener or sweetener a pie will need. Because fresh peaches are so welcome, we are inclined to forgive them if the pie they make is soupy or overly sweet or has a bottom crust that didn't bake properly.

But I wanted to remove the guesswork from this anthem to summer. I wanted to create a filling that was juicy but not swimming in liquid, its flavors neither muscled out by spices nor overwhelmed by thickeners. The crust would be buttery, flaky, and well browned on the bottom with a handsome, peekaboo lattice on the top.

I took my opening gambit from Christopher Kimball's *Cook's* article "How to Thicken Fruit Pies" (July/August 1995). The master recipe—a double-crust blueberry pie thickened with tapioca—was one I had made with great success in the past. But my first tests with peaches and a lattice-weave top crust left me with melting lattice strips and a migraine. I now knew that the crust of this particular pie would demand certain adjustments. My challenge was to find a crust that was buttery enough to be tender, tough enough to support a moist filling, and workable enough to be woven into a lattice. After the meltdowns of those first strips of top crust, I knew that I would need a dough with less fat than *Cook's* very tender version. So I decided to bounce the flour up to

The lattice crust can be woven right on the pie or assembled on parchment paper, frozen, then slid onto the pie.

three cups (from 2¼ cups), to leave the butter and shortening where they were (at 10 and seven tablespoons, respectively), and to up the ice water to about 10 tablespoons. With these adjustments in place, I had what I was looking for: a cooperative, flaky yet substantial dough.

My second challenge was to find a thickener that would, like tapioca, leave the fruit's color and flavor uncompromised but would not, like tapioca, leave undissolved beads that could be seen through the pie's open latticework design. A fruit pie should appear to be self-thickening, producing clear, syrupy juices, even when it is not. I knew I could lessen the problem by pulverizing the tapioca, but that seemed like an unnecessary bother for a simple pie. Our trials in the past demonstrated that flour and cornstarch were both too obvious. Then I found an old recipe that suggested potato starch as a thickener. I had never thought to try it in a pie. Working with proportions established in the earlier recipe, I conducted side-by-side tests with flour, cornstarch, Minute tapioca, and potato starch. Flour and cornstarch fared no better than expected. The tapioca, which I had pulverized to a

powder in my spice grinder, performed admirably, having no lumps. But the potato starch scored big: its clarity outshone flour but was less cosmetically glossy than cornstarch; its thickening qualities rivaled tapioca in their strength and neutrality; and, still better, there was no need for pulverizing. I also found that extra juicy peaches needed an additional tablespoon of starch.

Next I turned my attentions to the peaches themselves. Though a fuzzy peach makes a pleasant snack, only the satiny flesh is acceptable in a pie. After attempting to shave a ripe peach with a vegetable peeler, I resorted to traditional blanching and found that two full minutes in boiling water were necessary to humble even the ripest of peaches. A quick dip in an ice bath stabilized the temperature of the fruit and got the peels moving.

Experimenting with different sugars, I was surprised to discover that both light and dark brown sugar bullied the peaches, while white sugar complemented them. As with most fruit pies, lemon juice brightened the flavor of the fruit; it also kept the peach slices from browning before they went into the pan. A whisper of ground cinnamon and nutmeg and a dash of salt upped the peach flavor and added a note of complexity.

When it came to assembling the pie, I dealt with the dough first, fitting the bottom crust into a pan and chilling it in the fridge. The lattice strips behaved nicely when they were rolled out, cut, and then frozen for 30 minutes. A pizza cutter and a wide ruler worked more efficiently as cutting equipment than a knife.

Trying different oven rack levels and temperatures to satisfy the browning requirements of both the top and bottom crust brought me right back to *Cook's* earlier article on fruit pies, which recommended a low rack, initial high heat (425 degrees), and moderately high heat (375 degrees) to finish. I found that a glass pie dish and preheated sheet pan gave me a pleasantly firm and browned bottom crust. A quick prebaking spritz of the lattice top with water and a sprinkle of sugar brought this pie home.

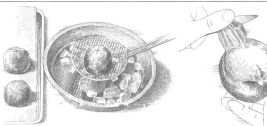

1. With a paring knife, score a small x at the base of each peach.

2. Lower the peaches into boiling water with a slotted skimmer. Cover and blanch until their skins loosen, about 2 minutes.

3. Use a slotted skimmer to remove the peaches to ice water and let stand to stop cooking, about 1 minute.

4. Cool the peaches, then, starting from the scored x, peel each peach, halve and pit it, and cut into ⅜-inch slices.

LATTICE-TOP FRESH PEACH PIE
SERVES 8

If your peaches are larger than tennis balls, you will probably need 5 or 6; if they're smaller, you will need 7 to 8. Cling and freestone peaches look identical; try to buy freestones, because the flesh will fall away from the pits easily. If you don't have or can't find potato starch, substitute an equal amount of pulverized Minute tapioca. Serve the pie with vanilla ice cream or whipped cream.

Pie dough
- 3 cups all-purpose flour
- 2 tablespoons sugar
- 1 teaspoon salt
- 7 tablespoons chilled all-vegetable shortening
- 10 tablespoons (1¼ sticks) chilled unsalted butter, cut into ¼-inch pieces and frozen for 30 minutes
- 10–12 tablespoons ice water

Peach filling
- 6–7 ripe medium-sized peaches (about 6 cups)
- 1 tablespoon juice from 1 lemon
- 1 cup sugar, plus 1 tablespoon
- Pinch ground cinnamon
- Pinch ground nutmeg
- Pinch salt
- 3–4 tablespoons potato starch (or substitute pulverized Minute tapioca)

1. Pulse flour, sugar, and salt in food processor workbowl fitted with steel blade until combined. Add shortening and process until mixture has texture of coarse sand, about 10 seconds. Scatter butter pieces over flour mixture; cut butter into flour until mixture is pale yellow and resembles coarse crumbs, with butter bits no larger than small peas, about ten 1-second pulses. Turn mixture into medium bowl.

2. Sprinkle 5 tablespoons ice water over mixture; with rubber spatula, use folding motion to evenly combine water and flour mixture. Sprinkle remaining 5 tablespoons ice water over mixture and continue using folding motion to combine until small portion of dough holds together when squeezed in palm of hand; add up to 2 tablespoons more ice water if necessary. (Dough should feel quite moist.) Turn dough onto clean, dry work surface; gather and gently press together in cohesive ball, then divide into 2 pieces, one slightly larger than the other. Flatten larger piece into a rough 5-inch square and smaller piece into a 4-inch disk; wrap separately in plastic wrap and refrigerate 1 hour, or up to 2 days, before rolling.

3. Remove dough from refrigerator (if refrigerated longer than 1 hour, let stand at room temperature until malleable). Roll larger dough piece to 11 by 15-inch rectangle, about ⅛ inch thick; transfer dough rectangle to cookie sheet lined with parchment paper. With pizza wheel, fluted pastry wheel, or paring knife, trim to even out long sides

of rectangle, then cut rectangle lengthwise into eight strips, 1¼ inches wide by 15 inches long. Freeze strips on cookie sheet until firm, about 30 minutes.

4. Roll smaller dough piece on lightly floured work surface or between two large sheets of plastic wrap to 12-inch disk. Transfer dough to pie plate by rolling dough around rolling pin and unrolling over 9-inch pie plate or by folding dough in quarters, then placing dough point in center of 9-inch pie plate and unfolding. Working around circumference of pie plate, ease dough into pan corners by gently lifting dough edges with one hand while pressing around pan bottom with other hand. Leave dough that overhangs lip of pie plate in place; refrigerate dough-lined pie plate.

5. Meanwhile, adjust oven rack to lower-middle position and heat oven to 425 degrees, bring 3 quarts water to boil in large saucepan, and fill large bowl with 2 quarts cold water and 2 trays ice cubes. Following illustrations 1 to 4, above, peel the peaches. Toss peach slices, lemon juice, 1 cup sugar, cinnamon, nutmeg, salt, and potato starch or Minute tapioca (3 tablespoons for moderately juicy peaches, 4 tablespoons for very juicy ones) in medium bowl.

6. Turn mixture into dough-lined pie plate. Remove dough strips from freezer; if too stiff to be workable, let stand at room temperature until malleable and softened slightly but still very cold. Following illustrations 1 to 4, below, form lattice top and place on top of peaches. Lightly brush lattice top with 1 tablespoon water and sprinkle with remaining 1 tablespoon sugar. Place pie on baking sheet and bake until crust is set and begins to brown, about 25 minutes. Rotate pie and reduce oven temperature to 375 degrees; continue to bake until crust is deep golden brown and filling is bubbly, 25 to 30 minutes longer. Cool on wire rack 2 hours before serving.

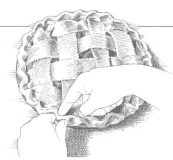

1. To make the lattice, lay out 4 strips of dough. Fold the first and third strips back, then place a long strip of dough slightly to the right of the center as shown.

2. Unfold the first and third strips over the perpendicular strip and fold the second and fourth strips back. Add a second perpendicular strip of dough. Now unfold the second and fourth strips.

3. Repeat this process with two more perpendicular strips (you will have a total of 8 strips of dough, four running in each direction).

4. Trim off the excess lattice ends, fold the rim of the shell up over the lattice strips, and crimp.

No Shortcuts to Good Fresh Pasta

When you want fresh egg pasta, do you have to make it yourself?
Or have supermarkets come up with decent alternatives?

⪼ BY MARYELLEN DRISCOLL ⪻

In recent years, the selection of pasta shapes, types, and sizes readily available to the American cook has become mind-boggling. One of the more beguiling options is the so-called fresh pasta found in the refrigerator cases of many supermarkets these days. With the growing enthusiasm among consumers for fresh, natural foods, these packages may cause shoppers to pause and take a second look. But the price of such products, usually about twice that of dried pasta, can provide enough impetus to push the shopping cart on.

At *Cook's,* we wanted to know when it is more appropriate or advantageous to cook with fresh egg pasta. And, in such instances, just how much work do you have to put into it? While you cannot get any fresher than homemade—the makings of which are surprisingly simple—few home cooks are willing to make pasta from scratch. The alternatives include shopping at a market that makes pasta fresh on-site or purchasing the "fresh" packaged pasta at the supermarket. You can also forgo the "fresh" approach and purchase dried egg pasta, which is manufactured under numerous brand names found in supermarkets and specialty stores. Which option, we wondered, is the best?

Fresh versus Dried

Typically, dried pasta is made with semolina flour and water. Made from a hard wheat called durum, semolina flour is high in protein, which makes it perfect for creating an elastic dough and springy, resilient noodles. This pasta is dried under specific humidity and temperature controls so that it is shelf-stable for up to or beyond one year. Like dried pasta, homemade fresh pasta is made of just two ingredients. Instead of semolina, however, it is made with softer all-purpose flour and is bound with egg instead of water. As a result, fresh pasta is more delicate than its resilient dried counterpart, with a texture that is not mushy but certainly soft. Fresh homemade egg pasta is rarely dried and is typically used within a couple of hours of being made.

The differences in resilience and texture between fresh egg pasta and dried semolina pasta translate into differences in the ways they are meant to be served. Fresh egg pasta is supposed to be porous as well as delicate, so that it absorbs the accompanying sauce. For this reason it is meant to be paired with a butter- or cream-based sauce, such as the famous Alfredo sauce. Dried semolina pasta is not absorbent, which makes it better suited to tomato- or oil-based sauces; each different dried pasta shape is better suited to different consistencies of sauce.

There is also a third option for those who want the flavor and softer texture of egg pasta—dried egg pasta. Made with ingredients similar to fresh pasta, this product might, we thought, be a more convenient way to benefit from the advantages of its fresh cousin.

For our blind tasting we purchased samples of "fresh" and dried egg pastas cut in the form of fettuccine noodles. We also made our own homemade fettuccine noodles with whole eggs and flour.

"Fresh" Is a Relative Term

As expected, the homemade pasta in our tasting stood out for its soft, delicate chew and clean flavor. It was the absolute favorite. Also relatively agreeable to our panel of tasters, which included magazine staff and several local chefs, were a couple of brands of fresh refrigerator pasta and a common supermarket brand of dried egg pasta. In the process of doing this tasting, though, we found that "fresh" is a very relative term.

Unlike homemade fresh pasta, with its two ingredients, the "fresh" refrigerator egg pasta found in supermarkets, as well as the dried egg pasta, are hybrids of a kind, made with semolina flour and water ordinarily used for dried pasta, but with eggs added in. The higher-protein semolina flour, which can absorb more liquid than all-purpose flour, automatically compromises the delicacy of the noodles' consistency. That is not to say, however, that they had the "chew" of eggless dried pasta; they simply could not compare with the delicacy of homemade. Also, the addition of water to these pastas (and the fact that some contain egg whites rather than whole eggs) seemed to dilute the fresh egg flavor usually associated with homemade pasta. This was particularly true with the dried egg pasta. One that we tasted was a surprising disappointment because it was inferior in taste and texture to the semolina pasta made by the same company, which is a favorite of many of our tasters.

Perhaps our biggest quibble with "fresh" refrigerator pasta, though, is the fact that these pastas are not really fresh at all. Unless your supermarket has a high rate of turnover, you may be buying a product that has been sitting on the shelf for weeks.

Fresh pastas are extremely perishable because they are high in moisture, which provides an ideal breeding ground for bacteria. Naturally occurring enzymes also exist that will over time discolor the pasta as well as modify its fats. These changes in the fats produce "off" flavors, according to Jim Jacobs, technical director at Northern Crops Institute, a learning center in Fargo, N.D., devoted to the study of the use of wheats, including durum, in food products. Consequently, the majority of "fresh" pasta products sold in supermarkets are both pasteurized and sealed in something called "modified atmosphere packaging" so as to extend their shelf life. This packaging method involves extracting air from inside the package and substituting it with another gas, typically a mix of carbon dioxide and nitrogen. This inhibits the growth of bacteria and helps to extend the pasta's shelf life by 25 to 120 days, depending on the product as well as the specific technologies used. Consequently, there is really no way of knowing the age of the pasta you buy.

Even though a "fresh" refrigerated pasta product can be safe to eat for as many as four months after its manufacture, that does not mean that time does not take its toll. So if you are not absolutely sure of the relative freshness of the supermarket product you are buying, it is possible that the pasta will have sat long enough for its texture to degrade from being somewhat tender and soft to being mushy.

One last point, regarding the price. The packaging size of "fresh" refrigerator pastas is curiously awkward. Most packages are just 9 ounces. Since most recipes call for either 12 or 16 ounces of fresh pasta, you end up buying two packages and spending nearly $6. Besides the expense, you inevitably have a few ounces left over. A 1-pound package of dried pasta serves four to six for about $1. If money is really a concern, set aside a few hours on a Saturday afternoon to make your own homemade noodles (the actual hands-on time is less than an hour), and serve your guests genuinely fresh pasta for just pennies.

TASTING FRESH EGG PASTA

The following pastas are listed in order of ranking based on scores for overall likeability. They were served plain immediately after cooking and evaluated for their flavor, surface texture, and degree of chew. The panel consisted of a dozen tasters, including magazine staff and professional chefs.

HIGHLY RECOMMENDED

HOMEMADE FETTUCCINE WITH EGG
➤ **About 50 cents for 16 ounces**

Made by hand shortly before the blind tasting, this pasta was preferred by tasters for its "good bite," which was described as "springy" and "resilient" yet tender. The flavor was decidedly clean, a "good pure flavor like real homemade pasta." The fact that it is homemade presents an obvious disadvantage: most home cooks don't have time to make their own pasta. The recipe used for this pasta was published in the *Cook's* September/October 1993 issue. It can also be found in *The Cook's Illustrated Complete Book of Pasta and Noodles*, available this summer.

RECOMMENDED WITH RESERVATIONS

CONTADINA BUITONI FETTUCCINE REFRIGERATOR PASTA WITH EGG
➤ **$2.29 for 9 ounces**

"Nice, but I wish there was more of a spring to it," one taster wrote in response to this refrigerator pasta. The majority of tasters agreed that these noodles were firm and chewy, "in between gummy and springy," which a few tasters perceived as "rubbery." Some, however, liked that trait, describing it as "fun to chew." The egg flavor was discernible but faint, making the noodles "bland" but pleasant enough if sauced. Available in supermarkets nationwide.

MONTEREY PASTA CO., FETTUCCINE REFRIGERATOR PASTA WITH EGG
➤ **$ 2.99 for 9 ounces**

There was "substantial heft to this noodle," which tasters found to be "thicker feeling than the others." It was also described as "in between too much bite and just right" and "a bit flabby at the core." The flavor was described as accented more with wheat than egg. It was a "hearty" tasting noodle "with a hint of sweetness." Tasters also noted that the noodles' surface texture was starchy, suggesting that "sauce would stick well." Available in Bay Area markets, nationwide wholesale stores, and online.

RONZONI FETTUCCINE DRIED PASTA WITH EGG
➤ **$1.69 for 12 ounces**

There was nothing delicate about this noodle. It had "decent tooth," which gave it a resilient bite. Its surface texture was more sticky than slick. The flavor was decidedly clean and slightly sweet, with nuances of egg and wheat. "This is a heavy, main course kind of pasta," wrote one taster. Available in supermarkets nationwide.

NOT RECOMMENDED

MALLARD'S FETTUCCINE REFRIGERATOR PASTA WITH EGG
➤ **$2.49 for 9 ounces**

This noodle was thin, with "not much to bite into." Tasters described it as "soft," "mushy," and "pasty." It was also described as dry. The flavor was wheaty, with a subtle unpleasant aftertaste that one taster likened to shrimp chips. "This is just blah," commented another taster. Available on the West Coast as well as in Texas and Florida.

RUSTICELLA D'ABRUZZO DRIED PASTA WITH EGG
➤ **$6.25 for 8.8 ounces**

Perhaps most outstanding was this pasta's bright yellow color. Most tasters were turned off by its markedly "gummy" texture. This porous texture made the pasta extremely starchy when tasted plain, suggesting a sauce would stick well. The flavor was described as clean but otherwise lacking. Of course, with such lackluster responses, it is hard not to be dismayed by the steep price. Available in specialty food stores.

DeCECCO EGG NOODLES DRIED PASTA WITH EGG
➤ **$1.99 for 8.8 ounces**

This was another bright, yolk-yellow noodle that took tasters by surprise. Its texture was tender and springy, perhaps slightly rubbery. What led to this product's demise, however, was its flavor, which many tasters described as "way too eggy," "like dirty eggs," "plasticky," "chemical," and "almost fishy." Available in specialty food stores and some supermarkets.

PREMIUM SELECT FETTUCCINE REFRIGERATOR PASTA WITH EGG
➤ **$1.99 for 9 ounces**

A Northeast supermarket brand of "fresh" noodles that was somewhat cheaper than the Contadina package it sat beside in the deli fridge, but the quality was also distinctly poorer. This pasta was disliked for being both "mushy and sticky." It "gets all doughy in the mouth," said one taster. "Sticks to my teeth," noted another. The flavor was "flour-y," a tad wheaty, and bland overall. Beware of refrigerator pasta like this one, which had condensation inside its packaging.

The Saw-Toothed Truth

Judge a bread knife by the length and shape of the blade and the type of serrations.

⇒ BY ADAM RIED ⇐

Serrated bread knives almost always seem sharp. Their aggressive blade design creates multiple cutting surfaces rather than the single, continuous cutting edge of other knives that can dull so quickly with use. Given their keen edges and longevity, we began to wonder if it mattered which bread knife you bought. To find out, we tested 10 different models by slicing 30 loaves of bread, five dozen bagels, and 25 pounds of tomatoes, whose surprisingly tough skin is a perfect subject for serrated knives. In the end, we were convinced that, yes, it does in fact matter which bread knife you buy. We also learned that while price and performance are only obliquely related, there are several key characteristics that can make a bread knife great.

Like the chef's knives and paring knives *Cook's* has tested in past issues, bread knives are manufactured by one of two methods, either forging or stamping. This, however, proved of little importance. Much more crucial was the type of serration on the blade, which in our group of knives was generally either pointed or wavy (see illustrations, next page).

Pointed serrations give the blade a good grip on the crust of a loaf of bread, allowing it to tear through the crust. The points also help preserve the blade's overall sharpness because they are the first part of the knife to touch all surfaces—be it a bread crust or a cutting board—thereby minimizing the surface contact by the rest of the edge. Our top-choice knives had pointed serrations. We did find, however, that pointed serrations can be too pronounced, as they were on both the LamsonSharp and the Progressive International knives. The distinct points on both of these blades caught on and ripped tomato skins and, in the case of the Progressive, even some of the softer breads.

In wavy serrations, the edge is reversed, an arrangement that allows more of the cutting surface to contact the food. In our tests on crusty bread, this blade type failed to get the same sure grip on the crust as did the pointy style. The wavy serrations slid a little more than we liked on the initial cut through a hard top crust.

In the process of cutting countless slices of bread with all of the knives, we developed a preference for textured plastic handles because they felt especially stable in the hand. A design we particularly liked was the offset LamsonSharp. Its raised handle kept fingers above the level of the cutting board, preventing scraping even when cutting through the bottom crust of each slice.

The Fine Points

Another factor that proved critical to the success of a bread knife was the length of its blade. Among the blades in our group, those measuring 10 inches, including the Forschner, the Wüsthof-Trident AvantGarde, the LamsonSharp, and the Chicago Cutlery, all cut through the entire width

The Bread Knives We Tested

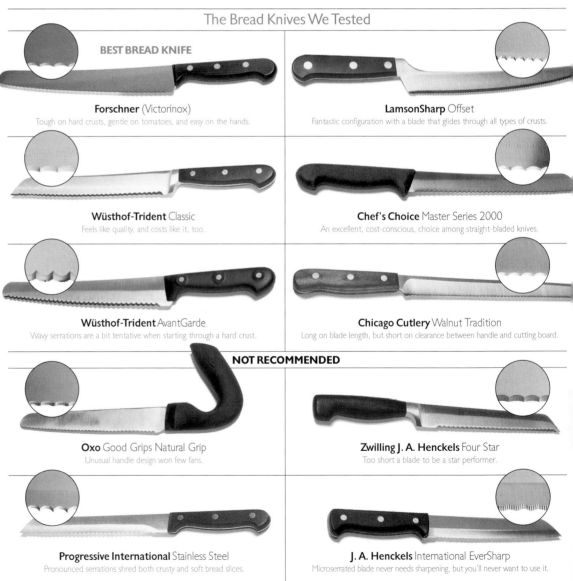

BEST BREAD KNIFE

Forschner (Victorinox)
Tough on hard crusts, gentle on tomatoes, and easy on the hands.

LamsonSharp Offset
Fantastic configuration with a blade that glides through all types of crusts.

Wüsthof-Trident Classic
Feels like quality, and costs like it, too.

Chef's Choice Master Series 2000
An excellent, cost-conscious, choice among straight-bladed knives.

Wüsthof-Trident AvantGarde
Wavy serrations are a bit tentative when starting through a hard crust.

Chicago Cutlery Walnut Tradition
Long on blade length, but short on clearance between handle and cutting board.

NOT RECOMMENDED

Oxo Good Grips Natural Grip
Unusual handle design won few fans.

Zwilling J. A. Henckels Four Star
Too short a blade to be a star performer.

Progressive International Stainless Steel
Pronounced serrations shred both crusty and soft bread slices.

J. A. Henckels International EverSharp
Microserrated blade never needs sharpening, but you'll never want to use it.

RATING BREAD KNIVES

We assessed 10 bread knives by cutting three types of bread—crusty peasant loaves, soft-crusted white sandwich loaves, and bagels—as well as soft, ripe tomatoes. Because crusty peasant bread was the biggest challenge, it was our most important test, followed by bagels, then sandwich bread, and last, tomatoes.

When testing the knives with each of the breads, we evaluated them on a combination of factors. First was the ease with which the knife broke through the top crust; second was how cleanly it sliced through the crumb; third was how well it cut through the bottom crust to free the slices from the loaf. Fourth and last, we also rated the knives on ease of use, which we based on whether the handle provided enough space for the fingers toward the bottom of the slice to avoid scraping knuckles on the cutting board, and on the length and design of the blade.

The prices listed are retail, paid in Boston-area stores and national mail-order catalogs. Generally, these prices reflect a standard 20–25 percent discount off full retail; expect prices in your area to vary depending on the discounts offered by local stores. See Resources, page 32, for specific price and availability of top choice models.

Brand	Price	Blade Type/ Length	Crusty Bread	Bagels	Soft Bread	Tomatoes	Ease of Use	Testers' Comments
BEST BREAD KNIFE **Forschner (Victorinox)** Model 40040	$36	Stamped/ 10 inches	★★★	★★★	★★★	★★★	★★★	A terrifically sharp blade with all the best traits—length, curvature, and serration design.
LamsonSharp Offset Bread Knife, Model 39556	$40	Stamped/ 10 inches	★★★	★★★	★★★	★★	★★★	High marks for ease of use on crusty bread, but the aggressive blade rips tomato slices. Some users found blade a little too flexible for their liking.
Wüsthof-Trident Classic Bread Knife, Item #4150	$70	Forged/ 9 inches	★★★	★★★	★★★	★★★	★★	Impressively sharp and smooth in action, but blade was a little too short and straight to be ideal.
Chef's Choice Master Series 2000 Bread Knife, Model 2000790	$32	Stamped/ 9 inches	★★★	★★★	★★★	★★★	★★	Nearly matches Wüsthof Classic, with great entry into a hard top crust and same problem—lack of knuckle clearance—when you get to the bottom.
Wüsthof-Trident AvantGarde Super Slicer, Item #4516	$48	Stamped/ 10 inches	★★	★★★	★★★	★★★	★★★	Love the long blade and heavy weight, but wavy serrations slip a little on tough crusts. Also available in an offset design with 7-inch blade.
Chicago Cutlery Walnut Tradition 10" Serrated Bread/Slicer, Item # BT10P	$25	Stamped/ 10 inches	★★	★★★	★★★	★★★	★★	Blade slips as it starts through a hard crust more than other models with pointed serrations.
NOT RECOMMENDED **Oxo Good Grips** Natural Grip Bread Knife	$12	Stamped/ 8 inches	★★	★★★	★★★	★★★	★	Handle limits the number of grip possibilities and forces the arms of shorter users into an uncomfortable angle. Oxo bread knives are also available in standard and offset configurations.
Zwilling J. A. Henckels Four Star, Model 31076-200	$50	Forged/ 8 inches	★★	★★★	★★★	★★★	★	The pointed tip of this knife's short blade got stuck in the crumb of bread loaves on forward strokes. Cutting through a tough bottom crust required considerable sawing and ripping.
Progressive International 8-Inch Stainless Steel Bagel Knife, Model GT-3610	$8	Stamped/ 8 inches	★★	★★	★	★★	★	Pronounced points on the blade make it difficult to begin cutting crusts on both rubbery bagels and delicate soft breads.
J. A. Henckels International EverSharp Pro 8-Inch Bread Knife	$10	Stamped/ 8 inches	★	★★	★★	★	★	Microserrations rip anything they touch to shreds and make for rough cutting action, too.

of our 9-inch peasant loaves much more easily than their shorter 9- and 8-inch counterparts. The 8-inch blades, including the Henckels Four Star (which is also available in a 10-inch length, though we couldn't find one in local stores or national mail-order catalogs), the Henckels International, the Progressive International, and the Oxo, were particularly frustrating because the tips of their blades tended to catch in the crumb of the loaves.

Another important aspect of blade design was curvature of the cutting edge. The edges of the Forschner, LamsonSharp, and Wüsthof-Trident AvantGarde blades were all slightly curved, which allowed for a gentle rocking motion to help cut through the peasant loaves' tough bottom crusts and separate each slice. By contrast, the knives with straight cutting edges required more manipulation—sometimes sawing with the tip of the blade, twisting, and even ripping—to get through the bottom crust and free the slice. Another advantage of a slightly curved blade was that it allowed a little extra room under the handle for fingers.

Last, we found that if a blade was too flexible, as were the LamsonSharp and Progressive blades, the knife felt less stable and sure while cutting through tough crusts.

After all this cutting, the features we came to prize in a bread knife included a blade that is rigid and long (10 inches is best), with a bit of curvature on the cutting edge, pointed serrations, and a handle design that gives the fingers room enough to clear the cutting board as you finish the cut. Among the knives we tested, any of the recommended models afford one or two of these traits and will do a good overall cutting job. But the

DESIGN | TYPES OF SERRATION

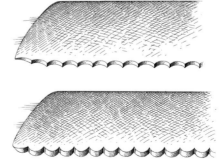

We preferred gently pointed serrations, top, which touch the food first, beginning the work for the beveled, arched cutting edges in between. Wavy serrations, bottom, are reversed: the arched cutting edges make up most of the blade edge.

Forschner has it all—and for a reasonable price in the mid-$30 dollar range to boot. If you opt for Forschner's textured black plastic handle, called Fibrox (this knife would be model #40547), as we would the next time, the price drops to below $30.

≥BY KAY RENTSCHLER≤

Tong-Tied

With barbecue season in full swing, we thought readers might be interested in the results of the tong testing our test cook Shona Simkin conducted over a hot grill recently. In testing nine different types of BBQ tongs (all at least 12 inches long), Shona wielded everything from a basic multi-purpose tong featuring a half-claw, half-spatula design, to tongs with serrated edges, long rounded teeth, and spoon grippers. She even tested a stiff, wooden-handled twin set—carving fork and tongs—that Dad waves around in the backyard. Shona put each pair through its paces, including moving hot coals, lifting and turning delicate asparagus spears, flipping slippery chicken thighs, and maneuvering slatted lengths of pork ribs. The results? Regular spring-loaded kitchen tongs do everything best—for about $8.

The Scent of a Lemon

In the past two decades the Meyer lemon, a hybrid made by crossing a lemon and an orange or mandarin, has become the chef's choice for desserts. Brought from China to California in 1980, the diminuitive Meyer has less acidity than a true lemon and is often called a sweet lemon. Yankee skepticism not-withstanding, we decided to pit the Meyer against a traditional Lisbon lemon in our lemon curd recipe (March/April 2000). Side-by-side comparisons (we reduced the sugar in the Meyer variant of the recipe by two tablespoons to level the field) produced mixed reactions.

Many tasters felt that the true lemon was more, well, lemony. The Meyer, with its floral notes, more complex flavor, and greener, grassy finish, took some getting used to. By midafternoon, following repeated spoonings, the Meyer had won a few converts. Judge for yourself: Meyer lemons are in season from August to March and are available from better produce vendors.

Nonplused by Nomenclature

Sleek, Japanese-made solid stainless Global knives come in numbers dazzling enough to place on a surgical cart. When we selected brands to deploy in our paring knife competition (January/February 2000), Global's entry resembled other candidates in name only. The 10-centimeter knife was long of handle, wide of blade, and difficult to wield around the contours of vegetables and fruits. As a result, it scored poorly against conventional rivals. Yet in subsequent months we found ourselves reaching for the Global again and again for other kitchen tasks. Though less fleet of foot than other paring knives, it is a fine little utility knife, holding a competitive edge and mincing and chopping with the best of them. Recently, to be fair, we purchased a Global "peeling" knife, an 8-centimeter specimen similar in appearance to traditional paring knives. Surgically sharp and scalpel-like in design, it is Global's paring knife par excellence, proving that a knife by any other name— might lose a contest.

The Meyer lemon (top) is about the size of an egg. It is sitting on a traditional Lisbon lemon.

A Hill of Beans

The vanilla flower, a member of the venerated orchid family, is in fact the only member of that extended clan that produces an edible product. Vanilla beans are picked green and flavorless, then cured over a period of several weeks. The result? A dark, intoxicating pod boasting 110 volatile flavor compounds. Most prized by chefs, certainly, is Tahitian vanilla, with its bewitching floral scent and stunning seed density (compared with traditional Madagascar beans). Tahitian vanilla (see Resources, page 32) made our panna cotta tasters weak in the knees. But vanilla beans dry out quickly when they are not stored in airtight containers. Even the sealed glass vials sold in grocery stores turn out snapping dry beans. Storage tips from our kitchen to yours: immerse whole, supple vanilla beans in a simple sugar syrup in a sealed glass jar or plastic container, then store in the refrigerator. (The syrup can be made by cooking equal parts granulated sugar and water together until the sugar is fully dissolved.) If the beans are already dry, grind them in a spice grinder and store them in sugar—the sugar will act as flavor ambassador in the desserts you make with it.

Sitting Pretty

If you read the story on grill-roasted chicken in this issue (see page 10) you may be intrigued by the beer can pedestal we recommend for the grill. An open, partially filled beer can supporting a whole chicken from the bottom up imparts moisture and a delicately hoppy flavor to the flesh, while keeping the bird a safe tanning distance from direct heat. We were all impressed by the ingenuity and grittiness of this technique, and didn't complain over the swigs of beer required to get the can level just right. But for indoor roasting, or for those of you who don't keep canned beer on hand, we would like to mention Willie's Chicken Sitter (see Resources, page 32). Our colleague, Jack Bishop, sent us one of these from Texas. Made of plain white ceramic, the Chicken Sitter looks like a cross between a vertical roaster and a travel mug. Pour your beer or lemonade into it, position the chicken over it (at which point it looks more like a potty seat), and dash it into the oven. You will be rewarded with a tender, juicy chicken that has managed to look after itself.

Where's the Worm?

A misty state of mind induced by margarita tasting got us curious about tequila trivia. Looking for the worm in the tequila bottle? You won't find one. Tequila is often confused with its worm-bearing cousin, mezcal. Though both tequila and mezcal are distilled from the agave plant—a cactuslike member of the lily family—strict government regulations require that tequila be distilled exclusively from blue agave, whereas any type of agave may be used to distill mezcal. Tequila comes in two general types: mixed, or "mixto," tequila often has added cane or corn sugar; superpremium tequila, on the other hand, is distilled from 100 percent blue agave sugar—and will say so on the bottle. Within these categories are five tequila styles. White or silver (*blanco* or *plata*) is a mixed tequila bottled immediately upon distillation or stored in steel tanks for up to 60 days. Gold (*joven abocado*) tequila, like silver, is also a mixed tequila but contains caramel coloring and flavoring to make it mimic the characteristics of an aged tequila. Rested (*reposado*) tequila is typically made from 100 percent agave and aged in oak casks for two to 12 months, which lends it a golden color and mellow flavor. Aged (*anejo*) or very aged (*muy anejo*) tequila are typically 100 percent agave products, aged between one and two, or two and six years, respectively. These rare and expensive tequilas have the softest of flavor and deepest amber color—superior for sipping, but a shame to waste in a margarita.

Bringing It All Back Home

Just what is American home cooking? Two new cookbooks try to answer that question—one notably more successfully than the other. BY CHRISTOPHER KIMBALL

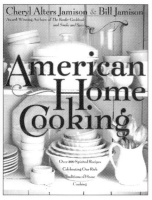

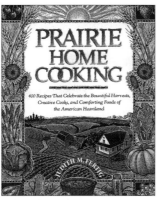

I once asked James Beard to define American home cooking, and he replied, "It's what your neighbor is making for dinner." Although glib, his comment accurately reflects the mongrel nature of American cuisine. This odd amalgam of local favorites, country classics, new technology, and the corrosive effects of mass production and marketing leaves us with a persistent question: Do we have a cuisine or simply a collection of recipes? When reviewing cookbooks devoted to American home cooking, one also wants to know whether the authors are merely digging up the past for one last viewing or providing recipes that have real currency for today's home cook. Put another way, is Country Captain Chicken a relic, or is it timely? Here are two books that try to get a handle on this elusive cuisine, attempting to meld the past with the present in an effort to make American home cooking relevant to this new century.

AMERICAN HOME COOKING
Cheryl Alters Jamison and Bill Jamison
Broadway Books, 470 pages

I still have my dog-eared copy of Nikka Hazelton's *American Home Cooking* (Penguin, 1980), a book I found comforting in the dark days of the 1980s, when American "cuisine" was redefined almost weekly. In this new volume of the same name, the Jamisons cast their net wide, including everything from cioppino to tomato soup and Lady Baltimore cake to biscochitos in an effort to present a fresh view of a familiar landscape. Their book includes 16 pages of color photographs and 300 recipes.
PROS: The Jamisons have successfully walked a fine line between yet another recipe for Johnnycakes and cultural revisionism. Their

choice of recipes is right on the money, providing many old favorites along with plenty of intriguing local specialties such as Honolulu Poke and Sugar Creek Fried Morels. *American Home Cooking* feels fresh and modern, yet at the same time comforting and solid. The design is simple and clean, making it easy to cook from, and the editorial asides are unusually well-chosen and informative. The Jamisons did their homework, and it shows.

CONS: If apt to quibble, one might point out that most of the recipes in this book are unlikely to be found in American homes in the year 2000 (after all, American home cooking is but a shadow of its former self). The authors might retort, however, (and I would agree) that most of these recipes *ought* to be included in a good cook's repertoire.

RECIPE TESTING: Holy Buckwheat Cakes! We tested 17 recipes and all but three of them were worth making again, a startlingly high percentage. The Jamisons know how to cook, their recipes are clear and well-tested, and the results are first-rate. There were many blue-ribbon winners, including Marinated Salmon Bits, A Bowl of Red, Maui Mango Bread, Banana Pudding, Chicken-Fried Steak, Iowa Skinny, New Orleans Bread Pudding, "Barbecued" Shrimp, and Onion and Olive Enchiladas. A few recipes got a thumbs-down, including the Broccoli-Rice Casserole and Saimin (a Hawaiian noodle soup), the latter being a lackluster interpretation of the real thing. (One of our editors grew up eating this soup in Hawaii.) We had a few quibbles with other recipes, including the need for seafood stock (we used bottled clam juice), mole paste, and $40 worth of clams for the chowder. Not all of the directions were on the money—some of the cooking and marinating times were off—but on the whole the recipe directions were clear and reasonably accurate.

PRAIRIE HOME COOKING
Judith M. Fertig
Harvard Common Press, 434 pages, paperback

Unlike the Jamisons, who took on the whole of American cuisine, Judith Fertig focuses on prairie food, having moved to Kansas in the early 1980s. This concentration on one region gives the book more focus but also necessitates a more idiosyn-

cratic collection of recipes, including such oddities as Hay-Smoked Grilled Steak (a fistful of hay is the first ingredient) and Swedish Knackebrod (homemade rye crisps). Fertig does mix the old with the new, calling for Maytag blue cheese in an up-to-date house dressing from the president of Maytag Dairy Farms, yet sticks to a more historical perspective with Shaker Poached Lake Fish. The recipe design is clean and readable, although the sidebar material is printed against a busy yellow and white pattern that makes it a bit hard on the eyes. There are plenty of recipes here, but all in all they seem less appealing than the selections in the Jamisons' book.

PROS: The author is knowledgeable about her subject, and the 400 recipes provide a lot of variety and depth. In addition, the ingredient lists and directions seem short enough for modern cooks.
CONS: Flipping through this book, one wishes for a bit more editing of the recipes. Many of the offerings seem to have been included more for historical accuracy than for modern implementation—most of us aren't going to make honeysuckle syrup or bake rye crisps from scratch. One also quickly gets the feeling that this food isn't designed for the uninitiated, since the directions are often cursory and the combination of ingredients seem to be an acquired taste, especially in the pairing of sweet and savory. Perhaps fewer recipes would have been preferable.

RECIPE TESTING: Our reservations about the recipes were borne out by our kitchen testing. We made 10 recipes, and nine of them were less than successful. The Mexican Fish Stew had virtually no flavor, containing no seasoning whatsoever, not even salt or pepper. A cornbread recipe had one-quarter cup each of honey and brown sugar, which produced a soggy, dense, and coarse bread. (The recipe introduction notes that the bread has a "hint" of sweetness!) The Heartland Choucroute Garni had a lopsided ratio of meat to sauerkraut, its ham hocks were given only one hour to cook, and the recipe called for a whopping two tablespoons of caraway seeds. The amount of flour recommended for the butter-almond cookies was vague at best, the Wild Mushroom Pot Pies with an Herb Crust were an astonishing purplish yellow color and virtually inedible, and a stuffed pork loin turned out dry and came with stuffing that was candylike. Either the recipes were poorly tested or prairie cooking is an acquired taste.

RESOURCES

Most of the ingredients and materials necessary for the recipes in this issue are available at your local supermarket, gourmet food store, or kitchen supply shop. The following are mail-order sources for particular items. Prices listed below were current at press time and do not include shipping and handling unless otherwise indicated. We suggest that you contact companies directly to confirm up-to-date prices and availability.

Bread Knives

Contrary to our assumptions about bread knives, they are not all created equal. Our ideal bread knife consists of a long, rigid blade with sharp serrations and a comfortable handle. Among the 10 knives tested for the story on page 28, the Forschner (Victorinox), model 40040, was the clear winner. The long, stable blade cut easily through the tough crusts of European bread and chewy bagels but didn't smash loaves of soft white bread, as some knives do. In addition, the Forschner sliced effortlessly into tomatoes without tearing the tender skin. The knife measures approximately 14¾ inches long and 1½ inches wide at its widest part. The stamped, high-carbon, stainless steel blade is 10 inches long and its comfortable handle is made of rosewood. The knife is also available with a black, textured plastic handle called Fibrox, which is model 40547. You can order both Forschner models from **Kitchen Arts (161 Newbury Street, Boston, MA 02116; 617-266-8701)**. Model 40040 sells for $37.80, and model 40547 sells for $27.95.

Finishing a close second to the Forschner bread knife was the LamsonSharp Offset Bread Knife, model 39556. This knife performed well in all of our tests but one. Its serrations sliced through even the most difficult of crusts, but the blade proved too aggressive for tomatoes, ripping their skin. The LamsonSharp features a stamped 10-inch offset blade that allows plenty of clearance for knuckles; its black synthetic handle has nickel silver rivets. It is available for $39.99 through **Professional Cutlery Direct (242 Branford Road, North Branford, CT 06471; 800-859-6994; www.cutlery.com)**. The purchase code is OCO7L.

Ramekins

Our panna cotta (page 23) is simplicity itself. For the most pristine appearance, we prefer to use straight-sided ramekins—not flared ones—as panna cotta molds. We found some that are not only the perfect size and shape, but also durable and lightweight. Made by Apilco, the white French porcelain ramekins are high-fired for maximum resistance to chipping. Each measures approximately 3½ inches in diameter and 1⅝ inches high and is safe for use in the oven, broiler, microwave, and dishwasher. These ramekins are also ideal for baking individual custards and soufflés. **Williams-Sonoma (Mail Order Department, P.O. Box 7456, San Francisco, CA 94120-7456; 800-541-2233; www.williams-sonoma.com)** carries a set of four Apilco porcelain ramekins, item 05-3426673, for $20.

Tahitian Vanilla

In addition to a panna cotta that unmolds beautifully, we also discovered the secret to intoxicating vanilla aroma and flavor: Tahitian vanilla beans. Though pricey ($3.00 per bean, or $7.50 for three), we think they're worth the price. They can be ordered from **The Spice House (1941 Central Street, Evanston, IL 60201; 847-328-3711; www.thespicehouse.com)**.

Hamburger Press

While developing the recipe for grilled hamburgers, we tested four burger-shaping devices. While all four were able to shape a patty, only one turned out a burger of our desired dimensions. The Hamburger Press is made of white plastic and has a plungerlike lid that tamps the meat into the mold and pushes the formed patty out for easy, mess-free shaping. In addition, we found the top of the plunger is the perfect size for making the depression in the center of the patty that prevents puffing during cooking. The Hamburger Press, model 5434, is made by Fox Run Craftsmen and measures 4⅜ inches in diameter and 2¾ inches high. It is available from **Kitchen Etc. (32 Industrial Drive, Exeter, NH 03833-4577; 800-232-4070; www.kitchenetc. com)** and sells for $3.99. Ask for item 643411.

Rustic Lattice Strips

Measuring and cutting straight, even lattice strips for our fresh peach pie (page 25) takes a little patience and precision. While testing the recipe, our test kitchen measured and cut the lattice strips with the aid of a stainless steel ruler. This ruler's length (15 inches) and width (1¼ inches) are identical to those of lattice strips, so measuring is a breeze. You can purchase the stainless steel ruler, item AMC-10416 (15 inches), for $5.39 by contacting **W. B. Mason's Office Supplies (888-926-2766; www.wbmason.com)**.

Though a paring knife works for cutting the lattice strips, a pizza wheel or fluted pastry wheel accomplishes the task quickly, smoothly, and precisely. Both worked flawlessly, although we preferred the pinking-sheared, rustic look created by the fluted pastry wheel. The choice is yours. It is important to have a sturdy pizza or fluted pastry wheel with a comfortable handle and a blade that can cut with ease. We recommend the Oxo Good Grips Pizza Wheel, item 5930, priced at $6.90, and the Wüsthof Fluted Pastry Wheel, item WT14, priced at $9.00. Both can be ordered from **A Cook's Wares (211 37th Street, Beaver Falls, PA 15010-2130; 800-915-9788; www.cookswares.com)**.

Wood Chunks

When developing the grill-roasted chicken recipe on page 11, senior writer Jack Bishop found wood chunks to be superior to wood chips. For the purposes of this recipe, wood chunks not only gave the chicken more smoky flavor but were necessary to help fuel the fire. We recommend chunks cut from hickory or mesquite. Make sure to soak the wood chunks for at least an hour before placing them on the hot coals. Wood chunks are sold in most hardware stores, but if you cannot find any, try **Armitage Hardware (925 West Armitage Avenue, Chicago, IL 60614; 773-348-3267; www.webergrills.com)**. They sell both hickory and mesquite chunks in 360-cubic-inch bags for $4.29 and in 720-cubic-inch bags for $7.79.

Chicken Sitter

For the grill-roasted beer can chicken recipe on page 12, Willie's Chicken Sitter has a 5-inch base that is a stable alternative to a sometimes wobbly beer can. Fill it up with your choice of potable—potent or not—then set your chicken on it and roast in the oven or on the grill. Some hardware and kitchen supply stores sell Willie's Chicken Sitter, but if you can't locate one, we recommend **Goode Company Barbeque Hall of Flame (5015 Kirby, Houston, TX 77098; 713-529-1212 or 800-627-3502; www.goodecompany.com)**. The Chicken Sitter item number is BBQ200 and the cost is $12.99.

Plimoth Plantation

For our "Harvesting, Using, and Storing Fresh Herbs" article on pages 16 and 17, we took a day trip to Plimoth Plantation in Plymouth, Mass., where we consulted with resident horticulturist John Forti. Plimoth Plantation, a "living museum," re-creates life in a 17th-century Pilgrim village. Visitors learn about the era by strolling through the village and interacting with its "residents." For directions, admission prices, and general information, contact **Plimoth Plantation (P.O. Box 1620, Plymouth, MA 02362; 508-746-1622; www.plimoth.org)**.

RECIPES

July & August 2000

PHOTOGRAPHY: CARL TREMBLAY & VAN ACKERE (MARGARITA)

Grilled Hamburgers

Grilled Pepper Salad

Curried Rice Salad

Grill-Roasted Chicken

Simple Sweet and Tangy Barbecue Sauce

Best Fresh Margarita

Stuffed Zucchini

Creamy Corn Pudding

Classic Panna Cotta

Fresh Peach Pie

www.cooksillustrated.com

Cook's Illustrated has just launched its new Web site, and we invite you to join us. Simply log on at www.cooksillustrated.com. Although much of the information is free, database searches are for site subscribers only. *Cook's Illustrated* readers can subscribe at a 20 percent discount.

Here is what you can do on our site:

Browse Web exclusives Find ratings, recipes, tips, and other material created exclusively for our Web site.

Search our recipes We provide a searchable database of all the recipes from *Cook's*.

Search tastings and cookware ratings You will find all of our reviews (cookware, food, wine, and cookbooks).

Find your favorite quick tips.

Get answers to your cooking questions Post questions for *Cook's* editors and fellow site subscribers.

Take a cooking course online Take online cooking courses from *Cook's* editors and receive personalized instruction.

Check your subscription Check the status of your subscription, pay a bill, or give gift subscriptions.

Visit our bookstore Purchase any of our cookbooks, hardbound annual editions of the magazine, or posters.

Subscribe to e-Notes Our free e-mail companion to Kitchen Notes offers cooking advice, test results, buying tips, and recipes related to a single topic each month.

Find out about our new television show Coming to public television later this year, *America's Test Kitchen* will take you behind the scenes in the *Cook's Illustrated* test kitchen.

Get all the extras The outtakes from each issue of *Cook's*—including step-by-step photographs, illustrations—are available at *Cook's Extra*.

White Currant

Red Currant

Cultivated Blueberry

Elderberry

Gooseberry

Strawberry

Blackberry

Mulberry

Golden Raspberry

Raspberry

Huckleberry

Wild Blueberry

BERRIES

NUMBER FORTY-SIX

SEPTEMBER & OCTOBER 2000

COOK'S
ILLUSTRATED

Chicken Cacciatore
Moist Meat, Rich Sauce

Garlic Mashed Potatoes
Toast the Garlic and Boil the Potatoes
in Their Skins

Best Caramel Sauce
Foolproof Method Produces
a Quick, Thick Sauce

Really Good Vegetable Stock
A Recipe That Holds Its Own
Against the Real Thing

Crisp Broiled Salmon
Two-Stage Cooking Is the Secret

Loaf Pan Testing
$4 Pan Beats Pricey Competitors

Chili Powder Taste Test
Perfect Stuffed Tomatoes
Steak Pan Sauces
Foolproof Dessert Soufflés

$4.95 U.S./$6.95 CANADA

62805

CONTENTS
September & October 2000

COOK'S
ILLUSTRATED
www.cooksillustrated.com

PUBLISHER AND EDITOR
Christopher Kimball

SENIOR EDITOR
John Willoughby

SENIOR WRITER
Jack Bishop

CORPORATE MANAGING EDITOR
Barbara Bourassa

TEST KITCHEN DIRECTOR
Kay Rentschler

ASSOCIATE EDITORS
Adam Ried
Dawn Yanagihara
Raquel Pelzel

ASSOCIATE EDITOR,
ONLINE EDUCATION
Becky Hays

RECIPE TESTING AND DEVELOPMENT
Bridget Lancaster
Julia Collin

WEB TEST COOK
Shona Simkin

ASSISTANT EDITOR
Shannon Blaisdell

CONSULTING FOOD EDITOR
Jasper White

CONSULTING EDITOR
Jim Dodge

CONTRIBUTING EDITORS
Maryellen Driscoll
Elizabeth Germain

ART DIRECTOR
Amy Klee

COPY EDITOR
India Koopman

EDITORIAL INTERN
Tammy Donroe

MARKETING MANAGER
Pamela Caporino

SALES REPRESENTATIVE
Jason Geller

MARKETING ASSISTANT
Connie Forbes

CIRCULATION DIRECTOR
David Mack

CIRCULATION MANAGER
Larisa Greiner

PRODUCTS MANAGER
Steven Browall

CIRCULATION ASSISTANT
Jennifer McCreary

INBOUND MARKETING
REPRESENTATIVES
Adam Dardeck
Jacqui Valerio

VICE PRESIDENT OPERATIONS
AND TECHNOLOGY
James McCormack

ASSISTANT PRODUCTION MANAGER
Jessica Lindheimer

PRODUCTION ARTIST
Daniel Frey

PRODUCTION COORDINATOR
Mary Connelly

SYSTEMS ADMINISTRATOR
Richard Cassidy

WEB MASTER
Nicole Morris

CONTROLLER
Mandy Shito

SPECIAL PROJECTS
Deborah Broide

For list rental information, contact The SpeciaLISTS, 1200 Harbor Blvd. 9th Floor, Weehawken, NJ 07087; (201) 865-5800; fax (201) 867-2450. Editorial office: 17 Station Street, Brookline, MA 02445; (617) 232-1000; fax (617) 232-1572. Editorial contributions should be sent to: Editor, *Cook's Illustrated*. We cannot assume responsibility for manuscripts submitted to us. Submissions will be returned only if accompanied by a large self-addressed envelope. Postmaster: Send all new orders, subscription inquiries, and change of address notices to: *Cook's Illustrated*, P.O. Box 7446, Red Oak, IA 51591-0446. PRINTED IN THE USA.

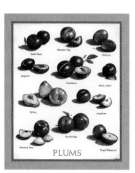

PLUMS

PLUMS: With more than 200 varieties and a growing season that lasts from May to September, plums are among the most widely distributed of all stone fruits. Each type has a distinct flavor, shape, and color. Santa Rosas have a classic sweet-tart taste, while Victorias are only semisweet but very juicy. Beautiful green Kelseys are sweet, with a spongy, pearlike texture, and both Howard Suns and Casselmans are floral, sweet, and aromatic. Royal Diamonds are light, sweet, and juicy. Scarlet Suns are mild and refreshing. Perhaps the most versatile of the plums we tasted are Angelenos, which are wonderful eaten raw or cooked. Black Ambers are also excellent for cooking, while the sour Empresses should be used only for cooking—with lots of sugar. Dinosaur Eggs are hybrids of apricots and plums.

COVER (*Cabbage*): ELIZABETH BRANDON, BACK COVER (*Plums*): JOHN BURGOYNE

BY HAND

I started thinking about hands as I was seated in a school auditorium, watching my 4-year-old son walk up the steps to the stage on his first day of school. He walked buoyantly over to the headmaster and extended his tiny right hand, which was immediately swallowed whole in a ceremonial shake. This pressing of flesh was perfunctory but nonetheless symbolic of his acceptance into a new community, one hand inviting another in a primitive ritual—an embrace, if you like—that is now taken for granted.

We all shake hands. We also use them for all sorts of mundane tasks, such as brushing teeth, pouring milk, picking up a coffee cup, scratching an itch, inserting a key, or typing on a keyboard, the task to which my hands are most often devoted. Fingers, the main attraction of hands, are particularly noteworthy. We stick them in our ears, my son puts them up his nose, and veterinarians use them for all sorts of things most of us would rather not know about. They bend or straighten to communicate a wide range of human emotions, including disdain, peace, life, death, invitations to come closer, or just a friendly Vulcan "hello" if you can muster sufficient muscle control. You can also paint with them, push a doorbell, or reach across the ceiling of the Sistine Chapel in an eternal gesture of longing.

Many cultures have a lot more respect for hands than we do. They cut them off if one is found guilty of stealing, which, in an odd way, accords their usefulness a large measure of respect. In many areas of the world, each hand has its own designated functions, and to get them mixed up is to gravely offend one's native hosts. (While traveling in North Africa, a left-handed friend of mine was always on the verge of making a terrible social gaffe.) However, the greatest example of the power of these appendages is the "laying on of hands," which is thought to transfer energy from healer to patient to effect a cure. I once published the story of a woman from Portland who was cured of a debilitating migraine by such a method while traveling in the Philippines. Once a skeptic, she went on to become a healer herself.

I note, with some measure of alarm, that hands are losing favor. Instead of being instruments of social contact—caressing, rubbing, soothing, massaging—our germ-averse modern culture has identified them as transmitters of disease. I first noticed this years ago when my dentist slipped on a pair of translucent surgical gloves before the annual cleaning. This trend has accelerated of late, and now naked digits no longer touch my tuna on rye at the local deli. Gardeners I know have wheelbarrows full of gloves, from tight-fitting deerskin to the oversized handyman variety. Even the simple art of shaking hands seems to be losing ground to the European smooch, which is performed on either one side or both sides of the person's face, the kiss always enacted in midair, lips never actually touching flesh. Even the verb "to touch" has taken on a sinister connotation in an age when a simple kiss can be grounds for legal action.

Over a lifetime, hands become invested with knowledge, if we allow it. The surgeon, the farmer, the gardener, the artist, and the mother all accrue a lifetime of skill in their hands. So, too,

Christopher Kimball

do cooks. We can fold egg whites by hand (skip the rubber spatula), knead bread, rub butter into flour for pie dough, mix ingredients, clean out bowls, rub in spices, unmold, shape, pat, and stuff. (We can even pick things up off the floor and throw them back in the pan when nobody is looking.) We can seek out pinbones with our fingers, pressing the flesh of the cool salmon as we work. We can caress the food as we prepare it, feeling its curves and inner spaces, and then use our sense of touch to determine when it is done. The cake springs back, the chicken leg wiggles freely, and our finger encounters just the right amount of resistance when the steak is ready to come off the grill.

The morning that my son shook hands on stage, I had put him on the school bus for the first time with his two older sisters. They held his hands as they walked to the bus, and when he turned to say goodbye I gave him a big wet kiss, not the fancy European kind. Then he looked up and said, "Daddy, can you wave goodbye to me?" He made his way like a rock climber up the huge, steep steps to the bus and took a window seat, his small round face pressed to the glass so he looked like a TV show host. With the bus standing still, I raised my hand and waved once, then twice, then frantically, like some lost soul, though neither of us had moved; we remained only a few feet apart. Since that September morning, I have used my hands for a thousand different things, but I often think that I have never used them better.

ABOUT COOK'S ILLUSTRATED

Visit our expanded Web site The new *Cook's* Web site features original editorial content not found in the magazine as well as searchable databases for recipes, equipment tests, food tastings, buying advice, step-by-step illustrations of cooking techniques, and quick tips. The site also features our online bookstore, cooking courses, a question-and-answer message board, and a sign-up form for *e-Notes*, our free online cooking newsletter. Join us online today at cooksillustrated.com.

The magazine *Cook's Illustrated* (ISSN 1068-2821) is published bimonthly (6 issues per year) by Boston Common Press Limited Partnership, 17 Station Street, Brookline, MA 02445. Copyright 2000 Boston Common Press Limited Partnership. Periodical postage paid at Boston, Mass., and additional mailing offices, USPS #012487. A one-year subscription is $29.70, two years is $55, and three years is $75. Add $6 postage per year for Canadian subscriptions and $12 per year for all other foreign countries. To order subscriptions in the U.S. call 800-526-8442; from outside the U.S. call 515-247-7571. Gift subscriptions are available for $24.95 each. Postmaster: Send all new orders, subscription inquiries, and change of address notices to *Cook's Illustrated*, P.O. Box 7446, Red Oak, IA 51591-0446.

Cookbooks and other products *Cook's Illustrated* also offers cookbooks and magazine-related items for sale through our bookstore. Products offered include annual hardbound editions of the magazine, a seven-year (1993–1999) reference index for the magazine, the How to Cook Master Series of single-subject cookbooks, as well as copies of other books from our editors, including *The Best Recipe, The Complete Book of Pasta*, and *365 Quick Tips*. Prices and ordering information are available by calling 800-611-0759 inside the U.S. or 515-246-6911 from outside the U.S. or by visiting our bookstore at www.cooksillustrated.com. Back issues of *Cook's Illustrated* are available for sale by calling 800-611-0759 inside the U.S. or 515-246-6911 from outside the U.S.

Questions about your book order? Visit our customer care page at www.cooksillustrated.com, or call 800-611-0759 inside the U.S. or 515-246-6911 from outside the U.S.

Reader submissions *Cook's* accepts reader submissions for Quick Tips. We will provide a one-year complimentary subscription for each tip that we print. Send your tip, name, address, and daytime telephone number to Quick Tips, *Cook's Illustrated*, P.O. Box 470589, Brookline, MA 02447. Questions, suggestions, or submissions for Notes from Readers should be sent to the same address.

Questions about your subscription? Visit our customer care page at cooksillustrated.com, where you can manage your subscription, including changing your address, renewing your subscription, paying your bill, or viewing answers to frequently asked questions. You can also direct questions about your subscription to *Cook's Illustrated*, P.O. Box 7446, Red Oak, IA 51591-0446, or call 1-800-526-8442.

Freezing Buttermilk

We occasionally use buttermilk in baking and in salad dressing and invariably have a lot left over. Rather than scrambling to use it up in other recipes or letting it sit too long and spoil, we freeze our leftover buttermilk in ice cube trays, then transfer the cubes to a freezer bag for storage. This makes us feel thrifty, and it's much easier to pull a few cubes from the freezer than it is to run out to the store the next time we need a small amount of buttermilk.

MITCH LEAVITT
RACINE, WIS.

➤ Like you, we have had to throw out spoiled buttermilk on occasion. Lured by the idea of saving a trip to the market, we were attracted to the idea of freezing leftovers. So we froze buttermilk in an ice cube tray and thawed it out seven days later to run some side-by-side baking and cooking tests using the previously frozen buttermilk and fresh buttermilk. The results of our tests were mixed.

We conducted our first test with our buttermilk doughnut recipe (March/April 1997, page 21). All of the tasters found the two batches to be identical in terms of both appearance and flavor, and the integrity of the doughnuts made with frozen buttermilk was what it should be—crisp on the outside and tender within. One taster did find the doughnuts made with frozen buttermilk marginally less fluffy than those made with fresh, but not so much that we'd pass on the option of pulling some buttermilk out of the freezer in a moment of need.

When we used frozen buttermilk to make a ranch salad dressing recipe from the *Joy of Cooking* (Simon & Schuster, 1997), however, our efforts fell flat. The dressing made with fresh buttermilk was thick and smooth, while the dressing made with frozen was thin and watery. In both the dressing and the thawed buttermilk itself, we noticed small, solid globules floating in the liquid. Dr. William LaGrange, a food scientist at the Iowa State University Extension Service, explained that when buttermilk is frozen, solid proteins coagulate, or clump, which accounts for the lumps we witnessed. When the buttermilk thaws, the bonds between the proteins break up and the liquid "wheys off"—that is, it separates from the rest of the emulsion. A quick spin in the blender returned the frozen buttermilk to its original, thick consistency. If you're going to make dressing, we absolutely recommend this step. Any flavor differences between fresh and frozen were relatively minor.

Dr. LaGrange also explained our success with buttermilk doughnuts. In that case, he said, the buttermilk blends with the other ingredients in the recipe, and this had the effect of masking the separation. In addition, the flour absorbs some of the liquid, which contributes to the masking effect. In our experience, then, freezing buttermilk is a fine idea. The thawed liquid can be used as is for baked goods or in other recipes containing flour, such as waffles or pancakes, but it's best to briefly whirl it in a blender before using it in salad dressing.

Using Styrofoam in the Pantry

I had to write regarding the quick tip on the homemade tiered shelf organizer in the September/October 1999 issue of *Cook's* (page 4). The reader who sent in the tip used lumber to make his tiers, whereas I've made them from pieces of the Styrofoam used as packing material. The Styrofoam is easier to cut than wood, especially for those with few tools. If you don't have any on hand, it can be purchased at most any good craft store.

JUDY BEYLERIAN
ALAMEDA, CALIF.

➤ Indeed, there often is Styrofoam lying around the office, and, just as you say, it was very easy to fashion into shelf tiers. (By the way, the original wooden tiered shelf is still in our test kitchen pantry, where we can now spot the right spice in seconds.)

Best Water Temperature for Coffee

Not being a coffee drinker myself, I am a bit in the dark about what constitutes a great cup of coffee. Your story on automatic drip coffee makers (November/December 1998, page 28) and a more recent mention in Kitchen Notes (January/February 2000, page 30) cite water temperature as an important concern. I'm not sure what the right temperature is. Please, for the sake of my husband's coffee, can you help?

LYNNE RINGQUIST
BURLINGTON, CONN.

➤ A number of factors contribute to a good cup of coffee: the origin and quality of the coffee itself, the degree to which it was roasted, the time elapsed since the beans were ground, whether they were ground coarse or fine, the duration of the brewing process, and, yes, the temperature of the water during brewing. In a number of previous conversations with Ted Lingle, executive director of the Specialty Coffee Association of America, we learned that hundreds of chemical compounds account for the flavor profile of a particular pot of coffee.

Generally, the best coffee results when 18 to 22 percent of the water-soluble flavor compounds have been extracted from the grounds. This can be accomplished only when the brewing time is no more than six minutes per pot of coffee and the temperature of the water is between 195 and 205 degrees. Longer brewing times or hotter water (a full 212-degree boil, for instance) will likely cause overextraction, in which case undesirable flavor compounds are released into the liquid.

To confirm this, we went into the test kitchen and brewed three pots of coffee using our favorite manual drip method and the same ratio of coffee grounds to water, varying only the temperature of the water. Coffee brewed with the coolest water, 180 degrees, tasted weak and tepid. Too few of the desirable flavor compounds had been released. At the other extreme, coffee brewed with water at a hard, 212-degree boil tasted somewhat bitter and scorched. The best cup was indeed brewed with water just short of a boil, at 200 degrees. The tasting panel unanimously judged this cup to have the most full, round, and balanced coffee flavor.

Failure to Fluff

A friend called recently to tell me that she could not get her egg whites to "fluff" and asked what she was doing wrong. I told her that the problem was most likely the result of oil residue on the surface of the mixing bowl or beaters or trace amounts of yolk in the separated whites. Am I correct? Is there any way to save a batch of egg whites that won't whip up properly?

WILLIAM WYTRWAL
LATHAM, N.Y.

➤ Egg whites are a finicky lot and demand optimal conditions for whipping. In the "failure to fluff" mystery experienced by your friend, fat, as you suspect, was the most likely culprit. A mere speck of yolk, oil, butter, or other fat captured in the whites will markedly reduce the maximum volume the foam can attain, as fats obstruct the bonding of the whites' protein molecules, inhibiting coagulation. It is essential to keep egg whites and all equipment that will come in contact with them—bowl, whip, spoons, and spatulas—fat-free. If fat is to blame when a batch of egg whites refuses to whip up, the damage done is irreversible. There's nothing to do but clean everything up and start over again.

This time make sure the equipment is scrupulously clean. Wash it in soapy, hot-as-you-can-stand-it water, rinse with more hot water, and dry with paper towels. A dish towel may have traces of oil within its fibers that could be transferred to the bowl.

Separating the eggs is the next important step. Eggs separate most easily and cleanly when refrigerator-cold because the yolk is firmer and so less likely to break. According to the *Encyclopedia* (American Egg Board, 1999), it is best to take the chill off the whites before whipping, but we found that the difference between whites that had been whipped cold versus warm was negligible—especially when they are to be used in baking.

Your choice of mixing bowl will also affect your success with whipped whites. Bowls made from plastic, a petroleum product with a porous surface, retain an oily film even when washed carefully and should not be used for whipping egg whites. The foam will never reach its optimal volume, no matter how long it is beaten. Glass and ceramic should be avoided as well, as their slippery surfaces make it harder for whites to billow up. Aluminum, which tends to gray whites, should also be avoided. The two best choices are stainless steel and, for those who have it, copper. (See "Do Copper Bowls Make a Difference?" page 25.)

Orange Liqueurs Explained

The *Cook's* recipe for sangría (May/June 1998, page 13) has become a favorite, and the margaritas in the July/August 2000 issue (page 21) have just joined its ranks. But I do have a question about both recipes. Each calls for Triple Sec orange liqueur, and I wondered why you didn't recommend an alternative such as Cointreau or Grand Marnier, which, though more expensive, are also better tasting—or so I always assumed. What's the difference between these liqueurs?

ANNE DEANER
PHILADELPHIA, PA.

➤ The different flavor profiles of Triple Sec, Cointreau, and Grand Marnier can best be explained by the way they are produced.

The orange essence in Cointreau and Grand Marnier is obtained by means of a similar production process. Oranges varying in character and degree of sweetness are harvested, pulped, and laid out to dry and ferment in the sun, which preserves the pungent oils in the skins. The skins are then shipped to their respective distilleries, where they are macerated, or softened, in alcohol to release the preserved flavors and aromas. Finally, the orange skins and alcohol are distilled to condense the natural sugars and remove some of the bitterness of the orange peels. That's where the similarities end.

Cointreau is an 80-proof orange liqueur from France. In 1849, attempting to improve upon the traditional opaque liqueurs and the so-called Triple Sec of the time, confectioner Adolphe Cointreau and his brother, Edouard-Jean, combined the peels of bitter Caribbean and sweet Spanish and Brazilian oranges with neutral spirits, cane sugar, and water. The mixture was distilled in steam-heated copper stills and filtered of any impurities before bottling. The result was a clear orange liqueur that was higher in alcohol and drier in flavor than the contemporary spirits.

Grand Marnier, another French liqueur, is cognac-based and aged in oak. It was developed in 1880 when Alexandre Marnier-Lapostolle, son of a wine and spirits merchant and son-in-law of the founder of a distillery, thought to combine the essence of orange with his father-in-law's reserves of cognac. Dried skins of bitter Haitian oranges macerated in eau de vie (a colorless, potent spirit distilled from fruit other than grapes) were blended with special oak-aged reserves of cognac and sugar, then finished with a secret ingredient that the manufacturer will not divulge to this day. The mixture was then temperature-treated to regulate the alcohol content, filtered, and aged in oak casks for at least 18 months. The result is a honey-colored, 80-proof spirit.

Triple Sec, like most flavored cordials, is a generic, vodka-based spirit. It is a simple mixture of vodka, artificial orange flavors, and fructose (a form of sugar found in fruits). Although we have read that some producers of Triple Sec use "all natural ingredients," all six of the local liquor stores we contacted were unfamiliar with any such brand. The syrupy concoction is lower in alcohol than Cointreau and Grand Marnier, available in 42 proof and 60 proof.

Having tried each product in drinks mixed with other ingredients, we conducted a tasting of Cointreau, Grand Marnier, and Triple Sec straight up. Cointreau, the tasters' least favorite, had the faintest orange flavor. Grand Marnier received slightly better marks as subtle hints of spice, citrus, and raisin were detected in the nose, and the taste was thought to be "smooth," "honeylike," and "mildly orangey." The cognac base was noticeable in that it rounded out the flavors. The 60-proof Triple Sec, although exceedingly sweet and orangey, was appreciated for its lower alcohol content, a factor in its successful blending with the other ingredients in sangría and margaritas.

Errata

➤ In the July/August 2000 Kitchen Notes we transposed a couple of numbers: the Meyer lemon was introduced to the United States in 1908, not 1980. We apologize for any confusion this may have caused. Speaking of confusion, we also referred readers to the wrong issue for the lemon tart recipe. The correct issue is January/February 2000. Again, our apologies.

WHAT IS IT?

I found this implement among the silverware at a beach house in Delaware last summer. I assume it is some kind of culinary device because it was in the kitchen. It is 7½ inches long and made of stainless steel. The handle is very similar to that of a dinner knife. The screw closes the mouth, which has sharp prongs on the inside, leading me to assume it was designed to attach to something.

JOSEPH MENG
BOSTON, MASS.

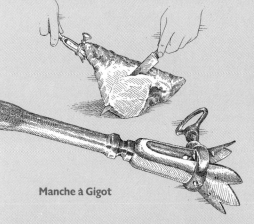

Manche à Gigot

You found a *manche à gigot*. Translated from French, manche means "sleeve" whereas gigot often refers to "leg of lamb." The device is designed to tastefully and neatly facilitate the carving of a bone-in roast leg of lamb. To use, slip the metal sleeve, with its six sharp interior teeth, over the frenched bone and screw tightly shut with the key, digging the teeth into the bone. Once firmly fastened, grasp the handle as if it were a carving fork, lift the leg of lamb at an angle to the carving surface for leverage, and slice the meat, almost parallel to the bone, into thin slices with a very sharp knife. Though seemingly practical, manches à gigot are no longer commonplace members of American carving sets. As noted by Fred Bridge in *The Well-Tooled Kitchen* (Hearst Books, 1991), "an inordinate number are sold in antique stores, testament to the old American tradition of giving the new bride any carving set that included a knife, fork and manche à gigot. In most instances she knew how to use the knife and fork, but not the manche, so it was often given away." Today they are primarily used in high-end, service-oriented restaurants and bought by home cooks interested in formal presentation. If your carving set isn't complete without one, contact Bridge Kitchenware (214 East 52nd Street, New York, NY 10022; 212- 688-4220; www.bridgekitchenware.com), which carries three styles: stainless steel (catalog code CKMG) for $136.95, faux ivory-handled (catalog code CKMG-1) for $75.95, and rosewood-handled (catalog code CKMG-R) for $70.

Quick Tips

Onion Mincing Streamlined

A sharp knife and good technique make mincing onions a quick, easy—even tear-free—task. One popular method dictates that you cut the peeled onion in half from pole to pole, then place the flat sides on the cutting board and make cuts parallel to the board, which can be tricky for some cooks. Kate Gardner of Lansdowne, Pa., recommends a fast method that eliminates the need to cut parallel to the board.

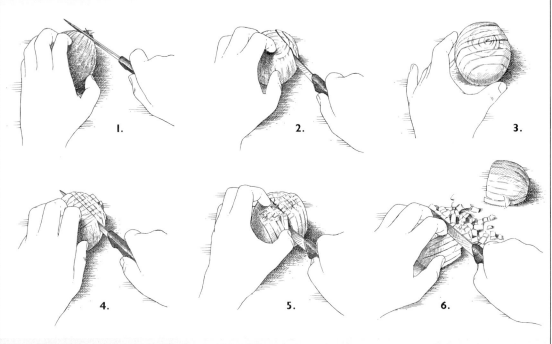

1. 2. 3.

4. 5. 6.

1. Cut off the ends of the onion and peel it.

2. Stand the onion on its root end and, moving from side to side, make parallel slices from the top pole down to, but not all the way through, the bottom pole.

3. Rotate the onion 90 degrees, or a quarter turn.

4. Holding the onion together as illustrated, again make slices from side to side, again without cutting all the way through the bottom. These slices will be perpendicular to the first set of slices. Make sure to keep your fingers clear of the knife blade.

5. Move the knife back to one of the slices at the middle of the onion, cut all the way through so the onion is separated into halves, and place each half, cut-side down, onto the cutting board.

6. Last, using a claw grip with your fingertips folded inward toward your palm to hold the onion in place, cut across the existing slices to make an even dice.

Rinsing Rice

In *Cook's* March/April 2000 story about rice pilaf, we found that we liked the effect rinsing has on the rice. The act of pouring the water off the rice can be tricky, however, sending some rice right down the drain. Denise Kuehner of Old Tappan, N.J., figured out a foolproof way to remove the water without losing a single grain. Put the rice in a wire mesh strainer or colander, and then put the strainer into a large, water-filled bowl. When you're done soaking, simply lift out the strainer and let the rice drain.

Draining Leafy Greens

Many recipes for large-leaved greens such as kale and collards recommend adding the greens to the cooking pot with a little water from their washing still clinging to the leaves. Finding a place to temporarily store the bulky, wet leaves without turning your work surface into a watery mess can be a challenge. Amy Yazbak of Fairfield, Conn., meets this challenge by placing the greens in the empty dish rack next to the sink.

Seasoning Raw Chicken

Many recipes call for seasoning raw chicken pieces with salt and pepper before they are browned or otherwise cooked. Touching other dishes—or the pepper mill—after you've handled raw chicken is a concern if you want to minimize the chances of cross-contamination. Eunice Taylor of Glasgow, Scotland has figured out a great way to avoid handling the pepper mill and saltshaker or saltcellar in this situation. Prior to handling the chicken, mix the necessary salt and freshly ground pepper in a ramekin or small bowl. This way, you can reach into that bowl with abandon and then just throw it in the dishwasher to be cleaned and sterilized when you're finished.

Send Us Your Tip We will provide a complimentary one-year subscription for each tip we print. See page 1 for information.

Best Tent for a Roast

Roasts need to rest for several minutes before being carved to give the juices a chance to distribute themselves throughout the meat. Most recipes instruct the cook to cover the roast with foil while it rests to retain the heat. Instead of using up a lot of foil, Ari Sugerman of Auchenflower, Queensland, Australia, uses a large, overturned mixing bowl. He finds that it's easier and does a better job of retaining the heat, too.

Drying Boiled Potatoes

Shaking just-boiled potatoes gently in the hot pan after pouring off the water is a common method of drying them a little before seasoning and dressing them. However, it's all too easy to break the potatoes apart this way. Enid Stubin of New York, N.Y., suggests an alternate method.

1.

2.

1. After pouring off the water, cover the potatoes with a clean dish or tea towel.
2. Replace the pot lid. After a minute or two, the towel will have absorbed the excess moisture from the potatoes.

Stabilizing Sandwiches

Be they grinders, hoagies, subs, or po' boys, overstuffed sandwiches in bulkie rolls are an American favorite. But they can be pretty sloppy, with fillings spilling out every which way. Gregory Goodhart of Thurmont, Md., neatens up these sandwiches by removing some of the interior crumb in the top and bottom halves of the bread. This creates a trough in the bottom half for meat fillings and a cap on the top for toppings.

Browning the Edges of Pork Chops

Last summer, while grilling thick pork chops, Bob Joseph of Somerville, Mass., found that it can be tricky to stand them up on their thinner sides to brown. Then he realized that the potatoes and onions he was grilling as a side dish suggested an easy solution to the problem: a potato or onion half, placed face-down on the grill, can be used as a prop to support the meat while it's standing on its side.

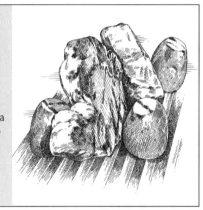

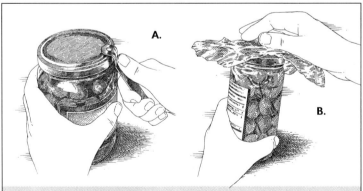

A.

B.

More Jar-Opening Tricks

If you don't happen to have a pair of rubber gloves handy to try Paul Marte's tip (above, right) for loosening stubbornly stuck jar lids, two other readers offer the following suggestions.
A. Sometimes the vacuum seal is to blame. Debra Collins of Ann Arbor, Mich., uses a bottle opener to gingerly (so as not to break the glass jar) pry the lid slightly away from the glass to let in air, which breaks the vacuum seal.
B. Stan Ivers of Dyer, Ind., gets a better grip on the jar lid by draping a piece of plastic wrap over it.

Rubber Gloves in the Kitchen

Even the simplest of kitchen tasks can be frustrating or messy or both. Several readers have found that rubber gloves can make such tasks less vexing.

A. Paul Marte of New York, N.Y., wears rubber gloves to open tightly sealed jars.

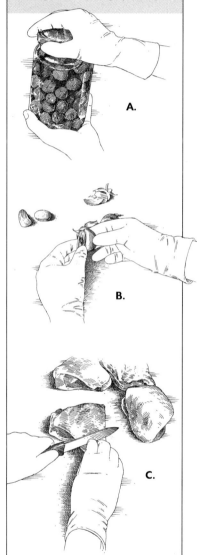

A.

B.

C.

B. Abby Koch of Chicago, Ill., uses gloves to handle and peel the hot toasted garlic cloves used in *Cook's* September/October 1999 recipe for Classic American Garlic Bread. Because the gloves protect her fingers from the heat, there's no need to wait for the cloves to cool, and because the gloves are a little tacky, the garlic peels stick and come right off the cloves. Koch also recommends the gloves for skinning roasted peppers and tomatoes.
C. Mary Lou Krauss of Harwinton, Conn., uses gloves to handle raw chicken.

How to Broil Salmon

Two-stage broiling yields perfect texture, and a surprise ingredient
makes the very best topping.

⇒ BY ADAM RIED WITH JULIA COLLIN ⇐

Our whole side of salmon with crisp crust cooks in just 12 minutes.

S almon is a surefire crowd pleaser, but it's not always easy to make for a crowd. Many cooks shy away from poaching, and our favorite indoor cooking method—pan-searing individual portions—can get cumbersome with too many pieces of fish. Our preferred outdoor cooking techniques—hot-smoking and straightforward grilling—can accommodate larger pieces of fish, but for denizens of the North, among whom we count ourselves, cooking outside is impractical, if not impossible, for almost half the year.

So we set out to beat the odds: to find the best way of cooking a whole side of salmon, enough to feed eight or more guests, in the oven. We wanted fish that was moist but not soggy, firm but not chalky, and nicely crusted, with golden, flavorful caramelization over its flesh. If we could work some interesting flavors and contrasting textures into the bargain, all the better.

Crust Is Key

Creating some flavorful caramelization on the flesh of the fish was a key goal, so we focused right away on high-heat cooking. Baking, though it seemed like a natural choice, was out because it

implies cooking in a moderate, 350-degree oven, which would never brown the fish. Heating things up from there, we tested roasting at oven temperatures of 400, 450, and 500 degrees. To our surprise, none of them worked well. Even at 500 degrees, on a preheated pan, the fish remained pale owing to the necessarily short 16-minute cooking time; any more time in the oven, and the fish would overcook. Another source of consternation was moisture—not the lack of it, as we might have expected, but an excess. The abundance of fat and collagen in the farmed Atlantic salmon we were using melted during cooking, giving the fish an overly wet, slippery texture and fatty mouthfeel.

Broiling was the next step up in heat, and here we met with some success. The salmon browned nicely under the intense broiler heat and, as a result, also developed better flavor. Some of the copious

moisture evaporated, leaving the fish with a much-improved texture, drier and more firm, yet still juicy. None of the broiling and roasting combinations we went on to try topped broiling from start to finish. We were on the right track to be sure, but plain broiled salmon was not terribly inspiring. If we were going to serve this to a crowd of people at a weekend dinner party, a flavor boost and some textural interest would be absolutely necessary.

Topping Antics

The addition of an interesting topping for the fish could, we thought, achieve both goals. Dried bread crumbs came immediately to mind—and left almost as quickly once we tasted them. The flavor was lackluster, and the texture akin to sawdust. Our favorite Japanese Panko bread crumbs were judged too light of flavor and feathery of texture. Fresh breadcrumbs were a crisp improvement, and toasted fresh breadcrumbs laced with garlic, herbs, and butter were better still. But there were more avenues to explore.

Dry spice rubs, similar to what we might apply to the fish if grilling, met with mixed results. Glazes and spice pastes won praise for their flavor, but since they themselves were wet, they added little in the way of texture.

Potatoes were another topping possibility. Potato crusts on fish are typically engineered by laying paper-thin slices of potato on the fish and sautéing it on the stovetop. Testing proved that the slices would not form a cohesive crust without the direct heat of a hot pan. In addition, we couldn't slice them thin enough without the help of a mandoline. But because tasters loved the potato flavor, we tried some other methods. A

STEP-BY-STEP | PREPARING THE SALMON

1. Run your fingers over the surface to feel for pinbones, then remove them with tweezers or needle-nosed pliers.

2. Hold a sharp chef's knife at a slight downward angle to the flesh and cut off the whitish, fatty portion of the belly.

We tried thick-cut Yukon Gold (Terra brand), kettle-cooked (Kettle brand), ridged (Ruffles), thin (Lay's), and molded (Pringles). The thick-cut and kettle-cooked served best, offering superior potato flavor and the sturdiest crunch. In a pinch, ridged chips will suffice.

crust of grated raw potatoes remained too loose and crunchy. Sautéing the grated potato before applying it to the fish helped some, but not enough, while completely precooking the potatoes robbed them of both flavor and texture.

Clinging tenaciously to the notion of potato flavor while groping for another way to build a crisp, crunchy texture, test cook Bridget Lancaster smirked and suggested, half in jest, that we try crushed potato chips. Everyone in the test kitchen at the time laughed, but after settling down we looked at one another and said, practically in unison, "Let's try it." Imagine our astonishment, then, at the chips' overwhelming success. Though a bit greasy and heavy on their own, they offered just what we were looking for in a crust: great potato flavor and crunch that wouldn't quit. After lightening the chips up by mixing in some fresh toasted breadcrumbs and adding dill for complementary flavor, we found ourselves with an excellent, if unorthodox, topping. We also found that the chips made a rich foil for some of the other flavors we wanted to add.

Because the chips brown under the broiler in just a minute—literally—we broiled the fish until it was almost cooked through before adding the topping. This gave us just the texture we wanted. After adding a flavorful wet element (mustard) to help the crumbs adhere to the fish, we knew we had it: a quick, oven-cooked, well-flavored, texturally interesting—and rather surprising—salmon dinner for eight.

BROILED SALMON WITH MUSTARD AND CRISP DILLED CRUST
SERVES 8 TO 10

Heavy-duty foil measuring 18 inches wide is essential for creating a sling that aids in transferring the cooked fillet to a cutting board. Use a large baking sheet so that the salmon will lie flat. If you can't get the fish to lie flat, even when positioning it diagonally on the baking sheet, trim the tail end. If you prefer to cook a smaller 2-pound fillet, ask to have it cut from the thick center of the fillet, not the thin tail end, and begin checking doneness a minute earlier.

> 3 slices high-quality sliced sandwich bread, crusts removed
> 4 ounces plain high-quality potato chips, crushed into rough ⅛-inch pieces (about 1 cup)
> 6 tablespoons chopped fresh dill
> 1 whole side of salmon fillet, about 3½ pounds, pinbones removed and belly fat trimmed (see illustrations, page 6)
> 1 teaspoon olive oil
> ¾ teaspoon salt
>   Ground black pepper
> 3 tablespoons Dijon mustard

1. Adjust one oven rack to uppermost position (about 3 inches from heat source) and second rack to upper-middle position; heat oven to 400 degrees.

2. Pulse bread in workbowl of food processor fitted with steel blade until processed into fairly even ¼-inch pieces about the size of Grape-Nuts cereal (you should have about 1 cup), about ten 1-second pulses. Spread crumbs evenly on rimmed baking sheet; toast on lower rack, shaking pan once or twice, until golden brown and crisp, 4 to 5 minutes. Toss together bread crumbs, crushed potato chips, and dill in small bowl; set aside.

3. Increase oven setting to broil. Cut piece of heavy-duty foil 6 inches longer than fillet. Fold foil lengthwise in thirds and place lengthwise on rimmed baking sheet; position salmon lengthwise on foil, allowing excess foil to overhang baking sheet. Rub fillet evenly with oil; sprinkle with salt and pepper. Broil salmon on upper rack until surface is spotty brown and outer ½ inch of thick end is opaque when gently flaked with paring knife, 9 to 11 minutes. Remove fish from oven, spread evenly with mustard, and press bread crumb mixture onto fish. Return to lower rack and continue broiling until crust is deep golden brown, about 1 minute longer.

4. Following illustrations below, transfer salmon and foil sling to cutting board, remove sling, and serve salmon from board.

BROILED SALMON WITH SPICY CITRUS– CILANTRO PASTE AND CRISP CRUST

In workbowl of food processor fitted with steel blade, process 1-inch piece fresh ginger, peeled; 3 medium garlic cloves, peeled; 3 medium shallots, peeled; 2 medium jalapeño chiles, stemmed and seeded; 2 teaspoons grated zest and 3 tablespoons juice from 1 or 2 medium limes; 2 tablespoons honey; and 2 cups loosely packed cilantro leaves until smooth, scraping down bowl as necessary, about 30 seconds. Follow recipe for Broiled Salmon with Mustard and Crisp Dilled Crust, omitting dill and substituting ½ cup spicy citrus-cilantro paste for Dijon mustard.

BROILED SALMON WITH CHUTNEY AND CRISP SPICED CRUST

We recommend smooth mango chutney. If you can find only chunky mango chutney, puree it in a food processor until smooth.

Heat 2 tablespoons unsalted butter in small skillet over medium heat until melted. Off heat, add 1 medium garlic clove, minced; ½ teaspoon each ground cumin and paprika; and ¼ teaspoon each ground cinnamon, cayenne, and salt. Set aside. Follow recipe for Broiled Salmon with Mustard and Crisp Dilled Crust, substituting 3 tablespoons chopped fresh parsley for dill, tossing butter-spice mixture into bread crumbs along with potato chips, and substituting 3 tablespoons prepared smooth mango chutney for Dijon mustard.

Serving the Salmon

1. Grasp foil overhang at both ends; lift carefully and set fish on cutting board.

2. Slide an offset spatula under the thick end. Grasp the foil, press the spatula down against the foil, and slide it under the fish down to the thin end, loosening the entire side of fish.

3. Grasp the foil again, hold the spatula perpendicular to the fish to stabilize it, and pull the foil out from under the fish. Use a moist paper towel to clean up the board, and serve immediately

Really Good Vegetable Stock

Too often, vegetable stocks are labor-intensive, drab, too-sweet stepchildren of chicken stock. Here is a recipe that can actually hold its own with "the real thing."

⇒ BY KAY RENTSCHLER ⇐

Vegetable stocks have always seemed to be a high-maintenance proposition, involving lots of work and little return. Trips to ethnic markets, miles of scrapes and peels, and what do you get? Hot vegetable bath water, hot sweet vegetable tea, or the sludge you pour off after the socks boil.

Nonetheless, I sensed there might be promise here, that a careful selection of ingredients and just the right technique could create a broth both nicely balanced and robust, with pleasing color and clarity—something, in short, worth making, even for people who aren't vegetarians. I felt certain, moreover, that a superior vegetable stock could not rise up from the remains in the vegetable drawer, be tossed into a pot with some water and a couple of laurel leaves, then subjected to death by boiling. I knew that it might be a time-consuming process and that I might end up with a long and complex ingredient list, but I believed I could come up with a truly good stock.

Clean Shot or Murky Mess?

To kick off, I made five stocks, using different techniques and vegetable combinations for each. In quick-simmered stocks, on the stove for less than an hour, most of the flavor was left locked in the vegetables. Vegetables simmered in water only—using no dry heat or reduction method—produced a spiritless stock. Roasting vegetables in the oven first did deepen the stock's color and flavor, but deglazing the pan and transferring the vegetables to a pot was a nuisance. We left this method behind. Sweating the aromatic vegetables (onions, garlic, shallots, celery, and carrots) in a small amount of water before adding the other vegetables and the water produced a stock of perfect clarity and increased flavor. But the best option was sautéing lightly oiled aromatics in the stockpot before adding water. This stock had rich flavor, only slightly compromised clarity, and very little oily residue.

My review of ingredient choices yielded fewer definitive results. I discovered, to no surprise, that the onion family brought depth and complexity to bear on flavor, that wine tasted out of

place, and that salt was essential to palatability. Otherwise, I gleaned no substantive ideas as to which vegetables were expendable, which essential, and which would play together nicely in a group. My travails were about to become, in fact, a lengthy treatise on what not to add.

Though I hoped to end up with a grocery list short enough to fit on a piece of scrap paper, lengthy testing lay in my path. Consequently, it seemed prudent to organize potential ingredients into broad categories, starting from the bottom, and to layer flavors one by one. Within the

A conical strainer with fine perforations, also known as a china cap, is ideal for straining this stock.

foundation group, for instance (those vegetables which enjoy a slow sauté and lengthy simmer to bring forth their aromatic qualities), I would test members of the onion cartel along with carrots, parsnips, celery, and celery root. Pungent or cruciferous vegetables—cabbage, cauliflower, turnips, peppers, and fennel, to name a few—would come next. Mushrooms and tomatoes had to be tested at some point, as did potential thickening agents such as potatoes, lentils, rice, and so on. Herbs would need to be tested and, at the end, anything from the condiment world I might to resort to if the vegetables alone proved inadequate.

I began by testing different mixes of yellow and red onions, shallots, garlic, and leeks to see which combination would be synergistic. (I was working toward a yield of a couple of quarts, sautéing the onions first and simmering a catholic selection of vegetables in water to finish.) As it happened, these alliums—except the red onion, which brought a dull bruised purple to the group—were most persuasive in concert. Yellow onions offered strong, pure onion presence, shallots were delicate and fragrant, garlic sultry and complex, leeks soft and bright. Sacrifice one, and the efficacy of the whole was diminished. I also learned that unpeeled onions are bitter but that unpeeled garlic is not; that leeks prefer to arrive late and stew a bit; and that their green, horsy tail ends taste horsy. Engaging the stock in a brisk businesslike simmer to get the job done proved a poor idea—the final product tasted boiled and frayed. I went with the old barbecue adage: low and slow.

I also found that while alliums are critical to flavor complexity, their high sugar content in combination with sustained simmering can result in something far too sweet. In fact, developing flavor while avoiding sweetness became the much sought-after (and nearly unattainable) goal of my testing.

Carrot and celery, both of which are likely to dominate canned or packaged vegetable broths, made enough of an impact with tiny, tiny contributions, and I selected them over their respective rivals, parsnip and celery root.

As I advanced to the next round—with the onion family, celery, and carrot on board for the duration—several vegetables dropped out of the running, one by one. Each addition, intended to improve the fragile foundation flavors, instead maligned them. White mushrooms, for instance, were a dastardly bunch, taking up space in the pot but contributing nothing. Red peppers and tomatoes, tested separately, were dismissed together. Both were differently, inscrutably, and distinctly unpleasant. Fennel bulb contributed what was perhaps the most unequivocally awful flavor to emerge from this mix. I was astounded by the fact that so many singularly tasty vegetables could fare so poorly in a group and that so many of my biggest flavor candidates had failed. "What does this need?" I would wail at tastings. "Some chicken," was the usual answer.

Out of this second tier of vegetables, only two had a strong and positive influence on those already in the pot: green cabbage and cauliflower. Minimal amounts contributed to the flavor-layering effect I was going for—the cabbage fragrant and nutty, the cauliflower earthy and nutty. Hoping they might prove interchangeable, I left each in place and moved on.

Next I approached the starchy candidates, thinking their flavor and body might reward the stock. Nothing could have been further from the truth. I made the basic recipe time and again, adding one by one bits of white rice, potatoes, potato skins, lentils, yellow split peas, and chick peas, straining them out with the other vegetables at the end. Rather than adding any real body to the stock—which remained stubbornly thin— these ingredients merely turned it murky. Those which added flavor—dry lentils, split peas, and chick peas— swathed the fresh vegetable flavor in a muddy legumey-ness. A half-hearted gesture toward the East obliged me to throw in some *kombu* (Japanese dried seaweed), which has gelatinous properties; a nod to the '70s, some nutritional yeast (thought to improve mouthfeel). Both were ghastly.

The Green Party

In addition to its other flavor problems, the stock was still damnably, persistently sweet. So I tested fresh ginger and lemon juice for their astringent properties. The ginger gave the stock too much of an ethnic flavor, and the lemon juice made it taste like it was going bad.

At this point, I felt as if I had crawled every inch of the produce section on my belly. A colleague then suggested that I might prevail upon leafy greens for flavor brightness. Why not? Another run to the market and I was back with collards, chard, and kale. Knowing they did not benefit from lengthy cooking, I added about a half pound of each to three separate stocks. Score! Here at last was a breakthrough. The greens brought both depth and brightness to the stock and helped correct the sweetness. Everyone liked the collards best: they were fresh and biting without being bitter.

A Fight to the Finish

I now began experimenting with finishing flavors. Fresh thyme and parsley went into the pot with the other greens to simmer briefly, bay leaf earlier, with the water. These simple ingredients alone made a substantial contribution to flavor. I did not care for miso (fermented soybean paste, used in Japanese cooking), as its particulate matter settled to the bottom and kicked up like a dust storm when stirred. But by now people were entering the test kitchen and asking what smelled so good. Sometimes it was my stock.

Buoyed by recent advances, I chopped on. Though lemon juice had been a failure, a bruised piece of lemon grass was a decisive success, adding bright new dimensions to the flavors. The finished stock had a golden, chickeny glow.

Reasonably confident, I put my new recipe to the test by making risotto.

I knew the technique of continued simmering used in making risotto would reveal any weaknesses in the ingredients and proportions. I made plain risotto with two kinds of stock—one with cauliflower, the other with cabbage. In this application tasters far preferred cauliflower over cabbage—it had more character and was less sweet. A risotto made with all ingredients (including Parmigiano Reggiano) had people going back for seconds and swearing it was just as good as chicken stock. Was I there? Not quite.

I offered a batch of my vegetable stock to a colleague and asked her to cook it for her vegetarian companion. In an Indian dish with a tangy-sweet direction, she gave my stock very good marks. But in a more savory braise with lentils and chard, it fared less well—though flavorful, it was still (what else?) too sweet.

Now I became ruthless, stripping the onion family of half its baggage and including only one small carrot. At my colleague's suggestion I added some chopped scallions to the stock along with the greens—a compensatory gesture to the onion family. They were piquant and crisp. A splash of rice wine vinegar and some peppercorns ended my efforts.

THE ULTIMATE VEGETABLE STOCK
MAKES ABOUT I QUART

It is important to use a heavy-bottomed Dutch oven or stockpot so that the vegetables caramelize properly without burning. A stalk of lemon grass, available in some grocery stores and most Asian markets, adds a clean, refreshing flavor to the stock. If you cannot find lemon grass, however, the flavor will still be very good. See Kitchen Notes, page 30, for how to make a vegetable stock reduction sauce.

2 medium onions (about 12 ounces), peeled and chopped coarse
10–12 medium garlic cloves from 1 head, each clove peeled and smashed
8 large shallots (about 8 ounces), sliced thin
1 celery rib, chopped coarse
 Vegetable cooking spray
1 small carrot, peeled and chopped coarse
4 large leeks, white and light green parts only, cleaned and chopped coarse (about 5 1/2 cups)
 Stems from 1 bunch fresh parsley
2 small bay leaves
1 1/2 teaspoons salt
1 teaspoon black peppercorns, coarsely cracked
1 pound collard greens, washed, dried, and sliced crosswise into 2-inch strips (about 10 cups packed)
1 small head cauliflower (about 12 ounces), chopped fine (about 4 cups)
8–10 sprigs fresh thyme
1 stalk lemon grass, trimmed to bottom 6 inches and bruised with back of chef's knife
4 medium scallions, white and light green parts, cut into 2-inch lengths
2 teaspoons rice wine vinegar

1. Combine onions, garlic, shallots, celery, and carrot in heavy-bottomed, 8-quart stockpot or Dutch oven; spray vegetables lightly with vegetable cooking spray and toss to coat. Cover and cook over low heat, stirring frequently, until pan bottom shows light brown glaze, 20 to 30 minutes. Add leeks and increase heat to medium; cook, covered, until leeks soften, about 10 minutes. Add 1 1/2 cups hot water and cook, partially covered, until water has evaporated to a glaze and vegetables are very soft, 25 to 35 minutes.

2. Add parsley stems, bay leaves, salt, peppercorns, and 7 cups hot water. Increase heat to medium-high and bring to simmer; reduce heat to medium-low and simmer gently, covered, to blend flavors, about 15 minutes.

3. Add collard greens, cauliflower, thyme, lemon grass, and scallions. Increase heat to medium-high and bring to simmer; reduce heat to low and simmer gently, covered, to blend flavors, about 15 minutes longer. Strain stock through large strainer into 2-quart bowl or container, allowing stock to drip through to drain thoroughly (do not press on solids). Stir vinegar into stock. (Stock can be covered and refrigerated up to 4 days or frozen up to 2 months.)

RISOTTO WITH VEGETABLE STOCK
SERVES 4

3 cups Ultimate Vegetable Stock
3 tablespoons unsalted butter
2 medium shallots, minced
1 cup Arborio rice
3 ounces grated Parmesan cheese (about 3/4 cup)

1. Bring vegetable stock and 1 cup water to simmer in small saucepan over medium-high heat; reduce heat to low and keep hot.

2. Meanwhile, heat butter in heavy-bottomed medium saucepan over medium-high heat until foaming; add shallots and sauté until softened, about 1 minute. Stir in rice and sauté until translucent, about 2 minutes. Using medium ladle, stir 1/2 cup hot stock into rice; simmer, stirring frequently, until rice has absorbed most of the liquid, about 3 minutes. Continue to stir in hot stock in 1/2-cup additions until all stock has been used and rice is tender and creamy, about 25 minutes. Off heat, stir in cheese, let stand, covered, 2 minutes. Serve immediately.

Garlic Mashed Potatoes

Cook the potatoes whole and in their skins, add the right dairy in the right order, and toast—don't roast—the garlic.

⇒ BY DAWN YANAGIHARA ⇐

Most of us who make mashed potatoes would never consider consulting a recipe. I customarily made them by adding chunks of butter and spurts of cream until my conscience—or a back-seat cook—told me to stop. Not surprisingly, I produced batches of mashed potatoes that were consistent only in their mediocrity. As for garlic mashed potatoes, matters were worse. Sometimes I'd go to the trouble of roasting whole heads of garlic and then have to perform the messy, insipid task of squeezing out the softened cloves. Other times, I'd just throw a few cloves into the water along with the potatoes and mash them right in. I've made some industrial-strength garlic mashed potatoes that could peel paint off the walls, and I've made others so lightly tinged with garlic that the flavor was all but undetectable.

To keep the potatoes hot, warm the half-and-half before adding it.

But there really was nothing to prevent me from making consistently great garlic mashed potatoes (or mashpots, as I have come to call them) at home. For me, the consummate garlic mashpots are creamy, soft, and supple, yet with enough body to stand up to sauce or gravy. As for flavor, the sweet, earthy, humble potato comes first, then the buttery richness, and finally that heady yet mild and nutty garlic flavor that keeps you coming back for more.

At Square One with Spuds

I needed first to address the simple matter of the best way to cook the potatoes. I started with russets (my favorite for mashed potatoes; see "I Say Potato," next page, for other possibilities), peeling and cutting some into chunks to expedite their cooking while simmering others unpeeled and whole. Even when mashed with identical amounts of butter, half-and-half (recommended by a number of trustworthy cookbooks), and salt, the two batches were wildly different. Those peeled and cut made mashed potatoes that were thin in taste and texture and devoid of potato flavor, while those cooked whole and peeled after cooking yielded mashed potatoes that were rich, earthy, and sweet. Dr. Alfred Bushway, professor of food science at the University of Maine, explained that peeling and cutting the potatoes before simmering increases the surface area through which they lose soluble substances, such as starch, proteins, and flavor compounds—to the cooking water. The greater surface area also enables lots of water molecules to bind with the potatoes' starch molecules. Combine these two effects and you've got bland, thin, watery mashpots.

Next were the matters of butter and dairy. Working with 2 pounds of potatoes, which comfortably serves four, I stooped so low as to add only 2 tablespoons of butter. The potatoes ultimately deemed best in flavor by tasters contained 8 tablespoons. They were rich and full and splendid.

When considering dairy, I investigated both the kind and the quantity. Heavy cream made heavy mashed potatoes that were sodden and unpalatably rich, even when I scaled back the amount of butter. On the other hand, mashed potatoes made with whole milk were watery, wimpy, and washed out. When I tried adding more butter to compensate for the milk's lack of richness, the mixture turned into potato soup. Half-and-half, which I'd used in my original tests, was just what was needed, and one cup was just the right amount. The mashed potatoes now had a lovely light suppleness and a full, rich flavor that edged toward decadent.

The issues attending butter and dairy did not end there. I had heard that the order in which they are added to the potatoes can affect texture and that melted butter makes better mashed potatoes than softened butter. Determined to leave no spud unturned, I threw several more pounds into the pot. As it turns out, when the butter goes in before the dairy, the result is a silkier, creamier, smoother texture than when the dairy goes first; by comparison, the dairy-first potatoes were pasty and thick. Using melted rather than softened butter made the potatoes even more creamy, smooth, and light.

With my curiosity piqued by the significant textural differences effected by minor differences in procedure, I again contacted Dr. Bushway, who explained that the water in the half-and-half, when stirred into the potatoes before the butter, works with the starch in the potatoes to make the mashpots gluey and heavy. When the butter is added before the half-and-half, the fat coats the starch molecules, inhibiting their interaction with the water in the half-and-half added later and thereby yielding silkier, creamier mashpots. The benefit of using melted butter results from its liquid form, which enables it to coat the starch molecules quickly and easily. This buttery coating not only affects the interaction of the starch molecules with the half-and-half, it also affects the starch molecules' interaction with each other. All in all, it makes for smoother, more velvety mashed potatoes.

A Smelly Matter

Getting the garlic right is the trickiest part of making garlic mashed potatoes. To tame the pungency of raw garlic and transform it into nutty sweetness, I tried several techniques: I sautéed whole cloves and minced cloves in butter, poached them in half-and-half, roasted whole cloves, roasted whole heads, poached cloves and then roasted them, and poached heads and then roasted them. But the simple technique of toasting whole unpeeled cloves in a dry skillet (first mentioned in "Chef's

Vegetable Preparation Tips," July/August 1998) took the prize in every contest. Plain old roasted garlic was close, but toasted garlic, mashed into the potatoes, contributed the truest, purest garlic flavor. What's more, removing the loosened skins from toasted garlic cloves is easier than either peeling raw cloves or squeezing the squishy roasted meat out of sticky skins.

The toasting technique was in need of refinement, however. If the garlic cloves were not completely soft, they marred the silky texture of the finished mashpots. I could detect their crunchy granules even after putting them through a ricer or food mill along with the potatoes. To eliminate this problem, I put a lid on the pan, turned down the heat as low as it could go, and let the garlic toast at a leisurely pace; once off the stove, a final covered rest ensured that all the cloves softened in the residual heat of the pan.

One average head of garlic weighs just over 2 ounces and contains 15 or so cloves. This is the amount I had been using in my testing, but my tasters voted unanimously in favor of more garlic

flavor. Proceeding with the premise that a person who doesn't like garlic would not be making garlic mashpots, I doubled the amount, but the resulting potency offended all but the biggest garlic fanatics. I reduced the amount to 22 cloves (about 1½ heads, or three ounces), which made everyone happy.

The Process of Processing

There is more than one way to mash potatoes. In my testing, I had been using either a ricer or a food mill. I preferred the food mill because its large hopper accommodated half of the potatoes at a time. A ricer, which resembles an oversized garlic press, required processing in several batches. Both, however, produced smooth, light, fine-textured mashed potatoes and made easy work of mashing the garlic—I simply processed the peeled cloves right along with the potatoes.

A potato masher is the tool of choice for making chunky mashed potatoes, but it cannot produce smooth mashed potatoes on a par with those processed through a food mill or ricer. With a masher, potatoes mashed within an inch of their lives could not achieve anything better than a namby-pamby texture that was neither chunky nor perfectly smooth. Since the sentiment among my tasters and I was that mashpots should be either smooth or coarse and craggy, a masher is best left to make the latter. Now, take a fork to some great garlic mashpots.

GARLIC MASHED POTATOES
SERVES 4

Avoid using unusually large garlic cloves, which will not soften adequately during toasting. Yukon Gold, red, russet, or white potatoes can be used—each turns out a different texture. For smooth mashed potatoes, a food mill or potato ricer fitted with the finest disk is the best choice. For chunky mashed potatoes, use a potato masher, decrease the half-and-half to ¾ cup, and mash the garlic to a paste with a fork before you add it to the potatoes.

22	small to medium-large garlic cloves (about 3 ounces, or ⅔ cup) from 2 medium heads garlic, skins left on
2	pounds potatoes, unpeeled and scrubbed
8	tablespoons (1 stick) unsalted butter, melted
1	cup half-and-half, warm
1½	teaspoons salt
	Ground black pepper

1. Toast garlic, covered, in small skillet over lowest possible heat, shaking pan frequently, until cloves are dark spotty brown and slightly softened, about 22 minutes. Off heat, let stand, covered, until fully softened, 15 to 20 minutes. Peel cloves and, with paring knife, cut off woody root end (see illustration 1, below). Set aside.

2. While garlic is toasting, place potatoes in large saucepan and cover with 1 inch water. Bring to boil over high heat; reduce heat to medium-low and simmer until potatoes are tender (a paring knife can be slipped into and out of center of potatoes with very little resistance), 20 to 30 minutes. Drain.

3. Set food mill or ricer over now empty but still warm saucepan. Spear potato with dinner fork, then peel back skin with paring knife (illustration 2, below). Working in batches, cut peeled potatoes into rough chunks and drop into hopper of food mill or potato ricer along with peeled garlic (illustration 3). Process or rice potatoes into saucepan.

4. Stir in butter with wooden spoon until incorporated; gently whisk in half-and-half, salt, and pepper to taste. Serve immediately.

GARLIC MASHED POTATOES WITH SMOKED GOUDA AND CHIVES

In this variation, smoked Gouda and chives give the garlic mashed potatoes an irresistible flavor.

Follow recipe for Garlic Mashed Potatoes, reducing salt to 1¼ teaspoons and stirring in 4 ounces grated smoked Gouda cheese (1 cup) along with half-and-half; set pot over low heat and stir until cheese is melted and incorporated. Stir in 3 tablespoons chopped fresh chives.

STEP-BY-STEP | MAKING GARLIC MASHED POTATOES

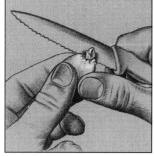 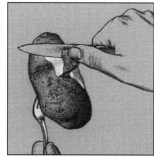 

1. After toasting and cooling the garlic, trim off the woody root end

2. Peel off the potato skins using a paring knife

3. Cut the potatoes into rough chunks

Grilling Portobello Mushrooms

The secret is marinating, wrapping in foil, then finishing over a hot fire.

⇒ BY RAQUEL PELZEL ⇐

As the end of the New England grilling season approaches and I've grilled what seems like my thousandth burger and chicken breast, portobello mushrooms step up to the plate, successfully reigniting my fire. Although I've eaten more than my share of flaccid fungi, I jumped into this venture stubbornly, holding out for the ideal grilled portobello: plump, juicy, and slightly charred.

With portobellos ranging from 4 to 6 inches in diameter, the first pitfall I encountered was how to develop an across-the-board grilling method for both smaller and larger mushrooms. This, I knew, would be difficult since I wanted to keep the grilling temperature relatively high; I wanted to be able to grill portobellos side by side with meat, which needs a hot fire.

Grilling directly on the rack over the fire proved problematic because the larger portobellos were charred to a black crisp by the time they had cooked through. Seeking refuge, I elevated the mushrooms on a grill rack, but now they took eons to cook through. I suspected that if I found a way to shield the mushrooms from the fire, I could grill them until entirely cooked through and also infuse them with a pure, smoky flavor without the bitterness associated with the direct-grilling method. I called upon an old campfire friend—aluminum foil—and loosely wrapped each mushroom in a handcrafted foil packet. I placed the portobellos gill-side up (through my endeavors I had learned that this method traps juices) on the grill. After about 10 minutes, my mushrooms were tender and juicy to the core, without sacrificing any of the grill's smoky attributes.

Pumping up flavor was my next concern, and I began brushing my way through a long list of marinades before finding that a simple combination of chopped garlic, lemon juice, olive oil, and salt worked best. After a one-hour marinade, the mushrooms, when grilled, developed a slightly tangy and complex flavor, with a tinge of garlicky oomph. At the end of cooking I stripped the portobellos of their foil jackets and seared them briefly, infusing them with the smoky essence of summertime grilling.

CHARCOAL-GRILLED MARINATED PORTOBELLO MUSHROOMS
MAKES FOUR 5- TO 6-INCH MUSHROOM CAPS

We prefer large 5- to 6-inch portobellos for grilling because they are sold loose—not prepackaged— and are typically fresher. However, if you cannot find large ones, use six 4- to 5-inch portobellos, which are usually sold three to a package; decrease their grilling time wrapped in foil to about 9 minutes.

- 1/2 cup olive oil
- 3 tablespoons juice from 1 lemon
- 6 medium garlic cloves, minced fine (about 2 tablespoons)
- 1/4 teaspoon salt
- 4 portobello mushrooms, each 5 to 6 inches (or about 6 ounces each), stems removed and discarded, caps wiped clean

1. Combine oil, lemon juice, garlic, and salt in large zipper-lock plastic bag. Add mushrooms; seal bag and gently shake to coat mushrooms with marinade. Let stand at room temperature until seasoned, about 1 hour. Meanwhile, cut four 12-inch-square pieces of foil (or six 9-inch-square pieces if using smaller mushrooms); begin building medium-hot fire (you can hold your hand 5 inches above grill surface for three to four seconds).

2. Remove mushrooms from marinade. Place a foil square on work surface and set mushroom on top, gill-side up; fold foil edges over to enclose mushroom and seal edges. Spread coals evenly over grill bottom, position grill rack; scrub rack with wire grill brush. Grill mushrooms, with sealed side of foil packet facing up, until juicy and tender, 10 to 12 minutes. Using tongs, unwrap mushrooms and discard foil; set unwrapped mushrooms on rack gill-side up and cook until grill-marked, 30 to 60 seconds. Remove from grill and use in one of following recipes.

GAS-GRILLED MARINATED PORTOBELLO MUSHROOMS

Follow recipe for Charcoal-Grilled Marinated Portobello Mushrooms; when mushrooms are almost done marinating, turn all burners on gas grill to high, close lid, and heat grill until hot, 10 to 15 minutes. Reduce grilling time of foil-wrapped mushrooms to 7 to 9 minutes.

GRILLED PORTOBELLO AND ARUGULA SALAD WITH BACON AND BLUE CHEESE
SERVES 4 AS A MAIN COURSE, 6 TO 8 AS A SIDE DISH

Cut the mushrooms while still hot and immediately add them to the arugula; their heat wilts the greens slightly for a yielding texture. There is also a slightly higher ratio of balsamic vinegar to olive oil than traditionally called for; this is to compensate for the richness of both the blue cheese and the bacon.

- 2 bunches arugula, washed, dried, stems trimmed, and leaves torn into bite-sized pieces (about 3 cups, loosely packed)
- 8 slices (about 8 ounces) bacon, cut into 1-inch pieces and fried until crisp
- 1 recipe Charcoal- or Gas-Grilled Marinated Portobello Mushrooms, cut into 1/2-inch cubes while still hot
- 1 tablespoon balsamic vinegar
- 1 medium shallot, minced
- 1 teaspoon salt
- 2 tablespoons olive oil
- 4 ounces blue cheese, crumbled (about 1 cup) Ground black pepper

1. Toss arugula with bacon and hot mushrooms in large bowl.

2. Combine vinegar, shallots, and salt in medium bowl. Whisk in olive oil in slow, steady stream. Sprinkle blue cheese over arugula mixture, and season with ground black pepper to taste. Pour dressing over salad and toss well to combine. Serve immediately.

GRILLED MARINATED PORTOBELLOS WITH TARRAGON
SERVES 4 TO 6 AS A SIDE DISH

This variation is great served with a grilled steak or a juicy hamburger.

- 2 teaspoons rice wine vinegar
- 1 medium garlic clove, minced
- 1 tablespoon chopped fresh tarragon leaves
- 1/4 teaspoon salt
- 2 teaspoons vegetable or canola oil
- 1 recipe Charcoal- or Gas-Grilled Marinated Portobello Mushrooms, cut into 1/2-inch cubes Ground black pepper

Combine rice wine vinegar, garlic, tarragon, and salt in medium bowl; stir in oil. Add mushrooms and ground black pepper to taste; toss to coat. Serve immediately or cover with plastic wrap and let stand at room temperature up to 30 minutes.

Better Stuffed Tomatoes

Say goodbye to bland, waterlogged stuffed tomatoes. The key is to draw out excess moisture by salting prior to stuffing.

⇒ BY RAQUEL PELZEL WITH EVA KATZ ⇐

M y past experiences with oven-baked stuffed tomatoes have not exactly been great. Still, when I am presented with one, the thought of its potential juicy tenderness and warmth is too tempting to ignore. I succumb to the hope that maybe this time the stuffed tomato will live up to its potential, only to be let down by my first bite into sodden mediocrity.

What irks me is that the stuffed tomato's singular components hold forth the promise of perfection. What could be better than a ripe, sun-drenched summer tomato, garden-fresh herbs, garlicky bread crumbs, and a sprightly bite of sharp cheese? When these elements are brought together into one vessel, however, their divinity dissipates. The once buxom tomato becomes mealy and bland, and the flavor of the stuffing is drowned within the waterlogged texture of the bread. Determined to save this traditional dish from the bland and watery depths, I set out to prove that an oven-baked stuffed tomato can actually taste as good as I'd always imagined.

Waterworld

I began my testing by following the directions called for in most cookbook recipes: stuff a hollowed-out, raw beefsteak tomato with a bread crumb filling and bake it at 375 degrees for 30 minutes. The outcome was a soggy mess. The tomato was bland and watery, and the stuffing tasted dull and overly moist. What's more, the tomato seemed to lack the structural strength to keep the filling intact. I concluded that perhaps the same element that lends majesty to a tomato—water—was the source of my failure.

Ridding the tomato of its excess liquid was my goal. At first I tested oven drying, rationalizing that the slow, low heat would concentrate the tomato's sweetness and vaporize the water. The dried tomato was laden with rich flavor notes, but it was also shriveled and shrunken, a collapsed vessel that was in no condition to hold any stuffing.

I then decided that if I chose a tomato with a naturally lower water content, such as a plum tomato, I might eliminate the water issue altogether. While I did end up with a meaty and sweet stuffed tomato, it lacked the complexity of flavor that the beefsteak possessed, and the effort required to stuff the smaller shell—coupled with the fact that I would have to make twice as many

if I were substituting for a beefsteak—turned me off the plum variety.

Light at the End of the Tomato

Recalling how salt is used to sweat an eggplant, I thought it might do the same for a tomato. So I cored and seeded a beefsteak, rubbed salt into its interior, and placed it upside down on a stack of paper towels. Within 30 minutes, my dry paper towels had absorbed a tremendous amount of liquid. Dr. Bill Morris, professor in the University of Tennessee's department of food science and technology, explained that when I salted the interior of the tomato, water passed through the cells' semipermeable membranes, moving from the inside of the cells to the outside, in effect, draining the tomato of its excess juices. In addition, the salt brightened and enhanced the tomato's flavor, as it did when we were testing tomato salads for our July/August 1998 issue.

Now that I had the moisture problem solved, I moved on to stuffing, baking times, and temperatures. For the stuffing, I tested store-bought bread crumbs, homemade bread crumbs made from stale French bread (as recommended in the May/June 1995 article, "The Virtues of Bread Crumbs"), and variations in the ratio of crumbs to cheese to herbs. The fine, store-bought crumbs were dry and gritty. Their homemade counterpart, on the other hand, absorbed the tomato's juices yet still provided an interesting chew and crunch, especially when paired with garlic, olive oil, and tangy Parmesan cheese.

My previous oven roasting experiment negated a low and long baking period, whereas experi-

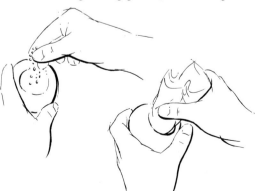

Salt the tomatoes, then stand them upside down on paper towels. After about 30 minutes, pat the interiors with several sheets of paper towels.

ments baking the tomato at an extremely high temperature (450 degrees) for a short time yielded burnt, crusty stuffing and a raw tomato. Baked at 375 degrees for 20 minutes, the tomatoes were tender and topped with a lovely golden crust. The result: a sweet—and savory—tomato triumph.

STUFFED TOMATOES WITH PARMESAN, GARLIC, AND BASIL
SERVES 6 AS A SIDE DISH

6	large (about 8 ounces each) firm, ripe tomatoes, 1/8 inch sliced off stem end, cored, and seeded
1	teaspoon kosher salt
3/4	cup coarse homemade bread crumbs
1	teaspoon plus 3 tablespoons olive oil
1/3	cup grated Parmesan cheese (about 1 1/2 ounces)
1/3	cup chopped fresh basil leaves
2	medium garlic cloves, minced (about 2 teaspoons)
	Ground black pepper

1. Sprinkle inside of each tomato with salt (see illustration, left) and place upside down on several layers of paper toweling; let stand to remove excess moisture, about 30 minutes.

2. Meanwhile, toss bread crumbs with 1 tablespoon olive oil, Parmesan, basil, garlic, and pepper to taste in small bowl; set aside. Adjust oven rack to upper-middle position and heat oven to 375 degrees; line bottom of 9 by 13-inch baking dish with foil.

3. Roll up several sheets of paper towels and pat inside of each tomato dry (see illustration, left). Arrange tomatoes in single layer in baking dish. Brush top cut edges of tomatoes with 1 teaspoon oil. Mound stuffing into tomatoes (about 1/4 cup per tomato); drizzle with remaining 2 tablespoons oil. Bake until tops are golden brown and crisp, about 20 minutes. Serve immediately.

STUFFED TOMATOES WITH GOAT CHEESE, OLIVES, AND OREGANO

Follow recipe for Baked Stuffed Tomatoes with Parmesan, Garlic, and Basil, substituting 3 ounces crumbled goat cheese for Parmesan, omitting basil, and adding 3 tablespoons minced fresh parsley, 1 1/2 teaspoons minced fresh oregano, and 3 tablespoons chopped black olives to bread crumb mixture.

Pan Sauces for Steak

Can you make a rich, thick, restaurant-style pan sauce for steak using canned broth?

⇒ BY ANNE YAMANAKA ⇐

Ever wonder how restaurants make that thick, rich red wine sauce that accompanies your filet or rib eye? Chances are it's a pan sauce, made with the delicious caramelized browned bits (called *fond)* that sit on the bottom of the pan after meat is sautéed or pan-seared.

Pan sauces are usually made by adding liquid (usually stock) to the pan and dissolving the fond (a process known as *deglazing)*, reducing this liquid, then enriching and thickening the sauce with butter. These sauces are heavenly when made well—full-bodied, complex, and balanced in flavor, rich in color, and thick enough to coat the steak and form a nice pool of sauce into which you can dip the meat. In other words, a good pan sauce can elevate the average steak dinner to the position of a luxurious, refined meal.

Making these sauces at home can be a challenge, however, since most home cooks don't have the rich beef or veal stock on hand that restaurant chefs count on as a base for the sauces. Canned broth is the obvious alternative, but because it lacks the body and beefy flavor of homemade beef stock, it usually makes sauces that are flat in flavor and watery and thin in consistency. I figured, though, that with the right technique and the right supporting ingredients I should be able to make pan sauces at home with restaurant-quality results using canned chicken broth. (Canned beef broth might seem to be the natural substitute for beef stock, but in previous tests we found it harsh and relatively flavorless.)

To achieve my goal, I knew that I must come up with a general technique for getting a good sear on the steaks and a flavorful fond to create a solid flavor base for the final sauce. In addition, I'd have to decide how far to reduce my liquid ingredients after deglazing the pan to achieve the desired thickness of sauce. Finally, I knew I'd have to determine which ingredients might boost the flavor and richness of the canned stock, making it suitable for a rich, meaty steak.

Flavor from the Sear
I got a head start by reading "The Secrets of Panfrying Steaks" (May/June 1997). The article

We found that adding acidic ingredients near the end of cooking gives sauces a livelier flavor.

recommends choosing cuts like rib eye or top loin (also known as strip steak), which brown better than leaner cuts of beef; preheating the pan before adding the steaks (to prevent the steaks from sticking to the pan); and using only sturdy pans for cooking steaks over high heat. I tried this approach and verified that it does indeed make for a good crust on steaks and contributes to the makings of a nicely flavored fond on the bottom of the pan.

But because I was making pan sauces in addition to the steak, there were other questions to consider. Because the steak and sauce are made in the same pan, I wanted to know if the type of pan used would make any difference in the sauce. I also wanted to know if cooking the steaks over high heat the whole time, as the article suggests, made sense for both the steaks and the sauce.

Many sources discourage the use of cast-iron pans when cooking foods that have a high acid content because of the iron's tendency to react with the food, giving it a metallic, "off" flavor. I put this theory to the test by cooking a red wine sauce in a cast-iron pan. The result: a sauce with a somewhat tinny aftertaste. As I suspected, a cast-iron skillet is not a good option for pan sauces.

When I tried a pan with a nonstick coating, the brown bits failed to form and cling to the cooking surface. This resulted in an anemic, weakly flavored

sauce. Pan sauces made in a regular nonreactive pan (I used All-Clad) were richer in both flavor and color. The best choice, then, is a heavy-bottomed, nonreactive pan without a nonstick coating.

Noticing that the sauces were slightly bitter when I cooked the steaks over high heat the entire time, I decided to turn down the heat a little to ensure that the drippings on the bottom of the pan didn't burn. By preheating the pan over high heat, then turning the heat down to medium-high once the steaks are added, I was able to get a good sear on the steaks and a nicely colored fond on the bottom of the pan with no burning. I also discovered that searing the steaks in a dry pan produced the same quality of browning as searing the steaks in oil.

Over the course of pan-searing dozens of steaks, I found a few other factors that helped ensure a good crust on the steak and a rich fond to flavor the sauce. First is the relationship of pan size to steaks. There should be at least 1/4 inch of space between each steak if they are to sear, not steam. At the same time, the pan should not be too large, because that encourages burning. I also noticed that it was not a good idea to move the steaks around in the pan. This interrupted the browning process and resulted in steaks that lacked good caramelization. The steaks browned much better when moved only once, just to turn them over to the other side.

Reducing It Right
At this point I was ready for the actual making of the sauce through deglazing and reduction. I wanted to know how much liquid I would need before reducing and how far I'd have to reduce the liquid to obtain sauce with the proper thickness and flavor.

Using a recipe for red wine pan sauce, I reduced one cup of liquid ingredients (one-half cup low-sodium chicken stock and one-half cup red wine) to one-half cup, one-third cup, and one-fourth cup, respectively, then finished each version with three tablespoons of butter.

   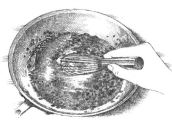

1. Pan-sear the steaks in a heavy-bottomed, nonreactive skillet.

2. Use the residual heat in the pan to sauté the aromatics until they just begin to caramelize.

3. Return the pan to the heat, add the liquids, bring to a boil, and reduce the total volume to about ⅓ cup.

4. Off heat, whisk in the butter until it is melted and incorporated, then add fresh herbs and season to taste.

Reducing to one-half cup produced a weak, watery sauce. The sauce reduced to one-third cup was thicker, but not as viscous as I thought it should be. When reduced to one-quarter cup, the sauce held just the right thickness, similar to heavy cream, and the flavor was better, not as watery as the others. (In my final recipe, the sauce is reduced to one-third cup, but this is because shallots are included in the reduction, so the liquid ingredients are actually reduced to about a quarter of the original volume.)

Now I turned to flavor. The pan sauces that I found most compelling in initial tests were those that included ingredients in addition to the basic mixture of wine or brandy, broth, and butter. I discovered, for example, that the flavor of my red wine pan sauce was vastly improved by a little brown sugar and a touch of mustard and vinegar. I also found that earthy flavors, such as mushrooms, added a needed boost of flavor.

I now had a technique for making full-bodied and flavorful pan sauces for steak at home, even when using canned broth.

PAN-SEARED STEAKS
SERVES 4

To cook two steaks instead of four, use a 10-inch skillet and halve the sauce ingredient quantities. Pan sauces cook quickly, so prepare the ingredients before you begin cooking the steaks. Use a heavy skillet with a nonreactive cooking surface.

- 4 boneless 8-ounce rib-eye or top loin steaks, I to I¼ inches thick, thoroughly dried with paper towels
   Salt and ground black pepper

1. Heat heavy-bottomed, 12-inch skillet over high heat until very hot, about 3 minutes. Meanwhile, season both sides of steaks with salt and pepper.
2. Lay steaks in pan, leaving ¼ inch of space between each; reduce heat to medium-high, and cook without moving until well browned, about 4 minutes. Using tongs, flip steaks; cook 4 minutes more for rare, 5 minutes more for medium-rare, and 6 minutes more for medium. Transfer steaks to large plate and tent with foil to keep warm while preparing one of the following sauce recipes.

RED WINE PAN SAUCE WITH MUSTARD AND THYME
MAKES ABOUT ½ CUP, ENOUGH TO SAUCE 4 STEAKS

- 2 medium shallots, minced (about ¼ cup)
- 2 teaspoons brown sugar
- ½ cup dry red wine, such as Cabernet Sauvignon
- ½ cup canned low-sodium chicken broth
- I small bay leaf
- I tablespoon balsamic vinegar
- I teaspoon Dijon mustard
- 3 tablespoons unsalted butter, cut into 6 pieces
- I teaspoon minced fresh thyme leaves
   Salt and ground black pepper

Follow recipe for Pan-Seared Steaks. To same skillet used to cook steaks (do not clean skillet or discard accumulated fat), add shallots and sugar off heat; using pan's residual heat, cook, stirring frequently, until shallots are slightly softened and browned and sugar is melted, about 45 seconds. Return skillet to high heat, add wine, broth, and bay leaf; bring to boil, scraping up browned bits on pan bottom with wooden spoon. Boil until liquid is reduced to ⅓ cup, about 4 minutes. Stir in vinegar and mustard; cook at medium heat to blend flavors, about 1 minute longer. Off heat, whisk in butter until melted and sauce is thickened and glossy. Add thyme and season to taste with salt and pepper. Remove bay leaf, spoon sauce over steaks and serve immediately.

COGNAC AND MUSTARD PAN SAUCE
MAKES ABOUT ½ CUP, ENOUGH TO SAUCE 4 STEAKS

- 2 medium shallots, minced (about ¼ cup)
- I teaspoon brown sugar
- ¼ cup cognac
- ¾ cup canned low-sodium chicken broth
- I tablespoon juice from I lemon
- I tablespoon plus I teaspoon whole grain mustard
- 3 tablespoons unsalted butter, cut into 6 pieces
- 2 teaspoons minced fresh tarragon leaves
   Salt and ground black pepper

Follow recipe for Pan-Seared Steaks. To same skillet used to cook steaks (do not clean skillet or discard accumulated fat), add shallots and sugar off heat; using pan's residual heat, cook, stirring frequently, until shallots are slightly softened and browned and sugar is melted, about 45 seconds. Return skillet to high heat, add cognac and broth; bring to boil, scraping up browned bits on pan bottom with wooden spoon. Boil until liquid is reduced to ⅓ cup, about 4 minutes. Add lemon juice and mustard; cook to blend flavors, about 1 minute longer. Off heat, whisk in butter until melted and sauce is thickened and glossy. Add tarragon and season to taste with salt and pepper; spoon over steaks and serve immediately.

PORCINI MUSHROOM AND MARSALA PAN SAUCE WITH ROSEMARY
MAKES ABOUT ¾ CUP, ENOUGH TO SAUCE 4 STEAKS

- ½ ounce dried porcini mushrooms
- ½ cup hot water
- 2 medium garlic cloves, minced (about 2 teaspoons)
- ½ cup sweet Marsala
- ½ cup canned low-sodium chicken broth
- 3 tablespoons unsalted butter, cut into 6 pieces
- 2 teaspoons chopped fresh rosemary
   Salt and ground black pepper

1. Cover mushrooms with hot water in microwave-safe bowl; cover bowl with plastic wrap, cut vents in wrap, and microwave on high for 30 seconds. Let stand to soften mushrooms, about 5 minutes. Lift mushrooms from liquid with fork; chop coarse and set aside. Strain mushroom soaking liquid through sieve lined with coffee filter or cheesecloth to remove grit; reserve ⅓ cup strained liquid and set aside.
2. Follow recipe for Pan-Seared Steaks. To same skillet used to cook steaks (do not clean skillet or discard accumulated fat), add garlic off heat; using pan's residual heat, cook, stirring constantly, until fragrant, 15 to 20 seconds. Return skillet to high heat, add Marsala, broth, chopped mushrooms, and reserved soaking liquid; bring to boil, scraping up browned bits on pan bottom with wooden spoon. Boil until liquid is reduced to ½ cup, about 3 minutes. Off heat, whisk in butter until melted and sauce is thickened and glossy. Add rosemary and season with salt and pepper to taste. Spoon sauce over steaks; serve immediately.

Anne Yamanaka lives and cooks in Torrance, Calif.

Garlic Tips and Techniques

With just a few garlic techniques under your belt, you can master this sometimes frustrating culinary staple. BY RAQUEL PELZEL

Garlic epitomizes the idea that good things come in small packages. Like a meticulously wrapped birthday gift, garlic reveals its true beauty only after its thin, paperlike shell has been removed: slightly sweet and pungent, with spicy undertones and a lingering finish. The types of garlic most people are familiar with are the white, pink, and purple sorts (the latter two being colored in skin only). Another variety often available that is great for roasting, owing to its larger-than-average size,

is the aptly named elephant garlic. Still, it is generally less potent than the smaller, standard-sized garlic. Regular garlic also varies widely in potency.

When buying garlic in the store, make sure to buy firm, tightly bound cloves. If your garlic has sprouted, it's still all right to use in a pinch. Just remove the green sprout—it can make your dish taste bitter. Here we present some tried-and-true tricks of the trade to help you work with garlic efficiently and effectively.

CLOVES OF GARLIC: Actual size

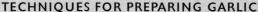

TECHNIQUES FOR PREPARING GARLIC

How to Peel Garlic with a Chef's Knife

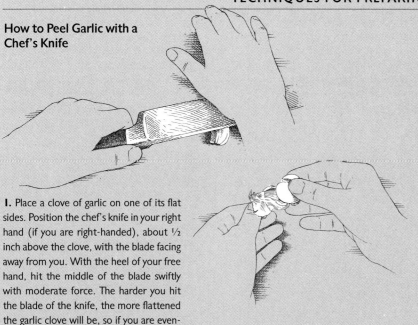

1. Place a clove of garlic on one of its flat sides. Position the chef's knife in your right hand (if you are right-handed), about ½ inch above the clove, with the blade facing away from you. With the heel of your free hand, hit the middle of the blade swiftly with moderate force. The harder you hit the blade of the knife, the more flattened the garlic clove will be, so if you are eventually planning to sliver the garlic, take care not to hit the blade with too much force.

2. The skin of the clove should crack open, enabling you to peel it away from the clove easily.

How to Peel Garlic with a Rubber Jar Opener

1. Place the unpeeled garlic cloves in the center of the jar opener.

2. Sandwich the cloves inside the jar opener, and, with the palm of your hand, roll the cloves around the inside of the "sandwich." The garlic skins should slip right off.

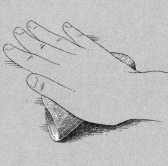

How to Mince Garlic

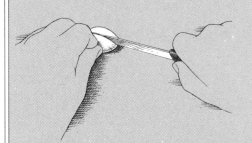

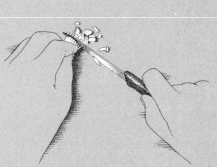

1. With a paring knife or a chef's knife (depending on what you feel most comfortable with), make pole-to-pole slices lengthwise along the clove, taking care not to cut through the root end.

2. Bring your knife back up and over the garlic and proceed to dice it into small bits.

3. Gather the diced garlic into a pile by dragging the knife blade toward you. Holding the chef's knife in your dominant hand, place your other hand flat over the upper-third portion of the blade. With your chef's knife, finely mince the chopped garlic with a firm, rocking motion, swiveling the blade across the chopped pieces. It may take several passes to get the garlic uniformly minced.

Illustration: John Burgoyne

MORE TECHNIQUES FOR PREPARING GARLIC

How to Puree Garlic with a Chef's Knife

1. After the garlic has been minced, sprinkle it with a generous pinch of kosher salt. (We prefer kosher salt since the large crystals help to puree the garlic).

2. Gently lay the top quarter of the flat portion of your chef knife's blade on top of the salted garlic. Place your free hand on top of the blade and drag the garlic toward you, then push it away in a small circular motion. Repeat this process until the garlic is smooth and partially liquefied.

How to Puree Garlic with a Fork

1. If you need a smaller quantity of garlic puree, this method may work best for you. Hold a fork with its tines facing down on a cutting board. Rapidly rub a peeled garlic clove back and forth against the tines, close to their points.

2. Mash any remaining chunks with the fork turned over.

How to Sliver Garlic

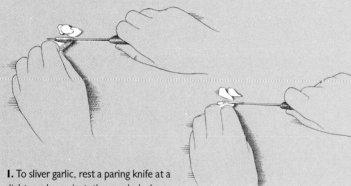

1. To sliver garlic, rest a paring knife at a slight angle against the peeled clove. Raise the paring knife above the clove, then bring it down on to the clove in a slow, even motion. Bring the knife back up again and make your next cut, barely moving to the left of your first slice. Continue to slice the garlic, working your way into the clove.

2. When you get to the end of the clove, turn it over so that the flat edge is resting on the cutting board and continue slivering the clove. (If you are making slivers to insert into meat or a portobello mushroom, cut them wider so they can be inserted more easily.)

How to Toast Garlic

When you want the sweet and caramel flavors of roasted garlic but don't have the time to roast, try toasting it. It's a great quick fix. You can substitute toasted garlic for roasted garlic in some recipes, such as in salad dressings.

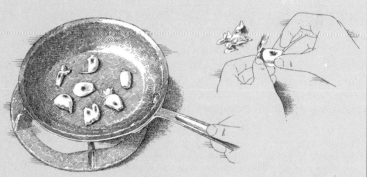

1. Heat the unpeeled cloves in a dry skillet over medium heat. Shake the pan occasionally until the garlic becomes fragrant and you notice small brown spots on all sides, about 8 minutes.

2. Remove the garlic from the pan. As soon as it is cool enough to handle, you can slip the skin right off.

How to Roast Garlic

Roasting brings out the sweet, mild flavor of garlic. To roast it, heat the oven to 400 degrees, then follow these steps.

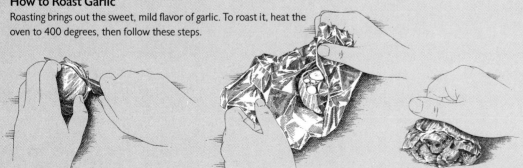

1. Take a large head of garlic and cut about ½ inch from the tip end so most clove interiors are exposed.

2. Place the garlic head, cut-side up, in the center of an 8-inch square of aluminum foil. Sprinkle the open end of the garlic with ½ teaspoon of olive oil and a pinch of salt, then gather the corners of the foil over the garlic and twist to seal.

3. Roast in a small baking dish until the garlic is soft and golden, about 45 minutes. When cool, squeeze the garlic out by hand or with the flat edge of a chef's knife, starting from the root end and working up.

How size affects flavor

We have heard that the way garlic is prepared—whether sliced, diced, or minced—can influence the flavor of a dish. To test this theory, we made three dishes—an uncooked vinaigrette, a quickly cooked olive oil pasta sauce, and a long-cooked meat sauce—using garlic cut in different ways. In each case, each particular "cut" of garlic affected flavor differently.

After some research, we discovered that what is behind these flavor differences is *allicin*, an enzyme that is released when garlic is cut. The intensity of garlic flavor in your dish depends on how finely you have chopped, minced, or pureed the garlic. If you want a bold garlic flavor, you should puree or mince your garlic, but if you want a more subtle essence, try slivering the clove. If you're not a true fan of garlic's bold flavors, you may want to roast or toast your garlic—the heat breaks down the allicin.

Improving Chicken Cacciatore

We found a way to make this Italian-American dish so it has moist meat
and a silken, robust sauce. The secret is in the skin.

⇒ BY BRIDGET LANCASTER ⇐

Cacciatore, which means "hunter-style" in Italian, originally referred to a simple method of cooking fresh-killed game. Game hen or rabbit would be sautéed along with wild mushrooms, onions, and other foraged vegetables and then braised with wine or stock. Unfortunately, when applied to chicken and translated by American cooks, cacciatore mutated into a generic pasty "red sauce" dish, often featuring sauces that were greasy and overly sweet along with dry, overcooked chicken.

I thought that it was time for a resurrection. I knew that there was a really good version of this dish to be found, and I was determined to discover it.

From the beginning I knew that I wanted a sauce that was just substantial enough to cling to the chicken; I didn't want the meat to be swimming in broth, nor did I want a sauce reminiscent of Spackle. Another thing I wanted was a streamlined cooking method. This cacciatore would be easy enough to prepare on a weeknight and, I hoped, would necessitate the use of only one pot.

As is the custom here at *Cook's*, I began my quest with a blind taste test. I gathered an abundance of recipes (seemingly, every "Italian" cookbook included some form of cacciatore), then selected what seemed to be the more "authentic" versions (no boneless, skinless chicken breasts, no jarred tomato sauces) written by prominent Italian cooks. All four of these recipes started with the same basic preparation, one that I would also use for my working recipe. Chicken (a whole chicken cut up, in all but one of the recipes) was dredged in flour and sautéed in olive oil, then removed from the pan, which was then deglazed with either wine or stock. Vegetables—most often tomatoes, onions, and mushrooms—were added to the braise, and the dish was then left to cook until the meat was fall-apart tender.

As I was reviewing the tasters' notes from this initial tasting, I noticed that two problems were common to all the recipes. For one, tasters found the dishes to be too greasy (nearly an inch of oil floated at the top of one dish), for another, they disliked the presence of chicken skin in the final product. The skin, which was crisp after the initial sauté, had become soggy and unappealing.

All of the recipes except one had other serious problems as well. One was too vegetal, another included black olives that proved too dominant a

If you can get hold of a Parmesan cheese rind, it adds a lavish flavor to the sauce.

flavor, and a third had no tomatoes, an omission that tasters thought took it too far from what Americans consider to be a classic cacciatore.

The fourth recipe was much more promising. It started off with chicken thighs rather than a whole, cut-up chicken and used a mixture made from equal parts flour and softened butter, known as a *beurre manié,* to thicken the sauce. The dark thigh meat remained much more moist and plump than the breast meat used in the other recipes, which became fibrous and flavorless while cooking. (It was also much easier to simply buy a package of thighs than to cut up a whole chicken.) The thighs also gave the braising liquid a more intense flavor. Unfortunately, the beurre manié overthickened the sauce, giving it a gravy-like consistency.

From the test results I was able to come to a few conclusions and devise a working recipe. Chicken

thighs were in. The flabby skin was out, and this, I hoped, would reduce the overabundance of grease in the dish. Wine (whether to use red or white was still to be determined) was the liquid of choice for braising, and the additional vegetables needed to be kept to a minimum—a combination of onions, mushrooms, and tomatoes was all that would be needed.

Skin Deep

I assumed that the flabby skin issue could be easily solved by using skinless chicken thighs. But that assumption proved to be untrue. A batch made with skinless thighs, while good, lacked the intense flavor of the batches made with skin-on chicken. The rendered fat and juice from the chicken skin caramelized on the pan bottom, which, when deglazed, made a big contribution to the flavor of the sauce. In addition, the skin protected the flesh of the chicken from direct contact with the high heat, thereby preventing the meat from forming a fibrous crust. I needed to lose the chicken skin after its fat had been rendered.

I found that pulling the skin off the thighs after the initial sauté cost the dish none of its flavor while allowing me to serve the dish sans skin. Removing the skin before braising also eliminated the problem of excess grease. The fat from the skin is first rendered at a high heat, which helps to keep the skin from sticking to the pan bottom. The extra fat is then disposed of, but the caramelized bits are left behind for deglazing.

Liquid Assets

Next came the braising medium. Preliminary testing suggested that red wine would prevail. Most tasters liked its bold presence, although some thought the hearty flavor of the wine was a bit too harsh. I tried cutting the wine with small amounts of water, dry vermouth, and chicken stock, and found that the latter buffered the strong presence of the wine and rounded out the flavors. (Since some tasters preferred the lighter, brothier taste of the version made with white wine, I decided to offer that as a variation on my final recipe.)

At this point the sauce was rich in flavor but lacking in substance. Truthfully, it was more like a broth; the vegetables and chicken were lost in the liquid. I remembered that the flour used to dredge the chicken thighs had been thrown away with the skin. I would have to introduce it somewhere else. A beurre manié was too complicated for my streamlined dish, so I ended up adding a little flour directly to the vegetables as they were finishing their sauté. The sauce was now silky and robust. On a whim I threw in a piece of a Parmesan cheese rind, an option I had noticed in one of the recipes tested earlier. The sauce, very good before, now surpassed all of our expectations. It was now substantial, lavish, and amply flavored.

I was finally down to the details of finishing. Portobello mushrooms, bursting with the essence of red wine, added an earthy flavor and meaty chew. I also found that just about any herb would complement the recipe; I chose sage for its mellow, woody flavor.

Don't Wine About It

When making a dish that uses red wine, our tendency is to grab whichever inexpensive, dry red is on hand, usually the leftover contents of a recently opened bottle. But we began to wonder what difference particular wines would make in the final dish, and decided to investigate.

We called on the advice of several local wine experts, who gave us some parameters to work with when selecting red wines to use in a braise such as cacciatore. When choosing a red wine look for one that is dry (to avoid a sweet sauce) and with good acidity (to aid in breaking down the fibers of the meat). Keep in mind that any characteristic found in the uncooked wine will be concentrated when cooked. From tests we ran in the test kitchen, we found that softer, fruity wines such as a Merlot tend to reduce and give a "grape jelly" flavor, which most tasters thought was too sweet for the cacciatore. Watch out for wines that have been "oaked," usually older wines; the oak flavor will tend to become harsh and bitter as it is cooked. —B.L.

CHICKEN CACCIATORE WITH PORTOBELLOS AND SAGE
SERVES 4

If your Dutch oven is large enough to hold all the chicken pieces in a single layer without crowding, brown all the pieces at once instead of in batches. The Parmesan cheese rind is optional, but we highly recommend it for the robust, savory flavor it adds to the dish. An equal amount of minced fresh rosemary can be substituted for the sage.

8	bone-in chicken thighs (about 3 pounds), trimmed of excess fat
	Salt and ground black pepper
1	teaspoon olive oil
1	medium onion, chopped
6	ounces (about 3 medium) portobello mushroom caps, wiped clean and cut into ¾-inch cubes
4	medium garlic cloves, minced
1½	tablespoons all-purpose flour
1½	cups dry red wine
½	cup chicken stock or low-sodium canned chicken broth
1	can (15 ounces) diced tomatoes, drained
2	teaspoons minced fresh thyme leaves
1	piece (2 inches) Parmesan cheese rind (about 1 ounce), optional
2	teaspoons minced fresh sage leaves

1. Season chicken with salt and pepper. Heat oil in Dutch oven over medium-high heat until shimmering but not smoking, about 2 minutes. Add four chicken thighs, skin-side down, and cook, not moving them until skin is crisp and well browned, about 5 minutes; using tongs, flip chicken and brown on second side, about 5 minutes longer. Transfer browned chicken to large plate; brown remaining chicken thighs, transfer to plate, and set aside.

2. Drain off all but 1 tablespoon fat from pot.

Add onion, mushrooms, and ½ teaspoon salt; sauté over medium-high heat, stirring occasionally, until moisture evaporates and vegetables begin to brown, 6 to 8 minutes. Meanwhile, remove and discard skin from browned chicken thighs. Add garlic to pot and sauté until fragrant, about 30 seconds. Stir in flour and cook, stirring constantly, about 1 minute. Add wine, scraping pot bottom with wooden spoon to loosen brown bits. Stir in stock, tomatoes, thyme, cheese rind (if using), ½ teaspoon salt (omit salt if using cheese rind), and pepper to taste. Submerge chicken pieces in liquid and bring to boil; cover, reduce heat to low, and simmer until chicken is tender and cooked through, about 45 minutes, turning chicken pieces with tongs halfway through cooking. Discard cheese rind, stir in sage, adjust seasonings with salt and pepper, and serve.

CHICKEN CACCIATORE WITH WHITE WINE AND TARRAGON

This variation is based on chicken chasseur, the French version of Italian cacciatore.

Mince 3 large shallots; clean 10 ounces white mushrooms and quarter if large, halve if medium, or leave whole if small. Follow recipe for Chicken Cacciatore with Portobellos and Sage, substituting shallots for onions, white mushrooms for portobellos, dry white wine for red wine, and 2 teaspoons minced fresh tarragon for sage.

Fresh Corn Chowder

This fresh-tasting chowder—which some may call a soup—uses grated corn as a thickener.

⇒ BY ELIZABETH GERMAIN ⇐

While it is most easily appreciated on the cob, fresh corn also lends itself well to another American favorite: corn chowder.

The ingredients in most corn chowder recipes are relatively standard and certainly simple enough. There are the corn and other vegetables, usually potatoes and onions at minimum; there are the liquids, water or corn or chicken stock enriched with some sort of dairy; and there's some sort of fat, be it butter, bacon, or the traditional favorite, salt pork. Most recipes also have in common a reliance on the time-honored technique of first cooking the onions in fat to develop flavor and then adding the liquids and vegetables. Comfortable with this basic approach, I decided to build my master recipe from the ground up. I would first test the fat, then the liquids, and finally the solids, determining how to season and thicken the chowder along the way.

Flavorful Fat

I knew from the outset that I wanted my chowder to be loaded with fresh corn flavor. What became apparent after testing a few recipes was that the texture and flavor of the base (the dairy-enriched liquid) is also critical to a great chowder. The first contributor to that flavor is fat. Because lots of people haven't cooked with salt pork and some shy away from bacon, I was hoping that butter or oil would prove to be adequate substitutes, but tests proved otherwise. Chowders prepared with corn oil were bland and insipid. Butter was better, but it failed to add complexity of flavor to the chowder. Somewhat surprisingly, rendered bacon fat also failed to add much interesting flavor.

Tradition, in the form of salt pork, served the chowder best, giving the base a deep, resonant flavor. Salt pork comes from the pig's belly and consists mostly of fat, striated with thin layers of meat. It can be confused with fatback, which is pure fat and comes from the pig's back. Make sure that what you buy at the market is salt pork; because it's both salted and cured and also contains meat, salt pork is more flavorful than fatback.

The next question concerning the fat was how to use it. What was the best way to render the fat? Was it necessary (or desirable) to cut the salt pork up into small pieces? Should the salt pork itself be removed from the pan after rendering, or is there an advantage to leaving it in the pot? The chowder developed a truly delectable flavor when the salt pork stayed in the pot throughout cooking.

We recommend using yellow corn varieties for this chowder because their "meatier" kernels create a thick pulp.

Cutting it in bits, though, proved to be undesirable; I found those little pieces to be tough and chewy. My solution was to use two big chunks that could easily be removed at the end of cooking. One shortcoming of this technique is that the same amount of salt pork cut into a couple of big pieces produces less fat than all of those small pieces, and it wasn't quite enough to sweat the onions. I compensated by adding a little butter to the pan.

Liquid Gold

With this first important building block of flavor in place, I could go on to consider how best to infuse the chowder base with the flavor of corn. Corn stock, corn puree, corn juice, and corn pulp were all possibilities.

I made two quick stocks with corn cobs and husks, using water in one and chicken stock in the other. Although both brews had some corn flavor, their overall effect on the chowder was minimal; making corn stock was clearly not worth the effort. I did learn, though, that water diluted the flavor of the chowder while chicken stock improved it; this would be my liquid of choice for the base.

Looking for a quick and easy solution, I next tried pureeing the corn kernels and dumping

them into the chowder. This wasn't going to work: the hulls made for an unpleasantly rough texture.

In an earlier *Cook's* article, "Corn Off the Cob" (July/August 1993, page 8), Rebecca Wood identified grating and scraping as a good means of extracting flavor from corn to be used for chowder (see illustrations, page 21). This approach is time-consuming and messy, but the result convinced me that it is worth the effort. Here was one of the secrets to great corn chowder. The pulp is thick, lush, smooth-textured, and full of corn flavor. When added to the chowder, it improved both flavor and texture dramatically. (For tips on how to freeze fresh corn to make chowder off-season, see "Extending the Corn Chowder Season," page 21.)

Hot Corn Ice Cream?

My next concern was the dairy, and, as it turned out, the thickener to be used. A problem with the dairy component of chowder is its tendency to curdle when heated, with lower-fat products such as 2 percent milk more likely to curdle than high-fat products such as heavy cream. It's the protein component of dairy that causes curdling, and heavy cream is not susceptible because it has so much (about 40 percent) fat; the protein molecules are thus completely surrounded by fat molecules, which keep the proteins from breaking down. But I would not be able to rely entirely on heavy cream to prevent curdling, as my tasters rejected this version. In their collective opinion, it tasted "like hot corn ice cream."

While some heavy cream was needed to give the base some depth of character, whole milk, which is wonderfully neutral and therefore capable of being infused with corn flavor, would make up the larger part of the dairy. This composition gave me some concern about curdling, which is where the thickening factor came in. I realized that the most practical thickener to use would be flour, which is known to help stabilize dairy proteins and so prevent curdling. Having a dual objective of both

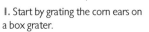

Extending the Corn Chowder Season

Midsummer through early autumn is prime time for fresh corn, but corn chowder's appeal continues into the cold months. I wondered if I could extend the fresh corn chowder season and what would be the best way to do it. Could I simply freeze the chowder I made in September? Or would I need to freeze the corn and make the chowder on the spot? If so, what was the best way to freeze my fresh corn?

For starters, I stocked the freezer with a quart of the chowder and three batches of just-harvested corn: one batch on the cob frozen raw; another batch of kernels, with the requisite amount of grated and scraped corn frozen separately, also raw; and another batch blanched on the cob before freezing.

Three months later, with winter now at hand, I removed what I hoped would be the sweet remains of summer from the freezer and got to work. The frozen chowder was easy to dismiss: its flavor was hollow and overly sweet, and the herbs tasted dried out and slightly moldy. In short, it was awful. Next, I made chowder from each of the batches of frozen corn. Chowder made from the corn frozen raw on the cob had a slightly stale freezer taste and looked curdled. Chowder made with pre-grated and scraped corn and kernels was worse. Its flavor was stale and dull, it had a plastic breath, and this chowder, too, looked curdled. The chowder prepared with corn blanched on the cob and then frozen was a different story altogether. It conveyed the clean, fresh flavor of summer corn, and its texture was completely pleasing.

John Rushing, professor of food science at North Carolina State University, explained the chemistry behind what seemed to me a small miracle. A good part of what gives fresh-picked corn its wonderful juiciness and flavor are its sugars. Once picked, however, these sugars start to break down, turning into starch. Primarily responsible for this unfortunate transformation, according to Rushing, are two groups of "marker" enzymes, peroxidase and catalase. Cold temperatures slow down the action of these enzymes considerably (which is why fresh-picked corn should go straight to the refrigerator and remain there till cooked), but the right amount of heat can stop them dead in their tracks. Blanching the corn completely disables the enzymes, thereby protecting the corn from decay. When I asked Rushing how long the blanched and frozen corn could be expected to maintain its quality, he said that deterioration from oxidation would become apparent after about six months.

Because freezing preserves quality but does not improve it, it makes sense to blanch the best just-picked corn you can find. Here's how to proceed when planning to use the corn for the chowder recipe: Husk 10 ears of corn and bring one gallon water to boil in large pot. Add half of the corn, return the pot to a boil, and then cook for five minutes. Remove the cobs and place immediately in a bowl of ice water for four minutes to stop the cooking action. Spread the cooled ears out on a clean kitchen towel to dry, and repeat blanching and shocking process with remaining corn. Place the dry corn in zipper-lock freezer bags, remove the air, seal the bags, then date and freeze. When preparing the chowder, cook the whole kernels in step 3 for just two to three minutes to obtain that wonderfully fresh corn crunch. —E.G.

---

thickening the base and stabilizing the dairy made my work easier. To prevent curdling, the flour has to be in the pot before the dairy is added. The logical choice of technique, then, would be to make a roux, stirring the flour into the fat and onions at the beginning of the cooking process.

The Solids—Easy as 1, 2, 3

Determining the chowder solids was a relatively simple matter. Onions, potatoes, and corn kernels were a given; the questions were what variety of onion and potato and how much of each? All-purpose onions and leeks were serviceable, but Spanish onions proved best, adding flavor without dominating the other ingredients. The favorite potatoes were red potatoes, which remained firm and looked great with their skins left on. I celebrated the symmetry of batch 41 when I realized that three cups of kernels, two cups of potatoes, and one cup of cooked onion (the volume of two cups raw) was perfect. Whole corn kernels add authenticity to the chowder, and I learned that adding the kernels after the potatoes have been cooked till tender, then cooking the kernels just briefly, results in a fresh-from-the-cob corn flavor. A bit of garlic added some depth and fullness, while thyme, parsley, and bay leaves helped to round out the flavors.

TECHNIQUE | MILKING THE CORN

1. Start by grating the corn ears on a box grater.

2. Finish by scraping any remaining kernels off the cob with the back of a knife.

FRESH CORN CHOWDER
MAKES ABOUT 2 QUARTS, SERVING 6

Be sure to use salt pork, not fatback, for the chowder. Streaks of lean meat distinguish salt pork from fatback; fatback is pure fat. We prefer Spanish onions for their sweet, mild flavor, but all-purpose yellow onions will work fine too.

- 10 medium ears fresh yellow corn, husks and silks removed
- 3 ounces salt pork, trimmed of rind and cut into two 1-inch cubes
- 1 tablespoon unsalted butter
- 1 large onion, preferably Spanish, chopped fine
- 2 medium garlic cloves, minced (about 2 teaspoons)
- 3 tablespoons all-purpose flour
- 3 cups chicken stock or canned low-sodium chicken broth
- 2 medium red-skinned potatoes (about 12 ounces), scrubbed and cut into 1/4-inch cubes (about 2 cups)
- 1 medium bay leaf
- 1 teaspoon minced fresh thyme leaves (or 1/4 teaspoon dried)
- 2 cups whole milk
- 1 cup heavy cream
- 2 tablespoons minced fresh parsley leaves
- 1 1/2 teaspoons salt
  Ground black pepper

1. Stand corn on end. Using chef's knife, cut kernels from 4 ears corn (you should have about 3 cups); transfer to medium bowl and set aside. Following illustrations below, grate kernels from remaining 6 ears on large holes of box grater, then firmly scrape any pulp remaining on cobs with back of knife (you should have 2 generous cups kernels and pulp). Transfer to separate bowl and set aside.

2. Sauté salt pork in Dutch oven or large heavy-bottomed saucepan over medium-high heat, turning with tongs and pressing down on pieces to render fat, until cubes are crisp and golden brown, about 10 minutes. Reduce heat to low, stir in butter and onions, cover pot, and cook until softened, about 12 minutes. Remove salt pork and reserve. Add garlic and sauté until fragrant, about 1 minute. Stir in flour and cook, stirring constantly, about 2 minutes. Whisking constantly, gradually add stock. Add potatoes, bay leaf, thyme, milk, grated corn and pulp, and reserved salt pork; bring to boil. Reduce heat to medium-low and simmer until potatoes are almost tender, 8 to 10 minutes. Add reserved corn kernels and heavy cream and return to simmer; simmer until corn kernels are tender yet still slightly crunchy, about 5 minutes longer. Discard bay leaf and salt pork. Stir in parsley, salt, and pepper to taste and serve immediately.

Foolproof Caramel Sauce

A no-stir method produces a user-friendly, rich caramel sauce.

≥ BY KAY RENTSCHLER ≤

What stirs the senses more than caramel? Pooling at the base of a flan, sitting smugly around an apple, spun into a fragile cage, or twisted in waxed paper, caramel is everything from high couture to Halloween. Part of what fascinates about caramel is its alchemy—the transformation of white, odorless sugar into aromatic gold. In fact, caramel is merely sugar that has been melted and then cooked until it reaches a temperature of about 235 degrees, at which point it colors. Caramel sauce is nothing more than caramel made fluid and soft with cream.

Still, many cooks are apprehensive about making caramel—and justifiably so. Once the sugar has melted, any foreign particle—even a sugar crystal—that finds its way into the liquid can cause it to recrystallize. For this reason, stirring is usually permissible only at the beginning, lest splashes of molten sugar hit the sides of the pot and form crystals that are then reintroduced into the liquid. There are other perils. Once the sugar caramelizes, the heat within will cause it to burn unless liquid is added or the pot is lowered into an ice bath. The addition of cream alone can spark a violent reaction.

My goal was to reduce the guesswork and remove the anxiety that seem inseparable from the process of making caramel sauce. And I wanted to accomplish these goals like a daring bicyclist—with no hands. I didn't want to worry about when to stir or whether to stir. And I wanted to know where I was headed in terms of time and temperature to ensure the caramel was the perfect color when I added the cream.

To establish some parameters, I made five caramel sauce recipes. Each involved preparing a simple caramel—granulated sugar dissolved in water and boiled until colored—and then adding cream, butter, and flavorings. None of the recipes suggested use of a thermometer to chart the syrup's progress, and most gave only rough time approximations—if any. I cooked the sugar to a rich mahogany before adding cream. Adding cold cream to the raging sugar provoked it to seize and clump—the pot had to go back on the flame, and the solid caramel stirred and dissolved. Too much butter produced a sauce with a butterscotch-like flavor; excess cream made the sauce thin and flat.

After this initial foray, I had an idea that I thought would simplify the whole process. So I selected proportions of ingredients that seemed promising and tried my technique.

Instead of adding water to sugar in a saucepan, I put the water in the pan first and then sprinkled the sugar over it. This step served to wet the sugar by the time it touched the bottom of the pot, making stirring unnecessary. Also, the relatively high proportion of water I used completely submerged the sugar, which made it unable to travel up the sides of pot, where it might crystallize. Determined to make this a hands-off project, I covered the pot and put it over high heat to get the sugar to dissolve quickly and let the condensation from the lid flow down the sides to dissolve any crystals.

After about five minutes I could see steam escaping from under the lid, and knew I had a rolling boil. Removing the lid, I hooked up a candy thermometer and watched the perfectly clear syrup boil along unimpeded. At the point when the ever-thickening syrup turned straw-colored (300 degrees), about 15 minutes, I reduced the heat. I then poured a cup of heavy cream into a small separate pot and brought it to a simmer over medium heat. The cream reached a simmer just as the syrup turned deep amber (350 degrees). I pulled the pot off the stove and gave the caramel 10 seconds to calm down before adding a quarter of the hot cream.

Bubbling and hissing violently, the cream brought the deepening color of the caramel to a dead halt. Adding cream in two steps and letting the bubbling subside, I was able to pour the entire cup into the caramel with no overflow and without stirring. I then whisked the sauce gently to make sure there was no sandbar of caramel on the bottom of the pot and stirred in two tablespoons cold butter. Top to bottom, 20 minutes. Three primary ingredients. No hands. Here was a perfect recipe for those of us who, given but one sweet tooth, would let it be solid gold.

CLASSIC CARAMEL SAUCE
MAKES ABOUT 2 CUPS

If you don't own a candy thermometer, spot-check the sugar syrup with an instant-read thermometer that can read temperatures in excess of 350 degrees. Otherwise, follow the time approximations in the recipe and watch the color of the sugar syrup; it should be a deep amber color before the cream is added. To keep the sauce from clumping, make sure the cream is hot before adding it to the sugar syrup; try to coordinate it

so that the cream reaches a simmer when the sugar syrup reaches 350 degrees.

2   cups sugar
1   cup heavy cream
     Pinch salt
2   tablespoons cold unsalted butter

1. Pour 1 cup water into 2-quart heavy-bottomed saucepan; add sugar to center of pot to keep granules from adhering to sides of pot. Bring to boil over high heat, covered. Uncover pot, insert candy thermometer, and continue to boil until syrup is thick and straw-colored, registering 300 degrees on candy thermometer, about 15 minutes. Reduce heat to medium; continue to cook until sugar is deep amber, begins to smoke, and registers 350 degrees on candy thermometer, about 5 minutes longer. Meanwhile, when temperature of syrup reaches 300 degrees, bring cream and salt to simmer in small, heavy-bottomed saucepan over high heat. (If cream reaches simmer before syrup reaches 350 degrees, remove cream from heat and set aside.)

2. Remove sugar syrup from heat. Pour about one quarter of hot cream into sugar syrup; let bubbling subside. Add remaining cream; let bubbling subside. Whisk gently until smooth; whisk in butter. Let cool until warm; serve. (Can be covered and refrigerated up to 1 month; reheat in microwave or small saucepan over low heat.)

CARAMEL SAUCE WITH DARK RUM

Follow recipe for Classic Caramel Sauce, whisking 3 tablespoons dark rum into finished sauce.

ORANGE–ESPRESSO CARAMEL SAUCE

Follow recipe for Classic Caramel Sauce, whisking 2 teaspoons finely grated orange zest, 1 tablespoon instant espresso, and 3 tablespoons Kahlùa into finished sauce.

COCONUT–GINGER CARAMEL SAUCE

Cut 1-inch piece fresh ginger, peeled, into thin rounds. Follow recipe for Classic Caramel Sauce, stirring ginger and 1/4 teaspoon coconut extract into finished sauce. Let stand to infuse flavors, about 10 minutes; strain.

COOK'S ILLUSTRATED
22

Creamy, Foolproof Dessert Soufflés

Many soufflés are foamy, flavorless, and temperamental. Here is a creamier, richer, more stable dessert that takes only minutes to prepare.

> BY CHRISTOPHER KIMBALL ≤

When was the last time you made a soufflé? Perhaps about the same time you prepared quiche, carved a swan out of an apple, or spent hours turning carrots into perfect miniature footballs. Many of us have never made one, relegating them to the category of "restaurant dessert," difficult to assemble and quick to deflate. The reality of soufflés, as I quickly learned, is entirely different. They are easy to make, unlikely to fall, and, when made properly, are nothing like the foamy, flavorless concoctions you may have had at third-rate ersatz French restaurants.

At its best, a soufflé rises dramatically above its rim to create a light but substantial and crusty top layer cushioned by a luxurious, creamy center that flows slowly across the tongue, richly saucing the taste buds. This contrast between exterior and interior is the essence of a great soufflé; lesser versions have a light, foamy texture throughout. A first-class soufflé must also convey a true mouthful of flavor, bursting with the bright, clear taste of the main ingredient rather than obscuring it with an eggy aftertaste. There are several types of soufflé—liqueur-flavored, chocolate, fruit, cheese, savory—and each requires a slightly different approach. For the purposes of this investigation, we decided to focus on a classic Grand Marnier soufflé, with variations to come after the initial recipe was perfected.

The first question was how to prepare the base, which is the thick, flavored mixture into which the beaten egg whites are folded. In a Grand Marnier soufflé, the base is often a béchamel, a classic French sauce made from butter, flour, and milk. Pastry cream is often used as a base as well, as is a bouillie, a paste made from flour and milk. It is similar to a béchamel without butter. The test kitchen prepared a blind tasting using each of these three methods. Although past experience led me to expect the béchamel version to win, the bouillie soufflé had the creamiest, richest texture. It did, however, taste a bit like scrambled eggs. To solve this problem, we added two tablespoons of butter to the bouillie, which eliminated the eggy aftertaste. (Although our bouillie now contained the same three ingredients as a béchamel, the two are made quite differently.)

Our tastings also confirmed that most recipes produce foamy rather than creamy soufflés. Part

When the aroma of a baking soufflé reaches your nose, it's time to remove it from the oven.

of the solution to this problem was to increase the amount of flour used in the base from 3 tablespoons per cup of milk to 5. We also wondered if milk was the right choice as opposed to heavy cream, half-and-half, or a mixture of milk and heavy cream. When all were tested, tasters preferred milk, which made for a livelier flavor than any of the other versions.

The next issue was determining the proper ratio of egg whites to egg yolks. We tried four variations, starting with 8 whites to 5 yolks, working our way down to 5 whites and 5 yolks.

The latter (5 each of whites and yolks) made the best soufflé, producing a rich and creamy mouthfeel rather than merely a mouthful of foam. As it turned out, however, the method of beating the whites would also be critical to our success.

It comes as no surprise that the technique used to beat egg whites is crucial to a successful soufflé. The objective is to create a strong, stable foam that rises well and is not prone to collapse during either folding or baking. Cookbooks often begin this discussion by warning against the use of cold egg whites, the theory being that

My Very Last Word on Egg Whites

Readily transformed from a gelatinous liquid state to something light and fluffy with just a bit of whipping, egg whites are perhaps the most mysterious of kitchen ingredients. To make whites even more incomprehensible, their whipping and baking properties are improved by the addition of granulated sugar and cream of tartar. For most of us, however, the rationale behind all of this is about as clear as the string theory of the universe.

Let's start with a few basics. Egg whites are 88 percent liquid (water) and 11 percent protein. (The remaining 1 percent consists of minerals and carbohydrates.) Beating an egg white relaxes its tightly wound protein molecules, which begin to unfold and stretch. With continued beating, the stretched proteins begin to overlap and bond together, creating a long, elastic surface. This is known as the soft peak phase, during which the air bubbles are relatively large and the foam unstable because the proteins have not sufficiently unwound and bonded to form a stable supporting structure. With continued beating, the proteins further bond and envelop the air bubbles, trapping and separating them. The trick here is to neither underbeat the whites (the mixture will not be stable) nor overbeat them (the foam will become too rigid and will rupture, squeezing out the liquid contained in the whites).

Adding sugar delays foam formation. It stabilizes the foam, particularly in the oven, because it attracts water and thus delays water evaporation, giving the protein structure more time to set up. Sugar also separates protein molecules, slowing the bonding process and thus guarding against the effects of overbeating. We also discovered that cream of tartar, an acid, makes it more difficult for the egg white proteins to bond too tightly. Why? Acids donate hydrogen ions, which interfere with the normal bonding pattern of proteins. With the addition of acid the proteins remain more elastic; while they do coagulate enough to maintain structure, they do so more slowly. Consequently, the air cells encounter less resistance as they expand under the influence of the heat, and this results in a higher rise.

What does all of this mean for the home cook? If you beat egg whites with sugar and cream of tartar, the resulting foam will be more stable as well as more moist, and it will rise better in the oven, be less prone to the symptoms of overbeating, and have a finer, more even texture once baked. Egg whites beaten without additional ingredients will be coarser in texture, more prone to collapse during folding and baking, more susceptible to the ills of overbeating, and will result in a drier, less appealing texture when used in a soufflé. —C.K.

cold whites do not whip up as well as those at room temperature. When I tested this, however, I discovered that the difference between egg whites that had been whipped when cold and when warm was negligible after they had been baked—so go ahead and use eggs right out of the refrigerator.

The next issue was whether sugar should be added to the whites during beating and, if so, how. We found that egg whites became more stable when beaten with even a small amount of sugar. This made them more resilient to a heavy hand during folding and less apt to fall quickly after being pulled from the oven. The question then became which is better, granulated or powdered? Granulated won this round because of its superior rise. Timing is also important. Most of the sugar, it turned out, must be added not at the outset of whipping but after the whites break up and become foamy. In addition, the sugar must be added gradually. Sugar added all at the outset produced a soufflé with an uneven, shorter rise and a bit of an overly sweet taste.

I wondered if any other ingredient should be added to the whites as they are beaten to improve stability and cooking properties. Knowing that cream of tartar is often recommended as an additive, we tested this and found it beneficial, producing a more stable soufflé with a bigger rise.

Just to satisfy my curiosity, I also made soufflés using powdered and pasteurized egg whites. The former produced a horrible-tasting soufflé, and the whites deflated quickly during the folding process. Pasteurized egg whites had a curious effect on the baked soufflé—the edges were crunchy and overcooked, yet the interior was almost raw. I also tried adding a bit of water to the whites during beating—a trick I use to increase the moisture content of certain sponge-style cakes—but there is insufficient fat in a soufflé recipe to support the water. The result? A dense, watery mess.

For perfectly whipped egg whites, then, you want to use granulated sugar and cream of tartar for stability and you want to add the sugar slowly. Neither powdered nor pasteurized egg whites are recommended, but you can use fresh eggs straight from the refrigerator; their temperature isn't much of a factor.

Next to be considered was oven temperature. Although I had been convinced that 375 degrees was the best temperature, when tested head-to-head against a 400-degree oven, the latter won hands down. The higher temperature provided for a more dramatic rise and more contrast between the cooked exterior and the creamy, saucy interior. If your oven runs a bit hot, though, beware that 400 degrees is pushing the outer envelope; the top crust can start to burn around the edges. I then tested the notion of using a water bath (the baking dish was placed in a roasting pan half-filled with hot water) with the hope that this might moderate the heat around the dish and result in a more delicate soufflé. In all cases the outside of the soufflé turned out wet and gelatin-like, a true disaster.

Now I had just a few more variables to test. I found that a 1½-quart dish works best; a 2-quart baking dish is so large that you don't get that nice, high rise and creamy, moist center. Freezing the buttered and sugared soufflé dish before adding the mixture and baking produced a dramatic high-rise soufflé, but the outside and top crust were inferior, so this idea was voted down. I also found that a soufflé should be baked in the upper-middle portion of the oven. When placed on the lowest rack, it burns on the bottom. When placed on the top rack, a soufflé can rise right up into the heating element or the top can simply overcook, turning black around the edges.

Finally, and most important of all, never overcook a soufflé. It should be very creamy in the middle and firm around the outside, almost like a pudding cake. The center should not be liquid but still quite loose and very moist. Once you can smell a soufflé baking in the oven, it's about ready to come out.

GRAND MARNIER SOUFFLÉ
SERVES 6 TO 8

Make the soufflé base and immediately begin beating the whites before the base cools too much. Once the whites have reached the proper consistency, they must be used at once. Do not open the oven door during the first 15 minutes of

TESTING | GETTING THE SOUFFLÉ JUST RIGHT

1. An underbaked soufflé will be wet and runny.

2. A perfectly baked soufflé will have a light, fluffy structure, but remain creamy.

3. An overbaked soufflé will be dry and cottony.

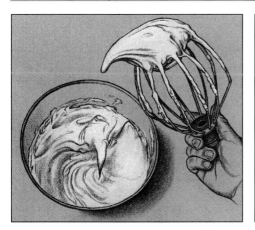 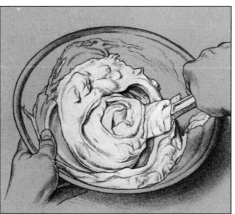 

1. The egg whites should be whipped until they have body and hold 2-inch peaks. Properly whipped peaks will be soft and graceful, not Styrofoam-like.

2. Stir one-quarter of the whites into the soufflé base to lighten it.

3. Turn the remaining whites into the lightened base. With a balloon whisk, use the same folding motion as with a rubber spatula, folding until no white streaks remain.

baking time; as the soufflé nears the end of its baking, you may check its progress by opening the oven door slightly. (Be careful here; if your oven runs hot, the top of the soufflé may burn.) A quick dusting of confectioners' sugar is a nice finishing touch, but a soufflé waits for no one, so be ready to serve it immediately.

3	tablespoons unsalted butter, room temperature
¾	cup granulated sugar
2	teaspoons sifted cocoa
5	tablespoons all-purpose flour
¼	teaspoon salt
1	cup whole milk
5	large eggs, separated
1	tablespoon grated zest from 1 medium orange
3	tablespoons Grand Marnier
⅛	teaspoon cream of tartar

1. Adjust rack to middle position and heat oven to 400 degrees. Grease a 1½-quart porcelain soufflé dish with 1 tablespoon butter, making sure to coat all interior surfaces. Stir together ¼ cup sugar and cocoa in small bowl; pour into buttered soufflé dish and shake to coat bottom and sides with thick, even coating. Tap out excess and set dish aside.

2. Whisk flour, ¼ cup sugar, and salt in small, heavy-bottomed saucepan. Gradually whisk in milk, whisking until smooth and no lumps remain. Bring mixture to boil over high heat, whisking constantly until thickened and mixture pulls away from sides of pan, about 3 minutes. Scrape mixture into medium bowl; whisk in remaining 2 tablespoons butter until combined. Whisk in yolks until incorporated; stir in orange zest and Grand Marnier.

3. In bowl of standing mixer fitted with whisk attachment, beat egg whites, cream of tartar, and 1 teaspoon sugar at medium-low speed until combined, about 10 seconds. Increase speed to medium-high and beat until frothy and no longer translucent, about 2 minutes. With mixer running, sprinkle in half remaining sugar; continue beating until whites form soft billowy peaks, about 30 seconds. With mixer still running, sprinkle in remaining sugar and beat until just combined, about 10 seconds. The whites should form soft peaks when beater is lifted, but should not appear Styrofoam-like or dry (see illustration 1, above).

4. Using rubber spatula, immediately stir one-quarter of beaten whites into soufflé base to lighten until almost no white streaks remain (see illustration 2, above). Scrape remaining whites into base and fold in whites with balloon whisk (see illustration 3, above) until mixture is just combined, gently flicking whisk after scraping up side of bowl to free any mixture caught in whisk. Gently pour mixture into prepared dish and run index finger through mixture, tracing circumference about ½ inch from side of dish, to help soufflé rise properly. Bake until surface of soufflé is deep brown, center jiggles slightly when shaken, and soufflé has risen 2 to 2½ inches above rim of dish, 20 to 25 minutes. Serve immediately.

GRAND MARNIER SOUFFLÉ WITH SHAVED CHOCOLATE

A rotary cheese grater is the perfect tool for grating the chocolate, though a box grater works well, too.

Finely grate ½ ounce bittersweet chocolate (you should have about ⅓ cup). Follow recipe for Grand Marnier Soufflé, folding grated chocolate into soufflé base along with beaten whites (see illustration 3, page 25).

KAHLÚA SOUFFLÉ WITH GROUND ESPRESSO

Espresso beans, ground fine in a coffee grinder, will make this dessert soufflé taste like a tawny cappuccino. If you do not have espresso beans, substitute an equal amount of instant espresso, adding it along with the milk in step 2 so that it dissolves.

Follow recipe for Grand Marnier Soufflé with Shaved Chocolate, omitting orange zest and substituting Kahlúa for Grand Marnier and 1 tablespoon finely ground espresso for the shaved chocolate.

Do Copper Bowls Make a Difference?

Despite the fact that almost nobody has large copper bowls anymore, I am a slave to any sort of investigation, so I decided to find out whether copper bowls are better for whisking egg whites. I discovered that while copper bowls do not produce a larger volume of beaten egg whites, they do have a contribution to make; the flavor of the baked soufflé is brighter, the soufflé is less eggy and dense, and the crust has a beautiful brown color. (Food scientists say that the copper ions combine with conalbumin, an egg white protein, to slow the coagulation process. This means that the foam can better tolerate expansion in the oven, which in turn results in greater volume in the final product.) I also discovered that best results were achieved by giving the bowl a spare coating of white wine vinegar and coarse salt before beating the whites. That said, very good results can also be achieved in stainless steel bowls using the techniques developed in this article, so copper is nice, but not necessary. —C.K.

Chili Powders Fail to Ignite Tasters

Commercial chili powders run the gamut, but few pack enough flavor punch for a knockout.

⋗ BY MARYELLEN DRISCOLL ⋖

Some culinary historians argue that if chili powder had not been developed as a commercial product (that is, if cooks had no option other than to make their own), chili con carne would never have become a common household dish.

Fortunately, chili powder did become a commercial product, and the rest is culinary history. In fact, home cooks now have so many chili powders to choose from that we decided it was time to give them a blind tasting here at *Cook's*. We sampled nine products, including those most widely available in supermarkets and a few popular mail-order products. Through the tasting we hoped to determine whether some chili powders were preferable to others. Through research, we sought to understand why.

Defining Chili Powder

Chili powder is a curious product, often misunderstood. For one thing, the kind you find in the supermarket on the A-to-Z shelf of single herbs and spices is not itself a single spice, made only from powdered dried chiles. While there is no established formula for making chili powder, it typically consists of about 80 percent chile pepper blended with garlic powder, oregano, ground cumin seed, sometimes salt, and occasionally monosodium glutamate. Some blends even include traces of clove, allspice, anise, and coriander. Although a number of powders made solely from chiles can now be found in ethnic and specialty markets, we stuck to blends because they are what most Americans cook with.

Another curious thing about chili powder is that it is usually not the source of the fiery heat for which much chili con carne is so beloved. Fresh chiles or additional dried chiles that are often soaked to make a chile tea are typically added to drive up the heat.

Balance versus Bravado

Before we held our tasting, I spoke to a number of chili experts—chefs, cookbook authors, manufacturers, and other aficionados—to gain a better understanding of the flavor profile we might be seeking from the ideal chili powder. I learned that the key to a successful chili powder is a careful blending of the chiles, spices, and seasonings. No one component is meant to stand out boldly. In other words, a successful chili powder should contribute a complexity of flavors that can be hard to pinpoint and that work on different levels. Here at *Cook's,* our idea of success was also an "independent" chili powder, capable of making a bowl of chili tasty with little or no help from other spices and seasonings. In other words, while we appreciated the idea of complexity of flavor, we also wanted some bravado.

For the most part, the results reinforced this estimation of an ideal chili powder. Those chili powders that delivered the most depth and assertiveness of flavor, otherwise described as "oomph," were the most highly rated. Unfortunately, only a few products were up to the task. Most were too subtle, leaving tasters wanting more spice and heat. A few tasters preferred the milder samples simply because they do not care for strong-flavored chili.

Acknowledging that there is no one way to make (or enjoy) chili and that not everyone likes their chili bold and spicy, we decided against categorizing the chili powders as "recommended" and "not recommended" in the chart on page 27. Instead, we listed them in order of ranking, with the top scorers at the head of the list. The experts we interviewed agreed that there is not necessarily a right or wrong flavor profile for chili powder. But they did say that there are some key elements that distinguish quality.

Measures of Quality

First and foremost, "fresh is flavor," said Park Kerr, founder of the El Paso Chili Co., which took a second-place finish for its chili powder. Because, like most spices, chili powder contains volatile flavor components, it is important to purchase it from a source that has steady turnover. A busy supermarket or specialty spice store is probably where you'll find the freshest product.

Our panel of experts also emphasized that good chili powder depends less on the type of chile or chiles used in the blend than on their quality. Manufacturers of the three top-ranked products in the tasting credited their product's success to careful selection of quality chiles. Pat Haggerty, president of Pendery's, likened chili powder to sausage making: the ingredients can be carefully selected or they can be mixed in with "scraps." Unfortunately, none of the manufacturers I contacted were willing to give us more information about the types of chiles they use in their powder or about how the chiles are treated, since they consider this proprietary information.

There is really no great secret, however, as to the general kind of chiles used to make chili powders. According to Paul Bosland, director of the Chili Pepper Institute in Las Cruces, New Mexico, the most common types are large pod-type red chiles, such as New Mexico, California, and pasilla chiles. On the heat level scale, these are at the dead bottom. (Most of the chiles used in chili powder average about 1,000 to 2,000 Scoville units, the standard measure for chile pepper heat. To compare, jalapeño chiles, which are not typically used in commercial chili powders, are rated at an average of 10,000 Scoville units.)

Most chili powder manufacturers buy the chiles for their chili powders dried and roasted to their specifications. Some manufacturers will have the chile seeds included in the grind, which is said to contribute a more nutty flavor, said Bosland. Others, such as Pendery's, insist that the seeds be removed, claiming that they dilute the chile flavor and act as mere filler. The ground chiles are then blended with spices according to a specific formula and technique the manufacturer develops.

A third aspect of quality concerned salt content. Most of the less expensive chili powders in the tasting contained twice as much sodium as the more expensive brands. While this didn't seem to make them taste salty, the potency of their flavor was decidedly less assertive.

Finally, serious chili cooks rate a chili powder for its ability to contribute to the famed rich, bright color of a "bowl of red." This may explain why Gebhardt's, which is a startlingly bright red, is a popular choice with chili cook-off competitors nationwide. While we found it lacking in flavor, this very lack may appeal to cooks who want to use it as a base on which to begin building a unique flavor profile. Ironically, the top-scoring product, by Spice Island, had a much deeper color, more like a rich rust. According to Donna Tainter, director of quality control and research and development for Spice Island, the rich color is attributed not so much to the blend of spices but to a caramelization process that occurs as the chiles and spices are blended This not only deepens the color but imparts a distinct, complex flavor that won tasters over easily.

TASTING CHILI POWDER

While there are numerous applications for chili powder, be it rubbed on fish and meats or sprinkled over hash browns and eggs, we chose to sample the following products as they are most likely to be used—in chili con carne. To keep the focus on the chili powders, we used a bare-bones recipe consisting only of onion, ground beef, crushed tomatoes, salt, and chili powder. The tasting panel consisted of 21 members of the magazine staff. The chili powders were rated for their aroma, depth of flavor, freshness, level of spiciness, and overall likability. The products are listed below according to their ranking, beginning with the highest scores.

Spice Island Chili Powder
$2.77 for 2.4 ounces

This well-known supermarket brand was the clear winner. "It's got a big flavor that stands out compared to the others." Some tasters noted a smoky character likened to chocolate and molasses. Brownish-red in color, it carried a "lingering heat after you swallow" and a more pronounced level of spiciness than most of the other products. Available in supermarkets, primarily on the West Coast.

The El Paso Chile Company's Chili Spices and Fixin's
$2.95 for 2.5 ounces

This blend was developed by Tex-Mex cookbook author and entrepreneur Park Kerr. Tasters liked it for its decent depth of flavor, freshness, and "pizzazz." The flavor was well balanced and well rounded with a "a nice progression—the after-taste is complete." Tasters described it as "deep yet sweet and complex—slightly smoky" and slightly earthy. This blend was deep red in color and contained no salt. Available by mail order.

Pendery's Top Hat Chile Blend
$4.73 for 3.2 ounces

Top Hat is one of the most popular blends at Pendery's, which carries more than 14 blends of chili powder. This blend had many fans, who cheered it on for its warmth, depth of flavor, and "definite character." "If I'm in the mood for spicy, this is good," commented one taster. It inarguably delivered a "broad spectrum of flavor notes" that were well balanced. One taster put it simply: "Very nice punch. Makes me sweat." Contains MSG. Available by mail order.

Schilling/McCormick Chili Powder
(sold in glass jar)
$4.49 for 2.12 ounces

Tasters' comments on this chili powder were brief owing to the overwhelming consensus that there just was not much flavor to discuss. "Vibrant at first bite—only," wrote one taster. Other comments included "a good base for improvement with other ingredients," "an even mix of not much," and "uninteresting, but not offensive." Available in supermarkets.

Schilling/McCormick Chili Powder
(sold in plastic jar)
$2.99 for 2.5 ounces

This chili powder was recommended by one taster as "good for people who don't like very spicy food." For many other tasters, however, this meant "bland" and "boring." Many tasters picked up on subtle garlic and smoky notes. A number also complained of it being "a bit salty, which makes it jump a bit more in flavor, but not enough." Available in supermarkets.

Tone's Chili Powder
$1.08 for .65 ounces

This product was deemed the spiciest but for all the wrong reasons, or, actually, just one reason—an excess of oregano. As one taster explained: "Oregano City... Next stop, Oregano... Oregano, fourth floor." Other flavors in the blend were faint if at all identifiable, making this sample taste primarily of oregano and tomato: "the Italian chili." Available in Midwest supermarkets.

Gebhardt Chili Powder
$4 for 3 ounces

This brand, which can be hard to find outside of Texas, is extremely popular among chili cook-off competitors. Our tasters were not as enamored. "Well rounded, but missing that *je ne sais quoi*—zip?" This product was remarkably bland but did give the chili a "nice, bright red color." Available in Texas or by mail order.

Pendery's Original
$4.14 for 2.88 ounces

"Original" does not always mean best. In this case, tasters thought there was room for improvement. This blend rated relatively well in terms of its depth of flavor but was weak in terms of spiciness. It was noticeably sweet, with an assertive cumin flavor that gave it an earthy, almost musty quality, knocking a number of tasters off guard. Available by mail order.

Durkee Chili Powder
$1.66 for .87 ounces

Most tasters agreed that this chili powder offered "nothing exciting and nothing off-putting." It was "comfortable but not impressive." "The more I taste it, the harder it is to find the flavor," commented one taster. A few tasters found this mild sample to contain "a ketchupy undertone," while others picked up a stale cornmeal aftertaste. In sum: "Needs oomph." Available in supermarkets.

$4 Loaf Pan Wins Top Rating

Finish, color, and a practical design helped a $4 pan outperform competitors that cost more than four times as much.

⇒ BY ADAM RIED WITH JULIA COLLIN ⇐

For most home cooks, the purchase of pots, pans, food processors, even relatively insignificant items such as a toaster, occasions some consideration, if not serious research. But how much thought have you ever given to the purchase of a loaf pan? If you're like any one of us here at *Cook's*, probably not much.

That changed recently when we went to buy some extra loaf pans for a recipe development project in the test kitchen. The wide range of pans available in the stores caught us off guard, so we responded with a decision to conduct a full testing. Could we get away with a $4 pan, or would parting with a few extra bucks make a real difference in our yeast and quick breads?

As usual, we rounded up all the contestants we could from local cookware stores and national catalogs. In a size as close to the standard 9 by 5 inches as we could get (depending on model availability), we chose pans of aluminum, insulated aluminum, tinned steel, ovenproof glass (Pyrex), and stoneware. Some pans were nonstick-coated, others were anodized or not coated

at all. The prices varied from a low of $2.99 for the Mirro aluminum pan to a high of around $16 for both the insulated WearEver CushionAire and heavy-gauge Calphalon pans. We had also heard of cast-iron loaf pans, but since none of the editors here had ever seen one in a store, we chose not to pursue it.

With the test kitchen ovens freshly calibrated, we set about baking loaves of white bread, corn bread, and lemon loaf cake in each pan in search of the performance differences that would distinguish the winners from the loafers. Those characteristics turned out to be browning, release of the loaf, and ease of handling the pan.

The Browning Derby

To be honest, the color differences among the loaves produced in each pan were less dramatic than we had imagined. All of the loaves browned adequately, though some minor variations in browning depth and evenness made some loaves slightly superior to others. The aluminum Mirro and Wilton pans produced loaves that were some-

what lighter than we liked, with areas of crust that were darker than other parts. This was surprising, because aluminum is known to be an even and efficient heat conductor. Each of these pans, though, had a relatively light-colored, shiny surface finish that we suspected was working against the aluminum's natural abilities by reflecting some of the heat the pans should have absorbed. We confirmed our suspicion with food scientist Harold McGee, author of *On Food and Cooking* (Collier Books, 1984), who said, "Bright surfaces reflect radiated heat, while dark surfaces absorb it. It's that straightforward. You can eventually get the same extent of heating with shiny pans, but it takes longer, and meanwhile the exposed top surface of the food may overcook."

Another problem pan was the insulated model, the WearEver CushionAire. Again, the exterior had a reflective silver finish, and the air layer sandwiched between the interior and exterior of the pan (both were aluminum) further inhibited conduction of heat to the dough, resulting in loaves with weak, thin, pale crusts.

The Loaf Pans We Tested

RECOMMENDED

Ekco Baker's Secret
Lightweight pan was easy to handle but picked up a small dent during testing.

Chicago Metallic SilverStone
Easy to grip, easy to clean, easy on the budget . . . a fine pan.

Kaiser Backform
Impressive in every regard, from loaf shape to browning.

Chicago Metallic Professional
Good pan, but not worth $8 more than our other Chicago Metallic entry.

Calphalon Nonstick
Produced beautifully shaped, beautifully browned loaves . . . for a hefty price.

NOT RECOMMENDED

Mirro Comet
Inexpensive, but not a star performer.

Corning Pyrex
Did not brown cornbread and sandwich bread loaves perfectly evenly.

Wilton Performance
Browning on the light side, and loaves have a wide, squat shape.

Stoneware
Bottom crusts of lemon cake and corn bread stuck in pan, causing loaves to break.

WearEver CushionAire
Browning was sub-par in terms of depth and evenness.

RATING LOAF PANS

We tested 10 standard-size loaf pans by baking at least three loaves, one each of *Cook's* American Loaf Bread (May/June 1996) and Golden Northern Cornbread (September/October 1995) and a lemon loaf cake, all baked to the same internal temperature and all in freshly calibrated ovens, and rated them according to the following criteria. For all tests, the pans were greased with a moderate coating of nonstick cooking spray.

RATINGS
★★★
GOOD
★★
FAIR
★
POOR

Performance differences among the pans that did well were so minor that we would recommend any of them. The pans are thus listed in two categories (in ascending price order in each): "recommended" and "not recommended." Depth and evenness of browning, loaf release performance, and design factors such as the presence of handles and the width of the pan (as it affected the loaves' appearance) were equally important criteria.

Brand	Price	Material/Finish	Size	Browning Degree	Browning Evenness	Release	Testers' Comments
RECOMMENDED **Ekco** Baker's Secret Non-Stick Large Loaf Pan	$3.99	Tinned steel/medium gray nonstick coating	9¹/8" l × 5¹/8" w × 2¹/2" d	★★★	★★★	★★★	Handles on both ends made this pan a breeze to manipulate. Browning was excellent, release was flawless, and cleaning was a breeze. Go for one size smaller, if you can get it.
Chicago Metallic SilverStone Bakeware Medium Loaf Pan	$5.99	Aluminum/medium gray nonstick coating	8¹/2" l × 4¹/2" w × 2³/4" d	★★★	★★	★★★	Handles make it easy to work with and performance was fine, though crust on the white bread was just a tad light.
Kaiser Backform Loaf Pan	$10.99	Tinned steel/medium gray nonstick coating	8¹/2" l × 4³/8" w × 2¹/2" d	★★★	★★★	★★	Exemplary browning, great release, and handles add up to a great pan.
Chicago Metallic Professional Loaf Pan	$13.99	Aluminum/dark gray nonstick coating	8¹/2" l × 4¹/2" w × 2³/4" d	★★★	★★★	★★	Slightly better browning of the white bread than its less expensive Chicago Metallic cousin, but no handles.
Calphalon Nonstick Professional Bakeware Medium Loaf Pan	$15.99	Aluminized steel/matte black nonstick coating	8¹/2" l × 4¹/2" w × 2³/4" d	★★★	★★★	★★★	Heavy pan with a high-quality feel, but tied for most expensive pan in test.
NOT RECOMMENDED **Mirro** Comet Loaf Pan	$2.99	Aluminum/brushed silver	9¹/4" l × 5¹/4" w × 2³/4" d	★	★	★★	With both breads and the cake, neither depth nor evenness of browning was up to our standards.
Corning Pyrex Originals Loaf Dish	$3.99	Ovenproof glass/clear	8¹/2" l × 4¹/2" w × 2³/4" d	★★	★★	★★	Handles make it easy to grab and move. Took a fair amount of gentle shaking to release lemon loaf cake.
Wilton Enterprises Performance Loaf Pan	$4.99	Aluminum/anodized matte silver	9" l × 5" w × 2³/4" d	★★	★★	★★★	Corners and edges of white bread loaves were noticeably light in their browning. Overall, browning was a hair lighter than perfect.
Stoneware Loaf Pan	$14.95	Stoneware/blue and white speckled glaze	8¹/4" l × 4³/4" w × 3" d	★★★	★★★	★	Browning was OK, but loaves stuck to the pan and broke, dropping its overall rating.
WearEver CushionAire Nonstick Insulated Bakeware Loaf Pan	$15.99	Sheets of aluminum with air in between/medium gray nonstick coating	9¹/4" l × 5¹/4" w × 2³/4" d	★	★	★	Browned poorly, felt bulky to handle, and produced wide, squat, unattractive loaves. White bread crust was thin and fragile, and quick breads tended to stick in pan.

The crusts of loaves baked in the stoneware and Pyrex glass pans were not as evenly browned as some, though they were acceptable. Excepting the WearEver CushionAire, the nonstick-coated pans, including the Ekco, both Chicago Metallics, the Calphalon, and the Kaiser, browned the loaves most evenly and to the deep, golden shade we desired. The trait this group of pans shared was their medium-dark, gray finish that, as McGee pointed out, helped them to absorb heat.

As noted in the chart above, the more expensive, "professional-grade" Chicago Metallic Professional and Calphalon pans, both made from thicker metal, turned in impressive browning performances. Though you could argue that the crusts on loaves from these pans were somewhat better than those on the loaves from less expensive, thinner pans, to us the improvement was sufficiently slight that we really didn't feel it justified the more than 400 percent price jump: $4 for the least expensive of our recommended pans, $16 for the Calphalon.

While we were at it, we also took note of the loaves' shapes. In the end, we preferred the tall,

classic stance of the loaves baked in the narrower, 4½-inch-wide pans in our group, including the Pyrex, both Chicago Metallics, Kaiser, Calphalon, and stoneware. Pans just ½ inch wider, with widths around 5 inches, including the Mirro, WearEver CushionAire, Wilton, and Ekco, turned out loaves that struck us as somewhat short and squat in appearance and therefore less attractive than we'd like. (Ekco also makes a smaller pan, measuring 8½ inches by 4½ inches, but we were unable to track one down in stores for this test.)

In addition to browning, the nonstick pans also excelled when it came to releasing the loaf, which, along with easy cleaning, was the raison d'être for the nonstick coating. Loaves literally slid right out.

The picture was far less rosy for our two last-place finishers, the stoneware and insulated WearEver CushionAire pans. Considerable fiddling was necessary to coax loaves out of these two pans, and both ultimately held on to big chunks of their loaves and were downgraded because of it.

It didn't take many loaves for us to notice one

design factor that made some pans much easier to grab and move into and out of the oven than others: handles. The Ekco, Kaiser, Chicago Metallic SilverStone, Pyrex, and stoneware pans all had handles, usually in the form of an extended lip at either end. The WearEver CushionAire did not have true handles, but it did have a wide rim that the cook could use to lift and move the pan.

And the Winners Are . . .

In choosing a loaf pan, more money buys thicker metal and a greater feeling of quality but not necessarily improved performance over similar, less expensive, models. Though the material a pan is made from turned out to be less important than we would have imagined, we do recommend pans with a moderately dark nonstick finish, a 4½-inch width, and handles, all of which come on the moderately priced pans from Ekco (in its smaller rendition), Chicago Metallic SilverStone, and Kaiser. If neither handles nor price are especially important to you, the other pans in our "recommended" category, from Chicago Metallic and Calphalon, will also serve you well.

⇒ BY KAY RENTSCHLER ⇐

Scallions Biting Back

Ever sipped a sudsy miso soup? The scallion garnish for Egg Lemon Soup in the March/April 2000 issue of *Cook's*, as well as the Vegetable Stock in this issue (page 9), reminded us anew of the drawbacks of prechopping. Yes, that spry scallion bite that adds mild green onion sweetness to soups, salads, and the like is supplanted by a dull, soapy flavor when the scallions are prechopped and left to await sprinkling or simmering. Though we have been unable to discover precisely what enzymatic reaction accounts for this change, despite calls to many of our favorite food scientists, we know it to be true empirically. Since scallions take but a moment to mince, it is best to have them cleaned and at the ready but whole until their moment arrives.

Hot Sugar Candy

During our development of Classic Caramel Sauce in this issue (page 22), we used a candy thermometer to check the progress of the sugar syrup. A candy thermometer, with its old-fashioned face, differs from an instant-read thermometer in a couple of crucial respects. Because sugar cooks in stages, it is helpful to keep track of advances in its temperature. As such, candy thermometers have clips that fasten to the pot, plus numerical markings and bands of mercury for easy readability. Digital instant-read thermometers, on the other hand, have heat sensors that relay signals to an electronic circuit and read out digitally. Though many instant-read thermometers are capable of registering the high temperatures necessary to cook caramel, readers have warned us that they will ultimately break if left dangling in the syrup. If you must use an instant-read thermometer when cooking sugar, remember that it is designed to endure spot checks only.

Equipment Update: Road-Testing Electric Coffee Makers

Our request for comments from readers on *Cook's* top-rated electric coffee maker, the Krups ProAroma (November/December 1998), prompted a number of responses. Though most letter writers found no fault with the flavor of the coffee brewed in the ProAroma, the overall performance and design of the machine drew more criticism than praise. Many letters mentioned that the coffee neither brewed up piping hot nor remained adequately hot once brewed and left on the heating platform (objections we shared and noted in our earlier testing).

Krups ProAroma 12 Time

Several readers were troubled by the dribbles the carafe left behind after coffee is poured from it; others by the location of the control panel; and others by the machine's top-loading feature, which requires that the entire coffee maker be hauled out from under a cabinet to pour water into the machine. No immediate structural or design changes are planned for the Krups ProAroma, which retails for $125.

In the Swim

If you're wondering why you would want to make vegetable stock (see page 9), let us offer a few suggestions. Take sauces, for instance. We reduced two cups of our vegetable stock down to three tablespoons, whisked in two tablespoons of butter, and ended up with a luscious, glazey pan sauce that could take on any chicken-based sauce. The sauce was outstanding on plain boiled red potatoes, grilled asparagus spears, and a humble broiled chicken breast. We also engaged our vegetable stock to braise endive spears right on stovetop—afterwards reducing the braising liquid to make sauce with butter and fresh herbs. Many French restaurants, in fact, feature dishes *à la nage* ("in the swim"), an upscale version of the very process we just described.

In preparations à la nage, an aromatic court bouillon (an infusion of vegetables and herbs, like our vegetable broth) is used to poach shellfish such as scallops or mussels. The poached shellfish is drained and kept warm, and the liquid reduced to a glaze with shallots and heavy cream or mounted with butter, then served over the fish.

A Question of Reduction

Speaking of sauce reduction, a few readers wrote with inquiries about our Meaty Tomato Sauce (March/April 2000). They commended the flavors of the dish but reported that by the end of the braising process the liquid had become a bit too thick to sauce the noodles. When a braising liquid or a sauce thickens too much on the stove or in the oven, it has overreduced. Put simply, too much liquid has been cooked or evaporated out of it. (This can happen despite careful testing and instructions because stoves and ovens vary in temperatures from household to household.) In a tomato sauce or a meat stew, for instance, overreduction will result in a solid, nonfluid sauce. The solution? Replace what was taken away: a splash of water and a couple of minutes over heat will restore the texture of your sauce. The same principle applies to an overreduced cream sauce for pasta. If your sauce looks thick and gluey, add a couple of tablespoons of fresh cream or plain water and some heat to the sauce. It will pull right back together. Added too much liquid? Reduce the sauce back to its desired consistency over medium heat.

Beg Your Pardon

In our rating of canned chicken broths (March/April 2000), a product made by the company More than Gourmet, labeled Glace de Poulet Gold, turned up at the bottom of the barrel. Tasters found it harsh and un-chickeny. Shortly after publication of the article, More than Gourmet Company President Bernard Leff contacted us to say we had tasted the wrong product. Though its packaging describes Glace de Poulet Gold as "Classic Roasted Chicken Stock," Leff characterized it as a reduced concentrate, designed to deglaze and finish pan sauces. Leff said its sibling, Fond de Poulet Gold, is lighter, less concentrated, and suitable for any basic preparation calling for chicken broth. We thought it only fair to give these products a second round of tests. To compare the flavors of the two More than Gourmet products, the test kitchen made two batches of chicken cacciatore, one using Glace de Poulet Gold and one using Fond de Poulet Gold. Tasters overwhelmingly preferred the dish made with Fond de Poulet Gold for its light, well-balanced flavor. But in a separate pan sauce test, the concentrated Glace de Poulet Gold won for the richer, more flavorful pan sauce it produced. Next we conducted a tasting with Fond de Poulet Gold and our top-rated canned broths, Campbell's and Swanson's regular and low sodium. The results left our top contenders unassailed, but we agree that Fond de Poulet Gold would have made the short list of "recommended" products had we entered it in the original tasting. More than Gourmet products are available at fine stores nationwide. They require no refrigeration until opened.

Italian Still Pleases

Two new cookbooks attempt to prove that there is still a lot to say about Italian food. With some reservations, we agree. BY CHRISTOPHER KIMBALL

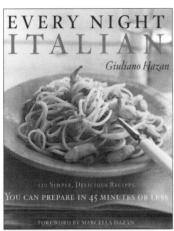

So what else can there possibly be to say about Italian food? I admit this is a rather glib question, but with the enormous glut of Italian cookbooks on the market, one wonders if there is anything new or interesting left to report about *spaghetti al pomodoro, salsicce e fagioli,* or *pollo alle olive verdi.*

Two new Italian cookbooks, *Simply Tuscan* and *Every Night Italian,* set out to prove that there is plenty left to say because the essential character of this cuisine is less about a rigid observance of technique than about an improvisational approach to food. Italian cooking, these authors would say, is like city politics, both local and constantly evolving.

SIMPLY TUSCAN
Pino Luongo
Doubleday, 292 pages

Luongo is the mastermind behind New York's Tuscan Square, an Italian market, restaurant, bakery, and espresso bar located in Rockefeller Center. Although currently a New Yorker, Luongo presents himself as a confirmed Tuscan in all things: food, wine, and lifestyle. He offers this book as an antidote to modern life, a road map to enjoying life more fully. The book is divided into sections according to the four seasons, and is comprised of seasonal menus such as Late Summer Buffet or A Tuscan Thanksgiving Dinner. This volume is beautifully produced with full color photographs throughout, including photos of Tuscany, recipe ingredients, many finished dishes, and working kitchen shots.

PROS: The philosophy of this book is well suited to the design: an uncoated ivory paper stock, a casual

typewriter-style typeface, and an abundant mix of color pictures. The food sounds great, with a nice mix of simple (Orange and Fennel Salad or Pastina with Milk and Eggs) and dinner party fare (Butternut Squash Cappellacci with Brown Butter and Nutmeg). Looking through *Simply Tuscan* makes you want to spend the day in the kitchen.

CONS: This is definitely not a cookbook for beginners. A lot of the recipes require serious cooking. A capon stuffed with sausage, for example, is wrapped in a towel, simmered for three hours, then served with a green sauce. Luongo also asks the reader to prepare chestnut gnocchi, make a whole menu based on truffles (both white and black—better extend your credit line at the bank), fry cream puffs, bake a savory baba, and so on.

RECIPE TESTING: A majority of the recipes were winners, but many were needlessly complex in either preparation or concept or both. The winners included Polenta with Wild Mushrooms and Spinach which, while giving only the vaguest directions about preparing the polenta (not even an approximate cooking time was provided), resulted in an excellent finished dish. We particularly liked the combination of milk and spinach. Cotechino (sausage) with Lentils was fussy, calling for tiny amounts of many ingredients, the use of three saucepans and one skillet, and a warning to select only "aceto balsamico tradizionale," which costs a small fortune; this rustic dish is then topped off with a savory zabaglione! Still, it worked and was delicious. The Black Olive and Zucchini Tart had a great filling but a tough, hard-to-handle crust made with room-temperature butter and water. Calamari in Zimino was simple and flavorful—a hands-down winner. Less successful were the Baked Salmon with King Crab and Black Truffle Mashed Potatoes (the salmon was seared, not baked, and the potatoes proved that too much of too many good things can be a bad thing). A potato salad with celery root, truffle oil, walnuts, and Gruyère was strange, ugly, and completely over the top.

EVERY NIGHT ITALIAN
Giuliano Hazan
Scribner, 256 pages

Yes, Giuliano is the son of cookbook author Marcella Hazan, and Giuliano's mission in *Every Night Italian* is to make Italian cooking accessible for folks cooking dinner Tuesday night. As he points out in the introduction, grilling a steak is cooking, too. The book is simply designed—usually one recipe per page—with 16 pages of color photographs. The food is simple and approachable, with modest ingredient lists and many familiar names. For example, the vegetable chapter includes Sautéed Carrots with Marsala, Tuscan Beans with Tomatoes and Rosemary, and Oven-Roasted Vegetables, none of these recipes being foreign to home cooks familiar with Italian cooking. The food sounds fresh, accessible, and well-suited to the needs of modern cooks.

PROS: The recipes are, for the most part, well constructed and reliable. Anybody can cook from this book. When Hazan is firing on all cylinders, his food is both simple and special—owing to interesting combinations of flavors and solid cooking skills.

CONS: One might question whether yet one more recipe for Florentine steak or linguine and shrimp is necessary. Yet there are plenty of interesting offerings here that appear practical for a quick midweek dinner, whether in Italy or the United States.

RECIPE TESTING: Although we encountered a few clunkers, more than half of the recipes we tested were worth making again. Big winners included Slow-Cooked Beef with Juniper Berries (great flavor, although the meat was a bit tough), Chicken Braised with Black Olives and Tomatoes (quick and easy, with great depth of flavor), Pineapple Ice Cream (a bit watery and a few curdled bits of cream but great tasting), Gratinéed Fennel with Parmesan Cheese (simple to make, unusual, and enthusiastically received), Devil's Shrimp with Brandy and Fresh Tomatoes (one of the simplest and best recipes in the book), and Shrimp and Beans. Less successful were a rather dull Bucatini with Sausage and Onions, Porcini Mashed Potatoes (too lean—more cream and butter please!), Orecchiette with Fresh Tomato, Basil, and Ricotta (make this only with fabulous tomatoes), a watery Cauliflower Gratin, and a greasy Chicken with Green Olives that made its way quickly to the disposal after one tough, acidic bite.

RESOURCES

Most of the ingredients and materials necessary for the recipes in this issue are available at your local supermarket, gourmet store, or kitchen supply shop. The following are mail-order sources for particular items. Prices listed below were current at press time and do not include shipping or handling unless otherwise indicated. We suggest that you contact companies directly to confirm up-to-date prices and availability.

Loaf Pans

It is no surprise that we favored practical design, even browning, and ease of release and cleaning when we rated loaf pans (page 29). What did come as a surprise—a pleasant one at that—is that our winners are inexpensive and easy to find. Ekco Baker's Secret Non-Stick Loaf Pan not only took the cake in all categories, but its suggested retail price is a mere $3.99. This loaf pan is made of tinned steel with a nonstick coating and easy-to-grip handles. It is available at most discount and grocery stores. You can call the manufacturer, **World Kitchen**, at **800-367-3526** and speak to a customer service representative to find the retailer nearest you that carries Ekco products. Our second-place finisher, the Chicago Metallic SilverStone Bakeware Medium Loaf Pan, was a great performer as well. This pan is made of aluminum and has a nonstick surface. A deal at $4.99, the pan is available through **Kitchen Etc. (32 Industrial Drive, Exeter, NH 03833; 800-232-4070; www.kitchenetc.com).** Ask for item #572133.

Chili Powder

As American as apple pie, chili powder evolved from a 19th-century concoction of herbs and vegetables—wild oregano, chile peppers, garlic, and onions—collected along the great cattle trails in Texas. Trail hands would collect the pungent, flavorful ingredients, hang them to dry on the sides of chuck wagons, and use them to flavor fresh-killed beef that was dinner. In the years to come, the dish, ultimately known as *chili con carne* ("chili with meat"), swept the nation, and the magic powder was jarred and distributed nationwide. Today, there are probably as many chili powder blends as there are recipes for the bowl of red itself.

Spice Island Chili Powder got the top rating in our chili powder tasting (page 26). Although the company's spices are available in most supermarkets in the West, they can be difficult to find on the East Coast. If your market doesn't sell Spice Island, call **800-635-6278** to locate a store near you. You can also mail-order the chili powder in cases of six 2.4-ounce jars from **Edge Distributing (800-373-372)** for $23.77. Orders are taken by phone only, Monday through Friday, 8 A.M. to 5 P.M., Central Standard Time. The second-place

winner, Chili Spices and Fixin's Powder, can be ordered from **El Paso Chile Company (909 Texas Avenue, El Paso, TX 79901; 800-27-IS-HOT; www.elpasochile.com).** It comes in a pack of two ½-ounce pouches for $2.95 (item #FECSPC01). If you prefer not to order it, customer service representatives will be happy to direct you to a store that sells the chili powder in your area. We rated two **Pendery's (1221 Manufacturing Street, Dallas, TX 75207-6505; 800-533-1870; www.penderys.com)** chili powders in our tasting as well. Both can be mail-ordered. The third-place powder, Top Hat Chile Blend, item #100001-25, comes in a 3.2 ounce jar for $4.73.

Candy Thermometer

When Test Kitchen Director Kay Rentschler developed the caramel sauce recipe on page 22, her aim was to take the guesswork out of this sometimes daunting process. Because the stages of sugar syrups are very texture- and temperature-specific, most chefs use water tests or candy thermometers to monitor them. The caramel stage in sugar cookery is the highest temperature stage, so to avoid potential problems we recommend using a candy thermometer to chart the progress of the syrup. Most candy thermometers record temperatures up to at least 400 degrees Fahrenheit. Since safety is a major concern when working at such high temperatures, insulated handles and pan clips are a must. **A Cook's Wares (211 37th Street, Beaver Falls, PA 15010-2130; 800-915-9788; www.cookswares.com)** carries an easy-to-read Candy/Jelly/Deep Fry Thermometer, item #7782, for $15.90. A Cook's Wares also sells the sturdy, heavy-bottomed saucepan we used to make the caramel sauce: the 2-quart All-Clad Stainless Steel with stay-cool handle, item #2707, which sells for $84.

China Cap

Clarity is one measure of a good vegetable stock (page 9). When it comes time to remove the flavor-exhausted vegetables from the savory liquid, your choice of strainer is an important consideration. By passing the stock through a common bowl-shaped colander or sieve you may create a mess as the liquid sloshes out the sides, and you will probably find that some small pieces of vegetables will find their way into the strained stock. The best tool to use for this purpose is a conical strainer with a functional funnel shape that draws liquid down through its pointed base. Of the two types of conical strainers available to us for straining our vegetable stock, we prefer a china cap. We use china caps in our test kitchen because it is more affordable and just as effective

as its counterpart, the fine mesh chinois. A china cap has a perforated metal body, a long handle for easy gripping, and a hook for resting on the rims of pots or bowls to facilitate use. The perforations come in two sizes, coarse and fine. We found the fine perforations best—they are small enough to allow the liquid to pass through relatively particle-free, leaving the mass of spent vegetables behind. If you can't find a reasonably priced fine conical strainer in your favorite kitchen store, you can order one from **A Cook's Wares (211 37th Street, Beaver Falls, PA 15010-2130; 800-915-9788; www.cookswares.com),** item #7255, for $23.

Yukon Gold Potato Chips

We tried a handful of potato chip varieties to top our broiled salmon (page 7). Searching for an ample, satisfying crunch and a superior potato flavor, we liked Terra Original Yukon Gold Potato Chips best. These chips, hearty-cut and full-flavored, are sold nationwide in natural and gourmet food stores and select supermarkets for a suggested retail price of $2.49. These chips are also very delicious eaten out-of-hand; the kitchen consumed many bags during testing. If you have trouble locating these chips, you can contact the manufacturer, **Terra Chips (50 Charles Lindbergh Boulevard, Uniondale, NY 11553; www.terrachips.com; customerservice@terrachips.com)** to locate a retailer near you. Be sure to include your name and full address in your inquiry so the company can contact you. Cases (12 bags) of Terra Chips of any flavor, including Original Yukon Golds, can be mail-ordered directly from the Terra Chips Web site.

Potato Ricer

Smooth, fine-textured garlic mashed potatoes (page 10) are a breeze to make if you've got the proper tools. Our "masher" of choice is a food mill because its large hopper accommodates more than one potato at a time, but a potato ricer also gets the job done. Both turn out lumpfree mashed potatoes every time. We used a Cuisipro Potato Ricer, manufactured by Browne & Company, in our test kitchen. Constructed of durable, dishwasher-safe stainless steel, this ricer means business. Its 9-inch handle offers sufficient leverage, and a ridge at the head of the bowl makes it easy to rest the ricer on saucepan. The Cuisipro ricer comes with three removable disks that allow you to control the coarseness or fineness of the mash. You can order the Cuisipro Potato Ricer from **Kitchen Arts (161 Newbury Street, Boston, MA 02116; 617-266-8701)** for $36, including shipping.

RECIPES

September & October 2000

Grilled Marinated Portobello Mushrooms

Broiled Salmon with Crisp Dilled Crust

Ultimate Vegetable Stock

Chicken Cacciatore

Stuffed Tomatoes

Fresh Corn Chowder

PHOTOGRAPHY: CARL TREMBLAY

Garlic Mashed Potatoes

Pan-Seared Steak with Red Wine Pan Sauce

Grand Marnier Soufflé

Classic Caramel Sauce over ice cream

---

www.cooksillustrated.com

Cook's Illustrated has just launched its new Web site and we invite you to join us. Simply log on at www.cooksillustrated.com. Although much of the information is free, database searches are for site subscribers only. *Cook's Illustrated* subscribers are offered a 20% discount.

Here is what you can do on our site:

Search Our Recipes: We have a searchable database of all the recipes from *Cook's Illustrated*.

Search Tastings and Cookware Ratings: You will find all of our reviews (cookware, food, wine, cookbooks) plus new material created exclusively for the Web site.

Find Your Favorite Quick Tips.

Get Your Cooking Questions Answered: Post questions for *Cook's* editors and fellow site subscribers.

Take a Cooking Course Online: Take online cooking courses from *Cook's* editors and receive personalized instruction.

Check Your Subscription: Check the status of your subscription, pay a bill, or give gift subscriptions online.

Visit Our Bookstore: You can purchase any of our cookbooks, hardbound annual editions of the magazine, or posters via the Internet.

Subscribe to e-notes: Our free e-mail companion to Kitchen Notes offers cooking advice, test results, buying tips, and recipes about a single topic each month.

Find Out About Our New Public Television Cooking Show: Coming to public television soon, America's Test Kitchen will take you into the *Cook's Illustrated* test kitchen.

Get All the Extras: The outtakes from each issue of *Cook's* are available at Cook's Extra, including step-by-step photographs.

Santa Rosa

Dinosaur Egg

Victoria

Empress

Casselman

Black Amber

Kelsey

Angeleno

Howard Sun

Scarlet Sun

Royal Diamond

PLUMS

NUMBER FORTY-SEVEN

NOVEMBER & DECEMBER 2000

COOK'S
ILLUSTRATED

Crisp-Skin Roast Turkey
We Discover an
Easy Technique

Cornbread Stuffing
Crisp on Top, Moist Inside

Pie Dough 101
Step-by-Step Guide to Perfect Crust

The Best Pasta all'Amatriciana

Bittersweet Chocolate Roulade
Great Chocolate Flavor, Easy Rolling

Do Electric Knives Really Work?
In a Word, Yes!

Roast Stuffed Pork Loin Perfected
Dutch Apple Pie
Great Turkey Soup
Roasted Pear Salads
Pommes Anna Simplified
Turkey Taste Test

$4.95 U.S./$6.95 CANADA

62805

12>

0 232817

CONTENTS
November & December 2000

COOK'S
ILLUSTRATED
AMERICA'S TEST KITCHEN
www.cooksillustrated.com

PUBLISHER AND EDITOR
Christopher Kimball

SENIOR EDITOR
John Willoughby

SENIOR WRITER
Jack Bishop

CORPORATE MANAGING EDITOR
Barbara Bourassa

TEST KITCHEN DIRECTOR
Kay Rentschler

ASSOCIATE EDITORS
Adam Ried
Dawn Yanagihara
Raquel Pelzel

ASSOCIATE EDITOR,
ONLINE EDUCATION
Becky Hays

RECIPE TESTING AND DEVELOPMENT
Bridget Lancaster
Julia Collin

ASSISTANT EDITOR
Shannon Blaisdell

ASSISTANT EDITOR, WEB SITE
Shona Simkin

CONSULTING FOOD EDITOR
Jasper White

CONSULTING EDITOR
Jim Dodge

CONTRIBUTING EDITORS
Maryellen Driscoll
Elizabeth Germain

ART DIRECTOR
Amy Klee

COPY EDITOR
India Koopman

EDITORIAL INTERN
Tammy Inman

MARKETING MANAGER
Pamela Caporino

SALES REPRESENTATIVE
Jason Geller

MARKETING ASSISTANT
Connie Forbes

CIRCULATION DIRECTOR
David Mack

CIRCULATION MANAGER
Larisa Greiner

PRODUCTS MANAGER
Steven Browall

CIRCULATION ASSISTANT
Jennifer McCreary

INBOUND MARKETING
REPRESENTATIVES
Adam Dardeck
Jacqui Valerio

VICE PRESIDENT OPERATIONS
AND TECHNOLOGY
James McCormack

ASSISTANT PRODUCTION MANAGER
Jessica Lindheimer

PRODUCTION ARTIST
Daniel Frey

PRODUCTION COORDINATOR
Mary Connelly

SYSTEMS ADMINISTRATOR
Richard Cassidy

WEB MASTER
Nicole Morris

CONTROLLER
Mandy Shito

OFFICE MANAGER
Juliet Nusbaum

SPECIAL PROJECTS
Deborah Broide

For list rental information, contact The SpecialISTS, 1200
Harbor Blvd. 9th Floor, Weehawken, NJ 07087; (201) 865-
5800; fax (201) 867-2450. Editorial office: 17 Station Street,
Brookline, MA 02445; (617) 232-1000; fax (617) 232-
1572. Editorial contributions should be sent to: Editor, *Cook's
Illustrated.* We cannot assume responsibility for manuscripts
submitted to us. Submissions will be returned only if accompanied by a large self-addressed envelope. Postmaster: Send all
new orders, subscription inquiries, and change of address
notices to: *Cook's Illustrated*, P.O. Box 7446, Red Oak, IA
51591-0446. PRINTED IN THE USA.

ORANGES AND TANGERINES The hundreds of varieties of oranges can be divided into three basic
categories: sweet, loose-skinned, and bitter. Among the best-known sweet oranges are seedless
navels, dark red-fleshed blood oranges, and Valencias. Most loose-skinned oranges are members of the
mandarin or tangerine family. They include the sweet honey tangerine, the highly fragrant and slightly
acidic clementine, and the seedless, mild satsuma. Many other oranges that fall into the loose-skinned
category are hybrids. The minneola, a cross between a mandarin and a grapefruit, has few seeds and a
distinctive sweet-tart taste, while the temple, another mandarin hybrid, is sweet and very juicy. The
best known bitter orange is the Seville. Ugli fruit, a Jamaican native, is thought to be a cross between a
mandarin and a grapefruit. It has extremely thick but loose yellow-green skin and a tangy flavor.

ORANGES
AND TANGERINES

COVER (*Pineapple*): ELIZABETH BRANDON. BACK COVER (*Oranges and Tangerines*): JOHN BURGOYNE

MEAT AND POTATOES

My first glimpse of Bozeman, Mont., came through the window of our plane from Minneapolis as it bumped and swayed out of the clouds and down into the valley, the shadowed sunlight spotlighting a crescent of mountains encircling a pale green high mountain plain. As the plane lined up on the runway, I recalled a trip to a dude ranch in Wyoming almost 40 years ago, where I discovered the vast expanse of the West as well as the 13-year-old girl in the cabin next door. Now I was traveling with my own family to a Montana ranch in search of adventure, realizing that family vacations are a risky business—pilgrimages often produce unexpected results.

Our first glimpse of the ranch as we drove past was promising. It looked simple enough; no fancy new construction, just a collection of modest log cabins set in a narrow valley headed past Snowflake Ridge and up toward the Taylor Hilgards, a snow-capped range that rises above 12,000 feet.

The ranch was purchased back in the 1920s by a couple who had little money but a lot of spirit. The husband used to stand on Wall Street, spinning tales of the Wild West to attract customers while his wife ran things back at home. As their granddaughter, Linda, who still heads up the ranch, told me, "He brought 'em, and she kept 'em." The most famous character employed at the ranch was Cruse Black, who showed up one day locked in a boxcar with a load of mules. He hailed from the Dakotas and couldn't read or write but made himself at home for the rest of his life. "Never hired, never fired" was his motto, and his photo still hangs on the wall of the office cabin.

Jim McGuiness, like his father before him, runs the dude operation, which boasts more than 100 geldings. Like most country folk, he takes his time

with most everything, words needing a bit of time to be introduced properly. He has been chased on horseback by a grizzly, he has a taste for Rocky Mountain oysters (strips of meat from animal testicles that are deep fried), and he grew up on a Norwegian diet of flatbread, potato dumplings, and meat, the latter still being the food of choice for the wranglers. Since they eat the same menu as the dudes, who prefer pasta and vegetables, there is a fair amount of grumbling around dinner time.

On the all-day rides up into the mountains, the fields are woven with Indian paintbrush, forget-me-nots, mule's ears, larkspur, elephant head, pussy toes, shooting stars, and lady-slippers. Up past 10,000 feet there are wild meadows with elk and sandhill cranes. A mule is spooked, a wrangler is thrown from his horse, we make lunch over a campfire and then head down a draw through Sage Valley to dinner, a cookout over a wagon wheel. Jim makes beer-batter buttermilk biscuits in two large Dutch ovens, heated over a fire, placed in a shallow pit, and then covered with coals. They are perfectly browned and fluffy, the best I have ever eaten. Steaks and brown trout are grilled and served with potato salad and beer. The sun starts to drop, it turns cool, and we saddle up and head through the valley at a lope under a robin's egg sky, down the trail toward camp. It's dusty, and you can smell the sagebrush and sweat from the horses. I'm sore, my knees ache from the long ride, but it has been a good day.

Things haven't changed much at the ranch. In October, they still herd the horses up through a

Christopher Kimball

mountain pass to their winter pasture and then move them back down in April. Sometimes the snow is "hat deep" in the spring, and they have to break trail just to get the horses through. There are wolverines, bobcats, mountain lions, coyotes, and bears nearby. The wranglers still wear chaps or chinks (short chaps) and, when they have time off, they take target practice on gophers or play tricks on the girls in the kitchen.

Back home in Vermont, I remember the trip: a week of cold mornings with a fire sparking in the cabin's wood stove; kids playing until dark, their voices echoing up the valley; a 16-inch rainbow trout stripping out line like a freight train one afternoon on the Madison River; and my 5-year-old son standing for a photograph in cowboy boots and hat with a group of wranglers by the corral, eyes squinting into the sun. I had traveled 3,000 miles in search of something new, but found, instead, the familiar. Sure, we have hardwoods instead of pine, black bears instead of grizzlies, and the fishing isn't half as good, but we are meat and potatoes folk all the same. I guess I trust a man who is happy eating meat and potatoes. He is the kind of guy who doesn't need to leave home in search of adventure. Like Cruse Black, who knew he had found paradise the moment he stepped out of that dark boxcar, he's smart enough to stay put when the grub is good, keep his head down at dinner, and take a second helping whenever it's offered. He doesn't need something new on his plate. He's been around long enough to just look for some more of the same.

ABOUT COOK'S ILLUSTRATED

Visit our expanded Web site The new *Cook's* Web site features original editorial content not found in the magazine as well as searchable databases for recipes, equipment tests, food tastings, buying advice, step-by-step illustrations of cooking techniques, and quick tips. The site also features our online bookstore, cooking courses, a question-and-answer message board, and a sign-up form for *e-Notes*, our free online cooking newsletter. Join us today at www.cooksillustrated.com.

The magazine *Cook's Illustrated* (ISSN 1068-2821) is published bimonthly (6 issues per year) by Boston Common Press Limited Partnership, 17 Station Street, Brookline, MA 02445. Copyright 2000 Boston Common Press Limited Partnership. Periodical postage paid at Boston, Mass., and additional mailing offices, USPS #012487. A one-year subscription is $29.70, two years is $55, and three years is $75. Add $6 postage per year for Canadian subscriptions and $12 per year for all other foreign countries. To order subscriptions in the U.S., call 800-526-8442; from outside the U.S. call 515-247-7571. Gift subscriptions are available for $24.95 each. Postmaster: Send all new orders, subscription inquiries, and change of address notices to *Cook's Illustrated*, P.O. Box 7446, Red Oak, IA 51591-0446.

Cookbooks and other products *Cook's Illustrated* also offers cookbooks and magazine-related items for sale through our bookstore. Products offered include annual hardbound editions of the magazine, an eight-year (1993–2000) reference index for the magazine, the How to Cook Master

Series of single-subject cookbooks, as well as copies of other books from our editors, including *The Best Recipe*, *The Complete Book of Pasta*, and *365 Quick Tips*. Prices and ordering information are available by calling 800-611-0759 inside the U.S. or 515-246-6911 from outside the U.S. or by visiting our bookstore at www.cooksillustrated.com. Back issues of *Cook's Illustrated* are available for sale by calling 800-611-0759 inside the U.S. or 515-246-6911 from outside the U.S.

Questions about your book order? Visit our customer care page at www.cooksillustrated.com, or call 800-611-0759 inside the U.S. or 515-246-6911 from outside the U.S.

Reader submissions *Cook's* accepts reader submissions for quick tips. We will provide a one-year complimentary subscription for each tip that we print. Send your tip, name, address, and daytime telephone number to Quick Tips, *Cook's Illustrated*, P.O. Box 470589, Brookline, MA 02447. Questions, suggestions, or submissions for Notes from Readers should be sent to the same address.

Questions about your subscription? Visit our customer care page at www.cooksillustrated.com, where you can manage your subscription, including changing your address, renewing your subscription, paying your bill, or viewing answers to frequently asked questions. You can also direct questions about your subscription to *Cook's Illustrated*, P.O. Box 7446, Red Oak, IA 51591-0446, or call 800-526-8442.

The Can That Could

I thought it was great that you included a recipe for beer can chicken in the July/August 2000 issue. One thing you didn't address in your article is whether there are any problems associated with using an aluminum can that has ink on it. I wonder about subjecting the can to that kind of heat.

KAREN GRAY
NEWARK, CALIF.

➤ Our recipe for Grill-Roasted Beer Can Chicken generated a lot of interest, and a handful of our readers, like you, were concerned about the safety of grill-roasting a chicken on top of a printed aluminum can. To find out about the possible hazards of doing such a thing, we contacted Dr. Barry Swanson, a professor in the department of food science and human nutrition at Washington State University. He assured us that the can could in no way contaminate the chicken.

After the body of an aluminum can is crafted, its exterior is sprayed with a base color and a protective coating approved by the Food and Drug Administration (FDA). The base color serves as the background of the final decorated product (think of the red color on a Coke can), and the coating permanently affixes the ink to the can. After both are applied, the cans are cured, or baked, in 400-degree Fahrenheit, gas-free, hot-air ovens to set and permanently bind the substances to the cans. Next, a second protective, FDA-approved lacquer is used to coat the cans' interior. This lacquer protects the aluminum from the corrosive action of the carbon dioxide in the beverage and helps keep the beverage fresh tasting. Finally, the finishing decorations are applied and adhered to the can in the same manner—sprayed on and then baked in the hot-air ovens.

According to Swanson, the lacquer and ink will not be disturbed unless the can comes into direct and continued contact with flames. As the recipe directs, the grill itself should get no hotter than 375 degrees and the chicken no hotter than about 175 degrees. During our tests, the can, semiprotected in the chicken's cavity, never registered more than 260 degrees.

Preserving Champagne's Effervescence, Continued

I read with interest your account of possible ways to preserve the effervescence of sparkling wine in opened bottles (March/April 2000). I share your skepticism regarding the spoon-in-the-mouth-of-the-bottle technique, but I was surprised that you did not specify the use of a silver spoon. Advocates of this method even insist on sterling rather than plate. If the spoon you used

was anything but sterling silver, the results may not have been entirely fair.

ERIK SUNDQUIST
MCLEAN, VA.

➤ The notion that the spoon should be made of sterling silver never arose in our previous testing. So, with this new information and to our great delight, it was back to the wine store for more champagne. Now armed with a sterling silver spoon as well as a stainless steel spoon and a champagne stopper (a plated steel bottle top with a gasket and two hinged wings that fold down to lock beneath the lip of the bottle, thereby expanding the gasket in the neck of the bottle to seal it tightly), we repeated our tests. After consuming half of three bottles of Moët et Chandon White Star champagne, we slipped the two spoon handles into the necks of two bottles and recorked the third with the stopper. The next day, approximately 20 hours later, we checked them.

The champagne in the bottle with the stopper had the largest, most active bubbles by far and tasted fresh, almost newly opened. As in our first round of tests, the champagne in the bottle with the stainless steel spoon had just a few small and sluggish bubbles, and tasters complained of a "vinegary" and "nail polish–like" taste. They found the champagne from the bottle with the silver spoon to be more palatable and at least a little more bubbly, but still nowhere near as effervescent as the champagne from the stoppered bottle.

We spoke to a host of wine experts, food chemists, and metallurgists, but no one had a specific explanation for our finding, though each speculated that the silver spoon "in some way" inhibited the loss of carbon dioxide, extending the life of the bubbles.

Mascarpone Et Al.

Two of your baked apple recipes (September/October 1995) call for mascarpone and crème fraîche. I've heard these are similiar to sour cream. Can you tell me more?

ANNIE WHITE
SAVANNAH, GA.

➤ Although made of the same basic ingredient—cream—mascarpone, crème fraîche, and sour cream are quite distinct. The differences lie mainly in their fat content, texture, taste, and range of use.

Mascarpone is a fresh temperature- and acid-treated Italian cheese made from cream with a butterfat content of 30 to 46 percent. Its texture is compact, but it is also supple and spreadable. Its flavor is unique—mildly sweet and refreshing. Usually distributed in small containers, mascar-

pone has a very short shelf life. Chefs often mix mascarpone with cocoa, coffee, liqueurs, or fruit to use as a spread or an accompaniment to fruit. Mascarpone is also used to make the filling for the popular Italian dessert tiramisu.

Crème fraîche is often considered the French equivalent of sour cream, but it is quite different. It is made from 30 to 40 percent butterfat cream that has been left out to mature and naturally sour without the addition of bacteria starters (which are generally added to sour cream). The final product is not sour or acidic, as is sour cream, but has a nutty flavor and is mildly tangy. The texture is often described as smooth, rich, and "spoonable, not pourable," and it has a creamy mouthfeel. Crème fraîche is used most often as a garnish for soups, fruit, and caviar.

Sour cream, an American product, is made from light cream (approximately 18 to 20 percent butterfat). It is pasteurized and then treated with lactic acid–producing bacteria. The bacterial action thickens the cream to a semisolid and gives it its recognizably piquant flavor. Sour cream has a markedly wet texture—the whey often floats atop—and a light, fleeting mouthfeel. Quite versatile, it may serve as a base for dips, a topping for potatoes, or a garnish for soups and is also used to moisten cakes and other baked goods.

In our minds, the three are not interchangeable. Mascarpone and crème fraîche, due to their high fat content, can be whipped into airy, satin-like peaks, but lower-fat sour cream does not really deviate from its wet, semisolid state. It gets smoother, but will not increase in volume. The tastes are also quite different.

Our Main Squeeze

Although I love the lemon tart recipe in your January/February 2000 issue, I found it very hard on my hands to squeeze the four to five lemons called for. Is there a way to make it easier?

ALLISON REYNOLDS
SARATOGA SPRINGS, N.Y.

➤ Most of us know that getting as much juice as possible out of a lemon—let alone what is asked for in a recipe—can be a mind- and hand-numbing experience. Supermarket lemons are especially troublesome, as they tend to be very young and hard. We use a wood citrus reamer to do the job (see "Citrus Secrets," January/February 1997), but we decided to determine the easiest way to juice a lemon whether you are using a reamer or your hands.

Two juice-releasing methods popular among professional cooks are rolling and microwaving. We put them to the test. Each lemon tested was relatively hard (that is, freshly harvested and thick-skinned), refrigerator-cold, cut in half through its equator, and juiced over a shallow, wide, glass bowl prior to measuring.

In the first test we rolled a lemon back and forth on a wooden cutting board until it felt markedly softer, about 10 times (the more it is rolled, the softer it gets), cut it in half, and squeezed it. Squeezing was fairly easy, though it did require extra pressure to release the last drops. This method produced 3½ tablespoons of pulpfree juice. Renee Goodrich, assistant professor of food science at the University of Florida's Citrus Research and Education Center, explained that rolling a lemon on a hard surface is effective because it bruises, breaks up, and softens the rind's tissues while it tears the membranes of the juice vesicles (tear-shaped juice sacs), thereby filling the inside of the lemon with juice even before it is squeezed.

Next, we zapped a whole cold lemon in the microwave on high for 10 seconds. When it came out, the rind was warm to the touch in spots but did not have the flaccid feel of the rolled lemon. It didn't produce as much juice, either. The juice membranes of this lemon were still intact and full of juice even after we squeezed the living daylights out of them.

In the end, despite the fact that hand cramps were not entirely eliminated, we found rolling lemons on a hard surface to be the best way to get the most juice out of a hand-squeezed lemon. The rind was malleable and the flesh juicer-friendly. Although we did not meet with much success in microwaving the lemons, you might find it worthwhile to take the chill off lemons before squeezing; squeezing cold lemons can do a number on your hands. And remember: if you have a reamer, by all means use it.

Rice Vinegar

Three of your recipes for crisp cabbage salad (September/October 1999) call for "rice wine vinegar." I have only been able to find plain rice vinegar. Can you explain the difference?

REBECCA GRAFTON
MILL VALLEY, CALIF.

➤ Your instinct to use rice vinegar for the cabbage salads was right on. We were actually mistaken in calling it rice wine vinegar, but it is apparently a common mistake. According to Lawrence Driggs of the International Vinegar Museum in Roslyn, S.D., the confusion arises from the fact that rice vinegar is essentially an acidic companion to Japanese sake. Sake is a rice beverage that stands on its own in the world of alcohol: it is not a spirit, though it is sipped from small glasses and has a strong, sweet taste, and it is not wine, though it is known colloquially as "rice wine." Flavor and carbonation aside, sake is most like beer—both are brewed from fermented

grains. Chinese rice wines are similar to sake, but most have added salt and are not taken by the glass—they are only used in cooking.

According to Linda J. Harris, professor of food microbiology at the University of California at Davis, rice vinegar is made in a three-step process. Steamed, glutinous, white rice is broken down into sugars, blended with yeast to ferment into alcohol, and, finally, aerated to form vinegar. We conducted a tasting of three brands of rice vinegar—the popular Japanese Marukan, another supermarket Japanese brand called Nakano, and the hard-to-find Chinese Foshan-Haitian—and all of our tasters preferred the Japanese brands to the Chinese Foshan brand. They commented on the overall clarity and the light, sweet taste of the Japanese varieties, but the extramild Marukan

WHAT IS IT?

I found this pan in my grandmother's basement and can't figure out what it could have been used for. The holes in the bottom make me think that whatever was cooked in it needed extremely high heat, but I am at a loss. Can you help?

SARAH ANDERSON
SEATTLE, WASH.

You have found a chestnut-roasting pan. Chestnuts can be braised, sautéed, or pureed, but they are more commonly boiled, steamed, or roasted. In the United States, roasting chestnuts traditionally involves cooking them over a gas or wood flame in a chestnut-roasting pan. The steel pan, which is broad (10 inches in diameter) and shallow with a long handle, accommodates 1½ pounds of chestnuts. The large perforations in the pan's bottom allow flames and smoke to come in contact with the chestnuts, enhancing their flavor.

To roast chestnuts, first cut a cross-hatch (an "X") into the shell with a chestnut knife (see "What Is It?" January/February 2000) or paring knife, so that steam can escape as the nuts heat up. (If you skip this step, the nuts will explode!) Toss the slashed nuts into the dry pan and shake them frequently over medium heat for 20 to 40 minutes, or until the shell begins to peel back at the "X." Just peel away the shell (you can use the chestnut knife for this, too) and enjoy them hot. The meat is yellow, sweet, and much softer than that of most other familiar nuts. If you plan on roasting some chestnuts this winter, you can order the Black Steel Chestnut Pan from Bridge Kitchenware (214 East 52nd Street, New York, NY 10022; 800-274-3435; item code APBS-CHES) for $19.95. Be sure to dry the pan well after washing; otherwise it will rust.

received a few more nods than the slightly tangy Nakano. The Chinese rice vinegar was not well received. Tasters were put off by its cloudiness and overly astringent taste. Driggs explained that the Japanese have a more highly developed production process and tighter quality control than the Chinese, so Chinese rice vinegars are usually of lesser quality.

I say Shrimp…

In my travels I have seen both "shrimp" and "prawns" on several menus, but when the dish is served, I can't detect any differences. Are they one and the same?

LEIGH SANDERS
CINCINNATI, OHIO

➤ To answer your question, we sought out the opinion of Sol Amon, long time fishmonger at Pure Food Fish Market in Seattle, Washington, and Susan Chamberlain, manager of the Global Aquaculture Alliance in St. Louis, Missouri. Both experts—one from the fishing industry, the other, the seafood farming industry—told us that while there are thousands of varieties of shrimp species, prawns and shrimp (both salt and freshwater) are indeed the same creatures. The words can be used interchangeably, though in the US, the word prawn is rarely seen or heard. Occasionally, it serves to describe what most Americans commonly know as jumbo shrimp. According to Mr. Amon, who sells both shrimp and prawns in his West Coast market, the word prawn is used as a marketing tactic to boost the mystique and interest of the larger crustaceans. In Canada and other English-speaking countries, the word shrimp is not used at all; all shrimp—jumbo, large, and medium—are known as prawns. Additional confusion may arise if you come across Dublin Bay Prawn on a menu. These so-called prawns, also called Norway Lobsters, lobsterettes, or scampi, resemble large shrimp but are really members of the lobster family. Unlike most common shrimp, Dublin Bay Prawns have hard, orange-red shells, bodies up to ten inches in length, and miniature pincer claws. And like lobster, they are usually cooked with heads and claws still attached for presentation—the claws are too small to yield any meat.

Errata

In the September/October 2000 *Resources* (page 32) the 2-quart All-Clad Stainless Steel saucepan from A Cook's Wares (item #2707) was listed at the wrong price. The price is $115. The last digit of the toll-free number for Edge Distributing in the chili powder item was left off. The number is 800-373-3726. Finally, if you call the toll free number listed to order Spice Island Chili Powder, don't be surprised when you reach Kmart, which can help you locate a Super Kmart store in your area that sells Spice Island spices. We apologize for the confusion.

Quick Tips

To celebrate the publication of our new book, *365 Quick Tips: Kitchen Tricks and Shortcuts to Make You a Faster, Smarter, Better Cook*, members of the magazine's editorial staff have chosen some of their favorite tips. Here are eight years' worth of our readers' best ideas, from the editors who use them.

Cutting Winter Squash

Pumpkins and winter squash are notoriously difficult to cut. The thick, tough skins and hard uncooked flesh resist the blade of even the best chef's knife. For butternut, the house favorite winter squash, Associate Editor Dawn Yanagihara hauls out a cleaver and mallet. It occasions a small ruckus, but the squash is quickly and easily cut.

1. Set the squash on a damp kitchen towel placed on top of a cutting board. Position the cleaver on the skin of the squash.
2. Strike the back of the cleaver with a mallet to drive the cleaver deep into the squash. Continue to hit the cleaver with the mallet until the cleaver cuts through the squash and opens it up.

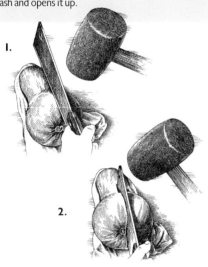

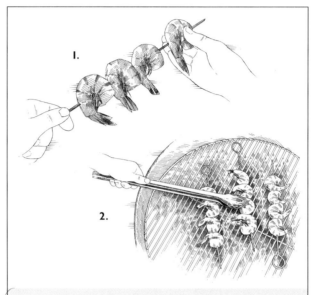

Preparing Shrimp for the Grill

Shrimp should be skewered before grilling to keep them from falling through the grate. However, every cook has been frustrated by shrimp that spin around on skewers and are impossible to turn. Senior Editor John Willoughby, who is addicted to grilled shrimp, adopted this approach to solve the problem.

1. Thread the shrimp by passing the skewer through the body near the tail, folding the shrimp over, and passing the skewer through the shrimp again near the head. Threading each shrimp twice keeps it in place (it won't spin around) and makes cooking the shrimp on both sides easier (the skewer needs to be turned just once).
2. Long-handled tongs make it easy to turn hot skewers on the grill. Lightly grab a single shrimp to turn the entire skewer.

Shredding Semisoft Cheese Neatly

Associate Editor Raquel Pelzel has a soft spot for interesting cheeses, such as raclette and smoked Gouda, especially in omelets and homemade pizzas. But grating such semisoft cheeses poses a unique challenge: How do you shred the cheese without mashing it onto the grater and clogging the holes? Here's how Raquel deals with this dilemma.

1. Use nonstick cooking spray to lightly coat the coarse side of a box grater.
2. Shred the cheese as usual. The cooking spray will keep the cheese from sticking to the surface of the grater.

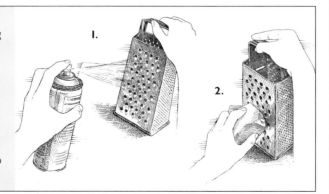

Improvised Mortar and Pestle

Senior Writer Jack Bishop often coats steaks with crushed peppercorns before grilling them. Stone, marble, wood, or porcelain mortars (bowls) and pestles (dowel-shaped grinding tools) are great for coarsely grinding peppercorns as well as chiles, spices, nuts, and herbs. Like many modern cooks, though, Jack doesn't own this handy tool. Here's how he makes a mortar and pestle with objects likely to be found in any kitchen.

Place the ingredients to be ground in a shallow, diner-style stoneware coffee cup (which will be the mortar) and use a heavy glass spice bottle as the pestle.

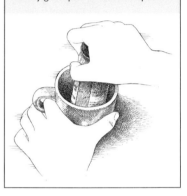

Releasing Basil's Flavorful Oils

Managing Editor Barbara Bourassa's husband, Marc, is addicted to pesto, so Barbara makes it just about every other week during the summer. It's easy to make pesto in a food processor or blender, but the fast grinding action of the blades doesn't create the richest tasting sauce. For the fullest flavor, Barbara finds it best to bruise the basil leaves before placing them in a food processor, thereby releasing all their flavorful oils. This trick also works with other soft herbs, especially mint and cilantro.

Place the basil leaves in a zipper-lock plastic bag and bruise with a meat pounder or rolling pin.

Preventing Scorched Pans When Steaming

Test Cook Julia Collin is sheepish to admit that on more than one occasion she has forgotten a pot of simmering water on the stove, allowing it to cook dry. The dry heat then ruins the pot and causes a dangerous situation. It's especially easy to forget a pot when steaming foods that take a long time to cook, such as artichokes. Here's a neat way to figure out when a simmering pot needs more water.

Before cooking, place a few glass marbles in the bottom of the pan. Add the water and steamer basket, cover, and cook as usual. When the water level drops too low, the marbles will begin to rattle around and the racket will remind you to add more water.

Measuring Brown Sugar

Although Assistant Editor Shannon Blaisdell doesn't mind getting her hands dirty while cooking, when a recipe calls for "firmly packed" brown sugar, she shuns the palm and finger method and instead uses two nested measuring cups to pack the sugar neatly, accurately, and quickly. The flat bottom of the smaller cup also helps to obliterate any hard clumps that may have developed in the bag.

For no-fuss measuring, fill the correct dry measure with brown sugar and use the next smallest cup to pack it down. For instance, if you need ½ cup firmly packed brown sugar, use the bottom of the ⅓ cup measure to pack it down.

Grating Butter into Flour

Editor Christopher Kimball found that many of his Vermont neighbors did not have food processors and were therefore unable to follow his directions for making the perfect pie pastry, which suggests cutting the butter into the flour by machine. Simply blending in the butter by hand or with a pastry blender is both difficult and unreliable, so he recommends the following method, which is more precise and can be done by hand.

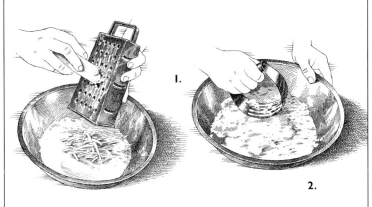

1. Rub a frozen stick of butter against the large holes of a regular box grater over the bowl with the flour.
2. Once all of the butter has been grated, use a pastry blender or two table knives to work the butter into the flour. Keep cutting the butter in until the flour turns slightly yellow and mealy.

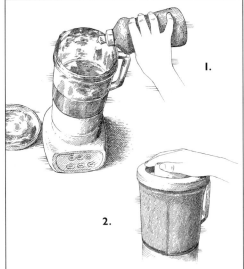

Quick-Cleaning a Blender

Embarrassing but true: Dishes often languish in Associate Editor Adam Ried's sink for a day before being washed. Hard remnants of this morning's smoothie stuck to the sides of the blender jar can make cleaning it a real chore, but things got a lot easier once Adam learned to get a head start on the cleaning process by following this method.

1. Fill the dirty blender halfway with hot water and add a couple of drops of liquid dish soap.
2. With the top firmly in place, turn the blender on high for 30 seconds. Most of the residue will pour right out with the soapy water, and the blender jar need only be rinsed or lightly washed by hand.

Cleaning the Grill Grate

There's nothing worse than having burgers or chicken pieces stick to the grill grate. To avoid this, we always let the cooking grate heat for several minutes and then clean it with a wire brush. But some foods, like fish, tend to stick to the grate more easily than others. To avoid a grilling catastrophe, Test Cook Bridget Lancaster dips a large wad of paper towels in vegetable oil, grabs the wad with tongs, and wipes the grid thoroughly to lubricate it and prevent sticking. This extra step also removes any remaining residue on the grate, which might mar the delicate flavor of fish.

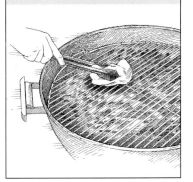

Judging Whipped Cream Status

Test Kitchen Director Kay Rentschler loves desserts—both making them and eating them! Nothing could be more central to desserts than whipped cream, whether used as an integral component of the dessert or as a simple garnish. But cream must be whipped to different stages for different applications. When it is folded into a dessert base, the recipe will generally call for "soft peaks." As a dessert garnish or piped decoration, cream is generally whipped enough to hold its shape, or "stiff peaks." Here is the trick Kay favors for determining when cream is perfectly whipped, whatever its ultimate destination.

1. Cream whipped to soft peaks will droop slightly from the ends of the beaters.
2. Cream whipped to stiff peaks will cling tightly to the ends of the beaters or whisk and hold its shape.

Better than Best Oven-Roasted Turkey

In our continuing search for the perfect roast turkey, we find a way to produce a bird with very crisp skin.

⊰ BY BRIDGET LANCASTER ⊱

You would think that by now we would have finished working on our roast turkey recipe. After all, it was back in November/December 1993 that we ran an article titled "The Holiday Turkey Perfected." The question we faced then was this: How do you produce a roasted bird with thoroughly cooked legs and moist, flavorful breast meat? Certainly, a tall order, but after roasting some 30 in a row, we had our answer.

First, we found that if we brined the turkey—that is, soaked it in a saltwater solution for an extended period—the breast meat stayed juicy throughout the allotted roasting time. In addition, we found that because the salt solution penetrates the meat, the meat was seasoned throughout, not just on the surface, as is the case with a traditionally seasoned bird.

Now we could concentrate on roasting the bird evenly. Turkeys roasted entirely breast-side up gave us overcooked breast meat. Butterflying the bird did nothing for aesthetics. We eventually found that using a rack to elevate the bird as well as starting the turkey breast-side down, turning it on either side, then finishing it breast-side up was the path to the most evenly cooked and nicely browned turkey.

Seven years later, this was the recipe we were still using—until recently. Here's what happened.

I was working on another turkey story and had one brined turkey left to roast, but the workday was coming to a close, so I decided to put off roasting it until the following morning. I placed the bird, uncovered, on a flat wire rack over a sheet pan and placed the pan in the refrigerator. The next morning I roasted the turkey according to the recipe, but the results were dramatically different. The skin was a deeper shade of brown and, more important, it was crackling crisp. The residual moisture left in the

An overnight stay in the refrigerator produced a bird with crackling crisp skin.

skin from brining had an opportunity to evaporate during the overnight rest in the refrigerator. The skin now crisped in the oven instead of steaming from the excess moisture.

This technique was similar to that used in our article on high-roast chicken (March/April 2000). Now, finally, we had the best-flavored, evenly cooked turkey with the crispiest skin.

So here is the updated version of our original turkey recipe. We've also updated the recipe for giblet pan gravy, finding that we preferred the taste and appearance of a sauce thickened with a dark roux (flour and melted butter cooked until it is rich brown) over our original cornstarch-thickened gravy. Last, we've included a stuffed turkey variation for those of you who prefer a stuffed holiday bird.

ROAST CRISPED-SKIN TURKEY
SERVES 10 TO 12

We prefer to roast small turkeys, no more than 14 pounds gross weight, because they cook more evenly than large birds. If you prefer, halve the amount of salt in the brine and brine 12 hours or overnight. When you remove the turkey from the oven to rotate it, be sure to close the oven door to prevent heat loss.

- 4 cups kosher salt or 2 cups table salt
- 1 turkey (12 to 14 pounds gross weight), rinsed thoroughly; giblets, neck, and tailpiece removed and reserved for gravy (see page 7)
- 3 medium onions, chopped coarse
- 2 small carrots, chopped coarse
- 2 celery ribs, chopped coarse
- 6 sprigs fresh thyme
- 6 tablespoons unsalted butter, melted

1. Dissolve salt in 2 gallons cold water in large stockpot or clean bucket. Add turkey and refrigerate or set in very cool spot (about 40 degrees) for 4 to 6 hours.

2. Remove turkey from salt water and rinse well under cool running water. Pat dry inside and out with paper towels. Place turkey breast-side up on flat wire rack set over rimmed baking sheet or roasting pan and refrigerate, uncovered, 8 to 24 hours.

3. Adjust oven rack to lowest position and heat oven to 400 degrees. Toss one-third of onions, carrots and celery with 2 sprigs thyme and 1 tablespoon butter in medium bowl; fill cavity with mixture. Tuck wings behind back; following illustrations 1 through 3, truss turkey.

4. Scatter remaining vegetables and thyme in shallow roasting pan; pour 1 cup water over vegetables. Prepare V-rack following illustration 4, page 7. Brush turkey breast with butter, then set turkey breast-side down on foil-lined V-rack. Brush back of turkey with butter. Roast 45 minutes.

5. Remove roasting pan with turkey from oven; brush back with butter. Using thick wads of paper towels or potholders, rotate turkey leg/wing–side up. If liquid in bottom of roasting pan has evaporated, add ½ cup water. Roast 15 minutes longer.

6. Remove roasting pan with turkey from oven, brush exposed surfaces with butter, and, using thick wads of paper towels or potholders, rotate turkey second leg/wing–side up; roast for 15 minutes longer.

7. Remove roasting pan with turkey from oven, brush exposed surfaces with butter and, using thick wads of paper towels or potholders, rotate turkey breast-side up. Roast until thickest part of

breast registers 165 degrees and thickest part of thigh registers 170 to 175 degrees on instant-read thermometer, 30 to 45 minutes longer. Move turkey from rack to carving board and let rest about 20 to 30 minutes. Carve and serve with gravy, if desired.

ROAST STUFFED CRISPED–SKIN TURKEY
SERVES 10 TO 12

Preheating in a microwave gives the stuffing a head start on cooking so that the turkey does not overcook as it waits for the stuffing to reach the proper internal temperature. A cheesecloth stuffing bag makes easy work of removing the stuffing when it's time to carve the bird.

    4   cups kosher or 2 cups table salt
    1   turkey (12 to 14 pounds gross weight), rinsed
        thoroughly, giblets, neck, and tailpiece removed
        and reserved for gravy
    2   medium onions, chopped coarse
    1   medium carrot, chopped coarse
    1   celery rib, chopped coarse
    4   thyme sprigs
    12 cups prepared stuffing
    4   tablespoons unsalted butter, melted, plus extra
        to grease baking dish

1. Follow recipe for Roast Crisped-Skin Turkey through step 2.

2. Adjust oven rack to lowest position and heat oven to 400 degrees. Scatter vegetables and thyme in shallow roasting pan; pour 1 cup water over vegetables. Prepare V-rack following illustration 4.

3. Place about 6 cups stuffing in medium microwave-safe bowl and cover with plastic wrap; microwave stuffing on high until stuffing registers 120 to 130 degrees on instant-read thermometer, about 6 minutes. Spoon hot stuffing into cavity of turkey; secure opening with turkey lacers or with skewers and kitchen twine. Tuck wings behind back; following illustrations 1 to 3, truss turkey. Brush breast with butter, then set turkey breast-side down on foil-lined V-rack; brush back with butter. Roast 1 hour, then reduce temperature to 250 degrees and roast 2 hours longer, adding more water to roasting pan if necessary. Meanwhile, place remaining stuffing in buttered 11 by 7-inch or 9-inch-square baking dish, cover with plastic wrap, and refrigerate until ready to use.

4. Remove roasting pan with turkey from oven; using thick wads of paper towels or potholders, rotate turkey breast-side up and brush with remaining butter. Increase oven temperature to 400 degrees; continue roasting until thickest part of breast registers about 165 degrees, thickest part of thigh registers 170 to 175 degrees, and stuffing registers 165 degrees on instant-read thermometer, 1 to 1½ hours longer. Remove turkey from oven and let rest until ready to carve.

5. While turkey is resting, unwrap baking dish with stuffing and bake until golden brown, about 35 minutes.

6. Carve turkey; serve with stuffing and gravy, if desired.

GIBLET PAN GRAVY
MAKES ABOUT 6 CUPS

To eliminate the rush to make gravy once the turkey emerges from the oven, you can make this gravy over several hours. Steps 1 and 2 can be completed while the turkey is brining. While the bird is roasting, proceed with step 3, then complete step 4 while the bird is resting.

    1   tablespoon vegetable oil
        Reserved turkey giblets, neck, and tailpiece
    1   onion, unpeeled and chopped
    6   cups turkey or chicken stock, or 4 cups canned
        low-sodium chicken broth plus 2 cups water
    2   sprigs fresh thyme
    8   parsley stems
    3   tablespoons unsalted butter
    ¼   cup all-purpose flour
    1   cup dry white wine
        Salt and ground black pepper

1. Heat oil in large heavy-bottomed saucepan over medium-high heat until shimmering but not smoking; add giblets, neck, and tail and sauté until golden, about 5 minutes. Add onion and cook, stirring occasionally, until softened, about 3 minutes. Reduce heat to low; cover and cook until turkey parts and onion release their juices, about 20 minutes. Add stock and herbs; increase heat to medium-high and bring to boil, then reduce heat to low and simmer, uncovered, skimming any scum that may rise to surface, until broth is rich and flavorful, about 30 minutes longer.

2. Strain broth (you should have about 5 cups), reserving heart and gizzard and discarding neck. When cool enough to handle, remove gristle from gizzard, then dice heart and reserved gizzard. Refrigerate giblets and broth until ready to use.

3. While turkey is roasting, bring reserved turkey broth to simmer in medium saucepan over medium heat. Heat butter in large heavy-bottomed saucepan over medium-low heat; when foam subsides, vigorously whisk in flour to make a roux. Cook slowly, stirring constantly, until nutty brown and fragrant, 10 to 15 minutes. Vigorously whisk all but 1 cup hot broth into roux. Increase heat to medium-high and bring to boil, then reduce heat to medium-low and simmer, stirring occasionally, until slightly thickened and flavorful, about 30 minutes longer. Set aside until turkey is done.

4. While turkey is resting on carving board, spoon out and discard as much fat as possible from roasting pan, leaving behind caramelized herbs and vegetables. Place roasting pan over two burners at medium-high heat (if drippings are not dark brown, cook, stirring constantly, until they caramelize). Return gravy in saucepan to simmer over medium heat. Add wine to roasting pan and scrape up browned bits clinging to pan bottom; boil until reduced by half, about 5 minutes. Add remaining 1 cup broth to roasting pan, then strain mixture into gravy, pressing on solids in strainer to extract as much liquid as possible. Stir in giblets, return to simmer. Adjust seasonings with salt and pepper; serve with turkey.

STEP-BY-STEP | PREPARING THE BIRD

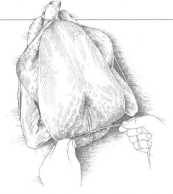
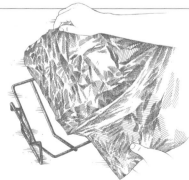

1. Using the center of a five-foot length of heavy kitchen twine, tie the legs together at the ankles.

2. Run the twine around the thighs and under the wings on both sides of the bird, pulling tightly.

3. Keeping the twine pulled snug, tie a firm knot around the excess flesh at the neck of the bird. Snip off excess twine.

4. Set V-rack in pan and line with heavy duty aluminum foil. Spray the foil with vegetable cooking spray, then pierce 20 to 30 small holes in the foil with a paring knife.

Improving Cornbread Stuffing

For best flavor and texture, dry the cornbread, add a little half-and-half,
and let it soak for at least an hour.

≥ BY JULIA COLLIN ≤

I come from upstate New York, where cornbread stuffing, like mint juleps and gumbo, always seemed an exotic, Southern culinary mystery. Recently, after leaving behind a pile of cornbread that should have been consumed along with the rest of my chili dinner, I decided to make a go of this classic dish. Though it did not measure up to my expectations, I was, frankly, interested. Banking on my innocent palate and unbiased heritage, I set out to make a cornbread stuffing with a toasted top, moist interior, and satisfyingly rich flavor.

After a few initial batches, I became aware of the principal problems with this dish. I found that most cornbread stuffings are much too dry. The cornbread turns into stale, loose nuggets that refuse to bind with any of the other ingredients. On the other end of the spectrum are stuffings that are too wet. They simply turn into a damp, sloppy mass. I wanted a moist and cohesive stuffing that wasn't soggy or greasy. While most recipes use stock, butter, and eggs to bind the stuffing ingredients together and add moisture, I wondered if there were any other options. Finally, there was quantity. None of the stuffings I had tried made nearly enough to handle a Thanksgiving crowd of 8 to 10 hungry people and to provide ample allowance for leftovers.

Letting the stuffing soak in a mixture of stock, eggs, and half-and-half ensures a rich, moist texture. A hot oven crisps the top.

Nailing Down the Cornbread

I decided it would be easiest to begin by finding out which type of cornbread is best suited for stuffing and then figure out how it should be prepared. Although there were differences of opinion, tasters generally preferred the rather fluffy, slightly sweet northern-style cornbread made with a recipe from our September/October 1995 issue.

Next I focused my attention on what to do with the cornbread once it was made. I made stuffings from cornbread that was whacked into small crumbs, cut into even-sized cubes, and torn into bite-sized pieces. The crumbs had a potent cornbread flavor, but the texture was mealy and unattractive. Although the cubed cornbread looked very tidy, it didn't carry the same flavorful punch as the crumbs. Tearing cornbread in bite-sized pieces, however, created enough crumbs to release the cornbread flavor, while the bigger pieces were toothsome and made for the most attractive dish.

I now made stuffings using fresh, toasted, and stale cornbread. The fresh cornbread turned soggy and bland, while the flavor of the toasted bread was overpowering. The hands-down winner of the lot was the stale bread, with its potent but not bullish flavor and pleasingly moist texture. (Drying fresh cornbread in a warm oven accomplishes the same thing.) With the main ingredient in the bag, I turned next to the binders.

Bind and Soak

Chicken stock, eggs, and pan drippings are the classic ingredients used to help moisten and bind a stuffing. After ruling out turkey drippings, which I use to make gravy, I tested stuffings made with stock and eggs on their own to see what exactly each did. As expected, the eggs thoroughly bound the ingredients so that each forkful of stuffing was cohesive. The stock added the necessary moisture and distinct poultry flavor. Obviously, a mixture of these two ingredients was key, but I also wanted to add something to the stuffing that would make it a bit richer and softer without turning it greasy or wet. Recalling an old cornbread pudding recipe, I tried pouring a little half-and-half into the mix. This was the missing link, turning a second-rate side dish into a medal winner. The stuffing took on an extraordinarily full, rich flavor without being oily or sodden.

Soaking stale bread is a classic technique. You are replacing the bread's lost moisture with something more flavorful. Wondering if an adaptation of this idea would move my stuffing along, I soaked the stale cornbread in the egg, stock, and cream mixture overnight. I then baked it and compared it with stuffings baked after an hour-long soak, a 30-minute soak, and no soaking at all.

As I had hoped, the differences in the stuffings were remarkable. The unsoaked stuffing tasted absolutely dull and lifeless when compared with the overnighter, and the 30-minute soaker was not nearly as good as the 60-minute one. While there was an obvious difference between the overnighter and the 60-minute version, it was far less than had I figured on. Because overnight soaking is inconvenient, I settled on one hour.

Now all I needed to do was round out the final flavors. Onions, celery, and fresh thyme and sage were a shoo-in. As I had expected, they all needed to be sautéed slightly before being mixed in with the cornbread. I tried adding a little wine or whiskey but found that their boozy flavor meddled with the rich flavor of the cornbread. Finally, some bulk pork sausage added nice pockets of texture and a meaty punch without overpowering the balance of flavors. Here was a cornbread stuffing that would match that of any southern grandmother. It almost seems a shame to hide it under a stream of gravy.

CORNBREAD AND SAUSAGE STUFFING
MAKES ABOUT 12 CUPS, SERVING 10 TO 12

In this recipe, the stuffing is baked outside of the turkey in a baking dish. If you want to stuff your turkey with it, prepare the stuffing through step 2, then follow the directions on page 7 for microwaving the stuffing. To make the stuffing a day in advance, increase both the chicken stock and half-and-half by ¼ cup each and refrigerate the unbaked stuffing 12 to 24 hours; before transferring it to the baking dish, let the stuffing stand at room temperature for about 30 minutes so that it loses its chill.

- 12 cups cornbread broken into 1-inch pieces (include crumbs), spread in even layer on 2 baking sheets, and dried in 250-degree oven 50 to 60 minutes
- 3   cups chicken stock or canned low-sodium chicken broth
- 2   cups half-and-half
- 2   large eggs, beaten lightly
- 8   tablespoons (1 stick) unsalted butter, plus extra for baking dish
- 1½ pounds bulk pork sausage, broken into 1-inch pieces
- 3   medium onions, chopped fine (about 3 cups)
- 3   ribs celery, chopped fine (about 1½ cups)
- 2   tablespoons minced fresh thyme leaves
- 2   tablespoons minced fresh sage leaves
- 3   garlic cloves, minced
- 1   tablespoon kosher salt
- 2   teaspoons ground black pepper

1. Place cornbread in large bowl. Whisk together stock, half-and-half, and eggs in medium bowl; pour over cornbread and toss very gently to coat so that cornbread does not break into smaller pieces. Set aside.

2. Heat heavy-bottomed, 12-inch skillet over medium-high heat until hot, about 1½ minutes. Add 2 tablespoons butter to pan and swirl to coat pan bottom. When foam subsides, add sausage and cook, stirring occasionally, until sausage loses its raw color, 5 to 7 minutes. With slotted spoon, transfer sausage to medium bowl. Add about half the onions and celery to fat in skillet; sauté, stirring occasionally, over medium-high until softened, about 5 minutes. Transfer onion mixture to bowl with sausage. Return skillet to heat and add remaining 6 tablespoons butter; when foam subsides, add remaining celery and onions and sauté, stirring occasionally, until softened, about 5 minutes. Stir in thyme, sage, and garlic; cook until fragrant, about 30 seconds; add salt and pepper. Add this mixture along with sausage and onion mixture to cornbread and stir gently to combine so that cornbread does not break into smaller pieces. Cover bowl with plastic wrap and refrigerate to blend flavors, at least 1 hour or up to 4 hours.

3. Adjust oven rack to lower-middle position and heat oven to 400 degrees. Butter 10 by 15-inch baking dish (or two 9-inch square or 11 by 7-inch baking dishes). Transfer stuffing to baking dish; pour any liquid accumulated in bottom of bowl over stuffing and, if necessary, gently press stuffing with rubber spatula to fit into baking dish. Bake until golden brown, 35 to 40 minutes.

SPICY CORNBREAD STUFFING WITH RED PEPPERS, CHIPOTLE CHILES, AND ANDOUILLE SAUSAGE

Andouille is a spicy smoked Cajun sausage. If you cannot find any, chorizo makes a fine substitute.

Follow recipe for Cornbread and Sausage Stuffing through step 1. In step 2, melt 4 tablespoons butter in heated skillet; when foam subsides, add 2 red bell peppers, cut into ¼-inch pieces, to skillet along with a third of the onion and celery. Sauté until softened, about 5 minutes, and transfer to medium bowl. Return skillet to heat and add remaining 4 tablespoons butter; when foam subsides, add remaining onion and celery and sauté, stirring occasionally, until softened, about 5 minutes. Stir in 4 to 5 chipotle chiles en adobo, chopped (about 4 tablespoons), along with thyme, sage, and garlic. Add this mixture, along with sautéed onions and celery and 1½ pounds andouille sausage, cut into ½-inch pieces, into cornbread and mix gently so that cornbread does not break into smaller pieces. Cover and refrigerate as directed in step 2; proceed with step 3 to bake stuffing.

GOLDEN CORNBREAD
MAKES ABOUT 16 CUPS CRUMBLED CORNBREAD

If you are using this cornbread for your stuffing, you will use about three-quarters of the recipe—the rest is for nibbling.

- 4   large eggs
- 1⅓ cups buttermilk
- 1⅓ cups milk
- 2   cups yellow cornmeal, preferably stone-ground
- 2   cups all-purpose flour
- 4   teaspoons baking powder
- 1   teaspoon baking soda
- 2   tablespoons sugar
- 1   teaspoon salt
- 4   tablespoons unsalted butter, melted, plus extra for greasing baking dish

1. Adjust oven rack to middle position and heat oven to 375 degrees. Grease 9 by 13-inch baking dish with butter.

2. Beat eggs in medium bowl; whisk in buttermilk and milk.

3. Whisk cornmeal, flour, baking powder, baking soda, sugar, and salt together in large bowl. Push dry ingredients up sides of bowl to make a well, then pour egg and milk mixture into well and stir with whisk until just combined; stir in butter.

4. Pour batter into greased baking dish. Bake until top is golden brown and edges have pulled away from sides of pan, 30 to 40 minutes.

5. Transfer baking sheet to wire rack and cool to room temperature before using, about 1 hour.

Tasting Boxed Cornbread Mixes

The Winner

We all are on the lookout for shortcuts around the holidays, and I was not about to overlook cornbread mixes. I tried my recipe with six well-respected mixes and liked the results I got with one of them.

Martha White's Yellow Cornbread Mix was the champion, achieving a beautiful, golden crust, a well-balanced cornbread flavor, and toothsome texture. Betty Crocker's Golden Corn Muffin and Bread Mix and Jiffy's Corn Muffin Mix were the sweetest of the bunch, inspiring comments such as "candy sweet" and "dessert stuffing." The other Martha White entries, including the Buttermilk and Cotton Pickin' Cornbread Mixes, along with White Lily White Cornbread Mix, resembled one another closely, with their sweet, pale crust and soggy, cakelike texture.

The problem with Martha White Yellow Cornbread Mix is that it is sold only in a few lucky states. Unless it graces the shelves of your local store, you'd best roll up your sleeves and put together a batch of our Golden Cornbread. –J.C.

Roasted Pear Salads

High heat, butter, and sugar transform underripe pears into
the centerpieces of unusual and delicious winter salads.

≥ BY RAQUEL PELZEL ≤

Clearly the carefree, melon-eating days of summer are long gone. But that doesn't mean you should give up fruit. Take pears, for example. Even hard and unfragrant specimens have the capacity to become juicy and butterscotch-brown after a brief spell in a blazing oven. Add them to bitter greens with some sharp cheese, and you have an impressive salad to either dress up a buffet table or serve as a side dish with a light meal.

My defining parameters for a simple roasted pear salad were elementary: the roasted pears should be slightly al dente, sweet but not syrupy, and caramel-colored on both sides. I first needed to narrow down my playing field—which pear would beget the best roasting results? I roasted one batch each of Anjou, Bartlett, and Bosc (chosen for their availability during the winter) and asked my colleagues to help me pare down the list. While tasters were torn between Anjou (delicate pear flavor with a grainy texture and good bite) and Bartlett (soft texture with a floral pear essence), the big loser was Bosc (mealy, dry, and flat-tasting).

Determining that either Bartlett or Anjou could be used, I turned to the question of slicing. Too thin a slice and the pear wouldn't hold up to the roasting process, but, if too thickly cut, the pear would be awkward to bite into, especially in a salad. I found my solution at a thickness of about ⅓ inch, or roughly five slices per half.

Next I tossed the thinly sliced, raw pears with various brews of fats, oils, wines, and broths and roasted them for 20 minutes at 425 degrees. Even though butter bestowed the highest glories on the pear, the flavor and color were still slack. So I upped the oven temperature to 500 degrees, decreased the roasting time by five minutes, and decided to turn the pears three-quarters of the way through roasting (at halfway through, the pears hadn't browned enough on their first side). To help draw out their untapped sweetness, I sprinkled some sugar onto the butter-coated pears prior to roasting. Not only were these roasted pears sweet and juicy, but, with the help of sugar to accelerate the caramelization process, they positively glistened.

The pears may be roasted up to three hours in advance, but keep them at room temperature till ready to serve; refrigeration adversely affects their texture.

ROASTED PEARS

- 4 firm Anjou or Bartlett pears (about 2 pounds)
- 1 tablespoon unsalted butter, melted
- 2 tablespoons sugar

1. Adjust oven rack to lower-middle position, place baking sheet or broiler pan bottom on rack, and heat oven to 500 degrees.

2. Peel and halve each pear lengthwise. With paring knife or melon baller, remove core. Set each half cut-side down and slice lengthwise into fifths.

3. Toss pears with butter; add sugar and toss again to combine. Spread pears in single layer on preheated baking sheet, making sure each slice lies flat on surface. Roast until browned on bottom, about 10 minutes. Flip each slice and roast until tender and deep golden brown, about 5 minutes longer. Let pears cool while preparing salad.

ROASTED PEAR AND BEET SALAD WITH WATERCRESS AND BLUE CHEESE
SERVES 4 TO 6

This salad is great served with warm pears. Roast the pears immediately after the beets and toss them into the salad while still warm.

- 3 small or 2 medium beets (about 12 ounces)
- 1½ tablespoons extra-virgin olive oil
- 1 teaspoon red wine vinegar
- ½ teaspoon salt
  Ground black pepper
- 4 ounces blue cheese, crumbled
- 1 recipe Roasted Pears
- 2 bunches watercress, washed, dried, and stemmed (about 6 cups)

1. Adjust oven rack to lower-middle position; heat oven to 350 degrees. Wrap each beet in foil and roast until fork can be inserted and removed with little resistance, 1 to 1½ hours; unwrap beets. When cool enough to handle, peel and cut beets lengthwise into quarters; cut each quarter in half into wedges.

2. Whisk together oil, vinegar, salt, and pepper to taste in small bowl.

3. Combine beets, blue cheese, and watercress in large serving bowl. Add pears and vinaigrette; toss gently to combine. Serve immediately.

ARUGULA AND ROASTED PEAR SALAD WITH WALNUTS AND PARMESAN CHEESE
SERVES 4 TO 6

Warm pears work nicely in this salad, too.

- 1½ tablespoons extra-virgin olive oil
- 2 teaspoons white wine vinegar
- ½ teaspoon salt
  Ground black pepper
- 2 bunches arugula, stems removed, washed, dried, and torn into bite-sized pieces (about 7 cups)
- 1 recipe Roasted Pears
- 4 ounces Parmesan cheese, shaved into thin strips with vegetable peeler
- 1 cup walnuts, chopped coarse and toasted in small dry skillet over medium heat until lightly browned and fragrant, about 3 minutes

1. Whisk together oil, vinegar, salt, and pepper to taste in small bowl.

2. Combine arugula, pears, and Parmesan in large serving bowl. Add vinaigrette and toss gently to combine; sprinkle with chopped walnuts. Serve immediately.

ROMAINE AND ROASTED PEAR SALAD WITH FENNEL AND LEMON–MINT VINAIGRETTE
SERVES 4 TO 6

- 1½ tablespoons extra-virgin olive oil
- 1 tablespoon minced fresh mint leaves
- 1 teaspoon grated zest plus 1½ tablespoons juice from 1 lemon
- ½ teaspoon salt
  Ground black pepper
- 1 head romaine lettuce, washed, dried, and torn into bite-sized pieces (about 8 cups loosely packed)
- 1 small fennel bulb (about 8 ounces), stems, fronds, and base trimmed; bulb halved, cored and sliced as thinly as possible (about 1¼ cups)
- 1 recipe Roasted Pears

1. Whisk together oil, mint, lemon zest and juice, salt, and pepper to taste in small bowl.

2. Combine romaine and fennel in large serving bowl. Add vinaigrette and toss gently to combine; scatter pears on top. Serve immediately.

Roast Stuffed Pork Loin Perfected

We solved the three classic problems with this holiday roast: tough, dry meat; dull, flavorless stuffing; and a sloppy, pale appearance.

≥ BY ADAM RIED ≤

In my decidedly foodie family, the debate over what to make for Christmas dinner usually begins while we do the Thanksgiving dishes. Both my sister and I consistently favor pork, but a simple roasted loin never seemed sufficiently celebratory. Fill the meat with a flavorful, interesting stuffing, however, and that roast is elevated to an opulent centerpiece for a holiday meal. With the stuffing nestled inside the meat, as opposed to sitting in a heap on the side, the flavors have a chance to mingle and embrace each other, and the presentation becomes truly impressive. After all, this is no quick Tuesday night supper — this is the holidays.

When most Americans think of a pork roast, it's a boneless center-cut loin roast that comes to mind. Though this cut is particularly well suited for stuffing and roasting because it is both tender and evenly shaped and cooks quickly, our past experiences with roast stuffed pork loin have been fraught with the same problems every time. First is the danger that the meat will become dry, tough, and overcooked by the time the stuffing is done. Second is a stuffing with dull flavor or poor texture. Third is a sloppy appearance and stuffing that oozes out from the ends of the roast during cooking, both the result of haphazard tying of the roast.

When I consulted the *Cook's* library for recipes that might deal with these problems, though, all I found was confusion. Methods for stuffing and cooking the meat were as disparate as the ingredients in the recipes, which varied wildly from meat to bread to fruit to nuts to greens—and countless combinations thereof. A few rounds in the *Cook's* test kitchen, I hoped, would clear the way to a tender, juicy, flavorful, substantial, and neat roast stuffed pork loin.

Meat Management

Boneless loin roasts are the typical and—according to our testing—best choice for stuffing because they consist largely of a single, uniformly shaped muscle that is easy to stuff and roast neatly. None of the other cuts the test kitchen considered for stuffing seemed as appropriate. These were the

Rather than a thin layer of stuffing rolled up inside the pork jelly-roll style, we wanted an ample stuffing suitable for the holiday table.

ham, either fresh or cured (but that's a different dish entirely), the shoulder (which is composed of too many separate muscles and fatty deposits), and the crown roast (which is truly an ordeal to form, fasten, and cook). When we started testing, though, our first few trips to the market revealed that not all boneless loin roasts are the same. We had to communicate clearly and specifically with the supermarket meat manager or butcher to get roasts with a large circumference, which was key for manageable stuffing and roasting (see "The Right Roast," page 12, for more information).

Even when we got the roast we wanted, though, our first few tests turned out dry, tough, tasteless meat. It's no secret that today's pork is considerably leaner, and therefore less flavorful and juicy, than that of a generation ago. The effects of this lack of fat are compounded in the loin, which is in any case one of the leaner cuts from the animal.

To solve our problems, we had to embrace two proven test kitchen techniques, while eschewing a third. Soaking the meat in a salt and sugar brine was one technique we welcomed. This treatment offered dual benefits: The salt and sugar seasoned the meat and helped to keep it juicy as it cooked. The second useful technique was butterflying and pounding. Butterflying, or cutting the roast in the center and opening it like a book, proved to be the best way to prepare it for stuffing. We were determined to provide every diner with a generous amount of stuffing, and butterflied loins hold more of the mixture than roasts stuffed by means of the other methods we tried, including boring a hole through the center of the roast with a knife and sharpening steel, making a "Y" cut to create space in the center, slitting the loin from the bottom, and studding the meat with its filling. Pounding the butterflied roast further maximized the amount of stuffing we could use by increasing the meat's surface area. Pounding also helped to even out the thickness of the meat and, in test after test, proved to tenderize it as well.

The one common cooking technique recommended for this recipe that we discarded was to sear the stuffed roast in a pan on the stovetop to brown the meat before roasting. Not only did the large roasts we were using complicate this process, but a series of tests revealed that putting this now-thin cut of meat in direct contact with a blazing-hot pan toughened it. Instead, we developed an alternative means of coloring the roast—brushing it with a sweet glaze that caramelized in the oven. The glaze also added flavor and moisture.

Our last hedge against tough pork was to avoid overcooking it. As we usually do in the test kitchen, we aimed for a final internal temperature of 145 to 150 degrees, at which point the meat would be fully cooked yet retain a slightly rosy hue inside.

Stuffing Studies

Having successfully completed our inquiries into matters of the meat, we turned our efforts to the stuffing. We tried all the usual stuffing bases, including ground meat, sausage, bread (fresh and dried, crumbs and cubes), fruit (dried and fresh, whole and pureed), ground nuts, greens, and herbs. Stuffings based on fruit, nuts, greens, or herbs struck us as unsubstantial. They didn't add the panache that the star of a holiday meal needs. We preferred to use dried fruit and nuts as accents in a heartier mixture.

We tried sausage, but found it was seasoned too assertively. Ground pork showed promise. The problem with the ground pork stuffing was that it had to reach an internal temperature of 160 degrees to eliminate the possibility of bacterial contamination. If harmful bacteria are present at all, they settle on the exterior of a cut of meat. When that cut is ground, however, the bacteria spread throughout the meat, inside and out. Hence the need for a high internal temperature. Unfortunately, by the time the stuffing was at 160 degrees, the meat around it had reached almost 195 degrees and was tough as a tire. We tried precooking the meat stuffing, but this caused it to develop an unpleasantly loose, crumbly texture and a gritty mouthfeel.

Undaunted, we developed a fresh bread stuffing with terrific flavor and a firm, sliceable, but still supple texture. This stuffing did its part for the roast's appearance, too, refraining from the leaking and oozing characteristic of many of the other mixtures we tried. Good as it was, though, safety concerns about its use of egg as a binder still necessitated a finished internal temperature of 160 degrees. When eggs are cooked alone, any bacteria present are killed at a lower temperature. In stuffing, however, other ingredients buffer the bacteria from the heat, so the final temperature must be higher (that is, 160 degrees). This was a problem because the dense bread stuffing heated more slowly than the meat stuffing had. No matter what oven temperature or rack position we tried, the stuffing lagged behind the pork by roughly 30 degrees. When

the stuffing had reached 140 degrees, the meat was overcooked at 170 degrees.

With a single bold move, we were able to eliminate that temperature differential completely. Looking back on the lessons we learned in the November/December 1997 article "How to Perfectly Roast a Stuffed Turkey," and recalling that the reason our previous efforts at precooking stuffing had failed was because of the meat, we decided to precook our bread stuffing. We used the time during which the pork was resting in its brine to mix up the stuffing and shape it into a log that would fit easily into the butterflied meat. We then baked the log for 45 minutes in a moderate oven.

This technique was a coup. The prebaked stuffing reached a temperature of 200 degrees with its flavor and texture undamaged, thus taking care of any safety concerns. Even though the idea of handling hot stuffing was off-putting, the reality of it was surprisingly easy. Because we had preshaped the stuffing into a cylinder, we could roll it right off the baking sheet and onto the meat without even touching it. And even though the temperature of the stuffing dropped about 70 degrees during the stuffing process, the meat and stuffing kept an almost equal pace when they began to heat up in the oven, finishing within just 5 degrees of each other. This technique makes careful timing an important element in the recipe, but the results are well worth the effort.

Fastening Fashion

The first few roasts we stuffed and tied looked more like something from a flaky midnight monster movie than dinner in a classic holiday rerun. For the uninitiated, packaging the stuffed roast into a neat cylinder can be quite the challenge. So we came up with an easier method.

We found that bamboo skewers, broken in half and used to fasten the sides of the meat around the stuffing, provided terrific temporary support. The skewers also helped to hold the stuffed roast together when we tied it.

Our final refinement came in the tying itself. I'm all thumbs when it comes to manipulating a single long piece of twine into a series of butcher's knots around a roast. But with the roast held together by its skewers, I could actually cut separate, shorter pieces of twine and tie them one at a time at even intervals along the length of the roast. The resulting professional look of my roasts was a happy shock.

At long last, my sister and I will get a show-stopping roast stuffed pork loin for Christmas dinner this year.

ROAST PORK LOIN WITH APRICOT, FIG, AND PISTACHIO STUFFING
SERVES 8 TO 10

Timing is important. The goal is to coordinate brining and stuffing so that the pork is out of the brine and ready to be stuffed when the pre-cooked stuffing comes out of the oven. To achieve this, begin preparing the stuffing ingredients immediately after setting the pork in the brine. Bamboo skewers, available in supermarkets (or see Resources, page 32), are our favorite way to fasten the roast around the stuffing. Alternatively, use poultry lacers (though they are generally sold only six to a package). The apricot preserves for the glaze can be melted in the microwave instead of on the stovetop. To do so, heat the preserves in a small, microwave-safe bowl, covered loosely with plastic wrap, at full power until melted, about 40 seconds.

Roast
- 1   4½ pound boneless pork loin roast, from the blade end

Brine
- ¾   cup sugar
- ¾   cup kosher salt (or 6 tablespoons table salt)
- 3   bay leaves, crumbled
- 1   tablespoon whole allspice berries, lightly crushed
- 1   tablespoon whole black peppercorns, lightly crushed
- 10   medium garlic cloves, lightly crushed and peeled

Stuffing
- 5   cups roughly torn 1-inch pieces baguette (not sourdough) (7 to 8 ounces), from one loaf
- ½   cup dried apricots (about 4 ounces)
- 1   medium garlic clove, peeled
-     Pinch ground cumin
-     Pinch ground coriander
-     Pinch ground cinnamon
-     Pinch cayenne

The Right Roast

The pork loin runs from the shoulder of the hog down the back to the ham in the rear. While every hog is different, most whole boneless loins measure roughly 30 inches long and weigh in the range of 8 to 12 pounds when they reach the butcher shop or supermarket meat department. There they are broken down into the 2- to 3-pound roasts typically available in the meat case. Most important for this recipe is the loin's shape, which is wide near the shoulder, or blade, end, and tapers to a thinner silhouette at the center.

In the process of cooking more than 50 loin roasts for this article, we learned from experience that boneless center loin roasts of the same weight can have entirely different dimensions, depending on the section of the loin from which they were cut. To be successful in our efforts, we had to use roasts cut from the wider blade end of the loin. These blade-end center loin roasts offered more surface area once butterflied and were much easier to stuff than those from the slender center section. Both of the roasts shown here, for example, weigh 4½ pounds, but the center-cut roast, right, has a circumference of 3 inches at its widest point and a whopping 19-inch length, making it a poor choice for stuffing. With its generous 4-inch circumference and shorter 13-inch length, the blade-end center loin roast, left, is a much better choice for this recipe. Because large, 4½-pound roasts are rare in the meat case, you'll probably have to ask the butcher to cut it for you. Ask for the blade end of the largest loin available. —A.R.

1. Using a boning knife, trim the tough silver skin from the pork loin.

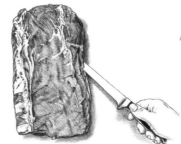

2. Lay the loin on the cutting board and begin to slice laterally through the center, starting at the thinner edge.

3. As you slice, open the meat as you would a book. Stop slicing 1 inch shy of the edge to create a "hinge."

4. Cover the surface with plastic wrap and pound the meat to a 1-inch thickness.

5. Cut eight 24-inch pieces of kitchen twine. Break nine 10- or 12-inch bamboo skewers in half.

6. Roll the hot stuffing onto the center of the butterflied pork, over the hinge.

7. Bring both sides of the meat together over the stuffing and fasten at the center with one skewer. Fasten the roast with the remaining skewers placed at regular intervals.

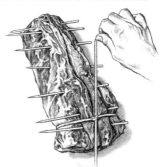

8. Shimmy lengths of twine one by one down the roast and tie them between the skewers, as shown. Trim the twine and remove the skewers before roasting.

---

2 tablespoons grated onion from 1 small onion
½ cup dried figs, halved lengthwise (about 3 ounces)
½ cup shelled pistachios (about 3 ounces), toasted in medium skillet over medium heat until color deepens slightly, 3 to 5 minutes, then cooled and chopped coarse
2 teaspoons minced fresh thyme leaves
2 tablespoons minced fresh parsley leaves
1½ teaspoons kosher salt (or 1 teaspoon table salt)
  Ground black pepper
2 large eggs
½ cup heavy cream

Glaze
½ cup apricot preserves

1. Following illustrations 1 through 4, trim, butterfly, and pound pork loin to even 1-inch thickness with mallet or bottom of heavy skillet.

2. *For the brine:* In a large, wide bowl, dissolve sugar and salt in 3 cups hot water. Add bay, allspice, peppercorns, garlic, and 5 cups cold water; stir to combine. Add butterflied and pounded pork; cover bowl with plastic wrap and refrigerate until fully seasoned, about 1½ hours. Remove pork from brine, pick spices off meat, and dry pork thoroughly with paper towels.

3. *For the stuffing and glaze:* Once the pork is in the brine, adjust oven rack to lower-middle position and heat oven to 325 degrees. Process half the bread pieces in workbowl of food processor fitted with steel blade until broken into crumbs with few pieces no larger than about ¼ inch, about 45 seconds; transfer to large mixing bowl and set aside. Repeat process with remaining bread pieces (you should have about 4 cups crumbs total).

4. In now-empty workbowl, process apricots, garlic, cumin, coriander, cinnamon, and cayenne until finely ground, about 30 seconds; add mixture to reserved bread crumbs. Add onion, figs, pistachios, thyme, parsley, salt, and pepper to taste to bread crumb and apricot mixture; toss until well distributed, breaking up any apricot clumps as necessary. Beat eggs and cream in small bowl; pour over bread and apricot mixture and toss with hands until evenly moistened and a portion of mixture holds together when pressed.

5. On parchment paper–lined cookie sheet or inverted rimmed baking sheet, form stuffing into log shape equal in length to butterflied pork. Cover stuffing with foil and bake until firm and cooked through and butterflied pork has been removed from brine and prepared for stuffing, about 45 minutes. Remove stuffing from oven; increase oven temperature to 450 degrees.

6. While stuffing bakes, heat apricot preserves in small saucepan over medium-low heat, stirring occasionally, until melted but not liquefied, 5 to 7 minutes. Strain through small strainer into small bowl (you should have about ⅓ cup) and set aside; discard solids in strainer.

7. *To stuff, roast, and glaze the roast:* Line shallow roasting pan or rimmed baking sheet with foil, position flat wire roasting rack over foil, and set aside. Following illustrations 5 through 8, stuff, roll, fasten, and tie pork loin. Place stuffed roast on rack, brush one-half apricot glaze evenly over exposed surface of meat and roast 20 minutes. Remove roast from oven and, with tongs, rotate roast so that bottom side faces up. Brush exposed surface with remaining apricot glaze; return roast to oven and roast 25 minutes longer (glaze should be medium golden brown and internal temperature of both meat and stuffing should register 145 to 150 degrees on instant-read thermometer). Transfer roast to carving board, tent with foil, and let rest 5 minutes. Cut off twine, slice, and serve.

ROAST PORK LOIN WITH APRICOT, CHERRY, AND PECAN STUFFING

Follow recipe for Roast Pork Loin with Apricot, Fig, and Pistachio Stuffing, substituting ½ cup dried tart cherries for figs and ½ cup coarsely chopped toasted pecans for pistachios in stuffing mixture.

ROAST PORK LOIN WITH APRICOT, PRUNE, AND PINE NUT STUFFING

Follow recipe for Roast Pork Loin with Apricot, Fig, and Pistachio Stuffing, substituting ½ cup pitted prunes, halved lengthwise, for figs and ½ cup toasted pine nuts for pistachios in stuffing mixture.

Shrimp Bisque Simplified

We take a circus of recipes and come up with a class act that relies on an unusual approach to extract flavor from the shrimp.

⋟ BY KAY RENTSCHLER WITH JULIA COLLIN ⋞

Shrimp bisque takes me into wintry midweek in Montreal, small basement restaurants and tables of dark suits. My mind must wander out of the country or back 20 years because Americans don't eat soups with shellfish and cream these days, let alone make them at home. Yet the first rush of brandy flaming over shrimp shells drew me back: that fine French fragrance reminded me of learning to cook and of how magical nearly forgotten smells and tastes can be.

Though a bisque by implication is any soup that is rich, velvety, and smooth, by definition it contains shellfish, cream, and the classic French aromatic trio of celery, carrot, and onion (known as *mirepoix)*. Shrimp bisque, in particular, should be a rich, blushing pastel—delicate in character but deeply intense—with an almost sweet shrimp essence and an elusive interplay of other flavors that couldn't be identified in a lineup. Its texture must run unfettered and silky over the tongue. If you are very lucky, there will be tender pieces of poached shrimp and shatteringly crisp, buttery croutons. As is the case with most French food, eating too much will make you feel sick.

I used to believe that a complicated recipe signaled an authentic recipe, a good recipe. Over the years, however, I have realized that while some culinary events require an odyssey of written words to accompany them, long recipes are often ill-conceived, poorly organized, or simply pompous. That was pretty much my take on the five different modern shrimp bisque recipes the test kitchen put together for this story. The recipes took hours. They featured a parade of kitchen tools, near-endless numbers of ingredients, and a cacophony of pots and lids. At the end of the day, we had dirtied every pot, spoon, and strainer in the kitchen—and were trying to give away five very average shrimp bisques to our colleagues.

The fundamental challenge in making a shrimp bisque is extracting flavor from the shrimp and shells. The recipes we tested did this in a couple of ways. Some pureed the shrimp meat into the

To flambé on a gas stove, add brandy to the reserved shrimp and shells, tilting the pan toward the flame to ignite it and then shaking the skillet.

base and left it there, others simmered the shrimp in the base until spent and then strained them out. The bisques made with pureed shrimp were grainy with shrimp curds; the ones in which the shrimp were strained out achieved the velvety texture properly associated with a bisque.

Because the shrimp flavor resides more in the shells than in the meat, a bisque made with shrimp alone is weak and unsatisfying. But trying to deal with shells and meat to the advantage of each tends to induce procedural overkill. The recipes that we tested got carried away by having several pots and pans active at once (here a little pot of simmering aromatics, here fish stock simmering with shells and rice, there a pan to sauté shrimp) rather than proceeding one step at

a time in logical sequence. One recipe, for example, sautéed shell-on shrimp to start and later simmered it in wine, broth, and previously sautéed aromatics. At that point the shrimp were peeled. Because the flavor from the shells had not been sufficiently extracted, a shrimp butter was advised. That involved crushing the shells to a paste, infusing them with butter, and straining them out. The resulting resolidified butter was stirred into the bisque at the end. Though arguably authentic, the technique was absurdly complicated and rendered a finished bisque far too rich for our tastes today.

My colleague and I talked strategy. The shrimp were key; other ingredients must add background depth and nuance. Fresh shell-on shrimp are virtually unavailable in the United States; those which are not frozen are usually not fresh but simply thawed. Size was not an issue because the shrimp are in effect sacrificed to the bisque. I thought it reasonable to recommend whatever variety of shell-on shrimp could be found in the freezer case. (Though brand differences did not prove overwhelming, as it turned out, the nicest bisques were produced with white Gulf shrimp.)

We began by taking two pounds of shrimp, shelling eight ounces worth, and putting them aside to use later as a garnish. We then heated a splash of oil in a heavy Dutch oven. Working in two batches, we sautéed the remaining shell-on shrimp until they reached a blistering pink. To wring every drop of flavor from the shells, we then flambéed the shrimp in brandy. Next we took the sautéed shrimp, dumped it into a food processor, and ground it to a pulp. Because we knew the shrimp and the shells were destined to be strained from the bisque, a food processor was the fastest way to unlock the shrimp's flavor potential.

Our next step was to sauté the shrimp pulp with a mirepoix in the same Dutch oven. After five minutes, we stirred in a bit of flour, preferring its convenience to rice or bread for thickening. Next came white wine, drained diced tomatoes, and some clam juice. After 20 minutes or so we strained the fragrant base through a cheesecloth-lined sieve, pressing to extract every drop. It looked like flowing silk Shantung.

Back on the stove we offered the soup base a bit of cream, sherry, fresh tarragon, and then the remaining shrimp, cut into pieces. A brief simmer poached the shrimp garnish and brought the flavors into harmony. We chucked the tarragon and added a couple of drops of lemon and a grain or two of cayenne. This bisque possessed everything we demanded of it: flavor in spades and a peerless texture and color.

And so it seemed we had a one-pot wonder. But we had to admit, a skillet would beat a Dutch oven at sautéing the shrimp and make the flambéing more manageable. OK. So now it was a two-pot wonder, but a very quick one—and a very good one. No one will ever suspect you used only two pots.

RICH AND VELVETY SHRIMP BISQUE
MAKES 6 CUPS, SERVING 4 TO 6

Shrimp shells contribute a lot of flavor to the bisque, so be sure to purchase shell-on shrimp. Large 21- to 25-count shrimp are a good size to use. If your food processor is small and your shrimp are extralarge, process them in two batches. For straining the bisque, if you do not own a chinois, use a china cap or large sturdy mesh strainer lined with a double layer of damp cheesecloth.

- 2 pounds shell-on shrimp, preferably Gulf or Mexican Whites
- 3 tablespoons olive oil
- 1/3 cup brandy or cognac, warmed
- 2 tablespoons unsalted butter
- 1 small carrot, chopped fine (about 3 tablespoons)
- 1 small rib celery, chopped fine (about 3 tablespoons)
- 1 small onion, minced (about 6 tablespoons)
- 1 medium garlic clove, minced
- 1/2 cup all-purpose flour
- 1 1/2 cups dry white wine
- 4 (8-ounce) bottles clam juice (4 cups)
- 1 (14 1/2-ounce) can diced tomatoes, drained
- 1 small sprig fresh tarragon
- 1 cup heavy cream
- 1 tablespoon juice from 1/2 lemon
  Pinch ground cayenne
- 2 tablespoons dry sherry or Madeira
  Salt and ground black pepper

1. Peel 1/2 pound shrimp, reserving shells, and cut each peeled shrimp into thirds. With paper towels, thoroughly pat dry remaining shrimp and reserved shells.

2. Heat 12-inch heavy-bottomed skillet over high heat until very hot, about 3 minutes. Add

The Princess and the Prawn

The first measure of a bisque's charm lies in its texture. Stray bits or fibers of food remaining in its base, however inscrutable, will give the tongue pause—what was that? If teeth must be enlisted to identify these bits, the relationship between soup and sipper is hopelessly compromised. No, a bisque must be luxuriously smooth to a fault. To make this fairy tale texture come true, I knew the means and methods of straining would be key. We set up a few tests in the kitchen to see what would produce the best results.

This chinois (1) with a mesh-protecting steel band is traditionally the preferred companion when producing flawlessly fine sauces and soups. Its silvery houndstooth screen is so fine that liquids must be forced through the solids with repetitive motions from the back of a ladle. But its woven mesh is supple, almost elastic, in fact, and takes a good pounding with aplomb—and no stress on the wrist. Its long conical shape is also a blessing when trying to concentrate a stream of liquid into the desired receptacle rather than out onto the counter. The puree it produced was immaculately fine.

This fine china cap (2) boasts a conical shape, like the chinois, but has perforations rather than a screen. This makes it ideal for straining hot, thin liquids through bones or vegetables. But its relatively small area of open spaces and rigid metal structure presents the ladle with quite a bit of resistance when up against the thicker bisque base. The resulting liquid contained myriad small bits of pureed shrimp and vegetables.

This fine-meshed strainer (3) is far shallower than the two conical strainers and had to be used accordingly. A circular motion with the ladle was most efficient for coaxing the liquid through the solids while keeping it within the perimeter of the strainer. Though it was not as easy to push the last few drops of liquid through the solids as with the chinois, the resulting puree was faultlessly smooth.

We lined this strainer (4) with a damp cheesecloth, arranged in layers throughout the interior of the strainer and overlapping its edges slightly. The cheesecloth trapped stray bits and sediment in its fibers, leaving a supersmooth base. But cheesecloth is not without its problems. It can slip and drag in the strainer, occasionally twisting into a bundle if you aren't careful. Cheesecloth is often packaged in stingy quantities and in widths so narrow that it is difficult to use. Try to buy it at a fabric store from large, wide bolts—and buy it in ample amounts, so you're not out every time you need it. —K.R.

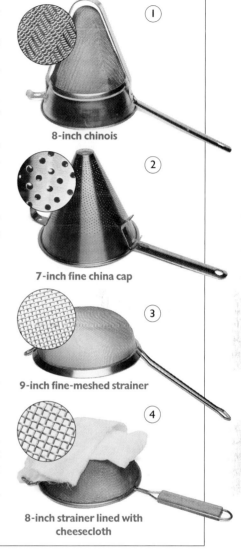

8-inch chinois

7-inch fine china cap

9-inch fine-meshed strainer

8-inch strainer lined with cheesecloth

---

1 1/2 tablespoons olive oil and swirl to coat pan bottom. Add half of shell-on shrimp and half of reserved shells; sauté until deep pink and shells are lightly browned, about 2 minutes. Transfer shrimp to medium bowl and repeat with remaining oil, shell-on shrimp, and shells. Return first browned batch to skillet. Pour warmed brandy over shrimp and wave lit match over pan until brandy ignites, shaking pan. When flames subside, transfer shrimp and shells to food processor bowl fitted with steel blade and process until mixture resembles fine meal, about 10 seconds.

3. Heat butter in large, heavy-bottomed Dutch oven over medium heat until foaming. Add carrots, celery, onion, garlic, and ground shrimp; cover and cook, stirring frequently, until vegetables are slightly softened and mixture is fragrant, about 5 minutes. Add flour and cook,

stirring constantly, until combined thoroughly, about 1 minute. Stir in wine, clam juice, and tomatoes, scraping pan bottom with wooden spoon to loosen browned bits, if any exist. Cover, increase heat to medium-high, and bring to boil; then reduce heat to low and simmer, stirring frequently, until thickened and flavors meld, about 20 minutes.

4. Strain bisque through chinois into medium container, pressing on solids with back of ladle to extract all liquid. Wash and dry now-empty Dutch oven; return strained bisque to Dutch oven and stir in tarragon, cream, lemon juice, and cayenne. Bring to simmer over medium-high heat; add reserved peeled and cut shrimp and simmer until shrimp are firm but tender, about 1 1/2 minutes. Discard tarragon sprig; stir in sherry, season to taste with salt and pepper, and serve hot.

Pie Dough 101

One of the hardest kitchen tasks for most home cooks is making and rolling out pie dough. Here are some surprising tips on making easy-to-roll-out dough and fitting it to a pie plate. BY CHRISTOPHER KIMBALL

If you have trouble working with pie dough you are in good company, since this is one of the home cook's most difficult tasks. The good news is that most of these problems can be solved with two pieces of advice: use a food processor to finely cut the shortening into the flour, and use plenty of water when forming the dough. Here is a complete illustrated course on how to make, roll, and fit pie dough perfectly. Our dough recipe can be found on page 23.

MAKING THE DOUGH

A food processor is the quickest and best tool for making a pie dough. Have butter cubes and shortening chilled and then proceed without delay. Refrigerate the finished dough for at least an hour before rolling it out.

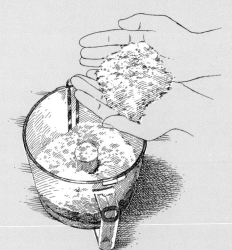

1. Pulse the flour, salt, and sugar in the bowl of a food processor. Add the cold butter and vegetable shortening in small pieces and then pulse until the butter pieces are no longer clearly visible.

2. When the mixture is properly processed, it will be slightly yellow, mealy in texture rather than floury, and it will ride up the sides of the bowl. At this point, transfer the mixture to a separate bowl.

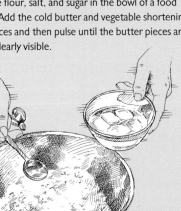

3. Add the ice water bit by bit, tossing and pressing the dry ingredients against the sides of the bowl with a rubber spatula. (The amount of water necessary to bring a dough together can vary up to 50 percent depending on how dry the flour is.)

4. Too much water is better than too little—a dry dough cannot be rolled out. The dough should clean the sides of the bowl and be wet to the touch. Form a ball, lightly flour, flatten into a 6-inch disk, wrap in plastic, and refrigerate for at least one hour.

Illustration: John Burgoyne

WHAT NOT TO DO

➤ Bakers are fearful of overprocessing the butter chunks. In fact, large or underprocessed butter chunks are more problematic. A dough made with inadequately processed butter pieces will be unevenly hydrated and difficult to roll out. The butter will stick to the rolling pin, the butter chunks will melt, and the dough may tear.

➤ A dough made without enough water will be difficult to form into a disk. It will tear and crumble when rolled out.

➤ The risk of overprocessing is high if water is not added by hand. An overprocessed dough will look like this.

ROLLING THE DOUGH

The goal when rolling out a pie dough is to get a thin, evenly rolled sheath into the pie pan in one piece quickly—before the dough becomes soft and unworkable. Frequent rotation—and flouring—of the dough will prevent sticking. If the dough is too soft, chill it in the fridge for 15 minutes.

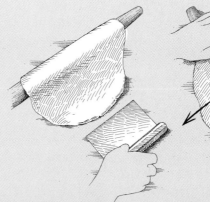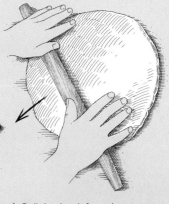

1. Using a tapered pin, roll a quarter turn, from about 2 o'clock to 5 o'clock, keeping your left hand stationary and moving the pin with your right hand.

2. Turn the dough a quarter turn and roll again as in step 1. Continue rolling until the dough is too thin to turn easily or when it is 8 or 9 inches in diameter. If necessary, lightly reflour the work surface.

3. Using a dough scraper, lift the dough onto the rolling pin, pick it up, reflour the counter, and replace the dough upside down.

4. Roll the dough from the center out and also along the edges to produce a uniform round of dough. The diameter of the circle should be 4 inches wider than the pie plate.

TRANSFERRING THE DOUGH

Once the dough is safely rolled out, it must be transferred to a pan.

Roll the dough over the pin, and unroll it evenly onto the pan.

FITTING THE DOUGH

Correctly fitted dough stays put when it is baked and doesn't shrink.

1. After draping the dough evenly over the pie plate, lift up the edges of the dough and ease it down into the lower creases of the pan. Press lightly to adhere the dough to the sides of the pan.

2. Use scissors to trim the dough overhang to within ¾ inch of the outer lip of the pan. (For a two-crust pie, trim the dough to the edge of the plate.)

3. Roll the trimmed overhang under so that it is even with the lip of the pan.

CRIMPING THE DOUGH

A graceful fluted edge is the crowning achievement of any pie dough. Be sure to chill or freeze the pie shell before baking it to avoid shrinking.

Use the index finger of one hand and the thumb and index finger of the other to create evenly spaced fluted edges. The edge of the dough should be vertical to the edge of the pie plate.

TROUBLESHOOTING

Occasionally, dough has a lopsided fit in the pan or it rips and tears. Here's what to do.

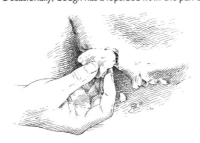

➤ If part of the edge of the rolled dough is too uneven to crimp, roll or flatten a leftover piece from the trimmings and patch it onto the overhang. Roll it under and crimp as usual.

➤ If the bottom dough tears in the pan, roll or flatten a small leftover piece from the trimmings and patch it over the crack. Bake as usual.

Pommes Anna for Home Cooks

The secrets of foolproof pommes Anna, the classic and elegant French potato cake, are to skip the clarified butter and use a nonstick skillet.

≥ BY DAWN YANAGIHARA ≤

I've spent years learning French verb conjugation. I've read Balzac, Zola, and Huysmans in their native language. I've gotten lost wandering the arrondissements of Paris and have found heaven in a plate of steak frites. Yes, I am a Francophile, particularly in matters gastronomic. In cooking school, though, I learned that while savoring French food is easy, preparing it is a labor of love. It took the regal, unsullied allure of pommes Anna to make me want to cook French at home.

Even if you think you are not familiar with pommes Anna, you are. Imagine thin potato slices layered meticulously in a skillet with nothing but butter, salt, pepper, and more butter, left to cook until the inverted dish reveals a potato cake with a lovely crisp, deep brown, glassine crust belying the soft, creamy potato layers within. She is the queen of potato cookery.

Legend has it that Anna was a fashionable woman who lived during the reign of Napoleon III. Whoever Anna was, the creator of this dish was, to be sure, a chef with an inordinate amount of time on his hands, as the recipe requires painstaking procedures and the patience of Job. Given that, it was particularly irritating when, in my preliminary recipe testing, the pommes Anna suffered a 50 percent rate of failure to cleanly release from the pan. It's no surprise, then, that pommes Anna is rarely seen on menus or home dinner tables and that recipes for it are sequestered in only the staunchest of French cookbooks.

I hoped to find a means of simplifying and foolproofing this classic. If I could do away with some of the maddening work and guarantee more than a crapshoot's chance of perfect unmolding, pommes Anna could find her way back onto the culinary map . . . and certainly onto my table.

First I needed a pan for the perilous pommes. Of the four different cooking vessels I employed in tests—a cast-iron skillet, a copper pommes Anna pan, a heavy-bottomed skillet with a stainless steel cooking surface, and a heavy-bottomed nonstick skillet—only the nonstick effortlessly released the potatoes onto the serving platter. As reluctant as I was to make such specific equipment requisite for pommes Anna, a nonstick skillet is essential to the dish's success. After all, once having expended the effort of slicing and arranging the potatoes, it is both enraging and mortifying to later witness them clinging hopelessly to the pan.

Once inverted, the bottom of the pommes Anna becomes the top, so arrange the most perfect potato slices in the skillet first.

Simplify, Not Clarify

Most, if not all, recipes for pommes Anna begin with clarified butter. To make it, butter is melted, the foamy whey is spooned off the top, and the pure butterfat is poured or spooned off of the milky casein at the bottom. Since it lacks solids and proteins, clarified butter has a higher smoking point (and so is more resistant to burning) than whole butter, but it also lacks the full, buttery flavor that those solids and proteins provide. I have always been annoyed by clarified butter because of the time required to make it, the waste involved (typically, about 30 percent of the butter is lost with clarifying), and the loss of flavor. But pommes Anna, which spends a substantial amount of time cooking at moderately high temperatures, is always made with clarified butter. My big coup, I thought, would be to circumvent its necessity, so I made a pommes Anna with whole butter to see if I couldn't prove false the centuries-old maxim that says clarified butter is a must. Sure enough, the surface of the potatoes was dotted with unappealing black flecks. Still, as a few tasters and I noticed, the whole butter gave the potatoes a richer, fuller flavor that we missed in the versions made with clarified butter.

I thought to replace the butter in the bottom of the skillet with oil, then drizzle melted whole butter between potato layers. This worked better than I could have hoped. My newfangled pommes Anna had a lovely crisp brown crust rivaling that of any made by the classic method.

Details, Details, Details

Thinly sliced potatoes are a defining characteristic of pommes Anna, as is the overlapping arrangement of the slices in concentric circles. In the early stages of my testing, I preferred to slice the potatoes by hand (for no good reason), but as numbers increased, I took to a food processor fitted with a fine slicing disk that could get the job done with effortless speed. If you own and are adept with a mandoline, it offers another quick means of slicing the potatoes.

Slicing wasn't the only obstacle presented by the potatoes. Because they will discolor if peeled and sliced and then kept waiting to be arranged in the skillet, they must be soaked in water, which in turn means that the slices must be dried before being layered. To avoid this incredible inconvenience, I opted to slice and arrange the potatoes in batches, making sure each group of slices was arranged in the skillet before slicing the next batch. This method prevented discoloration, but it was also awkward and inefficient. It was suggested that tossing the sliced potatoes in the melted butter might prevent them from discoloring. I tried this, and though the butter did not prevent the discoloration, it did slow it down to the extent that all slices could be layered in the skillet before severe discoloration set in. That the butter no longer required drizzling between each layer was a bonus.

Most pommes Anna recipes have the cook start layering potato slices in the skillet as it heats on the stovetop. It may sound dangerous, but it isn't, really, and it saves much time. After all the slices are in, the skillet is transferred to a hot oven or left on the stovetop to complete cooking. After many tests, I determined that the potatoes—

Seeing Rouge

My mother taught me that peeled burdock root had to be soaked in water to prevent discoloring. But she never said anything about potatoes. Consequently, I remember trying to make hash browns in the college dorm and being befuddled as I watched my grated spuds take on a brick-red hue.

Potato discoloration is of particular concern with pommes Anna since the peeled, sliced potatoes must wait to be layered into the skillet. I consulted spud expert Dr. Alfred Bushway, professor of food science at the University of Maine, to find out what causes potatoes to turn color. He explained that with peeling and slicing, potato cells are broken and enzymes and substrates are released. These enzymes and substrates combine with oxygen and react, causing discoloration. It's the same reaction that causes peeled apples to turn brown.

Tossing the potatoes with butter, as I do in the pommes Anna recipe, helps limit oxygen exposure and therefore retards discoloration. I had noted that certain potatoes discolor more rapidly than others. Dr. Bushway said from cultivar to cultivar and over the storage season, potatoes vary in their enzyme and/or substrate concentrations and enzyme activity, so differences in discoloration rates can be expected. In my experience, russet potatoes seem to discolor most rapidly, so if you're a slow hand, opt for Yukon Golds or white potatoes for pommes Anna. – D.Y.

started in a cold skillet—require 30 minutes on the stovetop at medium-low heat (if it takes you longer, next time try mashed potatoes), then—after a firm pressing with the bottom of a cake pan to compact the potatoes into a cohesive cake—25 minutes more in a 450-degree oven. The time on the stovetop gets the browning going on the bottom, and the oven time cooks through the potatoes' thickness while completing the bottom browning. Now, not only was a nonstick skillet necessary, but a nonstick ovenproof skillet was required to do the job.

The final step of pommes Anna is, of course, unmolding. If only it could be so easy as inverting a layer cake onto a cooling rack, but with a heavy, hot-handled skillet, the process is awkward and clumsy and can make an experienced cook feel like a bumbling one. Rather than trying to invert the potatoes directly onto a serving platter, where they cannot be unmolded in dead center because of the skillet's protruding handle, I lined the back of a baking sheet (a rimless cookie sheet will do) with lightly greased foil. I inverted the potatoes onto this surface, much as I would invert a cake onto a cooling rack, then slid them onto the serving platter. I found this technique a little less dangerous and much less complicated.

A last word on pommes Anna. Even simplified and streamlined, this recipe requires a good amount of patience, but she is no less a tour de force of culinary art and engineering than the classic rendition. Bring her to the holiday table and set her beside the bûche de Noël, where she will look and feel right at home.

POMMES ANNA
SERVES 6 TO 8

Do not slice the potatoes until you are ready to start assembling. Remember to start timing when you begin arranging the potatoes in the skillet—no matter how quickly you arrange them, they will need 30 minutes on the stovetop to brown properly.

- 3 pounds russet, Yukon Gold, or white potatoes, peeled and sliced ¹/₁₆ to ¹/₈ inch thick
- 5 tablespoons unsalted butter, melted
- ¼ cup vegetable or peanut oil, plus additional for greasing cookie sheet
  Salt and ground black pepper

1. Toss potato slices with melted butter in large bowl until potatoes are evenly coated. Adjust oven rack to lower-middle position and heat oven to 450 degrees.

2. Pour oil into 10-inch heavy-bottomed ovenproof nonstick skillet; swirl to coat pan bottom and set skillet over medium-low heat. Begin timing, and arrange potato slices in skillet, starting in center (see illustrations 1 and 2) to form first layer. Sprinkle evenly with scant ¼ teaspoon salt and ground black pepper to taste. Arrange second layer of potatoes, working in opposite direction of first layer (see illustration 3); sprinkle evenly with scant ¼ teaspoon salt and ground black pepper. Repeat, layering potatoes in opposite directions and sprinkling with salt and pepper, until no slices remain (broken or uneven slices can be pieced together to form a single slice; potatoes will mound in center of skillet); continue to cook over medium-low heat until 30 minutes elapse from the time you began arranging potatoes in skillet.

3. Using bottom of 9-inch cake pan, press potatoes down firmly to compact. Cover skillet and place in oven. Bake until potatoes begin to soften, about 15 minutes. Uncover and continue to bake until potatoes are tender when paring knife is inserted in center and edge of potatoes near skillet is browned, about 10 minutes longer. Meanwhile, line rimless cookie sheet or back of baking sheet with foil and coat very lightly with oil. Drain off excess fat from potatoes by pressing potatoes into skillet with bottom of cake pan while tilting skillet to pour off fat (see illustration 4).

4. Set foil-lined cookie sheet on top of skillet. With hands protected by oven mitts or potholders, hold cookie sheet in place with one hand and carefully invert skillet and cookie sheet together (see illustration 5). Remove skillet. Carefully slide potatoes onto platter (see illustration 6); cut into wedges and serve immediately.

STEP-BY-STEP | CONSTRUCTING AND UNMOLDING POMMES ANNA

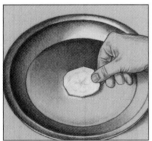
1. Use the nicest slices to form the bottom layer. Start by placing one slice in the bottom of the skillet.

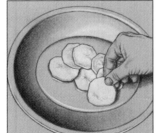
2. Overlap the slices in a circle around the center slice, then form the outer circle of overlapping slices.

3. Continue layering, alternating the direction of the slices in each layer.

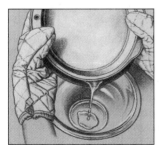
4. To drain off excess fat before unmolding, press a cake pan against the potatoes while tilting the skillet. Be sure to use heavy potholders or oven mitts.

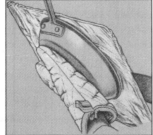
5. To invert, set a prepared baking sheet flat on top of the skillet. Invert the skillet and baking sheet together. Lift the skillet off the potatoes.

6. Carefully slide the pommes Anna from the baking sheet onto a serving platter.

The Best Pasta all'Amatriciana

Simpler is better when making this classic Italian sauce with tomatoes, bacon, and onion.

≥ BY JACK BISHOP ≤

I can still remember my first visit to Rome. I was 20, living in Florence, and had two grand passions—my girlfriend (who would eventually become my wife) and Italian cooking. On that first Roman holiday (and on all subsequent trips to the Eternal City), we made sure to order *bucatini all'Amatriciana* at least once.

This lusty pasta dish starts with *bucatini*, an extralong tube pasta that looks like a drinking straw. The sauce contains tomato, bacon, onion, dried chile, and Pecorino cheese. Like most Roman cooking, this dish is bold and brash. The recipe comes from Amatrice, a town outside of Rome, but it has become one of those classics, like pesto or carbonara, available in restaurants from Milan to Los Angeles.

What makes Amatriciana so popular? I have a few guesses. First, most cooks have all the ingredients on hand. Second, the sauce can be made in the time it takes to boil water and cook pasta. Third, although the recipe is simple, the flavors are complex and perfectly balanced—acidity from the tomatoes, sweetness from the sautéed onions, heat from the dried chile, meatiness and salt from the bacon, and tangy dairy from the cheese. My goal in developing my own version: Stay faithful to the Amatriciana my wife and I have eaten in Italy. The biggest challenge was the bacon. Romans use *guanciale*, bacon made from pork jowls. In the rest of Italy, pancetta (bacon made from pork belly) is used. I wondered how American bacon would compare.

My first tests revolved around the choice of bacon. I tested pancetta, American bacon, Canadian bacon, Irish bacon (both of the latter are cured pork loin), and salt pork (unsmoked pork belly). Tasters preferred the pancetta, which was the meatiest. The pure pork and salt flavors of the pancetta worked best with the sauce.

All three bacons were good, but most tasters felt that the smoke flavor and sweetness were distracting. The Canadian bacon and the Irish bacon (also called Irish back bacon) were meatier than the American bacon, although both were deemed a bit "hamlike." Regular American bacon was excessively fatty. If using it you will need to drain off the rendered fat (up to one-third cup), something not necessary when using pancetta, Canadian bacon, or Irish bacon.

The only product not recommended is the salt pork. Although it comes from the belly and is not smoked, it is much too fatty to use in a pasta sauce.

Whatever kind of bacon you use, make sure it is sliced thick. When I used thinly sliced pancetta or regular American bacon, the meat nearly disappeared in the sauce.

My next tests focused on technique. About half of the recipes I consulted called for sautéing the bacon and onion together and then building the tomato sauce on top of them. In the remaining recipes, the bacon was fried until crisp, removed from the pan, and then the onion was cooked in the bacon fat. Once the onion softened, it was time to make the tomato sauce. The crisped bacon was added back just before tossing the sauce with the pasta.

When I simmered the bacon with the tomatoes, it lost its crisp texture. By the time the sauce was done, the bacon was leathery and lacking in flavor. I much preferred bacon that was fried and then removed from the pan. It was crisp and chewy when tossed with the pasta and retained its salty, meaty flavor.

The next issue was the tomato. Crushed tomatoes made the worst sauce—the tomato flavor was weak and the consistency of the sauce was too thin. I missed the chunks of tomato, which give this sauce some character. Fresh tomatoes were good, but my tasters liked canned diced tomatoes even better. They were a tad juicier, and the preparation was certainly easier—no peeling, seeding, or chopping. Whole tomatoes packed in juice—which must be diced by hand or in a food processor—were just as good, but less convenient.

I tried simmering a small dried red chile in the sauce as well as adding hot red pepper flakes. The hot red pepper flakes won out, as they provide a more consistent heat level and are more likely to be on hand.

Some Amatriciana recipes call for Parmesan cheese, although Pecorino is traditional. I found the taste of Parmesan too subtle to stand up to the chile's heat. Sharp, robust Pecorino works better.

PASTA WITH TOMATO, BACON, AND ONION (PASTA ALL' AMATRICIANA)
SERVES 4

This dish is traditionally made with *bucatini*, also called *perciatelli*, which appear to be thick, round strands but are actually thin, extralong tubes. Linguine works fine, too. When buying pancetta, ask the butcher to slice it ¼ inch thick; if using bacon, buy slab bacon and cut it into ¼-inch-thick slices yourself. If the pancetta that you're using is very lean, it's unlikely that you will need to drain off any fat before adding the onion. Use 1½ small (14½ ounce) cans of diced tomatoes, or dice a single large (28 ounce) can of whole tomatoes packed in juice.

- 2 tablespoons extra-virgin olive oil
- 6 ounces ¼-inch-thick sliced pancetta or bacon cut into strips about 1 inch long and ¼ inch wide
- 1 medium onion, chopped fine
- ½ teaspoon hot red pepper flakes, or to taste
- 2½ cups canned diced tomatoes with juice
  Salt
- 1 pound bucatini, perciatelli, or linguine
- ⅓ cup grated Pecorino cheese (about 1½ ounces)

1. Bring 4 quarts water to rolling boil in large stockpot or Dutch oven.

2. Meanwhile, heat oil in large skillet over medium heat until shimmering, but not smoking. Add pancetta or bacon and cook, stirring occasionally, until lightly browned and crisp, about 8 minutes. Transfer pancetta or bacon with slotted spoon to paper towel–lined plate; set aside. If necessary, drain all but 2 tablespoons fat from skillet. Add onion to skillet; sauté over medium heat until softened, about 5 minutes. Add red pepper flakes and cook to release flavor, about 30 seconds. Stir in tomatoes and salt to taste; simmer until slightly thickened, about 10 minutes.

3. While sauce is simmering, add 1½ teaspoons salt and pasta to boiling water. Cook until pasta is al dente; drain and return pasta to empty pot.

4. Add pancetta to tomato sauce and adjust seasoning with salt. Add sauce to pot with pasta and toss over low heat to combine, about 30 seconds. Add cheese and toss again; serve.

BACON | ITALIAN PANCETTA

Pancetta and American bacon come from the same part of the pig—the belly—but the curing process is different. Pancetta is not smoked and the cure does not contain sugar—just salt, pepper, and cloves.

Great Turkey Soup

To make a great soup with the leftover Thanksgiving bird, add one unusual ingredient.

⋧ BY BRIDGET LANCASTER ⋦

There is a problem with turkey soup. While chicken soup usually begins with a raw, cut-up chicken carcass, turkey soup tends to start out with only the remnants of a fully roasted bird. Perhaps to compensate for the meager turkey flavor, some cooks load up the stockpot with every vegetable in the crisper drawer, but this only serves to overwhelm any remaining turkey flavor altogether. To boost the turkey flavor, some recipes call for simmering the carcass for up to 20 hours. I wanted a soup with big, rich turkey flavor, but I didn't want to spend a whole day making it.

I knew having a great stock was key. I began with the vegetables. After much testing and many rejections, I ended up with the components of a classic stock: carrots, onions, and celery, as well as garlic. But my stock was still a little stodgy. I wondered if adding a bit of white wine would brighten it up. I had not seen this in any of the many turkey soup recipes I had consulted, but I knew that it worked very nicely in certain classic fish stocks. When I tried it, the improvement was tenfold. The turkey flavor deepened greatly, and the flavor of the vegetables seemed clearer as well.

I then tested the amount of time it would take to extract the maximum flavor from the bones and meat. Were those day-long recipes really necessary? Thankfully, no. After a four-hour simmer, the wine-enriched stock was fully flavored—anything more made the soup too gelatinous, anything less and the stock was, pardon the expression, too soupy.

BASIC TURKEY STOCK
MAKES 3 QUARTS

Try not to use a barren carcass for the stock. The soup tastes best made with a carcass that has a good amount of meat clinging to it.

- 1   turkey carcass from 12- to 14-pound turkey, cut into 4 or 5 rough pieces to fit into pot
- 1   large onion, peeled and halved
- 1   large carrot, peeled and chopped coarse
- 1   large celery rib, about 4 ounces, chopped coarse
- 3   medium garlic cloves, unpeeled and smashed
- 2   cups dry white wine
- 1   bay leaf
- 5   sprigs fresh parsley
- 3   sprigs fresh thyme

1. Bring turkey carcass, onion, carrot, celery, garlic, wine, bay leaf, and 4½ quarts water to boil in 12-quart stockpot over medium-high heat, skimming fat or foam that rises to surface. Reduce heat to low and simmer, uncovered, 2 hours, continuing to skim surface as necessary. Add parsley and thyme; continue to simmer until stock is rich and flavorful, about 2 hours longer, continuing to skim surface as necessary.

2. Strain stock through large-mesh strainer into large bowl or container; remove meat from strained solids, shred into bite-sized pieces, and set aside; discard solids in strainer. Cool stock slightly, about 20 minutes; spoon fat from surface. Use stock in one of following recipes or cool to room temperature, cover, and refrigerate up to 2 days.

TURKEY NOODLE SOUP
MAKES ABOUT 3 QUARTS, SERVING 8 TO 10

- 1   recipe Basic Turkey Stock and reserved shredded meat
- 1   medium onion, diced medium
- 2   medium carrots, peeled and cut into ¼-inch-thick rounds
- 1   large celery rib, sliced ¼ inch thick
- 1   tablespoon fresh thyme leaves, minced
       Salt and ground black pepper
- 2–3 cups medium pasta shells or other medium-sized pasta shape
- 2   tablespoons minced fresh parsley leaves

Bring turkey stock to simmer in large stockpot or Dutch oven over medium-high heat. Add onion, carrot, celery, thyme, and 1 teaspoon salt; cover and simmer until vegetables are just tender, about 10 minutes. Add pasta and reserved shredded turkey meat from stock; simmer until pasta is al dente, 10 to 12 minutes. Stir in parsley, adjust seasonings with salt and pepper; serve.

TURKEY SOUP WITH POTATOES, LINGUIÇA, AND KALE

Linguiça is a garlicky Portuguese sausage. Chorizo sausage can be used instead.

- 1   recipe Basic Turkey Stock and reserved shredded meat
- 2   pounds boiling potatoes, unpeeled and cut into 1-inch pieces
- 2   teaspoons minced fresh savory leaves
       Salt and ground black pepper
- 12   ounces linguiça sausage, cut into ¼-inch-thick rounds
- 1   bunch kale (about 12 ounces), washed, stems removed, and leaves cut into ¼-inch strips (about 9 cups, packed)

Bring turkey stock to simmer in large stockpot or Dutch oven over medium-high heat. Add potatoes, savory, and 1 teaspoon salt; cover and simmer until potatoes are tender, about 15 minutes. Off heat, mash potatoes in broth with potato masher until no large chunks remain and potatoes thicken soup slightly. Return to medium-high heat, add sausage and reserved shredded turkey meat from stock; bring to boil, then reduce heat to medium-low, cover, and simmer to blend flavors, about 15 minutes. Add kale and simmer until tender, about 5 minutes longer. Adjust seasonings with salt and pepper; serve immediately.

SPICY TURKEY AND JASMINE RICE SOUP

- 1   recipe Basic Turkey Stock and reserved shredded meat
- 1   stalk lemon grass, trimmed to bottom 6 inches and bruised with back of chef's knife
- 1   ¾-inch piece fresh ginger, peeled, cut into thirds, and bruised with back of chef's knife
- 2   large garlic cloves, unpeeled and smashed
- 2   fresh jalapeño or Thai chiles, halved lengthwise and seeds removed
       Salt
- 1   cup jasmine rice
- 2   tablespoons minced fresh cilantro leaves
- 3   tablespoons minced fresh basil leaves
- 5   medium scallions, sliced thin

Bring turkey stock to simmer in large stockpot or Dutch oven over medium-high heat. Add lemon grass, ginger, garlic, chiles, and 1 teaspoon salt; cover and simmer until broth is fragrant and flavorful, about 10 minutes. With slotted spoon, remove and discard lemon grass, ginger, garlic, and chiles. Add rice and reserved shredded turkey meat from stock; bring to boil, then reduce heat to medium and simmer, covered, until rice is tender, 12 to 15 minutes. Adjust seasonings with salt and pepper; ladle soup into individual bowls and sprinkle each with a portion of cilantro, basil, and scallions. Serve immediately.

Improving Dutch Apple Pie

Many recipes for Dutch apple pie are lackluster, but this version, in which the filling and crust are handled separately, is well worth the time and effort.

⇒ BY RAQUEL PELZEL ⇐

Composed of tender, creamy apple filling, flaky pie crust, and buttery mounds of streusel, the Dutch apple pie of my youth was truly a pie to dream of. I would dive into my 2-inch-deep piece and not come up for air until the last crumbs had vanished from my plate. While this was years ago, when any amount of intense sugar consumption sent me into fits of glee, I've found that what I expect from a pie hasn't changed too much; I'm still looking for a burst of pie euphoria with every bite.

I readily accepted the challenge to create a Dutch apple pie that exceeded those lodged in memories of my youth. To get my bearings, I began by making five Dutch apple pies, each with a different recipe and technique. Surely one had to come close to my perhaps-romanticized-just-a-little version of Dutch apple pie? Not so. Each pie was a miserable failure. Variously soupy and void of crust, filled with undercooked apples or dotted with greasy, melted pools of butter, these pies were bad enough to induce laughter in the test kitchen. But I was stymied—why had they failed? What makes baking a Dutch apple pie any different from baking a standard American-style apple pie?

Before I could begin to solve the problems of Dutch apple pie, I needed to define just what it was. As it turns out, there are three components and one major omission that convert an ordinary apple pie into a Dutch apple pie. The additions consist of dried fruit (such as currants or raisins), dairy in the filling, and a streusel topping in lieu of the standard top crust. The major omission is lemon juice.

This omission was far from incidental, as it turned out. A standard apple pie is baked from start to finish with lemon juice, which helps to break down the apples and allows them to release their juices, making for a juicy as well as tender pie filling. But most of the recipes for Dutch apple pie that I had unearthed called for the addition of only one liquid ingredient—usually heavy cream—five minutes before the pie was done baking. When I sliced into these pies, I noticed two things: first, the interior was not creamy and golden; it was greasy and runny. Second, the apples didn't seem to have cooked through, despite the 45-minute-plus baking times.

. Knowing something was amiss, I made a call to Dr. Barry Swanson, a professor of food science at Washington State University. He explained that when the cream came into contact with the hot, acidic apples, the fat and water in the cream separated, giving my pies their lumpy, greasy, runny interiors. In addition, because these pies were undergoing dry-heat cooking (since there was no

When mixing the streusel topping, you want primarily large chunks with a few smaller, pea-sized pieces mixed throughout.

liquid, such as lemon juice, providing the apples with moisture), a much slower process than wet-heat cooking, the apples were remaining too crunchy. While a few recipes call for the dairy at the beginning of the baking sequence, they, too, produced pies with a coagulated filling.

At first I thought that I might doctor the situation by heating the cream before adding it to the almost-finished pie. But even if the cream didn't separate, five minutes in the oven wouldn't provide enough baking time for the cream to set amidst the layers of apples, and I would still be stuck with unevenly distributed amounts of cream in the pie. My next thought was to try adding some lemon juice and zest to the pie prior to

adding the cream. But the lemon-cream combination sent my tasters (and me) running for cover. The quickest fix I came up with was to cook off the water by reducing the cream, thereby preventing the fat from separating when it entered into a close encounter with the hot pie filling. This effectively remedied my dairy dilemma, but the apples were still too crunchy.

A Pie in Parts

It occurred to me that sautéing the apples (a mix of Granny Smith and McIntosh, as recommended in "All Season Apple Pie," September/October 1997) with some butter and sugar before they went into the pie might solve my crunch problem. So I prepared for a new experiment: precooking the apples as well as prebaking the pie shell. I ran through a number of pie dough recipes and chose one that stood out for its flakiness and flavor—the *Cook's* recipe for American pie dough (September/October 1996).

Choosing a Dutch oven for its size (as well as apropos name), I sautéed the apples until they were tender from exterior to interior and some of the softer McIntosh pieces began to break down. I strained the apples of their juices, packed them into the prebaked pie shell, and reduced one-half cup of heavy cream with the remaining apple juices (to give the cream reduction a flavor boost). The cream reduction was thick, glossy, and redolent with appley undertones. I spooned the sauce over the filling and topped the pie with streusel. After a mere 20 minutes in the oven, my Dutch apple filling was just right, and I had a perfectly crisp and flaky pie crust to boot.

Finessing the Pie

Now that the filling and crust met my expectations, I moved on to the streusel. I wanted it to be just crunchy enough on the outside to allow for some textural deviation from the flush and tender filling, but it also had to have enough fat to create a melt-in-your-mouth sensation. After trying all different ratios of brown sugar, light brown sugar, white sugar, honey, cornmeal, baking powder, flour, salt, spices, and butter, I found the streusel zenith to be a composition of melted butter with a touch of salt, just enough cornmeal to give it some snap, a combination of light brown sugar and white sugar, and an adequate amount of flour to bind everything together. By tossing the melted butter into the dry ingredients with a fork, I was able to create large chunks of streusel surrounded by smaller pea-sized morsels.

Now the only thing standing between me and a real Dutch apple pie was the dried fruit. The earliest recipe I found was published in 1667 and included currants. While currants far surpassed shriveled black raisins in terms of beauty, they did not contribute much flavor or chew. Dried cherries and cranberries were too sweet and too bold a shade of red for the subtle wheaty hue of the pie interior. I finally found solace in golden raisins, both sweet and plump, yet not too showy. No longer would I have to dream of the Dutch apple pie of my youth—now I had a better version I could actually sink my teeth into.

DUTCH APPLE PIE
SERVES 8

The most efficient way to make this pie is to use the dough's chill times to peel and core the apples and prepare the streusel, then cook the apples while the dough prebakes. We prefer ceramic or metal pie weights for prebaking the pie shell. If you don't own any, rice or dried beans can stand in, but since they're lighter than pie weights, be sure to fill up the foil-lined pie shell completely. For a finished look, dust the pie with confectioners' sugar just before serving.

Pie Dough
- 1½ cups (7½ ounces) all-purpose flour
- 1 tablespoon sugar
- ½ teaspoon salt
- 4 tablespoons vegetable shortening, chilled in the refrigerator for at least 30 minutes
- 4 tablespoons unsalted butter, cut into ¼-inch pieces, chilled in freezer for at least 30 minutes
- 4–6 tablespoons ice water

Apple Filling
- 2½ pounds (about 5 medium) Granny Smith apples
- 2 pounds (about 4 medium) McIntosh apples
- ¼ cup sugar
- ½ teaspoon ground cinnamon
- ⅛ teaspoon salt
- 2 tablespoons unsalted butter
- ¾ cup golden raisins
- ½ cup heavy cream

Streusel Topping
- 1¼ cups (6½ ounces) all-purpose flour
- ⅓ cup packed light brown sugar
- ⅓ cup granulated sugar
- 1 tablespoon cornmeal
- 7 tablespoons unsalted butter, melted

1. *For the pie dough:* Pulse flour, sugar, and salt in bowl of food processor fitted with steel blade until combined. Add shortening and butter and process until mixture is pale yellow, rides up sides of bowl, and resembles coarse crumbs with butter bits no larger than small peas, about ten 1-second pulses. Turn mixture into medium bowl.

2. Sprinkle 4 tablespoons ice water bit by bit over mixture; with rubber spatula, use folding motion to evenly combine water and flour mixture until small portion of dough holds together when squeezed in palm of hand (dough should feel rather wet). Add up to 2 tablespoons more ice water if necessary. Turn dough onto clean, dry work surface; gather and gently press together into cohesive ball and flatten into 4-inch disk. Wrap in plastic wrap and refrigerate 1 hour, or up to 2 days, before rolling.

3. Remove dough from refrigerator (if refrigerated longer than 1 hour, let stand at room temperature until malleable). Roll out on lightly floured work surface or between two large sheets of parchment paper to 12-inch disk. Transfer dough to pie plate by rolling dough around rolling pin and unrolling over 9-inch pie plate, or by folding dough in quarters, then placing dough point in center of 9-inch pie plate and unfolding. Working around circumference of pie plate, ease dough into pan corners by gently lifting dough edges with one hand while pressing around pan bottom with other hand. Trim dough edges to extend about ½ inch beyond rim of pan. Fold overhang under itself; flute dough as desired, refrigerate or freeze dough-lined pie plate until firm, about 1 hour in refrigerator or 30 minutes in freezer.

4. Adjust oven rack to lower-middle position and heat oven to 425 degrees. Remove dough-lined pie plate from refrigerator or freezer and press doubled 12-inch piece heavy-duty foil inside pie shell and fold edges of foil to shield fluted edge; distribute 2 cups ceramic or metal pie weights over foil. Bake, leaving foil and weights in place until dough looks dry and is light in color, 20 to 25 minutes. Carefully remove foil and weights by gathering corners of foil and pulling up and out. Continue to bake until pie shell is golden brown, 10 to 15 minutes longer. Remove from oven.

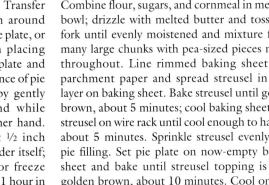

TESTING

IS IT DONE YET?

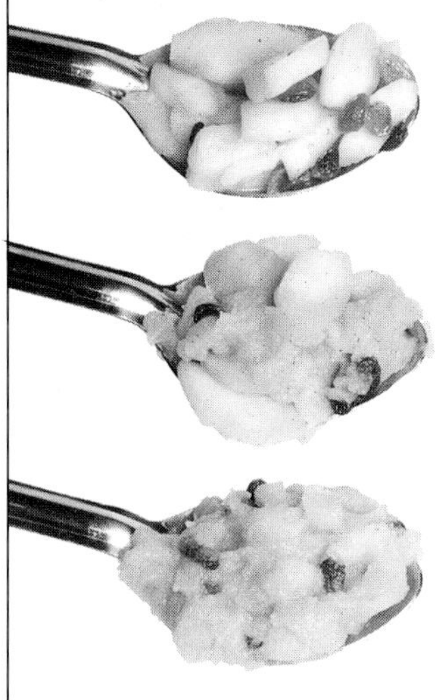

You'll know your pie filling is ready when the McIntosh apples just start to break down, as shown in the middle spoon. The filling shown in the top spoon is about halfway cooked; the filling in the bottom spoon is overcooked.

5. *For the apple filling:* Peel, quarter, and core apples; slice each quarter crosswise into pieces ¼ inch thick. Toss apples, sugar, cinnamon, and salt in large bowl to combine. Heat butter in large Dutch oven over high heat until foaming subsides; add apples and toss to coat. Reduce heat to medium-high and cook, covered, stirring occasionally, until apples are softened, about 5 minutes. Stir in raisins; cook, covered, stirring occasionally, until Granny Smith apple slices are tender and McIntosh apple slices are softened and beginning to break down, about 5 minutes longer.

6. Set large colander over large bowl; transfer cooked apples to colander. Shake colander and toss apples to drain off as much juice as possible. Bring drained juice and cream to boil in now-empty Dutch oven over high heat; cook, stirring occasionally, until thickened and wooden spoon leaves trail in mixture, about 5 minutes. Transfer apples to prebaked pie shell; pour reduced juice mixture over and smooth with rubber spatula.

7. *For the streusel topping:* Combine flour, sugars, and cornmeal in medium bowl; drizzle with melted butter and toss with fork until evenly moistened and mixture forms many large chunks with pea-sized pieces mixed throughout. Line rimmed baking sheet with parchment paper and spread streusel in even layer on baking sheet. Bake streusel until golden brown, about 5 minutes; cool baking sheet with streusel on wire rack until cool enough to handle, about 5 minutes. Sprinkle streusel evenly over pie filling. Set pie plate on now-empty baking sheet and bake until streusel topping is deep golden brown, about 10 minutes. Cool on wire rack and serve.

QUICK DUTCH APPLE CRISP
SERVES 8

This quick variation on our Dutch Apple Pie eliminates the pie crust, allowing you to have dessert on the table in less than an hour.

Follow recipe for Dutch Apple Pie, omitting pie dough and beginning with step 5. In step 6, pack cooked apples into 8-inch square baking dish and pour reduced juice mixture over. Continue with recipe at step 7.

Bittersweet Chocolate Roulade

We created a cake that is easy to roll but still moist, tender, and full of chocolate flavor.

⇒ BY KAY RENTSCHLER ⇐

Objects that sweep and spiral inward enchant the eye. I think of seashells, chignons, sweet rolls—each demure and voluptuous at the same time. Equally if not more appealing are spirals of sponge cake rolled inward around a creamy filling. A chocolate sponge cake roll—or *roulade*—is doubtless the most satisfying and versatile of this genre, its tender bittersweet shell home to a full spectrum of fillings, from pale creams to rich, dark mousses.

A chocolate roulade begins life as a thin sponge cake baked quickly on a jelly roll pan, unmolded, and rolled up. A sponge cake by definition contains little or no butter, and its (usually) separated eggs are whipped with sugar before the dry ingredients are folded in. Structurally speaking, a sponge cake sheet must be thin, even, and "rollable." Given the demands of its form, this cake cannot be fudgy, buttery, or rich. But it must pack serious chocolate flavor, remain moist, tender, and fine-pored, and refrain from being overly sweet. A knife should glide through a chocolate-glazed, cream-filled roulade seamlessly.

To begin, I made five chocolate roulade recipes. Several things were immediately evident: chemical leaveners were superfluous; cakes with more sugar failed to set the filling off to its advantage; and a rich, dark color was key to the cake's overall appeal. Only one of the cakes I baked used chocolate rather than cocoa, and that cake possessed by far the best flavor. Where every last cake fell from grace was in textural terms: we nibbled sheets of thick chocolate felt and soggy chocolate omelets. I wanted a texture that ventured in neither of these extremes.

Having chosen chocolate as the chief flavoring agent, I needed to determine which kind to use. I rejected unsweetened chocolate as too heavy-handed for this light, airy cake. Anything less than six ounces of semi- or bittersweet chocolate rendered a flavor too mild to suit me. One-third cup sugar tasted good with both semi- and bittersweet. I also added two tablespoons of butter to the melt-

This cake is easy to roll—but to prevent it from sticking to the cloth in which it is rolled, roll it when it is still quite warm.

ing chocolate. Though not enough to weigh the cake down, this small amount contributed to flavor and tenderness. One teaspoon vanilla extract and one-eighth teaspoon of salt satisfied my requirements for flavoring accents.

Because eggs are usually the sole liquid ingredient in a sponge cake—crucial for lightness of texture and ease of rolling—their number is key. Too few and the cake was not supple. Too many and I got either a wet chocolate sponge (if there was no flour in the recipe) or dry chocolate matting (if the proportion of eggs was too high). Six eggs provided the support necessary to blend the ingredients, the lift required to rise the cake, and the flexibility needed to roll it.

Still, even with chocolate contributing some structure, the fragile egg-and-sugar foam needed more support. I tested a quarter cup flour against the same amount of cocoa and ended up giving them equal partnership: the flour offered structural support, which kept the cake from becoming too moist after it was filled; the cocoa added a chocolatey undercurrent, which dramatically improved the overall flavor of the cake. Because the flavor of cocoa becomes more intense when it is mixed with water, I added two tablespoons of water to the recipe (adding it to the chocolate and butter

at the outset of melting rather than to the cocoa, which in my recipe was folded in as a dry ingredient). The water helped to deepen the chocolate flavor and made the batter glossy and beautiful.

Recipes offer several techniques for coaxing sheet cakes into their customary cylindrical shape. My cake responded best when cooled briefly in the pan on a cooling rack, and then unmolded onto a kitchen towel rubbed with cocoa to prevent sticking. The cake, still quite warm, was then rolled up, towel and all. Allowed thus to cool briefly, the roll could be unrolled, retain its rolled memory, then be filled and re-rolled.

The roulade was now delectable, with a yielding, melting texture and intense chocolate flavor. It needed a rich but adaptable filling. Not wanting to crack open the cupboards and make a big mess, I decided to use a modified tiramisu filling made with lightly sweetened mascarpone and some ground espresso. A glossy layer of dark chocolate ganache put the final flavor layer in place and made the cake beautiful to gaze upon. Those interested in a slice of chocolate tour de force can get in line.

BITTERSWEET CHOCOLATE ROULADE
SERVES 8 TO 10

We suggest that you make the filling and ganache first, then make the cake while the ganache is setting up. Or, if you prefer, the cake can be baked, filled, and rolled—but not iced—then wrapped in plastic and refrigerated for up to 24 hours. For directions on how to create the "branched" look of a bûche de Noël, or yule log, see Kitchen Notes on page 30. The roulade is best served at room temperature.

- 6   ounces bittersweet or semisweet chocolate, chopped fine
- 2   tablespoons cold unsalted butter, cut into two pieces
- 2   tablespoons cold water
- ¼   cup cocoa, sifted, plus 1 tablespoon for unmolding
- ¼   cup (about 1¼ ounces) all-purpose flour, plus more for baking sheet
- ⅛   teaspoon salt
- 6   large eggs, separated
- ⅓   cup granulated sugar
- 1   teaspoon vanilla extract
- ⅛   teaspoon cream of tartar

- 1   recipe Espresso-Mascarpone Cream (recipe follows)
- 1   recipe Dark Chocolate Ganache (recipe follows)

1. Adjust oven rack to upper-middle position and heat oven to 400 degrees. Spray 12 by 17½-inch jelly roll or half sheet pan with nonstick cooking spray, cover pan bottom with parchment paper, and spray parchment with nonstick cooking spray; dust surface with flour and tap out excess.

2. Bring 2 inches water to simmer in small saucepan over medium heat. Combine chocolate, butter, and water in small heatproof bowl and cover tightly with plastic wrap. Set bowl over pan, reduce heat to medium-low, and heat until butter is almost completely melted and chocolate pieces are glossy, have lost definition, and are fully melted around the edges, about 15 minutes. (Do not stir or let water boil under chocolate.) Remove bowl from pan, unwrap, and stir until smooth and glossy. While chocolate is melting, sift ¼ cup cocoa, flour, and salt together into small bowl and set aside.

3. In bowl of standing mixer fitted with whisk attachment, beat yolks at medium-high speed until just combined, about 15 seconds. With mixer running, add half the sugar. Continue to beat, scraping down sides of bowl as necessary until yolks are pale yellow and mixture falls in thick ribbon when whisk is lifted, about 8 minutes. Add vanilla and beat to combine, scraping down bowl once, about 30 seconds. Turn mixture into medium bowl; wash mixer bowl and whisk attachment and dry with paper towels. (If you have 2 mixer bowls, leave yolk mixture in mixer bowl; wash and dry whisk attachment, and use second bowl in step 4.)

4. In clean bowl with clean whisk attachment, beat whites and cream of tartar at medium speed until foamy, about 30 seconds. With mixer running, add about 1 teaspoon sugar; continue beating until soft peaks form, about 40 seconds. Gradually add remaining sugar and beat until whites are glossy and supple and hold stiff peaks when whisk is lifted, about 1 minute longer. Do not overbeat (if whites look dry and granular, they are overbeaten). While whites are beating, stir chocolate into yolks. With rubber spatula, stir one quarter of whites into chocolate mixture to lighten it. With a balloon whisk, fold in remaining whites until almost no streaks remain. Sprinkle dry ingredients over top and fold in quickly but gently with balloon whisk.

5. Pour batter into prepared pan; using an offset icing spatula and working quickly, even surface and smooth batter into pan corners. Bake until center of cake springs back when touched with finger, 8 to 10 minutes, rotating pan halfway through baking. Cool in pan on wire rack for 5 minutes.

6. While cake is cooling, lay clean kitchen towel over work surface and sift remaining tablespoon cocoa over towel; with hands, rub cocoa into towel. Run paring knife around perimeter of baking sheet to loosen cake. Invert cake onto towel and peel off parchment.

7. Following illustrations 1 through 3, below, roll and fill cake. Set a large sheet of parchment paper on overturned rimmed baking sheet and set cake seam-side down on top. Following illustrations 4 to 6, trim and ice cake. Refrigerate baking sheet with cake, uncovered, to slightly set icing, about 20 minutes.

8. Carefully slide 2 wide metal spatulas under cake and transfer cake to serving platter. Cut into slices and serve.

ESPRESSO–MASCARPONE CREAM

MAKES ABOUT 1¼ CUPS,
ENOUGH TO FILL BAKED CAKE

To learn more about mascarpone cheese see Notes from Readers, page 2.

- ¼ cup heavy cream
- 2 teaspoons whole espresso beans, finely ground (about 1 tablespoon ground)
- 3 tablespoons confectioners' sugar
- 8¼ ounces mascarpone cheese (generous 1 cup)

Bring cream to simmer in small saucepan over high heat. Off heat, stir in espresso and powdered sugar; transfer mixture to medium bowl and cool slightly. Whisk in mascarpone until smooth. Cover with plastic wrap and refrigerate until ready to use.

DARK CHOCOLATE GANACHE

MAKES ABOUT 1½ CUPS,
ENOUGH TO COVER FILLED ROULADE

Rose Levy Beranbaum, author of *The Cake Bible* (William Morrow, 1988), acquainted us with the technique of making ganache in a food processor, a method that beats all others, in our opinion, for ease and consistency. If your kitchen is cool and the ganache becomes too cold and stiff to spread, set the bowl over a saucepan containing simmering water, then stir briefly until smooth and icinglike.

- ¾ cup heavy cream
- 2 tablespoons unsalted butter
- 6 ounces high-quality semisweet or bittersweet chocolate, chopped
- 1 tablespoon cognac

Microwave cream and butter in measuring cup on high until bubbling, about 1½ minutes. (Alternatively, bring to simmer in small saucepan over medium-high heat). Place chocolate in bowl of food processor fitted with steel blade. With machine running, gradually add hot cream and cognac through feed tube and process until smooth and thickened, about 3 minutes. Transfer ganache to medium bowl and let stand at room temperature 1 hour, until spreadable (ganache should have consistency of soft icing).

STEP-BY-STEP | FILLING AND ICING THE ROULADE

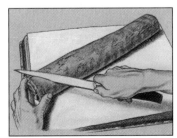
1. Roll cake—towel and all—into a jelly roll shape. Cool for 15 minutes, then unroll cake and towel.

2. Using an offset spatula, immediately spread the filling evenly over the surface of the cake, almost to the edges.

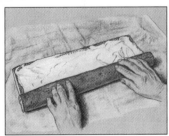
3. Roll the cake up gently but snugly around the filling.

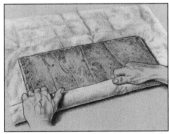
4. Trim both ends on the diagonal. Reserve the slices if making a yule log (see page 30).

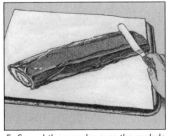
5. Spread the ganache over the roulade with a small icing spatula.

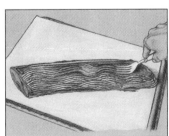
6. Use a fork to make wood-grain striations on the surface of the ganache before the icing has set.

Frozen Turkey Beats Out Fresh

A blind tasting of eight roasted turkeys revealed that we prefer brined or injected birds even if they have been frozen.

≽ BY MARYELLEN DRISCOLL ≼

While ground turkey and turkey cutlets have become common weeknight dinner options, most people purchase the whole bird just once during the year. Thanksgiving, of course, would be that occasion. When the moment of purchase arrives, however, the buyer may be somewhat befuddled. The options are many—this brand or that brand, fresh or frozen, hen or tom, flavor-enhanced or not. Then there is the growing number of product disclaimers to weed through—no antibiotics, no animal byproducts, minimal processing, and on and on it goes.

Everyone has priorities and standards when it comes to purchasing turkey. But what it all comes down to for most every cook is whether friends or relatives drive away after the big meal murmuring "That was the best turkey I've ever had" or "Thank goodness there was plenty of gravy and cranberry sauce."

To try to ensure the former response, we decided to do a blind turkey tasting. We corralled as many turkeys as we have ovens and cooked them all up. We roasted them using exactly the same method (starting breast-side up in a 400 degree oven, then rotating to one side, then the other side, and finally back to breast-side up to finish) and determined doneness at exactly the same internal temperature (175 degrees measured at the thigh). We then held a blind tasting, rating each of the nine birds for flavor, texture, and overall likability.

Because turkey is for the most part a regionally distributed product, few national brands are available. Consequently, our lineup consisted primarily of brands found on the East Coast. We selected them carefully, however, in order to represent the range of the types of turkeys found in stores nationwide. This included birds that were fresh and frozen, flavor-enhanced (or "basted," to use the industry term) and minimally processed, brined and unbrined.

The Results

From this magazine's perspective, the best way to cook a turkey is to brine it first—that is, to immerse the turkey overnight in a strong solution of water and salt. Recognizing that not everyone brines their turkey, though, we did not brine any of the turkeys for the tasting. But a few of the turkeys in the tasting came prepared in a manner that is similar to brining. These had either been injected with a salt solution or, in the case of the kosher bird, treated as described in "Turkey Talk," below.

All the turkeys in the tasting that were brined, basted, or rubbed with salt as part of their manufacturer's processing method were remarkably moist and tender and placed high in our ratings. This is because as the basting solution penetrates the turkey, the salt unravels the coiled proteins in the uncooked muscle, trapping water between the protein strands. As the meat cooks, the proteins set and form a barrier that prevents moisture from leaking out. The salt also helps to enhance the natural flavors of the turkey.

Commercially basted turkeys can also "fool" you into thinking a turkey is juicier than it is. This is because the basting solutions often contain some kind of fat—butter or oil. "In small amounts, fat makes the salivary glands produce saliva, which tricks you into thinking there's more juiciness in the meat," says Dr. Sarah G. Birkhold, assistant professor of poultry science at Texas A & M University.

While the success of the basted and kosher turkeys was not unexpected, what did surprise us was that tasters found no discernible difference between frozen and fresh birds. That came as no surprise to Birkhold, however. She explained that improved technology permits manufacturers to "flash freeze" birds in freezers where temperatures range around 30 degrees below zero and cold air is blasted at about 60 miles per hour. This prevents the development of large ice crystals that can damage the tissue, causing moisture loss. Home freezers, of course, cannot replicate this process. So if you are buying a turkey in advance of Thanksgiving, you are much better off buying a frozen one than buying and freezing a fresh one.

While prebasted birds might conveniently deliver juicy, tender meat, we still advocate brining a turkey on your own whenever possible. As our results show, a standard United States Department of Agriculture (USDA) grade A turkey is a good choice; it can only get better with brining. Note, however, that when brining at home, you should avoid kosher or "basted" birds, which have already been treated with salt. A final advantage is that basted birds often contain additives that you can avoid when brining a turkey at home.

Turkey Talk

Perhaps one of the most difficult elements of buying a turkey nowadays is making sense of the labels. Here is a rundown of what the most basic terms mean.

Fresh versus Frozen: This is perhaps the primary decision that most of us make with regard to turkeys. A bird labeled "fresh" is kept at a refrigerated temperature that is not allowed to fall below 26 degrees Fahrenheit, so that its flesh remains supple. These days, fresh turkeys tend to be the more popular choice because of their convenience, with no advance thawing time needed. Convenience, however, comes at a price. Fresh turkeys tend to cost about 50 cents per pound more than frozen. A frozen turkey must be at a rock-solid temperature of 0 degrees Fahrenheit or below. Of course, there is a gap between 0 and 26 degrees. While no specific labeling is required for birds stored within this temperature range, some manufacturers opt to label them "hard-chilled" or "refrigerated." These birds are considerably less common in stores, but we tracked one down in Utah and had it shipped for the tasting (see Norbest in the chart on page 27).

Grade A: The USDA grade A label is the one most common to supermarket turkeys. This rating indicates that the bird is intact—in other words, that it has no bruises, torn flesh, discoloration, or broken bones. While the USDA requires that turkeys be inspected for "wholesomeness," USDA grading for quality is optional.

Basted or Self-Basted: The next thing you might notice when purchasing a bird is that some are labeled "basted" or "self-basted." Such birds are injected or marinated with a solution commonly containing butter or some other fat along with broth, stock, or water, plus spices and flavor enhancers. When a bird is sold basted, its label must clearly state the total quantity of the solution added, which cannot exceed 8 percent of the weight of the raw turkey before processing. It must also list the ingredients in the solution.

Kosher: Kosher turkeys are rubbed with salt, left to rest so that the salt penetrates, and then rinsed during processing. They are also prepared under rabbinical supervision.

TASTING TURKEY

Last December, when turkeys were in abundance in grocery stores, we held a blind tasting of the nine products below. A panel of 21 tasters, including members of the *Cook's Illustrated* staff and Boston-area culinary students, rated each sample for its flavor, tenderness, texture, and overall likability. Tasters took into account both white and dark meat for each sample. The turkeys are listed below in order of their overall rating. At the end of each product description we have reprinted the terms appearing on the product's packaging.

BEST TURKEY

Marval FROZEN, BASTED
➤ **79 cents per pound**

"Best of tasting." This turkey was full-flavored yet tasted "very clean, like spring water." "This is real, succulent turkey—tender but not oily; flavorful, and distinct." As for tenderness, it outscored all the other turkeys by a good margin. A couple of tasters noted that it tasted a bit salty.

LABELING: Basted with approximately 6 percent solution of turkey broth, salt, sodium phosphate, sugar, and flavoring.

Empire Kosher FRESH, KOSHER
➤ **$1.69 per pound**

"Another winner," commented one taster. "Very tender and juicy, with flavor immediately clean on the palate." The "white meat in particular held its true flavor and tenderness." "Clean, sturdy, and full-bodied."

LABELING: All natural, no preservatives, no artificial ingredients, minimally processed—soaked, salted, and rinsed.

Shady Brook Farms FRESH
➤ **$1.29 per pound**

This standard fresh supermarket turkey was "a good bird, but not something to write home about." It was somewhat moist—more moist than many—but could have been more so. The flavor was "good" and the texture "quite nice," all adding up to "perfectly OK." This turkey "could be great with brining," one taster duly noted.

LABELING: None

Butterball FROZEN, BASTED
➤ **$1.39 per pound**

As one taster appropriately summed it up: "This reminds me of turkey I grew up with." This nationally known brand of turkey ranked medium-well in all categories. It carried a strong flavor that rang slightly of salt and butter—"like movie popcorn," noted one taster who preferred her turkey on the bland side. It was not quite as moist as the higher-scoring turkeys, but it could not be categorized as dry.

LABELING: 3% of a self-basting mixture added—vegetable oil, water, salt, emulsifiers, sodium phosphate, annatto color, and artificial flavor.

Butterball FRESH
➤ **$1.39 per pound**

What was unique to this turkey was the "visibly high" fat content, which made the meat greasy yet somewhat dry. It received an overall average rating for tenderness. What did not help this turkey was that the meat was "devoid of any flavor." "Never ate anything quite so bland and boring," commented one taster.

LABELING: All natural, no artificial ingredients, minimally processed.

Norbest "REFRIGERATED," BASTED
➤ **99 cents per pound**

Tasters' responses to this product were mixed. Some found it moist, some dry. Others said the texture was spotty—dry in some spots, moist in others—which might explain the mixed results. The overall tenderness of the meat was respectable but not striking. The dark meat was unpopular, strong in flavor, like that of liver, and stringy in texture. The white meat was clean but bland.

LABELING: Basted with 5.5% turkey broth, salt, sodium phosphate, and natural flavorings.

Plainville Farms FRESH
➤ **$1.89 per pound**

One taster said it all: "This sample was very tender, and if one discounted the flavor, it would be great." The downfall was a gamey flavor, described as sour and likened to liver. The texture, however, received high scores in terms of both tenderness and moistness.

LABELING: No artificial ingredients, minimally processed, "veggie grown," "animal friendly."

Bell & Evans FRESH, ALL-NATURAL, FREE-RANGE
➤ **$1.79 per pound**

This turkey was spongy—moist, tough, and stringy. "Requires much chewing," noted one taster. The worst part, however, was the flavor. The overwhelming consensus was that the turkey tasted "old" and slightly metallic, although a few tasters said "at least this turkey has flavor."

LABELING: All natural, no antibiotics administered, no animal products, all vegetable diet, minimally processed, naturally lite—contains 55 percent less fat than other uncooked turkeys based on USDA data of standard turkey fat content.

Do Electric Knives Really Work?

Chefs and home cooks alike are rediscovering electric knives
for everything from slicing meat to cutting pecan pie. Here's how they work,
what they are good for, and which models to buy.

⇒ BY ADAM RIED ⇐

Often overlooked since their heyday in the 1960s, electric knives remain eminently useful for cutting every course of a holiday meal, from appetizers right on through to dessert. Instigated and encouraged by test kitchen director Kay Rentschler, a stalwart electric knife fan, we gathered seven models in a single sweep through local discount and hardware stores and put them through their paces on a variety of foods. Passersby from other departments in our company all had the same reaction when they saw what we were up to: "I haven't seen one of those *in years.* Does anybody still use them?" Indeed, we do. Let us tell you why, and which of the current models is best.

Design, Comfort, and Performance

Electric knives operate by the quick mechanized sawing action of two serrated blades. Clipped together at one end, the blades fit so snugly against each other that they function, in effect, as a single blade. With the two blades thus connected, you insert their bases into the motor unit (which also serves as the handle), switch the motor on, and let the slices fall where they may.

Contemporary electric knives offer improved comfort and balance and more efficient performance than their predecessors, according to David Arnott, marketing manager for food preparation products at Applica Consumer Products, exclusive North American licensee for Black & Decker food preparation products. "The original knives were designed primarily to carve meat, and they performed reasonably well," said Arnott. "With current models, though, there has been an increased focus on consumer interaction with the product—design, comfort of use, and safety. The knives fit better in the hand, so they are more comfortable and therefore perform better."

To see for ourselves if this was the case, we got our hands on a 1960s vintage electric knife courtesy of Kay Rentschler's mother, who kindly shipped us her pristine Riviera Electric Slicing Knife, a gift from her father almost 40 years ago. Our observations confirmed Arnott's comments. At 26.6 ounces, the Riviera weighed a full 6 ounces more than our leading knife. In addition, its balance was terrible because the motor was positioned at the far rear of the unit, making the grip much less comfortable than any of the current models in our lineup.

This group included units from Black & Decker, White Westinghouse, Rival, Hamilton Beach, Sanyo, Toastmaster, and Krups. We tested each of them by carving large holiday roasts (stuffed pork loin and roasted turkey, in our case) and by serving up a number of delicate dishes.

We quickly came to some general conclusions about the usefulness of these knives. We found, for example, that they are better suited for uniformly shaped roasts than for poultry. Aside from the Krups OptiSlice, which tattered slices of roasted stuffed pork loin very slightly near the bottom edge, every knife carved thin, even slices. Turkey was another matter. None of our contestants was nimble enough to negotiate the curves and inner spaces of a whole roasted turkey, so we judged them on how well they sliced the breast alone. We used our preferred carving strategy of removing the breast as a whole, laying it flat on

The Electric Knives We Tested

BEST ELECTRIC KNIFE

Black & Decker Ergo Electric Knife
Our top pick for balance and control. Comes with long and short blades.

RECOMMENDED

BEST BUY
White Westinghouse Electric Knife with Slicing Guide
A solid performer at a rock-bottom price.

Rival Electric Knife
A pretty good knife with a couple of flaws.

Hamilton Beach Easy Slice
Smooth and reasonably balanced in operation, but on the noisy side.

Sanyo Cordless Kitchen Knife Set
Cordless and exceptionally quiet, but you have to pay.

NOT RECOMMENDED

Toastmaster Electric Carving Knife
Slipped in ratings because it fell short in terms of balance and comfort.

Krups OptiSlice Electric Knife
Noisy and shaky, with a touchy power switch.

RATING ELECTRIC KNIVES

Knives were rated according to their overall comfort and ability to cut through the foods listed in the chart below. Price indicates amounts paid in Boston-area stores. Comfort assessments were made by different users with both large and small hands. They were based on the ease with which the unit could be gripped and held, the precision with which it could be maneuvered, the position and engagement qualities of the power switch, and the amount of noise and vibration. With regard to food tests, we placed more importance on

RATINGS
★★★ GOOD
★★ FAIR
★ POOR

a knife's ability to cut through pommes Anna, pecan pie, quesadilla, and roulade than turkey breast and pork roast.

While most of the knives were comfortable to use and performed well, one in particular, the Black & Decker, stood out as the best and so is distinguished from the others in the "Recommended" category below. The remaining models in both the "Recommended" and "Not Recommended" categories appear in ascending price order.

Brand	Price	Blade Length (Actual Cutting Area)	Comfort & Design	Pommes Anna	Pecan Pie	Quesadilla	Roulade	Turkey/ Pork Roast	Testers' Comments
BEST ELECTRIC KNIFE **Black & Decker** Ergo Electric Knife, Model EK600	$24.88	6⅝" (long); 4½" (short)	★★★	★★★	★★★	★★★	★★★	★★★	Great balance and feel, no matter what size the user's hands. Power-switch lock feature offers extra safety. Knife stand particularly well designed. Two blades.
RECOMMENDED **White Westinghouse** Electric Knife with Slicing Guide, Model WEK9430	$12.99	6¾"	★★½	★★★	★★★	★★★	★★★	★★★	Well balanced and comfortable with a lockable power switch. We weren't crazy for the design of the knife stand, though.
Rival Electric Knife, Model 1205	$14.97	6½"	★★½	★★★	★★	★★★	★★★	★★★	Similar in feel and performance to the White Westinghouse, with a little more vibration and the same flawed knife stand design. Squished slices of pecan pie slightly.
Hamilton Beach Easy Slice, Model 74150	$16.99	5¾"	★★½	★★★	★★★	★★★	★★★	★★★	Reasonably comfortable and precise. Loved the on-unit blade storage but not the handle design.
Sanyo Cordless Kitchen Knife Set, Model NHP-SKEK	$29.99	7¼" (long); 5" (short)	★★½	★★★	★★★	★★★	★★★	★★★	Pecan pie slices less crisp than with other knives in this category, but certainly acceptable. Cordless model comes with two blades, a block, and a battery charger.
NOT RECOMMENDED **Toastmaster** Electric Carving Knife, Model 6104	$15.00	6⅝"	★	★★	★★	★★★	★★	★★★	Not a bad knife, but judged less evenly balanced and comfortable than other choices by most users.
Krups OptiSlice Electric Knife, Model 371	$19.99	6"	★	★	★	★★	★★★	★★	Vibrated a great deal in use, and the power switch required exceptional pressure to remain engaged. This was the case on both of the two units we tried.

the carving board, and cutting it crosswise into thin slices, each with a small piece of crisp skin still attached. Just try that with a regular knife.

Where electric knives really excel, however, is in cutting foods made up of different layers with distinctly firm and soft textures. Consider pecan pie, for example. The top layer is all crunchy, caramelized nuts. Beneath that is a soft, custardy gel. In a well-executed slice of pecan pie, the soft bottom layer should not become mashed and oozy because of the pressure exerted to cut through the firm, nutty, top layer. If everything goes right, both layers will remain separate and defined so that each slice has a crisp, neat presentation. Just try that with a regular knife.

Other delicate, layered foods with the same dynamic at play include quesadillas (like a Mexican grilled cheese sandwich made with tortillas), pommes Anna (see page 18), and roulade, a rolled cake with a soft, creamy filling (also in this issue, see page 24). We tested the knives on them all, and in every case they outperformed nonelectric knives.

Another quick point: For a holiday party, when presentation really counts, there's nothing like a good electric knife for cutting small, uniform, neat pieces of appetizers such as a savory phyllo pastry or pissaladière (a French onion pizza of crisp dough topped generously with soft caramelized onions).

Sorting Out the Winners

Although most of the knives proved very useful, there were clear differences among them. To begin with, some were far more comfortable to use than others. We judged this aspect of their performance just as we would with regular knives. Cooks with different hand sizes and strength levels assessed each model in terms of balance; the size, weight, and texture of the grip; and overall feel.

There were two different grip configurations among the knives. The Hamilton Beach, Toastmaster, and Sanyo all had loop handles molded into the top of their motor units. On the Black & Decker, White Westinghouse, Rival, and Krups knives, the motor unit itself served as the grip. This arrangement allowed users to choke up on the grip, which led to a better feeling of balance and therefore improved control while cutting. Without exception, all testers preferred the more "natural feel" of the integrated handles in this group, in part because the way you hold them comes closer to the way you hold a regular knife.

The placement of the power switch was another design consideration. All but one of the knives with our preferred grip, the Krups, had trigger-type power switches located on the bottom of their handles. Users favored this position over top-mounted power buttons, especially when the top-mounted buttons were positioned

near the blade-release buttons, which could lead to some dangerous confusion. The knives with both integrated handles and trigger-type power switches—Black & Decker, White Westinghouse, and Rival—were our top three picks.

Overall, the Black & Decker Ergo was our favorite by far. Little design touches pushed the Ergo into first place. The stand that keeps the Ergo stable and upright when you set it down, for instance, is designed so that the cutting edge of the blade can rest almost flush on the work surface. By contrast, the knife stands on the Westinghouse and Rival elevate their blades off the work surface by a full inch or more, so as you reach the bottom of whatever you're slicing, you have to tilt the blades down at the tip to prevent the handle, and your knuckles, from hitting the cutting board. Because its blade is lower to begin with, the Black & Decker requires no such tilting.

Another factor that set the Black & Decker apart was its softly rounded, textured grip. Compared with the slick, hard grips on the other knives, the Black & Decker was a pleasure to hold—and, therefore, secure and precise in use. But if picture-perfect pie slices can't lure you to spend $25 on an electric knife, the White Westinghouse model, which costs just over half as much, is also a fine choice.

⇒ BY KAY RENTSCHLER ⇐

Bowled Over

In the process of working on vegetable stock for the last issue and shrimp bisque for this one, we ran into the problem of what kind of receptacle to use to collect the strained liquid. Wide-mouthed mixing bowls are a poor choice: not only are they too wide to offer most strainers stationary support, but liquids slosh readily over their broad, shallow edges. Deep cylindrical containers are ideal, but what if you don't have one? Look no farther than your baking cupboard: The KitchenAid mixing bowl is sturdy, deep, and relatively narrow at the top. Its stainless steel imparts no residual off odors (as plastic can), and hot fridge-bound liquids cool more quickly than in a plastic container. Once in the fridge, the KitchenAid bowl takes up far less room than a conventional mixing bowl. A minor note of caution: Because its base of support is relatively narrow, be sure to position your KitchenAid bowl securely across the rungs of the refrigerator shelf. Better yet, stabilize the bowl on a small plate.

Warming Thoughts

Everyone agrees that mashed potatoes taste best when they are hot, freshly mashed, and still in the pot. As they cool, and their starches harden, mashed potatoes sacrifice much of their creamy fluffiness, becoming, over the space of a couple of hours, positively leaden. Yet it's not always possible to make them at the last minute, especially during the holidays, when other dishes demand equal time and attention. During development of the Garlic Mashed Potatoes recipe for the September/October 2000 issue, we experimented with a few warming techniques (low oven, rewhipping with hot milk, etc.) and got the best results with a water bath, or *bain marie*. Here's what to do: Make the potatoes with one-quarter cup additional hot half-and-half, then turn them into a glass serving bowl or whatever vessel can be fit snugly over a pot containing about 3 inches of barely simmering water. Cover them flush with a damp, lintfree kitchen towel, a layer of plastic wrap, and a pot lid or tight band of aluminum foil. The potatoes will hold beautifully for up to two hours.

So Fine

Isn't it annoying to find recipes that call for superfine sugar when you've just sprinkled the last few crystals from the tiny box? Worse yet is when you can't find superfine sugar in any store and have to take your regular sugar for a spin in the food processor. Well, the folks at C&H Sugar Company have a little something for you. They are launching a professional grade ultrafine granulated baker's sugar in hefty 4.4 pound bags, retailing at $3.19 each. We put this fairy dust to the test against regular granulated by making a meringue, creaming butter, and mixing our favorite margaritas. The baker's sugar disappeared magically into everything, leaving no trace of grit or unmelted sugar sludge. Made of pure cane sugar, baker's sugar weighs the same per cup as regular granulated sugar. The two can be used interchangeably. Though C&H products sell in supermarkets west of the Mississippi only, baker's sugar will be available on the Web at www.bakerssugar.com and www.igourmet.com and from the King Arthur *Baker's Catalogue*. Look for it in time for your holiday baking.

Crispiest Streusel

We often wondered how the Germans and Austrians manage to get crispy streusel topping to flock their cakes, while the same sweet crumbs back home are often soft and pasty. In a simple recipe with only three basic ingredients— flour, sugar, and butter—we guessed that the differing results must have to do with the fact that European butter has more fat and less water than American butter. That would give our streusel a higher water content and softer texture, right? Well, so we thought. We were pleasantly surprised but also confounded, then, when our Associate Editor Raquel Pelzel produced a streusel recipe for her Dutch Apple Pie (see page 22) that contained standard American butter yet was as crispy as its European counterparts. It turned out that Raquel, in addition to adding a tablespoon of cornmeal to the flour, used melted instead of whole butter. When she made an identical streusel with whole butter, its texture was predictably mushy.

To understand this phenomenon, we contacted Dr. Chuck Walker, a professor of bakery science at Kansas State University, who explained that when butter is melted, the crystalline structure of its fat breaks down, thereby allowing the fat to soak into the core of the flour. While whole butter coats the dry ingredients, melted butter penetrates them. The result is a crispier streusel.

Air Blossoms

Quite a few readers have written us to inquire about the tiny pockmarks that can mar the top of a baked custard, wondering what accounts for them and how they can be avoided. Those little pits come from overwhisking eggs with milk or cream, thus introducing air into the equation and creating foam. The bubbles rise to the surface, where they break as the custard heats and bakes. Less vigorous agitation when mixing will reduce the foam and inhibit formation of bubbles.

Bumps on a Log

Some of you may want to gussy up your chocolate roulade for the holidays (page 24). Here's the way to create a traditional yule log: Reserve the two diagonally sliced endpieces. Frost the cake with ganache as described in the illustrations on page 25. Before the icing has set, affix the reserved slices on the cake as illustrated. Using a small offset or icing spatula, ice over and around the cake stumps, smoothing the surface to create a contiguous line between cake and stumps. Etch wood grain–like striations on the surface of the log with fork tines. If your holiday schedule is not fraught with last-minute crises, you might even want to make meringue mushrooms and some green marzipan holly leaves and....Oh, never mind.

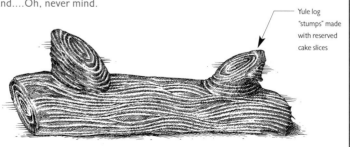

Yule log "stumps" made with reserved cake slices

Cooking across the Pond

Three cookbooks from London restaurants bode well for the resurrection of good food in England. BY CHRISTOPHER KIMBALL

The fact that London restaurants offer good, even great, food is certainly not newsworthy, as their culinary revolution is already 20 years old. London is also known for its wide variety of ethnic cuisines, offering up, for example, some of the best Indian cuisine in the world. If you wish to spare the expense of a round-trip ticket, though, the easiest solution is to seek out a few good London restaurant cookbooks. We assembled three such books, all published within the last three years and available here in the United States. Then we headed off to the test kitchen to find out how well these London restaurant recipes would work for the American home cook and to see if the Brits have anything to add to the food scene on this side of the Atlantic.

SALLY CLARKE'S BOOK
Sally Clarke

Macmillan, 310 pages

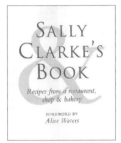

The first thing one notices about Sally Clarke's cookbook is that it is drop-dead gorgeous, with lots of Vermeer-inspired still-life photographs, expensive coated paper, and a classic, easy-to-read design. It exudes a reverential tone, which Alice Waters does her best to promote in her heartfelt foreword, thereby placing an extra burden on the recipes. But the recipes stand up, perhaps a testament to Clarke's long, eclectic career, which includes stints in Paris and Santa Monica as well as London. She opened her own place, Clarke's Restaurant, in late 1984.

PROS: Clarke presents a wide selection of recipes in a very singular personal voice. At their best, the recipes are interesting but straightforward. The Goat's Cheese and Thyme Soufflé and the Carrot, Cumin, and Coriander Soup are examples.

CONS: Like most restaurant chefs, Clarke includes some recipes that have no place in the home kitchen. One example is Courgette-Flower Fritters, the title of which suggests another occasional problem: ingredients that will be unfamiliar to, and perhaps unobtainable by, the American home cook. Another complicating factor is that many ingredients are measured in grams or milliliters. Still, most ingredients are simple, and substitutions require only a small bit of improvisation.

RECIPE TESTING: Of the three books tested, Clarke's had the highest ratio of winning recipes, fresh in terms of both concept and flavor and straightforward in execution. A salad of basil-roasted aubergine (eggplant) with mozzarella was simple, elegant, and delicious. The spiced pineapple chutney was fabulous (although it made 5 pounds!). A spiced corn soup with chiles and crème fraîche was easy and excellent, a wonderful change from the run-of-the-mill American versions. Finally, grilled scallops with kale and sprouting broccoli made for a bit of an odd combination, but we liked the dish nonetheless.

THE CAFE COOK BOOK
Rose Gray and Ruth Rogers

Broadway Books, 350 pages

The subtitle of this book, Italian Recipes from London's River Cafe, tells you what it is really about: pasta, polenta, risotto, pizza, bruschetta, and other Italian dishes. The book's design has much more wattage than Clarke's, using primary colors in chapter openings and bold, modern type. The color photography is excellent and abundant, and the book also features a good selection of black-and-white working shots of everything from cheese makers to mud-splattered pigs. Clearly, the authors want us to have some fun at the café.

PROS: The recipes give the cook a lot to choose from, and a good percentage have short ingredient lists. What's more, along with the usual collection of Italian restaurant offerings, the authors give us more intriguing dishes, such as wet polenta with kale and chicken stock, marinated lobster spaghetti, and zucchini carpaccio.

CONS: Like Clarke's book, this one includes some recipes best suited for a professional kitchen and some ingredients that are not available to American home cooks. Dover sole, if you can find it, will cost you half of next month's rent, a simple summer pudding had $50 worth of fruit in it, and not too many home cooks will be braising pigeons anytime soon.

RECIPE TESTING: We would make half of the dozen or so recipes we tested again, which is a good percentage. An apricot, nectarine, and plum bruschetta was unusual, gorgeous, sweet, and tangy all at the same time. The tagliatelle with walnut sauce worked fine and delivered as promised. On the downside was a frittata of wild mushrooms, which was so thick that the sides and bottom dried out before the center cooked properly; a plum ice cream that tasted more like frozen yogurt; and a crab risotto with sketchy directions that would be impractical for home cooks.

CAFÉ SPICE NAMASTE
Cyrus Todiwala

Soma, 144 pages

The author states that this is a cookbook about "modern Indian cooking," and his recipes back him up. Unusual dishes such as Monkfish Tikka, Instant Semolina Cakes, and Apple and Potato Bhajee will be fresh offerings for most cooks from Key West to Seattle. Like the other two books reviewed here, this one has plenty of beautiful color food shots, but Café Spice Namaste also saturates many of its pages with color.

PROS: Looking for new recipe ideas? You won't be disappointed. This book feels like London at its best—thoroughly modern ethnic food with lots of spice and energy.

CONS: You will have to make more than one trip to a specialty market to find some of the recipe ingredients, which include chickpea flour, asafetida (a spice), and Greek-style yogurt, and the recipes can be time-consuming, with some calling for condiments or other basic preparations that must be prepared ahead of time. The recipe instructions assume some familiarity with this style of cooking and so provide insufficient commentary for amateur Indian cooks.

RECIPE TESTING: Ethnic recipes are often hard to translate for use in the American kitchen, but this book was a pleasant surprise. Chicken with Fenugreek had a nightmarish ingredient list and the preparation was time-consuming, but the outcome was satisfying. Scallops with Ginger, Garlic, and Chili was a two-minute stir-fry: quick, easy, and quite good. Green beans with cumin and tomatoes was both beautiful and tasty. Less successful were banana fritters, which seemed more like bananas Foster; pulao, a spiced rice dish that was made by means of an imprecise cooking method (our rice ended up sticky); and a yogurt curry, which never thickened properly (perhaps our yogurt was not "Greek-style").

RESOURCES

Most of the ingredients and materials necessary for the recipes in this issue are available at your local supermarket, gourmet store, or kitchen supply shop. The following are recommended sources for particular items. Prices listed below were current at press time and do not include shipping or handling unless otherwise indicated. We suggest that you contact companies directly to confirm up-to-date prices and availability.

Electric Knives

In our testing on page 28, we found that electric knives definitely have a place in modern kitchens. From slicing roasts to divvying up quesadillas, the knives matched—and in most cases even surpassed—the ease and efficacy of a well-sharpened chef's knife. The overall winner, the Black & Decker Ergo Electric Knife, model EK600, is perfect for cooks of all (hand) sizes. The soft, ergonomic handle and unique blade angle give it great balance and control, and the trigger-guard safety lock is a plus. You can buy the Black & Decker EK600 exclusively at Wal-Mart, Target, Sears, and Service Merchandise stores. The suggested retail price is $32.99, but most sell it for considerably less. Our second favorite, the White Westinghouse Electric Knife with Slicing Guide, model WEK9430, is available at Kmart stores only. We bought ours for $12.99, but prices will vary from store to store. The Rival Electric Knife, model 1205, suggested retail price $23.95, can be found at Wal-Mart, Kmart, Home Depot, Target, and Sears. Again, the stores sell it for much less.

Turkey

This year we have supplied you with the tools for a successful Thanksgiving meal, right down to which brand of turkey to buy. Flavor, texture, and tenderness were our guidelines in this year's turkey tasting. Our number one turkey was the frozen Marval. Marval turkeys are raised, processed, and marketed by Rocco, and contain no artificial ingredients or preservatives. We were pleasantly surprised by this frozen bird's full-flavored, succulent, and extremely tender meat. Marval turkeys are readily available in most major supermarkets on the East Coast and in Texas. At this time, however, no mail-order option is available for residents of the central or western United States. For more information, go to **www.rocco.com** or call **800-336-4003**. Our second-place winner, the fresh Empire Kosher turkey, was esteemed for its juicy, tender meat and clean flavor. To meet the requirements of the kosher label, these turkeys must be free-roaming and all-natural. No antibiotics, growth hormones, or steroids are used to promote growth. Empire Kosher turkeys are widely available in all 50 states and in Canada. Check the company's Web site (**www.empirekosher.com**) for a listing of retailers by state. The birds can also be ordered online or over the phone (**www.koshersupermarket.com; 888-425-6743**). Prices vary per retailer.

Gearing Up for Roulade

As Test Kitchen Director Kay Rentschler discusses in her article "Bittersweet Chocolate Roulade" (page 24), time is of the essence when baking and putting together this dessert. It is important to make sure you have all of your ingredients and equipment ready to go before you begin. The first item we suggest you have at the ready is a fine sieve for presifting the cocoa. Because cocoa has a higher fat content and is denser than flour, it will pass through a regular sifter in small beads, rather than mixing perfectly with the flour. Pressing the cocoa through the mesh of a very fine sieve with the back of a spoon is a great presifting method. **A Cook's Wares (211 37th Street, Beaver Falls, PA 15010-2103; 800-915-9788; www.cookswares.com)** carries a highly polished stainless steel, fine-mesh strainer, 5½ inches in diameter, item #8497, for $20, that is perfect for the job. We also found it extremely convenient to have an extra KitchenAid mixer bowl on hand while preparing the sponge cake batter. With an extra bowl, there's no need to decant the beaten yolks and sugar before scrupulously cleaning the bowl for whipping the whites. A Cook's Wares also sells replacement bowls, 4½ and 5 quarts (designed for different mixers), both for $39.99, item #5100 and #5101, respectively. Finally, because the flatter and more even a cake, the easier it is to roll, we suggest using a large offset spatula to smooth the batter in the sheet pan. The crook in the blade of this spatula, averaging about 55 degrees, raises its handle, offering the leverage needed to level out the batter evenly without scarring it. A small offset spatula is also the perfect tool with which to ice the roulade. You can buy both the large and small offset spatulas from **Different Drummer's Kitchen (374 Pittsfield Road, Lenox, MA 01240; 800-375-2665)**. The large spatula has a 9½-inch blade and sells for $5.99 (item #17696). The small spatula has a blade 4¼ inches long and costs $2.49 (item #17175).

Bamboo Skewers and Twine

To meet the challenge of safely and neatly packaging our stuffed pork roast (page 11) in cylinder form, Associate Editor Adam Ried and Test Cook Julia Collin found it helpful to secure the meat around the stuffing with bamboo skewers before tying it. They favored 10-inch skewers broken roughly in half, which provided ample length and strength to hold the meat together. The 10-inch bamboo skewers, item #90309, come in a package of 100 for 99 cents from **The Oriental Pantry (423 Great Road, Acton, MA 01720; 800-828-0368; www.orientalpantry.com)**. When the meat is firmly supported, tying it is simple, but be sure to use heavy cotton or linen twine, as both are natural and won't burn or fray in the oven. If you can't find either one in your favorite kitchen store, **Bridge Kitchenware (214 East 52nd Street, New York, NY 10022; 800-274-3435; www.bridgekitchenware.com)** sells 370 feet of fine cotton butcher's twine, item code BBTW, for $2.95.

Broiler Pan

While developing the recipes for roasted pear salads (page 10), we were reminded that the broiling pan is often the victim of caked-on, hard-to-clean food debris, leaving one thinking how nice it would be to throw out the pan and start anew. The slotted tray/underlying drip pan combination is great to use when cooking with an electric coil broiler (which equips the ovens in our test kitchen) or with a gas oven broiler that is tucked away in a drawer under the oven. The slots in the pan's removable tray allow for some heat to reach the underside of what is broiling, and they also channel away rendered fats and juices, minimizing splattering and smoking. If you are missing or have had it with your current broiling pan, **Cooks Corner (P.O. Box 220, 836 South Eighth Street, Manitowoc, WI 54221-0220; 800-236-2433; www.cookscorner.com)** carries two sizes. The smaller of the two, item #28629, is 13 inches long by 8½ inches wide and 1¼ inches deep. It sells for $14.99. The larger pan, item #28630, runs 17 inches long by 12¾ inches wide and 1½ inches deep and sells for $24.99. Both are coated with a nonstick surface, inside and out, for quick release and easy cleanup, and can be used in electric or gas ovens. Be sure to measure your oven before ordering.

Ceramic Pie Weights

When prebaking the pie crust for the Dutch Apple Pie on page 22, we found that ceramic pie weights conduct heat more efficiently than metal beads or dried beans. We used two cups of the unglazed ceramic balls, and our crust came out of the oven evenly browned, flat, and bubblefree. If you don't have ceramic pie weights, you can order them in 13-ounce packages (enough for 1¼ cups) from **The Baker's Catalogue (King Arthur Flour, P.O. Box 876, Norwich, VT 05055-0876; 800-827-6836; www.kingarthurflour.com)** for $5.95, item #9238. Be sure to order two packages so you have enough for two cups.

RECIPES
November & December 2000

Roasted Pear and Beet Salad

Rich and Velvety Shrimp Bisque

Roast Stuffed Pork Loin

Pasta all'Amatriciana

Cornbread and Sausage Stuffing

Roast Crisped-Skin Turkey

PHOTOGRAPHY: CARL TREMBLAY

www.cooksillustrated.com

Cook's Illustrated has just launched its new Web site and we invite you to join us. Simply log on at www.cooksillustrated.com. Although much of the information is free, database searches are for site subscribers only. *Cook's Illustrated* readers are offered a 20% discount.

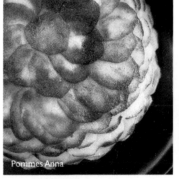

Pommes Anna

Spicy Turkey and Jasmine Rice Soup

Here is what you can do on our site:

Search Our Recipes: We have a searchable database of all the recipes from *Cook's Illustrated*.

Search Tastings and Cookware Ratings: You will find all of our reviews (cookware, food, wine, cookbooks) plus new material created exclusively for the Web site.

Find Your Favorite Quick Tips.

Get Your Cooking Questions Answered: Post questions for *Cook's* editors and fellow site subscribers.

Take a Cooking Course Online: Take online cooking courses from *Cook's* editors and receive personalized instruction.

Check Your Subscription: Check the status of your subscription, pay a bill, or give gift subscriptions online.

Visit Our Bookstore: You can purchase any of our cookbooks, hardbound annual editions of the magazine, or posters via the Internet.

Subscribe to e-notes: Our free e-mail companion to Kitchen Notes offers cooking advice, test results, buying tips, and recipes about a single topic each month.

Find Out About Our New Public Television Cooking Show: Coming to public television soon, America's Test Kitchen will take you into the *Cook's Illustrated* test kitchen.

Get All the Extras: The outtakes from each issue of *Cook's* are available at Cook's Extra, including step-by-step photographs.

Dutch Apple Pie

Bittersweet Chocolate Roulade

Temple Orange

Minneola

Valencia

Clementine

Ugli Fruit

Honey Tangerine

Navel Orange

Blood Orange

Satsuma

Seville Orange

ORANGES
AND TANGERINES